CW00969783

Apple Pro Training Series

AppleScript 1-2-3

Sal Soghoian and Bill Cheeseman

Apple
Certified

Apple Training Series: AppleScript 1-2-3
Sal Soghoian and Bill Cheeseman

Published by Peachpit Press. For information on Peachpit Press, contact:

Peachpit Press
1249 Eighth Street
Berkeley, CA 94710
510/524-2178
510/524-2221 (fax)

Find us on the Web at: www.peachpit.com

To report errors, please send a note to errata@peachpit.com

Peachpit Press is a division of Pearson Education

Copyright © 2009 by Apple Inc. and Bill Cheeseman

Project editor: Clifford Colby
Production coordinator: Lisa Brazieal
Copyeditor: Kim Wimpsett
Compositor: WolfsonDesign
Indexer: Rebecca Plunkett
Cover design: Mimi Heft
Cover illustration: Mimi Heft; source photo by Derrick Story
Cover photo: Derrick Story

ISBN 13: 978-0-321-14931-2
ISBN 10: 0-321-14931-9

9 8 7 6 5 4 3 2 1

Printed and bound in the United States of America

I dedicate this book to my wife, Naomi, and Mosby, without whose support and understanding it would not have been written.

And to my family, Avedis, Laura, Stephen, and Christopher, and the tapestry of relatives who add color to my life.

And finally to the Apple engineers and staff whose vision and dedication to AppleScript have been such a benefit to me and thousands of others. I thank them for their work and their unwavering belief that the power of the computer should rest in the hands of those that use it.

—Sal Soghoian

For my wife, Sharon, with love.

Thanks to AppleScripters everywhere for the extraordinary good will and high spirits of our community all these many years.

—Bill Cheeseman

Contents at a Glance

Table of Contents

Essential Topics

Foreword

I think we owe my Aunt Sarah a big thank you. After all, she's the one who inspired the book that's about to change your computer life forever.

It was at one of those big get-togethers that occur frequently in ethnic families like mine. Hundreds of relatives gather, taking over the neighborhood and local markets to play, feast, and talk for days. Kids with parents and elders clustered around an ongoing buffet of Armenian goodness (my stomach still is full to this day), making the joyous racket that is life in motion.

Anyway, I wander into the kitchen, and there is Sarah, standing with her belly pressing against the edge of the sink, her dark hair pulled back into a bun of sorts, sleeves rolled up, elbows deep in a tub of dishes, with pile upon pile of plates on the counter next to her. Moved by her toil, I approach and offer to show her an easier way to clean the day's plates, pans, and cups, to which she immediately quips "I don't have time to learn how to use the dishwasher, I'm busy washing dishes."

At some point in our lives, we've all felt like that. There's no time to try something new, even if it can help us. We know what we know, learned on the job, and it works for us. It might not be the best or fastest way, but it's what we know how to do. And so we labor harder and longer than we need to, missing any opportunity to make things easier for ourselves.

Until one day, something happens. Maybe you pick up a book. *This* book. And you decide you're finally going to take a chance and spend a little time—just half an hour or so—to follow the first chapter, to see what's possible and if it's right for you. That's when magic happens. The magic of AppleScript and its power to make the computer do what you want and need it to do *for you*.

It Was a Dark and Stormy Night...

My name is Sal Soghoian, and since January 13, 1997, I've had the honor to be the product manager for automation technologies at Apple. To paraphrase a famous lawyer, "for me, AppleScript is a living breathing reality." AppleScript been a big part of my life since a moment of inspiration in 1992: While working at a service bureau in Charlottesville, Virginia, I wrote my first script and changed the course of my life. It was this simple script for QuarkXPress:

```
set the color of the current box to "Blue"
```

And when the color of that selected text box changed from white to blue, I knew nothing would be the same. In an instant, the power to control the computer was no longer just in the hands of companies whose software I purchased: It was in mine as well.

By writing English-like statements, I could automate the many redundant tasks I performed over and over, all day long, at the service bureau. It was liberating! I quit my job, and for the next three months spent every waking hour teaching myself to master this wondrous technology. It took that long because there were no books, no videos, no podcasts, no Web sites to turn to for assistance—just a dedicated group of individuals in online communities who shared a passion to automate and accomplish the impossible.

How some things have changed for the better.

As time went on, my automation skills matured and grew (like most "scripters") and people noticed, asking (and paying) me to write scripts for them. And for the next years, I wrote magazine articles, presented at trade shows, and taught individuals and classes how to take advantage of AppleScript and make it an essential part of their computer lives.

About This Book

This book is based on years of hands-on classes and contains many of the scripts developed for those sessions.

But the task of documenting and teaching a technology such as AppleScript is daunting (especially while you're employed at a busy company like Apple), and it could not have been accomplished without the assistance and contribution of an exceptional individual with laser-like focus and deep knowledge of AppleScript: Bill Cheeseman. A lawyer of considerable renown, Bill leads a double-life as a talented programmer who has written extensively on the subject. He also is a master scripter and someone who I've learned from time and again. It was very fortunate that he made time in his schedule to contribute to this book.

For this book, Bill and I agreed that we were writing for those individuals without any programming or coding experience, just the same type of "normal folks" who take my classes at the Macworld Conference each year. People who work hard and are looking for an "easier way" to do things on the computer. They've heard about AppleScript and the promise that it holds but have never had the time or the means to learn it. And perhaps they looked at some of the excellent books on the subject but thought they were written for geeks and not for themselves. If you're one of these "normal Mac users," we designed this book for you (although scripters and programmers may find it useful too).

The book is divided into three sections (it is named AppleScript 1-2-3 after all), and is very step by step, hands-on, and easy to follow. You learn by writing short scripts that demonstrate principles, ideas, and techniques. Start with the first chapter, "The First Step," in the first section, "Instant AppleScript," and proceed in order through chapter 12. This first section teaches the basics and fundamentals to writing AppleScript. When you're done with it, you'll be a very dangerous person with a great foundation to build upon.

The remainder of the book, chapters 13 through 30, serve as a reference to specific AppleScript tasks and capabilities. Explore the subjects covered in those chapters as you need to. You'll find they contain interesting topics such as manipulating image files, running scripts on a schedule, connecting to networks, and creating dynamic scriptable databases. There's plenty to explore.

The third section of the book is not actually "in" the book: It's on the book's companion Web site, `www.peachpit.com/applescript123`. Here you'll find updated information, downloadable examples and scripts, and other training materials.

Think Big. Start Small.

So let me close this forward with a word about believing in yourself: You can do this. You can learn how to automate the computer and the applications that run on it. Over the years, I have seen countless people—people just like you—spend a few hours, a few days, and even a few weeks, committing themselves to stretching and expanding their knowledge and skills, to grow, to learn, and in so doing, to change their computer lives forever. I've seen it happen. And I've seen their faces when the light goes on and they discover the power in their hands. It's your turn now.

Part **I**

Instant AppleScript

1

Lesson **1**

The First Step

Consider this chapter a "book within a book." If you don't read any other chapter, read this one. It has been designed to give you a quick but thorough introduction to AppleScript through a short, fun, hands-on tutorial. In 25 minutes you'll learn what AppleScript is, how it works, and how to write basic, functional AppleScript scripts with confidence.

To accomplish this goal, you'll learn the fundamentals of AppleScript and then put them to use as we step through the creation of a Finder toolbar script. You can use the script on your own computer to reset a cluttered Desktop display to a predefined window set instantly.

NOTE ▶ The scripting examples in this book are written for Mac OS X 10.5 (Leopard) and 10.4 (Tiger), so they may not work with earlier systems. Because AppleScript is always updated and improved with each OS release, it's important to keep your system current to take advantage of the many new features and tools.

What Is AppleScript?

AppleScript is a language used to automate the actions of the Macintosh operating system and many of its applications.

Whether a task is as simple as copying a file or as complex as building a real estate catalog, AppleScript can perform the requisite actions for you with intelligence, controlling applications and making decisions based on its observations or information provided by its interaction with the person running the script.

Every day, businesses and individuals alike use AppleScript to create newspapers and books, manage networks, build DVDs, process images, generate Web pages, back up files and folders, make videos, and do much more. AppleScript is the most powerful, easy-to-use automation tool available on any platform. Best of all, this technology is free and is built into every copy of the Mac OS!

How It Works...

To automate the actions of applications, the computer reads the sequential instructions contained in AppleScript scripts written by you and others, and then it communicates those instructions to targeted applications. The targeted applications interpret the communicated instructions and perform the actions listed in the scripts.

Motivated users like yourself compose AppleScript scripts in AppleScript, an English-like language containing many of the verbs, nouns, adjectives, articles, and other English-language elements we use every day. The AppleScript language is designed to be easily understandable, and it has a syntax or grammatical structure similar to the one we use to create normal sentences.

You write scripts in the Script Editor application, a free utility included with every copy of the Mac OS. You can run scripts from within the Script Editor application or save them either as script files or as script applications.

Saved scripts are available for use at any time from within any application. You launch script files from an application's script menu or from the Mac OS system-wide Script Menu utility. You launch script applications, or applets, like any other application—by double-clicking their icons in the Finder or by clicking their Dock or Finder toolbar and sidebar icons.

The Big Picture

AppleScript is based on the concept of scriptable objects that belong to or are contained in other scriptable objects, such as a file contained in a folder that belongs to the hard disk, or a word being part of a paragraph belonging to a story. Understanding the relationship between scriptable objects is an essential step in learning how to write scripts. It can be summarized in the following statements:

▶   On the computer, everything is an object.

The computer, the Desktop, the disks it displays, the folders on the disks, and the files in those folders—all of these items are objects. So are applications, their documents, and the data in those documents.

▶   Everything belongs to, is related to, is contained in, or is part of something else.

The file is in the folder that is in the disk that is on the Desktop that is on the computer. This same relationship can apply to text as well. The character is in the word that is in the line that is part of the paragraph that is contained in the story.

This relationship between objects is referred to as hierarchical or, in military terms, following a "chain of command." AppleScript uses this hierarchical containment structure to identify specific scriptable objects. All the scripts you write will contain hierarchical references.

Just remember this:

▶   Scriptable objects are described by their positions in their object hierarchy, or where they are in their "chain of command."

NOTE ▶ Don't be put off by the term hierarchical. We often use hierarchical references to identify objects in our lives. For example, you refer to your home as being on a specific street in a specific city in a specific county in a specific state in a specific country. Or you refer to your advanced pottery class as being in room 128 on the third floor of the west wing of the Creative Arts building. Object references in AppleScript work the same way.

Properties and Values

Disks, files, folders, alias files, document files, application files, clippings, font suitcases, packages, Internet location files, application files, windows, and Finder windows are all objects, or elements, belonging to the Finder application. They are the items the Finder application uses in its organization and display of information. Each of these items has properties that define or describe the particular item. Some of these properties are unique to each item, while others are shared by all Finder items.

For example, while an Internet location file is the only Finder element that has a property describing a location on the Internet, it still shares some properties common to all Finder elements, such as its icon display size or its position in a folder window or on the Desktop. And like other Finder elements, such as a folder or document file, an Internet location file has a `name` property whose value is text that can be edited by the user of the computer.

FIGURE 1.1 An Internet location file is a file that, when opened, displays its target URL in the default browser window.

An important rule to remember about scriptable objects is this:

▶ Scriptable objects have properties with values that can be read and sometimes manipulated.

This rule applies to the Finder application and to all scriptable applications
as well. All elements of the Finder application have properties, such as their
name, size, and location. All of these properties have values, some of which can
be edited, some which can only be read.

Think Big...Start Small

Your exploration of AppleScript is about learning the fundamental principles
of the AppleScript language and how to apply them in writing scripts. No
matter how complex a script is, the fundamental principles applied within the
script remain the same. The lessons learned in scripting a common object such
as a Finder window pertain to all scriptable objects and applications. They can
be used to create more complex and powerful automation tools later.

You'll begin the process of becoming a scripter by examining the properties of
a Finder window and learning how to manipulate them with scripts.

The Script Editor

Since this tutorial is very "hands-on," you'll be writing scripts right away.
To write a script, you'll use the Script Editor application installed on your
system. You can find this application in the AppleScript folder located in the
Applications folder on your computer's main hard drive. Navigate to this
folder now, and double-click the Script Editor icon to launch the application.

Script Editor

FIGURE 1.2 The Script Editor application icon.

NOTE ▶ The following description and illustrations are for the Script
Editor application included in Mac OS X 10.5 (Leopard). Earlier versions
have a slightly different design.

After starting up, the Script Editor application displays a multipaned window
known as a script window. This script window contains two panes, the top
pane containing the script text and the bottom pane containing either the
script description, the script result, or the script log, depending on which tab
below the pane has been selected.

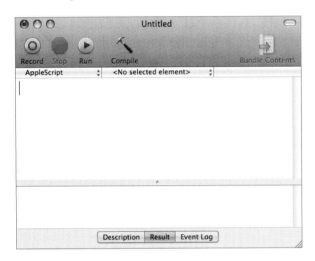

FIGURE 1.3 A script window in the Script Editor application.

By default, the script window is rather small, so you may want to expand its
size before proceeding with this tutorial. Note that the Script Editor and other
AppleScript tools are covered in detail in Chapter 13, Script Editor, and in
Chapter 14, AppleScript Utility.

Your First Script

You'll begin the process of learning AppleScript by writing a series of simple script commands in the form of a `tell` statement. A `tell` statement is a single-line script beginning with the verb `tell`. This verb is used to direct script actions at a specific application or scriptable object. A `tell` statement is composed of two parts:

- ▸ A reference to the object to be scripted

- ▸ The action to be performed

Using this grammatical format, or syntax, you can write scripts instructing the Finder to perform whatever actions you desire. Script 1.1 is your first script.

```
tell application "Finder" to close every window
```
SCRIPT 1.1

Enter Script 1.1 in the top pane of Script Editor's script window exactly as shown (be sure to enclose the word `Finder` in straight quotation marks). Click the Compile button in the script window to confirm that it has been written correctly and to prepare the script for use.

Next, click the Run button to play your script. The operating system reads the script and sends the appropriate commands to the Finder application, which then follows the instruction to close any open windows.

Congratulations, you've written and run your first AppleScript script!

Note that the word `Finder` is enclosed in quotation marks in the script. Names and textual data are always quoted in scripts. This is done to indicate to Script Editor that the quoted material is textual data and not to be considered a command or instruction when the script is compiled in preparation for execution.

Delete the previous script from the script window, and then enter, compile, and run Script 1.2.

```
tell application "Finder" to open the startup disk
```
SCRIPT 1.2

A new Finder window now appears on the Desktop displaying the contents of the startup disk, as shown in Figure 1.4. You'll use this newly opened window as you examine the properties of a Finder window.

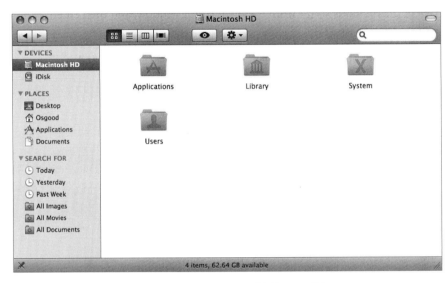

FIGURE 1.4 Finder windows display the contents of folders or disks.

A Word About Finder Windows

Finder windows are different from other windows used by the Finder application in that they display the contents of folders and may contain a toolbar and sidebar. The remaining script examples in this chapter will use the term Finder window instead of the generic term window when referring to Finder windows.

The name Property

The first property of a Finder window we'll examine is its name property.

A window's name is the window title displayed in the title bar of the window. In the case of Finder windows, the value of the name property is the name of the folder or disk whose contents are displayed within the Finder window.

To retrieve the value of the name property of a window, use the command get. This verb is used when you want to extract information or data from a scriptable element or object.

Delete the previous script from the open script window, and then enter, compile, and run Script 1.3.

```
tell application "Finder" to get the name of front Finder window
```
SCRIPT 1.3

To see the result of your request, look in the Result pane at the bottom of the script window. To activate the Result pane, click the tab titled Result. In the Result pane you'll see the result, if any, of the last script action. In Script 1.3, the result is the title of the open Finder window, which also happens to be the name of your start-up disk. As shown in Figure 1.5, this is Macintosh HD on Sal's computer.

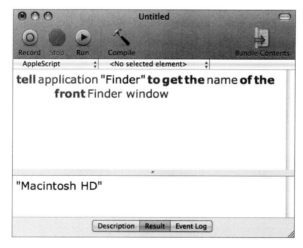

FIGURE 1.5 A script window displays the result of the last script action in the Result pane at the bottom of the window.

For Finder windows, the name property is a read-only property. It can be used to refer to a Finder window, but its value cannot be changed by a script. The value of the name property of a Finder window is always the name of the folder or disk whose contents it displays.

Delete the previous script from the script window, and then enter, compile, and run Script 1.4. Be sure to replace Macintosh HD with the name of the open Finder window if it is different on your computer.

```
tell application "Finder" to close Finder window "Macintosh HD"
```
SCRIPT 1.4

As Script 1.4 demonstrates, you can use the name property as a means to refer to a specific Finder window. When the script is run, the Finder window named Macintosh HD closes.

Script 1.4 worked because it is a fully qualified tell statement. It refers to the object receiving the commands, in this case the open window, and it indicates the desired action to be performed, closing the window. All tell statements are constructed in this manner.

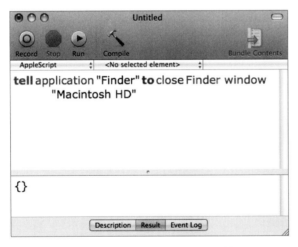

FIGURE 1.6 A script consisting of a single tell statement targeting a Finder window.

Also note that the result of the script action is a set of curly brace characters. This is an AppleScript list. We'll talk more about that in a couple pages.

The index Property

If you're writing a script that will be used on multiple computers, using the name property to refer to Finder windows is not always the most reliable way to locate a specific window. It's possible that two windows may have the same name. A more generic way to refer to an open Finder window is through its index property.

The value of this read-only property is a number corresponding to the window's layer in the stacking order of open Finder windows. On the computer, no two windows can occupy the same layer. One window is always on top of or in front of another window. The index property reflects this fact.

For example, the front Finder window always has an index value of 1, since it is the first window in the stack of open windows, while the last Finder window always has an index value equal to the number of open Finder windows.

Let's see how the index property can be used to refer to Finder windows.

First, reopen the previous window using Script 1.5.

```
tell application "Finder" to open the startup disk
```
SCRIPT 1.5

Now delete Script 1.5 from the script window, and then enter, compile, and run Script 1.6. Again, be sure to replace Macintosh HD with the name of the open Finder window if it is different on your computer.

> **IMPORTANT:** Note the use of the special character (¬) in the script text in the following example. This character, generated by pressing Option+L or Option+Return, is used by Script Editor to indicate that a single-line statement has been placed on multiple lines in order to make it easier to read. Because of the space restrictions involved in displaying scripts in a book, this character will be used in all script examples containing long statements. Script Editor has an autowrapping feature that makes using this character unnecessary. If you are using the Script Editor, you can ignore the special character and continue entering the script on the same line.

```
tell application "Finder" to ¬
    get the index of Finder window "Macintosh HD"
```
SCRIPT 1.6

The result of this script, shown in the Result pane, is the numeric value **1**, since there is only one window currently open on the Desktop.

Let's open a second window. Instead of deleting Script 1.6 from the script window, simply edit it by deleting **the startup disk** and entering in its place **home**, so it reads **tell application "Finder" to open home**. Then compile and run it.

A second window displaying the contents of your home directory now appears on the Desktop, as shown in Figure 1.7.

FIGURE 1.7 Two Finder windows with one window overlapping the other. No two windows can occupy the same position in the order of stacked windows.

TIP ▶ Note the use of the words home and startup disk in the two versions of Script 1.6. startup disk and home are special terms, reserved by the Finder application, to identify important locations. These terms are generic and will work regardless of how drives and folders are named on the computer.

Now, let's see whether the addition of the new window on the Desktop has affected the `index` value of our previously targeted window. Delete the existing script from the script window, and then enter, compile, and run Script 1.7.

```
tell application "Finder" to ¬
    get the index of Finder Window "Macintosh HD"
```
SCRIPT 1.7

The result is now the numeric value 2 since the target window is the second window in the stack of open windows on the Desktop.

The `index` property can also be used to refer to any open window. Try the two versions of Script 1.8 one at a time and note their results.

```
tell application "Finder" to get the name of Finder Window 1
    --> returns the name of your home directory


tell application "Finder" to get the name of Finder Window 2
    --> returns the name of your startup disk
```
SCRIPT 1.8

Descriptive index Values

As you've seen in the previous scripts, the AppleScript language is designed to be "English-like" and can be written in a conversational manner. Because of this, the value of the `index` property can also be described using descriptive terms as well as numeric values. For example, try the two versions of Script 1.9.

```
tell application "Finder" to ¬
    get the index of the first Finder window
    --> returns: 1


tell application "Finder" to ¬
    get the index of the second Finder window
    --> returns: 2
```
SCRIPT 1.9

Note the use of the words `first` and `second` for the value of the `index` property instead of the numbers `1` and `2`. The AppleScript language accepts the terms `first`, `second`, `third`, `fourth`, `fifth`, `sixth`, `seventh`, `eighth`, `ninth`, and `tenth` in place of the corresponding numeric character equivalents.

As a matter of fact, the value of the `index` property could also be written using the terms shown in these additional versions of Script 1.9:

```
tell application "Finder" to get the index of the 1st Finder window
--> returns: 1
```

```
tell application "Finder" to get the index of the 2nd Finder window
--> returns: 2
```

The use of descriptive terms works with any number, not just the first ten, for example, `22nd`, `312th`, `3rd`, and so on.

Relative Position

In addition to recognizing `index` values written as text, AppleScript also accepts `index` values described in terms of a window's position relative to other windows. For example:

```
tell application "Finder" to ¬
    get the index of the front Finder window
    --> returns: 1
tell application "Finder" to ¬
    get the index of the back Finder window
    --> returns: 2
tell application "Finder" to ¬
    get the index of the last Finder window
    --> returns: 2
tell application "Finder" to get the index of the ¬
    Finder window before the last Finder window
    --> returns: 1
tell application "Finder" to get the index of the ¬
    Finder window after the front Finder window
    --> returns: 2
```

The `index` values in these examples were written using the terms `front`, `back`, and `last`. AppleScript accepts the terms `middle` and `some` as well. Also note that the additional terms `before` and `after` were used to further define the target window's location.

Finder Window index References

The value of the `index` property can be expressed using any of the previous methods. All are valid and can be used freely and interchangeably. Here's a summary of the ways a Finder window can be referenced:

By name:

```
Finder window "Documents"
```

By numeric index:

```
Finder window 1
```

By descriptive index:

```
the first Finder window
the second Finder window
the fifth Finder window
the 1st Finder window
the 23rd Finder window
```

By relative position:

```
the front Finder window
the middle Finder window
the back Finder window
the last Finder window
```

Randomly:

```
some Finder window
```

Changing a Finder Window's index Value

So far we've examined the name and index properties by using them to refer to specific Finder windows. The name property is a read-only property; in other words, its value can be gotten but not changed. However, the index property of a Finder window is an editable property, meaning its value can be altered.

Next, you'll change the value of the index property of the open Finder windows. To change the value of a property, use the verb set. The set verb is the command used to change the value of a property.

Delete the previous script from the script window, and then enter, compile, and run Script 1.10.

```
tell application "Finder" to ¬
    set the index of the last Finder window to 1
```
SCRIPT 1.10

The last Finder window, the one displaying the contents of the startup disk, is now in front of all other windows. The script moved the last Finder window to the front by changing the value of its index property.

Now let's write a script that will move the front Finder window behind all other Finder windows. This seems simple enough. Just set the value of the index property of the front Finder window to 2—right? That will work with the current setup of windows in the Finder since there are only two windows open, but what if you didn't know how many windows were open? What would you use for the index value? Here's a simple solution that moves the front Finder window to the back no matter how many windows are open. Enter, compile, and run Script 1.11.

```
tell application "Finder" to ¬
    set the index of the first Finder window to ¬
        the index of the last Finder window
```
SCRIPT 1.11

The Finder window displaying the contents of your home directory is now the front Finder window again. The script accomplishes this by using the value of the index property of the last Finder window as the value for the index property of the front Finder window.

> **NOTE ▶** When you change the value of the index property of a Finder window, you may change the index value of some of the open Finder windows behind it.

The target Property

The value of the target property is a reference to the folder or disk whose contents are displayed in the Finder window. This value can be both read and changed. Let's examine both actions.

First, let's get the value of the target property of the frontmost window using Script 1.12.

```
tell application "Finder" to get the target of the front window
--> returns: folder "<name of your home directory>" of folder "Users" of
startup disk of application "Finder"
```
SCRIPT 1.12

FIGURE 1.8 A script getting the value of the target property of a Finder window.

As you can see in Figure 1.8, the result of this script is a reference to the folder whose contents are displayed in the Finder window, in this case your home directory. This reference describes the target folder in terms of its location in its object hierarchy, or where it is in its "chain of command."

The returned object reference clearly shows, through the use of the possessive of, that the target folder is contained by the Users folder, which is on the startup disk, which is an element of the Finder application. You'll use this hierarchical reference structure often in the scripts you write.

Next, we'll change the targets of the open Finder windows. To change the value of a property, we'll use the verb set. The verb set is the command used to change the value of a property.

Delete the previous script from the script window, and then enter, compile, and run Script 1.13.

```
tell application "Finder" to ¬
    set the target of the front Finder window to the startup disk
```
SCRIPT 1.13

You'll notice as shown in Figure 1.9 that the frontmost Finder window now displays the contents of the startup disk.

FIGURE 1.9 The frontmost Finder window now displays the contents of the startup disk.

Now try Script 1.14.

```
tell application "Finder" to ¬
    set the target of the last Finder window to home
```
SCRIPT 1.14

The second Finder window now displays the contents of your home directory, as shown in Figure 1.10.

FIGURE 1.10 The rear Finder window now displays the contents of the home directory.

In summary, the **target** property of a Finder window has a value that is a reference to a specific folder or disk whose contents are displayed within the Finder window. This value can be changed by using the verb **set** in conjunction with a reference to a new target folder. A reference describes an object in terms of its location in its object hierarchy, or in the case of a folder object, where it is on its parent disk.

Finder References

Since you'll often use object references in the scripts you write, here's a short overview of how to create an object reference for use with the Finder application.

First, in the front Finder window, navigate to your Documents folder in your home directory. In the Documents folder, create a new folder named Smith Project. We'll use this folder in the following examples.

To construct an object reference to a specific Finder disk item, simply start with the item to be referenced, and list each folder or containing item of the object hierarchy until you've reached the disk containing the item.

For example, to create a Finder reference to the folder named Smith Project in the Documents folder in your home directory, begin the Finder reference with the name of the referenced item preceded by a class identifier indicating the type of object it is, such as a `folder` or `document file`.

```
folder "Smith Project"
```

Next, add the class identifier and name of the object's parent or containing folder or object, preceded by the possessive `of` to indicate its ownership of the previous item:

```
folder "Smith Project" of folder "Documents"
```

Again, add the class identifier and name of the last object's parent or containing folder or object, preceded by the possessive `of` to indicate ownership:

```
folder "Smith Project" of folder "Documents" of ¬
    folder "<name of your home directory>"
```

Continue this process until you've reached the disk containing the referenced object:

```
folder "Smith Project" of folder "Documents" of ¬
    folder "<name of your home directory>" of ¬
        folder "Users" of disk "Macintosh HD"
```

Note the use of the class identifier `disk` for the `disk` object.

You've now constructed an object reference to the Finder item Smith Project located in the Documents folder in your home directory.

Object references to Finder items can sometimes be very long. To shorten the example reference and make it more generic and easier to write, you can replace the section of the reference pertaining to your home directory and its parent containers with the special Finder term home mentioned earlier:

```
folder "Smith Project" of folder "Documents" of home
```
This shortened version will function the same as the longer reference.

If you wanted to use this object reference as the value for the target property, the script would be written like this:

```
tell application "Finder" to set the target of ¬
    the front Finder window to folder "Smith Project" of ¬
    folder "Documents" of home
```

Of course, this script will not work if there is no folder named Smith Project in the referenced location.

> **TIP ▶** To view the object hierarchy of a Finder disk item, click the title in its Finder window or its parent Finder window while holding down the Command key. Each segment in the object hierarchy will be listed on the pop-up menu.

FIGURE 1.11 Click a Finder window's title with the Command key held down to reveal a navigation menu displaying the folder's location.

Before continuing our tutorial, reset the front Finder window so it displays the contents of the startup disk by running Script 1.15.

```
tell application "Finder" to set the target of ¬
    the front Finder window to the startup disk
```
SCRIPT 1.15

That's a short explanation and demonstration of Finder disk item references. This topic is covered in greater detail in Chapter 3, Identifying Objects. For now, it is enough to understand the following:

▶   Scriptable objects are referred to by their positions in their object hierarchy or where they are in their "chain of command."

Now let's continue our overview of the properties of a Finder window.

The toolbar visible Property

In Mac OS X, Finder windows were redesigned for greater functionality and ease of use. One of the new window features is the toolbar area located at the top of a Finder window. This area contains display, navigation, and action tools available in the sheet that appears when you choose Customize Toolbar from the Finder's View menu.

The `toolbar visible` property, introduced in Mac OS X 10.3 (Panther), has a value of `true` or `false` to indicate whether the toolbar is visible in the targeted Finder window. If the value is `true`, then the toolbar is visible. If the value is `false`, then the window is displayed without a toolbar.

As a read-write property, meaning its value can be accessed and edited, the value of the `toolbar visible` property can be changed to toggle the display of a Finder window's toolbar. Try Scripts 1.16 and 1.17, and see the results in Figures 1.12 and 1.13.

```
tell application "Finder" to ¬
    set toolbar visible of the front Finder window to false
```
SCRIPT 1.16

FIGURE 1.12 A Finder window without a toolbar.

```
tell application "Finder" to ¬
    set toolbar visible of the front Finder window to true
```
SCRIPT 1.17

FIGURE 1.13 A Finder window with a toolbar.

Property values that are either **true** or **false** are called Boolean values. You'll see this term used throughout this book.

The statusbar visible Property

Introduced in Mac OS X 10.4 (Tiger), the statusbar visible property determines whether the Finder displays a status bar. Like the toolbar visible
property, this property also has a value that is a Boolean, in other words,
true or false.

Alter the previous script to set the toolbar visible property to false, as shown
in Script 1.18.

```
tell application "Finder" to set toolbar visible of ¬
    Finder window 1 to false
```
SCRIPT 1.18

Now, write and execute Script 1.19.

```
tell application "Finder" to set statusbar visible of ¬
    Finder window 1 to true
```
SCRIPT 1.19

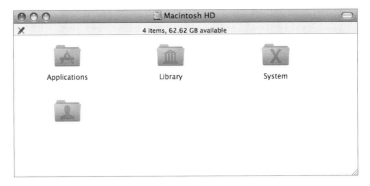

FIGURE 1.14 A Finder window without a toolbar but displaying a status
bar below the title bar.

As shown in Figure 1.14, the Finder window now displays a status bar beneath
the title bar. This status bar can only be made visible when the window's toolbar is not showing.

Return the window to normal by setting the value of the toolbar visible property back to true using Script 1.20.

```
tell application "Finder" to set toolbar visible of ¬
    Finder window 1 to true
```
SCRIPT 1.20

The sidebar width Property

Another new Finder window property introduced in Mac OS X 10.4 (Tiger) is the sidebar width property. The value of this property is an integer, indicating the width of the sidebar in pixels. Not only can you read it, but you can set it.

Try Script 1.21, which sets the sidebar width to 240 pixels, and see the result in Figure 1.15.

```
tell application "Finder" to set the sidebar width of ¬
    Finder window 1 to 240
```
SCRIPT 1.21

FIGURE 1.15 The sidebar width of the front Finder window has been set to 240 pixels.

Now, set the width of the sidebar in the second window using Script 1.22, and see the result in Figure 1.16.

```
tell application "Finder" to set the sidebar width of ¬
    the second Finder window to 240
```
SCRIPT 1.22

FIGURE 1.16 Both Finder windows have their sidebar width set to 240.

Now, set the sidebar width to the minimum value for both windows at the same time using Script 1.23, and see the result in Figure 1.17.

```
tell application "Finder" to set the sidebar width of ¬
    every Finder window to 0
```
SCRIPT 1.23

FIGURE 1.17 Both Finder windows have their sidebar width set to the minimum value.

NOTE ▶ In Mac OS X 10.4 (Tiger), the sidebar could be completely closed by setting the value of the sidebar width to 0. In Mac OS X 10.5 (Leopard), the sidebar has a minimum width of 135. Any value less than 135 is ignored and 135 is used instead.

You can even set the value of the sidebar width property of one window to match another window using a script like this:

```
tell application "Finder" to set the sidebar width of ¬
    Finder window 1 to the sidebar width of Finder window 2
```

The current view Property

The next Finder window property we'll examine is the current view property. You set the value of this property to display the contents of the Finder window in one of four enumerated views, icon view, list view, column view, and, in Leopard, flow view. Like the target and toolbar visible properties, you can both read and edit this property. Script 1.24 shows how to read it.

```
tell application "Finder" to ¬
    get the current view of the front Finder window
    --> returns icon view, list view, column view, or flow view
```
SCRIPT 1.24

Try these versions of Script 1.25, and watch as the front Finder window
changes its method of display. The last, flow view, is shown in Figure 1.18.

```
tell application "Finder" to ¬
    set the current view of the front Finder window to list view


tell application "Finder" to ¬
    set the current view of the front Finder window to column view


tell application "Finder" to ¬
    set the current view of the front Finder window to icon view


tell application "Finder" to ¬
    set the current view of the front Finder window to flow view
    -- flow view is new in Mac OS X v10.5 (Leopard)
```
SCRIPT 1.25

Window management is an issue that most of us deal with on a daily basis.
We're often moving, resizing, and adjusting windows to facilitate the access
and control of information. The current view property controls how the contents of Finder windows are displayed. The next two properties pertain to the
placement and sizing of Finder windows on the Desktop.

> **TIP** ▶ If you're the kind of person who likes all folders to open in the
> same view mode, here's a simple tell statement that changes the view
> display mode of every folder within a designated folder, such as your
> home directory:
>
> tell application "Finder" to set the current view of the window of
> every folder of home to icon view

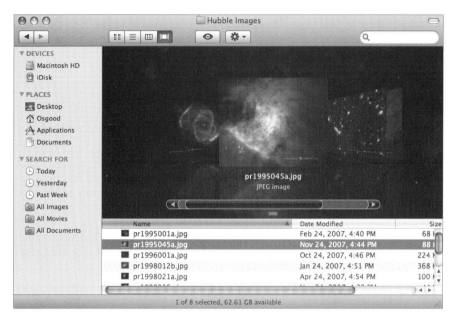

FIGURE 1.18 The flow view in Mac OS X 10.5 (Leopard)

The position Property

The value of the `position` property indicates where a Finder window is placed on the Desktop. Its value is displayed as a list of two numbers describing the position of the top-left corner of the Finder window in relation to the top-left corner of the Desktop display. The value of the `position` property can be both read and edited.

Delete the previous script from the script window, and then enter, compile, and run Script 1.26.

```
tell application "Finder" to ¬
    get the position of the front Finder window
--> returns a list of two numbers, similar to: {97, 364}
```
SCRIPT 1.26

The result of the script is a list of two numbers describing the window's position relative to the top-left point of the Desktop display.

In AppleScript, lists are enclosed in curly braces with each list item separated by a comma. Lists begin with the open brace character ({) and end with the close brace character (}). AppleScript lists can contain any kind of information, such as text, numbers, references, or any combination of data types.

In a position list, the first list item is a number describing the horizontal distance in pixels from the left side of the Desktop display. The second list item is a number describing the vertical distance in pixels from the top of the Desktop display. Together, these two numbers describe the specific point on the screen where the top left of the window begins.

Let's change the value of the position property of the front Finder window to move the window near the top left of the screen.

Delete the previous script from the script window, and then enter, compile, and run Script 1.27.

```
tell application "Finder" to ¬
    set the position of the front Finder window to {94, 134}
```
SCRIPT 1.27

The front Finder window has been moved so that its top-left corner is now 94 pixels from the left side of the Desktop and 134 pixels from the top of the Desktop.

To move the window toward the right side of the Desktop, increase the horizontal offset by adding to the first value in the position list, as shown in Script 1.28.

```
tell application "Finder" to ¬
    set the position of the front Finder window to {300, 134}
```
SCRIPT 1.28

To move the window toward the bottom of the Desktop, increase the vertical offset by adding to the second value in the position list, as shown in Script 1.29.

```
tell application "Finder" to ¬
    set the position of the front Finder window to {300, 240}
```
SCRIPT 1.29

Vertical Offset Exception

Unlike most other scriptable applications that use the distance from the top of the screen to the top of a window to determine its vertical position, the Finder uses the distance from the top of the screen to just below the title bar of the window, thus adding the height of the title bar, an extra 22 pixels, to the measurement. This applies whether the Finder window is displaying its toolbar or not. This exception applies only to the Finder application.

In Figure 1.19, the vertical offset of both Finder windows is 44, which consists of 22 pixels for the height of the Desktop's menu bar plus 22 pixels for the height of the Finder window's title bar, for a total vertical offset of 44 pixels. As shown, the tops of the two windows are located in the same position vertically, immediately below the bottom of the menu bar.

FIGURE 1.19 The vertical offset of a Finder window must include the height of its title bar, which is 22 pixels.

The bounds Property

If you find yourself always resizing windows, you will probably write many scripts using the `bounds` property.

The value of the `bounds` property describes both the size and the position of the target window. This is accomplished by specifying two points: the top-left point of the window and the bottom-right point of the window. These two coordinates, combined into a four-item list, are used to outline the rectangular shape of the window.

Like the `position` property, the value of the `bounds` property can be read and edited. First, let's get the bounds of the frontmost window using Script 1.30.

```
tell application "Finder" to get the bounds of the front window
--> returns something like: {72, 90, 512, 481}
```
SCRIPT 1.30

The value of the `bounds` property is returned as a four-item list of integers representing the area of the window like this:

▶ List item 1: the distance in pixels from the left side of the screen to the left side of the Finder window

▶ List item 2: the distance in pixels from the top of the screen to the top of the Finder window

▶ List item 3: the distance in pixels from the left side of the screen to the right side of the Finder window

▶ List item 4: the distance in pixels from the top of the screen to the bottom of the Finder window

By changing the value of the `bounds` property, you can resize and reposition a Finder window anywhere on the Desktop. For example, Script 1.31 places the front Finder window near the top left of the Desktop and resizes it to 500 pixels in width and 300 pixels in height. Again, the verb `set` is used to change the value of the property.

```
tell application "Finder" to ¬
    set the bounds of the front window to {24, 96, 524, 396}
```
SCRIPT 1.31

The Finder window is now repositioned to the top left of the Desktop and resized.

By the way, if you want to know the size of the current computer display, access the value of the **bounds** property for the Desktop window as shown in Script 1.32. It returns the bounds of the entire Desktop, even if you have more than one monitor.

```
tell application "Finder" to ¬
    get the bounds of the window of the desktop
    --> returns something like {0, 0, 1440, 900} or {-1280, 0, 1680, 1050}
```
SCRIPT 1.32

Verbs Used with Windows

In addition to properties, Finder windows respond to a specific set of verbs or commands. Some of these have been incorporated into our previous scripts:

▶ get: used to access the current values of a window property

▶ set: used to apply a new value to a window property

▶ open: causes a window to display in the Finder

▶ close: causes a window to close

With these commands we've been able to manipulate the size, position, and display of Finder windows. Now we'll add another command for controlling windows to our vocabulary, select.

Although the select verb can be applied to other scriptable objects, it can be used to make a window active so that it moves in front of any other open windows:

select: causes a window to come to the front

Delete the previous script from the script window, and then enter, compile, and run Script 1.33.

```
tell application "Finder" to select the last Finder window
```
SCRIPT 1.33

The Finder window that was behind the front Finder window now moves to the front of the open windows.

The Desktop Setup Script

Using all the properties and verbs we've covered so far, you now have the tools to create a script you can use to quickly return a cluttered Desktop to a default window configuration. Follow these steps for preparing the script.

First, set up the Desktop to what you want to be the finished state. For the purposes of this tutorial, follow the example shown in Figure 1.20.

Close all the open Finder windows on your Desktop. Open two Finder windows and arrange them as shown in the following illustration. Note that the window on the left is displaying its toolbar, while the window on the right is not. Don't worry about setting the target folders in each window; just set the shape and position of the two windows. Leave the window on the left selected as the frontmost window.

> **NOTE** ▸ The display mode for the Documents folder in the Desktop Setup script example uses the new flow view introduced in Mac OS X 10.5 (Leopard). If you are currently using an earlier version, substitute `list view` for `flow view`.

FIGURE 1.20 An example window arrangement for the Desktop Setup script.

Next, use both versions of Script 1.34 to extract the **bounds** of both windows, and write them down for later use in the Desktop Setup Script.

```
tell application "Finder" to get the bounds of Finder window 1
    --> returns something like: {36, 116, 511, 674}


tell application "Finder" to get the bounds of Finder window 2
    --> returns something like: {528, 116, 1016, 674}
```

SCRIPT 1.34

The tell Block

To set the Desktop window display to the arrangement you have set up, the
script performs a series of 12 commands that open and manipulate the two
windows, as shown in Script 1.35.

```
tell application "Finder" to close every window
tell application "Finder" to open home
tell application "Finder" to ¬
    set toolbar visible of the front Finder window to true
tell application "Finder" to ¬
    set the sidebar width of the front Finder window to 135
tell application "Finder" to ¬
    set the current view of the front Finder window to column view
tell application "Finder" to ¬
    set the bounds of the front Finder window to {36, 116, 511, 674}
tell application "Finder" to open folder "Documents" of home
tell application "Finder" to ¬
    set toolbar visible of the front Finder window to false
tell application "Finder" to ¬
    set statusbar visible of the front Finder window to true
tell application "Finder" to set the current view ¬
    of the front Finder window to flow view
tell application "Finder" to set the bounds ¬
    of the front Finder window to {528, 116, 1016, 674}
tell application "Finder" to select the last finder window
```

SCRIPT 1.35

Don't bother entering this script in Script Editor. As you see, it is rather long,
is very dense, and would take some effort to type into Script Editor. There's an
easier way to compose your scripts.

Notice that the script is a series of tell statements targeting the same application, namely, the Finder.

Instead of writing a group of 12 `tell` statements, each beginning with `tell application "Finder" to`, we'll shorten the time it takes to write the script and make it easier to read by enclosing the commands within a single `tell` block.

A `tell` block is used to target multiple actions at a single scriptable object, in this case the Finder application, which makes scripts easier to understand. You'll always want to use a `tell` block in your scripts when addressing more than one action at one scriptable object.

A `tell` block begins with the verb `tell` followed by a reference to a target object. The various actions to be performed by or to that object are then listed, each on its own line. After all the actions have been entered, the `tell` block ends with the closing statement **end** `tell`. All actions inside the `tell` block target the object referenced in the first line of the `tell` block.

Enter, compile, and run the following script as shown, except you may optionally substitute the **bounds** values you previously wrote down, as shown in Script 1.36.

```
tell application "Finder"
    close every window
    open home
    set toolbar visible of the front Finder window to true
    set the sidebar width of the front Finder window to 135
    set the current view of the front Finder window to column view
    set the bounds of the front Finder window to {36, 116, 511, 674}
    open folder "Documents" of home
    set toolbar visible of the front Finder window to false
    set the current view of the front Finder window to flow view
    set the bounds of front Finder window to {528, 116, 1016, 674}
    select the last finder window
end tell
```

SCRIPT 1.36

You should now see two Finder windows placed side by side on the Desktop, one in column view, the other in flow view, with your home directory the active window and your Documents folder displayed in the other window. Instant Desktop organization!

We'll do more with this script in a moment, but first let's return to the subject of `tell` blocks. A `tell` block is much cleaner, more concise, and easier to read than a series of separate `tell` statements. Compare Script 1.36 to the same script written as a series of `tell` statements, Script 1.35.

It is not only easier to write the script using a `tell` block, but you can clearly see the relationship between scriptable objects and the commands that target them, because of the indentations automatically placed in the script text by Script Editor when you compile the script. It's very easy to see where a section of a script targeting a specific object begins (`tell`) and ends (`end tell`).

In summary, `tell` blocks are easy to use if you remember these simple rules:

▶   If you begin a `tell` block, you must end a `tell` block.

▶   Commands within a `tell` block target the object addressed in the `tell` block's opening statement.

Nested tell Blocks

`tell` blocks can contain other `tell` blocks that target scriptable elements or objects belonging to the scriptable element or object targeted in the outermost `tell` block. For example, Script 1.36 can be rewritten so that the actions targeting the front window are enclosed within their own `tell` blocks within the outer Finder `tell`, as shown in Script 1.37.

```
tell application "Finder"
    close every window
    open home
    tell the front Finder window
        set toolbar visible to true
        set the sidebar width to 135
        set the current view to column view
```

```
        set the bounds to {36, 116, 511, 674}
    end tell
    open folder "Documents" of home
    tell the front Finder window
        set toolbar visible to false
        set the current view to flow view
        set the bounds to {528, 116, 1016, 674}
    end tell
    select the last finder window
end tell
```

SCRIPT 1.37

The technique of placing `tell` blocks within other `tell` blocks is referred to
as nesting tell blocks and is found quite often in scripts. And, since scripts are
read from top to bottom and from left to right, the use of `tell` blocks makes it
very easy to quickly see how a script is designed.

For example, Script 1.37 starts with two commands to the Finder followed by
four commands to the front Finder window followed by a single command to
the Finder followed by four commands to the front Finder window again and
then finishes with a single command to the Finder.

Since you'll often edit your scripts later (perhaps a long time later), it's important to write your scripts in a manner that is easy to understand and review.
Using `tell` blocks and nested `tell` blocks in your scripts enables you to write
scripts that are readable and that make sense to yourself and others.

If you entered Script 1.36, edit it now to match the version with the nested
`tell` blocks, Script 1.37. Be sure to remove the possessive phrase `of the front
Finder window` when you create the nested `tell` blocks. The function played
by that phrase in defining the containment hierarchy of the `front Finder
window` object is now played by the nested `tell` statement, `tell the front
Finder window`.

Notice there are two nested `tell` blocks addressing the front Finder window
in the Desktop Setup script. Why? Shouldn't the second nested `tell` block be
addressing the second Finder window?

No, when the second Finder window is opened, it automatically becomes the
frontmost Finder window in the stack of open Finder windows. Therefore, it is
now the front Finder window and can be targeted in the same manner as the
previous window.

> **TIP** ► As you continue to develop your scripting prowess, you'll probably
> start writing scripts for others to use. One of the challenges in writing
> scripts that work on a variety of computers is that applications may have
> been renamed by users. In those situations, the `tell` blocks in uncompiled
> scripts would have to be revised to use the new application names.
>
> In Mac OS X 10.5 (Leopard), AppleScript has made this unnecessary
> by adding the ability to refer to applications by means other than their
> names. You can now use an application's `id` (its bundle identifier or its
> creator code) instead of its `name` as a generic way to address an application
> regardless of what a particular user has named it or which language the
> operating system is set to.
>
> For example, this script addressing the Finder:
>
> ```
> tell application "Finder" to open the startup disk
> ```
>
> could be made generic by addressing the Finder by its bundle identifier:
>
> ```
> tell application id "com.apple.finder" to open startup disk
> ```
>
> To get an application's `id` in Leopard, write a script statement that asks for
> the value of the application's `id` property:
>
> ```
> get id of application "Finder"
> --> returns: "com.apple.finder"
> ```
>
> This topic and the other new features of the intrinsic application object in
> Leopard are covered in detail in Chapter 6, Information Tools.

Saving the Desktop Setup Script

Now back to our script. Since this script is a useful mechanism for resetting the Desktop display, let's save the script as a script application, or applet, and install it in the Finder toolbar for easy accessibility from within any open Finder window.

Choose Save from Script Editor's File menu. In the sheet, navigate to the Library folder in your home directory. Click the New Folder button, and create a new folder in the Library folder named Toolbar Scripts.

Next, save the script as a self-running application named Setup by choosing Application from the File Format pop-up menu in the sheet. Do not select any of the Options check boxes at the bottom of the sheet. Click the Save button, and the new applet is saved in the newly created folder in the Library folder in your home directory.

FIGURE 1.21 The Script Editor Save sheet.

Open the Toolbar Scripts folder you just created. Drag the Setup script applet icon to the Finder window toolbar, and release the mouse once the cursor changes to include a plus sign (+).

FIGURE 1.22 Add items to a Finder window's toolbar by dragging them onto the toolbar.

FIGURE 1.23 A script application in the Finder toolbar.

The script is now available from within any open Finder window. Anytime you want to return your Desktop to your default setup, just click the script icon in the toolbar!

Be sure to customize the properties of the Setup script to your preferences for open windows, view methods, and window sizes and positions.

Chapter Summary

Congratulations, you've finished your initial foray into the world of AppleScript. You've learned what AppleScript is, how it works, and how to script the Finder application to control the display of Finder windows.

In addition to creating a useful script tool, you've learned these important AppleScript concepts:

- On the computer, everything is an object.

- On the computer, everything belongs to, is related to, is contained in, or is part of something else. For example, the Finder application contains windows and folders.

- Scriptable objects are referred to by their positions in their object hierarchy or where they are in their "chain of command." For example:

    ```
    file "cars.pdf" of folder "Documents" of folder "sal" of ¬
        folder "Users" of startup disk
    ```

- Scriptable objects have properties with values that can be read and sometimes manipulated. For example, a Finder window has `name`, `position`, and `bounds` properties.

- The AppleScript verb get is used to retrieve the value of a property, as in `get the name of the front window`.

- The AppleScript verb set is used to alter the value of editable properties, as in `set the position of the front window to {0, 44}`.

- Scripts are written using single-line `tell` statements or multiple-line `tell` blocks that target one or more actions at a scriptable object.

- Textual content used in a script is placed within straight quotation marks ("").

- Lists in AppleScript begin with the opening brace character ({), contain items separated by commas, and end with a closing brace character (}).

Finder Window Properties

For reference, the following is a summary of the Finder window properties and commands used to create the Desktop Setup script. Review these items, keeping in mind that the principles you've learned here apply to all scriptable applications, not just the Finder.

Read-Only Properties

Read-only properties are properties whose corresponding values can be accessed or read only; they cannot be changed.

name: the text displayed in the title bar of the window

```
tell application "Finder" to get the name of the front window
```

Editable Properties

Editable properties are properties whose corresponding values can be both read and changed.

index: an integer (number) indicating the position of the window in the stack of open windows

```
tell application "Finder" to ¬
    get the index of the front window
```

bounds: a list of coordinates defining the top-left and bottom-right corners of a window

```
tell application "Finder" to ¬
    set the bounds of Finder window 1 to {0, 44, 400, 300}
```

collapsed: a true or false value indicating whether the window has been minimized to the Dock

```
tell application "Finder" to ¬
    set collapsed of every window to false
```

current view: the method currently used to display content in the window. Values for this property are one of the following: icon view, list view, column view, and, in Leopard, flow view

```
tell application "Finder" to ¬
    set the current view of Finder window 1 to icon view
```

position: a list of coordinates indicating the horizontal and vertical offset of the window from the left and top sides of the screen

```
tell application "Finder" to ¬
    set the position of the front Finder window to {0, 22}
```

target: a reference to the folder or directory whose contents are displayed in the window

```
tell application "Finder" to ¬
    set the target of the front Finder window to home
```

toolbar visible: (Mac OS X 10.3) a true or false value that indicates whether the Finder window displays a toolbar

```
tell application "Finder" to ¬
    set toolbar visible of the front Finder window to false
```

statusbar visible: (Mac OS X 10.4) a true or false value that indicates whether the Finder window displays a status bar. This works only when the toolbar is not visible.

```
tell application "Finder" to ¬
    set statusbar visible of the front Finder window to false
```

sidebar width: (Mac OS X 10.4) an integer value that indicates the width of the Finder window's sidebar in pixels. To close the sidebar in Mac OS X 10.4 (Tiger) without hiding the toolbar or the status bar, assign this property a value of 0. In Leopard, setting the sidebar width property to 0 reduces it to a width of 135 pixels.

```
tell application "Finder" to ¬
    set the sidebar width of the front Finder window to 0
```

`zoomed`: a `true` or `false` value that indicates whether the window has been expanded

```
tell application "Finder" to ¬
    set zoomed of the front Finder window to true
```

Referring to a Finder Window

Finder windows, and other scriptable objects as well, can be referenced in a variety of ways:

By name:

```
Finder window "Documents"
```

By index:

```
Finder window 1
Finder window 23
```

By descriptive index:

```
the first Finder window
the second Finder window
the fifth Finder window
the 1st Finder window
the 23rd Finder window
```

By position relative to other windows:

```
the front Finder window
the middle Finder window
the back Finder window
the last Finder window
the Finder window before the last Finder window
the Finder window after the first Finder window
```

Randomly:

```
some Finder window
```

Verbs Used with Finder Windows

AppleScript verbs are the commands targeted at scriptable objects to retrieve or manipulate property values and to perform actions with the scriptable objects.

Accessing the Values of a Window's Property

get: used to access the current values of a window property

```
tell application "Finder" to ¬
    get the target of the front Finder window
```

Changing the Values of a Window's Property

set: used to apply a new value to a window property

```
tell application "Finder" to ¬
    set the target of the front Finder window to home
```

Controlling Windows

open: causes a window to become visible in the Finder

```
tell application "Finder" to ¬
    open the Finder window of the startup disk
```

```
tell application "Finder" to open the startup disk
```
close: causes a window to close

```
tell application "Finder" to close every Finder window
```
select: causes a window to come to the front

```
tell application "Finder" to select the last Finder window
```

The tell Statement

A `tell` statement is a single AppleScript statement, beginning with the verb `tell`, that contains a reference to the target object and the action to be performed:

```
tell application "Finder" to ¬
    set the target of the last Finder window to home
```

The target object in this example is the last Finder window displayed on the Desktop. The action to be performed is to change the contents of the window by altering the value of the window's `target` property to be the user's home directory.

The tell Block

Use `tell` blocks replace multiple `tell` statements and target multiple actions at a scriptable object or objects. All `tell` blocks begin with the verb `tell` followed by a reference to a target object or parent application. Statements defining the actions to be performed are placed after the opening line, with each statement getting its own line. The `tell` block is closed with the statement `end tell`.

```
tell application "Finder"
    set the target of the front Finder window to home
    set the current view of the front Finder window to icon
    set the position of the front Finder window to {0, 22}
end tell
```

`tell` blocks within other `tell` blocks are called nested `tell` blocks. When compiled, the hierarchy of the scriptable objects is revealed by the indentation applied to the formatted script text.

```
tell application "Finder"
    tell the front Finder window
        set the target to home
        set the current view to icon
        set the position to {0, 22}
    end tell
end tell
```

The Principles Remain the Same

In this chapter, you've been introduced to the fundamental principles and structures of the AppleScript language. These principles include the following essential concepts:

▶ Scriptable objects have properties with corresponding values.

▶ Scriptable objects can also contain other scriptable objects that also have properties with corresponding values.

▶ The values of the properties of scriptable objects can be read and sometimes altered.

In learning to apply these principles, you wrote scripts to control the appearance of Finder windows in the Finder application by accessing and changing the values of their properties and by using standard verbs, such as `close` and `open`, to control their display. As stated earlier in this chapter, the principles used in those scripts apply to all scriptable applications, not just the Finder application.

Let's see whether that statement is indeed true.

In a new Finder window, navigate to your Applications folder, and launch the Safari application. After it has finished starting up, enter, compile, and run Script 1.38 in a new script window in Script Editor.

```
tell application "Safari" to close every window
```
SCRIPT 1.38

Any open browser windows in the Safari application are immediately closed. As with the scripts you used with the Finder, note that this script is a `tell` statement containing the necessary two elements: a reference to the targeted objects (in this case the open browser windows) and the action to be performed (`close`).

Next, open a Web page with Script 1.39 (assuming your computer is connected to the Internet).

```
tell application "Safari" to open location "http://automator.us"
```
SCRIPT 1.39

A new browser window containing the specified Web site is displayed. Let's see whether we can use the properties of the browser window to control where the window appears on the screen. Enter and run Script 1.40 to get the position coordinates of the new window.

```
tell application "Safari" to get the position of the front window
```
SCRIPT 1.40

Instead of getting a list of the horizontal and vertical offsets of the window, the Script Editor selects the word `position` and displays the error message shown in Figure 1.24.

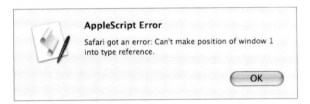

FIGURE 1.24 An error dialog displayed as a sheet attached to a script window in Script Editor.

The error message states (in a slightly convoluted way) that a script can't refer to the position of a window in Safari. This is because, like many Mac OS X applications, Safari does not support the use of the `position` property for windows in the same manner as the Finder does. Instead, try using the `bounds` property to get the coordinates of the browser window. Enter and run Script 1.41.

```
tell application "Safari" to get the bounds of window 1
--> returns something like: {184, 36, 924, 857}
```
SCRIPT 1.41

Most scriptable Mac OS X applications support the `bounds` property for getting and setting window dimensions. You can use it to change the position and shape of the browser window. Try Script 1.42.

```
tell application "Safari" to ¬
    set the bounds of the front window to {0, 22, 800, 1024}
```
SCRIPT 1.42

The Safari browser window is now sized and positioned to fit in the left section of the computer screen. Note that if you provide a vertical coordinate that is larger than the screen is tall, Safari automatically adjusts the vertical display of a browser window so that it doesn't go below the Dock or the bottom of the screen. Very convenient.

So as you've now seen, you can use AppleScript to close, open, and resize Safari windows. And the point is?

▶   The principles you learned scripting Finder windows apply to other scriptable applications and objects as well.

Just as the Finder application has scriptable window elements, so does the Safari application. And as with Finder windows, windows in Safari have properties that have corresponding values that can be read and sometimes changed. A browser window has a `bounds` property, just like a Finder window, whose value is a list of four numbers describing the location of its top-left corner and bottom-right corner on the screen.

TIP ▶ If you've ever wanted to be able to make your browser window fill your computer's display, here's a script that uses the result of a `tell` statement that gets the bounds of the Finder Desktop to resize the frontmost Safari window to fill the screen:

```
tell application "Finder" to ¬
    get the bounds of the window of the desktop
tell application "Safari" to ¬
    set the bounds of the front window to ¬
        {0, 22, (3rd item of the result), (4th item of the result)}
```

You'll learn more about how to pass information between script statements in Chapter 8, Data Containers, Operators, and Coercions.

Principles Remain Constant?

Let's continue validating the universal nature of AppleScript principles. Navigate to the Applications folder, and open the QuickTime Player application.

Next, open a movie file by choosing Open Movie in New Player from the File menu and locating a movie file on your computer. Any standard QuickTime movie will do.

Like the Finder application, QuickTime Player contains other scriptable elements besides windows, one of which is the movie object. As with the scripts you wrote to query Finder windows, you can use the get verb to access the values of the properties of the scriptable objects or elements of QuickTime Player.

> NOTE ▶ The terms object and element are used interchangeably in describing scriptable items that belong to other scriptable items, such as Finder windows belonging to the Finder application or movie windows belonging to the QuickTime Player application.

Try Script 1.43.

```
tell application "QuickTime Player" to get name of the front movie
--> returns: "New iMac Ad" (or the name of the movie you opened)
```
SCRIPT 1.43

> NOTE ▶ In QuickTime 7.2 the term movie was replaced by the term document, and any scripts written using movie will be changed when they are compiled. They will run the same, but the term document will appear instead of movie. For compatibility with Tiger, the term movie is used in these example scripts.

The result of the script is the value of the name property of a movie.
Try Script 1.44.

```
tell application "QuickTime Player" to ¬
    get the duration of the front movie
--> returns: 17998 (the number of frames comprising the movie)
```
SCRIPT 1.44

The result of the script is the value of the duration property of a movie expressed as a number indicating the number of frames in the movie.

As with other scriptable applications, you can use the set verb to change the value of the property of an object. Script 1.45 changes the value of the current `time` property of a movie to move the playback cursor to a specified point in the movie.

```
tell application "QuickTime Player" to ¬
    set the current time of the front movie to 1500
```
SCRIPT 1.45

QuickTime Player also responds to other commands as well.

Try Script 1.46.

```
tell application "QuickTime Player" to play the front movie
```
SCRIPT 1.46

And try Script 1.47.

```
tell application "QuickTime Player" to stop the front movie
```
SCRIPT 1.47

The AppleScript principles that work with the Finder application work for the QuickTime Player application as well. Let's try applying them to one more application.

Quit QuickTime Player without saving any changes, and open the iTunes application.

Like the other scriptable applications, iTunes contains scriptable elements or objects that contain other scriptable elements. If you are familiar with iTunes, you know the application has playlists, which are collections of tracks or songs. The master playlist for the application, containing all tracks, is the Library playlist.

Here's the basic object hierarchy for the iTunes application:

`iTunes Application > playlist > track`

In other words, tracks are contained in playlists that are contained in the iTunes application.

As with the Finder and QuickTime Player applications, each one of the scriptable elements of iTunes has properties with corresponding values. Let's try accessing some of the properties of the **track** object with the **tell** statement shown in Script 1.48.

```
tell application "iTunes" to ¬
    get the name of the last track of the first library playlist
--> returns: "Ave Maria" (whatever you have in your iTunes database)
```
SCRIPT 1.48

Remember, a **tell** statement has two components: a reference to the target object and the action to be performed. In this example, the target object is the **last track of the first library playlist**, and the action to be performed is to get the value of its **name** property.

Now extract the value of other track properties using Script 1.49.

```
tell application "iTunes"
    tell the first library playlist
        get the duration of the last track
        --> returns: 281 (the length of the track in seconds)
    end tell
end tell


tell application "iTunes"
    tell the first library playlist
        get the artist of the last track
        --> returns: "Aaron Neville"
    end tell
end tell
```
SCRIPT 1.49

As these examples demonstrate, playlists contain tracks that have properties, such as **name**, **duration**, **artist**, **album**, and so on.

The iTunes application, like the Finder and QuickTime Player, responds to commands to perform actions with its scriptable objects. See, for example, Script 1.50.

```
tell application "iTunes" to ¬
    play the last track of the first library playlist
```
SCRIPT 1.50

In this example, the verb `play` is used to initiate the playing of the `track` referenced as its target. To stop the iTunes application, use the `stop` verb. It doesn't require a reference to a particular track because only one track can play at a time in iTunes.

```
tell application "iTunes" to stop
```
SCRIPT 1.51

What's Next?

Congratulations on completing your introduction to the world of AppleScript. As you've seen, it's an easy but powerful way to control the actions of applications.

If you've understood the concepts presented in this chapter, you're well on your way to becoming a powerful scripter, because the lessons presented here will be used to create even more interesting and useful automation tools.

In the next chapter, you'll discover how to access all of the scriptable objects, properties, and commands of any scriptable application by reading its terminology dictionary. See you there!

2

Dictionaries

"The greatest lesson I learned in school was how to teach myself."

Too often we confuse learning with the memorization and recall of facts and figures, instead of the mastery of how something is done and how to do it for ourselves. It's a concept succinctly captured in the old Chinese proverb "Give a man a fish and he will eat for a day. Teach him how to fish and he will eat for a lifetime."

Maybe that's why so many scripters are musicians. With music, you learn the basic rules and techniques (harmony and scales) and then apply them to make something magical happen. In the world of AppleScript, you learn the fundamental principles of writing scripts and then apply them to various situations to make magical things happen on your computer. Ah, the Zen of AppleScript—the emphasis on practice and experiential wisdom. LOL!

Speaking of wisdom, in the first chapter you learned some of the basic tenets of AppleScript:

▶ On the computer, everything is an object.

▶ On the computer, everything belongs to, is related to, is contained in, or is part of something else.

▶ Scriptable objects are referred to by their positions in their object hierarchy or where they are in their "chain of command."

▶ Scriptable objects have properties with values that can be read and sometimes manipulated.

Using verbs such as `get`, `set`, `open`, `close`, and `select`, with properties such as `name` and `bounds`, you wrote useful scripts that controlled Finder windows and then applied those commands to other applications as well.

However, up to this point, the various terms used in your scripts, such as property names and commands, have been given to you. Now comes the time to learn where to find them for yourself. Let's go fishing.

Noah Webster Knew What He Was Doing

Whether you're writing a book, a blog entry, a letter to the editor, or even a missive to your mother, there's usually one place to look to find a word or phrase that encapsulates what you want to say—a dictionary. It's the master reference book for languages.

Well, the same situation applies to AppleScript. Every scriptable application carries within its bundle its own dictionary describing every term, every verb, and every property that can be used to write AppleScript scripts to query and control the application. And most conveniently, an application's internal scripting dictionary can be opened and perused using the same program you use to write scripts, the Script Editor.

In the File menu in Script Editor, choose the Open Dictionary menu item or use its keyboard shortcut Command+Shift+O. A special dialog appears listing all the scriptable applications and scripting additions installed on your computer, shown in Figure 2.1.

FIGURE 2.1 The Open Dictionary dialog.

Most of the items listed in the Open Dictionary dialog are applications; however, some are special plug-ins called scripting additions that add commands and abilities to the core set of AppleScript tools. Although applications have a name extension of "app," Scripting Additions have a name extension of "osax," which stands for Open Scripting Architecture Extension. We will examine their use later in this chapter.

Note that the Open Dictionary dialog also contains a Browse button. If the application you want to script is not listed in the Open Dictionary dialog, you can open its dictionary by clicking this button and locating the application on your system. Unfortunately, not all applications are scriptable. Many are, but some are not, even some belonging to Apple! If an application appears in the browsing dialog but is not selectable, it is not scriptable.

> **TIP** ▶ A quick way to open an application's scripting dictionary is to drag its icon onto the Script Editor application. If the application is scriptable, its dictionary will open; otherwise, you'll be presented with a dialog informing you that the application is not scriptable.

Let's explore the wonders of the scripting dictionary using an application you're somewhat familiar with already—the Finder. Select it in the list of items in the Open Dictionary dialog, and click the OK button to display the Finder's scripting dictionary in a new Dictionary Viewer window.

FIGURE 2.2 The default Dictionary Viewer window displaying the Finder's dictionary.

The first thing to notice about the Dictionary Viewer window shown in Figure 2.2 is the green button at the top left of the window's title bar. It's the third button from the left for those whose monitors are set to grayscale. Clicking this button expands the dictionary window to fill your screen. Do that! Don't rely on scrolling in a small window area. It's important you have room to view all the elements of a dictionary so you can get the big picture. Don't be afraid to move the dividers and expand the window partitions as you proceed through this chapter. Go crazy—you can't break the window!

By default, the Dictionary Viewer window is divided into three horizontal segments: the toolbar across the top of the window, a three-column browser pane in the center of the window, and the dictionary pane occupying the bottom section of the window.

The browser pane displays information grouped in one of three possible arrangements, determined by the button selected in the three-segment view control in the toolbar. Dictionary entries can be browsed by suites (the default), by containment, or by inheritance. We'll examine these methods as we proceed, but for now, leave the view control set to suites (the first button).

In the leftmost column of the browser view, select the Window classes suite. The various objects contained in the suite, in this case the several kinds of windows used by the Finder, are now listed in the adjacent column, as shown in Figure 2.3.

FIGURE 2.3 The Dictionary Viewer window displaying the items contained in the selected Window classes suite.

> **NOTE** ▶ The term classes is often used to refer to scriptable objects in the abstract. It comes from the world of programming where a specific type of object is thought of as an instance of a class. If you see the term class, just think of it as referring to a specific type of scriptable object, like a track in a movie, a box on a page, or even a window in the Finder.

As a visual aid to help you easily identify items in the dictionary, a small square icon containing a letter is placed to the left of each item. A browser item that is a suite (meaning a group of related terms) is preceded by a yellow box containing the letter S for suite. A browser item that is a class (meaning a type of scriptable object) is preceded by a purple box containing the letter C for class. And as you'll shortly see, item properties are preceded by a purple box containing the letter P for property.

The Window classes suite in the Finder dictionary contains the various kinds of scriptable windows used by the Finder application. There's a generic `window`, a `Finder window`, the `desktop window`, an `information window`, a `preferences window`, and a `clipping window`.

Note that the `Finder window` class has a small right-pointing arrow next to it in the list. This arrow indicates that selecting this list item will reveal more information. Select the `Finder window` class in the middle browser column, and you'll see that its related properties are listed in the adjacent column to the right, as shown in Figure 2.4.

Note that the dictionary pane at the bottom of the window now shows the dictionary entry for the `Finder window` class, beginning with a single-line definition of a `Finder window`, followed by a list of definitions for each of its properties.

The `Finder window` class definition begins with the name of the class followed by the letter n indicating that the term is used as a noun. This means it is a scriptable object that can be the target of various script operations.

```
Finder window n [inh. window] : every Finder window
```

The next part of the entry—enclosed in brackets and beginning with the abbreviation `inh.`—indicates that the `Finder window` class inherits some properties from the `window` class. We'll talk more about that in a moment.

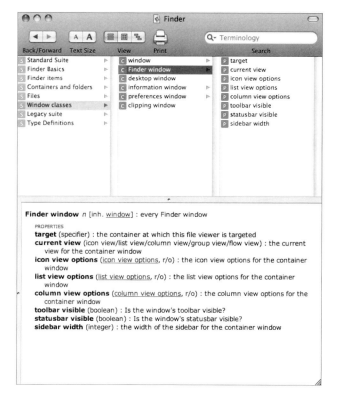

FIGURE 2.4 The Finder window class is selected to display its properties.

The last part of the class definition follows a colon character and is a description of the object being defined. In this case the description is "every Finder window." What? That's not very helpful. A better description would be "a window in the Finder displaying the contents of a container, such as a disk or folder. The title of a Finder window is the name of the container whose contents are displayed within the window."

That's a much more informative description; too bad it's not the one used in the dictionary. That brings up a point: you'll find that dictionaries, like the applications they are part of, vary in their quality and usefulness. Some are very sparse, while others are verbose. Usually, the more you know about the application you're scripting, the easier it can be to understand its dictionary.

TIP ▶ This chapter examines scripting dictionaries using the Script Editor application included in the default installation of Mac OS X. Although the Script Editor is a good basic editor for accessing dictionaries and creating and editing scripts, some excellent third-party editors provide much more detail and visual tools for parsing dictionaries. One of these is Script Debugger from Late Night Software at `http://www.latenightsw.com`. For those of you who want to take your scripting prowess to the next level, we strongly recommend trying this excellent scripting and debugging tool.

Property Definitions

Let's examine how properties are defined in a scripting dictionary. Click the `toolbar visible` property in the third column of the dictionary's browser pane, and its property definition is highlighted in the dictionary pane, as shown in Figure 2.5.

The format of a property definition is similar to that of a class definition. It begins with the name of the property being defined, followed by a type descriptor enclosed in parentheses, a colon, and the description of the defined property.

```
toolbar visible (boolean) : Is the window's toolbar visible?
```

A type descriptor indicates the type of data used for the property's value. Some common types are integers (whole numbers), real numbers (numbers with decimal fractions), strings (text), object specifiers (references to scriptable objects), and enumerations (lists of possible values).

For the `toolbar visible` property, its type descriptor is `boolean`, meaning the property has a logical value that is expressed as either `true` or `false`. So, an example script changing the value of this property would look like this:

```
set toolbar visible of the front Finder window to false
```

The property below the `toolbar visible` property in the definition display, `statusbar visible`, also has a value expressed as `boolean` and could be changed using a script statement like this:

```
set statusbar visible of the front Finder window to true
```

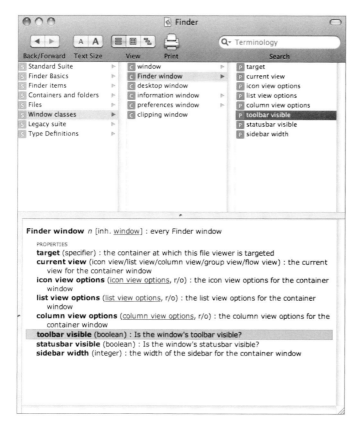

FIGURE 2.5 The toolbar visible property is selected.

The last property in the list, `sidebar width`, has a value that is expressed as an `integer` (a whole number). So, you could set the width of a Finder window's sidebar using a script statement containing an integer, like this:

```
set the sidebar width of the front Finder window to 160
```

Now take a look at the first property in the list of properties for the Finder window, `target`. It has a value that is expressed as a `specifier`. This term is an abbreviation for object specifier, which is a reference to a scriptable object, like the Finder references you used in the previous chapter:

```
folder "Auto Photos" of folder "Pictures" of home
```

The value of the `target` property of a Finder window is a reference to the folder whose contents are displayed in the window. So, a script statement to change the `target` of a Finder window would look like this:

```
set the target of front Finder window to folder "Documents" of home
```

When you see specifier in the dictionary, just think object reference or object specifier. Remember one of the tenets of AppleScript:

▸   Scriptable objects are referred to by their locations in their object hierarchy or where they are in their "chain of command."

The second property in the property list for Finder windows, `current view`, has as its type descriptor a list of terms that can be used as its value. The items in the list are called enumerations and are the only accepted options for the value of the property. So, an example script setting the value of the `current view` property would use one of these enumerations, like this:

```
set the current view of the front Finder window to flow view
```

or perhaps this:

```
set the current view of the front Finder window to icon view
```

We'll examine the three remaining Finder window properties in a moment, but have you noticed that some of the Finder window properties you used in the first chapter are missing from the list of properties in the definition display area? Where are the `name`, `bounds`, and `index` properties you used, and why aren't they listed?

You Got That from Your Mother

In the "real world," it's not unusual to find objects that are similar in function but are not quite the same. Motor vehicles are a good example. Although a Volkswagen Beetle and a Toyota Tundra are both motor vehicles that can be used to transport you from location A to location B, they are drastically different in their design and purpose. One is used to carry passengers, and the other is used to carry cargo. One is a car, and the other is a truck.

However, even though they have differences in functionality, the two motor vehicles share some common features, such as their turning radius, horse-power, and miles per gallon—properties common to all motor vehicles.

But since the two vehicles are designed to perform different tasks, they have some properties that are particular to their class of motor vehicle. For example, trucks have properties that cars don't, like bed size (a bed is the part of the truck used for hauling), payload, and towing torque coefficient. When we talk about cars, we don't ask about their bed size; instead, we ask about the size of the passenger compartment.

Think of motor vehicles as being a type or class of object, possessing a fundamental set of properties defining what it is and how it works. In this scenario, you can correctly make the observation that both cars and trucks have properties in common—properties they inherit as motor vehicles.

Cars and trucks are motor vehicles, but they can be further defined or categorized as subclasses, based on the parent class of objects called motor vehicles. And since they are motor vehicles, cars and trucks automatically inherit the properties of the parent class of object on which they are based.

As a matter of fact, you could even divide cars and trucks into more classes, each with their own properties. For example, cars could be divided into subclasses such as sports car, family sedan, and passenger van. Trucks could be divided into sports utility, heavy duty, and light duty—each with its own set of properties.

See how this works? Well, scripting dictionaries work the same way. Applications can have classes that are based upon other classes and inherit the properties of the class from which they are derived.

In the definition of the `Finder window` class, within the brackets following the defined term, is the abbreviation `inh.` followed by the class `window`, indicating that a Finder window inherits some properties from the `window` class.

```
Finder window n [inh. window]: every Finder window
```

Notice that in this definition, the term `window` is displayed as a hyperlink. Click the link to access the properties of the `window` class the `Finder window` class is based upon.

FIGURE 2.6 The properties of the `window` class.

Once the link is clicked, the dictionary pane of the dictionary window changes to show the definition and properties for the `window` class of Finder objects shown in Figure 2.6.

In this list, you'll recognize some of the `window` properties as ones you used in the previous chapter, terms such as the following: `position`, `bounds`, `name`, and `index`. And you'll see some new properties such as `id`, `closable`, `floating`, `modal`, `resizable`, `zoomable`, `zoomed`, and `visible`. Let's try using some of the new properties.

Open a new script window in Script Editor, type Script 2.1, and run it.

```
tell application "Finder"
    close every window
    open home
end tell
```
SCRIPT 2.1

A single Finder window displaying the contents of your home directory should now be open on the Desktop.

Examine the `visible` property in the list of `window` properties:

```
visible (boolean, r/o) : Is the window visible (always true for open
Finder windows)?
```

According to the property's definition, this property has a value that is `boolean` (`true` or `false`). Let's see whether that is correct. Run Script 2.2.

```
tell application "Finder"
    get visible of the front Finder window
end tell
```
SCRIPT 2.2

The result returned by the script and displayed in the Result pane of the script window, is `true`, a boolean value. Let's see whether we can make the Finder window invisible by setting the value of its `visible` property to `false`. Run Script 2.3.

```
tell application "Finder"
    set visible of the front Finder window to false
end tell
```
SCRIPT 2.3

Oops! Something didn't work as expected and caused the script to error. Since the script is being executed in the Script Editor application, Script Editor handles the process of informing you of the problem by displaying an error message in a drop-down dialog sheet attached to the script window, shown in Figure 2.7.

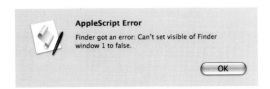

FIGURE 2.7 A sheet attached to a script window displaying an error message.

According to the error message, there's a problem when you try to make a Finder window invisible by setting the value of its **visible** property to **false**. Hmm, wonder why?

Well, if we had read the property definition, it would have warned of this issue—twice!

```
visible (boolean, r/o) : Is the window visible (always true for open
Finder windows)?
```

Notice that the property's type descriptor contains two items of information within its enclosing parentheses: the type of the value (**boolean**) and the abbreviation **r/o**, which stands for—you guessed it—read-only, meaning the property value can only be read, not set.

Also, the property description implies that the property value is read-only by stating that the value of the property is always **true** for open windows. Sometimes it pays to read a definition thoroughly!

So if we can't make the Finder window invisible, can we at least get it out of our way using some other **window** property?

The next-to-last property in the list of **window** properties is a property named **collapsed**. According to its definition, this property has a boolean value that determines whether the window is collapsed—whatever that means. Let's try setting this property for the currently open Finder window. Run Script 2.4.

```
tell application "Finder"
    set collapsed of the front Finder window to true
end tell
```
SCRIPT 2.4

The front Finder window has now been miniaturized and placed in the Dock, as shown in Figure 2.8!

FIGURE 2.8 A Finder window miniaturized to the Dock by changing its `collapsed` property.

That's very cool, but where does the term `collapsed` come from, and why isn't it named `miniaturized` or something that better describes what happens to the window?

The answer comes from a Mac OS 9 Finder feature that was discontinued when Mac OS X was introduced: collapsing windows. Finder windows in Mac OS 9 could be scripted to hide their content view and be reduced to a title bar. This process was referred to as collapsing a window. To maintain as much consistency as possible in the Finder's scripting dictionary during the transition from Mac OS 9 to Mac OS X, the term was kept but revised to apply to the process of miniaturizing windows to the Dock.

Return the window to its previous place on the Desktop by reversing the status of the `collapsed` property. Run Script 2.5.

```
tell application "Finder"
    set collapsed of every Finder window to false
end tell
```
SCRIPT 2.5

TIP ▶ As shown in the previous script, you can use the term every when you set the value of the collapsed property to miniaturize or restore all the currently open Finder windows:

```
tell application "Finder"
    set collapsed of every Finder window to true
end tell
```

One more thing about the collapsed property: the term is specific to the Finder application. In other applications that support using scripts to send windows to the Dock, you'll find the term miniaturized is used instead.

Batch? Natch.

Counting its 8 direct properties and the 15 inherited properties of the base window class, the Finder window class has a total of 23 properties whose values you can retrieve. That's quite a bit of useful information available to you. But how do you extract all that information easily without having to write a series of script statements asking for the value of each property and then clicking the Event Log tab in the script window to see the results of each script statement? Script 2.6 shows the roundabout way to do it.

```
tell application "Finder"
    tell the front Finder window
        get target
        get current view
        get its icon view options
        get its list view options
        get its column view options
        get toolbar visible
        get statusbar visible
        get sidebar width
        get id
        get position
        get bounds
        get titled
```

```
            get name
            get index
            get closeable
            get floating
            get modal
            get resizable
            get zoomable
            get zoomed
            get visible
            get collapsed
        end tell
    end tell
```

SCRIPT 2.6

The Event Log shows the following running record of the results of all the commands in Script 2.6:

```
tell application "Finder"
    get target of Finder window 1
        --> folder "sal" of folder "Users" of startup disk
    get current view of Finder window 1
        --> icon view
    get icon view options of Finder window 1
        --> icon view options of Finder window id 221
    get list view options of Finder window 1
        --> list view options of Finder window id 221
    get column view options of Finder window 1
        --> column view options of Finder window id 221
    get toolbar visible of Finder window 1
        --> true
    get statusbar visible of Finder window 1
        --> true
    get sidebar width of Finder window 1
        --> 135
    get id of Finder window 1
        --> 221
```

script continues on next page

```
get position of Finder window 1
    --> {18, 84}
get bounds of Finder window 1
    --> {18, 84, 704, 671}
get titled of Finder window 1
    --> true
get name of Finder window 1
    --> "sal"
get index of Finder window 1
    --> 1
get closeable of Finder window 1
    --> true
get floating of Finder window 1
    --> false
get modal of Finder window 1
    --> false
get resizable of Finder window 1
    --> true
get zoomable of Finder window 1
    --> true
get zoomed of Finder window 1
    --> false
get visible of Finder window 1
    --> true
get collapsed of Finder window 1
    --> false
end tell
```

The easy way to get the values of the properties of a `Finder window` object is to access the value of one of its properties, which is a special property and the last one in the list of properties for the `window` class: the `properties` property, as shown in Script 2.7.

```
tell application "Finder"
    get the properties of the front Finder window
end tell
```

SCRIPT 2.7

The result of this script is a collection of property information, looking like this:

```
{class:Finder window, id:221, name:"sal", position:{18, 84}, bounds:{18,
84, 704, 671}, index:1, zoomed:false, closeable:true, titled:true,
floating:false, modal:false, resizable:true, zoomable:true, visible:true,
collapsed:false, target:folder "sal" of folder "Users" of startup disk
of application "Finder", current view:icon view, icon view options:icon
view options of Finder window id 221 of application "Finder", list
view options:list view options of Finder window id 221 of application
"Finder", column view options:column view options of Finder window id 221
of application "Finder", toolbar visible:true, statusbar visible:true,
sidebar width:135}
```

In some respects, the value of the **properties** property resembles an AppleScript **list**. If you remember from the previous chapter, lists are one or more items placed within curly braces and delimited by commas, like this:

```
-- A list of text strings
{"Sal", "Sue", "Bob", "Wanda"}
-- A list of numbers
{234, 12.5, 4321234, 0.23}
-- A list of mixed data types
{23, "Sid", false, {65535, 0, 0}}
```

The value of the **properties** property of a window is a list of the individual properties of the window by name or label, and each label is paired with the current value of the property, with a colon acting as the delimiter between the property's label and its corresponding value, like this:

```
{property:value, property:value, property:value, property:value,
property:value, property:value, property:value}
```

This type of data structure is called a record, and it is used quite extensively in the AppleScript language, especially when referring to the properties of scriptable objects.

Also note that the first pairing in the properties record for a Finder window is a property called `class`, paired with the title of the class of the scriptable object whose properties are listed in the record.

```
{class:Finder window}
```

Although it does not appear in the list of properties for windows or Finder windows, the `class` property is a fundamental component of the AppleScript language and can be used to find out the type of any scriptable object or data. As an example, try Script 2.8.

```
tell application "Finder"
    get the class of the front Finder window
--> returns: Finder window
end tell
```
SCRIPT 2.8

The result of the previous script is the name of the `class` of the scriptable object targeted by the script statement, which in this case is a Finder window. However, the `class` property can also be used to determine the type of any specific data:

```
get the class of 12
    --> integer
get the class of 12.345
    --> real
get the class of "Sal"
    --> text
get the class of {"Sal", "Sue", "Bob"}
    --> list
get the class of {id:123}
    --> record
```

Clean and Wax

If you examine the definition for the `properties` property, you'll notice that there is no `r/o` in its type descriptor to indicate that it is read-only. Therefore, we should be able to use the `set` verb to change its value, which in this case is a record of the window's properties and their corresponding values. Let's try.

To change the value of the `properties` property, you create a record containing the writable `window` and `Finder window` properties you want to change, along with their corresponding new values. You don't have to include all the writable properties. Run Script 2.9 as an example.

```
tell application "Finder"
    set the properties of the front Finder window to {bounds:{22, 66,
700, 600}, index:1, zoomed:false, collapsed:false, current view:icon
view, toolbar visible:true, statusbar visible:true, sidebar width:135,
target:(path to documents folder)}
end tell
```
SCRIPT 2.9

The Finder window on the Desktop now displays the contents of your Documents folder as icons!

The `properties` property provides quick access to the information about a scriptable object. In addition, the property can often be used to set the values of a group of properties in a single script statement. However, there are a couple of caveats to be aware of when setting this property.

The order in which the properties are changed does not necessarily match their order in the properties record. When the properties property is used to set the property values of a visible object such as a Finder window, the result may not be what you intended, because of the way the properties may interact with each other. In the cases where you are dramatically changing the appearance of a Finder window, it is best to set the properties in individual script statements in the order you want them executed, like this:

```
tell application "Finder"
    tell the front Finder window
```
script continues on next page

```
        set current view to icon view
        set toolbar visible to true
        set statusbar visible to true
        set sidebar width to 135
        set zoomed to false
        set collapsed to false
        set bounds to {22, 66, 700, 600}
        set target to (path to documents folder)
        set index to 1
    end tell
end tell
```

Because of an issue with how the Finder processes script commands, when you set the value of the target property of a Finder window using a typical Finder item reference, make sure the script statement is within a `tell` block directly referencing the Finder, like this:

```
tell application "Finder"
    set the target of the front Finder window to ¬
        folder "Documents" of home
end tell
```

and not within a nested `tell` block, like this:

```
tell application "Finder"
    tell the front Finder window
        set the target to folder "Documents" of home
    end tell
end tell
```

When setting the value of the **target** property using a properties record, or when the statement setting the **target** property value is within a `tell` block other than a Finder `tell` block, use a reference to the targeted folder in a format other than the typical Finder item reference. Usually an alias reference works well. These types of references are covered later in this book.

```
tell application "Finder"
    -- setting the value of the target within a nested tell block
```

```
    tell the front Finder window
        set the target to (alias "Mac OS X:Users:sal:Documents:")
    end tell
end tell


tell application "Finder"
    tell the front Finder window
    -- setting the value of the target within a property record
        set properties to ¬
            {target:alias "Mac OS X:Users:sal:Documents:"}
    end tell
end tell
```

What's a Window Without a View?

Let's return to the properties definition for Finder windows and examine the remaining properties in its list.

As you probably inferred by clicking the hyperlink to view the window properties, the dictionary pane of the dictionary window is designed to display information that has been formatted using the standard HTML coding used to build Internet Web pages. In that regard, the dictionary viewer functions very much like a Web browser.

To return to viewing the properties of the Finder window class, click the Back button located at the left side of the Dictionary Viewer toolbar, shown in Figure 2.9.

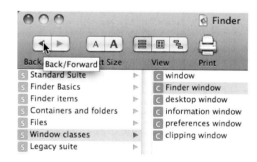

FIGURE 2.9 Back/Forward buttons used to navigate the pages displayed in the dictionary pane of the Dictionary Viewer window.

There are three remaining `Finder window` properties to examine: `column view options`, `icon view options`, and `list view options`. Click the `column view options` property in the third browser column to highlight its definition in the dictionary pane, as shown in Figure 2.10.

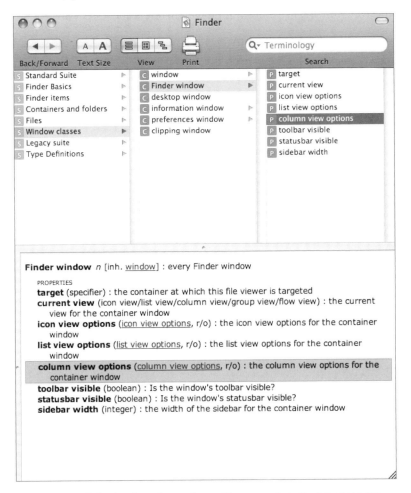

FIGURE 2.10 Selecting the `column view option` property in the browser pane.

The definition for this property is fairly sparse, but it provides some useful information:

```
column view options (column view options, r/o) : the column view options
for the container window
```

This property, as with the other `view options` properties, is marked as read-only (`r/o`), meaning its values cannot be set when setting the properties of a Finder window. However, its values can be set when it is addressed directly.

Notice the type descriptor for this property is a class of object titled the same as the property: `column view options`. In the Finder's scripting dictionary, the term `column view options` is both a property and a class.

Click the link to view the definition for this class:

```
column view options n : the column view options
    properties
    text size (integer): the size of the text displayed in the column view
    shows icon (boolean): displays an icon next to the label in column view
    shows icon preview (boolean): displays a preview of the item in
        column view
    shows preview column (boolean): displays the preview column in
        column view
    discloses preview pane (boolean): discloses the preview pane of
        the preview column in column view
```

The definition indicates that the class `column view options` is a scriptable object (notice the n for noun) that has its own properties.

Up to now, the scriptable objects you've written scripts for have had a physical representation on the computer—Finder windows that you can open, view, and close. However, the `column view options` scriptable object is a collection of properties controlling a specific view mode of a window. Some scriptable objects don't have to be visible to be scriptable.

Let's get the properties of this object using Script 2.10.

```
tell application "Finder"
    get the properties of the column view options of ¬
        the front Finder window
end tell
```
SCRIPT 2.10

The result, displayed in the Result pane of the script window, is a `properties` record containing the various properties and their corresponding values:

```
{class:column view options, text size:12, shows icon:true, shows icon
preview:true, shows preview column:true, discloses preview pane:true}
```

Note that the `column view options` object exists regardless of what the current view is for its parent Finder window! You can change the view mode of the front Finder window and rerun the script, and the results will be the same. Remember:

▶ Some scriptable objects don't have to be visible to be scriptable.

Also notice that all the properties of the `column view options` object are writable (there's no `r/o` in their definitions), meaning their values can be set. You can set the values of the properties of the `column view options` object individually, as we do in Script 2.11.

```
tell application "Finder"
    activate
    tell column view options of the front Finder window
        set text size to 12
        set shows icon to true
        set shows icon preview to true
        set shows preview column to true
        set discloses preview pane to true
    end tell

    tell the front Finder window
        set current view to column view
    end tell
end tell
```
SCRIPT 2.11

Or you can set them all at once by setting the value of its **properties** property, as we do in Script 2.12.

```
tell application "Finder"
    tell column view options of the front Finder window
        set the properties to {text size:12, shows icon:true, shows icon ¬
            preview:true, shows preview column:true, discloses preview ¬
                pane:true}
    end tell

    tell the front Finder window
        set current view to column view
    end tell
end tell
```
SCRIPT 2.12

To summarize, when the term `column view options` is used as a property, its value cannot be set. However, when the term `column view options` is used as a class, the values of its properties can be set. The same scenario is true for the other view options properties.

Color My World

Click the Back button in the Dictionary Viewer window to return to the definition for `Finder window`. Then, select `icon view options` in the third column of the browser pane to highlight its definition in the dictionary pane.

The definition for the `icon view options` property is similar to the definition for the `column view options` property:

```
icon view options (icon view options, r/o) : the icon view options for the
container window
```

Like the column view options property, the icon view options property has a value that is a class named the same as the property. Click the class name in the type descriptor to view the class definition for the icon view options object:

```
icon view options n : the icon view options
    properties
    arrangement (not arranged/snap to grid/arranged by name/arranged by
modification date/arranged by creation date/arranged by size/arranged by
kind/arranged by label) : the property by which to keep icons arranged
    icon size (integer) : the size of icons displayed in the icon view
    shows item info (boolean) : additional info about an item displayed in
icon view
    shows icon preview (boolean) : displays a preview of the item in icon
view
    text size (integer) : the size of the text displayed in the icon view
    label position (right/bottom) : the location of the label in reference
to the icon
    background picture (file) : the background picture of the icon view
    background color (RGB color) : the background color of the icon view
```

As you can see, these properties determine how information is displayed in a Finder window when its current view property is set to icon view.

Enter and run Script 2.13 to access the current values of the properties of the icon view options for the front Finder window.

```
tell application "Finder"
    get the properties of the icon view options of ¬
        the front Finder window
end tell
```

SCRIPT 2.13

As with the `column view options` object, the result of getting the value of the `properties` property of the `icon view options` object is a record listing its properties with their corresponding values:

```
{class:icon view options, arrangement:arranged by name, icon size:64,
shows item info:false, shows icon preview:true, text size:12, label
position:bottom, background color:{65535, 65535, 65535}}
```

We'll be writing a script to set these properties in a moment, but first, notice the returned value for the `background color` property. It is a list of three numbers. What are these numbers? Well, according to the type descriptor in the dictionary entry for the `background color` property, it has a value that is an RGB color.

RGB is an acronym that stands for Red, Green, Blue. On the computer, all colors are defined as a combination of these colors. So, an RGB color is a list of three integers, representing in order the red, green, and blue values for a particular color, in this case the color used as the background for the folder whose contents are displayed in the front Finder window.

Each of the RGB values can be an integer between 0 and 65535. If all the numbers are the same, then the color is either white, black, or a shade of gray. Try Script 2.14.

```
tell application "Finder"
    activate
    tell the icon view options of the front Finder window
        set the background color to {32765, 32765, 32765}
    end tell

    set the current view of the front Finder window to icon view
end tell
```
SCRIPT 2.14

The background of the folder displayed in the front Finder window is now 50 percent gray (32765 is halfway between 0 and 65535).

Note that we said the background color of the folder had been changed. Finder windows themselves don't really have a background color; they just display the contents of whatever folder is the value of their **target** property. So even though this property pertains to Finder windows, it actually sets the background color of the Finder window on an individual folder-by-folder basis. To prove this, run Script 2.15 to change the folder displayed by the front Finder window.

```
tell application "Finder"
    activate
    set the target of the front Finder window to home
end tell
```
SCRIPT 2.15

The background color of the front Finder window now shows white (or whatever color is the default on your computer). Run Script 2.16 to return to the previous displayed Documents folder.

```
tell application "Finder"
    activate
    set the target of the front Finder window to ¬
        folder "Documents" of home
end tell
```
SCRIPT 2.16

The Documents folder, with a gray background color, is again displayed in the front Finder window.

Speaking of colors, would it be possible to write a script that lets you choose the color to use for the background of this folder? Would we ask such a question if it weren't possible?

To write a script to let a user choose a color, we'll use a command that's found in another scripting dictionary. Leaving the Finder dictionary window open, go to the Window menu in Script Editor, and choose the Library menu item or press its keyboard shortcut, Command+Shift+L. A small palette appears, shown in Figure 2.11.

This is the Library palette. It provides quick access to the dictionaries of applications you script often. The palette also provides access to important dictionaries used by AppleScript that are "hidden" within the System folder on the computer. Database Events, Image Events, and System Events are three such applications used only by AppleScript and run invisibly to users.

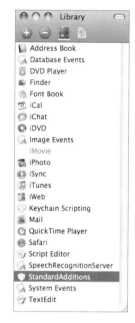

FIGURE 2.11 The Script Editor Library palette.

> **TIP** ▶ You can add applications to the Library palette by dragging them from the Finder into the palette or by clicking the + button and choosing the applications in a dialog. To remove an application, select it and click the minus button. As a shortcut for creating scripts, select an application from the palette, and click the script icon in the palette's toolbar to generate a new script containing a `tell` block targeting the selected application.

One particularly important dictionary is called Standard Additions. It is a collection of commands designed to be used in any script regardless of the application it may be addressing. Select Standard Additions in the Library palette, and open its dictionary by clicking the library icon in the palette's toolbar. (You can also open a dictionary by double-clicking an application icon in the palette.) The dictionary is shown in Figure 2.12.

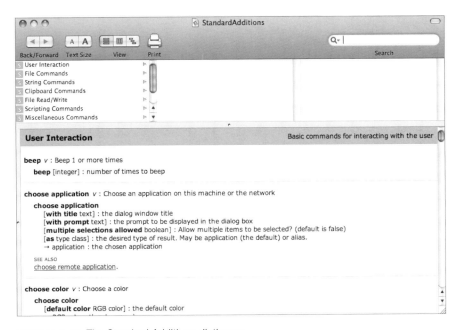

FIGURE 2.12 The Standard Additions dictionary.

The Standard Additions dictionary contains hundreds of commands and classes that add to the native abilities of the AppleScript language. Like the Finder dictionary, they are grouped in suites in the left column of the dictionary browser.

Instead of searching through the various suites by hand looking for a command dealing with color, place the cursor in the Search field at the top right of the window, and enter the term color. Instantly the entire contents of the Standard Additions dictionary are searched, and any matching items are displayed in a list view that temporarily replaces the browser view.

Two matches appear in the list, a command named choose color and a property named default color. Select the choose color command in the list to display its definition in the Dictionary pane at the bottom of the window, as shown in Figure 2.13.

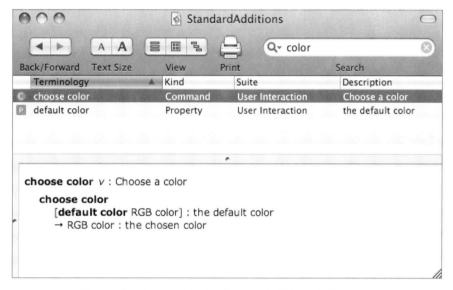

FIGURE 2.13 The results of a search in the Standard Additions dictionary.

The definition for the choose color command begins with a line identifying the term, followed by the letter v to indicate it is a verb, and then provides a description of what the command does:

```
choose color v : Choose a color
```

The next lines of the dictionary entry show how the command is written. First is the command, choose color, followed by any direct parameters required for its use. In this case, there are none. A simple script using this command is Script 2.17, which you should enter and run in a script window.

```
choose color
```

SCRIPT 2.17

When the script is run, it causes the standard Mac OS X color picker dialog to appear, shown in Figure 2.14.

By default, the color picker displays the color black as the current color. Click the OK button to close the dialog. Notice that the script result is the chosen color, which is the RGB color value for black: {0, 0, 0}.

The last line in the dictionary entry for the choose color command confirms that the command returns a result as an RGB color value:

```
RGB color : the chosen color
```

Run the script again to summon the color picker. Move the tint slider on the right side of the window to the top, and click a color within the color wheel on the left, as shown in Figure 2.15.

FIGURE 2.14 The system color picker dialog.

FIGURE 2.15 Selecting a shade in the color picker dialog.

Click the OK button and note the resulting RGB color value, perhaps something like {18623, 65535, 30351}. This is the RGB color value for the color you chose.

Using this command is very simple, but how do you get the color picker to open with some color besides black selected? The answer is in the next line in the definition for this command:

```
[default color RGB color] : the default color
```

The definition for a command (verb) is always followed by whatever parameters can be used to adjust how the command is executed. Parameters that are not required for use with the command are displayed in the definition enclosed in square brackets and are referred to as optional parameters. That makes sense.

The command choose color has one optional parameter, default color, whose value is an RGB color that is the one preselected when the color picker dialog appears. To use this parameter, place it after the choose color command in a script, and follow it with the RGB color value to use as the default color. Try Script 2.18, which summons the color picker dialog preselected to red.

FIGURE 2.16 The color picker dialog with the default color set to red.

```
choose color default color {65535, 0, 0}
```
SCRIPT 2.18

The color picker dialog now appears with red set as the default color value, as shown in Figure 2.16.

Now that you've learned how to use the `choose color` command, write a script that will enable you to choose the background color of a folder displayed in a Finder window. In a new script window, run Script 2.19.

```
tell application "Finder"
    activate
    choose color default color {65535, 65535, 65535}
    set the background color of the icon view options of ¬
        the front Finder window to the result
end tell
```
SCRIPT 2.19

The script will present the color picker dialog and then change the background color of the front Finder window to the color chosen in the dialog. Let's examine how this script works.

The first line of the script after the `activate` statement presents the color picker and returns its result, the chosen RGB color value, to the script. The next line of the script uses the resulting value of the previous script statement to set the `background color` of the folder displayed in the front Finder window to the chosen color.

You can use the term `result` in your scripts in this manner to capture the result of the previous script statement's execution.

Back to the Icon View

Now that you understand RGB color values, you can construct scripts to set the value of the `icon view options` of a Finder window.

As with the `column view options`, you can set the values of the properties of the `icon view options` of a Finder window, individually, as shown in Script 2.20.

```
tell application "Finder"
    activate
    tell icon view options of the front Finder window
        set arrangement to arranged by name
        set icon size to 64
        set shows item info to false
        set shows icon preview to true
        set text size to 12
        set label position to bottom
        set background color to {65535, 65535, 65535}
    end tell

    tell the front Finder window
        set current view to icon view
    end tell
end tell
```
SCRIPT 2.20

Or you can do it by setting the value of its **properties** property, as shown in Script 2.21.

```
tell application "Finder"
    activate
    tell icon view options of the front Finder window
        set the properties to {arrangement:arranged by name, icon size:64,
shows item info:false, shows icon preview:true, text size:12, label
position:bottom, background color:{65535, 65535, 65535}}
    end tell

    tell the front Finder window
        set current view to icon view
    end tell
end tell
```
SCRIPT 2.21

If you want to set the `icon view options` of a Finder window and you want the user to pick the folder's background color, try Script 2.22 where the `choose color` command is placed within parentheses and used as the value for the `background color` property.

```
tell application "Finder"
    activate
    tell icon view options of the front Finder window
        set the properties to {arrangement:arranged by name, icon size:64,
shows item info:false, shows icon preview:true, text size:12, label
position:bottom, background color:(choose color default color {65535,
65535, 54000})}
    end tell

    tell the front Finder window
        set current view to icon view
    end tell
end tell
```
SCRIPT 2.22

Remember, script statements and calculations placed within parentheses are executed first and then are replaced with the results of their execution.

A Picture Is Worth...

There is one more property of the `icon view options` class that is worth mentioning, simply because it is fun—the `background picture` property, as shown here:

```
background picture (file) : the background picture of the icon view
```

This property can be used to set the background picture of a folder displayed within a Finder window. Like the `background color` property, this property is set on a per-folder basis.

Its type descriptor indicates that its value is a `file`, or more correctly a reference to a file. Ordinarily, we'd use the `get` verb to get the current value of the property, but because of a bug in the current version of the Finder dictionary, this property can be `set` only, and its value cannot be retrieved.

Script 2.23 uses a Finder file reference to set the picture for the front Finder window's folder.

```
tell application "Finder"
    activate
    set background picture of the icon view options of ¬
        the front Finder window to document file "Maple.jpg" of ¬
        folder "Plants" of folder "Desktop Pictures" of ¬
        folder "Library" of the startup disk

    tell the front Finder window
        set current view to icon view
    end tell
end tell
```
SCRIPT 2.23

Once the script is executed, the background of the folder is the specified picture, as shown in Figure 2.17.

FIGURE 2.17 A folder with an image background.

We know what you're thinking…"Hmmm. I wonder whether there's a command to choose a file so the user could pick the image to use for the folder background?" The answer, of course, is "Yes, there is such a command." And you can find it by doing a search in the Standard Additions dictionary for the term `choose file`, shown in Figure 2.18.

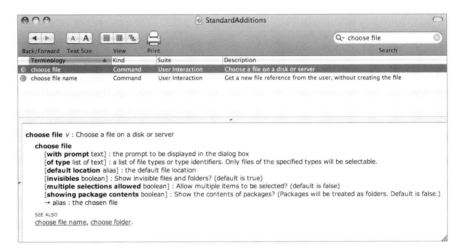

FIGURE 2.18 The `choose file` command from the Standard Additions dictionary.

To save some time here Script 2.24 sets the `background picture` of a folder by jumping ahead and using the `choose file` command to prompt the user to pick an image from the Desktop Images directory. The `choose file` command is covered in detail in Chapter 9, Communicating with the User.

```
tell application "Finder"
    activate
    choose file of type "public.image" default location ¬
        (path to desktop pictures folder) with prompt ¬
        "Pick an image for the folder background:" without invisibles
    set the background picture of the icon view options of ¬
        the front Finder window to the result
end tell
```

SCRIPT 2.24

When the script is run, it uses the `choose file` command to present a file picker dialog where the user can choose the image to use as the background for the folder displayed in the front Finder window, as shown in Figure 2.19.

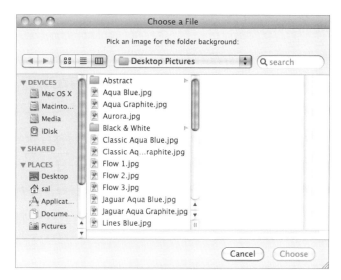

FIGURE 2.19 The file picker dialog displayed by the `choose file` command from the Standard Additions dictionary.

Here's one last thing about the `background image` property: the current version of the Finder scripting dictionary doesn't support removing the background image via a script. You have to use the View Options dialog in the Finder to reset the background to white or another color.

Doric, Ionic, Corinthian, Egyptian, Romanesque...

The last of the three view options properties for Finder windows is the `list view options` property. In the Finder dictionary window, click the Back button to return to the Finder's `window` properties, and then select `list view options` in the last browser column to highlight its definition in the dictionary pane.

```
list view options (list view options, r/o) : the list view options for the
container window
```

As with the previous view options properties, the `list view options` term is used as both a property and a class. As a property, it is read-only; as an object, its property values can be set.

Click the hyperlink to view the definition of the `list view options` class, shown in Figure 2.20.

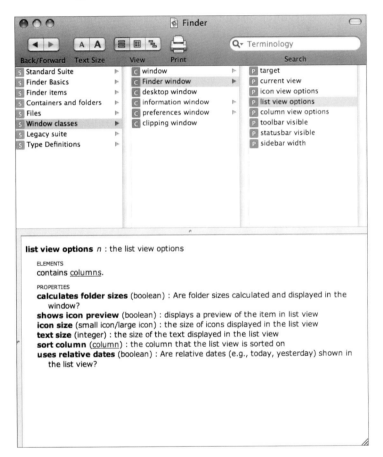

FIGURE 2.20 The Finder dictionary window displaying the definition for the `list view options` class.

Like the other view option class definitions, the `list view options` class definition begins with a statement indicating it is a scriptable object by identifying it as a noun (note the n for noun). But unlike the other view option classes, this definition is broken into two groups: elements and properties.

Properties we are already familiar with, but what are elements? The answer is contained in one of the fundamental principles of AppleScript you're already familiar with:

▶   On the computer, everything belongs to, is related to, is contained in, or is part of something else.

In other words, scriptable objects can belong to or be contained by other scriptable objects, and scriptable objects can contain other scriptable objects. Elements is another term used to describe scriptable objects contained by other scriptable objects. A scriptable object contained by a scriptable object is an element of the containing object.

The elements group of the `list view options` class definition begins with the identifier elements followed by the word contains, which is then followed by a list of the elements belonging to the defined class. In this case, the `list view options` class contains only one element, `columns`.

That makes sense. When the value of the `current view` property of a Finder window is set to `list view`, the window displays its contents as a list of items whose disk information is organized in columns to the right of each item's name, as shown in Figure 2.21.

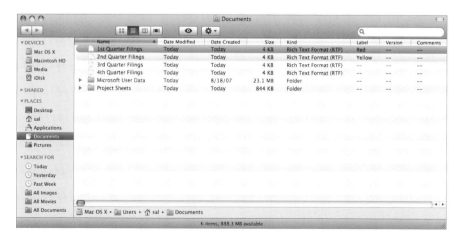

FIGURE 2.21 A Finder window displaying the contents of its target folder in list view.

So, the definition for the `list view options` class is telling us that columns belong to, or are contained by, the `list view options` object.

Let's find out about columns. Click the `columns` hyperlink in the elements list to view the class definition for the `column` class, shown in Figure 2.22.

---

column *n* : every list column

ELEMENTS
contained by <u>list view optionss</u>.

PROPERTIES
index (integer) : the index in the front-to-back ordering within its container
name (name column/modification date column/creation date column/size column/kind column/label column/version column/comment column, r/o) : the column name
sort direction (normal/reversed) : The direction in which the window is sorted
width (integer) : the width of this column
minimum width (integer, r/o) : the minimum allowed width of this column
maximum width (integer, r/o) : the maximum allowed width of this column
visible (boolean) : is this column visible

FIGURE 2.22 The definition for the `column` class.

The definition for the `column` class is similar to the previous class definitions. It is identified as a noun or scriptable object. And like the `list view options` class definition, it is broken into two sections: elements and properties. However, instead of the elements list beginning with the term contains, it begins with the term contained by followed by a list of the objects that contain columns.

The elements section of a class definition displays information about the defined class's relationship to other scriptable objects. An elements list can identify objects contained by the class, as well as objects that contain the class—sometimes both in the same list.

So if columns are contained by a `list view options` object, then a script that gets or sets the value of `column` properties will have to reflect their object hierarchy, like Script 2.25, which gets the name of every column of the front Finder window.

```
tell application "Finder"
    activate
    tell list view options of the front Finder window
        get the name of every column
    end tell
end tell
```
SCRIPT 2.25

The result is an AppleScript list of enumerations representing the name of
every column, whether it is visible and whether the `current view` of the front
Finder window is `list view`:

```
{name column, modification date column, creation date column, size column,
kind column, label column, version column, comment column}
```

Script 2.26 uses the `set` verb to change the value of the `width` property of a
column. Notice how the `tell` blocks in the script follow the same containment
hierarchy as the `list view option` and `column` classes—the `tell` block addressing the `column` is placed within the `tell` block addressing the `list view`
`options` object.

```
tell application "Finder"
    activate
    tell list view options of the front Finder window
        tell column name column
            set its width to 180
        end tell
    end tell
    tell the front Finder window
        set the current view to list view
    end tell
end tell
```
SCRIPT 2.26

The principle of the containment of objects is fundamental to the way AppleScript functions and the way AppleScript scripts are written. Remember:

▶ Scriptable objects are referred to by their positions in their object hierarchy or where they are in their "chain of command."

This rule applies not only when creating object references but also when writing scripts. The "chain of command" must always be apparent.

Mighty Column Magic

Using our `properties` property trick with the containment hierarchy of the Finder's `window` class, we can write Script 2.27, which not only sets the value of the properties of the Finder window's `list view options` object but also sets the values of the properties for the various list `columns` as well as shown in Figure 2.23.

```
tell application "Finder"
    activate
    tell list view options of the front Finder window
        set properties to {calculates folder sizes:false, shows icon
preview:false, icon size:large icon, text size:12, uses relative
dates:true, sort column:name column}


        tell column name column
            -- No need to set visiblility, column is always visible
            set properties to ¬
                {index:1, sort direction:normal, width:280}
        end tell
        tell column size column
            set properties to ¬
                {index:2, sort direction:normal, width:72 ¬
                    , visible:true}
        end tell
        tell column modification date column
            set properties to ¬
                {index:3, sort direction:normal, width:120 ¬
                    , visible:true}
```

```
        end tell
        tell column creation date column
            set properties to ¬
                {index:4, sort direction:normal, width:120 ¬
                    , visible:true}
        end tell
        tell column kind column
            set properties to ¬
                {index:5, sort direction:normal, width:120 ¬
                    , visible:false}
        end tell
        tell column label column
            set properties to ¬
                {index:6, sort direction:normal, width:72 ¬
                    , visible:false}
        end tell
        tell column version column
            set properties to ¬
                {index:7, sort direction:normal, width:72 ¬
                    , visible:false}
        end tell
        tell column comment column
            set properties to ¬
                {index:8, sort direction:normal, width:240 ¬
                    , visible:false}
        end tell
        set sort column to size column
    end tell

    tell the front Finder window
        set current view to list view
        set zoomed to false
    end tell
end tell
```

SCRIPT 2.27

FIGURE 2.23 The window after running the Script 2.27.

Inheritance

During the process of learning about dictionaries, we've touched upon the concepts of property inheritance and object containment. Let's explore these a bit more, starting with property inheritance, while having even more fun with windows.

First, close the open dictionary windows for the Finder and Standard Additions dictionaries. Next, select Preferences from the Script Editor application menu to open its Preferences window.

In Leopard, Script Editor has a new preference in the General preferences pane that enables inherited properties to be displayed in the Dictionary Viewer along with an object's direct properties. Select the checkbox labeled "Show inherited items in dictionary viewer," and then close the Preferences window as shown in Figure 2.24.

From the Library palette, double-click the Finder item to reopen the Finder in the Dictionary Viewer.

In the Dictionary Viewer window, select the third button of the view control in the toolbar to switch the browser view to Inheritance mode. A single entry named item appears in the left column. Select that entry to display its definition in the dictionary pane, as shown in Figure 2.25.

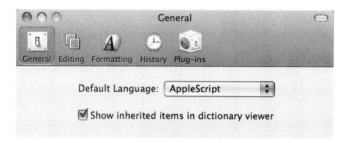

FIGURE 2.24 The new Script Editor preference to display inherited properties with an object's direct properties.

FIGURE 2.25 The Finder dictionary, set to display Inheritance, with the item base class selected.

The class definition for `item` indicates that it is a noun and therefore a scriptable object. The definition's element list indicates that items are contained by many other scriptable objects, including the Finder application, containers, disks, folders, the Desktop, and the Trash.

The `item` class does not contain any other classes or objects and does not inherit any properties from any other class of object. Because the item class does not inherit or contain, it is referred to as being a base class—the bottom-level object from which other objects inherit.

The definition description for the `item` class, every item, is not very helpful and would be much more informative if it pointed out that the `item` class actually refers to the various tangible things found on hard drives, such as files, folders, and other special containers such as the Desktop and the Trash.

As you can see, `item` objects have an extensive list of properties, many of which you are already familiar with through daily computer use, such as `name`, `comment`, `kind`, `size`, and `modification date`.

Second-Level Objects

The objects listed in the second browser column are scriptable objects that inherit the properties of the `item` class. One of them is `container`. Click the `container` class to reveal its class definition and its inherited objects and properties as shown in Figure 2.26.

You can see that this definition contains an element list for objects that the `container` class contains, as well as an element list for objects that it is contained by. The definition displays the direct properties of the `container` class, as well as properties inherited from the `item` base class.

Two direct properties of the `container` class that are worth noting are the `entire contents` property, which is a list of objects within the entire hierarchy of the container, and the `container window` property, which has a value that is a reference to the window that displays the contents of this container. We'll be using this property in a moment.

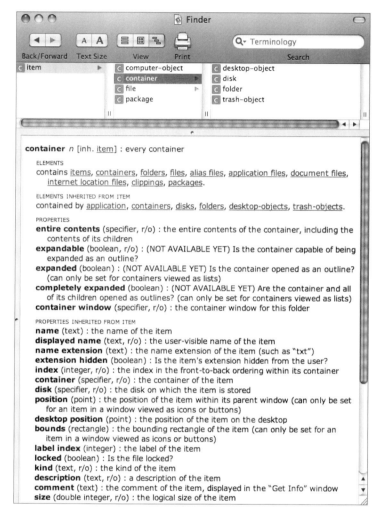

FIGURE 2.26 The `container` class definition, including properties and
objects inherited from the `item` class.

The description of the `container` class is just as sparse as the one for the `item`
class: every container. A more informative description would be this: "an
object used to store or hold another object." The various Finder containers are
listed in the last browser column: the `desktop` container, `disks`, `folders`, and the
`trash` container. Basically, a container is just a fancy way to say folder.

Third-Level Objects

Finally, select the `disk` class in the last browser column to display its definition in the dictionary pane, as shown in Figure 2.27.

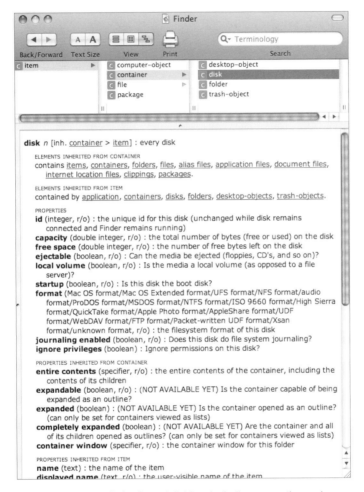

FIGURE 2.27 The `disk class` definition, including properties and objects inherited from both the `container` and `item` classes.

As you can see, the `disk` class definition contains both elements lists and property lists inherited from the `item` and `container` classes on which it is based.

It has its own set of unique properties, such as id, capacity, free space, ejectable, local volume, startup, format, journaling enabled, and ignore privileges. The disk class also inherits properties from the classes it is based on, including the property mentioned earlier: container window.

It's All in the Preparation...

For scripters (like yourself) who write scripts that open and display Finder windows, the container window property of container objects, such as folders and disks, is your best friend.

According to the type descriptor in its definition, its value is a reference to a scriptable object, in this case a window. Actually, it's not a visible window, but the default properties record for the window of its parent container, folder, or disk.

For example, enter and run Script 2.28, which gets the default properties that will be used to draw the window displayed when your start-up disk is opened.

```
tell application "Finder"
    get the properties of the container window ¬
        of the startup disk
end tell
```

SCRIPT 2.28

The result is a record containing properties you are familiar with—position, bounds, and current view—and the view option properties—icon view options, list view options, and column view options:

{class:container window, position:{136, 244}, bounds:{136, 244, 899, 702}, current view:icon view, icon view options:icon view options of container window of startup disk of application "Finder", list view options:list view options of container window of startup disk of application "Finder", column view options:column view options of container window of startup disk of application "Finder"}

So, why is this important? Well, since the properties property of a container window object is a collection of properties for a window that will be opened, you can set the properties of a window that your script is about to open, before it opens. When it opens, it opens with the correct view and look already in place. Very slick!

Enter and run Script 2.29 targeting the container window of the start-up disk.

```
tell application "Finder"
    activate
    tell icon view options of container window of the startup disk
        set properties to {arrangement:arranged by name, icon size:72,
shows item info:false, shows icon preview:true, text size:14, label
position:bottom, background color:{65535, 65535, 46000}}
    end tell
    tell the container window of the startup disk
        set properties to ¬
            {current view:icon view, bounds:{72, 104, 835, 542}}
    end tell
    open container window of the startup disk
end tell
```
SCRIPT 2.29

Containment

Remember these AppleScript principles?

▶ On the computer, everything belongs to, is related to, is contained in, or is part of something else.

▶ Scriptable objects are referred to by their positions in their object hierarchy or where they are in their "chain of command."

They really are fundamental to understanding how AppleScript works and how to write scripts. But the concept of containment hierarchy can be difficult to grasp when it gets to be more than one or two items long. Sometimes when you can visualize a concept it is easier to comprehend. So, to help you "see" what a containment hierarchy looks like, the dictionary window has a view mode that highlights how objects are contained within each other.

In the dictionary window, click the center button in the view control in the toolbar to set the browser to display information in containment view, as shown in Figure 2.28.

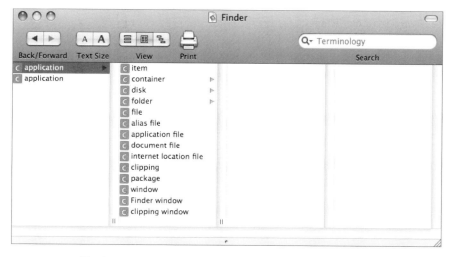

FIGURE 2.28 The browser view set to display containment hierarchy.

When scripting an application, the top level is always the `application` class, and it is always the first entry in the left browser column when the browser is set to containment view. Usually, there is only one `application` class entry, but in this case there is a second that lists a single legacy `application` property or one that is not really part of the Finder's dictionary but has been included for legacy support of older scripts. The `application` class entry that contains its object hierarchy is the one that is followed by a right-facing arrow indicating it contains other items. Click that one to reveal the top-level objects belonging to the Finder application.

As you can see, the Finder application class contains 14 other classes of scriptable objects, most of which you are familiar with from your day-to-day use of the Finder.

The `item` class is the base class from which many of the other classes inherit properties. However, the `item` class contains no other classes (note there is no arrow next to its entry). There is a difference between inheritance and containment. An object that acts as a source of inherited properties for another object doesn't necessarily contain the other object. In this section, we're talking strictly about ownership, or objects containing other objects.

According to the dictionary viewer, there are only three Finder objects that act as containers for other objects: containers, disks, and folders.

Note that Finder windows are not portrayed in the dictionary as objects that contain other objects (those with an arrow next to their entries). Instead, they are thought of as views into the contents of their target folders. The files and objects they display don't reside in them but rather "live" on a hard drive or disk.

But if that's so, why does Script 2.30 work?

```
tell application "Finder"
    get the name of the first item of Finder window 1
end tell
--> returns:  2007 Tax Summary.rtf
```
SCRIPT 2.30

Doesn't it look like the Finder window contains the object? It might appear that way, but it's an illusion. The script is actually asking for the first item of the list of viewable items displayed by the Finder window. The item doesn't live in the window; it lives somewhere else. To prove it, run Script 2.31.

```
tell application "Finder"
    get the first item of Finder window 1
end tell
```
SCRIPT 2.31

The result is a reference, in typical Finder format, to the item's location on disk:

```
document file "2007 Tax Summary.rtf" of folder "Documents" of folder "sal"
of folder "Users" of startup disk of application "Finder"
```

This confirms that scriptable items are always referred to by their position in their object hierarchy, or where they live.

However, referring to an item by its position in a window list works because the Finder understands your intent and will convert your list reference to a reference to the item on disk when processing script commands, as shown by Script 2.32.

```
tell application "Finder"
    activate
    set the label index of every folder of ¬
        the front Finder window to 3
end tell
```
SCRIPT 2.32

All the folders displayed in the front Finder window are now labeled yellow!

So, to summarize, Finder windows list the objects of their target folders; they don't actually contain them. If it were possible to use the following syntax (which won't compile), this concept would be more obvious:

```
tell application "Finder"
    activate
    set the label index of every folder ¬
        displayed by the front Finder window to 3
end tell
```

Now let's return to the containment view in the dictionary window.

You Say "Potato," I Say "Tomato"

According to the dictionary viewer, only three objects act as containers for other objects: `containers`, `disks`, and `folders`. For practical purposes, they all function as objects that contain other objects.

Click the **disk** class in the second browser column to reveal what objects it contains, as shown in Figure 2.29.

FIGURE 2.29 Disks contain a variety of other Finder items.

As you can see, **disk** objects can contain all Finder items except the various **window** classes and other disks. Those classes belong only to the application object and must be referenced only within a Finder **tell** block.

For example, write and run Script 2.33, where a command targeting a **disk** is placed within a **tell** block targeting a **folder**.

```
tell application "Finder"
    tell folder "Documents" of home
        get the properties of the startup disk
    end tell
end tell
```
SCRIPT 2.33

When the script is executed, Script Editor displays an error message on a sheet attached to the window, as shown in Figure 2.30.

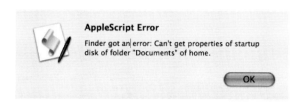

FIGURE 2.30 An error message indicated the requested
action could not be performed.

The script failed because script statements or nested `tell` blocks must be
placed within each other to reflect a target object's position in its object hierarchy. The previous script does not have a valid object hierarchy because disks
aren't contained within folders.

To prove this, select the `folder` class in the second browser column (just above
the `disk` entry) to see what objects it can contain. Now do the same for the
`container` class in the second browser column, as shown in Figure 2.31.

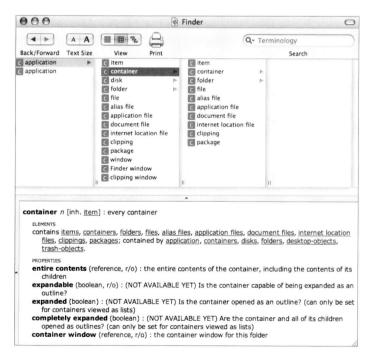

FIGURE 2.31 The `container` class selected.

All three classes, `disks`, `containers`, and `folders`, contain the same set of Finder elements, which are all the Finder elements except windows and disks. Disks and windows can be addressed only within statements or `tell` blocks directly targeting the Finder application.

So, to resolve the error in the previous script, move the offending statement outside the `tell` block targeting the Documents folder but still within the outer `tell` block targeting the Finder, and the script will run fine. The new version is Script 2.34.

```
tell application "Finder"
    tell folder "Documents" of home

    end tell
    get the properties of the startup disk
end tell
```

SCRIPT 2.34

As you just viewed in the dictionary window, the classes `container` and `folder` hold the same set of objects. In practical terms, they are the same thing, the difference being that the `container` class has a small but important set of properties that the `folder` class inherits from it. In practical terms, the two classes can be used interchangeably in scripts.

The Never-Ending Containment Hierarchy?

As you know from years of working with the Mac OS, folders can contain other folders that can contain other folders that can contain other folders that can contain other folders that can contain other folders that can contain other folders...and so on, and so on. This Russian-doll-within-a-doll metaphor is reflected in the dictionary browser as well.

Select the `disk` class in the second column in the browser pane to reveal in the adjacent column the objects it can hold. In the next column, select the `folder` class to reveal in the adjacent column the objects it can hold. And do the same thing again, as shown in Figure 2.32.

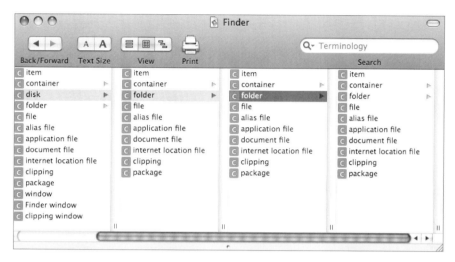

FIGURE 2.32 A containment chain.

This containment chain can continue forever until you select a Finder object that does not contain other objects, such as a `document file`, as shown in Figure 2.33.

FIGURE 2.33 A containment chain ending with a document file.

This containment chain displayed by the browser pane exactly matches how we refer to scriptable objects in scripts; only the syntax used by a Finder object reference goes from the end of the chain to the beginning of the chain or from the bottom up:

```
document file "Car Stereos.pdf" of folder "sal" of folder "Users" of the
startup disk
```

Most applications don't have the "elastic" object model used by the Finder application. Instead, they have well-defined containment paths to objects. For example, as you can see in this illustration of the iTunes dictionary, the `artwork` class has a well-defined containment hierarchy: `artwork` belongs to `tracks`, which are contained by `playlists`, which are contained by a `source` object, which are contained by the `application`, as shown in Figure 2.34.

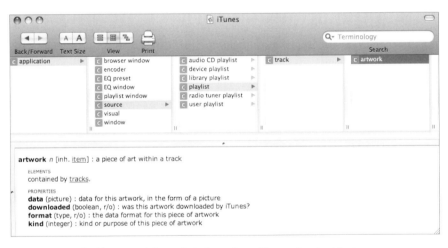

FIGURE 2.34 An iTunes containment chain ending with an artwork object.

Using the visual trail in the dictionary browser as a guide, you can create a script, matching a nested `tell` block for each of the chain objects, to get the value of one of the properties of the `artwork` class, as shown in Script 2.35.

```
tell application "iTunes"
    tell source "Library"
        tell playlist "Music"
```

```
            tell track "Should've Known Better"
                get the format of its first artwork
                --> returns: JPEG picture
            end tell
        end tell
    end tell
end tell
```
SCRIPT 2.35

That's what containment is all about!

Walking Back Up the Chain

Sooner or later in your career as a script writer, you'll have the need to locate the container that is holding a certain object and perform some action with it. So, how do you find the container of an object? Ask for it!

Try this experiment:

1. In the Documents folder in your home directory, create a new folder named Parent folder.

2. Within the newly created folder, create another folder named Child folder.

3. Run Script 2.36 to find the Child folder.

```
tell application "Finder"
    get the first folder of the entire contents of ¬
        folder "Documents" of home whose name is "Child folder"
    get the container of the result
end tell
```
SCRIPT 2.36

The result of the script will be a Finder object reference to the folder that contains the folder Child folder:

```
folder "Parent folder" of folder "Documents" of folder "sal" of folder
"Users" of startup disk of application "Finder"
```

To get an object reference to the container holding a scriptable object, ask for the `container` of the object, and you will get a reference to the folder or disk that holds the object. As a matter of fact, you can ask for the `container` of the `container` of the `container` of an object and walk back up the object's containment hierarchy.

Just the Disk, Ma'am

Should you ever want to know what `disk` a Finder object is on, just ask for the `disk` of the object, and the Finder will provide you with the correct information. Try Script 2.37.

```
tell application "Finder"
    get the disk of folder "Child folder" of ¬
        folder "Parent folder" of folder "Documents" of home
end tell
--> returns: startup disk of application "Finder"
```
SCRIPT 2.37

Containment is not a difficult concept to understand and use if you just remember:

▶ On the computer, everything belongs to, is related to, is contained in, or is part of something else.

▶ Scriptable objects are referred to by their locations in their object hierarchy or where they are in their "chain of command."

(Notice how we snuck in one more repetition?)

Making Things Happen

The lynchpin of the AppleScript language is the verb or command. Verbs make things happen. As you've seen many times over, even simple verbs such as `get` and `set` can be used to create scripts that take control of your computer and applications. This power becomes even stronger and more focused when you start using the other available verbs in an application's dictionary.

One of the basic concepts behind the creation of AppleScript is that applications would share a standard collection of verbs, with their dictionaries occasionally augmented with other verbs that addressed functionality unique to that specific application.

For example, verbs such as `open`, `close`, `print`, and `quit` address tasks commonly performed by most scriptable applications. Rather than each scriptable application making up their own versions of these verbs, they implement the same basic set of verbs so that scripters are more comfortable scripting various applications—a concept similar to the way common keyboard shortcuts are implemented in Macintosh applications, such as Command+Q for quit, Command+O for open, and Command+P for print.

So, the basic design behind AppleScript is to use a standard set of verbs (commands) targeting a large variety of scriptable nouns (classes) in order to create endless combination of script statements and to make magic happen. And most of the time, this design works well. Although the language's looseness is at once both its strength and its weakness, you'll find over time that the more experience you get, the easier it will be to recognize this dichotomy and write scripts that work correctly.

So, What's Standard About "Standard?"

Verbs are defined in script suites, with the standard set of verbs being found in—you guessed it—the Standard Suite. Almost all scriptable applications incorporate the Standard Suite.

In the Finder's dictionary window, select the Suites button in the View control in the toolbar to set the browser pane to display the dictionary by script suites. Select the first suite in the left browser column—the `Standard Suite`, as shown in Figure 2.35.

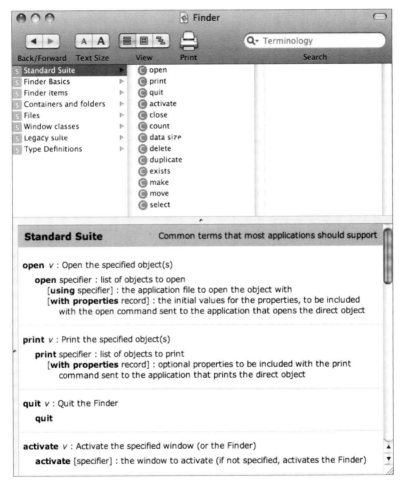

FIGURE 2.35 The Finder dictionary window, set to view by script suites, with the Standard Suite selected.

Although the Standard Suite can contain classes in addition to verbs, the Finder's implementation of it is all verbs. Let's examine how this standard set of verbs is implemented in the Finder application.

The first verb is the most fundamental—open. Select it in the second browser column to reveal its definition:

```
open v : Open the specified object(s)
    open specifier : list of objects to open
        [using specifier] : the application file to open the object with
        [with properties record] : the initial values for the properties,
to be included with the open command sent to the application that opens
the direct object
```

According to the definition, the verb open takes a direct parameter that is a specifier, meaning a reference to the object to open. Use it as shown here:

```
tell application "Finder"
    open <the object specifier of object to open>
end tell
```

You've used this command in previous scripts to open a folder or disk, like this:

```
tell application "Finder" to open home
```

There, the special term home acts as a shortcut for the object specifier, instead of using the full path reference, as shown here:

```
tell application "Finder"
    open folder "sal" of folder "Users" of the startup disk
end tell
```

The open command can be used to target any Finder disk item, including files belonging to other applications, as in Script 2.38.

```
tell application "Finder"
    open document file "Report.rtf" of folder "Documents" of home
end tell
```

SCRIPT 2.38

In the previous script, the file "Report.rtf" will be opened with the application assigned as its owner in its Information window, as shown in Figure 2.36.

FIGURE 2.36 The Information window for a document file showing the default application assigned to open it.

If you want to open the document with an application other than the one assigned as its default application, the Finder's implementation of the open command has provided the optional parameter using, which takes as its value a specifier or bundle identifier of the application file with which the file is to be opened, like this:

```
tell application "Finder"
    open <the object specifier of object to open> ¬
        using <the object specifier of the application used to open>
end tell
```

It looks like this when used in a functioning script such as Script 2.39.

```
tell application "Finder"
    open document file "Report.rtf" of folder "Documents" of home ¬
        using application file id "com.barebones.textwrangler"
end tell
```

SCRIPT 2.39

In Script 2.39, the Finder accepts the bundle identifier of the target application file, preceded by the term `id`, as its specifier rather than the normal Finder object specifier describing the location of the application file. When you reference an application by its bundle identifier, the Finder automatically locates the application file no matter where it is on your computer. This is handy for writing scripts that will run on computers where you don't know where the applications have been placed!

If you want to know what the bundle identifier is for a particular application, ask the Finder for the value of the `id` property of the `application file`, as shown in Script 2.40.

```
tell application "Finder"
    id of application file "TextWrangler.app" of ¬
        folder "Applications" of the startup disk
end tell
```
SCRIPT 2.40

The result is usually a period-delimited string like this, containing the "com" prefix and the name of the company followed by the application name:

```
"com.barebones.textwrangler"
```

The last optional parameter of the `open` command is `with properties`. It takes a record as its value. The record is supposed to contain the initial values to be used for the properties of the opened object. The only problem is that it doesn't work.

Run Script 2.41, and you'll see that a Finder window is created displaying the contents of the startup disk, but none of the provided properties is applied.

```
tell application "Finder"
    activate
    open the container window of the startup disk with properties ¬
        {current view:list view, bounds:{0, 44, 500, 500}}
end tell
```
SCRIPT 2.41

This script example points up two issues to be aware of about AppleScript:

▶ Applications vary in the depth and quality of their implementation of the Standard Additions commands.

▶ You can compose and compile scripts that seem like they should work, without any warning from AppleScript or the Script Editor application that they will not execute. You will find out there's a problem only when the script is run and an error is displayed.

The second issue applies even to scriptable applications with excellent implementations. It is this loose nature of the AppleScript language that makes it both easy to write yet sometimes difficult to use. Another example of this dichotomy is in the use of the next command in the Standard Additions suite: `print`.

Select the `print` verb in the second browser column to reveal its definition:

```
print v : Print the specified object(s)
    print specifier : list of objects to print
        [with properties record] : optional properties to be included with
the print command sent to the application that prints the direct object
```

According to the definition, the verb `print` takes a direct parameter that is a single specifier, or a list of specifiers, of the objects to print, in this form:

```
tell application "Finder"
    print <the object specifier(s) of object(s) to print>
end tell
```

So, according to the definition, shouldn't we be able to print the front Finder window using a script like Script 2.42?

```
tell application "Finder"
    print the front Finder window
end tell
```
SCRIPT 2.42

You can enter and compile the script without a problem. Run the script, and you get error alert shown in Figure 2.37.

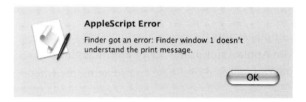

FIGURE 2.37 An error dialog triggered by trying to print a Finder window.

The error message says that the front Finder window doesn't understand the `print` command. In other words, the `print` command can't target the `window` class of Finder objects.

Instead, the Finder uses the `print` command only to print files, not to print windows. Unfortunately, the only way to learn this lesson is through instruction or trial and error when you actually run your scripts. Such is the nature of the AppleScript language and AppleScript dictionaries. Many current scripting dictionaries do not list which classes can be the target of the defined commands, and this omission presents a challenge to those new to AppleScript. The best solution is to spend time exploring and experimenting by writing short scripts with dictionaries that are new to you. Every great scripter has done the same thing. Of course, reading books like this one can save time too.

Back to the `print` command. Although it is used to print files, the Finder doesn't actually print them; instead, it passes the `print` command and the file(s) to the application that "owns" them or is set as the default application to process them, as in Script 2.43.

```
tell application "Finder"
    print document file "Report.rtf" of folder "Documents" of home
end tell
```
SCRIPT 2.43

The optional `with properties` parameter is not supported by the Finder, although some other applications such as TextEdit do support passing the `print settings` record with the `print` command, as shown in Script 2.44.

```
tell application "TextEdit"
    print the front document with properties {copies:2, collating:true,
starting page:3, ending page:9, pages across:1, pages down:1, error
handling:standard, target printer:"HP Color Laserjet 3600"} without print
dialog
end tell
```
SCRIPT 2.44

You can script the Printer Setup Utility application to get the status of a printer or print job or to get and set the default printer. To have the application print a file, you can choose one of two methods:

Have the Finder open the file using the Printer Setup Utility, as shown in Script 2.45.

```
tell application "Finder"
    open document file "Report.rtf" of folder "Documents" of home ¬
        using application file id "com.apple.print.PrintCenter"
end tell
```
SCRIPT 2.45

Or script the Printer Setup Utility directly, as we do in Script 2.46.

```
tell application "Printer Setup Utility"
    set the current printer to printer "HP Color Laserjet 3600"
    open (alias "Mac OS X:Users:sal:Documents:Report.rtf")
end tell
```
SCRIPT 2.46

Make sure to use the `open` command rather than the `print` command. You'll need to provide the `open` command a file reference in alias format rather than as a nested Finder reference. Alias references are covered later in this book.

TIP ▶ The scriptable Printer Setup Utility application that was included with Mac OS X 10.4 (Tiger) has been changed for Leopard. It no longer has a user interface. It has been redesigned to respond only to AppleScript commands. In addition, it has been moved from the Applications > Utilities folder to System > Library > CoreServices, and it now runs as an invisible background application. Any scripts you wrote for it in Tiger should continue to work in Leopard.

Creating Objects

Creating useful scripts not only involves controlling and manipulating scriptable objects but also involves creating new objects for use by the script. Having the Finder create folders and files is a common task that scripts perform.

The make command is used to create scriptable objects. Select it in the second browser column to reveal its definition:

```
make v : Make a new element
    make
        new type : the class of the new element
        at location specifier : the location at which to insert the
element
        [to specifier] : when creating an alias file, the original item to
create an alias to or when creating a file viewer window, the target of
the window
        [with properties record] : the initial values for the properties
of the element
    specifier : to the new object(s)
```

The make command has no direct parameter, but it does have two required parameters, new and at, for creating a functional script statement. Optional parameters for commands are shown in square brackets; required parameters are not.

So, according to the definition, the format for using the make command is this:

```
tell application "Finder"
    make new <class of object to create> at <location specifier>
end tell
```

The parameter new is followed by the name of the class of object the script is creating, followed by the parameter at, whose value is an object specifier to a location or container that will hold the newly created object. For example, Script 2.47 creates a new folder on the Desktop.

```
tell application "Finder"
    make new folder at desktop
end tell
```
SCRIPT 2.47

According to the definition, the result of the command is an object specifier to the newly created object, which appears in the Result pane in the script window once the script is executed:

```
folder "untitled folder" of folder "Desktop" of folder "sal" of
folder "Users" of startup disk of application "Finder"
```

Notice that the newly created folder has the default name of untitled folder. If you want to create a folder with a specific name, you use the optional with properties parameter. It has as its value a record containing the initial values for the folder's properties. Run Script 2.48.

```
tell application "Finder"
    activate
    make new folder at desktop with properties {name:"Created Items"}
    open the result
end tell
```
SCRIPT 2.48

Since the make command returns an object specifier referring to the newly created object, we can follow the make statement with the open command using the returned result as the direct parameter of the open command, thereby leaving the newly created folder open on the Desktop.

So, you can use the make command to create folders. But to save you the time spent "exploring and experimenting" to find out what class of Finder objects can be created, let's just say straight out that there are four: folders, plain text documents, Internet link files, and alias files. Here are script examples for each.

Using the make verb to create plain-text documents uses the same syntax as you use to create a folder. Run Script 2.49, which will create a new text file in the folder you just created on the Desktop.

```
tell application "Finder"
    activate
    make new document file at folder "Created Items" of desktop ¬
        with properties {name:"My Text Document"}
end tell
```
SCRIPT 2.49

A new empty text file will appear in the previously created folder.

Using the make verb to create Internet link files requires the addition of the parameter to followed by the URL targeted by the link. Run Script 2.50, which creates a new Internet link file in the folder you just created on the Desktop.

```
tell application "Finder"
    activate
    make new internet location file ¬
        to "http://www.automator.us" at ¬
        folder "Created Items" of desktop ¬
        with properties {name:"Automator Link"}
end tell
```
SCRIPT 2.50

A new Internet link file appears in the previously created folder. Double-clicking an Internet link file opens its stored URL in the default browser.

TIP ▶ For those who want a quick way to screen-share a computer using the built-in screen sharing in Leopard, use the make verb to create an Internet link file that you can add to your login items list. Whenever you log into your computer, a sharing window to another computer will automatically open. In Script 2.51, replace "sharing-name.local" with the target computer's sharing name as it appears beneath the Computer Name text input field in the Sharing system preference pane on the target computer.

```
tell application "Finder"
    activate
    make new internet location file ¬
        to "vnc://sharing-name.local" at desktop ¬
        with properties {name:"Shared Screen Link"}
end tell
```
SCRIPT 2.51

The last object for the make verb is an alias file. An alias file is a file that acts as a link to another file, folder, or disk. Its icon usually has a curved arrow badge to indicate its status as a link. To create an alias file, use the optional parameter to in a manner similar to the syntax used to create an Internet link file. Run Script 2.52 to create an alias file to the Applications folder.

```
tell application "Finder"
    activate
    make new alias file ¬
        at folder "Created Items" of desktop ¬
        to folder "Applications" of startup disk ¬
        with properties {name:"Applications Link"}
end tell
```
SCRIPT 2.52

The previously created folder now contains a text file, an Internet link file, and an alias file, as shown in Figure 2.38.

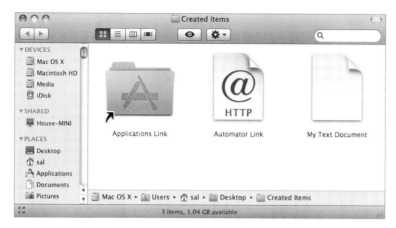

FIGURE 2.38 The created folder containing an alias file, an Internet link file, and a text document.

What Goes Up...

If the make verb is used to create objects, it stands to reason that there's a verb for the opposite process, deleting objects. The Standard Suite provides the appropriate verb for removing scriptable objects, delete. Select the term in the second browser column to reveal its definition:

```
delete v : Move an item from its container to the trash
    delete specifier : the item to delete
        specifier : to the item that was just deleted
```

According to the definition, the delete verb takes the direct parameter of a single object specifier, or a list of object specifiers, to the item or items to delete. Run Script 2.53, which deletes the text document you recently created.

```
tell application "Finder"
    activate
    delete document file "My Text Document" of ¬
        folder "Created Items" of the desktop
    open the trash
end tell
```

SCRIPT 2.53

Unlike most other applications, which simply remove deleted objects from their parent container, the Finder has a two-stage process for removing objects: move the items to delete to the Trash container, and then empty the Trash container. This process helps prevent unintended deletion of Finder items.

To empty the Trash container, we'll use a verb from the Finder items suite. This suite contains commands that are specific to the Finder application and that deal with the management of Finder disk items. Select the suite in the leftmost browser column, and then select the term empty from the middle column to reveal its definition, as shown in Figure 2.39.

FIGURE 2.39 The Finder Items suite contains commands specific to the Finder application.

According to the definition, the empty verb takes a single object specifier, which is a reference to the Trash container. Run Script 2.54.

```
tell application "Finder" to empty the trash
```

SCRIPT 2.54

The text file you previously created has now been erased. But, as you probably know, erased files can sometimes be retrieved by special software. If you want to ensure that the items you erase with your scripts stay erased, use the optional `security` parameter to have the computer erase the disk area occupied by the deleted items multiple times.

The security parameter has a boolean value, so enter and compile this script:

```
tell app "Finder"
    activate
    delete folder "Created Items" of the desktop
    empty the trash security true
end tell
```

When the script is compiled, the term `security true` will be replaced by the more English-like phrase `with security`. If the `security` parameter's value were `false`, the terms would compile to the dignified phrase `without security`. That's just one of the many cool things about AppleScript.

Now run the compiled script, shown in Script 2.55, to delete the remaining items you previously created.

```
tell application "Finder"
    activate
    delete folder "Created Items" of the desktop
    empty the trash with security
end tell
```
SCRIPT 2.55

The items have now been securely erased from the hard drive.

It's Here Somewhere...

Have you ever had to call your cell phone to find out where it is in your house? Be honest, of course you have. Well, here's a handy command for showing where a disk item lives in the Finder—`reveal`.

Select the term in the middle browser column to display its definition:

```
reveal v : Bring the specified object(s) into view
    reveal specifier : the object to be made visible
```

The verb takes a direct parameter that is a single object specifier or a list of object specifiers of the items to show to the user. Try Script 2.56.

```
tell application "Finder"
    activate
    reveal every document file of folder "Documents" of home
end tell
```
SCRIPT 2.56

The Documents folder on your computer will be opened and the documents it contains will be selected for your perusal. How quaint!

Chapter Summary

As you have seen in this chapter, scripting dictionaries are packed with interesting and powerful constructs. Learning to use them takes time and involves exploration and experimentation. Although articles and books like this one can reduce some of the time and frustration involved in figuring things out for yourself, nothing can replace your dedication, patience, and desire to "learn how to fish." Don't be afraid to try, and try again if necessary. The rewards are great. With a bit of effort you'll soon become Master of Your Computer Universe.

Approach the process of learning an application's dictionary in steps. Begin by gathering an understanding of an application's object hierarchy—what objects belong to or are contained in what other objects? Doing so will enable you to correctly target an object in your scripts.

Next, explore the dictionary by writing simple short scripts, one- or two-line snippets, that perform tasks such as getting and setting the values of properties. You've already taken this approach with many of the scripts in the first two chapters. This incremental approach familiarizes you with the various scriptable objects and what they can do.

And remember, most complex creations can be broken down into a series of smaller blocks put together to accomplish more than what they could do individually. This concept applies to everything from music to DNA—and even AppleScript. Complex scripts are most often a series of short scripts and routines strung together.

The point we're trying to make is that you can do this. AppleScript is the programming language for the rest of us.

Inheritance

While you worked your way through this chapter, delving deeper into the fascinating world of Finder windows, you were actually learning very important concepts and tools, such as inheritance, that will apply throughout your use of AppleScript.

Your explorations showed not only that scriptable objects are contained within other scriptable objects but that many of them inherit properties from the other objects upon which they are based. Remember, both cars and trucks are motor vehicles, and they both inherit and share some the properties of motor vehicles.

The same relationship applies to windows in the Finder or objects in any scriptable application.

Containment

Another important concept about relationships is the way objects belonging to applications are placed within each other to form containment hierarchies that are mirrored in scripts to describe an item's ownership and location. You saw examples of this in the Finder with folders within folders and items within folders—all within disks that are contained by the Finder application.

Hey, we didn't create the formula—it's just the way the universe works:

"Hi! I'm Sal, a person living in the city of Cupertino, located in the state of California, part of the United States of America, of the North American continent, of the planet Earth, of our small solar system, of the galaxy Milky Way…."

Properties Property

Definitely one of the coolest things about writing scripts for a good scriptable application is that you can—sometimes—use the `properties` property to quickly `get` or `set` the values of the properties of an object. It's kind of like "clean and wax" in one motion. What a concept!

Verbs

A great aspect of the AppleScript language is the use of standardized verbs such as `make`, `move`, `delete`, `exists`, `open`, `close`, `print`, and `save` to manipulate scriptable applications and objects. Well-constructed scripting dictionaries use these terms for standard procedures instead of commands made up by an application developer.

And So...

That brings up a reality of scripting on the Mac OS X. Not all scripting dictionaries are equal. Some are excellent. Some are pathetic and frustrating to try to parse. It all depends on the developer's understanding and commitment to their customers and meeting their needs. Providing good AppleScript support in an application is the best way to add abilities to applications without adding complexity to their user interface.

In that regard, it is important to communicate your needs to the developers of the applications you use. Contrary to what you may believe, developers do pay attention to what customers say—they may not act upon their suggestions, but they do listen. Ask for and demand good AppleScript support in the applications you purchase.

What's Next?

In the first two chapters of this book we've given you a thorough introduction to the most basic techniques used to write AppleScript scripts. We've used the Finder almost exclusively as the vehicle for instruction, but the techniques you've learned apply to every scriptable application. You're now ready to move more deeply into the world of AppleScript. In the next chapter, you'll begin by learning more about how to use AppleScript to identify various kinds of objects in applications.

3

Lesson 3
Identifying Objects

Nearly all scripts have one thing in common: they contain *references* to scriptable objects. For example, a script that rotates all the images in a folder contains references to the image files to be rotated. A script that adds annotations to a group of QuickTime movies contains references to the movie files to be edited. A script that applies formatting to the paragraphs in a story contains references to the targeted paragraphs.

To AppleScript, every item or thing it encounters is an *object*. Referring to scriptable objects is an essential technique that all good scripters understand and use daily. This chapter will provide you with a thorough understanding of how to refer to scriptable objects using various kinds of AppleScript *object references*.

Because the Finder is so familiar, we'll focus on it. In particular, we'll discuss those objects that the Finder knows as *items* and that the System Events application knows as *disk items*. For this reason, we'll sometimes call references to them *item references*.

This chapter and the four chapters following it explore the tasks of identifying, finding, and manipulating objects using AppleScript. These chapters are meant to be read in sequence, with each chapter building on the ideas presented in the previous chapters. Although most of the examples use Finder items such as files and folders, many of the principles described pertain to all scriptable objects, not just disk items.

Object References

Every scriptable object has a *location* within a hierarchy of objects. Whether it's the third word in the second paragraph of a story, a PDF file in your Documents folder in your home directory on the startup disk, or a track in an iTunes playlist, scriptable objects exist within or belong to other scriptable objects.

Describing an item's location on a disk or an object's location in a document or in some other object is the method scripts use to "point" to it. An object reference is a description of a scriptable object's location. Although there is more than one way to describe an object's location, one important principle of scripting remains constant:

> **NOTE** ▸ Scriptable objects are referenced by describing their location in their object hierarchy, or where they are in their "chain of command" relative to other objects.

This principle is true whether the scriptable object is a movie, image, paragraph, text container, circle, music track, document file, application file or folder, or anything else.

Scripters can use five types of *item references* in Mac OS X to refer to items on disk. We call them *nested references*, *path references*, *alias references*, *POSIX paths*, and *file URLs*. We'll begin the coverage of item references by showing how to identify and refer to files and folders on your hard drive using each of these five item reference types.

Nested References

In the first chapter of this book, you learned AppleScript basics by manipulating the properties of Finder windows. One of the properties examined was the `target` property. Its value was a reference to the folder or directory whose contents were displayed in the Finder window.

Here's a quick review. Enter and run Script 3.1 in a new script window in the Script Editor application:

```
tell application "Finder" to open home
```
SCRIPT 3.1

Your home directory should now be the frontmost window on your Desktop. Leave it there for now. Next, get the value of the `target` property of the front window with Script 3.2:

```
tell application "Finder" to get the target of the front window
```
SCRIPT 3.2

In the Result pane at the bottom of the script window is a reference to the folder whose contents are being displayed in the frontmost Finder window. This reference should look something like this (naturally, the home folder will have your name instead of Sal's):

```
folder "sal" of folder "Users" of startup disk of application "Finder"
```

We call this kind of item reference a *nested reference* because, like a set of Russian dolls, the objects "nest" inside each other.

A nested reference uses the possessive "of" to indicate that an object is contained by or belongs to a parent object. In this example, the folder sal is in the folder Users, which is on the startup disk, and it is displayed in the Finder application.

All scriptable applications, by default, use the nested reference form to describe their scriptable objects. Scripts 3.3 through 3.6 show some examples.

QuickTime Player:

```
text frame 12 of track 3 of movie 2 of ¬
    application "QuickTime Player"
```
SCRIPT 3.3

QuarkXPress:

```
word 5 of paragraph 4 of story 1 of ¬
    document "Newsletter" of application "QuarkXPress"
```
SCRIPT 3.4

iDVD:

```
button 3 of menu 4 of application "iDVD"
```
SCRIPT 3.5

Finder:

```
document file "car.pdf" of folder "Documents" of ¬
    folder "sal" of folder "Users" of startup disk of ¬
    application "Finder"
```
SCRIPT 3.6

When the Finder, or any scriptable application, returns the requested location of a scriptable object to a script, it is usually in the form of a nested reference.

> **NOTE ▶** If you are typing these scripts into Script Editor as you follow along, be sure to use your own short user name instead of sal, and use the name of your startup disk instead of the name of Sal's startup disk, which is Macintosh HD. Otherwise, the scripts won't work correctly, and several of them won't even compile. To compile and run them successfully, you also have to enclose each statement in a tell block addressed to the application, and the referenced object, such as `document "Newsletter"`, must exist.

Path References

To request information about a specific object and to perform actions with it, scripts pass the object to the item's parent application for processing in the form of a reference. When manipulating specific files and folders, scripts pass references to them to the Finder application, which is the traditional application in Mac OS X for dealing with disk items, or to the System Events application.

As you've seen, nested references to disk items can sometimes be very long and wordy. A shorter reference form, often used to pass references to disk items to the Finder application, is the *path reference*. Like a Finder nested reference, a path reference is used to refer to a scriptable object on disk. However, a path reference takes a different approach to point to the scriptable object.

Nested references begin with the targeted scriptable object and proceed *up* its object hierarchy or chain.

Path references take the opposite approach, beginning at the top of the object hierarchy and proceeding *down* to the target object. And, instead of using the possessive "of" to indicate containment, the "path" in a path reference is represented as a colon-delimited list of the names of the chain's objects displayed as a "string" or series of text characters read from left to right.

As an example, let's ask the Finder for a reference to the Documents folder in your home directory. Enter and run Script 3.7.

```
tell application "Finder" to get folder "Documents" of home
```
SCRIPT 3.7

The result, displayed in the Result pane at the bottom of the script window, is a nested reference that looks like this:

```
folder "Documents" of folder "sal" of folder "Users" of ¬
    startup disk of application "Finder"
```

Next, convert the nested reference into a *path* by adding as string to the existing script. The words as string are read by the script as an instruction to *coerce* the result of the previous action from its default format to the indicated format, or in this case a text string.

```
tell application "Finder" to get folder "Documents" of home as string
```
SCRIPT 3.8

When the script is run, the result will look similar to this:

```
"Macintosh HD:Users:sal:Documents:"
```
This is a *path*. It is a colon-delimited list of the names of the objects in the target object's chain of command, presented as a string of characters, read from left to right, with the leftmost name being the name of the topmost object in the object hierarchy, in this case the hard drive containing the Documents folder. Each segment in the chain is separated, or *delimited*, by a colon character.

A path begins with the name of the drive containing the target object, followed by each descending object in the hierarchy and ending with the name of the target item. Each container or folder name in the path is followed by a colon character. If the last item in the chain is a folder, it is followed by a colon. If the last item in the chain is a file, no colon is added.

For example, the path to a Cars folder in the Documents folder would look like this:

```
"Macintosh HD:Users:sal:Documents:Cars:"
```

but the path to a file named "cars.pdf" in the Documents folder would look like this:

```
"Macintosh HD:Users:sal:Documents:cars.pdf"
```

Remember:

> **NOTE** ► Paths to folders end with a colon; paths to files do not.

Also note that the entire path string is enclosed in straight quotation marks. As you learned in the first chapter, text, whether a name or path, is always enclosed in straight quotation marks to indicate to Script Editor that it is not to be interpreted as a command.

To complete the creation of a path reference, you need only to place the class of the target object before the path string.

For example, Script 3.9 shows the path reference to the Documents folder as you would enter it when addressing commands to the Finder.

```
tell application "Finder"
    folder "Macintosh HD:Users:sal:Documents:"
end tell
```
SCRIPT 3.9

Since a folder is an object of the class `folder` in the Finder's dictionary, the word `folder` precedes the path.

Script 3.10 shows a path reference to a document file in the Documents folder.

```
tell application "Finder"
    document file "Macintosh HD:Users:sal:Documents:cars.pdf"
end tell
```
SCRIPT 3.10

Since a file is an item of the class `document file` in the Finder's dictionary, the words `document file` precede the path.

If you're not sure of the class of the target object, you can use the Finder's class name for generic objects, `item`:

```
tell application "Finder"
    item "Macintosh HD:Users:sal:Documents:"
    item "Macintosh HD:Users:sal:Documents:cars.pdf"
end tell
```
SCRIPT 3.11

All the previous examples are path references and are used by the Finder application to refer to files, disks, and folders.

To demonstrate that the Finder understands and responds to path references, enter and run Script 3.12 (be sure to replace Sal's name with the name of your home directory and to replace `Macintosh HD` with the name of your startup disk):

```
tell application "Finder" to ¬
    open folder "Macintosh HD:Users:sal:Documents:"
```
SCRIPT 3.12

Since the Finder has no problem understanding a path reference, the Documents folder is now open on your Desktop.

Alias References

Nested references are easy to follow and understand because they have a syntax that is very "English-like." However, nested references are valid only when used within their host application. They cannot be passed between applications.

For example, QuickTime Player does not understand the command in Script 3.13, and Script Editor won't compile it:

```
tell application "QuickTime Player"
    open document file "trailer.mov" of folder "Movies" of ¬
        folder "sal" of folder "Users" of the startup disk
end
```
SCRIPT 3.13

QuickTime Player doesn't know what a folder or document file is. The nested reference in the example uses terms from the Finder's dictionary, such as *document file* and *folder*, which are not part of QuickTime Player's scripting vocabulary.

Path references won't work in most other applications either, because they are unique to the Finder application and a few others.

For references to files and folders to be usable in most applications, they must be in a generic format, recognized by all applications, called an *alias reference*.

A reference in alias format looks like a path reference, except the path string is preceded by the word `alias` rather than `document file`, `item`, or `folder`.

Scripts 3.14 and 3.15 are references to the Documents folder in path and alias formats.

Path reference:

```
folder "Macintosh HD:Users:sal:Documents:"
```
SCRIPT 3.14

Alias reference:

```
alias "Macintosh HD:Users:sal:Documents:"
```
SCRIPT 3.15

The Finder, and all other applications that can handle files, understands and accepts disk item references in alias format. Close any open Finder windows, and try Script 3.16, a modified version of the previous scripts.

```
tell application "Finder" to ¬
    open alias "Macintosh HD:Users:sal:Documents:"
```
SCRIPT 3.16

Requesting an Alias Reference

Since the Finder recognizes alias references, it will, upon request, supply a reference to an item in alias format. This is done by adding an `as alias` coercion at the end of the request.

For example, to have the Finder return an alias reference to the Documents folder in your home directory, enter and run Script 3.17.

```
tell application "Finder" to get folder "Documents" of home as alias
```
SCRIPT 3.17

The result of this request is an alias reference to the Documents folder:

```
alias "Macintosh HD:Users:sal:Documents:"
```

Although you can use alias references with any application that is able to handle files, there is a caveat regarding their use in versions of Mac OS X before Leopard.

For an alias reference to be valid for use in a pre-Leopard script, it must refer to an *existing* item. You can't even compile a script containing an alias reference to a nonexistent item. For example, if you're running Mac OS X 10.4 (Tiger), enter the alias reference in Script 3.18 into a script window, and click the Compile button.

```
alias "Macintosh HD:Users:sal:Documents:zippydodah"
```
SCRIPT 3.18

Script Editor reports an error stating that the file could not be found, since this alias reference points to a file that does not exist on your computer. This limitation makes it awkward to write a script that uses an item you know will be available later, when you're ready to install and run the script, but which isn't available while you're writing it.

In Leopard, you can now compile a script containing alias references to nonexistent items. It will fail with an error if a referenced item still doesn't exist when you run the script, but now you can write the script, compile it, and save it even if the actual item isn't yet available.

UNIX References

Mac OS X's UNIX underpinnings have brought great stability and many enhancements to Macintosh computing. Mac OS X has successfully combined the capabilities of UNIX with the traditional Mac user experience, providing Mac users with additional controls and ways of navigating and manipulating the file system. For example, the Go to Folder command in the Finder's Go menu accepts only UNIX-style item references.

Item references in UNIX are displayed as *POSIX paths* (POSIX stands for Portable Operating System for UNIX). An item reference in POSIX format is similar to the path part of alias references and path references, but the delimiter character is a forward slash (/) instead of a colon (:). These two paths point to the same file:

```
"/Users/sal/Documents/cars.pdf"
"Macintosh HD:Users:sal:Documents:cars.pdf"
```

As you see, the initial forward slash in the POSIX path refers to the startup disk without using its name.

Alias Reference to POSIX Path

Occasionally, your scripts may need to communicate with the UNIX aspect of Mac OS X. Fortunately, AppleScript provides the means to convert alias references to POSIX paths and POSIX paths to alias references, making it possible for scripters to script both the traditional Mac and UNIX worlds.

Here's an example that derives a POSIX path from the Finder.

First, get the Finder to return a reference to your Documents folder by entering and running Script 3.19.

```
tell application "Finder" to get folder "Documents" of home
```
SCRIPT 3.19

The result is a nested reference similar to this:

```
folder "Documents" of folder "sal" of folder "Users" of ¬
    startup disk of application "Finder"
```

Next, add a coercion to the end of the script to convert the returned *reference* from a nested reference to an alias reference, as in Script 3.20.

```
tell application "Finder" to get folder "Documents" of home as alias
```
SCRIPT 3.20

The result is now a reference to the Documents folder in alias format:

```
alias "Macintosh HD:Users:sal:Documents:"
```

Now that the script is returning a reference in alias format, you can extract a POSIX path from the result by placing `POSIX path of` before the alias reference, as shown in Script 3.21.

```
tell application "Finder" to ¬
    get the POSIX path of (folder "Documents" of home as alias)
```
SCRIPT 3.21

Note that the section of the script that generates the initial reference and coerces it to an alias reference is enclosed in parentheses. This is done to indicate to the script that it should perform the actions in the parentheses first and replace the actions with their result, in this case an alias reference, and only then perform the other script actions in the `tell` block.

The result of the previous example looks like this:

```
"/Users/sal/Documents/"
```

This is the POSIX path to the Documents folder.

To see the Mac OS X UNIX underpinnings in action, enter the path that was just returned by the previous script (without the quotation marks) in the dialog presented when you switch to the Finder, close all windows, and select Go to Folder from the Go menu. Your Documents folder instantly appears on the Desktop!

We pointed out earlier that the name of the startup disk is missing from the beginning of the path. In POSIX paths, the name of the startup disk is omitted in paths that point to items on the startup drive. Drive names are included when the target volume is not the startup disk. For example, here's a POSIX path to a file on a mounted server:

```
"/Volumes/Backup Drive/Clients/Smith Varney/new pamphlet.pdf"
```

POSIX Path to Alias Reference

To convert a POSIX path to an alias reference, you use two coercions, the first to a file reference and then to an alias reference.

For example, replace the existing script in the script window with the POSIX path returned from the previous script. Place the words `as POSIX file` after the path, and run Script 3.22.

```
"/Users/sal/Documents/" as POSIX file
```
SCRIPT 3.22

The result is a file reference in this form:

```
file "Macintosh HD:Users:sal:Documents:"
```

To complete the conversion in Script 3.23, add a second coercion to the end of the statement by adding the term `as alias`.

```
"/Users/sal/Documents/" as POSIX file as alias
```
SCRIPT 3.23

Since scripts are executed from the top down and from the left to the right, the POSIX file coercion is performed first, and its result is then coerced to an alias reference:

```
alias "Macintosh HD:Users:sal:Documents:"
```

We'll explain how to use POSIX paths in scripts in later chapters. For now, it's important to understand what they are and how to convert between alias references and POSIX paths.

> **NOTE** ▶ Coercing a path string in POSIX path format to a POSIX file works even if the file doesn't exist on the disk. However, if you try to coerce it to an alias reference, the script will generate an error if you run it when the file does not exist.

File URLs

The last kind of item reference is the *file URL.*

The robust integration of the Internet with Mac OS X has made the difference between items on your drive and items on the Internet less visible. For example, choosing iDisk from the Go menu in the Finder mounts your iDisk as if it were just another folder on the Desktop.

In addition to supporting item references in nested, path, alias, and POSIX path formats, the Finder supplies references in the same standard URL format that is used to link to items from Internet web pages.

For example, enter and run Script 3.24.

```
tell application "Finder" to ¬
    get the url of folder "Documents" of home
```
SCRIPT 3.24

The result is an item reference in HTML format, like this:

```
"file://localhost/Users/sal/Documents/"
```

To see how closely the Internet and the Mac OS X file system are related, enter this URL (without quotes) in Microsoft Internet Explorer, and you'll be able to browse your hard drive! (This doesn't work in Safari, because Safari opens your Documents folder in the Finder.)

Chapter Summary

In this chapter you examined five types of item references used by the Finder in Mac OS X: nested references, path references, alias references, POSIX paths, and file URLs. You'll use these references in the following chapters as you examine how to find specific items.

Before continuing to the next chapter, review this summary to make sure you understand the various types of object references.

Item References

Scriptable disk items are referenced by their location in their object hierarchy or where they are in their "chain of command." A reference to an item is a description of its location.

Nested References

A nested reference is the default reference format returned by most scriptable applications. The location of a scriptable item in its object hierarchy is described from the bottom of the chain to the top using the possessive "of" to indicate the containment of one item in another.

```
tell application "Finder"
    folder "Documents" of folder "sal" of ¬
        folder "Users" of startup disk
end tell
```
SCRIPT 3.25

Path References

Path references are used in scripts to pass a reference to a scriptable item to the Finder application. Path references end with text strings, read from left to right, that contain the name of each item in the object hierarchy from the top down delimited by a colon character. Path references begin with the name of the class of the target item, such as `folder` or `document file`, or the generic term `item`.

```
tell application "Finder"
    folder "Macintosh HD:Users:sal:Documents:"
    item "Macintosh HD:Users:sal:Documents:"
    document file "Macintosh HD:Users:sal:Documents:1028.pdf"
    item "Macintosh HD:Users:sal:Documents:1028.pdf"
end tell
```
SCRIPT 3.26

Alias References

Alias references are recognized by all applications that can handle files. They are used when item references are passed between applications.

```
alias "Macintosh HD:Users:sal:Documents:"
alias "Macintosh HD:Users:sal:Documents:1028.pdf"
```

SCRIPT 3.27

POSIX Paths

The UNIX aspects of Mac OS X accept references to objects in POSIX path format. This reference type lists the names of the items in the object hierarchy separated by forward slash characters.

```
"/Users/sal/Documents/Projects/Cars/new.txt"
```

POSIX paths can be derived from alias references in this manner:

```
POSIX path of alias "Macintosh HD:Users:sal:Documents:"
--> returns: "/Users/sal/Documents/"
```

SCRIPT 3.28

Alias references can be coerced from POSIX paths in this manner:

```
"/Users/sal/Documents/" as POSIX file as alias
--> returns: alias "Macintosh HD:Users:sal:Documents:"
```

SCRIPT 3.29

File URLs

Every item in the Mac OS X file system can be described in the *URL format* (Uniform Resource Locator format) similar to the one used to reference items on the Internet.

```
tell application "Finder" to ¬
    get the url of folder "Documents" of home
--> returns: "file://localhost/Users/sal/Documents/"
```

SCRIPT 3.30

What's Next?

In this chapter, you learned how AppleScript identifies scriptable objects in the object hierarchy. Using Finder items as the focus, you learned all about the several types of object reference that AppleScript uses. You'll put this knowledge to use in the next chapter, where you'll learn how to find particular objects using AppleScript.

4

Lesson **4**
Finding Objects

This chapter is the second in a series of five chapters about identifying, finding, and manipulating scriptable objects in applications.

Finding specific scriptable objects is a task common to most scripts. For example, a script might locate all the TIFF image files in a given folder that were modified today. Or a script might locate all the occurrences of a specific phrase in a story and replace them with another phrase. Finding scriptable objects is a common task and something that AppleScript and scriptable applications do exceptionally well. In this chapter, we'll cover the techniques used to locate specific scriptable objects.

Location or Property

Imagine you're standing in front of a group of people seated in a small auditorium that contains five rows of seats separated into two groups by an aisle that runs down the center of the room to where you are standing.

Each row contains five seats, with five on each side of the center aisle, and every seat contains a person. Your job is to choose five of the assembled people to take with you on a vacation to Mexico.

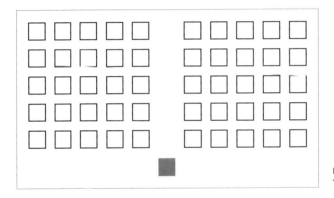

FIGURE 4.1
The full auditorium.

You could make the selection process easy by choosing to take all the people seated in the first row to your left:

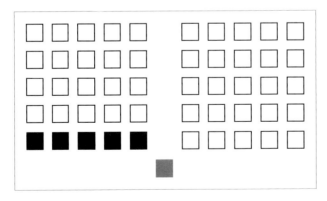

FIGURE 4.2
Everybody in the first row on the left.

Or you could choose to take the people seated in the second row to your right:

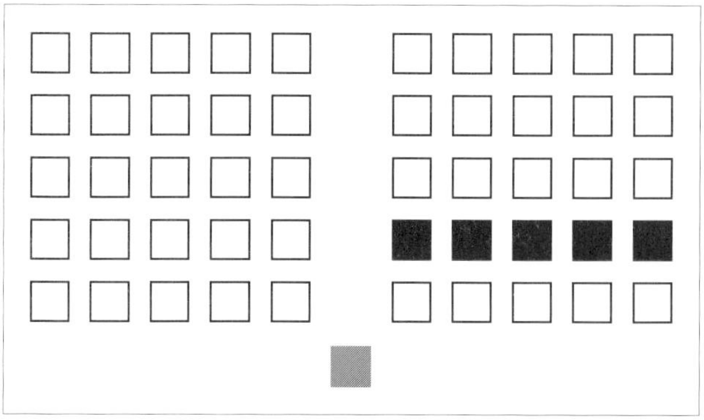

FIGURE 4.3
Everybody in the
second row on the right.

Or you could choose to take the people seated in the last row on the right:

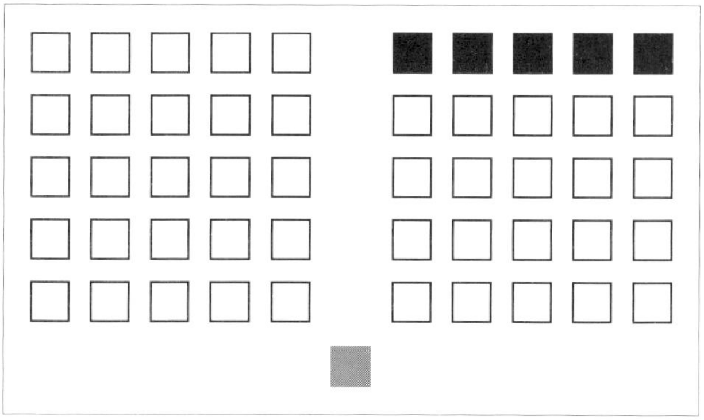

FIGURE 4.4
Everybody in the last
row on the right.

Or even the row before the last row on the left:

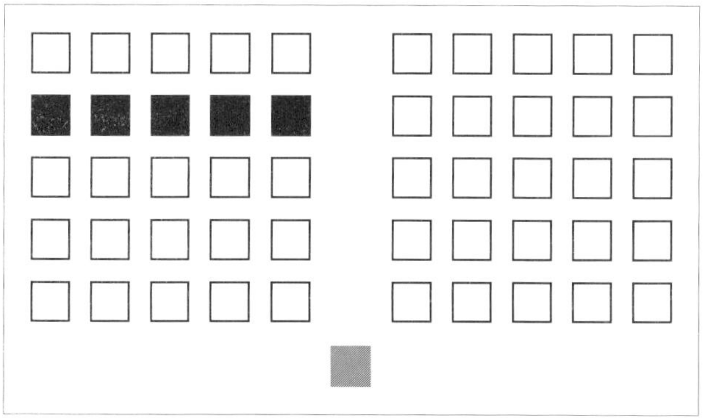

FIGURE 4.5
Everybody in the row
before the last row on
the left.

You might choose to take the last person in each row on your left:

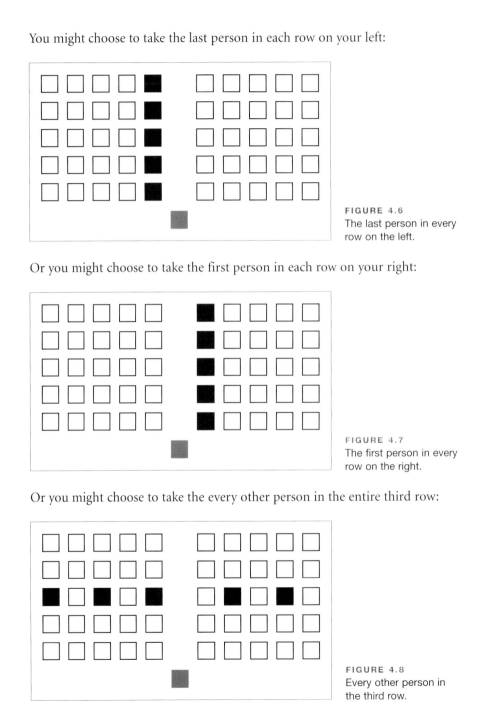

FIGURE 4.6
The last person in every
row on the left.

Or you might choose to take the first person in each row on your right:

FIGURE 4.7
The first person in every
row on the right.

Or you might choose to take the every other person in the entire third row:

FIGURE 4.8
Every other person in
the third row.

Or you might choose to take the every other person in the entire fourth row starting with the second person in that row:

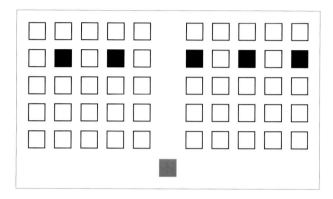

FIGURE 4.9
Every other person in the fourth row, starting with the second person.

You could even use a geometric pattern for selecting by choosing the first person in the first row, the second person in the second row, and so on.

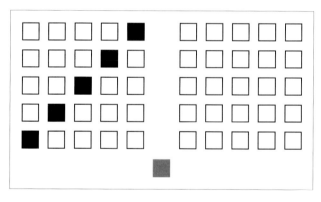

FIGURE 4.10
The first person in the first row, second person in the second row, and so on.

Or you could just take the first five random people chosen by drawing tickets containing their seat numbers out of a hat.

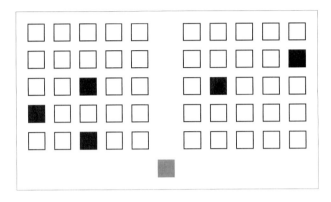

FIGURE 4.11
Five people chosen at random.

Now, if you don't mind traveling with strangers who have nothing in common with you, choosing people by where they are seated might be an acceptable solution. However, if you'd like to share your exotic vacation with those more like yourself, you could try another approach.

For example, if *age* is an important consideration to you, you could ask everyone whose age is within five years of yours to stand up and then choose five people from amongst those standing.

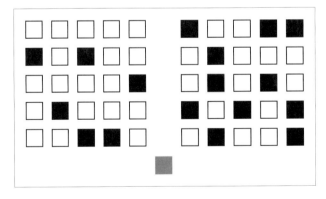

FIGURE 4.12
Everybody whose age is within five years of yours.

If *gender* is your most important consideration, you could ask all men or women to stand up and then choose five people from among those standing.

You could even make your selection very specific by asking all people of a specific gender whose age is within five years of yours and who like to dance to salsa music to stand up and then choose five people from among those standing.

As you see from this scenario, there are two ways to find items: by location and by property.

▶ *Location* in this example is a person's place in the order in which people were seated.

▶ *Property* is a person's age, gender, and so on.

You will use these two techniques in most of the scripts you write that locate and process scriptable objects.

Finding Items by Location

In the previous chapter, you learned that every scriptable object is contained in a parent object. Now, consider that there might be any number of objects that are also contained by the same parent object. The topic for this chapter is how you refer to any of the objects that are contained in the one parent object, all at the same level of the containment hierarchy.

Finding Items by Index

Every scriptable item on disk, like every scriptable object belonging to an application, occupies a specific place among all the items in its parent container. There is a first item, a second item, and so on. In other words, they have an *ordered* relationship among themselves. The numeric value representing an item's location in an ordered group of items is called its *index*.

For example, the second paragraph in a story consisting of ten paragraphs of text has an index value of 2. The third paragraph has an index value of 3, and so on. So, if you asked for the contents of paragraph 5 of the story, you would receive the text of the fifth paragraph in the story. The same principle applies to files and folders in the Finder, as demonstrated in the following examples.

The results of the queries in the following examples are based on the standard Mac OS X installation as it comes on a newly purchased computer. The scripts, when run on your computer, may return answers different from those shown here.

Enter and run Script 4.1.

```
tell application "Finder" to get item 1 of the startup disk
```
SCRIPT 4.1

An item reference in nested format is returned by the script:

```
folder "Applications" of startup disk of application "Finder"
```

The returned item reference may not refer to the first item displayed in a Finder window showing the contents of the startup disk, because the display may be arranged, for example, in order of modification date or in reverse alphabetical order. Instead, it refers to the first item in the Finder's internal list of items belonging to the startup disk. This internal list is usually alphabetical by default.

Let's get the second item in the startup disk. Don't enter the line beginning with `--> returns: in Script 4.2` because we added this only to show you the result as it is displayed in the Result pane at the bottom of the script window. The result shown on your computer may differ, depending on the folders that exist on your startup disk.

```
tell application "Finder" to get item 2 of the startup disk
--> returns: folder "Library" of startup disk of application "Finder"
```
SCRIPT 4.2

And here's the third item in Script 4.3:

```
tell application "Finder" to get item 3 of the startup disk
--> returns: folder "System" of startup disk of application "Finder"
```
SCRIPT 4.3

Here's a simple exercise to demonstrate using index values to specify the locations of items. Enter and run Script 4.4:

```
tell application "Finder" to open the startup disk
```
SCRIPT 4.4

A Finder window displaying the contents of the startup disk now opens on the Desktop. Switch to the Finder, and make a new folder in that window named Aardvark. Once you've made the folder, enter and run Script 4.5.

```
tell application "Finder" to get item 1 of the startup disk
--> returns: folder "Aardvark" of startup disk of application "Finder"
```
SCRIPT 4.5

Notice that the first item of the startup disk is no longer the Applications folder. Its index value has been increased by 1 because an item with a name that alphabetically precedes its name has been added to the folder. In other words, the Applications folder is now the *second* folder of the startup disk.

For proof of this, let's ask the Finder for the new index of the Applications folder in Script 4.6.

```
tell application "Finder" to ¬
    get the index of folder "Applications" of the startup disk
--> returns: 2
```
SCRIPT 4.6

Based on the result of the previous example, you can see the following:

▸ Although the index of an item is always unique (there is only one item 2, one item 3, and so on), its value may change if other items are added to or removed from the parent container.

Now, let's return the startup disk to the way it was. Delete the Aardvark folder from the startup disk, and then run Script 4.7.

```
tell application "Finder" to get item 1 of the startup disk
--> returns: folder "Applications" of startup disk of application "Finder"
```
SCRIPT 4.7

Since the top level of the startup disk no longer contains any items that alphabetically come before the folder Applications, it is once again the first item in the startup disk.

Negative Index Values

When working with multiple items, it may be useful to address the last item in the list of scriptable items. AppleScript provides a variety of means to do this. We'll now continue our coverage of index values by showing how to get the index of the last item in a group of items.

One method is to get the total number of items in the container. After all, the index value of the last item in a folder must be equal to the total number of items in the folder, right? Try Script 4.8.

```
tell application "Finder" to count the items of the startup disk
--> returns: 4
```
SCRIPT 4.8

The result is the total number of items contained in the top level of the startup disk. Incidentally, you can also use the word **count** as a *noun* instead of a *verb*, as in Script 4.9.

```
tell application "Finder" to ¬
    get the count of items of the startup disk
--> returns: 4
```
SCRIPT 4.9

So, if you want to get a reference to the last item in a container, you can use the result of the item count as your index by placing the count request in parentheses, as in Script 4.10.

```
tell application "Finder" to ¬
    get item (the count of items of the startup disk) of ¬
    the startup disk
```
SCRIPT 4.10

When the script is run, the section in the parentheses is executed first and is replaced with the result of its action, in this case the total number of items in the folder, and then the rest of the script is processed, returning this:

```
folder "Users" of startup disk of application "Finder"
```

Although the previous script returns the correct result, it is a rather wordy way to request a reference to the last item. There is a more concise way to accomplish the same result using negative index values.

Enter and run Script 4.11.

```
tell application "Finder" to ¬
    get the name of every item of the startup disk
--> returns: {"Applications", "Library", "System", "Users"}
```
SCRIPT 4.11

The result is a list of the names matching the items in the top level of the startup disk. Reading from left to right, item 1 in the list of names is Applications, item 2 is Library, and so on, with the last item in the list being Users. Make sense? Try Script 4.12.

```
tell application "Finder" to ¬
    get the name of item 4 of the startup disk
--> returns: "Users"
```
SCRIPT 4.12

However, AppleScript supports not only indexing lists from *left to right* but also from *right to left*! When indexed in reverse order, index values are *negative* numbers beginning with -1. In other words, a list of items referenced from left to right would be as follows:

```
{item 1, item 2, item 3, item 4}
```

The same list of items, referenced in the same order but using negative numbers, is as follows:

```
{item -4, item -3, item -2, item -1}
```

The ability to reference items in either direction allows you to locate the last item without knowing how many items are in the group. Just use index value -1.

Try Script 4.13.

```
tell application "Finder" to ¬
    get the name of item -1 of the startup disk
--> returns: "Users"
```
SCRIPT 4.13

If you want a reference to the item before the last item in the startup disk, you write it as shown in Script 4.14.

```
tell application "Finder" to get item -2 of the startup disk
--> returns: folder "System" of startup disk of application "Finder"
```
SCRIPT 4.14

Finding Items by Range

Another use of the index value is to locate or reference a *range* of items. For an example, see Script 4.15.

```
tell application "Finder" to get items 2 thru 4 of the startup disk
```
SCRIPT 4.15

The result is a three-item list of nested references to a range of items located in the top level of the startup disk.

Note the use of the term **thru** instead of **through**. Although they have the same meaning and either spelling can be used, scripters often prefer to use the shorter version.

Negative index values can also be used in requests targeting a range of items. For example, to retrieve references to a range of items starting with the second item and ending with the last item, follow the example of Script 4.16:

```
tell application "Finder" to get items 2 thru -1 of the startup disk
```
SCRIPT 4.16

To get a list of references to *all* items in a container or folder, you could start with the first item and end with the last item, as in Script 4.17.

```
tell application "Finder" to get items 1 thru -1 of the startup disk
```
SCRIPT 4.17

However, it is much clearer to use the term every, as in Script 4.18.

```
tell application "Finder" to get every item of the startup disk
```
SCRIPT 4.18

Finding Items by Descriptive Index

As you've seen, the index property is an excellent means for finding or referring to specific items or a range of items in a container. Simply follow the class name of the target item with a number, and you have an index reference, as in item 5, folder 3, or Finder window 2.

However, since AppleScript is designed to be written in a "conversational" style, you may optionally choose to write index values in a more descriptive manner.

For example, instead of using item 5, you could write your index value as the fifth item, because AppleScript supports the descriptive indexes for the numeric values 1 through 10, as in first, second, third, fourth, fifth, sixth, seventh, eighth, ninth, and tenth.

Or you can use descriptive suffixes for any integer value, as in the 1st item, the 23rd item, or the 4064th item.

Although using these optional index forms can make your scripts very easy to read and understand, there is one caveat regarding their use. When describing a range of items, you must use only integers, as in items 56 thru 112.

Items can also be identified by other synonyms that stand in for numeric indexes. For example, to get the first item in a group of items in a container, you can use the term front as in Script 4.19.

```
tell application "Finder" to get the front item of the startup disk
--> returns: folder "Applications" of startup disk of application "Finder"
```
SCRIPT 4.19

Correspondingly, to get the final item in a container, you can use the terms back or last as in Script 4.20,

```
tell application "Finder" to get the last item of the startup disk
--> returns: folder "Users" of startup disk of application "Finder"
```
SCRIPT 4.20

or Script 4.21.

```
tell application "Finder" to get the back item of the startup disk
--> returns: folder "Users" of the startup disk of application "Finder"
```
SCRIPT 4.21

Although the terms front and back are usually used to reference windows, they work to reference any object type.

Location references can also be used for items within the outer boundaries of a group. For example, you can use the term middle to get the centermost item in a group of items:

```
tell application "Finder" to get the middle item of the startup disk
```
SCRIPT 4.22

Finding Items by Relative Location

In addition, you can use the terms before and after to locate items in relation to other items of the group, as shown in Scripts 4.23 and 4.24.

```
tell application "Finder" to ¬
    get the item before the last item of the startup disk
--> returns: folder "System" of startup disk of application "Finder"
```
SCRIPT 4.23

```
tell application "Finder" to ¬
    get the item after the first item of the startup disk
--> returns: folder "Library" of startup disk of application "Finder"
```
SCRIPT 4.24

Finding Random Items

Occasionally a script may require the selection of a random item. AppleScript offers support for random selection through the use of the term some as in Script 4.25.

```
tell application "Finder" to get some item of the startup disk
--> returns a random reference to one of the items in the startup disk
```
SCRIPT 4.25

Finding Items by Property

The previous section describes all the methods used to locate or reference items by their *location* in their parent container or in *relation* to each other. Although a useful and valuable means of locating items, finding items by location is not the only way to find the items you need to process.

As you learned in the example at the start of this chapter, referring to items by the value of their *properties* is more useful when you know *what* you want but not *where* it is. AppleScript has an excellent built-in means of finding the items you need by using an easy-to-understand query syntax.

For example, how would you write a script to locate *every item of the startup disk whose name begins with* S? The answer is that you just wrote it! Script 4.26 shows that it is exactly what you would say in conversation.

```
tell application "Finder" to ¬
    get every item of the startup disk whose name begins with "S"
--> returns: {folder "System" of startup disk of application "Finder"}
```
SCRIPT 4.26

The result of this query is a list of references to the items at the top level of the startup disk whose name begins with the letter *S*. If no items match the query, an empty list is returned. If many items match the query, a reference to each of them is returned in the list.

The Structure of a Query

Let's examine the various components that make up the previous query. It begins with a keyword that identifies how many or which items are to be referenced. Examples are `every`, `first`, `last`, and `some`.

This query:

```
every item of the startup disk whose name begins with "S"
```

returns a list of references to *all* the items whose properties match the request, while this query:

```
the first item of the startup disk whose name begins with "S"
```

returns a single reference to the *first* item whose properties match the request. Likewise, this query:

```
the last item of the startup disk whose name begins with "S"
```

returns a single reference to the *last* item whose properties match the request.

Another way to request references to all matching items is to use the plural form of the class of the objects you are searching for, such as this:

```
items of the startup disk whose name begins with "S"
```

or this:

```
folders of the startup disk whose name begins with "S"
```

The plural `items` is equivalent to the term `every item`, and you can use them interchangeably.

The next component of the query begins with the term whose and specifies the target property and the target property's value.

This specification is composed of the title of the target property (in this case, the name property), a comparison operator (in this case, begins with), and the value of the target property (in this case, the letter *S*). Each of the elements can be changed to suit the needs of the query. Here are some examples.

Original query:

```
every item of the startup disk whose name begins with "S"
```

Changing the location indicator:

```
the first item of the startup disk whose name begins with "S"
the last item of the startup disk whose name begins with "S"
some item of the startup disk whose name begins with "S"
```

Changing the comparison operator:

```
every item of the startup disk whose name ends with "S"
every item of the startup disk whose name contains "S"
every item of the startup disk whose name does not contain "S"
```

Changing the value of the target property:

```
every item of the startup disk whose name ends with "q"
every item of the startup disk whose name ends with ".zip"
```

As with the English language, innumerable variations are available for the syntax of the query, providing the ability to search for exactly the items you desire.

For your reference, the following sections are partial lists of the operators used by the AppleScript language:

Containment Operators

Here are the containment operators:

```
start with
starts with
begin with
begins with
end with
ends with
contains
does not contain
doesn't contain
is in
is contained by
is not in
is not contained by
isn't contained by
```

Comparison Operators (Equality)

Here are the comparison operators (equality):

```
=
equal
equals
equal to
is equal to
g
does not equal
doesn't equal
is not
is not equal
is not equal to
```

Comparison Operators (Precedence)

Here are the comparison operators (precedence):

```
<
comes before
is less than
is not greater than or equal
is not greater than or equal to
isn't greater than or equal
isn't greater than or equal to
less than
>
comes after
greater than
is greater than
is not less than or equal
is not less than or equal to
isn't less than or equal
isn't less than or equal to
≠
<=
does not come after
doesn't come after
is less than or equal
is less than or equal to
is not greater than
isn't greater than
less than or equal
less than or equal to
≤
>=
does not come before
doesn't come before
greater than or equal
greater than or equal to
is greater than or equal
is greater than or equal to
≥
is not less than
isn't less than
```

Script 4.27 gives a few examples of Finder queries using the various operators.

```
tell application "Finder"
    every item of folder "Documents" of home whose ¬
        name contains "Smith Project"
    every document file of folder "Pictures" of home whose ¬
        file type is in {"JPEG", "TIFF", "GIFf"}
    every document file of folder "Pictures" of home whose ¬
        name extension is not in {"jpg", "tif"}
    every folder of folder "Documents" of home whose ¬
        size is greater than 10000000
    every item of home whose name comes before "P"
end tell
```
SCRIPT 4.27

Compound Property Queries

You can limit the scope of searches by incorporating additional or optional search parameters in your queries.

For example, to add another property value to a query, use the term **and** followed by the new parameter, as in Script 4.28 (this example assumes Leopard is installed on your computer):

```
tell application "Finder"
    get 1st item of folder "Applications" of the startup disk whose ¬
        name begins with "T" and name contains "Machine"
end tell
--> returns: application file "Time Machine.app" of folder "Applications"
of startup disk of application "Finder"
```
SCRIPT 4.28

Each additional comparison must be complete in itself. It cannot be a continuation of the previous comparison. Script 4.29 is an example that won't compile:

```
tell application "Finder"
    get 1st item of folder "Applications" of the startup disk whose ¬
        name begins with "Q" and contains "Player" --> SYNTAX ERROR
end tell
```
SCRIPT 4.29

The proper syntax is shown in Script 4.30.

```
tell application "Finder"
    get 1st item of folder "Applications" of the startup disk whose ¬
        name begins with "Q" and name contains "Player"
end tell
--> returns: application file "QuickTime Player.app" of folder
"Applications" of startup disk of application "Finder"
```
SCRIPT 4.30

There is no limit to the number of additional search parameters that can be added. For example, the query in Script 4.31 contains a search specification that has four comparisons.

```
tell application "Finder" to ¬
    get every document file of folder "Pictures" of home whose ¬
    kind is "JPEG image" and name contains "Account" and ¬
    size is greater than or equal to 50000 and ¬
    size is less than or equal to 100000
```
SCRIPT 4.31

Optional search specifications can be added to a query by using the term or, as in Script 4.32.

```
tell application "Finder"
    get every document file of folder "Pictures" of home whose ¬
    file type is in {"JPEG", "TIFF"} or ¬
    name extension is in {"jpg", "tif", "tiff"}
end tell
```
SCRIPT 4.32

Any items meeting either of the search specifications are returned from the query.

Searches can contain both additional and optional specifications by using both the `and` and `or` terms.

The example in Script 4.33 encloses the additional specifications in parentheses so the logic of the query is easier to see. This is a good habit to develop, because it will help ensure that you've written your queries properly.

```
tell application "Finder"
    get every document file of folder "Pictures" of home whose ¬
        (kind is "JPEG image" or kind is "TIFF image") and ¬
        name contains "Smith Project"
end tell
```
SCRIPT 4.33

The previous query returns a reference to every TIFF or JPEG image whose name contains the phrase *Smith Project*. Both conditions, the kind of the image and its name, must match before a reference is returned.

In addition to `whose`, the term `where` can be used whenever it will help make the statement read more smoothly. For an example, see Script 4.34.

```
tell application "Finder"
    get every document file of folder "Pictures" of home where ¬
        its kind is "JPEG image"
end tell
```
SCRIPT 4.34

Note the use of the possessive term `its` to indicate ownership of the `kind` property. You can also use `of it`, as in `where kind of it is "JPEG image"`.

Chapter Summary

In this chapter, you learned how to locate items in the Finder by referencing their numeric location in their parent container or by searching for items based on the value of their properties.

In upcoming chapters, you'll put these principles to use when you write scripts that perform Finder actions based on queries.

The following are the important concepts from this chapter regarding creating queries.

Index or Property

Items in a container can be located by numeric location (index) or by the values of their properties.

Index

Every item in a container is represented by a numeric value corresponding to its location in the list of items in the parent container. This value is the item's index.

```
item 4 of folder "Documents" of home
```

Positive or Negative Index

Items in a list of items can be referenced incrementally using positive numeric values counting from left to right or using negative numeric values counting from right to left. For example, a list of four items when indexed from left to right would be as follows:

```
{item 1, item 2, item 3, item 4}
```

The same list of items referenced in the same order but counting from right to left would be as follows:

```
{item -4, item -3, item -2, item -1}
```

Item -1 is always the last item in a list.

So, in the following list of planets, Venus has an index value of either 2 or –8, depending on whether it is referenced from the left or right of the list (and assuming you think Pluto is a planet and all those other Kuiper belt objects aren't):

```
{"Mercury", "Venus", "Earth", "Mars", "Jupiter", "Saturn", "Uranus",
"Neptune", "Pluto"}
```

Range

Index values can be used to describe a subset of items in a larger list of items. Ranges can be described with either positive or negative indexes or a combination of both methods:

```
items 2 thru 4 of {"Mercury", "Venus", "Earth", "Mars", "Jupiter",
"Saturn", "Uranus", "Neptune", "Pluto"}
--> returns: {"Venus", "Earth", "Mars"}
```
SCRIPT 4.35

```
items 2 thru -6 of {"Mercury", "Venus", "Earth", "Mars", "Jupiter",
"Saturn", "Uranus", "Neptune", "Pluto"}
--> returns: {"Venus", "Earth", "Mars"}
```
SCRIPT 4.36

Descriptive Index

Because AppleScript was designed to be written in a "conversational" manner, you can use more descriptive names for index values.

AppleScript supports location word indexes for the numeric values 1 through 10, like so:

```
first, second, third, fourth, fifth, sixth, seventh, eighth, ninth,
and tenth
```

You can also use descriptive numeric suffixes for any index value, like so:

```
1st, 23rd, 4064th
```

Items can be referenced in terms of synonyms for their place in the list:

```
front, first, back, last, middle
```

Relative Location

The terms `before` and `after` can be used in relative location references:

```
item after the front item
item before the last item
item after the middle item
```

Random

Items can be referenced at random by using the term `some`:

```
Some item of {"Venus", "Earth", "Mars"}
```

Property

Items can be referenced by comparing the value of their properties to a desired set of values. For example:

```
every paragraph whose first character is "A"
```

or for example:

```
the first document file whose name contains "Smith Project"
```

A query using a property reference begins with a term indicating how many or which items are to be referenced.

This is followed by the term `whose` or `where`.

This is then followed by a comparison operator determining the manner in which the item's property value is compared.

The desired property value completes the query.

Here are variations of each component of the property reference query.

Location indicator:

```
the first document file whose name contains "Smith Project"
the last document file whose name contains "Smith Project"
every document file whose name contains "Smith Project"
```

Comparison operator:

```
every document file whose name begins with "Smith Project"
every document file whose name ends with "Smith Project"
every document file whose name contains "Smith Project"
every document file whose name does not contain "Smith Project"
```

Property value:

```
every document file whose name contains "Smith Project"
every document file whose name contains "Revised"
```

Compound Property Queries

The scope of queries can be made more specific or broader by using the term **and** to add search parameters and the term **or** to specify optional search parameters:

```
every document file whose name contains "Revised" and ¬
    kind is "JPEG image"

every document file whose kind is "JPEG image" or ¬
    name extension is "jpg"
```

Both terms can be combined to create complex search queries:

```
every document file whose (kind is "JPEG image" or ¬
    name extension is "jpg") and ¬
    name contains "Smith Project"
```

What's Next?

In this chapter, you learned how to find items in specified locations within ordered containers such as lists and how to find items by specifying desired values when the locations of items aren't known. You'll be putting these lessons to use in an upcoming chapter about identifying, finding, and manipulating scriptable objects in the Finder and other applications. But first, in the next chapter, you'll learn how to locate and refer to the special folders on your computer.

5

Lesson 5
Special Folders

This chapter is the third in a series of five chapters about identifying, finding, and manipulating scriptable objects in applications.

It's inevitable that sooner or later you'll want to share scripts you've written with others. And it's just as inevitable that a script that worked perfectly on your computer won't work as expected on your friend's computer. This sometimes happens because your script contains references to folder and file locations on your computer that do not exactly match those on another computer.

For example, a reference to a file named "cars.pdf" in the Documents folder would appear on Sal's computer as follows:

```
item "Macintosh HD:Users:sal:Documents:cars.pdf"
```

Although this reference works fine on Sal's computer, it cannot be used to refer to a file named "cars.pdf" in the Documents folder on Bill's computer. Not only will Bill's home directory be named differently than Sal's (cheeseb, as it happens, instead of sal), but Bill has also named his startup disk something other than Macintosh HD. On Bill's computer, the target file might actually have a file reference like this:

```
item "G5:Users:cheeseb:Documents:cars.pdf"
```

In addition, the task of correctly referencing files could be made much more difficult if the host computer's default language is not the same. Given all these possible differences, can scripts be designed to work on multiple computers?

Yes. AppleScript solves this problem by providing the means to locate just about any standard system folder on any Mac OS X system, regardless of the default language, the user's name, or the name of the startup disk. In this chapter, we'll demonstrate this by using the `path to` command, but you should be aware that similar features are available in the Finder, in the System Events application, and in some other applications.

The `path to` command is part of the Standard Additions scripting addition installed with every copy of Mac OS X. This handy command generates paths to—at last count—about 45 specially designated Mac OS X folders such as the home or Applications folders. Using these folders as starting points, you can easily generate paths to files and other folders within these special folders. By not relying on "absolute" paths (those written for a specific computer), your scripts will become more generic and able to work on most systems.

To use the `path to` command in your scripts, simply follow the command with a four-character string or a special enumeration constant that identifies the desired folder. When the script is run, the path to the designated folder is returned as a file reference in alias format that can be stored in a variable for use later in the script.

For example, to locate the Documents folder on your computer, enter Script 5.1 in a script window, and run it.

```
path to "docs"
--> returns: alias "<your_drive_name>:Users:<your_name>:Documents:"
```
SCRIPT 5.1

An alias reference containing the name of your startup disk and your home directory appears in the Result pane. If the same script were run on another computer, the result would contain the name of the startup disk and home directory on that computer. The same command yields results specific to the host computer.

Now, in Script 5.2, use the `path to` command to locate the Movies folder.

```
path to "mdoc"
--> returns: alias "<your_drive_name>:Users:<your_name>:Movies:"
```
SCRIPT 5.2

And, in Script 5.3, the Pictures folder.

```
set the target_folder to path to "pdoc"
--> returns: alias "<your_drive_name>:Users:<your_name>:Pictures:"
```
SCRIPT 5.3

In each of these examples, you used a four-character string that the system understands as a code for one of the special folders. These codes aren't exactly plain English, however, and you have to know a professional developer to find out what all of them are (or look at Table 4.1 later in this chapter). Shortly, we'll show you a much simpler technique that is also readily understandable. But first...

Domains

Being UNIX-based, Mac OS X is by nature a multiuser operating system, even if you happen to be the only person who uses your computer. Each user of the computer gets a personal home directory in the Users folder on the startup disk. This folder contains private documents, pictures, movies, songs, preferences, and other files that are available only to the user who is currently logged into the computer. Using multiple home directories also allows the files essential to the operating system to be kept separate from the user's files, thereby avoiding any accidental deletions or overwriting of essential system components.

Mac OS X divides the computer environment into four areas, or *domains*, each with its own files and folders. (We aren't covering a fifth domain available in older versions of Mac OS X, the Classic domain, in this book.) This multiple domain structure is particularly evident in the use of Library folders.

For example, the Library folder containing the preferences for your individual setup, such as your Desktop picture, preferred icon size, and folder display, is in your home directory. However, the preferences for the computer itself, applicable to all users, are kept in a different Library folder at the root level of the startup disk. And system settings such as the default preference panes displayed by the System Preferences application are kept in yet another Library folder in the System folder on the startup disk. Each of these individual Library folders belongs to a specific domain.

The four Mac OS X domains are as follows:

▶ *System domain*: Contains items specific to the operating system

▶ *Local domain*: Contains the support files and preferences for the general computer setup and other files that are available to all users

▶ *User domain*: Contains files and preferences for each user

▶ *Network domain*: Contains the items used over networks

Since each domain has its own resources and files, separate from those used by other domains, locating specific folders with the `path to` command could be complex if it weren't for the optional `from` parameter. The `from` parameter allows you to locate any special folder regardless to which domain it belongs.

For example, to locate the Library folders for each domain, you just use the appropriate `from` parameter.

Use Script 5.4 to locate the current user's Library folder.

```
path to "dlib" from user domain
--> returns: alias "<your_drive_name>:Users:<your_name>:Library:"
```
SCRIPT 5.4

Use Script 5.5 to locate the computer's local Library folder.

```
path to "dlib" from local domain
--> returns: alias "<your_drive_name>:Library:"
```
SCRIPT 5.5

Use Script 5.6 to locate the System Library folder.

```
path to "dlib" from System domain
--> returns: alias "<your_drive_name>:System:Library:"
```
SCRIPT 5.6

Use Script 5.7 to locate the network Library folder.

```
path to "dlib" from network domain
--> returns: alias "<your_drive_name>:Network:Library:"
```
SCRIPT 5.7

The last script, using the network domain, won't work if your computer is not connected to a network server configured to expose it.

Enumeration Constants

In addition to possessing a special four-character code, many special folders also have an assigned enumeration constant, a simple word or phrase that can be used in place of the code. These constants are much easier to remember than the codes because they are descriptive—they're often similar to the target item's name. For example, the constant for the Folder Action Scripts directory is `Folder Action scripts folder`.

```
path to Folder Action scripts folder from user domain
--> alias "<your_drive_name>:User:<your_name>:Library:Scripts:Folder
Action Scripts:"
```
SCRIPT 5.8

Special folder constants are often added to the Standard Additions scripting addition in new versions of Mac OS X, sometimes for familiar folders and sometimes for folders that didn't even exist in earlier versions. For example, Leopard adds `downloads folder` for the new standard Downloads folder in every user's home folder. For those using an earlier version of the OS, use the four-character code if no constant is available.

Special Folders List

Each special folder is tagged by the operating system with its own unique four-character code and often with its own enumeration constant. The code or the constant is used by the `path to` command to locate a specific folder.

Table 4.1 lists all the special folders we are aware of, showing the folder description (which is not necessarily the name of the folder), the four-character code, any constant that can be used instead of the code, which domains can contain the folder, and which of them (if any) is the default domain (marked by an asterisk).

If no domain is specified when using the `path to` command, the default domain is used to determine the path to the special folder. If no default is indicated in the table, the domain must be specified.

Some special folders are useful only for a particular domain, even if the code is valid for other domains. Experiment to find the one you can use.

Some special folders have different names depending on the domain or the current user. For example, the User Temporary Folder defaults to the local domain, where its name is "Caches," while its name in the other domains is something like "folders.501". If you want the Caches folder in any domain, use the Cached Data Folder, instead. The Current User folder name is the short name of the current user in all domains; that is, it's the home folder name.

The System special folder is especially interesting. It can be accessed by the four-character code "dtop" or the enumeration constant `system folder`. However, when using the "dtop" code, what it actually returns is an alias reference to whatever folder is at the top of the domain designated in the `from` parameter. In the default domain, the system domain, its name is System. In the user domain, its name is the name of the current user; that is, it's the home folder name. In the network domain, its name is Network. The Root special folder is similar.

TABLE 4.1 Special Folder Codes and Constants

Folder	Code	Constant	Domains
Appearance	`appr`		user, local
Apple Extras	`aexf`		local,* system
AppleShare Authentication	`auth`		user, local*
AppleShare Support	`shar`		user, local, system*
Applications	`apps`	applications folder	user, local,* system
Application Support	`asup`	application support	user, local*
Assistants	`astf`		user
Audio Alert Sounds	`alrt`		user, local*
Audio Components	`acmp`		user, local*
Audio Support	`adio`		user, local*
Audio Plug-Ins	`aplg`		user, local*
Audio Presets	`apst`		user, local*
Audio Sound Banks	`bank`		user, local*
Audio Sounds	`asnd`		user, local*
Autosave Information	`asav`		user,* local
Cached Data	`cach`		user, local,* system
Carbon Library	`carb`		user, local
Cleanup at Startup	`flnt`		user, local,* system network
ColorSync	`sync`		user, local, system*
ColorSync CMMs	`ccmm`		user, local
ColorSync Profiles	`prof`		user, local, system*
ColorSync Scripting	`cscr`		user, local, system*
Components	`cmpd`		user, local, system*
Contextual Menu Items	`cmnu`		user, local*
Core Services	`csrv`		user, local, system*
Current User	`cusr`		user,* local, system network
Desktop	`desk`	desktop	user*
Desktop Pictures	`dtpf`	desktop pictures folder	user, local*

* Default domain, ° Folder name differs depending on domain, † ADC Reference Library

TABLE 4.1 Special Folder Codes and Constants *(continued)*

Folder	Code	Constant	Domains
Developer Docs†	ddoc		user, system*
Developer†	devf		user, system
Developer Help†	devh		user, system*
Directory Services	dsrv		user, local*
Directory Services PlugIns	dplg		user, local*
Documentation	info		user, local,* system
Documents	docs	documents folder	user*
Downloads	down	downloads folder	user,* local
Favorites	favs	favorites folder	user,* local
File System Support	fsys		user, local, system*
Find By Content Indexes	fbcx		user,* local
Find Support	fnds		user, local, system*
Folder Action Scripts	fasf	Folder Action scripts	user,* local
Fonts	font	fonts	user, local, system*
Framework Folder	fram		user, local, system*
Help	fhlp	help	user, local,* system
Home	cusr	home folder	user,* local, system network
Index Files	indx		user, local*
Installer Logs (Receipts)	ilgf		user, local*
Installer Receipts	rcpt		user, local*
Internet Plug-Ins	fnet	Internet plugins	user, local
Internet Search Sites	issf		user,* local
Kernel Extensions	kext		user, local, system*
Keyboard Layouts	klay		user, local, system*
Keychain Folder	kchn	keychain folder	user,* local, system
Library	dlib	library folder	user, local, system*
Managed Items	mang		user,* local
MIDI Drivers	midi		user, local*
Modem Scripts	fmod	modem scripts	user, local, system*
Movies	mdoc	movies folder	user*

* Default domain, ° Folder name differs depending on domain, † ADC Reference Library

TABLE 4.1 Special Folder Codes and Constants *(continued)*

Folder	Code	Constant	Domains
Music	μdoc	music folder	user*
Pictures	pdoc	pictures folder	user*
Preferences	pref	preferences	user,* local
Printers	impr		user, local, system*
Printer Descriptions	ppdf	printer descriptions	user, local, system*
Private Frameworks	pfrm		user, local, system*
Public	pubb	public folder	user*
Quicktime Components	wcmp		user, local, system*
Quicktime Extensions	qtex		user, local, system*
Recent Applications	rapp		user,* local
Recent Documents	rdoc		user,* local
Recent Servers	rsvr		user,* local
Root	root		user, system,* network
Scripts	scrf	scripts folder	user,* local
Scripting Additions	ƒscr	scripting additions	user, local, system*
Shared User Data	sdat	shared documents	user,* local, system network
Shared Libraries	ƒlib	shared libraries	user, local, system*
Sites	site	sites folder	user*
Sound Sets	snds		user, local
Speakable Items	spki	speakable items	user, local
Speech	spch		user, local, system*
Spotlight Searches	spot		user,* local
Startup Items	empz	startup items	user, local,* system
Startup Disk	boot	startup disk	user,* local, system network
Stationery	odst		user, local
System (Top Level Folder)°	dtop	system folder	user, system,* network
System Preference Panes	sprf	system preferences	user, local, system*
System Sounds	ssnd		user, local, system*
Temporary Items	temp	temporary items	user, local,* system network

* Default domain, ° Folder name differs depending on domain, † ADC Reference Library

TABLE 4.1 Special Folder Codes and Constants *(continued)*

Folder	Code	Constant	Domains
Text Encodings	`ftex`		user, local
Theme Files	`thme`		user, local
Trash	`trsh`	trash	user*
User Temporary Items°	`utmp`		user, local,* system network
Users	`usrs`	users folder	user,* local, system network
Utilities	`utif`	utilities folder	user, local,* system
Workflows	`flow`	workflows folder	user,* local
Voices	`fvoc`	voices folder	user, local, system*

* Default domain, ° Folder name differs depending on domain, † ADC Reference Library

Special Folders in Classic

Mac OS X 10.3 (Panther) added support for the Classic domain parameter. Certain special folders contained within the Mac OS 9 System Folder could be referenced via the `path to` command prior to Leopard. Script 5.9 shows an example:

```
path to apple menu items folder from Classic domain
--> returns: "<your_drive_name>:System folder:Apple Menu Items:"
```
SCRIPT 5.9

We don't cover the Classic domain in this book, because it is no longer supported in Leopard.

Creating References to Items in Special Folders

Using the destinations provided by the `path to` command as starting points, it's possible to create a reference to any file or folder within those special folders. As an example, let's create a reference to a file in a folder in the Documents folder in your home directory.

For this example to function properly, you'll need an actual file on disk. Create a new folder in your Documents folder in your home directory named Path Example. Next, duplicate a file into that folder, name the duplicated file *test* (making sure to delete any name extension), and proceed with these steps to create a reference to this file:

1. Use the `path to` command as shown in Script 5.10 to get the path to the special folder containing the target item, in this case the user's Documents folder. Coerce the returned alias reference into a text string, and place the result into a variable.

```
set the target_item to path to documents folder as string
--> returns: "<your_drive_name>:Users:<your_name>:Documents:"
```
SCRIPT 5.10

2. On a new line in the script, add the name of each of the subfolders containing the file to the end of the returned path, remembering that folder names in a path are separated by and end with a colon character (`:`). To join two text strings, use the concatenation operator; that is, use the ampersand character (`&`):

```
set the target_item to path to documents folder as string
set the target_item to the target_item & "Path Example:"
--> returns: "<your_drive_name>:Users:<your_name>:Documents:Path Example:"
```
SCRIPT 5.11

3. The next line adds the name of the target file to the end of the path, as shown in Script 5.12.

```
set the target_item to path to documents folder as string
set the target_item to the target_item & "Path Example:"
set the target_item to the target_item & "test"
--> returns: "<your_drive_name>:Users:<your_name>:Documents:Path Example:test"
```
SCRIPT 5.12

4. Now that you've created a proper colon-delimited path to the file, you coerce the path from a string to an alias reference by adding `as alias` after the string. The result, shown in Script 5.13, is an alias reference to the target file.

```
set the target_item to path to documents folder as string
set the target_item to the target_item & "Path Example:"
set the target_item to the target_item & "test"
set the target_item to the target_item as alias
--> returns: alias "<your_drive_name>:Users:<your_name>:Documents:Path
Example:test"
```

SCRIPT 5.13

Alias references refer to existing items. If the targeted item is not in the expected location, an error will occur when the coercion is attempted. You'll need to use an error handler in your script if it's possible the targeted item won't be in the expected location. Replace the last line in the script with the **try** block shown in Script 5.14.

```
set the target_item to path to documents folder as string
set the target_item to the target_item & "Path Example:"
set the target_item to the target_item & "test"
try
    set the target_item to the target_item as alias
on error
    display dialog "The targeted item was not found."
end try
```

SCRIPT 5.14

You'll learn more about **try** blocks in Chapter 12, *Error Handlers*.

Folder Creation

Mac OS X 10.3 (Panther) added a new parameter to the `path to` command: `folder creation`. By default, the `path to` command attempts to create a folder if one does not exist in the designated location. The optional `folder creation` parameter takes a true or false value to determine whether a folder should be created. Script 5.15 shows how it is used.

```
path to documents folder from local domain without folder creation
```
SCRIPT 5.15

Note that if the designated folder does not exist, running that script returns an error reporting "Folder does not exist."

Special Forms of path to

The `path to` command returns two locations that are not folders. The first, shown in Script 5.16, is the path to the application file of the application process that is currently running in the foreground.

```
path to frontmost application
--> returns: alias "<your_drive_name>:Applications:AppleScript:Script
Editor.app"
```
SCRIPT 5.16

The second special location is the path to the application executing the script or to the script itself. In this situation, use the term `me` as the value for the required parameter.

The behavior of `path to me` has changed in Leopard. Formerly, Script Editor returned the path to Script Editor itself if Script Editor was running the script, except that it returned the path to the script it was running if the script had been saved as a script application, or *applet*. Now, in Leopard, Script Editor returns the path to Script Editor itself only if the script it is running has not been saved. It returns the path to the script document if it has been saved, even if it is saved as a compiled script rather than a script application.

Other applications that run scripts may implement different behavior for `path to me`. Any script saved as a script application and run by itself in the Finder returns the path to the applet.

When you type Script 5.17 into Script Editor and run it from within Script Editor, without saving the script, it returns the path to the Script Editor application both in Tiger and in Leopard.

```
path to me
--> returns: alias "<your_drive_name>:Applications:AppleScript:Script
Editor.app:"
```
SCRIPT 5.17

> **NOTE** ▶ The last character of the path string in the returned alias reference is a colon because Script Editor is an application package, or bundle. Like all bundles, it is actually a folder. In the next example, if you save the script as an application instead of an application bundle, its path string will not end with a colon.

When you run Script 5.18 as a script application, or *applet*, saved on the Desktop and named My Applet Script, it returns the path to the applet. In Leopard, it will also return the path to the script file if you save it as a compiled script or an applet and run it from Script Editor.

```
path to me
display dialog (result as string)
--> displays: "<your_drive_name>:Users:<your_name>:Desktop:My Applet
Script.app"
```
SCRIPT 5.18

In the script example above, you use the `display dialog` command to display the resulting path by coercing the path to the string format used by the dialog.

You're done with these examples now, so you can trash the My Applet Script applet on your Desktop and the Path Example folder and its contents in your Documents folder.

TIP ▶ The `path to me` command is useful for those times when a script needs to know where it's located on the computer in order to find items within its parent directory, such as templates or support files. For an example of this technique, type Script 5.19 in Script Editor and run it without saving it. It returns a list of references to every item in the AppleScript folder in your Applications folder, because the `path to me` command returns the path to the Script Editor application.

```
set my_path to the path to me
tell application "Finder"
    set the parent_folder to the container of my_path
    get every item of the parent_folder
end tell
```

SCRIPT 5.19

A third `path to...` command is the `path to resource` command. As you will see in Chapter 9, *Communicating with the User*, sometimes you want to save a script as a bundle so you can ship it to users with resources inside it, such as custom sounds or icons that the script needs. When you do this, use the `path to resource` command in the script to obtain whichever resource file the script needs. This command takes the name of the desired resource as its direct parameter. There are two optional parameters: `in bundle`, which takes an alias or file reference to some other bundle that contains the resource, and `in directory`, which takes the name of a particular subfolder in the script bundle's Resources folder. The `path to resource` command returns an alias reference to the resource file.

Chapter Summary

In the default Mac OS X installation, the system recognizes special folders for accessing specific files and items. These special folders are invisibly tagged with unique four-character codes.

Scripts can locate these special folders by passing the code to the `path to` command or, in some cases, by passing an enumeration constant. The result of this command is an alias reference to the special folder. Using the code or an enumeration constant makes your scripts more portable, since they work on any computer no matter what the special folders are named or what the folders in their paths are named.

By coercing these alias references to strings and adding folder names and file names to the end of them, you can create paths to files and folders contained within the special folders. These paths can then be coerced to alias references, which can be used elsewhere in your scripts.

What's Next?

In this chapter, you learned about a number of special folders that AppleScript can refer to without knowing their names or paths. The next chapter continues the topic of identifying, finding, and manipulating objects by introducing special commands for accessing information about the system and specific features of Mac OS X.

6

Lesson 6
Information Tools

This chapter is the fourth in a series of five chapters about identifying, finding, and manipulating scriptable objects in the Finder and other applications.

In the previous chapters, you learned how to refer to scriptable objects; how to locate specific items using several reference forms, including every and whose clauses; and how to refer to important directories in the file system.

In addition to the methods described in the previous three chapters, there are other important commands for locating items in the file system and accessing information about them. These commands are also part of the Standard Additions scripting addition. They are global in scope, and they can be used anywhere in a script, even outside of a tell block or a statement targeting an application.

This is also a good place to discuss a new feature in Mac OS X 10.5 (Leopard) that makes it easy to get information about any application on your computer. Beginning with Leopard, every application object has a number of properties that allow you to get important information about an application. These properties are built into AppleScript; they do not require the use of a scripting addition. However, as with the scripting addition commands discussed in this chapter, you can get information about an application object without using a `tell` block.

Get Information About Disks

The traditional method to get a list of the names of all mounted volumes in AppleScript has been the `list disks` command. It is still available in Leopard, but the Standard Additions scripting addition dictionary identifies it as a legacy command in Leopard. This means that, although it still works, there is a new way to obtain this information that is preferred in Leopard and future versions of Mac OS X. You are advised to write new scripts to use the new techniques recommended for Leopard, described later in this section, unless your scripts must be able to run on older systems where the new technique is not available.

We will describe the `list disks` command first, because it is in common use. Then we will discuss the recommended technique to obtain the same information in Leopard using the System Events application.

The `list disks` command provides a simple way to get the names of all mounted volumes or disks. Shown in Script 6.1, the command has no parameters and returns a list of the names of the mounted volumes.

```
list disks
--> returns: {"Macintosh HD", "Mac OS X", "Client Backup"}
```
SCRIPT 6.1

Of course, you will probably see a different list of names on your computer.

In the case of a disk, its name is its path because it is at the top of the containment hierarchy. For this reason, you can easily convert a disk name to an alias reference to use with other commands to obtain information about the disk. Simply place the `as alias` coercion after the disk name, as in Script 6.2. Change the disk's name to the name of a disk on your computer before running it.

```
set the target_disk to "Macintosh HD" as alias
--> returns: alias "Macintosh HD:"
```
SCRIPT 6.2

The result is an alias reference to the named disk.

Like references to folders, the path component of a reference to a disk or volume ends with a colon. This indicates the referenced item is a container for other items.

Starting with Leopard, the preferred way to obtain a list of the names of all mounted volumes is to use the System Events application instead of the Standard Additions scripting addition. System Events is a powerful scriptable application located in the CoreServices folder of the System Library folder, along with the Finder and some other important scriptable applications, at System > Library > CoreServices. You will learn more about it later in this book, especially in Chapter 21, *Folder Actions*, and Chapter 28, *GUI Scripting*. For now, just try this simple script, which returns the same result as the `list disks` command:

```
tell application "System Events" to get the name of every disk
--> returns: {"Macintosh HD", "Mac OS X", "Client Backup"}
```
SCRIPT 6.3

This script also works on Mac OS X 10.4 (Tiger), so you can use this technique in scripts meant to run on both Tiger and Leopard. System Events was also available in even older versions of Mac OS X, but its scripting dictionary has evolved over time. In Leopard, for example, the System Events dictionary adds the new properties `server` and `zone` to the `disk` class for use with AppleShare volumes. If you write scripts that address System Events on older versions of the OS, test them carefully.

One reason why the System Events application is now preferred over the `list disks` command is that System Events is much more flexible. What you usually want is a list of *references to* the disks, instead of a list of their *names*, because you can use a reference to obtain more information about each disk. Using System Events, you can do this without having to derive an alias from a disk's name. Script 6.4 shows how to get a list of useful disk references:

```
tell application "System Events" to get every disk
--> returns: {disk id "Macintosh HD,-100,2" of application "System
Events", disk id "Mac OS X,-101,2" of application "System Events", disk id
"Client Backup,-102,2" of application "System Events"}
```
SCRIPT 6.4

The same script works in the previous version of Mac OS X, Tiger, but in Tiger, it returns a list of disk references by `name` instead of by `disk id`. The use of `disk id` in Leopard allows the script to distinguish between disks having identical names.

Either way, in Tiger or in Leopard, you can use a disk reference to obtain information about the disk from the System Events application. For example, in Leopard, Script 6.5 informs you that the disk identified by the reference is not a removable disk.

```
tell application "System Events" to get ejectable ¬
    of disk id "Macintosh HD,-100,2"
--> returns: false
```
SCRIPT 6.5

Get Information About Folders

The `list folder` command is also considered a legacy command in Leopard. It has been the usual way to obtain a list of the contents of a folder in previous versions of Mac OS X. It still works in Leopard, but there is now a preferred way to do it. Again, update your existing scripts to use the new technique recommended for Leopard, described later in this section. As with the `list` `disks` command, the new technique using System Events is much more flexible because it doesn't limit you to a list of names.

The `list folder` command provides a simple way to get the names of all items in a folder. To use it, follow the command with an alias reference to the folder whose contents are to be listed, as shown in Script 6.6.

```
list folder (path to startup disk)
```
SCRIPT 6.6

As you see, this command treats a volume as a folder.

The result is a list of the names of all the items in the targeted directory. The list includes any invisible items that are contained in the folder, even though they are not displayed in Finder windows or on the Desktop.

```
--> returns: {".DS_Store", ".hidden", ".immkb", ".Trashes", ".vol",
"Applications", "automount", "bin", "cores", "Desktop DB", "Desktop DF",
"Desktop Folder", "dev", "etc", "Library", "mach", "mach.sym", "mach_
kernel", "Network", "private", "sbin", "System", "TheFindByContentFolder",
"TheVolumeSettingsFolder", "tmp", "Trash", "Users", "usr", "var",
"Volumes"}
```

On Mac OS X, invisible disk items usually have names beginning with a dot (.) or a special flag in the Finder marking them as invisible. To restrict the result of the `list folder` command to items that are visible in the user interface, use the optional `invisibles` parameter, which you can set to `true` or `false`:

Type this statement into the script window:

```
list folder (path to startup disk) invisibles false
```

When you compile it, Script Editor automatically changes it to the form shown in Script 6.7.

```
list folder (path to startup disk) without invisibles
--> returns: {"Applications", "Library", "System", "Users"}
```
SCRIPT 6.7

The term `without` indicates a Boolean value of `false`; conversely, `with` indicates a Boolean value of `true`.

When the script is run, the resulting list contains the items that are visible to the user in the Finder.

> **NOTE** ▶ In some versions of Mac OS X, the list may include some files that are not visible in the Finder, even though the `without invisibles` parameter is used.

Starting with Leopard, the preferred way to obtain a list of the contents of all folders is, again, to use the System Events application instead of the Standard Additions scripting addition, as illustrated by Script 6.8.

```
tell application "System Events" to get ¬
    the name of every item of folder "Applications" of startup disk
--> returns: {".DS_Store",".localized","Address Book.app",...}
```
SCRIPT 6.8

To access properties that are unique to items on a disk, use `disk item` instead of `item`. This script works in both Tiger and Leopard to obtain a list of the names of all visible disk items in the Applications folder:

```
tell application "System Events" to get ¬
    the name of every disk item of folder ¬
        "Applications" of startup disk whose visible is true
--> returns: {"Address Book.app","AppleScript", "Automator.app"...}
```
SCRIPT 6.9

As you saw in the previous section, it is usually preferable to get a list of references, instead of a list of names. Script 6.10 returns the same result in both Tiger and Leopard:

```
tell application "System Events" to get every disk item ¬
    of folder "Applications" of the startup disk ¬
        whose visible is true
--> returns: {file package "Macintosh HD:Applications:Address Book.app" of
application "System Events",...}
```
SCRIPT 6.10

Get Information About Disk Items

A third traditional Standard Additions command, the `info for` command, is considered a legacy command in Leopard. Perhaps one of the most useful commands in AppleScript, `info for` has always been an excellent way to access the important properties of a disk item. As with other commands in the Standard Additions scripting addition, it is global in scope and can be used anywhere in a script, both inside and outside of application `tell` blocks. Because it still works in Leopard, we will describe it first, and then we will describe the recommended replacement for Leopard using System Events.

File Information Record

Table 6.1 shows the properties of the `file information` record returned by the `info for` command in Leopard. The values of all these properties are read-only. They cannot be altered using `info for`. Some of them are not available for certain kinds of disk items; for example, you can't get the short name of a file unless it is an application file.

TABLE 6.1 The File Information Record

Property	Value Type	Definition
name	text	Name of the item.
displayed name	text	User-visible name.
short name	text	Short name, if an application.
name extension	text	Name extension.
bundle identifier	text	Bundle identifier, if a package.
type identifier	text	Uniform type identifier (UTI).
kind	text	Kind.
default application	alias reference	Application that opens it.
creation date	date	Date the item was created.
modification date	date	Date the item was last modified.
file type	text	File type of the item.

TABLE 6.1 The File Information Record *(continued)*

Property	Value Type	Definition
file creator	text	Creator type of the item.
short version	text	Short version string from Get Info.
long version	text	Long version string from Get Info.
size	integer	Size of the item in bytes.
alias	Boolean	Is this an alias file?
folder	Boolean	Is this a folder or volume?
package folder	Boolean	Is this a package?
extension hidden	Boolean	Is the name extension hidden?
visible	Boolean	Is the item visible?
locked	Boolean	Is the item locked?
busy status	Boolean	Is the item currently in use?
icon position	point	Coordinates of the item's icon.
folder window	bounding rectangle	Coordinates of window, if a folder.

To use the `info for` command, place an alias reference to a disk item after the command, as shown in Script 6.11, which gets the properties of a folder.

```
info for (path to home folder)
```
SCRIPT 6.11

The result of the `info for` command is a `file information` record. In AppleScript, a *record* is a comma-delimited set of *properties* enclosed in curly braces, where each property consists of a *label* and its corresponding *value*. A record is displayed in this format in Script Editor:

```
{label 1:value 1, label 2:value 2, label 3:value 3}
```

You will learn more about records in Chapter 18, *Working with Lists and Records*.

Here is the `file information` record returned by Script 6.11 for the home folder in Leopard (the result would be slightly different in Tiger):

```
--> returns: {name:"cheeseb", creation date:date "Saturday, July 28, 2007
9:06:05 AM", modification date:date "Saturday, August 11, 2007 6:14:06
PM", size:81949770, folder:true, alias:false, package folder:false,
visible:true, extension hidden:false, name extension:missing value,
displayed name:"cheeseb", default application:alias "MyDisk:System:Libra
ry:CoreServices:Finder.app:", kind:"Folder", folder window:{0, 0, 0, 0},
file type:" file creator:"}
```

Script 6.12 is an example extracting the `file information` record for a file. Be sure to change the alias so it refers to an existing file somewhere on your computer before running this script:

```
info for alias "MyDisk:Users:cheeseb:Desktop:Special Folders.scpt"
--> returns: {name:"Special Folders.scpt", creation date:date "Sunday,
March 5, 2006 5:17:42 PM", modification date:date "Monday, March 6, 2006
7:41:57 AM", size:13756, folder:false, alias:false, package folder:false,
visible:true, extension hidden:true, name extension:"scpt", displayed
name:"Special Folders", default application:alias "MyDisk:Applicatio
ns:AppleScript:Script Editor.app:", kind:"script", file type:"osas",
file creator:"ToyS", type identifier:"com.apple.applescript.script",
locked:false, busy status:false, short version:"", long version:""}
```
SCRIPT 6.12

In Leopard, the preferred technique to get all available information about any disk item is, again, to use the System Events application. Script 6.13 works in Tiger and Leopard to get the properties of the home folder (although the result will be slightly different depending on which version of Mac OS X you use). The result contains almost all the information returned by the `info for` command in Script 6.11 but sometimes in slightly different form.

```
tell application "System Events" to get properties of home folder
--> returns: {package folder:false, size:missing value, busy
status:false, creation date:date "Saturday, July 28, 2007 9:06:05
AM", physical size:missing value, container:folder "MyDisk:Users:"
of application "System Events", POSIX path:"/Users/cheeseb",
path:"MyDisk:Users:cheeseb:", URL:"file://localhost/Users/cheeseb/",
name:"cheeseb", visible:true, volume:"MyDisk", name extension:"",
class:folder, displayed name:"cheeseb", id:"cheeseb,-100,557051",
modification date:date "Saturday, August 11, 2007 6:14:06 PM"}
```

SCRIPT 6.13

Script 6.14 gets the properties of a file, which are similar to the properties
returned by Script 6.12.

```
tell application "System Events" to get properties ¬
    of disk item "Special Folders.scpt" of desktop folder
--> returns: {physical size:20480, container:folder
"MyDisk:Users:cheeseb:Desktop:" of application "System Events",
POSIX path:"/Users/cheeseb/Desktop/Special Folders.scpt", default
application:alias "MyDisk:Applications:AppleScript:Script Editor.
app:" of application "System Events", product version:"", name:"Special
Folders.scpt", visible:true, volume:"MyDisk", displayed name:"Special
Folders", modification date:date "Monday, March 6, 2006 7:41:57 AM",
package folder:false, creator type:"ToyS", size:13756, busy status:false,
stationery:false, type identifier:"com.apple.applescript.script",
creation date:date "Sunday, March 5, 2006 5:17:42 PM", version:"", short
version:"", file type:"osas", path:"MyDisk:Users:cheeseb:Desktop:Special
Folders.scpt", kind:"script", URL:"file://localhost/Users/cheeseb/Desktop/
Special%20Folders.scpt", name extension:"scpt", class:file, id:"Special
Folders.scpt,-100,694505"}
```

SCRIPT 6.14

Accessing Specific Properties

Use the get verb to extract an individual property's value from the returned
file information record using the info for command, as in Script 6.15. Don't

forget to change the alias reference so it refers to a file that exists somewhere on your computer—we won't remind you again.

```
get the name extension of ¬
    (info for alias "Macintosh HD:Users:sal:Desktop:attributes.tif")
--> returns: "tif"
```
SCRIPT 6.15

The `info for` command provides an easy means for extracting all the properties of an item in a single command. Scripters often place the `file information` record returned by the `info for` command in a variable and then extract individual property values from the record contained in the variable. It can take a few moments for the command to finish gathering all the information. Getting it once and then referring to the variable is more efficient than getting all the properties several times in a row.

The example shown in Script 6.16 uses this technique to determine whether a specific file is a TIFF or JPEG image file. The first statement gets the `file information` record for the targeted item and copies it into the variable `item_info`. The next statement checks the values of the `file type` and `name extension` properties of the `file information` record stored in the variable to see whether they match any items in lists of desired values:

```
set the item_info to the ¬
    (info for alias "Macintosh HD:Users:sal:Desktop:attributes.tif")
if the file type of the item_info is in {"TIFF", "JPEG"} or ¬
    the name extension of the item_info is in ¬
    {"tif", "tiff", "jpg", "jpeg"} then
    -- the file is an image, so place more statements here
end if
```
SCRIPT 6.16

Use the same approach to get an individual property's value from the System Events application, as shown in Script 6.17.

```
tell application "System Events" to get ¬
    kind of disk item "Special Folders.scpt" of desktop folder
--> returns: "script"
```
SCRIPT 6.17

Use the system info Command

A new command, `system info`, was added in Mac OS X 10.4 (Tiger) to give scripts access to important information about the computer and the system on which they are running. Most of the items of information that this command returns in the `system information` record have been requested by scripters for a long time. Table 6.2 shows the properties of the `system information` record returned by the `system info` command.

Like the `info for` command, `system info` is defined in the Standard Additions scripting addition. Its scope is global, and it can be used anywhere in a script, both inside and outside of application `tell` blocks.

TABLE 6.2 The System Information Record

Property	Value Type	Definition
AppleScript version	text	AppleScript version
AppleScript Studio version	text	AppleScript Studio version
system version	text	System version
short user name	text	Current user's short name
long user name	text	Current user's long name
user ID	integer	Current user's ID
user locale	text	Current user's locale
home directory	alias	Current user's home directory
boot volume	text	Boot volume
computer name	text	Computer name
host name	text	Host name
IPv4 address	text	IPv4 address
primary Ethernet address	text	Primary Ethernet address
CPU type	text	CPU type
CPU speed	integer	Clock speed of the CPU in MHz
physical memory	integer	Amount of physical RAM in MB

System Information Record

The system info command has no parameter. Just call it as shown in Script 6.18.

```
system info
```
SCRIPT 6.18

The result of the system info command is a system information record. Like the file information record returned by the info for command, it is a set of comma-delimited properties consisting of labels and their corresponding values.

Here is the system information record returned for one computer (altered slightly to ensure anonymity):

```
system info
--> returns: {AppleScript version:"2.0", AppleScript Studio
version:"1.5", system version:"10.5", short user name:"cheeseb", long
user name:"Bill Cheeseman", user ID:501, user locale:"en_US", home
directory:alias "MyDisk:Users:cheeseb:", boot volume:"MyDisk", computer
name:"Bill's PowerBook G4", host name:"Bills-PowerBook-G4.local", IPv4
address:"10.0.1.2", primary Ethernet address:"00:15:50:22:25:70", CPU
type:"PowerPC 7450", CPU speed:1666, physical memory:1024}
```

Accessing Specific Properties

As with the file information record, extract the values of various properties of the system information record by using the get command, as shown in Script 6.19.

```
get the long user name of (system info)
--> returns: "Bill Cheeseman"
```
SCRIPT 6.19

Get Information About Applications

In Leopard, every application object has four new properties that give you useful information about the application without requiring you to run it first or to tell it to do anything. Although much of this information was previously available to scripts using more convoluted techniques, it is now available directly. Because you don't have to run the application or use a `tell` block to get this information, you can obtain and use it in advance to help you decide whether to run the application or to make running it easier. The four new properties of the application object are `running`, `frontmost`, `version` and `id`.

These new properties do not require the use of a scripting addition. They are built into AppleScript.

We'll give you a quick summary of these properties here with a few examples of their use.

First, however, we'll explain an important change in the way applications are launched by AppleScript in Leopard. Applications that are automatically launched by an AppleScript `tell` statement are hidden by default in Leopard, whereas they were visible when launched in Mac OS X 10.4 (Tiger) and older versions of the Mac OS. Until now, a `tell` statement addressed to an application has typically launched the application and displayed an untitled window, but now in Leopard it launches the application with any new, untitled window hidden. To be precise about what *hidden* means, you will see the application's icon in the Dock and when you use the Command-Tab keyboard shortcut, but you won't see any of the application's windows until you send it an `activate` command.

This change is helpful because a script can now launch a supporting application without fear that its new, untitled window will become visible and distract you from whatever the script is showing you. But it does mean that you should always include a statement to `activate` the target application at the beginning of a `tell` block if you want it to be visible and frontmost. This isn't a significant burden, and most scripters already do this anyway. As alternatives to activating an application at the beginning of a `tell` block, you can use the `run` or `launch` command. The `run` and `launch` commands both make the application visible, but `launch` does not open a new, untitled window as `run` does with most applications.

Now let's discuss the new application object properties.

The running Property

You might sometimes want to know whether an application is already running before you try to use it. For example, if an application is not currently running, you might not want to take the extra time required to launch it, or the simple fact that it isn't running may tell you that you don't have to change its state in order to clear the way for some other action that your script will perform. You can learn whether the application is running by using the new `running` property. To see this feature in action, make sure TextEdit isn't running on your computer, then run Script 6.20. Notice that it returns the result `false` without having to launch TextEdit, which would have defeated the purpose of finding out whether it is running.

```
get running of application "TextEdit"
--> returns: false
```
SCRIPT 6.20

The frontmost Property

Even if you know an application is running, you might sometimes want to know whether it is currently the active application. To find out, use the new `frontmost` property, as shown in Script 6.21.

```
get frontmost of application "TextEdit"
--> returns: false
```
SCRIPT 6.21

If TextEdit isn't running, or if it is running but isn't the frontmost application, Script 6.21 returns `false`. Even if TextEdit is running, if you run Script 6.21 in Script Editor or by saving it as an applet and double-clicking it in the Finder, it always returns `false` because Script Editor or the applet is frontmost while the script is running, and the target application is therefore in back. However, if you save Script 6.21 as a compiled script in the Scripts folder of your user Library folder and run it from the Script menu in the menubar, it returns `true` if TextEdit is running and frontmost.

The `frontmost` property always returns `false` for applications that are designed to run only in the background, even though some of them, known technically as *UI element applications*, are capable of being activated to show alerts and other user interface elements.

The `frontmost` property is useful even when you run a script in Script Editor or as an applet, because you can test it and, if it returns `false`, activate the target application to bring it to the front. The script can then cause the target application to perform any actions that require it to be frontmost. Run Script 6.22 in Script Editor to see how this works. Normally, however, it is sufficient to activate the target application without testing the `frontmost` property first, because the `activate` command does nothing if the target application is already frontmost.

```
if frontmost of application "TextEdit" is false ¬
    then activate application "textEdit"
```
SCRIPT 6.22

The version Property

Most applications have a `version` property that you can read when the application is running. To get an application's version when it is not running and you don't want to launch it, use the new `version` property of the application object. Run Script 6.23 twice, once with TextEdit not running and once when it is running. It always returns TextEdit's version, but it does not launch TextEdit in the first case.

```
get version of application "TextEdit"
--> returns: "1.5"
```
SCRIPT 6.23

The id Property

A perennial issue for scripters has been how to write bullet-proof scripts that will run as intended on someone else's computer. One of the problems is that computer users have a habit of renaming their applications to suit themselves. Your carefully crafted script to `tell application "Goldmine" to make new nugget` works perfectly well on your computer, but it might fail if your best buddy has renamed the application "Silvermine" on his computer.

Mac OS X was originally able to identify an application both by its name and by its *signature*, or *creator code*. A signature is a four-character code that uniquely identifies an application, such as "ToyS" for Script Editor. In recent versions of Mac OS X, application signatures have slowly been phased out and a more powerful and reliable feature, known as a *bundle identifier*, has taken over. The bundle identifier for Script Editor is "com.apple.ScriptEditor2".

Neither the signature nor the bundle identifier of an application is easily changed by the average user. Wouldn't it be nice if you could write `tell` blocks that used the signature or bundle identifier of an application instead of its name? Well, now you can. In Leopard, AppleScript `tell` blocks can do just that using the new `id` property.

Unless the application you're targeting is an old-fashioned single-file application and doesn't have a bundle identifier, you should always use its bundle identifier in `tell` blocks in scripts that you will distribute to other users who have Leopard installed. For single-file applications without a bundle identifier, use the signature. An easy way to find an application's bundle identifier is to run a script like Script 6.24 on your own computer. Then use the returned `id` as the `id` in the `tell` blocks in your final script.

```
get id of application "TextEdit"
--> returns: "com.apple.TextEdit"
```
SCRIPT 6.24

Script 6.25 shows how you use the `id` to tell TextEdit to do something.

```
tell application id "com.apple.TextEdit" to make new document
--> returns: document "Untitled 2" of application "TextEdit"
```
SCRIPT 6.25

What's Next?

This chapter and the previous three chapters covered essential lessons of identifying, finding, and manipulating specific scriptable items. In the next chapter, you'll use these lessons to find and process scriptable items in the Finder and other applications.

7

Lesson **7**

Actions with Items

This chapter is the fifth in a series of five chapters about identifying, finding, and manipulating scriptable objects in applications. This final chapter in the series can best be summarized with the single phrase *find and do*. It's the chapter where you apply all the lessons and concepts from the previous four chapters by creating scripts that make you a very dangerous person.

In prior chapters, you examined and absorbed the concepts of *object hierarchy containment* and *inheritance,* and you learned how to construct *search queries* to locate items based on their position in a group of items or the value of their properties. Now that you can *find* items, the logical next step is to learn how to *do* something with the items you've found. We're going to have some fun combining the process of finding items with the process of doing something with them. In other words: *find and do.*

Action Statements

Complex does not always mean *powerful*. Sometimes the simplest approach provides the most concise and direct way of expressing action. For example, the statement "Tom, fetch the groceries from the car" elegantly combines two actions into a single sentence, targeted at a specific individual:

1. Find or locate the groceries.

2. Fetch them.

Where are the groceries? *In the car*. What to do with them? *Bring them in*. Who is to perform these actions? *Tom*. It's very neat, concise, and to the point—a classic example of a *find and do action statement*.

In AppleScript, an *action statement* is a single-line script command that both identifies a set of scriptable objects and performs an action with them, in other words, *find and do*.

Although we use the concept of *find and do* every day, we often syntactically reverse the order of the two actions when speaking or communicating the commands. And we also imply some actions without stating them directly. For example, instead of saying this:

```
Tom, locate the groceries in the car, and then bring them in.
```

we shorten the statement by placing the verb that represents the action to be performed with the items *before* the references identifying the items themselves and then assume or imply that the process of locating the items will be done first:

```
Tom, fetch the groceries from the car.
```

In this case, the action verb or phrase is `fetch`, and the target of the action term is `the groceries in the car`. Naturally, we assume that Tom will *locate* the groceries before attempting to *fetch* them. So, the syntax of the shortened action statement is as follows:

```
<verb> <object(s) targeted by the verb>
```

In other words, the identified objects become the *direct parameter* of the verb or command.

So, even though the *syntax* of the *find and do* concept is reversed when speaking or writing scripts, like so:

```
<do> <find>
```

the actions are still performed in sequence as *find and do*:

1. *Find* or identify the items to process.

2. And then *do* or perform an action with the found items.

This simple reverse syntax is the bread and butter of scripts and scripters. In keeping with the focus of the previous chapters, you'll learn to implement the action statement syntax by writing scripts that find and manipulate Finder items. However, as with most AppleScript principles, the concepts used in writing scripts containing *find and do* statements for Finder items apply to all scriptable applications.

Manipulating Objects

We will be demonstrating how to perform actions on objects and their properties in this chapter, so you need to begin by setting up some objects on your computer that you can manipulate. For use with the example scripts in this chapter, create a folder on your Desktop containing copies of a couple of dozen image and movie files. We used files downloaded from the HubbleSite. org website, a fantastic resource for information and media gathered by the Hubble Telescope over its many years of invaluable work.

You may use your own images and movie files if you like. Just make sure you place them in a folder on your Desktop. Also, be sure to replace the name of the folder used in the example scripts with the name of your folder, or instead simply name your folder to match ours. Figure 7.1 shows our folder.

FIGURE 7.1 Image and movie files to use as the target of the example scripts.

The last step of preparation is to close any open Finder windows and open the folder containing your demonstration files. Set the view mode of the Finder window to icon view, and you're now ready to explore the power of *find and do*.

The Syntax of "Find and Do"

The Finder's scripting dictionary contains the standard verbs, such as `count`, `delete`, `duplicate`, `move`, and `open`, in addition to Finder-specific verbs such as `select`, `reveal`, `eject`, `sort`, and `update`. All of these verbs work well in action statements since they take references to Finder items as their direct parameters. We'll begin examining how to create *find and do* scripts, using the basic verb `count` that is used to determine how many items are in a group of items.

Run Script 7.1.

```
tell application "Finder"
    count (every document file of the front Finder window ¬
        whose kind ends with " movie")
end tell
```

SCRIPT 7.1

The script follows a classic *find and do* format, with the *find* section of the script placed within parentheses:

```
do (find)
```

Placing a search query within parentheses indicates that the enclosed section of the script (the *query*) should be executed first and then replaced with the results of its execution, in this case a list of Finder item references to the movies displayed in the Finder window:

```
do (result of find)
```

The resulting list of references to the movie files on disk becomes the direct parameter of the verb count, which generates a numeric total of the items in the list. The result of the count verb is an integer representing the number of movie files contained in the folder whose contents are displayed in the front-most Finder window. In abstract terms:

```
count (result of find)
--> returns: an integer, such as 8
```

All *find and do* scripts follow this same format. Now, try a new version of the same script, Script 7.2.

```
tell application "Finder"
    count (every document file of the front Finder window ¬
        whose kind ends with " image")
end tell
```

SCRIPT 7.2

As in the previous script, the result of Script 7.2 is an integer, in this case representing the number of image files contained in the folder whose contents are displayed in the frontmost Finder window.

Allow us to insert a quick explanation about the `kind` property of Finder items, which is used to locate specific types of objects. The value of the `kind` property of Finder items is a text string describing what the object is. It is displayed in the information window for a selected Finder item, as shown in Figure 7.2.

FIGURE 7.2 The General pane of the information window for Finder items displays the value of the Kind property, in this case *QuickTime Movie*.

Usually, the value of the `kind` property is a short phrase like *QuickTime Movie*. It is also common that Finder items of a specific genre have `kind` strings that are similar, such as *PICT image*, *TIFF image*, and *JPEG image*, where the specific file type of the image is followed by the common term *image*. You can use this shared term to focus your search on all the Finder items whose `kind` strings end with the same term, as in Script 7.2.

However, if you want to search for specific Finder items, you can use the value of the `name extension` property to be more focused, as we do in this variant of Script 7.2 that searches for only TIFF and JPEG images:

```
tell application "Finder"
    count (every document file of the front Finder window ¬
        whose name extension is "jpg" or name extension is "tif")
end tell
```

Here's a quick note about the term count. In the English language, it is used as both a verb (to *count* items) and a noun (the *count* of items). The same applies to its use in AppleScript. It can be used as a *verb*:

```
tell application "Finder"
    count (every document file of the front Finder window ¬
        whose size is greater than 300000)
end tell
```

or as a *noun*:

```
tell application "Finder"
    get the count of (every document file of front Finder window ¬
        whose size is greater than 300000)
end tell
```

Either way, the result is the same.

More "Find and Do" Verbs

Now, back to writing *find and do* script statements. Here's another verb that takes references to Finder items as its direct parameter: reveal. It is most often used to display and highlight Finder items so the user can see them.

Close the Finder window containing your demo content, and then run Script 7.3.

```
tell application "Finder"
    reveal (first document file of folder "Hubble Media" whose ¬
        kind ends with " movie" and name begins with "G")
end tell
```
SCRIPT 7.3

The folder containing the found item is opened, and the first item that matches the search parameters is highlighted, as shown in Figure 7.3. (Naturally, you'll have to adjust the script to work with your own demo content.)

FIGURE 7.3 The found item selected and displayed in the Finder window showing the contents of its containing folder.

Although it can be used to display multiple Finder items in differing locations, the reveal verb is most often used to show a *single* item to the user.

Another verb often used with *find and do* script statements to highlight items is select. Run Script 7.4. It sorts the contents of the front Finder window by kind, sets the current view of the window to flow view (introduced in Leopard), and then selects the first movie in the list.

```
tell application "Finder"
    set current view of the front Finder window to list view
    set sort column of list view options ¬
        of the front Finder window to kind column
    set current view of the front Finder window to flow view

    select (first document file of the front Finder window ¬
        whose kind ends with " movie")
end tell
```

SCRIPT 7.4

After you run the script, the frontmost Finder window is set to flow view and
ready for you to review the listed movie files, as shown in Figure 7.4.

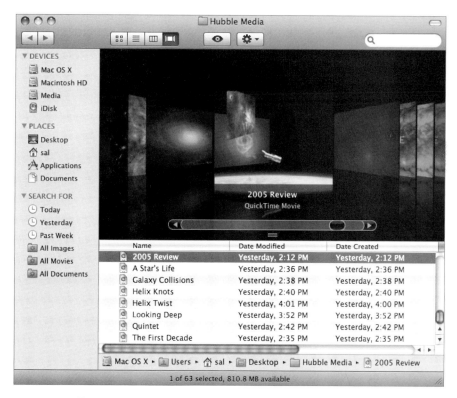

FIGURE 7.4 The front Finder window in flow view, sorted by kind, and ready to review the
movie files.

The `select` verb also works very well in conjunction with another feature introduced in Leopard, Quick Look. Quick Look provides instant browsing of *selected* documents on your computer without having to open them in their originating or designated default applications. Using AppleScript, you can apply the `select` verb to select the objects to review and then invoke the Quick Look view in the Finder.

Although Quick Look can be activated on Finder items selected and displayed in a Finder window set to any view mode, for demonstration purposes, let's first change the value of the `current view` property of the front Finder window to `icon view` with Script 7.5.

```
tell application "Finder"
    set the current view of the front Finder window to icon view
end tell
```
SCRIPT 7.5

Next, run Script 7.6. It selects all the images in the front Finder window and uses a Finder File menu keyboard shortcut to trigger Quick Look.

```
tell application "Finder"
    activate
    select (every document file of the front Finder window ¬
        whose kind ends with " image")
    tell application "System Events" to ¬
        keystroke "y" using command down
end tell
```
SCRIPT 7.6

After running Script 7.6, a Quick Look window opens displaying the first image in the collection of image files selected in the Finder window, as shown in Figure 7.5.

You can navigate the list of selected images by clicking the left/right arrows located at the bottom of the Quick Look window, or you can choose to view a collection of selected images by clicking the collection icon at the bottom of the Quick Look window to have it display the selected images in a grid, as shown in Figure 7.6.

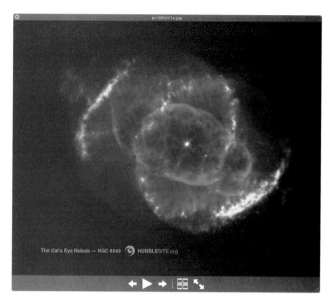

FIGURE 7.5 A Quick Look window displaying the first of the selected images.

FIGURE 7.6 A Quick Look window displaying a grid of the selected images.

> **NOTE** ▸ The Finder's scripting dictionary does not currently provide a way to invoke the Quick Look view with selected items. However, the Finder does provide a menu item with keyboard shortcut Command+Y for doing so. In scenarios like this, the scriptable System Events application can be used to trigger the keystrokes necessary to mimic a user interacting with the computer by selecting a menu item. We cover the topic of scripting the user-interface in Chapter 28, GUI Scripting.

"Getting Physical" with Finder Items

So far in this chapter, the actions performed with the designated Finder items have involved passive actions such as *counting* or *selecting*. Now it's time to start shaking things up a bit. Let's write a script that adds a new folder to the front Finder window and places all the movie files displayed by the front Finder window into that new folder. Run Script 7.7.

```
tell application "Finder"
    set the current view of the front Finder window to list view
    set this_folder to make new folder at front Finder window ¬
        with properties {name:"Movies"}
    move (every document file of the front Finder window ¬
        whose kind ends with " movie") to this_folder
end tell
```
SCRIPT 7.7

Like the previous verbs, the move verb takes as its direct parameter a single reference or list of references to the Finder items to be moved to a new location. In addition, it requires that the second parameter **to** be followed by a reference to the container that is the destination for the moved items. The result of an action statement using the move command is a list of references to the moved items in their new location.

Your frontmost Finder window now should look something like Figure 7.7.

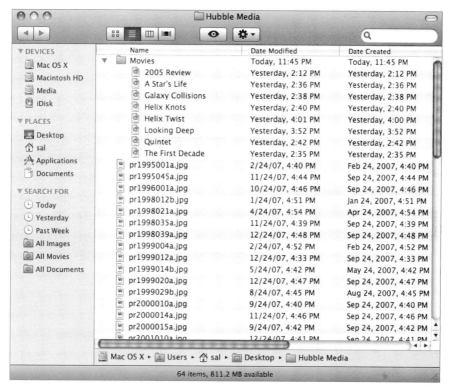

FIGURE 7.7 The movie files have been moved into a newly created folder.

Another action command often used in AppleScript scripts is `duplicate`. This verb creates clones of the Finder items targeted as its direct parameter. Script 7.8 is a simple *find and do* example that duplicates all the image files displayed in the front Finder window.

```
tell application "Finder"
    duplicate (every document file of the front Finder window ¬
        whose kind ends with " image")
end tell
```

SCRIPT 7.8

When Script 7.8 is executed, it locates the image files in the folder whose contents are displayed in the front Finder window and duplicates them into the same container. The term *copy* is added to each duplicate item name, and the duplicated items are selected. The result of the script is a list of Finder item references to the duplicated items. The Finder window now looks something like Figure 7.8.

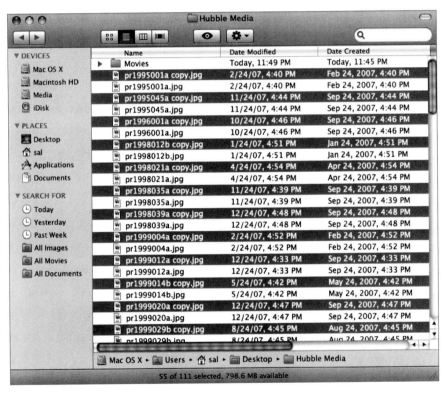

FIGURE 7.8 The duplicate image files are selected in the Finder window.

The image files targeted in Script 7.8 were duplicated into the same container as the original files. The `duplicate` command can duplicate items to other locations as well. We'll write a script to demonstrate this ability shortly, but first let's use another verb to clean up the window by removing the selected duplicate image files.

The delete verb is used to remove scriptable objects from their containers. So, to move the selected duplicate files to the Trash, Script 7.9 seems like it should do the job—give it a try.

```
tell application "Finder"
    delete the selection of the front Finder window
end tell
```
SCRIPT 7.9

When you run the script, an error sheet is displayed and attached to the script window, as shown in Figure 7.9.

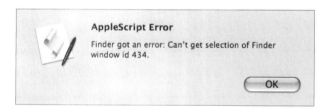

FIGURE 7.9 The error alert presented when you run Script 7.9.

The error states that the script can't get the *selection* of the front Finder window. That seems odd, since the selected items are right there in the window. However, if you look in the Finder's scripting dictionary, you'll see that the class selection belongs only to the *application* object, not to *windows* or any other object. In the Finder application, there is only one selection; it's the items selected in the frontmost container of the application.

So to delete selected Finder items, make their parent container the frontmost window (in this case, it is already), and then use the delete command within the application's tell block, as shown in Script 7.10.

```
tell application "Finder"
    delete the selection
end tell
```
SCRIPT 7.10

Of course, you could always choose not to target the items based on their selection but rather use the good ol' *find and do* technique to locate and manipulate the Finder items that have the term *copy* in their name:

```
tell application "Finder"
    delete (every document file of the front Finder window ¬
        whose name contains " copy")
end tell
```

Now back to the `duplicate` command. As stated before, this command can be used to copy Finder items to locations *other* than the container of the original items (the scripting equivalent to holding down the Option key when dragging items from a folder). When using the duplicate command in this manner, add the optional `to` parameter followed by a reference to the destination container for the copied items.

Run Script 7.11. It will create a new folder on the Desktop and duplicate the image files displayed in the front Finder window to the newly created folder.

```
tell application "Finder"
    set this_folder to make new folder at desktop ¬
        with properties {name:"Hubble Image Copies"}
    duplicate (every document file of the front Finder window ¬
        whose kind ends with " image") to this_folder
    open this_folder
end tell
```

SCRIPT 7.11

When run, Script 7.11 opens a new Finder window to the folder containing the duplicated items, as shown in Figure 7.10.

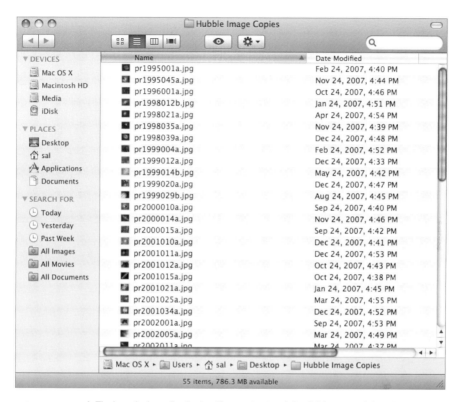

FIGURE 7.10 A Finder window displaying the contents of the folder containing the duplicated items.

> **NOTE ▶** Script 7.11 uses the variable `this_folder` to store and retrieve the references to the found Finder items. The use of variables in scripts is covered in detail in Chapter 8, Data Containers, Operators, and Coercions.

The `duplicate` command can be used multiple times without issue when it is duplicating items into *the same container as the original items*. In that scenario, the Finder simply keeps adding the term *copy* and a numeric increment to each of the duplicated items, yielding a name such as `pr2002005 copy 5.jpg`.

However, when the `duplicate` command is used to duplicate items to another location, an error can be caused if the destination folder already contains files named the same as the items being duplicated. Figure 7.11 shows the error alert.

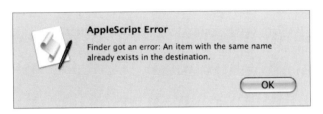

FIGURE 7.11 An error alert warning that duplication is not possible because items with the same name are already in the destination container.

To replace the existing items in the destination container with the new duplicates, use the optional boolean parameter `with replacing`. Run Script 7.12, which closes the Finder window displaying the duplicates, thereby making the folder behind it the new front window, and replaces them with new duplicates of the original image files.

```
tell application "Finder"
    close the front Finder window
    duplicate (every document file of the front Finder window ¬
        whose kind ends with " image") ¬
        to folder "Hubble Image Copies" with replacing
end tell
```
SCRIPT 7.12

By the way, the `with replacing` parameter can also be used with the `move` command.

Other Finder Items

Files are not the only type of Finder item that can be the target of action statements. `disk` objects and the Finder's `eject` verb can be combined to create useful script tools.

First, a bit of demo preparation. If you have a .Mac account, mount your iDisk by selecting My iDisk from the Go > iDisk menu (or press the keyboard short-cut Command+Shift+I). If you don't have a .Mac account, mount some other network volume if one is available.

To eject volumes that are not hard drives connected to your computer, run Script 7.13, a classic *find and do* script that searches for nonlocal disks and unmounts them.

```
tell application "Finder"
    eject (every disk whose local volume is false)
end tell
```
SCRIPT 7.13

Here's a variation on Script 7.13 that ejects only nonlocal volumes that use the WebDAV networking protocol, such as iDisks:

```
tell application "Finder"
    eject (every disk whose local volume is false ¬
        and format is WebDAV format)
end tell
```

Again, this is another classic use of the *find and do* technique. By the way, mounting and unmounting various types of volumes via scripts is covered in detail in Chapter 27, *Connecting to Network Servers*.

Setting Properties

Up to now, the example action statements in this chapter have used Finder items themselves as the direct parameter of the script actions. You've *revealed*, *selected, moved, duplicated*, and *deleted* files using verbs from the Standard Suite and application-specific verbs from other suites. But you can also use the set verb with action statements to alter the values of the *properties* of found items.

Set the view mode of the frontmost Finder window to list view, and run Script 7.14. It sets the value of a single property of multiple items in a single action statement.

```
tell application "Finder"
    set label index of (every document file of front Finder window ¬
        whose name extension is "jpg") to 2
end tell
```
SCRIPT 7.14

When run, Script 7.14 locates the items displayed in the frontmost Finder window matching the search parameters and then changes the value of the `label index` property of each of them to display a colored label in the Finder window, as shown in Figure 7.12.

FIGURE 7.12 Labeled image files.

Action statements like the one in Script 7.14 can be used to change the values of many properties of objects.

Most of the time, action statements that address the properties of items begin with the set verb. However, properties are sometimes objects that respond to other verbs. In the case of the Finder application, for example, there is a property of the item class that doesn't respond to the set verb but rather is targeted by the open command: information window. Run Script 7.15. It causes the information windows for a group of items to be displayed for five seconds.

```
tell application "Finder"
    open information window of (every document file of ¬
        folder "Movies" of the front Finder window)
    delay 5
    close every information window
end tell
```
SCRIPT 7.15

Setting Multiple Properties for Multiple Objects

In the first chapter you learned how to write tell statements, which are single-line scripts targeting a specific application or object and performing a single task. When you wanted the script to perform more than one process with a *single* object, you wrote tell blocks that began with an opening tell statement targeting a scriptable object and closed with an end tell statement, like this:

```
tell application "Finder"
    tell the front Finder window
        set the current view to list view
        set its position to {144, 144}
    end tell
end tell
```

Well, you can also use `tell` blocks to set the values of one or more properties of items found by a search query. Just make the object references returned by the search query the target of the `tell` block's opening `tell` statement, as in this abstract template:

```
tell (<results of search query>)
    --> set property value
    --> set property value
end tell
```

Run Script 7.16, which sets the values of multiple properties for each of the items identified by the query in the opening `tell` statement.

```
tell application "Finder"
    tell (every document file of front Finder window ¬
            whose name extension is "jpg")
        set label index to 0
        set modification date to (current date)
        set extension hidden to true
        set locked to false
        set comment to "Image taken by the Hubble Space Telescope"
        set group privileges to read write
        set everyones privileges to read write
    end tell
end tell
```

SCRIPT 7.16

Open the information window for one of the image files displayed in the front Finder window, and you can see that the values of the properties were indeed set, as shown in Figure 7.13.

FIGURE 7.13 The information window showing the status of various properties set by Script 7.16. Note that the modification dates displayed in the Finder window have been set for all the images.

Targeting multiple objects with a single `tell` block is a powerful technique for quickly changing the values of one or more properties of the targeted items. However, this technique works only for setting properties. If you want to perform more involved procedures with the items located by search queries, you'll have to process them individually, one at a time. Does that sound slow? It's not. In fact, you'll find it to be very quick and efficient.

Processing Multiple Items Individually

Action statements are great when you want to perform a *single* action with a group of items. When you want to perform *multiple* actions with multiple items, you use loops. Let's turn to repeating mechanisms in scripts.

Let's say you'd like to add a numeric prefix to the name of each of the image files displayed in the front Finder window so that the number reflects the sorting order of each file according to its creation date. This way, the files would be displayed in their creation order even if the name column is used as the sort column for the Finder window.

Determining the sort order of the various image files and adding a corresponding numeric prefix to each of their names will require multiple steps, more than can be done in batches using an action statement.

Run Script 7.17, which sorts and renames the several image files displayed in the front Finder window.

```
tell application "Finder"
    set these_items to sort (get every document file ¬
        of the front Finder window) by creation date
    repeat with i from 1 to count of these_items
        set this_item to item i of these_items
        set the name of this_item to ((i as string) & "-" & ¬
            (the name of this_item))
    end repeat
end tell
```
SCRIPT 7.17

When run, Script 7.17 renames the image files so that they are displayed in order of their creation date even when the sort column in the Finder window is set for alphabetical display by name, as shown in Figure 7.14.

> **NOTE ▶** In older versions of Mac OS X, the prefix for the first few files would have to be "01," "02," and so on, so that they would sort alphabetically in numerical order. The leading zero is no longer necessary.

Let's examine the script in more detail.

Even though Script 7.17 uses more complex constructs, it is still basically a *find and do* script. The difference is that instead of finding and processing items in a single action statement, it uses a series of steps to find and process the found items one at a time.

First, the *find* part: the targeted items, each of them an image file, are located with an action statement using the Finder's **sort** verb. The result of the action statement is a list of Finder references to the found items, sorted by creation date, stored in the variable these_items. All this is accomplished with one script statement. For more on using variables such as these_items, see Chapter 8, *Data Containers, Operators, and Coercions.*

```
set these_items to sort (get every document file ¬
    of the front Finder window) by creation date
```

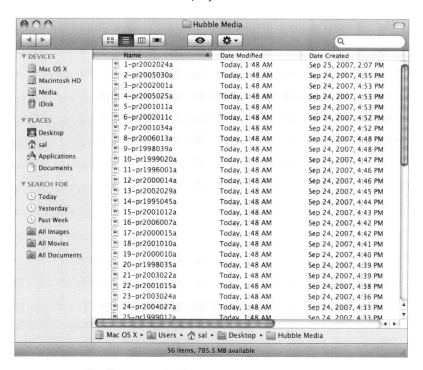

FIGURE 7.14 The files renamed with numeric prefixes.

Next, the *do* part: the resulting list of references to the sorted image files is processed using a **repeat** loop that processes the list incrementally, one item at a time, renaming each file using the value of the *loop index placeholder* to reflect the item's position in the list of image files sorted by their creation date:

```
repeat with i from 1 to count of these_items
    set this_item to item i of these_items
    set the name of this_item to ((i as string) & "-" & ¬
        (the name of this_item))
end repeat
```

For more information regarding **repeat** loops, see Chapter 11, *The Repeat Loop*.

Instead of combining the *find* and *do* steps in a single statement, Script 7.17 performs them separately. This way, each processed item is able to get the unique individual attention it requires.

> **NOTE ▶** When using the Finder's **sort** verb in an action statement, always begin the query, the part enclosed in parentheses, with the **get** verb. Most of the time the **get** verb is implied and doesn't have to be added to a query. When used in an action statement with the Finder's **sort** verb, it needs to be there.

Now, let's restore the item names to their original titles by removing the numeric prefix that begins each name. This will require extracting the original name from the new name. This should be easy, since the original name is everything after the first hyphen, which has been placed as a delimiter between the ordering number and the original name, as in `14-pr1995045a.jpg`.

Script 7.18 processes the image files to restore their original filenames:

```
tell application "Finder"
    set these_items to ¬
        (every document file of the front Finder window)
    repeat with i from 1 to count of these_items
        set this_item to item i of these_items
        set this_name to the name of this_item
        set the hypen_offset to (the offset of "-" in this_name) + 1
        set the original_name to ¬
            text from the hypen_offset to -1 of this_name
        set the name of this_item to the original_name
    end repeat
end tell
```

SCRIPT 7.18

When the script is run, the image files have the same names they had before the numeric prefix was added. Note that the `document file` class was used in the first statement without specifying a kind of document file, because the only documents displayed in the window are the image files we want.

Script 7.18 is basically a *find and do* script. The first statement locates (the *find* part) the image files. Next, the `repeat` loop processes each of the found items (the *do* part) to alter its name. You'll discover that many of the most useful scripts are really just *find and do* scripts.

Find and Do with Multiple Applications

When creating *find and do* scripts, you're not limited to working within a single application. Various parts of the script can be performed by other applications or by AppleScript itself.

Script 7.19 is an example where the *find* part of the script uses the Finder application, and the *do* part of the script uses AppleScript and the TextEdit application.

Run Script 7.19. It generates a list of the names of the image files displayed in the frontmost Finder window, sorted by their file size, and then it creates a new document in TextEdit containing the list of names.

```
tell application "Finder"
    -- generate a list of file references sorted by size
    set these_items to sort (get every document file ¬
        of the front Finder window) by physical size
    -- generate a list of names
    set these_names to {}
    repeat with i from 1 to the count of these_items
        set the end of these_names to ¬
            the name of (item i of these_items)
    end repeat
end tell
-- convert the list of names to a paragraph-delimited text block
set AppleScript's text item delimiters to return
set the item_list to these_names as string
set AppleScript's text item delimiters to {""}
-- make a new document with the text
tell application "TextEdit"
    activate
    make new document
    set text of document 1 to the item_list
end tell
```

SCRIPT 7.19

Running the script creates a printable document in TextEdit listing the names of the image files displayed the front Finder window, sorted by the file size of their corresponding image files (smallest to largest), as shown in Figure 7.15.

FIGURE 7.15 A printable list of file names in TextEdit.

Script 7.20 is a variation of the same script. It reverses the sort order of the image file references so that they are ordered from largest to smallest and inserts the list of file names into a new e-mail message.

```
tell application "Finder"
    -- generate a list of file references sorted by size
    set these_items to sort (get every document file ¬
        of the front Finder window) by physical size
    -- reverse the order of the list of references
    set these_items to the reverse of these_items
    -- generate a list of names
    set these_names to {}
    repeat with i from 1 to the count of these_items
        set the end of these_names to ¬
            the name of (item i of these_items)
    end repeat
end tell
-- convert the list to paragraph-delimited text
set AppleScript's text item delimiters to return
set the item_list to these_names as string
set AppleScript's text item delimiters to ""
-- make a new outgoing message with the text
tell application "Mail"
    set this_message to make new outgoing message
    tell this_message
        set content to the item_list
        set visible to true
    end tell
end tell
```
SCRIPT 7.20

After running Script 7.20, there is a new mail message in Mail listing the names of the image files displayed in the front Finder window, sorted by the file size of their corresponding image files (largest to smallest), as shown in Figure 7.16.

FIGURE 7.16 A list of file names in an outgoing mail message.

A Physical Sort

The previous scripts used the Finder's **sort** verb to generate a list of ordered file references. The items on disk were unaffected, remaining in place in their parent container. Only the file references were sorted.

Sometimes you may want to sort the files themselves into folders based on the value of some property. Script 7.21 locates and sorts the files displayed in the front Finder window into a set of folders based on the month each file was created. In other words, files created in May are moved into a folder titled 05 May, files created in November are moved into a folder titled 11 November, and so on. The script is still basically a *find and do* operation but with some statements to create folders inserted at the beginning.

```
tell application "Finder"
    -- get reference to folder whose contents are shown in the window
    set the target_folder to the target of front Finder window

    -- make a set of folders, one for each month
    set the month_titles to ¬
        {"01 January", "02 February", "03 March", "04 April", "05 May",
"06 June", "07 July", "08 August", "09 September", "10 October", "11
November", "12 December"}
    repeat with i from 1 to 12
        set the month_title to (item i of month_titles)
        if not (exists folder month_title of the target_folder) then
            make new folder at the target_folder ¬
                with properties {name:month_title}
        end if
    end repeat

    -- find the documents in the folder
    set these_files to (every document file of the target_folder)

    -- move each document to its corresponding folder
    repeat with i from 1 to the count of these_files
        set this_file to item i of these_files
        set the creation_month to ¬
            (the month of (get creation date of this_file)) as string
        move this_file to (the first folder of the target_folder ¬
            whose name ends with the creation_month)
    end repeat
end tell
```
SCRIPT 7.21

After you run the script, a set of ordered folders exists on disk, each containing files whose month of creation corresponds to the title of the folder, as shown in Figure 7.17.

FIGURE 7.17 A set of ordered folders.

When the Finder window is displayed in list view, it does not show how many items reside in each folder. To make this information visible for all the folders at once, Script 7.22 inserts the number of items each folder contains into its Finder comment and displays the comment column.

```
tell application "Finder"
    -- get reference to folder whose contents are displayed in window
    set the target_folder to the target of front Finder window

    -- generate a list of references to folders displayed in window
    set these_folders to every folder of the target_folder

    -- count the number of items in each folder and add to comment
    repeat with i from 1 to the count of these_folders
        set this_folder to item i of these_folders
        if the name of this_folder is not "Movies" then
            set the item_count to the count of document files ¬
                of the entire contents of this_folder
            set the comment of this_folder to ¬
                (item_count & space & "images") as string
        end if
    end repeat

    -- make comments visible in front window
    tell list view options of the front Finder window
        set properties to {calculates folder sizes:false, shows icon
preview:false, icon size:large icon, text size:12, uses relative
dates:true, sort column:name column}

        tell column name column
            set its width to 180
        end tell
        tell column comment column
            set properties to ¬
                {index:2, sort direction:normal, width:100 ¬
```

```
                , visible:true}
        end tell
    end tell
    tell the front Finder window
        set the current view to list view
    end tell
end tell
```

SCRIPT 7.22

The result of running Script 7.22 is a Finder window similar to Figure 7.18.

FIGURE 7.18 Using the comments field of a folder to display the count of items it contains.

Chapter Summary

Script 7.22 incorporates several scripting techniques you've learned over the course of the previous chapters and a couple you'll discover in the chapters that follow.

In this chapter, you saw that powerful, useful scripts can be simple *action statements*, or they can be more complex scripts that contain *loops*, *conditionals*, and other constructs to expand the scope and abilities of the script.

However, regardless of their complexity, most scripts still basically follow the concept of finding or identifying items to be processed and then processing the identified items. In other words, *find and do*. Keep that concept in mind as you develop your own scripts.

And one more thing…

It's always a good practice to clean up after yourself when you've been experimenting as we have in this chapter. So here's one last script for you to write, analyze, and run. Script 7.23 restores the Finder window to its initial configuration at the beginning of the chapter by moving the items out of the sorting folders and back into the parent folder and then deleting the emptied sorting folders. See the result in Figure 7.19.

```
tell application "Finder"
    set the target_folder to the target of front Finder window

    set these_folders to (every folder of the target_folder)

    repeat with i from 1 to the count of these_folders
        set this_folder to item i of these_folders
        move (every item of this_folder) to the target_folder
        delete this_folder
    end repeat

    set current view of front Finder window to icon view
end tell
```

SCRIPT 7.23

FIGURE 7.19 The frontmost Finder window restored to its original look.

Ah, the magic of AppleScript!

What's Next?

This was the fifth in a series of five chapters about identifying, finding, and manipulating scriptable objects in applications. Now that you've mastered the basics, the next chapter will start you on your way to truly powerful scripting by showing you how to preserve and manipulate data in your scripts using variables, operators and coercions.

8

Lesson 8

Data Containers, Operators, and Coercions

Now that you know how to find your way around your computer using AppleScript, you're ready to start doing something useful with the information that's available to you. To do real work with AppleScript, you need to be able to hold onto the data you're interested in while you're working with it, to manipulate it in various ways to produce new data, and sometimes to change its type so you can combine it or compare it to other data.

To perform these tasks with data in AppleScript, you need to learn about containers, operators, and coercions:

▶ Data containers are known to scripters as *variables*. Variables are terms that you define in a script, such as `my_name` or `return_value`, and that hold a piece of information of any type. They are called *variables* because the data they hold can vary from time to time as a result of the statements executed by your script.

▶ *Operators* are terms in a script that modify, combine, or compare information. They include arithmetic operators such as + (add) and - (subtract), and comparison operators such as < (less than) and `comes after`.

▶ *Coercions* are expressions that convert one type of data to another type; for example, `Monday as string` converts the enumeration constant `Monday` to the string `"Monday"` so it can be concatenated with another string or displayed in a dialog.

A great many operators and coercions are available in AppleScript. Learning them is simply a matter of looking them up and remembering them.

Data Containers (Variables)

You already know how to get data, but you haven't yet explored in any depth how to keep it around for use elsewhere in a script. You'll take that important step now.

You get data by executing a statement that creates or returns a value. Some examples are shown in Scripts 8.1, 8.2 and 8.3.

```
92
--> returns: 92
```
SCRIPT 8.1

```
"758"
--> returns: "758"
```
SCRIPT 8.2

```
tell application "Finder" to get name of window 1
--> returns: "Data Containers"
```
SCRIPT 8.3

Sometimes getting data is all you need to do, either because you won't use the data again or because it is simplest just to execute the statement again, as in the first two examples. But often you need to do several things with the data, and your script therefore needs to remember what it is. You can't just execute the same statement to get the data again from its original source, because the source might have changed behind your back in the meantime. For example, the window whose name you got a while ago might have closed since then. Also, getting the value from the variable in which you stored it is often much faster and more efficient than getting it from an application again.

To remember data in a script, you simply give it a name. From then on, you can get the value of the data back again and again by executing the name. The name is called a *variable*, and it is said to "contain" or "refer to" the data. You give data a name by using the **set** or **copy** command. Scripts 8.4 and 8.5 are some examples.

```
set today to date string of (current date)
get today
--> returns: "Sunday, August 12, 2007"
```
SCRIPT 8.4

```
copy last word of "Sal Soghoian" to last_name
return "Author: " & last_name
--> returns: "Author: Soghoian"
```
SCRIPT 8.5

In the first example, we used the **set** command to set the value of the variable **today** to a string representing today's date, and then we used the **get** command with the name of the variable to get the same value back. In the meantime, the value remained stored in the variable, and it remains stored there no matter how many times you get it, until you set it to something else. This would have worked even if there were dozens of other statements lying between these two statements, unless any of the intervening statements set **today** to a new value.

In the second example, we used the **copy** command to copy Sal Soghoian's last name into the variable `last_name`, and then we got the value of `last_name` back simply by executing the variable. We got a little ahead of ourselves by using the concatenation operator, **&**, to combine the result, "Soghoian," with the literal string "Author: " and return the combination.

Nothing stops you from setting the value of a variable once and then changing it to some other value later. In fact, this is often useful if you don't need to keep the original value. For example, Script 8.6 increments the `counter` variable using the addition operator, +.

```
set counter to 0
set counter to counter + 1
return counter
--> returns: 1
```
SCRIPT 8.6

You can even assign data of a different type to a variable after first setting it to data of one type, as shown in Script 8.7.

```
set counter to 1
set counter to "one"
return counter
--> returns: "one"
```
SCRIPT 8.7

There are a few simple rules about how to name variables. You can use any letters and numerals and the underscore character, but variable names must start with a letter, and they must not be an AppleScript reserved word such as **get** or **string**. You can use uppercase and lowercase letters, but variable names are not case sensitive. In other words, the variables `my_Name`, `My_Name`, and `my_name` are the same variable. (In fact, when you compile a script, all instances of a variable are changed to the capitalization of the first instance. This can be surprising if you accidentally name a variable with capitalization you didn't intend, but it doesn't affect how your script works.) You can't use punctuation or white space in a variable name, which means variable names must always consist of one word. This is why so many variable names in this book use underscore characters: the underscores stand in for spaces to make variable names more readable. Many scripters prefer to use intercaps to call out individual words, like this: `myName` or `valueOfResult`.

You can use reserved words and names containing illegal characters if you enclose the name in vertical bars, also called pipe characters. This is sometimes useful as an advanced technique. In Script 8.8, the variable's name is `123 & 4`.

```
set |123 & 4| to 1234
return |123 & 4|
--> returns: 1234
```
SCRIPT 8.8

The set and copy Commands (Data Sharing)

Most of the time, you can use the **set** and `copy` commands interchangeably. However, if the type of the data is an object—specifically, in AppleScript, if it is a *list*, *record*, *date*, or *script object*—these two commands work very differently.

When used with an object, the set command stores a *reference* to the object in the variable, while the `copy` command makes a separate copy of the object and stores the copy in the variable. Suppose you assign an object to a variable and then assign that variable to another variable. If you later change any of the object's values using one of the variables, the value returned by the other variable will differ depending on which command you used to give it a value in the first place, set or copy. It is important to understand this difference, because your scripts may produce unexpected results if you use the wrong command.

When we say the set command stores a *reference* to an object in a variable, we mean that the value of the object itself is not assigned to the variable. Instead, the variable *points* to the object, which resides somewhere else in the computer's memory. When you assign the variable to another variable using the set command, both variables now point to the same object at the same location in memory. The object is *shared* between the variables. As a result, any change you make using one of the variables changes the object itself, and the second variable's value changes, too, because it refers to the same object. In essence, you've given one object two different names, and changes you make using one of the names affect the object no matter which of its names you use to get it back.

Script 8.9 shows an example. Suppose the current date is August 12, 2007.

```
set today to current date
set tomorrow to today
set day of tomorrow to (day of today) + 1
return date string of today
--> returns: "Monday, August 13, 2007"
```
SCRIPT 8.9

What?!? You probably didn't mean to change today's date when you set the value of tomorrow to the next day, but that's what happened because you used the set command to assign the same date object to both variables. A single modification of the script, shown in Script 8.10, gets the result you intended:

```
set today to current date
copy today to tomorrow
set day of tomorrow to (day of today) + 1
return date string of today
--> returns: "Sunday, August 12, 2007"
```
SCRIPT 8.10

The copy command creates a separate copy of the object. The two variables now refer to different objects at separate locations in the computer's memory, and changes to one do not affect the other. Script 8.11 shows another example.

```
set line_1 to {"A", "rose", "by", "any", "other", "name"}
set line_2 to line_1

tell line_2
    set {item 1, item 2, item 3, item 4, item 5, item 6} ¬
        to {"would", "smell", "as", "sweet", "", ""}
end tell

return line_1
--> returns: {"would", "smell", "as", "sweet", "", ""}
```
SCRIPT 8.11

Oops! The script is easily fixed by changing the second line to:

```
copy line_1 to line_2
```

Sometimes you want data sharing, and in those cases it is appropriate to use the **set** command with object references. For one thing, it allows you to use different descriptive variable names in different parts of a script without using extra memory. In the first example, if you had named the second variable now instead of tomorrow, it would be perfectly appropriate to make sure a change to the value of now also changes the value of today.

Smart Variables

You can even define a variable as a reference to an object in the first place, by using the a reference to operator. When you do this, the variable doesn't permanently acquire the current value of the object, like it does with the copy command. Instead, it points to the object, and afterward it assumes whatever value the object might have from time to time. The variable acts like the "smart folders" that have become so popular in recent versions of Mac OS X. The value contained in the variable changes whenever the value of the object changes. You can use the contents property at any time to get the current value of the object.

The examples shown in Scripts 8.12, 8.13 and 8.14 illustrate the concept of smart variables.

```
set my_names to "Sal"
set his_name to a reference to my_name
return his_name
--> returns: my_name of "script"
```
SCRIPT 8.12

As you see, the returned value is not the name contained in the my_name variable, but a reference to the my_name variable of the script. To get the current value contained in the my_name variable, get the contents property of the his_name variable, as in Script 8.13.

```
set my_name to "Sal"
set his_name to a reference to my_name
return contents of his_name
--> returns: "Sal"
```
SCRIPT 8.13

To see the "smart" aspect of the a reference to operator at work, assign a different name to the my_name variable *after* the his_name variable is set to a reference to the my_name variable and *before* getting the contents property of the his_name variable. Script 8.14 shows that the value of his_name keeps up with changes to the value of my_name.

```
set my_name to "Sal"
set his_name to a reference to my_name
set my_name to "Bill"
return contents of his_name
--> returns: "Bill"
```
SCRIPT 8.14

Local and Global Variables

You can assign a value to a variable anywhere in the main body of a script and then get its value anywhere else in the main body. You just do it. You don't have to *declare* the variable in advance explicitly, as you do in some programming languages.

However, you are *allowed* to declare any variable before using it, if you want. Declaring a variable lets you control the *scope* within which the variable is accessible in the script. A variable is available either locally or globally. You declare a *local variable* by using the term `local` followed by the variable name, and you declare a *global variable* by using the term `global` followed by the variable name, as in these examples:

```
local my_name
global your_name
```

To understand the concept of a variable's scope, you first need to know that you can break any script into separate groups of commands by writing *subroutine handlers*. Looking ahead, you will learn in Chapter 16, *Subroutines*, that *subroutines* are named groups of statements that usually perform a single function. Subroutines are called by name from the main body of a script or from other subroutines, almost as if they were AppleScript commands on their own. When they are called, the statements they contain are executed. The idea of *scope* has to do with whether a variable in one subroutine is available in another subroutine or in the main body of the script.

When you use a variable without explicitly declaring it, you normally can get and set its value only within the same level of the script where you first used it. The variable is considered to be a *local variable*. For example, if you first use an undeclared variable in a subroutine, it is considered local to that subroutine, and you can't get or set its value in the main body of the script (sometimes called the *top level*) or in any other subroutine. Similarly, if you use an undeclared variable in the main body of a script that has subroutines, it is local to the top level, and you can't get or set its value in any subroutine. (This is because the top level of a script is actually a subroutine handler itself, sometimes called an *implicit run handler*.)

This is not to say that you can't use the same variable name anywhere you like. You can use a variable having the same name elsewhere in a script, outside the scope of the local variable, and Script Editor will happily compile the script without error. However, AppleScript will see it as a different variable when you run the script, even though it has the same name, and the script may therefore give the same name different values in different parts of the script. This can become very confusing if you don't pay attention to how you name and scope your variables. As a general rule, if you use a variable with the same name in multiple subroutines, or in the main body of a script and also in one or more subroutines, you should think about declaring it explicitly to make sure you're using it correctly.

When you use subroutines, you will find that it is often a good idea to use the same variable both in the main body of the script and in one or more of its subroutines. This gives the entire script easy access to the same value everywhere in the script. You do this by explicitly declaring the variable *global* before you use it. You declare it global either in the main body of the script or in every subroutine where you need to use it. Either way, once you declare it global, you can set and get its value at any level of the script, including the top level, and you will get the same value everywhere.

If you declare a variable global in a subroutine and not at the top level, its scope will not extend to other subroutines where you did *not* declare it global. In other words, declaring a variable global in a subroutine instead of in the main body requires that you repeat the declaration in every subroutine where you use it. Otherwise, a variable of the same name in another subroutine will be treated as a different variable, local to that subroutine.

To use a global variable in all the subroutines where you declared it global but simultaneously treat a variable having the same name at the top level of the script as a separate variable, declare it local at the top level. You can also declare a variable local within any subroutine to make it a separate variable within that subroutine, even if a variable of the same name is declared global at the top level or in other subroutines.

If these rules seem confusing now, don't worry about it. You will learn all about subroutines and see examples of local and global variable declarations when you get to Chapter 16, *Subroutines*.

Persistence of Variables

The value of global variables is persistent. This means that if you change the value of a global variable the first time you run the script, it will retain the new value the next time you run it—if you haven't closed the script in the meantime.

You will notice that a global variable's value is persistent only if the script does not store a new value in the variable every time you run it. It is hard to write a script that doesn't set a global variable to a new value, however, and a myth has therefore grown saying that global variable values are not persistent. It's a tall tale, and you shouldn't believe it.

There is another kind of data container in AppleScript called a *property*. We won't discuss properties in detail until Chapter 15, *Script Properties*. We'll mention here, however, that properties are designed to make persistence easy. If you want a value in a script to persist, use a property instead of a global variable for convenience and clarity. Chapter 15 shows you how.

Operators

An *operator* is used in an AppleScript expression to perform an operation on data. Scripts operate on data all the time, so this is an important concept to get straight. It isn't difficult. When you add 2 + 2, the + sign is an operator that tells the script to add the second value to the first value. Most operators work the same way.

An operator is called a *binary operator* if it operates on two values and a *unary operator* if it operates on a single value. The values on which an operator operates are called *operands*. An example of a binary operator is the addition operator, which is used like this: `return x + y`. An example of a unary operator is `not`, which returns the opposite, or negation, of a single Boolean value. Most operators are binary.

Operators are pervasive in scripts, so you will see examples of their use throughout this book. This section therefore describes the rules for using them in general terms, without many examples.

Most operators built into AppleScript have multiple synonyms. To compare two values for equality, for example, you can write `x = y`, `x is y`, `x equals y`, or `x is equal to y`, among others. In these examples, the operators are `=`, `is`, `equals`, and `is equal to`. You can choose whatever synonym strikes you as the most likely to produce an understandable English-like sentence or whatever form takes the least space. In some situations, you need to take into account whether a synonym will print in recognizable fashion, such as when formatting a script for display on a Web page where some AppleScript operators are illegal characters.

Operations are sometimes performed by AppleScript and sometimes by an application. You shouldn't have to worry about this normally, because operations usually just work. If it becomes important to you for any reason—for example, because an operator doesn't seem to perform its job the way you expected it to—you should know the rules. The general rule is that the object to the left of the operator determines who tries to perform the operation in the first instance. If it is a reference to an application object, the application is given an opportunity to try to perform the operation. Otherwise, or if the application can't perform it, AppleScript tries to perform it. There are a few exceptions to this rule. For example, the `is contained by` operator is evaluated right to left.

Operators generally act on specific classes of data and not on others. Division, for example, works with real and integer operands, but not with strings. If an operator encounters a class it can't handle, AppleScript attempts to coerce the value to an equivalent class that it can handle. It usually looks at the value to the left of the operator first, attempting to coerce it to a class that is legal for that operator. If successful, it attempts to coerce the value to the right to a compatible class, if necessary. The `is contained by` operator is, again, an exception, and equality operations do not invoke coercion. If coercion fails, an error is generated. Coercion is discussed in more detail in the next section.

The type of the result of an operation sometimes depends on the class of the values on which it operates. Concatenating two lists returns a list, for example, while concatenating two strings returns a string. Comparison operations always return a Boolean value.

Operators can be combined to form compound expressions. Rules of *operator precedence* dictate when it is necessary to enclose some of the component expressions in parentheses to force the operators to operate in a particular order to achieve the result you want. Parentheses can always be used to override the precedence rules, because parentheses are themselves operators, and they have the highest precedence of all. You can be safe by always using parentheses to group operations. Operations in inner parentheses are performed before operations in outer parentheses.

> **NOTE** ▶ Parentheses also affect the automatic formatting of scripts when they're compiled. The examples throughout this book often use parentheses strictly to force line breaks to fall where they will make it easier for you to read a script, even though they aren't necessary to ensure correct operator precedence.

You saw a list of containment operators such as `starts with` and `contains`, as well as lists of comparison operators such as `equals` and `comes before`, in Chapter 4, *Finding Objects*. Here are some others, for your convenience.

Logical Operators

Here are some logical operators:

▶   and

▶   or

▶   not

Concatenation Operator

Here is a concatenation operator:

▶   &

Arithmetic Operators

Here are some arithmetic operators:

- ▶ * (multiplication)

- ▶ + (addition)

- ▶ - (subtraction or unary negation)

- ▶ / (division)

- ▶ div (integral division)

- ▶ mod (remainder)

- ▶ ^ (exponentiation)

Coercions

We touched briefly on coercion of data types earlier in the chapter. Coercion is necessary whenever you attempt to perform an operation that is not designed for the type of data you're feeding to the operator.

Some kinds of data can be coerced to almost anything. For example, a list containing a single item can be coerced to the item itself, no matter what its type. The reverse is also true: data of any type can be coerced to a list containing the original value as its only item. Each of the number types, real and integer, can be coerced to the other. When a real is coerced to an integer, the result is rounded off. (In older versions of AppleScript, a real could be coerced to an integer only if it had no fractional part.) An integer or real can be coerced to its string equivalent (not the word, but the digits and any decimal point enclosed in straight quotation marks) and a string of digits, with or without a decimal point, can be coerced to a real or integer. Dates can be coerced to strings, and vice versa. The string format depends on your settings in the Date & Time pane of System Preferences. Strings can be coerced to a list of words, and a list of words can be coerced to a string. Constants can be coerced to strings (this wasn't always true). There are other rules too numerous to list here.

AppleScript often performs required coercions automatically, without your intervention. It looks as if the operator was designed to work with the type of data you're using in the first place.

When working with classes created by applications, appropriate coercions may also be supplied by the application. Sometimes, however, an application returns something that looks like a familiar AppleScript data type, but operations that normally work on that data type don't seem to work. In such cases, it might actually be an application-specific data type that doesn't support the operation. To operate on it, you might first have to use the `as` operator to coerce the application type to the AppleScript type.

There are other situations where you may want to control the coercion, to ensure that it yields data of a specified type. You do this using the coercion operator, `as`. For example, the expression `123 as string` returns `"123"`, while the expression `123 as list` returns `{123}`. When you tell an application to `get` a value `as` a data type, you are in effect asking the application to perform the coercion, but the application may hand the job off to AppleScript.

What's Next?

In this chapter, you learned how to hold onto data using variables, how to manipulate data using operators, and how to change the type of data using coercions. In the next chapter, you'll learn how to make your scripts smart using conditionals, which are `if` statements that allow your scripts to make decisions and to act on them.

9

Communicating with the User

Although scripts can be designed to run unattended, many scripts require interaction with the person running the script. For example, a script that adds a suffix to the names of selected files might require the user to provide the suffix. A script that converts images from one file format to another may require the user to select a folder in which to place the duplicated images. And a script that is processing a large number of items may need to keep the user informed of the script's progress.

This chapter contains a detailed overview of the most widely used script commands for communicating with the person running the script. We examine the dictionary listing for each command, and we provide short example scripts for each communication method.

The examples provided in this chapter are for Mac OS X version 10.5 (Leopard). Some commands and optional parameters in Leopard were not available in prior system releases.

The beep Command

The most basic user interaction command is beep. Macs have been beeping at us since 1984 and they still do today, but instead of a *beep*, it's now called an *alert sound*. Unlike in the early days of computing, there's now a wide variety of alert sounds to choose from in the Sounds preference pane of Mac OS X.

Scripts trigger the current system alert sound by using the beep command. Like almost all the user interaction commands described in this chapter, this command is part of the Standard Additions scripting addition. It is global in scope, and it can be used inside or outside of any tell blocks in your scripts.

To use it, place the command on its own line in the script, as shown in Script 9.1.

```
beep
```
SCRIPT 9.1

When the script is executed, it plays the current system alert sound. Optionally, you can make the script beep multiple times by placing an integer, representing the number of consecutive beeps to sound, after the beep command as shown in Script 9.2.

```
beep 3
```
SCRIPT 9.2

Typically, you should play an alert sound just before displaying unexpected dialogs and alerts or when an error has occurred, as in Script 9.3 where the attempt to coerce a string containing a word to an integer generates an error:

```
try
    set x to "hello" as integer
on error
    beep
end try
```
SCRIPT 9.3

There is currently no built-in AppleScript command to play a specific alert sound other than the one the user has set as the system alert sound. One alternative is to script the QuickTime Player application to open, play, and close another alert sound in the background, but this doesn't work very well. Another alternative is to use a third-party scripting addition.

Script 9.4 runs QuickTime Player and tells it to play the Submarine sound. Although it has the advantage of playing a sound other than the current system sound, it has several disadvantages. For example, the script takes a few moments to start QuickTime Player if it isn't already running, and a QuickTime Player window appears briefly on the screen every time it plays a sound. Also, if QuickTime Player's "Show Content Guide automatically" preference is turned on, the Content Guide window opens automatically when QuickTime Player runs (this setting can't easily be turned off using AppleScript).

```
set this_sound to ¬
    (((path to library folder from System domain) as string) ¬
    & "Sounds:Submarine.aiff") as alias
tell application "QuickTime Player"
    open this_sound
    set close when done of movie 1 to true
    play movie 1
end tell
```
SCRIPT 9.4

The first statement in the script creates an alias reference to the Submarine sound and assigns it to the `this_sound` variable. It locates the system's Library folder using the `path to` command, and then it appends the rest of the path to the Submarine sound in the Sounds folder. This uses a technique you learned in Chapter 5, *Special Folders*, for getting the path to standard folder locations. After opening the sound, the script sets its `close when done` property to `true` to make QuickTime Player close the sound file right after it finishes playing.

Script 9.5 is a version of the script that plays a random alert sound.

```
set the sounds_folder to ¬
    (((path to library folder from System domain) as string) ¬
    & "Sounds:") as alias
tell application "System Events"
    set this_sound to (some item of the sounds_folder) as alias
end tell
tell application "QuickTime Player"
    open this_sound
    set close when done of movie 1 to true
    play movie 1
end tell
```

SCRIPT 9.5

This is identical to the previous script, except it gets an alias reference to the Sounds folder and then tells the System Events application to get some item from that folder. Every time you run the script, it chooses some other sound at random.

To avoid the disadvantages that come with QuickTime Player, use the free Play Sound scripting addition written by David Blache, which lets you play any available sound with a simple AppleScript command. It's available at http://microcosmsoftware.com/playsound/. As you become more experienced with AppleScript, you will want to keep an eye out for good third-party scripting additions. They can add a lot of power to your scripting toolbox.

The display dialog Command

The most commonly used communication tool in AppleScript is the `display dialog` command. This command is generally used to do the following:

▶   Provide the user with information, such as explaining the result of a script action or the current status of the script.

▶   Ask the user to make a decision regarding the further actions of the script.

▶   Prompt the user to enter text such as a password.

When run, the `display dialog` command presents a small window containing text messages, various buttons, and, optionally, a text field to receive text entered by the script's user.

Like all the user interaction commands described in this chapter, this command is part of the Standard Additions scripting addition. It is global in scope, and it can be used inside or outside of any `tell` blocks in your scripts.

Here is the Standard Additions dictionary listing for the `display dialog` command. You learned how to read a dictionary in Chapter 2, *Dictionaries*. The command requires a direct parameter, and it has ten optional parameters, each of which is discussed in this chapter.

```
display dialog v : Display a dialog box, optionally requesting user
    input
    display dialog text : the text to display in the dialog box
        [default answer text] : the default editable text
        [hidden answer boolean] : Should editable text be displayed
            as bullets? (default is false)
        [buttons list of text] : a list of up to three button names
        [default button text or integer] : the name or number of
            the default button
        [cancel button text or integer] : the name or number of the
            cancel button
        [with title text] : the dialog window title
        [with icon text or integer] : the resource name or ID of the
            icon to display…
        [with icon stop/note/caution] : …or one of these system
            icons…
        [with icon file] : …or an alias or file reference to a
            '.icns' file
        [giving up after integer] : number of seconds to wait
            before automatically dismissing the dialog
        --> dialog reply : a record containing the button clicked and
            text entered (if any)
```

The entries in the `dialog reply` record may not always be included. The `button returned` entry is empty text if the `giving up after` parameter was supplied and the dialog timed out. The `text returned` entry is present only if the `default answer` parameter was supplied. It returns empty text if the user entered no text. The `gave up` entry is present only if the `giving up after` parameter was supplied. It returns true if the dialog timed out and false if the user supplied an answer in time.

Our first example script employs the command with none of its optional parameters. The only parameter used in the script is the mandatory direct parameter, which is the text message to be displayed by the dialog. To use the `display dialog` command in a script, type the command followed by the message as shown in Script 9.6. Remember that text and item names used in a script are always enclosed in straight quotation marks.

```
display dialog "You left the iron on. Should this script continue?"
```
SCRIPT 9.6

Here's the resulting dialog:

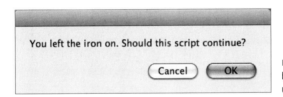

You left the iron on. Should this script continue?

Cancel   OK

FIGURE 9.1 The dialog displayed by the `display dialog` command using no optional parameters.

By default, the dialog contains two buttons: Cancel and OK. The dialog is dismissed when the user chooses either of them. The Cancel and OK buttons are special in several ways, but you can also create ordinary buttons using the `display dialog` command, as you will see in the next section.

The OK button serves as the default button, which can be chosen by clicking it with the mouse or pressing the Return key on the keyboard. When the user chooses the OK button, the script resumes running.

The Cancel button can be clicked with the mouse or chosen by pressing the Escape key on the keyboard. When the user chooses the Cancel button, the script stops running. The same applies for any dialog presented by the `display dialog` command that contains a Cancel button, as explained in more detail next.

NOTE ▶ Prior to Mac OS X version 10.3 (Panther), the display dialog command had a limit of 255 characters that could be displayed. That limit was removed in the 10.3 release.

display dialog: The buttons Parameter

The display dialog command has an optional parameter, buttons, to specify the number, order, and titles of buttons that appear in a dialog. Using this parameter, you can create up to three buttons for a dialog.

The value for the buttons parameter, placed after the parameter name buttons in the script statement, is a list of strings displayed as the titles for the buttons. The title for the leftmost button is the first item in the list, and the title for the rightmost button is the last item in the list.

Here are examples of button options.

A One-Button Dialog

Since they present only one option for the script's user, dialogs containing a single button are usually used simply to convey a message. To use the buttons parameter with the display dialog command, place it after the message text, and follow it with a list of strings representing the button titles. Since our first example dialog will have only one button, the title of the button is entered as the sole item in the button list, as in this example:

```
display dialog "Today is Tuesday." buttons {"OK"}
```
SCRIPT 9.7

When the script is run, the following dialog is presented:

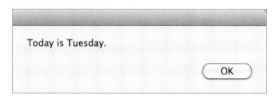

FIGURE 9.2 The dialog displayed by the display dialog command using a single name in the buttons parameter.

In this example, the dialog's purpose is to provide information. The user's only option is to click the OK button.

> **TIP** ▸ You don't have to include the curly braces when you create a dialog having a single button, and scripters often don't. AppleScript automatically coerces the string ("OK" in the example) to a single-item list before passing it to the `display dialog` command.

▶ About Dialog Messages

As long as we're discussing messages, here's a tip about message formatting. Sometimes dialog messages are composed of multiple sentences or sections, as in Script 9.8.

```
display dialog "Today is Tuesday. Although every day is a good
day to learn more about AppleScript, Tuesdays are especially
good for expanding your horizons. Keep up the good work!"
buttons {"Right On!"}
```
SCRIPT 9.8

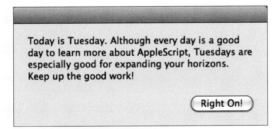

FIGURE 9.3
An unformatted `display`
`dialog` message.

As you see in Figure 9.3, the message fills the dialog, appearing to the user as a blob of text requiring a bit of concentration to read completely. To make the dialog more attractive, easier to read, and quickly comprehensible, separate the sections of the message with carriage returns by inserting the term **return** (meaning carriage return) in the message text, and use the concatenation operator (**&**) to join the message sections, as shown in Script 9.9.

```
display dialog "Today is Tuesday." & return & return &
"Although every day is a good day to learn more about
AppleScript, Tuesdays are especially good for expanding your
horizons." & return & return & "Keep up the good work!" buttons
{"Right On!"}
```
SCRIPT 9.9

Figure 9.4 shows the result.

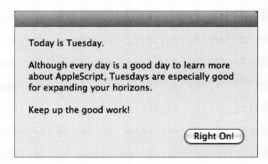

FIGURE 9.4 A formatted display dialog message.

The resulting dialog has a much cleaner, simpler appearance and can be read by the script's user with little effort.

Note that each section of text in the script is enclosed in straight quotation marks and joined to the next section by the concatenation operator (&).

Two-Button and Three-Button Dialogs

Dialogs containing two or three buttons are used to prompt the script's user to make a decision regarding the future action of the script. The titles of the buttons identify the available choices. For example:

```
display dialog "Who should get the money?" buttons {"Sal", "Bill"}
```
SCRIPT 9.10

When the script is run, the dialog shown in Figure 9.5 appears:

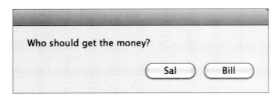

FIGURE 9.5 The dialog displayed by the `display dialog` command using two names in the `buttons` parameter.

In this example, the user is presented with a dialog containing a question and two options represented by buttons. The user indicates a choice by clicking one of the buttons, thereby dismissing the dialog and returning the choice to the script.

The result of the `display dialog` command, shown in Figure 9.6 in the Result pane of the script window in Script Editor, is a *record* containing one or more properties, including one with the label `button returned` and a corresponding value. The value is the title of the button that was clicked by the user.

FIGURE 9.6 The Script Editor window showing the result of clicking the first button.

Scripts use the property values in the `dialog reply` record to determine the action to take next. To extract the value of a property from the `dialog reply` record, such as the value of the `button returned` property, for use in the remainder of the script, use the `set` command to assign the value to a variable. Script 9.11 shows an example:

```
display dialog "Who should get the money?" buttons {"Sal", "Bill"}
set the chosen_person to the button returned of the result
display dialog "You chose " & the chosen_person & " to get the money!"
```
SCRIPT 9.11

▶ **A Tip from Sal**

Having written scripts for more than a decade, I'm a firm believer in defensive scripting, which is the practice of not assuming the script's user will follow the obvious path or choose the obvious action. Two or three choices often aren't enough to anticipate everything the user might want to do. When possible, therefore, you should allow users an opportunity to stop the script, just in case they're not prepared to continue the process.

Accordingly, when you start to write a script that displays a two-option dialog to the user, use three buttons instead. Designate one of the buttons as the Cancel button, giving the user the option to stop the script. This practice has saved me countless times!

Script 9.13 shows an example.

```
display dialog ("Rotate the image in which direction?") ¬
    buttons {"Cancel", "Left", "Right"}
```
SCRIPT 9.13

FIGURE 9.7 A dialog with two choices and a Cancel button.

Furthermore, my personal preference is to place the Cancel button on the left side of the dialog, leaving the right side for the query options.

You'll find more examples of extracting values from the `dialog reply` record later in this chapter.

Continuing our examination of buttons, here's another example in Script 9.12. It presents a dialog asking the user to choose one of three options.

```
display dialog ("The money should be spent on which item?") ¬
    buttons {"Movies", "Food", "Disneyland"}
```
SCRIPT 9.12

FIGURE 9.8 The dialog displayed by the `display dialog` command using three names in the `buttons` parameter.

display dialog: The default button Parameter

The optional `default button` parameter is used to indicate which button should be accessible from the keyboard by pressing the Return or Enter key. In Mac OS X, the default button has a solid color and pulses slowly to mark its status as the default button for the dialog.

The `default button` parameter is invoked by placing the parameter name after the button list and following it with a value that is either the default button title or a number representing the numeric position of the button's title in the button list.

Scripts 9.14 and 9.15 demonstrate both options and present the same dialog. The first script identifies the default button by name.

```
display dialog ("Translate the selected text to which language?") ¬
    buttons {"English", "French", "German"} default button "German"
```
SCRIPT 9.14

The second script identifies the default button by its index in the list.

```
display dialog ("Translate the selected text to which language?") ¬
    buttons {"English", "French", "German"} default button 3
```
SCRIPT 9.15

In both examples, the default button is the last button in the list. Users generally expect the default button to appear at the bottom-right corner of the dialog.

FIGURE 9.9 A dialog with a
default button.

TIP ▶ Making your scripts easy to use is the goal of every good scripter.
The default button parameter can help you achieve this. If possible, make
sure all the user interaction dialogs in your script can be controlled via the
keyboard. Select the option that is most often used to be the one associated with the default button.

display dialog: The cancel button Parameter

A similar parameter, the cancel button parameter, was added in Mac OS X
10.4 (Tiger).

If you don't use this new parameter, the only convenient way to have a button
in a dialog that behaves like a cancel button is to name it "Cancel." Now, however, you can name the cancel button anything you like and then provide its
number or name in the cancel button parameter to make it accessible via
the keyboard.

Script 9.16 is an example, naming the cancel button "Quit." If you click the
Continue button, the script resumes execution and plays the system alert
sound. But if you click the Quit button, the script stops immediately, without
playing the sound.

```
display dialog "Continue?" buttons {"Quit", "Continue"} ¬
    default button "Continue" cancel button "Quit"
beep
```
SCRIPT 9.16

Just as you can choose the default button by pressing the Return key, you can choose the cancel button by pressing the Escape key instead of clicking the button. It normally stops script execution, giving the script's user the option to bail out immediately. Try running Script 9.16 and press the Return or Escape key instead of clicking a button.

Why does a script stop running when the user clicks the cancel button or presses the Escape key? Well, the `display dialog` command deliberately generates an error, error -128, to signal that the user wants to stop. This behavior is common to several of the user interaction commands in the Standard Additions scripting addition, as you will see shortly. It is a convenient design, because it allows you to intercept the error and do something else before script execution stops. For example, you might want to give the user some information before quitting, as in the modified version of Script 9.16 shown in Script 9.17.

```
try
    display dialog "Continue?" buttons {"Quit", "Continue"} ¬
        default button "Continue" cancel button "Quit"
    beep
on error number -128 -- user canceled
    display dialog ("Run me again for a second chance.") ¬
        buttons {"OK"} default button "OK"
end try
```
SCRIPT 9.17

You'll learn more about the **try** block and error handler shown here in Chapter 12, *Error Handlers*.

display dialog: Timed Dialogs

As mentioned earlier, defensive scripting, or the practice of writing your scripts to allow for all possible user responses, will drastically reduce the time spent troubleshooting problems with your users or customers.

A commonly overlooked user option is the *nonaction,* where a script's user walks away from the computer without responding to a dialog. As a scripter, you can choose not to allow for this possibility, but doing so may have the unwanted consequence of leaving a dialog hanging, which may interfere with other processes running on the computer. Fortunately, AppleScript provides a useful mechanism for resolving this problem.

The optional `giving up after` parameter to the `display dialog` command provides the following:

▶   The means for a script to gracefully continue or stop on its own

▶   A mechanism for periodically communicating the status of a script process to the script's user

The `giving up after` parameter is placed at the end of the `display dialog` command and is followed by an integer indicating the number of seconds the dialog should remain on display before automatically closing. The `dialog reply` record returned to the script after the dialog closes contains a `gave up` property with a value of either `true`, if the user did not make a timely choice, or `false`, if the user answered the dialog before it closed.

Here are two scenarios using this parameter. Both examples, Scripts 9.18 and 9.19, show the same script, but the return values are different because the user responds to the dialog differently. In the first example, the user responds by clicking OK within the indicated time limit of ten seconds. The `dialog reply` record contains the `gave up` parameter with a value of `false`.

```
display dialog "Do you want to continue?" giving up after 10
--> returns: {button returned:"OK", gave up:false}
```
SCRIPT 9.18

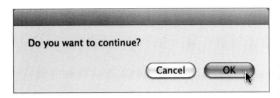

FIGURE 9.10 Clicking a button in a dialog with a `giving up after` parameter.

In the second example, the user has not responded to the dialog within the indicated time span. The corresponding `dialog reply` record contains the `gave up` parameter with a value of `true`, indicating the dialog closed itself. As with the previous example, the `dialog reply` record also contains the `button returned` property but with a value of an empty string (`""`) since no button was clicked.

```
display dialog "Do you want to continue?" giving up after 10
--> returns: {button returned:"", gave up:true}
```
SCRIPT 9.19

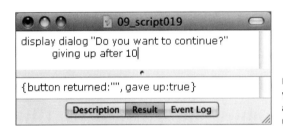

FIGURE 9.11 The Script Editor window after letting a dialog with a `giving up after` parameter give up by itself.

Scripts can use the value of the `gave up` property in the `dialog reply` record to determine what action, if any, the script should take.

Simply including the `giving up after` parameter in your script does not automatically stop the script after the indicated time. Instead, it closes the dialog. To stop the script if the dialog goes unanswered, include a conditional statement as in the second line of Script 9.20.

```
display dialog "Do you want to continue?" giving up after 5
if gave up of the result is true then error number -128
display dialog "OK, here we go!"
```
SCRIPT 9.20

The script resumes execution if the user clicks the OK button. The script stops if the user clicks the Cancel button or does not respond to the dialog. To stop the script, the second line uses the AppleScript verb `error` to generate an error. It assigns –128 as the error number because that is the same error number a script returns when any cancel button is clicked in a dialog.

Another common use of the `giving up after` parameter is to provide periodic feedback to the script's user about the progress of the script as shown in Script 9.21 and Figure 9.12. Typically, these status dialogs display only for one to two seconds, and they may or may not contain a `cancel` button allowing the user to stop the current processing cycle.

```
display dialog ("Processing image 550 of 2000...") ¬
    buttons {"•"} default button 1 giving up after 2
```
SCRIPT 9.21

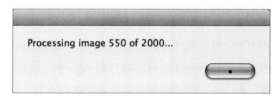

FIGURE 9.12 A progress dialog.

To help convey the concept that the progress dialog does not require a user response, use an ellipsis character (…) (Option+;) or three periods at the end of the message to indicate that more action is forthcoming. It also uses a bullet character (Option+8) as the title of the default button.

display dialog: Icons

During the course of a busy day, it's easy to forget to read a dialog and instead confirm the default button out of habit. To call your attention to important messages, Mac OS X uses icons in its special dialogs.

AppleScript dialogs can display one of three standard Mac OS alert icons: note, caution, and stop. These icons visually alert the user to important information or upcoming events that might cause severe damage.

To add an icon to a dialog, place the optional `with icon` parameter at the end of the `display dialog` statement and follow it with either the icon's name or its number.

Here are the three standard icons and examples of their use:

Note (icon number 1): Use this icon to provide information about a situation that has no drastic effects, as shown in Script 9.22 and Figure 9.13. The user usually responds by clicking the OK button. The note icon is the icon of whatever application is running the script.

```
display dialog "This script encountered a file naming problem. " & ¬
    "The problem has been fixed." buttons {"OK"} default button 1 ¬
    with icon note
```
SCRIPT 9.22

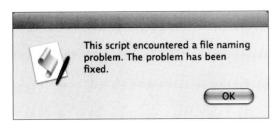

FIGURE 9.13 A dialog with the note icon.

Caution (icon number 2): Use this icon to call attention to an operation that may have undesirable results if allowed to continue, as shown in Script 9.23 and Figure 9.14. Usually, the user is given the option to continue or stop.

```
display dialog ("One of the images may not be complete.") ¬
    buttons {"Continue", "Cancel"} default button 2 ¬
    with icon caution
```
SCRIPT 9.23

FIGURE 9.14 A dialog with the caution icon.

Stop (icon number 0): Use this icon to call attention to a serious problem that requires the user to choose from alternative courses of action, as shown in Script 9.24 and Figure 9.15.

```
display dialog ("The target file is corrupted and can not be used.") ¬
    buttons {"Restart", "Cancel"} default button 2 ¬
    with icon stop
```
SCRIPT 9.24

FIGURE 9.15 A dialog with the stop icon.

New in Mac OS X 10.4 (Tiger) is the ability to include a custom icon in the dialog by providing an alias or file reference to it. The icon must be an icon file with the ".icns" name extension, which you can create using various utilities or obtain from other sources. You can package custom icons in a script bundle and refer to them using the `path to resource` command described in Chapter 5, *Special Folders*.

Icons add spice to dialogs, but as with any good spice, use icons sparingly and only when appropriate. In fact, all three of the script examples in this section are in the nature of alerts, rather than dialogs. When you are scripting for Leopard or Mac OS X 10.4 (Tiger), it would be better to use the new `display alert` command in situations like these. It uses a different icon scheme, described later in this chapter, which is more consistent with current user interface guidelines from Apple.

display dialog: Requesting Text from the User

It is not uncommon for scripts to require the user to name a file or an object or to provide a password or ID. The optional `default answer` parameter of the `display dialog` command displays a dialog containing a text input field into which the user types text that is returned to the script.

To use this optional parameter, place it after the message string, and follow it with any text you want to display within the text input field itself. To have the text input field appear empty, use an empty text string ("") as the parameter's value.

Script 9.25 and Figure 9.16 show a dialog with an empty text input field.

```
display dialog "Please enter your name:" default answer ""
```
SCRIPT 9.25

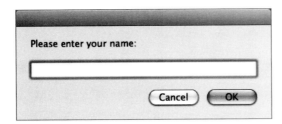

FIGURE 9.16 A dialog requesting text from the user.

By default, the text input field is selected and ready to receive keyboard input. Script 9.26 and Figure 9.17 show an example of a dialog with a default answer string.

```
display dialog ("Please enter your name:") ¬
    default answer "last name, first name"
```
SCRIPT 9.26

FIGURE 9.17 A dialog requesting text and providing a default answer.

A dialog containing a text input field accepts a text reply up to 255 characters in length. The text reply is returned to the script as part of the `dialog reply` record generated by the `display dialog` command.

When the `default answer` parameter is used, this record contains another name-value pair in addition to the `button returned` property. It now includes the `text returned` property, the value of which is the text string entered by the user in the dialog.

Here's the `dialog reply` record for Script 9.26 after the user types Sal's name:

`{text returned:"Soghoian, Sal", button returned:"OK"}`

Scripts can use the returned text in a variety of ways. In Script 9.27, the user is prompted to enter a name in the text input field. The script extracts the text entered from the result, which is the `dialog reply` record, by using the `set` command to assign the value of the `text returned` property of the result to a variable, which is then used in a response dialog.

```
display dialog "What is your name?" default answer ""
set the user_name to the text returned of the result
set the response_text to "Hello " & the user_name & "!"
display dialog response_text buttons {"OK"} default button 1
```
SCRIPT 9.27

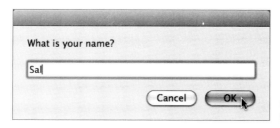

FIGURE 9.18 A dialog showing the user's answer.

FIGURE 9.19 A dialog making use of the user's answer.

Remember, the `dialog reply` record of a dialog containing a text input field is composed of at least two elements: the text input by the user and the title of the button the user clicked.

As a matter of fact, scripts can incorporate both button and text input options to require the user to make multiple decisions in the same dialog. Script 9.28 is an example of this technique:

```
display dialog ("Name the article and indicate its position.") ¬
    default answer "" buttons {"Cancel", "Left Page", "Right Page"}
```
SCRIPT 9.28

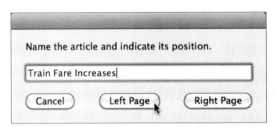

FIGURE 9.20 A dialog showing the user's answer and chosen button.

The `dialog reply` record for the dialog pictured in Figure 9.20 is this:

```
{text returned:"Train Fare Increases", button returned:"Left Page"}
```

display dialog: Text Input Filter Routines

The following scripts use the `display dialog` command, the `default answer` parameter, and AppleScript language elements such as conditionals, repeat loops, and error handlers to extract specific information from the user. You may find them useful in your scripts. The techniques used here are described in more detail in Chapter 10, *Conditionals*; Chapter 11, *The Repeat Loop*; and Chapter 12, *Error Handlers*.

▶ **A Tip from Sal**

Here's an easy way to quickly extract and store both the text and the button information provided by the `dialog reply` record of a dialog that contains a text input field.

The line after the `display dialog` command in Script 9.29 first converts the `dialog reply` record to a list of property values by using the `as list` coercion, and then it copies those values into a corresponding list of variable names:

```
display dialog ("Name the article and indicate its position.") ¬
    default answer "" buttons {"Cancel", "Left Page", "Right Page"}
copy the result as list to {the article_title, the article_position}
```
SCRIPT 9.29

The variables `article_title` and `article_position` now contain the text input by the user and the name of the button clicked by the user, respectively. Incorporate this dual-action technique in your scripts that use a `display dialog` command with text input (be sure to change the variable names to names appropriate for your script). You'll learn more about coercing records to lists in Chapter 18, *Working with Lists and Records*.

Requesting Numeric Input

Script 9.30 prompts the user to enter a number in the dialog's text input field. The dialog is presented repeatedly until the user has entered a valid numeric value or clicked the Cancel button.

The `as number` coercion is used to convert the entered text into a numeric value. If the coercion fails because the user enters non-numeric characters, the dialog is redisplayed to give the user an opportunity to get it right.

Decimal, positive, and negative numbers can be entered successfully.

```
repeat
    display dialog "Enter a number:" default answer ""
    try
        if the text returned of the result is not "" then
            set the requested_number to ¬
                the text returned of the result as number
            exit repeat
        end if
    on error
        beep
    end try
end repeat
```
SCRIPT 9.30

Requesting a Whole Number

Script 9.31 prompts the user to enter a whole (nonfractional) number into the dialog's text input field. The dialog is presented repeatedly until the user has entered a valid numeric value or clicked the Cancel button.

```
repeat
    display dialog "Enter a whole number:" default answer ""
    try
        set this_text to the text returned of the result
        if this_text is not "" then ¬
            set the this_number to this_text as number
        if this_number mod 1 is equal to 0 then
            set this_number to this_number div 1
            exit repeat
        end if
```

```
    on error
        beep
    end try
end repeat
```
SCRIPT 9.31

To check whether the entered value is a whole number, the script uses two arithmetic operators: `div` and `mod`. Additional examples of these operators are shown in Scripts 9.32 and 9.33.

▶   The `div` operator is a binary arithmetic operator that divides the number to its left by the number to its right and returns the integral (nonfractional) part of the answer as its result.

▶   The `mod` operator is a binary arithmetic operator that divides the number to its left by the number to its right and returns the remainder as its result.

For example:

```
5 div 2
--> returns: 2
```
SCRIPT 9.32

And for example:

```
5 mod 2
--> returns: 1
```
SCRIPT 9.33

As you remember from math class, when a number is taken modulo 1, a result of 0 indicates that the number does not have a fractional part; that is, it's a whole number.

Requesting a Number Within a Range

Script 9.34 prompts the user to enter a number in the dialog's text input field that is within a specified range of numbers. The dialog is presented repeatedly until the user has entered a valid numeric value or clicked the Cancel button.

You can change the range that the routine uses by editing the `low_value` and `high_value` values.

```
set the low_value to 1
set the high_value to 10
repeat
    display dialog ("Enter a number between ") ¬
        & low_value & " and " & high_value & ":" default answer ""
    try
        if the text returned of the result is not "" then ¬
            set this_number to ¬
                the text returned of the result as number
        if this_number is greater than or equal to low_value and ¬
            this_number is less than or equal to high_value then
            exit repeat
        end if
    on error
        beep
    end try
end repeat
```
SCRIPT 9.34

Requesting Non-numeric Characters

Script 9.35 prompts the user to enter text containing no numeric characters in the dialog's text input field. The dialog is presented repeatedly until the user has entered valid text or clicked the Cancel button.

You can adapt this routine to disallow any characters by editing the `disallowed_characters` list.

An empty string ("") is assigned to the `this_text` variable before the script enters the repeat loop, and then `this_text` is passed to the `default answer` parameter the first time the `display dialog` command is called inside the repeat loop. This ensures that the input text field appears empty the first time the dialog is displayed. The user's answer is then assigned to `this_text` inside the repeat loop. As a result, the user's most recent incorrect answer will be displayed every time the dialog is displayed thereafter.

The inner repeat loop tests each character of the user's answer in turn to ensure that each character is a number.

```
set the disallowed_characters to ¬
    {"0", "1", "2", "3", "4", "5", "6", "7", "8", "9"}
set this_text to ""
repeat
    display dialog ("Enter text (no numbers):") ¬
        default answer this_text
    try
        set this_text to the text returned of the result
        if this_text is "" then error
        repeat with this_character in this_text
            if this_character is in disallowed_characters then
                error
            end if
        end repeat
        exit repeat
    on error
        beep
    end try
end repeat
```
SCRIPT 9.35

display dialog: Requesting a Hidden Password from the User

A new parameter to the display dialog command introduced in Mac OS X 10.4 (Tiger) is hidden answer. It takes a Boolean value, which is taken to be false by default if you omit this parameter. If you include the default answer parameter in the display dialog command and set the value of the hidden answer parameter to true, the text the user types appears in the text input field as bullet characters. This is important because it lets your script hide secret values such as passwords from prying eyes.

Script 9.36 prompts the user to enter a password in the dialog's text input field. The dialog is presented up to three times if the wrong password is entered. The password, which is stored in the script, is case sensitive since the script invokes the `considering case` action clause when performing the string comparison. You will learn more about action clauses in Chapter 19, *Action Clauses.*

Do not use this routine to safeguard valuable data, because it offers only minimal security. Thanks to the new `hidden answer` parameter, however, the password is displayed as bullet characters rather than regular text when entered in the dialog. Type **Frogger**, and press Return to gain access.

```
set this_password to "Frogger"
considering case
    repeat with i from 1 to 3
        display dialog ("Enter password:") ¬
            default answer "" with hidden answer
        if the text returned of the result is this_password then
            exit repeat
        end if
        if i is 3 then return "access denied"
    end repeat
end considering
```
SCRIPT 9.36

Figure 9.21 shows what the dialog looks like while the user is entering a password.

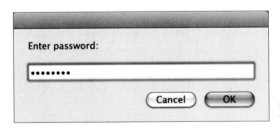

FIGURE 9.21 A dialog showing the user's answer using bullets.

display dialog: Giving the Dialog a Title

Usually, the dialog presented by the `display dialog` command does not have a title but only a blank title bar that you can use to drag the dialog around the screen.

Beginning with Mac OS X 10.4 (Tiger), however, you can use the `with title` parameter to give the dialog a meaningful title. Script 9.37 shows an example.

```
display dialog ("Give the guy a break, please.") ¬
    with title ("Gimme a break!") ¬
    buttons {"Cancel", "Break"} default button "Break"
display dialog ¬
    "Thanks, I needed that!" buttons {"OK"} default button "OK"
```
SCRIPT 9.37

Figure 9.22 shows the resulting dialog with its title.

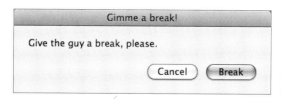

FIGURE 9.22 A dialog showing a title in the title bar.

The display alert Command

The `display alert` command was introduced in Mac OS X 10.4 (Tiger) to allow scripts to display alerts that conform to current Macintosh human interface guidelines. Until now, script writers had to resort to the `display dialog` command, which was able to fill the role well enough. But the `display alert` command makes it easier to present alerts that look right by today's standards.

The `display alert` command presents a small window containing an alert message in a large, bold font to draw the user's attention to the nature of the problem quickly, an explanatory or informational message in a smaller font to explain what went wrong in more detail and advise the user what to do, and various button choices. It does not include the optional text input field that the `display dialog` command offers, because alerts aren't intended to obtain textual information from the user.

Like all the user interaction commands described in this chapter, this command is part of the Standard Additions scripting addition. It is global in scope, and it can be used inside or outside of any `tell` blocks in your scripts.

Here is the Standard Additions dictionary listing for the `display alert` command. The command requires a direct parameter, and it has six optional parameters.

```
display alert v : Display an alert
    display alert text : the alert text (will be displayed in
        emphasized system font)
        [message text] : the explanatory message (will be displayed
            in small system font)
        [as critical/informational/warning] : the type of alert
            (default is informational)
        [buttons list of text] : a list of up to three button names
        [default button text or integer] : the name or number of
            the default button
        [cancel button text or integer] : the name or number of the
            cancel button
        [giving up after integer] : number of seconds to wait
            before automatically dismissing the alert
    --> alert reply : a record containing the button clicked
```

The entries in the `alert reply` record may not always be present. The `button returned` entry is an empty string if the `giving up after` parameter was supplied and the alert timed out. The `gave up` entry is present only if the `giving up after` parameter was supplied. It returns `true` if the alert time out or `false` if the user clicked a button in time.

The `buttons`, `default button`, `cancel button`, and `giving up after` parameters all work the same as the corresponding parameters to the `display dialog` command, so we won't discuss them here.

The proper use of the mandatory direct parameter and the optional message parameter is vital to provide a user-friendly alert. The direct parameter should be a brief, eye-catching summary of the nature of the problem, while the message parameter should take a few more words to explain the problem in more detail and describe the user's options.

The direct parameter should be short and punchy. It's all that many users will bother to read before they click a button, so you have to convey the essential nature of the problem in as few words as possible—three or four at most, if you can manage it. Don't make it insulting; make it informative. The message parameter is for users who are a little more at sea. Make it more detailed, and unless it's obvious, give the user some suggestions about what to do next.

Script 9.38 and Figure 9.23 show an example. When you run the script, first enter a number such as **123**. The script successfully coerces the text you typed into the text input field to a number, and the script completes execution without incident. Second, enter your first name or some other word or phrase. Since your entry can't be coerced to a number, the error handler is executed, and it runs the `display alert` command.

```
try
    display dialog ("Enter a number:") ¬
        default answer ("") ¬
        buttons {"OK"} default button "OK"
    set user_entry to text returned of result
    return user_entry as number
on error
    set alert_string to "Not a Number"
    set message_string to ¬
        ("\"" & user_entry & "\" is not a number. ") & ¬
        "Run the script again and use only the number keys."
    display alert alert_string message message_string ¬
        buttons {"OK"} default button "OK" giving up after 5
end try
```
SCRIPT 9.38

Figure 9.23 shows the alert the script displays. You'll probably agree that this alert strikes the right combination of crispness and helpfulness.

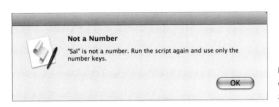

FIGURE 9.23 A well-designed error message using the `display alert` command.

The `as` parameter should be used rarely, if ever. In fact, the `critical` and `informational` constants present alerts with the identical appearance, because Apple's human interface experts believe any attempt to distinguish them by using different icons only adds to users' confusion. Both of them remain in the dictionary for backward compatibility with older scripts. Use the `warning` constant rarely, only when the user's choice might risk loss of data or other destructive consequences. If you overuse it, its power to attract the user's attention when it's really important will be diluted.

Figure 9.24 shows an alert that is justified in using the `warning` constant:

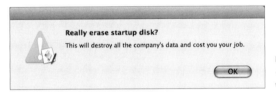

FIGURE 9.24 An alert using the `display alert` command's as `warning` parameter.

The choose folder Command

Another common script interaction is to ask the script's user to select a folder, whether it's a source folder containing files to be processed by the script or a destination folder that will contain items that have been processed by the script.

The `choose folder` command enables a user to select a folder from a disk or volume connected to the host computer. As with the other user interaction commands, this command is part of the Standard Additions scripting addition, and it can be used within or outside of any `tell` blocks.

Here is the Standard Additions dictionary listing for the choose folder command. The command has no direct parameter and five optional parameters.

```
choose folder v : Choose a folder on a disk or server
    choose folder
        [with prompt text] : the prompt to be displayed in the
            dialog box
        [default location alias] : the default folder location
        [invisibles boolean] : Show invisible files and folders?
            (default is false)
        [multiple selections allowed boolean] : Allow multiple
            items to be selected? (default is false)
        [showing package contents boolean] : Show the contents of
            packages? (Packages will be treated as folders. Default is
            false.)
        --> alias : the chosen folder
```

Script 9.39 is a simple example of the choose folder command in use.

```
set the source_folder to choose folder
```
SCRIPT 9.39

This script presents the standard operating system dialog for selecting directories, shown in Figure 9.25.

FIGURE 9.25 The dialog displayed by the choose folder command.

This window displays in column view by default and can be resized by the user to show more columns and list items. The New Folder button allows the user to create a new directory.

Once the user navigates to the desired folder and clicks the Open button, the script returns an alias reference to the chosen folder, as in Script 9.40.

```
set the source_folder to choose folder
--> returns: alias "Macintosh HD:Users:sal:Pictures:"
```
SCRIPT 9.40

In this example, the verb set is used to assign the result of the choose folder command to the variable source_folder, which can then be used elsewhere in the script. It is common scripting practice to invoke the choose folder command in this manner. Just remember to change the name of the variable to something appropriate for your script!

choose folder: The with prompt Parameter

The dialog displayed by the choose folder command usually does not contain a prompt, as you can see in Figure 9.25. The optional with prompt parameter provides text to display instructions or requirements for choosing a specific folder. The with prompt parameter is placed after the command and is followed by the text message to be included in the dialog, as shown in Script 9.41.

```
set the source_folder to choose folder with prompt ¬
    "Pick the folder containing the images to process:"
```
SCRIPT 9.41

As you see in Figure 9.26, the prompt message is displayed just below the title bar.

The message is optional in the choose folder command, while it is mandatory in the display dialog command. This allows you to omit an instructional message if the purpose of the choose folder dialog is obvious in context, as is often the case.

FIGURE 9.26 The choose folder dialog showing a prompt.

choose folder: The default location Parameter

Good scripters write their scripts anticipating the user's needs and possible actions, since well-designed scripts require less time to execute and support.

The optional `default location` parameter to the `choose folder` command is used to specify the directory that is to be selected when the dialog is presented. This often saves time and confusion by making it easier for the user to navigate to a desired location.

This parameter is placed after the `choose folder` command and is followed by an alias reference to the folder you want to be selected when the dialog opens. To compile Script 9.42, you must change the path of the alias reference to include the name of your hard drive and home folder.

```
set the source_folder to ¬
    choose folder with prompt ¬
        ("Choose the folder containing the songs to process:") ¬
            default location alias "MyDisk:Users:cheeseb:Music:"
```
SCRIPT 9.42

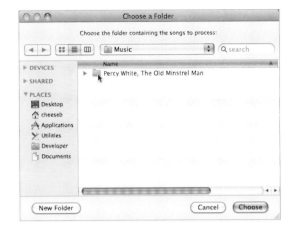

FIGURE 9.27 The choose folder dialog opened to the folder specified by the default location parameter.

To make your script generic and able to run on most computers, use the path to command described in Chapter 5, *Special Folders*, to generate the alias reference for the default location parameter. For example, the previous example targeting the user's Pictures folder as the default location would best be written as shown in Script 9.43.

```
set the source_folder to ¬
    choose folder with prompt ¬
        ("Choose the folder containing the songs to process:") ¬
            default location (path to the music folder)
```
SCRIPT 9.43

choose folder: The invisibles Parameter

The optional invisibles parameter to the choose folder command is used to control whether directories and files not usually visible to the script's user are displayed in the choose folder dialog.

The parameter has a Boolean value of either true or false. False is the default value, since invisible folders are invisible for a reason: users aren't supposed to mess with their contents. It is placed after the `choose folder` command. In AppleScript, parameters with values of true are written as `with theParameterName`, and parameters with values of false are written as `without theParameterName`. If you type a script using the true or false form, Script Editor automatically changes it to the canonical `with` or `without` form when you compile the script. Scripts 9.44 and 9.45 show the compiled form.

```
set the source_folder to ¬
    choose folder with prompt ¬
        ("Pick the folder containing the files to process:") ¬
            without invisibles
```

SCRIPT 9.44

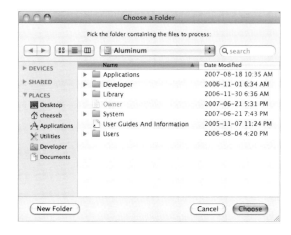

FIGURE 9.28 The choose folder dialog using the `without invisibles` parameter.

```
set the source_folder to ¬
    choose folder with prompt ¬
        ("Pick the folder containing the files to process:") ¬
            with invisibles
```

SCRIPT 9.45

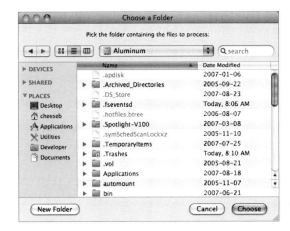

FIGURE 9.29 The choose folder dialog using the with invisibles parameter.

choose folder: The multiple selections allowed Parameter

The optional `multiple selections allowed` parameter to the `choose folder` command is used to allow the script's user to select more than one folder at a time from the `choose folder` dialog.

The parameter has a Boolean value of either true or false (false is the default value). It is placed after the `choose folder` command, as shown in Script 9.46.

```
set the source_folder to choose folder with prompt ¬
    "Pick the source folders:" with multiple selections allowed
--> -returns: {alias "Macintosh HD:Users:sal:Documents:", alias "Macintosh
HD:Users:sal:Pictures:", alias "Macintosh HD:Users:sal:Music:", alias
"Macintosh HD:Users:sal:Movies:"}
```
SCRIPT 9.46

The result of the `choose folder` command `with multiple selections allowed` is a list of alias references to the chosen folders, even if the user selects only a single folder.

FIGURE 9.30 The choose folder dialog showing multiple selections.

choose folder: The showing package contents Parameter

The new showing package contents parameter introduced in Mac OS X 10.4 (Tiger) is part of a group of AppleScript features, new in Tiger, supporting Mac OS X bundles and application packages.

Although the Finder displays a bundle or an application package as if it were a single file, it is actually a folder. This standard feature of Mac OS X allows applications and documents to contain additional files that are inaccessible by the user in everyday use. It was common in the past to place these resources loose in a folder, where careless users could inadvertently lose them while moving files and folders around. Bundles overcome this danger, making it much easier and safer to install applications and other resources. You simply drag what looks like a single file to the desired location, and everything inside the bundle comes along for the ride.

The showing package contents parameter to the choose folder command gives AppleScript scripts access to the resources inside bundles and application packages. As a result, scripts can now let the user navigate inside a bundle or application package to choose a folder of interest.

Script 9.47 lets you choose any folder inside any application package, and then it reports how many icon files it found in the chosen folder. You'll find it most rewarding if you navigate to the Resources subfolder of the Contents folder in just about any application package, because that's where application icon files are usually stored. We'll put this concept to better use in the discussion of the `choose file` command next.

```
choose folder with prompt ¬
    ("Choose a Resources folder in any application package:") ¬
        default location (path to applications folder) ¬
    with showing package contents
tell application "Finder"
    count (every file of result whose name extension is "icns")
end tell
display dialog "Icon files in chosen folder: " & result ¬
    buttons {"OK"} default button "OK"
```

SCRIPT 9.47

FIGURE 9.31 Choosing the Resources folder in the Address Book application package.

choose folder: Filter Routines

The following scripts use the `choose folder` command and AppleScript language elements, such as conditionals, repeat loops, and error handlers to extract specific information from the user. You may find them useful in your scripts. The techniques used here are described in more detail in Chapter 10, *Conditionals*; Chapter 11, *The Repeat Loop*; and Chapter 12, *Error Handlers*.

Choosing a Folder on the Start-up Disk

Script 9.48 prompts the user to choose a folder located on the startup disk. It beeps and displays the dialog again if you choose a folder on the wrong disk. The script may not function properly if there is another disk on the Desktop named the same as the chosen disk.

```
repeat
    set the chosen_folder to ¬
        choose folder with prompt ¬
            ("Choose a folder on the startup disk:") ¬
                default location (path to the startup disk)
    tell application "Finder"
        if the disk of the chosen_folder is ¬
            the startup disk then exit repeat
    end tell
    beep
end repeat
```
SCRIPT 9.48

Choosing a Volume (Disk)

Although AppleScript does not currently have a `choose volume` command, the `choose folder` command can be adapted to perform the same function.

Script 9.49 encloses the `choose folder` command in a repeat loop and uses the Finder to check the properties of the chosen directory. If it is a volume, the script continues; otherwise, it repeats the `choose folder` command.

```
repeat
    set the chosen_disk to ¬
        (choose folder with prompt "Choose a volume:")
    tell application "Finder"
        if kind of the chosen_disk is "volume" then
            exit repeat
        end if
    end tell
    beep
end repeat
```
SCRIPT 9.49

Choosing a Network Volume

Script 9.50 adds an extra Finder check to the previous example to determine whether the chosen volume is a local disk or a mounted network volume such as an iDisk.

```
repeat
    set the chosen_disk to ¬
        (choose folder with prompt "Choose a network volume:")
    tell application "Finder"
        if kind of the chosen_disk is "volume" and ¬
            local volume of the chosen_disk is false then
            exit repeat
        end if
    end tell
    beep
end repeat
```
SCRIPT 9.50

The choose file Command

The choose file command enables a script to ask a user to select a file from a disk or volume connected to the host computer.

Like the choose folder command, the choose file command is part of the Standard Additions scripting addition. It can be used within or outside of tell blocks.

Here is the Standard Additions dictionary listing for the choose file command. The command has six optional parameters.

```
choose file v : Choose a file on a disk or server
    choose file
        [with prompt text] : the prompt to be displayed in the
            dialog box
        [of type list of text] : a list of file types or type
            identifiers. Only files of the specified types will be
            selectable.
        [default location alias] : the default file location
        [invisibles boolean] : Show invisible files and folders?
            (default is true)
        [multiple selections allowed boolean] : Allow multiple
            items to be selected? (default is false)
        [showing package contents boolean] : Show the contents of
            packages? (Packages will be treated as folders. Default is
            false.)
        --> alias : the chosen file
```

Script 9.51 is a simple example of the choose file command in use:

```
set the target_file to choose file
```
SCRIPT 9.51

This script presents the standard operating system dialog for selecting files, shown in Figure 9.32.

FIGURE 9.32 The dialog displayed by the choose file command.

Once the user navigates to a directory, selects a file, and clicks the Choose button, the script returns an alias reference to the chosen item, as shown here:

```
alias "Mac OS X:Users:sal:Pictures:cat.tiff"
```

As with previous examples, the choose file command is often used with the set verb to assign the result of the command, which is an alias reference to a chosen file, to a variable that can then be used elsewhere in the script.

choose file: The with prompt Parameter

The optional with prompt parameter to the choose file command provides text to display instructions or requirements for choosing a specific file. The with prompt parameter is placed after the choose file command and is followed by the text message to be displayed in the dialog, as shown in Script 9.52.

```
set the template_file to choose file with prompt ¬
    "Pick the template file to use:"
```

SCRIPT 9.52

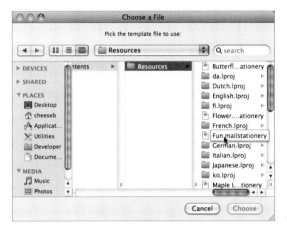

FIGURE 9.33 The choose file dialog showing a prompt.

choose file: The default location Parameter

The optional default location parameter to the choose file command is used to specify the folder that is selected when the dialog is presented. This often saves time and confusion by making it easier for the user to navigate to a desired file.

This parameter is placed after the choose file command and is followed by an alias reference to the folder you want to be highlighted in the dialog or an alias reference to any file in the folder. The script errors if the default item is not an existing directory or item.

As Script 9.53 demonstrates, providing an alias reference to a file does not leave the file selected in the dialog, but only the folder containing it. Nevertheless, unlike the choose folder command, the Choose button is not enabled until the user selects a file. After selecting a file and clicking Choose, the command returns an alias reference to the chosen file. To compile this script, change the name of the drive and home folder to names that exist on your computer.

```
set the target_file to ¬
    choose file default location ¬
        (alias "G5:Users:cheeseb:Sites:index.html") ¬
            without invisibles
--> returns: alias "G5:Users:cheeseb:Sites:index.html"
```
SCRIPT 9.53

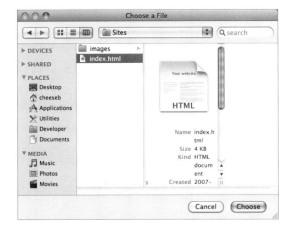

FIGURE 9.34 The choose file dialog opened to the folder containing the file specified by the default location parameter.

To make your script generic and able to run on most computers, use the path to command described in Chapter 5, *Special Folders*, to generate the alias reference for the default location parameter. The previous example targeting the "index.html" file in the user's Sites folder as the default location could be written as shown in Script 9.54, since the specified file is not actually selected:

```
set the target_file to ¬
    choose file default location (path to the sites folder) ¬
        without invisibles
--> returns: alias "G5:Users:cheeseb:Sites:index.html"
```
SCRIPT 9.54

choose file: The invisibles Parameter

The optional `invisibles` parameter to the `choose file` command is used to control whether directories and files not usually visible to the script's user are displayed in the `choose file` dialog.

The parameter has a Boolean value of either true or false. Unlike the `choose folder` command, true is the default value. The parameter is placed after the `choose file` command. Because the default value is true, Script 9.55 shows invisible items just as in the earlier Figure 9.32.

```
set the target_file to choose file with invisibles
```
SCRIPT 9.55

Script 9.56 hides invisible files, just as in the earlier Figure 9.34.

```
set the source_folder to choose file without invisibles
```
SCRIPT 9.56

choose file: The multiple selections allowed Parameter

The optional `multiple selections allowed` parameter to the `choose file` command is used to allow the script's user to select more than one file from the `choose file` dialog.

The parameter has a Boolean value of either true or false (false is the default value). It is placed after the `choose file` command, as shown in Script 9.57.

```
set these_files to ¬
    choose file with prompt ("Pick the images to process:") ¬
        default location (path to pictures folder) ¬
        with multiple selections allowed without invisibles
--> returns: {alias "MyDisk:Library:Application Support:Apple:iChat
Icons:Flowers:Sunflower.gif", alias "MyDisk:Library:Application
Support:Apple:iChat Icons:Flowers:Dandylion.gif"}
```
SCRIPT 9.57

The result of the `choose file` command `with multiple selections allowed` is a list of alias references to the chosen files, even if the user selects only a single file.

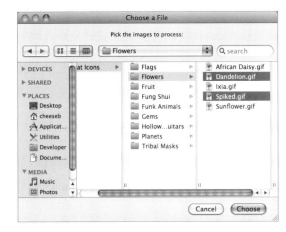

FIGURE 9.35 The `choose file` dialog showing multiple selections.

choose file: The of type Parameter

An essential tenet of the philosophy of defensive scripting is keeping your scripts easy to use. Doing so reduces the possibility of user errors and enables workflows to run smoothly. Reducing clutter in dialogs can do much to achieve this goal by limiting the user's options to those relevant to the task at hand.

The `invisibles` parameter, mentioned earlier, reduces dialog clutter by hiding invisible files and folders. The `of type` parameter further reduces confusion by limiting the files that can be selected to files of a specified file type, such as TIFF images. All other files, while visible, are grayed out in the dialog and not selectable.

When writing scripts, the `of type` parameter is placed after the `choose file` command. Until recently, it was always followed by either a single file type code or a list of file type codes. File type codes are text strings of four characters each, representing a specific file format. For example, `TIFF` is the file type code for TIFF images, `JPEG` is for JPEG images, `PDF` is for PDF files, and so on. In Leopard, it is recommended that you always use Uniform Type Identifiers

(UTIs) instead, as described in the next section, because many files no longer contain the old-style Macintosh type metadata.

> TIP ▶ Don't forget to supply spaces as needed to pad a shorter file type string out to the required four characters. If you supply a three-character string by accident, the of type parameter won't work, and all files of all types will be selectable in the dialog.

Script 9.58 is an example that does not use the of type parameter.

```
set these_files to choose file default location ¬
    (path to desktop pictures folder) without invisibles
```
SCRIPT 9.58

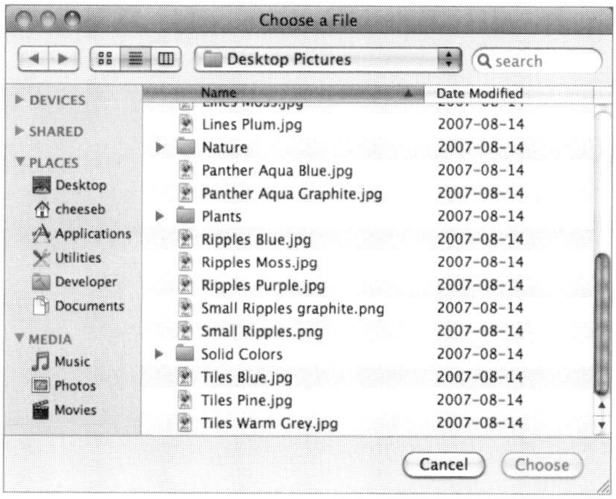

FIGURE 9.36 A dialog allowing selection of all types of files when the choose file command is used without the of type parameter. Both JPEG and PNG files are selectable.

The selected folder may contain images in JPEG, BMP, PNG, TIFF, PDF, and other formats. Since the of type parameter is not used in the script, all files, regardless of their type, are selectable.

The example shown in Script 9.59 uses the of type parameter to limit the script's user to PNG files, passing the "public.png" UTI:

```
set these_files to choose file of type {"public.png"} ¬
    default location (path to desktop pictures folder) ¬
        without invisibles
```
SCRIPT 9.59

TIP ▶ The of type parameter is supposed to be given a list, as shown here, but you can omit the curly braces when providing a single type. AppleScript automatically coerces it to a list containing that type as its only item.

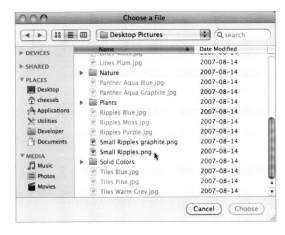

FIGURE 9.37 A dialog allowing selection of PNG files when the choose file command is used with the of type parameter set to "public.png".

Although all the image files are visible, only the PNG images can be selected. Other image files are dimmed and unselectable.

In earlier versions of Mac OS X, the of type parameter expected a list of old-style file types. In Mac OS X 10.4 (Tiger) and Leopard, this is discouraged and you should use UTIs. Script 9.60 is an example that allows the user to select JPEG and TIFF images:

```
set these_files to choose file of type {"public.jpeg", "public.png"} ¬
    default location (path to desktop pictures folder) ¬
        without invisibles
```
SCRIPT 9.60

Although images of other types would be visible, if there were any in this folder, only the JPEG and PNG images can be chosen from the dialog.

The four-character file type string originated in the classic Mac OS. In Mac OS X, file types in the old style became optional, and Mac OS X 10.1 and newer increasingly relied on other metadata, such as name extensions like "tif" or "pdf," to identify file types. However, the of type parameter to the choose file command has never responded to name extensions, and this has led to problems using this parameter in the modern world, where many files have no internal type information.

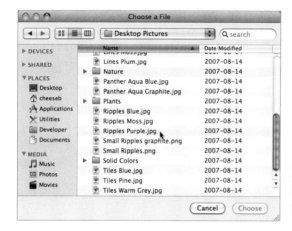

FIGURE 9.38 A dialog allowing selection of JPEG and PNG files when the choose file command is used with the of type parameter set to "public.jpg" and "public.png".

In Mac OS X 10.4 (Tiger), all files now have a UTI. These are strings such as "public.jpeg", "public.png", "public.tiff", and " "com.apple.pict". UTIs solve the problems created by the proliferation of file type metadata in older versions of the system. We'll discuss the use of UTIs in the of type parameter next and then follow up with some workarounds for use in older versions of Mac OS X.

Uniform Type Identifiers (UTIs)

For the modern world of UTIs, the of type parameter optionally takes a list of UTIs in Leopard and in Mac OS X 10.4 (Tiger). Because the algorithm used to determine a file's UTI automatically takes into account old-style file types and name extensions, if they are present in a file, as well as other information, scripts running under Leopard and Tiger should always use UTIs instead of file types. If you use file types, some files may not be selectable in the dialog because they don't have internal file type information.

UTIs are based on a hierarchical structure where, for example, a specific type identifier such as `"com.compuserve.gif"` may also have a higher-level or more general type identifier to which it *conforms*, like `"public.image"`. The `of type` parameter to the `choose file` command recognizes general UTIs like `"public.image"`, as well as more specific UTIs like `"com.compuserve.gif"`. It knows whether a specific UTI conforms to a more general UTI. Thus, for example, a script can pass `"public.image"` to the `of type` parameter of the `choose file` command, and files of any type conforming to the `"public.image"` UTI will be selectable in the dialog. Script 9.61 shows an example. Try it, and you'll see that all image files, no matter their specific type, are selectable, while text and other files are not.

```
set these_files to choose file of type {"public.image"} ¬
    default location (path to pictures folder) without invisibles
```
SCRIPT 9.61

FIGURE 9.39 A dialog allowing GIF files to be selected when the `choose file` command is used with the `of type` parameter set to `"public.image"`.

The list of recognized public and private UTIs is long, and it grows longer daily as developers invent new file types and give them new UTIs. Duplication of UTIs is prevented because new public types can be created only by Apple, and private types always include the developer's name, as in `"com.compuserve.gif"`. The system is very robust, and it brings great flexibility and reliability to file typing in Tiger and Leopard.

The topic of UTIs is too big to take on in this book in more detail. For an introduction, read the *Uniform Type Identifiers Overview* document on the Apple developer Web site at `http://developer.apple.com`. It includes several tables listing all the common UTIs and explains their hierarchical structure.

File Types and Name Extensions

You can't use UTIs in the `of type` parameter for scripts running under Mac OS X 10.3 (Panther) and older. You have to use four-character file types, but this runs the risk of overlooking files that don't have an internal file type indicator. A workaround, if you find the `of type` parameter to be inadequate, is to avoid the `of type` parameter altogether and allow all file types to be displayed in the `choose file` dialog. Your script should then check the `file type` and the `name extension` of the items in the user's selection to see whether they match the allowed types. (This technique will work on Leopard and Mac OS X 10.4 (Tiger), too, and you could even add a test for the `type identifier` property of the `info for` command. But it would be wasteful to do it this way under Leopard and Tiger, because the `of type` parameter to the `choose file` command recognizes UTIs, and they automatically take old-style file types and name extensions into account.)

Script 9.62 is an example of this strategy for checking the file type of a single selected item:

```
repeat
    set this_file to ¬
        choose file with prompt ("Pick a JPEG or TIFF image:") ¬
            default location (path to pictures folder) ¬
            without invisibles
    set this_info to the info for this_file
    if the file type of this_info is in {"JPEG", "TIFF"} or ¬
        the name extension of this_info is in ¬
        {"jpg", "jpeg", "tif", "tiff"} then
        exit repeat
    else
        beep
        display dialog "The selected file is not the correct type."
    end if
end repeat
```
SCRIPT 9.62

In this example, if the script's user selects a file that is not a JPEG or TIFF file, the script beeps, displays a dialog explaining the mistake, and displays the choose file dialog again. Only when a JPEG or TIFF file is selected will the script dismiss the choose file window and continue.

The file type and name extension of the chosen item are checked using the info for command to access information about the chosen file. The script then uses a conditional (if statement) to determine whether the file information record returned by the info for command has an acceptable file type or name extension property. You learned about the info for command in Chapter 6, *Information Tools*. To bring Script 9.62 up to Leopard standards, replace the info for command with appropriate calls to the System Events application, as described in Chapter 6.

Script 9.63 is an example that checks the file types and name extensions of multiple items.

```
repeat
    set these_items to ¬
        choose file with prompt ("Pick JPEG and/or TIFF images:") ¬
            default location (path to pictures folder) ¬
            with multiple selections allowed without invisibles
    set the item_count to the count of these_items
    set the exit_flag to false
    repeat with i from 1 to number of items in these_items
        set this_item to item i of these_items
        set this_info to the info for this_item
        if the file type of this_info is in {"JPEG", "TIFF"} or ¬
            the name extension of this_info is in ¬
            {"jpg", "jpeg", "tif", "tiff"} then
            if i is the item_count then set the exit_flag to true
        else
            set the item_name to the name of this_info
            beep
            display dialog "File "" & item_name & ¬
                "" is not the correct type."
        end if
    end repeat
    if the exit_flag is true then exit repeat
end repeat
```

SCRIPT 9.63

▶ **A Tip from Sal**

Mac OS X still supports, and will likely continue to support, files
that are typed in the traditional manner and have file type and creator codes. You can use a droplet, such as Script 9.64 shown here, to
read a file's name extension and apply corresponding file types to
files dropped on it. Save this example as an applet, and place it on
your Desktop or in the Dock.

```
on open these_items
    try
        repeat with i from 1 to number of items in these_items
            set this_item to item i of these_items
            set this_info to the info for this_item
            tell application "Finder"
                if the name extension of this_info ¬
                    is in {"jpg", "jpeg"} then
                    set file type of this_item to "JPEG"
                else if the name extension of this_info ¬
                    is in {"tif", "tiff"} then
                    set file type of this_item to "TIFF"
                else if the name extension of this_info ¬
                    is in {"pdf"} then
                    set file type of this_item to "PDF "
                end if
            end tell
        end repeat
    end try
end open
```

SCRIPT 9.64

choose file: The showing package contents Parameter

The showing package contents parameter to the choose file command was
introduced in Mac OS X 10.4 (Tiger), along with the corresponding showing
package contents parameter to the choose folder command discussed earlier.

Like the showing package contents parameter to the choose folder command,
this parameter gives AppleScript scripts access to the resources inside bundles
and application packages. Instead of letting the script's user choose a folder
inside a bundle or application package, it lets the user choose one or more files
of interest. This can be useful, as the next example shows.

Script 9.65 lets you choose one or more icon files inside any application package, and then it duplicates them on the Desktop where you can use them for
your own purposes. Most applications' icon files are in the Resources subfolder
of the Contents folder of the application package.

```applescript
choose file with prompt ¬
    ("Choose one or more icon files in any application package:") ¬
        default location (path to applications folder) ¬
    with multiple selections allowed and showing package contents without
invisibles
tell application "Finder"
    repeat with a_file in result
        if name extension of a_file is "icns" then
            duplicate a_file to desktop with replacing
        end if
    end repeat
end tell
```

SCRIPT 9.65

The choose file name Command

Scripts not only manipulate or process existing files; they can also create new files. The `choose file name` command is designed to give your scripts a standard user interface to specify the name and location where a new file will be saved. It displays a dialog in which the user enters the name of the new file and navigates to the folder in which it will be saved. The familiar New Folder button is available to create a folder to hold the new file. The dialog's default button is always named "Save."

The `choose file name` command returns a reference to a file, which may not yet exist. Because the file might not exist, the command cannot return an alias reference, as many of the other user interaction commands do. Instead, it returns a file reference.

The most important thing to remember about the `choose file name` command is that it does not actually create or save the file. Your script is expected to use the file reference to create and save the file using some other command. Examples are provided next.

This command is part of the Standard Additions scripting addition. It can be used within or outside of `tell` blocks.

Here is the Standard Additions dictionary listing for the `choose file name` command. The command has three optional parameters.

```
choose file name v : Get a new file reference from the user,
    without creating the file
    choose file name
        [with prompt text] : the prompt to be displayed in the
            dialog box
        [default name text] : the default name for the new file
        [default location alias] : the default file location
        --> file : the file the user specified
```

Script 9.66 and Figure 9.40 show the `choose file name` command in use.

```
Set the new_file to choose file name
```
SCRIPT 9.66

FIGURE 9.40 The dialog displayed by the choose file name command, collapsed.

Figure 9.40 shows the expanded version of the dialog:

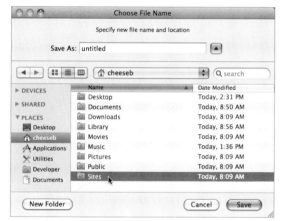

FIGURE 9.41 The dialog displayed by the choose file name command, expanded.

Once the user navigates to the destination folder, enters a name for the new file, and clicks the Save button, a file reference for the new file is returned to the script:

```
file "Macintosh HD:Users:sal:Desktop:IMAGE.001.JPG"
```

As with the `choose folder` and `choose file` commands, the `choose file name` command is most often used with the `set` verb to assign the result of the command, in this case a file reference to the new item, to a variable that can be used elsewhere in the script.

If the script's user enters a name and location for an existing file, the warning dialog shown in Figure 9.42 automatically appears asking the user to confirm the replacement of the existing file.

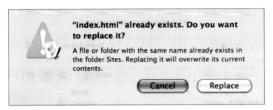

FIGURE 9.42 A warning dialog displayed when the user chooses a file name that is the same as an existing file in the selected location.

choose file name: The with prompt Parameter

The optional `with prompt` parameter to the `choose file name` command provides text to display instructions or requirements for choosing a name and selecting a location. The `with prompt` parameter is placed after the `choose file name` command and is followed by the message to be displayed at the top of the dialog, as shown in Script 9.67.

```
choose file name with prompt ¬
    "Choose a name and location for the new file:"
```
SCRIPT 9.67

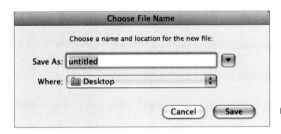

FIGURE 9.43 The `choose file name` dialog with a custom prompt.

If you do not provide a prompt, the dialog displays the default prompt "Specify new file name and location."

choose file name: The default location Parameter

The optional `default location` parameter to the `choose file name` command is used to specify the folder that is selected when the `choose file name` dialog is presented.

Like previous examples, the `default location` parameter accepts an alias reference to an existing destination folder. In Script 9.68, the `path to` command is used to generate an alias reference to the Pictures folder that is passed to the `default location` parameter.

```
choose file name default location (path to pictures folder)
```
SCRIPT 9.68

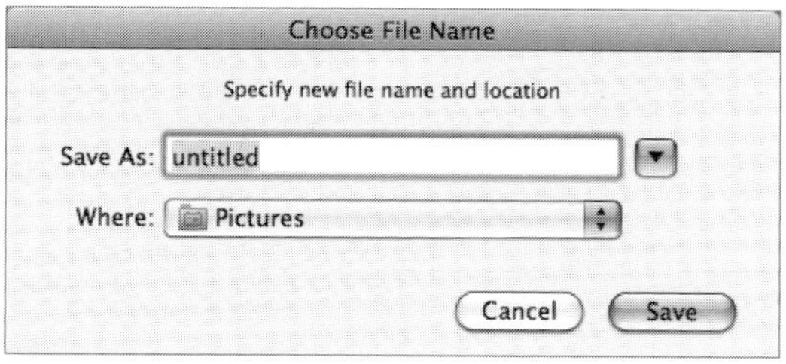

FIGURE 9.44 The choose file name dialog displayed with a default location.

choose file name: The default name Parameter

Often scripts process a large number of files. Helping the script's user keep track of item names is essential for making scripts easier to use. The `default name` parameter to the `choose file name` command provides the user with a suggested name for the new file.

Scripters use a variety of methods for deriving the default name. It can be an example for the format of a file name, or it can be derived from document names, sequential increments of a project name, or any combination of factors.

To use the `default name` parameter, place it after the `choose file name` command followed by the text string representing the suggested name, as shown in Script 9.69.

```
choose file name default name "IMAGE.001.JPG"
```
SCRIPT 9.69

The default name now appears in the Save As text input field in the dialog. The script's user can then choose to accept or alter the suggested name. The portion of the name before the name extension is selected automatically to make it easy to edit the name without affecting the name extension.

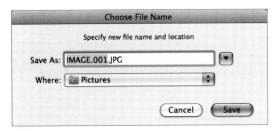

FIGURE 9.45

▶ A Tip from Sal

Another tenet of defensive scripting is to always check any information provided by the user, because even the most conscientious users make mistakes. Adding error-checking routines to your scripts is a good practice to develop.

Script 9.70 is an example that ensures the user adds a name extension to the entered file name. Since the `choose file name` dialog is enclosed within a repeat loop, it appears repeatedly until the entered file name ends with ".JPG", thereby triggering the `exit repeat` command.

```
repeat
    set the new_file to ¬
        (choose file name default name "IMAGE.001.JPG")
    if (the new_file as string) does not end with ".JPG" then
        display dialog ¬
            ("File names must have a ".JPG" name extension.")
    else
        exit repeat
    end if
end repeat
```
SCRIPT 9.70

Using the choose file name Command

Novice scripters are often surprised to discover that the `choose file name` command doesn't actually create and save a new file. In fact, its only function is to give the user a familiar interface for specifying a name and location for a new file. It is up to the script to create the file and save it, using the file reference that the `choose file name` command returns.

It usually isn't necessary to use this command with scriptable applications that support the AppleScript Standard Suite. Those applications already have a `make` command to create a new document and `close` and `save` commands that let a script present a standard Save dialog and save it.

The real purpose of the `choose file name` command is to provide a user interface to specify how to save a file that is created and saved by applications or commands that don't supply these capabilities themselves. One example is the `say` command in the Standard Additions scripting addition, which we'll explore later in this chapter. It has a `saving to` parameter that needs a *file reference* just like the file reference returned by the `choose file name` command, and it creates the file automatically if it doesn't already exist. The `choose file name` command is useful whenever you want to provide a standard user interface to get the file name and location from the user.

Another good use for the `choose file name` command is to provide a user interface for the File Read/Write commands in the Standard Additions scripting addition. The File Read/Write commands are advanced AppleScript features beyond the scope of this book, but we will show a couple of them in use here to illustrate the use of the `choose file name` command. All you need to know about the File Read/Write commands is that the `open for access` command automatically creates an empty file and that you should always close the file when you're done with it, using the `close access` command. The beauty of the `open for access` command, for our purposes, is that it creates a new file automatically when given a file reference like the file reference returned by the `choose file name` command. Script 9.71 shows this technique in use.

```
set file_ref to ¬
    choose file name with prompt ¬
        ("Create a new file for your secret code:") ¬
            default name "Code Book.txt"
open for access file_ref -- creates file
close access file_ref
tell application "TextEdit"
    activate
    open file_ref
    set text of document 1 to "Type your secret code: "
end tell
```
SCRIPT 9.71

Run the script to see how it works in practice. When prompted, click the disclosure triangle if necessary to expand the choose file name dialog, navigate to the Desktop in the dialog's browser view, enter a file name of your choice (with or without a name extension, although ".txt" would be good), and click Save. You'll instantly see a new file created on the Desktop, thanks to the open for access command, and its name is the name you specified in the choose file name dialog. The new document then opens in TextEdit and asks you to enter your secret code, because the script tells TextEdit to do all that with the new file. Notice that the name in the title bar of the document window is the name you specified in the dialog. Type something into the document, and click the window's close box. Click Save when prompted by TextEdit. After the document has closed, double-click it in the Finder. It opens in TextEdit showing you (and anybody looking over your shoulder) what your secret code is. Close the document again in preparation for the next test.

Run the script again, and specify exactly the same name, name extension, and location. When you click Save, the choose file name command presents an alert asking you whether you want to replace the original file. Click OK. Now enter a different code, and then close and save the document. Double-click it on the Desktop, and you'll see that the script really did replace the original file with the new file. (It does not replace the original file if you don't enter a new code.)

The choose from list Command

Scripts often require the user to select a particular item from a group of items or to choose an action from more than the three options provided by the buttons in a `display dialog` command.

The `choose from list` command presents a dialog displaying a list from which the user can select one or more items.

The `choose from list` command returns a list of chosen items. If a single item is chosen, a list containing a single item is returned. If multiple items are selected, the result is a multiple-item list.

The `choose from list` command is part of the Standard Additions scripting addition. It can be used within or outside of any `tell` blocks.

Here is the Standard Additions dictionary listing for the `choose from list` command. The command requires a direct parameter specifying the list of available choices, and it has seven optional parameters.

```
choose from list v : Choose one or more items from a list
    choose from list list of text or number : a list of items to
        display
        [with title text] : the dialog window title
        [with prompt text] : the prompt to be displayed in the
            dialog box
        [default items list of text or number] : a list of items to
            initially select (an empty list if no selection)
        [OK button name text] : the name of the OK button
        [cancel button name text] : the name of the Cancel button
        [multiple selections allowed boolean] : Allow multiple
            items to be selected?
        [empty selection allowed boolean] : Can the user make no
            selection and then choose OK?
    --> list of number or text : the list of selected items
```

To use the command in a script, place a list of numbers or strings after the command as in Script 9.72, where a list of names is provided:

```
choose from list {"Sal", "Sue", "Yoshi", "Wayne", "Carla"}
```
SCRIPT 9.72

When the command is executed, a dialog containing the items from the list is presented to the script's user. By default this dialog displays two buttons: OK and Cancel, as shown in Figure 9.46.

FIGURE 9.46 The dialog displayed by the choose from list command.

If the user selects a list item and clicks the OK button, a single-item list containing the selected item is returned to the script. Selected items, whether a single item or multiple items, are always returned in a list.

```
--> returns: {"Wayne"}
```

Unlike the other user interaction commands, clicking the Cancel button in the choose from list dialog does not stop the script with an error but instead returns a Boolean value of false. The choose from list command is the only user interaction command with this response to the Cancel button.

```
--> returns: false
```

▶ Handling the Cancel Button

The choose from list command is unique among the AppleScript user interaction commands in that it returns false instead of generating an error when the user clicks the Cancel button. This behavior requires scripts to adopt a different approach than handling the Cancel button in the choose from list dialog.

A common technique is to test the result first to determine whether it is false, using a conditional (`if` clause). If the result is not false, then the script can go on to determine which list item the user chose. Although the result of the `choose from list` command might be false, it can never be true. Either the result is false or it is a list containing the chosen items. It therefore makes no sense to test whether the result is true. Script 9.73 is an example showing this technique.

```
choose from list {1, 2, 3, 4}
if result is false then
    display dialog "You didn't choose an item"
else
    set choice to result
end if
```
SCRIPT 9.73

Another technique forces the `choose from list` command to act like other user interaction commands when the user clicks the Cancel button. To do this, use the same `if` clause shown in the previous example, but if the result is false, simply generate error -128 yourself. From then on, your script can use the same error-handling techniques that are used to handle the Cancel button in other user interaction commands. You already saw this technique once before, in the earlier "*display dialog: Timed Dialogs*" section. Script 9.74 is an example using the `choose from list` command:

```
set choice to choose from list {1, 2, 3, 4}
if choice is false then error number -128
display dialog "You chose " & item 1 of choice
```
SCRIPT 9.74

You'll learn more about the `try` block and error handlers in Chapter 12, *Error Handlers*.

To capture the returned value of the `choose from list` command, scripts often use the `set` command to assign the value to a variable, as shown in Script 9.75.

```
set the dialog_result to ¬
    choose from list {"Sal", "Sue", "Yoshi", "Wayne", "Carla"}
```
SCRIPT 9.75

After the command has completed, the variable can be used in a comparison (`if` clause) to determine the user's choice and respond accordingly. Since the variable `dialog_result` in the example contains a single-item list, another step is required to extract the user selection from this list. The next example, Script 9.76, does this by asking for the first item of the returned list.

```
set the dialog_result to ¬
    choose from list {"Sal", "Sue", "Yoshi", "Wayne", "Carla"}
if the dialog_result is false then
    error number -128
else
    set the chosen_friend to item 1 of the dialog_result
    display dialog the chosen_friend & " is my friend too!"
end if
```
SCRIPT 9.76

An easier way to extract the user selection is to coerce the resulting single-item list to a string. A list can always be coerced to a string, as in Script 9.77.

```
{"Sal", "Sue", "Yoshi", "Wayne", "Carla"} as string
```
SCRIPT 9.77

The result is a text string composed of all the list items pushed together like this:

```
SalSueYoshiWayneCarla
```

That's what happens when a list is coerced into a string. The resulting blob of text may not appear to be very useful for our purposes, but the list-to-string coercion works just fine if the list has only one item, as in Script 9.78.

```
{"Wayne"} as string
--> returns: "Wayne"
```
SCRIPT 9.78

So, we can change the statement in Script 9.78 from this:

```
    set the chosen_friend to item 1 of the dialog_result
```

to a statement like this:

```
    set the chosen_friend to the dialog_result as string
```

As a matter of fact, we can streamline our entire script by adding the coercion at the end of the `choose from list` statement in order to coerce the result before it is assigned to the variable. To do this, place parentheses around the `choose from list` command, as shown in Script 9.79. The parentheses force the script to execute the code in the parentheses first, before it performs the coercion. Finally, the script assigns the result of the coercion to the variable. As in algebra, statements in parentheses are executed first.

```
set the chosen_friend to ¬
    (choose from list {"Sal", "Sue", "Yoshi", "Wayne", "Carla"}) ¬
        as string
if the chosen_friend is "false" then error number -128
display dialog the chosen_friend & " is my friend too!"
```
SCRIPT 9.79

Since the coercion from list to string is done in the same statement as the `choose from list` command, we no longer need more than one variable to store and manipulate the result. The variable `chosen_friend` now stores either the list item chosen by the user or the string `"false"` if the user clicked the Cancel button. The Boolean value false is coerced to a string automatically.

choose from list: Giving the Dialog a Title

Like the `display dialog` command, the `choose from list` command usually does not have a title, but only a blank title bar that you can use to drag the dialog around the screen.

Beginning with Mac OS X 10.4 (Tiger), however, you can use the `with title` parameter to give the dialog a meaningful title. Script 9.80 shows how.

```
choose from list {1, 2, 3, 7} ¬
    with title ("Pick the lucky number")
if result is {7} then display dialog ¬
    "You win!" buttons {"OK"} default button "OK"
```
SCRIPT 9.80

FIGURE 9.47 A `choose from list` dialog with a title.

choose from list: The with prompt Parameter

The optional `with prompt` parameter to the `choose from list` command provides the text for the message displayed at the top of the dialog. To use it, place the parameter after the `choose from list` command, and follow it with a short text message, as shown in Script 9.81.

```
set the dialog_result to ¬
    (choose from list {"Sal", "Sue", "Yoshi", "Wayne", "Carla"} ¬
        with prompt "Choose your new teammate:") as string
```
SCRIPT 9.81

FIGURE 9.48 A choose from list dialog with a custom prompt.

The `choose from list` dialog is small and looks best with one or two lines of text, necessitating a little creativity in the phrasing of user prompts.

If you do not provide message text using the `with prompt` parameter, the `choose from list` command displays the default "Please make your selection:" message. This is often sufficient, especially if you make good use of the new `with title` parameter. To suppress the default message, pass an empty string in the parameter.

choose from list: The default items Parameter

Using the `default items` parameter, a script can present a list dialog with one or more items preselected. The value for this parameter is a list of the items contained in the full list.

Script 9.82 is an example of a single selection dialog.

```
set the members_list to {"Sal", "Sue", "Yoshi", "Wayne", "Carla"}
set the favorite_member to ¬
    (choose from list members_list ¬
        with prompt ("Pick your favorite club member:") ¬
        default items {"Wayne"}) as string
if the favorite_member is false then error number -128
return favorite_member
```
SCRIPT 9.82

FIGURE 9.49 A choose from list dialog with a single item preselected.

Script 9.83 shows a multiple selection dialog.

```
set the members_list to {"Sal", "Sue", "Yoshi", "Wayne", "Carla"}
set the chosen_members to ¬
    (choose from list members_list with prompt ¬
        "Pick your favorite club members:" default items ¬
        {"Sue", "Carla"} with multiple selections allowed)
if the chosen_members is false then error number -128
return chosen_members
```

SCRIPT 9.83

FIGURE 9.50 A choose from list dialog with multiple items preselected.

The two previous examples started with a **set** statement assigning the list of names to a variable and then using the variable as the value for the **choose from list** command. This technique makes for simplicity and readability when dealing with a long list of items.

choose from list: Renaming the Buttons

Unlike the `display dialog` command, the `choose from list` command always presents a dialog that contains two buttons. By default, these buttons are named "Cancel" and "OK." Use the `OK button name` and `cancel button name` parameters to give them different names. No matter what names you give them, the left button always behaves like a cancel button, and the right button always behaves like a default button. For example, you can press the Escape key instead of clicking the left button, and you can press the Return key instead of clicking the right button.

Setting either of these parameters to an empty string (`""`) does not suppress the button but instead presents a blank button. This looks ridiculous and certainly isn't user-friendly, so don't do it!

These two parameters do not work the same as the `default button` and `cancel button` parameters to the `display dialog` command. You cannot use them to switch the positions of the Cancel and OK buttons, but only to rename them.

Script 9.84 is an example:

```
choose from list {1, 2, 3} ¬
    OK button name "Choose" cancel button name "Quit"
```
SCRIPT 9.84

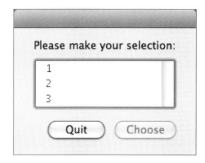

FIGURE 9.51 A `choose from list` dialog with custom button names.

choose from list: Choosing Multiple Items

By default, the choose from list command permits the selection of a single list item. The optional multiple selections allowed parameter enables users to select multiple list entries by clicking them while holding down the Command or Shift key. To include this parameter, place it at the end of the command preceded by the word with indicating a value of true, as shown in Script 9.85.

```
set the dialog_result to ¬
    (choose from list {"Sal", "Sue", "Yoshi", "Wayne", "Carla"} ¬
        with prompt ("Choose your new teammates:") ¬
        with multiple selections allowed)
if the dialog_result is false then error number -128
return dialog_result
```
SCRIPT 9.85

The result of the choose from list command with multiple selections allowed is a list containing the chosen items, even if the user selects only a single item. The previous example does not coerce the dialog's result to a string value as was done in a previous example. Because we want to obtain a list of multiple choices from the user, we must retain the result, if it is not a value of false, in list format in order to use it later in the script.

Many novice Macintosh users don't know they can hold down the Command key when selecting noncontiguous items in a dialog or on the Desktop. Script 9.86 is an example of a short dialog prompt to inform the user of this technique and the better-known use of the Shift key to extend a selection.

```
set the dialog_result to ¬
    (choose from list {"Sal", "Sue", "Yoshi", "Wayne", "Carla"} ¬
        with prompt "Choose your new teammates:" & return & ¬
        ("(Hold down the ⌘ or Shift key ") & ¬
        ("to select multiple items)") ¬
            with multiple selections allowed)
if the dialog_result is false then error number -128
return dialog_result
```
SCRIPT 9.86

Instead of calling it the "Command" key, you can display the Apple character that identifies the Command key on most Macintosh keyboards. The Apple character is Shift+Option+K.

Choose your new teammates:
(Hold down the or Shift key to select multiple items)

| Sal |
| Sue |
| Yoshi |
| Wayne |
| Carla |

Cancel   OK

FIGURE 9.52 A `choose from list` dialog with multiple items selected.

choose from list: Choosing No Items

In some circumstances, it is appropriate to let a user click the OK button in the `choose from list` dialog without selecting any items. To do this, include a `with empty selection allowed` parameter in the `choose from list` command.

In your script's logic, treat a return value that consists of an empty list as an invisible "none of the above" choice. Although clicking the Cancel button indicates that the user decided not to make a choice at all, clicking the OK button without selecting an item in the list allows the user to indicate that a choice is being made—it's just a choice that isn't included in the list.

Script 9.87 shows an example.

```
set Macs_owned to choose from list {0, 1, 2, 3} ¬
    with prompt ("How many Macs do you own?") ¬
    with empty selection allowed
if Macs_owned is false then error number -128
display dialog "More than 3!"
```
SCRIPT 9.87

choose from list: Related Lists

On occasion, the information presented to the script's user for selection may not be the data that will be used in the script, but instead words describing the data. In this situation, the items chosen by the user must be matched to the data in a related list that the script will actually use.

For example, consider a script where the user selects the name of a Web site from a list of Web sites and the script then opens the chosen Web site in a browser. When designing the script, would you present the user with a list of URLs? Or would it be better to display a list of Web site names to the user and then match the chosen site name with its corresponding URL invisibly to the user? It's more likely the latter, because URLs can be long, complex, and too technical for the average user to parse at a glance.

Here's how to match content from related lists using the `choose from list` command:

1. Create a list of the entries from which the script's user will select an item. In this example, it is a list of Web site names.

2. Create another list of entries that correspond to the items in the first list. In this example, the second list is a list of URLs corresponding to the Web site names in the first list. It is essential that the two lists be synchronized so that the first item in the first list relates to the first item in the second list, and so on.

3. Present the first list to the user using the `choose from list` command.

4. After the user has made a selection, determine the chosen item's index in the first list. To do this, run through all the items in the list in a repeat loop, in order, until an item in the list is equal to the chosen item. If you increment a counter each time through the repeat loop, you will end up with the offset of the matched item in the first list.

5. Use this index value to extract an item with the same index from the second list.

6. Exit the repeat loop, and perform the related actions.

Script 9.88 is an example of this technique.

```
set the website_names to ¬
    {"ABC News", "CNN", "TIME Magazine"}
set the website_URLs to ¬
    {"http://www.abcnews.go.com", ¬
        "http://www.cnn.com", ¬
        "http://www.time.com/time/"}
set the chosen_website to ¬
    (choose from list website_names with prompt ¬
        "Pick a web site to visit:") as string
if the chosen_website is "false" then error number -128
repeat with i from 1 to the count of the website_names
    -- determine the offset of the web site name in the names list
    if item i of the website_names is the chosen_website then
        -- use offset to extract the corresponding URL
        set the target_URL to item i of the website_URLs
        -- stop comparing items by exiting the repeat loop
        exit repeat
    end if
end repeat
open location the target_URL
```
SCRIPT 9.88

The choose color Command

The `choose color` command lets you choose a color value from the standard Mac OS X color picker dialog. The result returned by the command is an RGB value, a standard list containing three integers representing the intensities of the red, green, and blue components of the color. This RGB value can be used in any application command that takes an RGB list value as a parameter.

This command is part of the Standard Additions scripting addition. It can be used within or outside of `tell` blocks.

Here is the Standard Additions dictionary listing for the choose color command. The command has one optional parameter.

```
choose color v : Choose a color
    choose color
        [default color RGB color] : the default color
        --> RGB color : the chosen color
```

Script 9.89 shows how the command is used.

```
set this_color to choose color
```

SCRIPT 9.89

A completed choose color dialog returns an RGB value of the color chosen by the script's user. RGB values are a list of three integers, ranging from 0 to 65535, representing the individual values for red, green, and blue.

```
--> returns: {65535, 0, 0}
```

Here are some sample values:

```
red = {65535, 0, 0}
green = {0, 65535, 0}
blue = {0, 0, 65535}
yellow = {65535, 65535, 0}
cyan = {0, 65535, 65535}
purple = {32768, 0, 32768}
salmon = {65535, 26214, 26214}
```

FIGURE 9.53 The color picker dialog displayed by the choose color command.

choose color: The default color Parameter

The optional default color parameter determines the color that is preselected when the color picker opens. To use it, place it after the choose color command followed by the RGB value for the default, as shown in Script 9.90.

```
set this_color to choose color default color {31270, 38327, 65535}
```

SCRIPT 9.90

Script 9.91 is a useful subroutine that converts an RGB value to an HTML color tag:

```
set the HTML_tag to my RGB2HTML(choose color)
--> returns: "#FF8000"
on RGB2HTML(RGB_values)
    -- NOTE: this subroutine expects RGB values from 0 to 65535
    set the hex_list to ¬
        {"0", "1", "2", "3", "4", "5", "6", "7", "8", ¬
            "9", "A", "B", "C", "D", "E", "F"}
    set the hex_value to ""
    repeat with i from 1 to the count of the RGB_values
        set this_value to (item i of the RGB_values) div 256
        if this_value is 256 then set this_value to 255
        set x to ¬
            item ((this_value div 16) + 1) of the hex_list
        set y to ¬
            item (((this_value / 16 mod 1) * 16) + 1) of hex_list
        set the hex_value to (the hex_value & x & y) as string
    end repeat
    return ("#" & the hex_value) as string
end RGB2HTML
```

SCRIPT 9.91

Talking Scripts!

Every once in a while you discover things on the Mac that are unusual, powerful, and just plain fun. Speech technology is just such a wonder.

Often overlooked, speech is one of the best ways to communicate to the script's user in a pleasant, nonintrusive manner. Although available only on English systems, Mac OS X contains powerful built-in text-to-speech and speech recognition engines that can be controlled directly by AppleScript. Your scripts can speak to the user, and they can listen for and understand a user's response to a spoken query.

In Mac OS X, the settings for speech technology are located in System Preferences. Use Script 9.92 to open the Speech preference pane so you can change the settings while you try the following examples.

```
tell application "System Preferences"
    activate
    set the current pane to pane "com.apple.preference.speech"
end tell
```

SCRIPT 9.92

There are two AppleScript commands for accessing the Mac OS X Speech engines: say and listen for. We'll begin our foray into "aural-AppleScript" with a brief examination of the say command. For now, disable speech recognition by making sure the Speakable Items control at the top of the Speech Recognition pane of the Speech preference pane is set to Off, as shown in Figure 9.54.

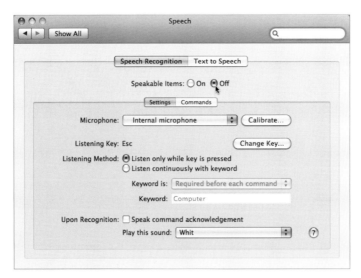

FIGURE 9.54 The Speech pane of the System Preferences window.

The say Command

The **say** command causes the computer to speak words or phrases to the
script's user.

This command is part of the Standard Additions scripting addition. It can be
used within or outside of `tell` blocks.

Here is the Standard Additions dictionary listing for the **say** command. The
command has a mandatory direct parameter, the text to be spoken aloud, and
four optional parameters.

```
say v : Speak the given text
    say text : the text to speak, which can include intonation
        characters
    [displaying text] : the text to display in the feedback
        window (if different). Ignored unless Speech Recognition
        is on.
    [using text] : the voice to speak with.
    [waiting until completion boolean] : wait for speech to
        complete before returning (default is true). Ignored
        unless Speech Recognition is on.
    [saving to any] : the alias, file reference or path string
        of an AIFF file (existing or not) to contain the sound
        output.
```

To use the **say** command, simply follow the command with the text you want
to have the computer speak, as in Script 9.93.

```
say "Hi! I'm your computer. I've been waiting for someone to talk to!"
```
SCRIPT 9.93

The computer uses the voice currently set as the system default to speak the
text. On Leopard, the default voice is Alex, a wonderfully natural-sounding
new voice. Optionally, you can indicate another voice to speak the text by placing the `using` parameter at the end of the statement followed by the full name
of the voice to use, as shown in Script 9.94.

```
say "Attention! Your file transfer has been completed." using "Kathy"
```
SCRIPT 9.94

You can even simulate a dialog by switching between voices as in Script 9.95. Note that the delay command is used to place a slight pause after each person has spoken.

```
say "I just came back from a trip to France!" using "Victoria"
delay 0.5
say "I'm so jealous. What cities did you visit?" using "Bruce"
delay 0.5
say "I spent a week in Paris, and then a week in Cannes." using "Victoria"
delay 0.5
say "Wow! I'll bet the food was superb." using "Bruce"
delay 0.5
say "The movies were even better!" using "Victoria"
```
SCRIPT 9.95

Incorporating speech into your scripts is easy, and sometimes you may want the script's user to choose a voice to use in the script. Script 9.96 is a routine, containing a list of some of the better Mac OS X voices, for prompting the user to pick a voice.

```
set the voices_list to ¬
    {"Alex", "Bruce", "Fred", "Kathy", "Vicki", "Victoria"}
set this_voice to ¬
    (choose from list voices_list with prompt ¬
        "Pick the voice to use:") as string
if this_voice is "false" then error number -128
say "Testing, one, two, three" using this_voice
```
SCRIPT 9.96

Scriptable speech is an excellent means for providing the script's user with the ongoing status of a script's actions. Script 9.97 parses a chosen folder of JPEG images and repeats an action (not provided) with each of the matching files. The user is informed of the progress of the script by a **say** command placed inside the repeat loop.

```
tell application "Finder"
    activate
    set this_folder to ¬
        choose folder with prompt "Pick a folder to process:"
    set these_items to every file of this_folder whose ¬
        kind is "JPEG image"
    if these_items is {} then
        say "The chosen folder contains no images."
    else
        set the image_count to the count of these_items
        say "Beginning processing " & image_count & ¬
            " images."
        delay 1
        repeat with i from 1 to the image_count
            say "Processing image " & (i as string)
            -- ADD YOUR PROCESSING STATEMENTS HERE
        end repeat
    end if
end tell
```
SCRIPT 9.97

Converting Text to a Sound File

Not only can you use the **say** command to speak text; you can use the optional **saving to** parameter to convert the spoken text to an AIFF sound file that can be used as a system alert sound or voice track for a movie!

To use the **saving to** parameter, place it after the **say** command, and follow it with a path string, a file reference, or an alias reference to the file that will contain the rendered sound data. If the file doesn't yet exist, it will be created automatically. Script 9.98 uses the `choose file name` command to prompt the script's user to name and locate a new file.

```
set this_string to "AppleScript and speech work well together!"
set the target_file to ¬
    choose file name with prompt ¬
        ("Name and location for the sound file:") ¬
            default name "example.aiff"
say this_string using "Bruce" saving to the target_file
tell application "QuickTime Player"
    activate
    open the target_file
    play the front movie
end tell
```
SCRIPT 9.98

The say Command: The displaying Parameter

The **say** command has an optional parameter, available when speech recognition is active, that displays a short text message to the user. Before trying these example scripts, enable speech recognition in the Speech Recognition pane of the Speech preference pane by setting the Speakable Items control to On.

A small floating round feedback window appears on the screen.

FIGURE 9.55 The Speech Recognition feedback window.

To display a text message along with spoken text, add the `displaying` parameter to the end of the script statement followed by the message to display, as in Script 9.99. The displayed text is independent from the spoken text and is often a condensed version of the spoken message.

```
say ("Attention, you've just received a call from Bob.") ¬
    displaying "Bob wants to talk to you."
```
SCRIPT 9.99

FIGURE 9.56 The Speech Recognition feedback window displaying textual feedback.

To display text without speaking a message, pass a string composed of a single space to the **say** command followed by the displaying parameter and the message to display, as in Script 9.100.

```
say " " displaying "You have new mail!"
```
SCRIPT 9.100

Scripts That Listen?

Scriptable voice recognition is an entire universe waiting for you to explore. The topic could easily fill its own book, but for brevity's sake we'll just give you the basic tools necessary for you to start your exploration of this fun and powerful technology.

Here's how it works. When you activate speech recognition, also called Speakable Items, a special application known as the *speech recognition server* is launched and runs invisibly as a background process on your computer. It is the job of this application to interpret spoken commands and perform any corresponding tasks. These tasks are accomplished using special scripts stored on your computer.

The speech recognition server is actually an application named SpeechRecognitionServer that is buried deep in the operating system; it's buried so deep we won't even try to reproduce its path here. It has a small AppleScript dictionary that provides scripts with the means to present the user with a question and listen for a reply that matches a set of possible answers. The `listen for` command is the only command you'll need to converse with any Mac OS X computer. It has a mandatory direct parameter and four optional parameters to enhance the performance of the command.

```
listen for v : Listen for a spoken phrase
    listen for list of text : list of possible phrases to listen for
        [with prompt text] : text computer will speak as a prompt
        [giving up after integer] : how many seconds to wait before
            giving up
        [filtering boolean] : whether to skip phrases with special
            characters
        [displaying list of text] : an optional list of commands to
            be displayed
        --> text : the recognized phrase
```

To use the command, simply follow it with a list of words or phrases that are possible answers to the question spoken to the user. When the computer detects a match with any of the list items, it returns the matched text string to the script. As with the other user interaction commands covered in this chapter, it's best to use the **set** verb to store this returned value into a variable for later use.

Before using scriptable speech recognition, make sure you have a microphone attached to the computer and selected in the Input tab of the Sound preference pane in System Preferences. When you activate Speakable Items for the first time, it automatically opens the Speech Help System to inform you of the various available control options. It's also a good idea to click the Calibrate button in the Speech Recognition tab of the Speech pane in System Preferences and perform the exercise you find there.

TIP ▶ It may be necessary to use the Speech preference pane to change the default listening key from Escape to some other key or key combination (such as F5). Holding down the Escape key can interfere with AppleScript control of the speech recognition server.

▶ **Sal Remembers**

One of the most profound moments of innovation I've witnessed at Apple was the day that members of the AppleScript and Speech teams announced they had given AppleScript the ability to listen to and understand spoken commands. From that moment on, I've never looked at or used the computer in the same way.

For a while, those is the office close to me thought I had a special assistant named "Victoria" doing my work for me, since they heard our "conversations" all day, every day, and it seemed I could get tasks done so easily. Speech recognition can truly be that extra pair of hands you sometimes need. For months, all my presentations were done with me across the room from my computer until my "remote control" was getting more attention than what I was showing!

Script 9.101 is a simple example for you to try. Be sure to hold down the listening key (Escape by default) for a second before speaking.

```
tell application id "com.apple.speech.recognitionserver"
    set user_response to listen for {"Sal", "Sue", "Bob", "Wanda"} ¬
        with prompt "Who's your friend?"
end tell
say the user_response & " is my friend too!"
```
SCRIPT 9.101

When you run the script, the computer speaks the specified prompt message and then waits 60 seconds for a user response that matches one of the items in the list of names. The recognized response appears above the feedback window, and the script's response via the **say** command appears at the bottom.

FIGURE 9.57 The Speech Recognition feedback window displaying a recognized response and textual feedback.

It can be hard to restrict yourself to asking only one question when you write a script using voice recognition. Naturally, you want your script to be conversational, mimicking the normal give and take of human interaction. Instead of writing voice recognition routines over and over in your script, use the subroutine in the script shown next to query the script's user and get the responses, and call the subroutine for every query.

The `voice_query` subroutine has parameters to set the message spoken to the script's user, the list of acceptable replies, and the number of seconds to wait for a reply. It also has the ability to stop when the user says "Cancel." Place the subroutine at the bottom of your script, outside of any `tell` block, as shown next.

To call the subroutine, use the name of the subroutine followed by opening and closing parentheses. In the parentheses, place the values for the three parameters. The values can be placed in the parentheses or passed to the subroutine in variables placed in the parentheses. Precede the command with the term `my` if the command is called inside a `tell` block addressed to an application to indicate to the script that the routine is part of the script body and not a term used by the application.

Script 9.102 shows how Script 1.101 would be written if it called the subroutine. Note that the essential values are passed to the subroutine in the parentheses.

```
set my_friends to {"Sal", "Sue", "Bob", "Wanda"}
set the user_response to ¬
    voice_query("Who's your friend?", my_friends, 30)
if the user_response is false then error number -128
say user_response & " is my friend too!"


on voice_query(user_prompt, these_items, timeout_value)
    set the cancel_commands to {"Cancel"}
    set the match_items to cancel_commands & these_items
    try
        tell application "SpeechRecognitionServer"
            set the user_response to listen for match_items ¬
                with prompt user_prompt ¬
                giving up after timeout_value ¬
                displaying these_items
        end tell
        if the user_response is in the cancel_commands then
            error "user cancelled"
        end if
        return user_response
    on error
        return false
    end try
end voice_query
```

SCRIPT 9.102

One last item. Note that the subroutine also implements the `displaying` parameter to the `listen for` command. You notice the effect of this parameter only when you click the disclosure triangle at the bottom of the speech feedback window to open the speech commands palette. Usually, the palette lists all the commands the speech recognition server is prepared to recognize at the moment, which can be helpful when a large number of possible words or phrases are available for the user's reply. Using the displaying parameter, you can limit the commands displayed in the palette to a subset of those the server can actually recognize. In the previous example, the word "Cancel" is omitted from the list of available commands in the palette, but the server and the script still respond when you speak "Cancel."

FIGURE 9.58 The Speech Commands window displaying available spoken responses.

The choose application Command

The choose application command gives the script's user an easy way to select an application. Like the other user interaction commands (except listen for), this command is part of the Standard Additions scripting addition. It can be used anywhere in your scripts, both inside and outside of any tell blocks.

Here is the Standard Additions dictionary listing for the command. It has four optional parameters.

```
choose application v : Choose an application on this machine or the
    network
    choose application
        [with title text] : the dialog window title
        [with prompt text] : the prompt to be displayed in the
            dialog box
        [multiple selections allowed boolean] : Allow multiple
            items to be selected? (default is false)
```

```
[as type class] : the desired type of result. May be
    application (the default) or alias.
--> application : the chosen application
```

When the `choose application` command is executed, Mac OS X generates a list of all applications on the start-up disk and connected disks, which is presented in a single-pane scrollable window. When the user selects an item from the list and clicks the Choose button, the selected application is launched, and the command returns a reference to it. Try running Script 9.103.

```
choose application
--> returns: application "Address Book"
```

SCRIPT 9.103

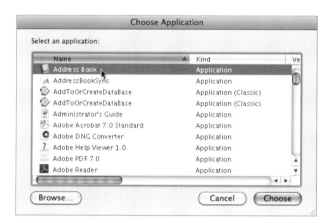

FIGURE 9.59 The dialog displayed by the `choose application` command.

The `choose application` dialog includes a Browse button that allows the user to navigate to a specific application. The search can include mounted network volumes, even though the list does not include applications on mounted network volumes.

Multiple versions of an application may be listed in the window if more than one partition or drive is connected to the computer. The `choose application` dialog can also be expanded horizontally to reveal column data regarding a listed application's version, kind, and file path in POSIX format.

choose application: The with title and with prompt Parameters

The optional `with title` and `with prompt` parameters can be used to provide a title for the `choose application` dialog and to provide a prompt to the script's user, as shown in Script 9.104.

```
choose application with title "Browser Picker" with prompt ¬
    "Choose the preferred browser for viewing HTML data:"
```
SCRIPT 9.104

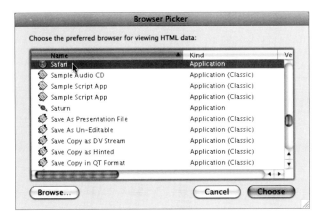

FIGURE 9.60 The `choose application` dialog with custom title and prompt.

choose application: The as Parameter

By default, the result of the `choose application` command is a reference to the chosen application. To get an alias reference to the chosen application file without launching it, place the `as` parameter after the command followed by the term `alias`.

As with other user interaction commands, you can capture the returned alias reference by using the `set` verb to assign the value to a variable, as shown in Script 9.105.

```
Set this_app to choose application as alias
--> returns: alias "Macintosh HD:Applications:Address Book.app:"
```
SCRIPT 9.105

To coerce the alias reference to a path, place the command within parentheses, and add the **as text** coercion to the end of the statement, as shown in Script 9.106. (If you coerce the returned application reference to text, as in (choose application) as text, you get the name of the application instead of its path string.)

```
set this_app to (choose application as alias) as text
--> returns: "Macintosh HD:Applications:Address Book.app:"
```
SCRIPT 9.106

To coerce the alias reference to a POSIX path, place the command within parentheses, and add the **POSIX path** property to the beginning of the statement, as in Script 9.107.

```
set this_app to the POSIX path of (choose application as alias)
--> returns: "/Applications/Address Book.app/"
```
SCRIPT 9.107

Add the **quoted form** parameter to enclose the POSIX path in single quotes, as in Script 9.108. This is useful when using the **do shell script** command.

```
set this_app to the quoted form of POSIX path of ¬
    (choose application as alias)
--> returns: "'/Applications/Address Book.app/'"
```
SCRIPT 9.108

Opening Files with Other Applications

In Mac OS X, most document files have an assigned default application that opens the file when it is double-clicked in the Finder. Script 9.109 shows how to use the **choose application** command to open selected files with an application that is not the file's default application.

```
set this_file to choose file of type ¬
    "TEXT" with prompt "Pick a file of type TEXT to open:"
set this_app to ¬
    choose application with prompt ¬
        "Pick the application to open the chosen file:" as alias
tell application "Finder"
    open this_file using this_app
end tell
```

SCRIPT 9.109

The choose remote application Command

Mac OS X 10.4 (Tiger) saw the introduction of a companion to the choose application command, the choose remote application command. It fills a gap in the choose application command, giving the user a list of applications on mounted network servers. The list is limited to applications that are currently running on the remote volume.

Like the other user interaction commands, this command is part of the Standard Additions scripting addition. It can be used anywhere in your scripts, both inside and outside of any tell blocks.

Here is the Standard Additions dictionary listing for the command. It has two optional parameters.

```
choose remote application v : Choose a running application on a
    remote machine or on this machine
    choose remote application
        [with title text] : the dialog window title
        [with prompt text] : the prompt to be displayed above the
            list of applications
        --> application : the chosen application
```

The with title and with prompt parameters work exactly as they do in the choose application command.

The return value of the command is a reference to a remote application. It looks something like this:

```
--> returns: application "Finder" of machine "eppc://10.0.1.52/?uid=501&p
id=266"
```

This reference can be used to tell the remote application to respond to AppleScript commands. When you do this, be sure to use the `using terms from` action clause described in Chapter 20, *Action Clauses*, to get the target application's terminology. Script 9.110 is an example. When you try it, enter the IP address or Bonjour name of a remote machine currently mounted on your network, and choose the Finder on that machine. The script returns the name of the start-up disk of the remote machine.

```
set remote_application to choose remote application
tell remote_application
    using terms from application "Finder"
        get name of startup disk
    end using terms from
end tell
```

SCRIPT 9.110

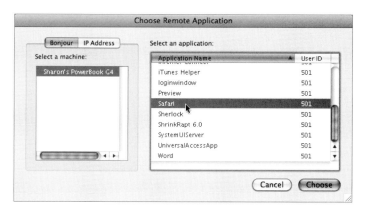

FIGURE 9.61 Using the `choose remote application` dialog to choose Safari on Sharon's PowerBook.

The Remote Apple Events setting in the Sharing preference pane of System Preferences must be enabled on the remote machine.

The choose URL Command

To round out the user interface commands, we'll describe the choose URL command. It is used to obtain an address of a service on the Internet or a local network. It returns an URL in a form appropriate to a designated service and leaves you to do something with it using other AppleScript techniques. The dialog that it presents in Leopard has been greatly simplified from the Mac OS X 10.4 (Tiger) dialog, including a change in the name of its default button from Connect to OK.

Like most of the other user interaction commands, this command is part of the Standard Additions scripting addition. It can be used anywhere in your scripts, both inside and outside of any tell blocks.

Here is the Standard Additions dictionary listing for the command. It has two optional parameters.

```
choose URL v : Choose a service on the Internet
    choose URL
        [showing list of Web servers/FTP Servers/Telnet hosts/File
            servers/News servers/Directory services/Media
            servers/Remote applications] : which network services to
            show
        [editable URL boolean] : Allow user to type in a URL?
        --> URL : the chosen URL
```

The value that it returns is not a URL object, but a simple string in URL format.

The choose URL command is similar to the choose file name command, in the sense that clicking the default button in the choose URL dialog doesn't actually connect you to anything. Instead, the command returns the URL as a string, and your script must then execute an appropriate command using the string to open or mount the service. In Leopard, the default button's name has changed from Connect to OK, presumably to give you greater freedom of choice as to the action you want to take.

The `choose URL` dialog in Tiger was a bit complex. It contained a variety of controls to help the user choose an existing service. These might come from remembered Internet services previously accessed and saved as favorites, or from currently mounted servers on the local network, depending on the value you pass in the `showing` parameter. In Leopard, the dialog is clean and simple: you see a list of services, and when you select one you see its address. Click OK, and that's the end of the story.

choose URL: The showing Parameter

The optional `showing` parameter takes a list of enumeration constants, such as `File Servers` or `Remote applications`. The complete list appears in the dictionary for the command.

If you omit the `showing` parameter, the dialog that was presented in Tiger contained a Show pop-up menu that let the user choose which service to show. The values you could pass in the `showing` parameter corresponded to the menu items in the Show pop-up menu. If you provided one of the available constants in the `showing` parameter, the dialog did not contain a Show pop-up menu, and it was limited to showing services of the kind indicated.

In Leopard, there is no Show menu. If you omit the `showing` parameter, the command defaults to `File servers, showing a list of available servers` and returning a URL string in afp:// format. If you provide a service constant to the showing parameter, it shows available services of that kind and returns a URL string in appropriate format, such as eppc:// for remote applications.

For example, if you pass `Remote applications` in the `showing` parameter, a list of currently mounted network servers appears in the dialog. Run Script 9.111 and select one of them, and its network address, such as eppc://10.0.1.54:3031, appears in the Address field. Click the OK button, and this address is returned as the result of the command. In Tiger, the user can click the dialog's Add to Favorites button to keep a record of the selected URL for future invocations of the command. The Add to Favorites button is not available in Leopard.

```
choose URL showing Remote applications
```
SCRIPT 9.111

Figure 9.62 shows the Tiger dialog, and Figure 9.63 shows the Leopard dialog.

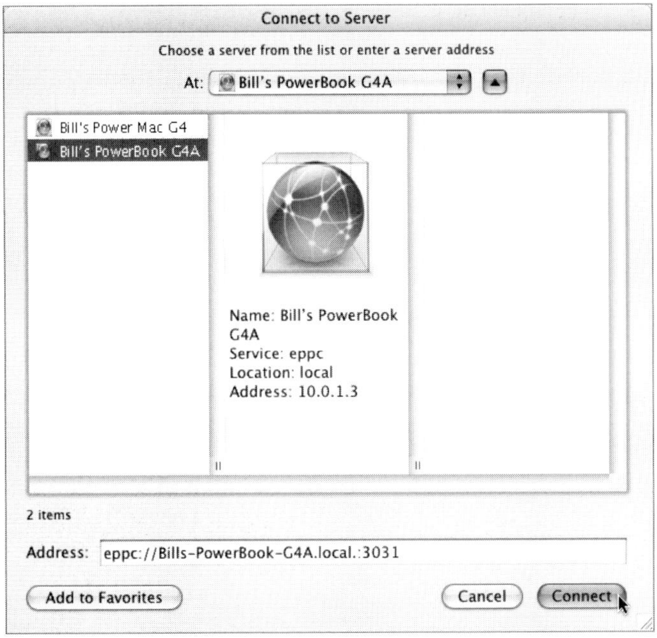

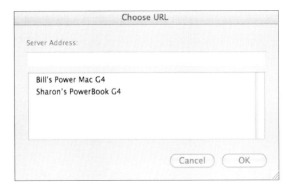

FIGURE 9.62 The dialog displayed by the choose URL command with a showing Remote applications parameter in Mac OS X 10.4 (Tiger).

FIGURE 9.63 The dialog displayed by the choose URL command with a *showing Remote applications* parameter in Leopard.

choose URL: The editable URL Parameter

Pass false in the optional `editable URL` parameter to prevent the user from typing a new URL. The dialog that is presented omits the URL text field. Pass true or omit the parameter to show the URL text field and let the user type in any URL.

Mounting a Service or Server

Once the `choose URL` command returns a URL, use an appropriate command to mount it.

The example shown in Script 9.112 mounts a local network file sharing server when the user chooses it, presenting an authentication dialog as appropriate. It uses the `open location` command in the Standard Additions scripting addition to mount the server.

```
set my_server to choose URL showing File servers
open location my_server
```
SCRIPT 9.112

The example shown in Script 9.113 mounts an FTP server on the Internet, using whatever application is currently set as the user's default FTP client.

```
set my_server to choose URL showing FTP Servers
open location my_server
```
SCRIPT 9.113

What's Next?

In this chapter, you've learned pretty much all there is to know about basic user interaction commands in the Standard Additions scripting addition, plus a little about listening for spoken commands. We spent a lot of time on these commands because they play a central role in most scripts. In the next chapter, you'll learn about conditionals—if clauses and their variants—with which you can begin to give your scripts the intelligence they need to make choices.

10

Conditionals

You've learned a lot about the nuts and bolts of AppleScript, including how to store and manipulate data. But you haven't yet learned much about how to make your scripts smart. You'll take the first step toward writing intelligent scripts in this chapter.

What is the most important criterion of intelligence? We think it's the ability to make decisions and to act on them. In AppleScript, the key to making decisions is the `if` statement and its variants. With an `if` statement, your script takes a quick look at the world around it, notices the current state of some condition it's interested in, and responds appropriately based on what it sees. The script's response can be simple or complex. It can make a simple decision to do something or not do it, it can decide to do one thing or another thing, or it can choose one course of action from a long list of alternatives. The responses from which the script chooses are set out in separate groups of statements, and the script executes the appropriate statements by *branching* to them based on the result of a *test*.

The Simple if Test

The simplest form of the simplest `if` test is a one-liner. It checks a condition and, if the condition exists, performs a specific operation. If the condition doesn't exist, the script bypasses that operation and moves on to the next part of the script, or it quits if there are no further statements to execute. To ask whether a condition exists is to ask whether a statement about it is true. Here's an example, in Script 10.1.

```
set winner to "7"
display dialog "Pick a number from 1 to 10:" default answer ""
if (text returned of result) is winner then beep
```
SCRIPT 10.1

When you first run this script, it has no idea what number you might choose. Once you make a choice, it has to look at the answer you provided and decide whether you picked the winner. It does this by looking at the `text returned` property of the `dialog reply` record returned by the `display dialog` command in the Standard Additions scripting addition and then comparing it for equality to the `winner` variable, which it sets to `"7"` at the outset. If the result is `true`—that is, if the user typed the character 7—it beeps. If the result is not true, but `false`—the user typed something else—it does not beep but instead moves on, which in this case means it quits because there are no statements following the `if` test.

A slightly more complex version of the simple `if` test is one that executes a group of statements, instead of a single statement, when the test returns `true`. It still tests a condition and moves on if it is not true, but if the condition is `true`, it executes several statements contained in an `if` block. Using this technique, the first example can be modified to do several things when you guess the right answer. Script 10.2 shows the modified version of Script 10.1.

The simple `if` test does not limit you to checking a single condition. You can test any number of conditions with any combination of operators, and all of the statements in the `if` block will be executed as long as the final result of evaluating all of the conditions is true. Script 10.3 shows an example.

```
set winner to "7"
display dialog "Pick a number from 1 to 10:" default answer ""
if (text returned of result) is winner then
    beep
    display dialog "You guessed it!"
    beep
end if
```

SCRIPT 10.2

```
set winner to "7767"
display dialog "Pick a number from 1000 to 9999:" default answer ""
set answer to text returned of result
if (first character of answer is "7") ¬
    and (character 2 of answer is equal to character 1 of answer) ¬
    and ((character 3 of answer comes before character 1 of answer) ¬
    and (character 3 of answer comes after "5")) ¬
    and (last character of answer is (3 + 4) as string) then
    beep
    display dialog "WOW! You're really lucky!"
end if
```

SCRIPT 10.3

In Script 10.3, the parentheses were used only to make the complex Boolean statement easier to read. Although the script would run correctly without them, using parentheses is a good idea when writing complex logical tests.

The Two-Value if Test

Often you don't want to bypass a block of statements when a test doesn't pan out. A more complex script might need to execute one block if the result of the test is true and another block only if the result is false.

If the script has nothing to do after the test statements are executed, you can achieve your objective by using a simple if test and placing a return statement at the end of the if block, like this:

```
set winner to "7"
display dialog "Pick a number from 1 to 10:" default answer ""
if (text returned of result) is winner then
    display dialog "You guessed it!"
    return
end if
display dialog "You lose."
```
SCRIPT 10.4

When you guess right, the `return` statement at the end of the `if` block causes the script to quit immediately, without displaying the final dialog. When you guess wrong, the body of the `if` block is not executed, and only the final dialog is displayed when execution jumps to the first statement after the `if` block.

But what if your script needs to do something more after the game is completed, win or lose? For that case, you need a two-value `if` test. It has two blocks, the usual `if` block and a second block, which is the `else` block. One or the other is always executed, depending on whether the result of the test is `true` or `false`, and the script then always goes on to execute any statements following the two blocks of the complex `if` statement. Script 10.5 shows how this is done.

```
set winner to "7"
display dialog "Pick a number from 1 to 10:" default answer ""
if (text returned of result) is winner then
    display dialog "You guessed it!"
else
    display dialog "You lose."
end if
beep
display dialog ("Run me again to play another game.") ¬
    buttons {"OK"} default button "OK"
```
SCRIPT 10.5

The Multi-Value if Test

Complex `if` tests can be chained together as many times as you like to handle more numerous potential outcomes. Script 10.6 shows an example.

```
display dialog "What's your favorite number?" default answer ""
set answer to text returned of result
if answer is "1" then
    set response to "One is singular and odd."
else if answer is "2" then
    set response to "Two is plural and even."
else if answer is "3" then
    set response to "Three's a crowd."
else if answer is "4" then
    set response to "I can barely count to four."
else
    set response to "I'm speechless."
end if
display dialog response buttons {"OK"} default button "OK"
```
SCRIPT 10.6

As you see, you test multiple conditions by using chained else if clauses. The final else clause is optional. If present, its block is executed whenever all of the other blocks return false. Think of it as a catchall or "otherwise" case. If you omit it, the script simply moves on to the rest of the script following all the clauses of the complex if test.

Script 10.6 illustrates a useful technique when you're using chained if else clauses. The script stores a unique string in the response variable in each clause and then calls the display dialog command only once, after the entire if block, using the value of the variable as the message to display.

What's Next?

In this chapter, you learned how to give your scripts some smarts, empowering them to test a variety of conditions, and perform different operations depending on the results. Where if tests really shine is in a *repeat loop*, which is what you'll study in the next chapter.

11

The Repeat Loop

Now that you've learned about conditionals, you're ready to get into really powerful scripting.

Most information you encounter in the workaday world comes in the form of collections of individual items of data, all of which have some sort of standardized organization or structure, such as the telephone book with its gigantic collection of names, addresses, and telephone numbers. These collections cry out for management in a repetitive process, where each item in succession is run through the same mill. It wouldn't be very useful if you had to run a script separately, over and over again, once for each item in the collection. Instead, AppleScript offers you the *repeat loop*, in which you can process successive items in a collection one at a time using the same group of statements repeatedly.

In AppleScript, a repeat loop is a block beginning with the reserved word
repeat and ending with the reserved word end. You place as many statements as
you like within this block. When you run the script, the statements within the
block are executed repeatedly. Script 11.1 is a simple example.

```
set counter to 0
repeat 10 times
    set counter to counter + 1
end repeat
return counter
--> returns: 10
```
SCRIPT 11.1

There are many variants of the repeat loop in AppleScript. You saw one of
them in this example: the repeat [number] times statement. In this chapter,
you'll learn about the most useful of the repeat statements. We'll just touch
upon the others.

repeat (Forever)

The simplest form of the repeat statement is, simply, repeat. When you run a
script with a simple repeat statement, the repeat loop repeats forever, without
stopping. This is, of course, useless by itself. If you run Script 11.2, it appears
to freeze up because it just keeps on churning away at the arithmetic until the
counter reaches the maximum legal value for an AppleScript integer. It never
gets to the return statement.

> **TIP ▸** If you actually run this script, you can break out of it at any time by
> pressing Command+. (that's Command+period) on your keyboard. This
> is a useful trick to remember when your scripts get stuck.

```
set counter to 0
repeat
    set counter to counter + 1
end repeat
return counter
```
SCRIPT 11.2

Termination Conditions

If it's so useless, why does the **repeat** statement exist in this simple form? You can find the answer in Chapter 10, *Conditionals*. By using an **if** test within the repeat loop, you can force the repeat loop to terminate when some condition, often called a *termination condition*, occurs. Depending on what you tell the script to do in the conditional, the script may then move on to the statements following the repeat loop, if there are any, or it may quit immediately.

The return Statement

Script 11.3 modifies the previous example slightly by adding just such a termination condition, causing the script to return the counter value and terminate immediately after the counter reaches 10.

```
set counter to 0
repeat
    set counter to counter + 1
    if counter is 10 then return counter
end repeat
--> returns: 10
```
SCRIPT 11.3

As this example demonstrates, a **return** statement can be used to terminate a script immediately, even if it is in the middle of executing statements inside a repeat loop. If the repeat loop had been inside a subroutine handler, it would have caused the subroutine to return the **counter** value, and the script would have resumed execution at the next statement after the subroutine call. You can even do this with a bare **return** statement, one that does not return a value at all.

The exit Statement

The **return** statement can be useful, but it is often better to break out of a repeat loop without terminating the script so that additional work can be done before the script quits. AppleScript has a special statement that is used only to break out of repeat loops and to go on with the rest of a script. It is the **exit** statement. Script 11.4 recasts the previous example slightly to use an **exit** statement.

```
set counter to 0
repeat
    set counter to counter + 1
    if counter is 10 then exit repeat
end repeat
return counter
--> returns: 10
```
SCRIPT 11.4

In this example, the `exit` statement could have been placed at the beginning of the repeat loop, as could the `return` statement in the previous example. It can be placed anywhere within a repeat loop, as long as the logic of your script does the right thing. Sometimes placing it at the beginning of a repeat loop prevents unnecessary additional processing after the termination condition has come into existence; on other occasions, it results in one extra iteration through the repeat loop that could have been avoided by placing it at the end of the repeat loop. Which technique is appropriate often depends on the antic-ipated state of the script at the time the repeat loop is first entered.

The point to remember is that the `exit` statement terminates execution of the repeat loop immediately, but it does not cause the script to quit or a subrou-tine handler to return a value. Instead, the flow of execution exits the repeat loop and resumes with the first statement following the end of the repeat block.

The continue Statement—Not!

There is one more point to understand about repeat loops in general, before we move on to their other forms. AppleScript does not have a `continue` state-ment for repeat loops, as many programming languages do. If it did, you could tell a repeat loop to skip the rest of the statements within the current iteration of the loop, without exiting the repeat loop as a whole, and move immediately to the next iteration. Suppose, for example, you wanted to report only an even-numbered result. You can't do it this way in AppleScript; Script 11.5 won't even compile.

```
set counter to 0
repeat
    set counter to counter + 1
    if counter mod 2 is not 0 then continue repeat --> BAD SYNTAX
    if counter is greater than 8 then return counter
end repeat
```
SCRIPT 11.5

Not to worry. You can always accomplish the same result by enclosing the part of the repeat block that you don't want to execute in an `if` block, as shown in Script 11.6.

```
set counter to 0
repeat
    set counter to counter + 1
    if counter mod 2 is 0 then
        if counter is greater than 8 then return counter
    end if
end repeat
--> returns: 10
```
SCRIPT 11.6

That script returns 10 instead of 9 because the statement testing whether the counter is greater than 8 is executed only when the counter's value is an even number.

> **NOTE** ▸ There actually is a `continue` command in AppleScript, but it has nothing to do with repeat loops and it's beyond the scope of this book.

There is no reason to avoid the `repeat (forever)` statement if it serves your purposes, but other forms are usually more useful.

repeat [number] times

Most of the previous examples used a counter variable to determine when the script should terminate, breaking out of the infinite loop with a `return` or `exit` statement. AppleScript provides several more direct and efficient ways to do this. The first one we'll examine is the `repeat [number] times` statement. You already saw one example at the beginning of this chapter. It used a counter variable, too, but not to control when the repeat loop terminated. Script 11.7 shows another example:

```
display dialog "Make three wishes."
repeat 3 times
    display dialog "I wish that..." default answer ""
end repeat
display dialog ("Just fooling!") ¬
    buttons {"Too Bad"} default button "Too Bad"
```
SCRIPT 11.7

The `repeat [number] times` statement is appropriate when you know in advance how many times you want the loop to repeat. You learned as a child that you get only three wishes, and the genie will find the `repeat [number] times` statement perfect for his job.

This form of the `repeat` statement is also useful when you're performing repetitive operations on items in a list. You will learn all about lists in Chapter 18, *Working with Lists and Records*, but the simple example shown in Script 11.8 should be clear to you now.

```
set my_list to {"one", "two", "three"}
repeat length of my_list times
    beep
    delay 1
end repeat
```
SCRIPT 11.8

As you see, you can use the `repeat [number] times` statement to repeat an operation once for each item in a list by using the `length` property of the list as the number of times to repeat.

What you can't do with this form of the `repeat` statement, however, is to know which iteration of the loop is currently running, unless you use a counter variable. For example, to beep a number of times equal to the current iteration count, you would have to keep track of the iteration count, as shown in Script 11.9.

```
set my_list to {"one", "two", "three"}
set counter to 1
repeat length of my_list times
    beep counter
    set counter to counter + 1
    delay 1
end repeat
```
SCRIPT 11.9

You've probably already guessed that this example is the lead-in to the next form of the **repeat** statement.

repeat with [loop variable] from [start value] to [stop value]

An even more useful form of the **repeat** statement is the **repeat with [loop variable] from [start value] to [stop value]** statement. It builds a counter variable into the repeat loop itself, where it is called a *loop variable*. You provide start and stop values in the form of integers or expressions that return integer values. The statement starts with the loop variable set to the start value, it increments the loop variable by 1 on each pass through the loop, and it stops after the loop variable has reached the stop value. The loop variable can be used within the loop to get its current value, and it remains valid after the loop has finished executing, holding its value from the last iteration of the loop (if it wasn't changed inside the loop). Script 11.10 shows the previous example rewritten to use this form of the **repeat** statement:.

```
set my_list to {"one", "two", "three"}
repeat with counter from 1 to length of my_list
    beep counter
    delay 1
end repeat
```
SCRIPT 11.10

That example works exactly like the previous example, but it is more compact and easier to understand at a glance.

We said that the loop variable increments by 1 on each pass through the loop, but this is true only by default. You can use an optional **by** parameter to increment by other values. You can specify **by** `1`, but that would be redundant because it is the default.

Harking back to an earlier script in the section about the missing `continue` statement, we reported a return value only if it was even. Script 11.11 is a new version using this form of the repeat loop with a **by** parameter to increment the loop counter by 2 on each pass. Because the loop variable increments by 2, we know it is always even, and we needn't use the `mod` command.

```
repeat with counter from 2 to 10 by 2
    if counter is greater than 8 then return counter
end repeat
--> returns: 10
```
SCRIPT 11.11

Notice also that the start value was not 1, but 2, because we are interested only in even values. The start value in this form of the repeat loop can be any integer value. It doesn't have to be 1.

The value of the **by** parameter can be negative instead of positive. In this case, the loop variable decrements on each pass, instead of incrementing. For this reason, you had better remember that the start value must be larger than the stop value when you use a negative value.

If the loop is processing items in a list or words in a string with a negative **by** parameter, you are processing them backward. Processing a list backward can be essential if, for example, you might delete items as you go. If you delete from the end first, the positions of items earlier in the list will remain unchanged, and you can refer to them correctly using an index. If you were to delete them from the beginning, the index of the next item would have changed by the time you got to it, and your script won't work as expected.

It is not an error to use a start value that is larger than the stop value with a positive **by** parameter or one that is smaller with a negative **by** parameter. The statements in the loop will simply execute once, and the script will move on. Sometimes this is what you want.

In the previous examples, the loop variable was used for the first time in the repeat statement itself, where AppleScript created it for you as a local variable. You can use a preexisting variable from earlier in the script, if you like, and its value is reset to the start value specified in the repeat statement. Its value will still be valid after the loop completes, holding its value from the final iteration, but you can assign a new value outside the loop and continue using it, if that is convenient.

The initial values of any variables or expressions used for the start value, the stop value, and the by parameter value in the repeat statement are always used to control the behavior of the loop, for all of its iterations. AppleScript evaluates them before it enters the loop and then socks away the resulting integers for repeated use to control the loop. For this reason, it is safe to specify initial values using expressions that depend upon conditions that might change during execution of the loop. Also, using a complex expression in the repeat statement will not bog the script down, because it will be evaluated only once, at the beginning.

You will learn why this behavior is important in later chapters, where you'll see that you can set up the initial parameters of the repeat loop based on the properties of a list, such as its length, even though the script will alter the list within the repeat loop.

Despite this, any variables used in the repeat statement can be changed within the loop, and if you use them within the loop, their new values will be honored. The silly little ditty shown in Script 11.12 beeps three times even though the value of the variable used to establish the initial stop value is changed to 1 every time it goes through the loop.

```
set x to 3
repeat with counter from 1 to x
    set x to 1
    beep
    delay 1
end repeat
```
SCRIPT 11.12

Even the value of the loop variable can be changed within the loop, because the next value will be reset automatically on the next iteration. Script 11.13 will play only three sets of beeps, but each set will consist of two beeps because the value of `counter` was set to `2` in each iteration. The value of counter will remain `2` after the loop completes.

```
repeat with counter from 1 to 3
    set counter to 2
    beep counter
    delay 1
end repeat
return counter
--> returns: 2
```

SCRIPT 11.13

repeat with [loop variable] in [list]

Another useful form of the repeat loop is `repeat with [loop variable] in [list]`. In this version, the loop variable doesn't necessarily evaluate to an integer but might refer to any type of value at all. Instead of counting iterations, the loop variable acquires a reference to the next item in the list on each iteration, and the loop iterates once for each item in the list. Within the loop, your script statements can use this reference for any purpose.

Recasting the first example from the previous section to use this form of the `repeat` statement, it works as shown in Script 11.14.

```
set my_list to {1, 2, 3}
repeat with my_item in my_list
    beep my_item
    delay 1
end repeat
```

SCRIPT 11.14

This form often yields the most readable scripts of all, and it can be quite convenient when writing the statements within the loop.

You can use a record instead of a list with this form of the repeat statement. AppleScript coerces the record to a list, removing the labels. You'll learn more about lists and records in Chapter 18, *Working with Lists and Records*.

There is one gotcha when using this form of the repeat statement, but it is easy to guard against if you keep it in mind. The loop variable always contains a *reference* to the next item in the list, not its *value*. For example, in the first iteration, the value of the loop variable is not `1` but `item 1 of (list)`. Therefore, in order to perform valid comparisons to the loop variable within the loop or to use its value in other ways, you may first have to evaluate the loop variable to get the value of the reference. You do this by getting the contents of the loop variable. It is often best to do this at the beginning of each iteration of the loop, as shown in the next example, but in any event you must do it somewhere within the loop in order to use the value represented by the loop variable reference.

You already know that it is not always necessary to use the contents of operator, because the previous example beeped the correct number of times even though my_item was only a reference to the first item in the list. AppleScript often evaluates references for you, without your knowledge, so that you don't have to worry about it.

When a script using this form of the repeat statement doesn't work as you expected, the first thing to look at is the possibility that you might need to get the contents of the loop variable. This problem usually crops up in the context of comparisons. The defect will be subtle and all too easy to overlook, because it usually does not generate an error. Instead, the comparison simply returns false. If you don't test for cases where it should return true, your script probably won't fail with an error, but it sure won't work right. Script 11.15 is an example of a comparison properly done.

```
set employees to {"Bob", "Ted", "Carol", "Alice"}
repeat with employee in employees
    set employee to contents of employee
    if employee is "Carol" then beep
end repeat
```
SCRIPT 11.15

The first thing you do in the repeat loop in this example, before you forget, is to reassign a value to the loop variable, `employee`, so that it contains the actual value instead of a reference to an item in the list. Since the actual value is a string, you can compare it with `"Carol"`, another string, in the body of the loop and get the correct answer. The script beeps once, because the comparison returns `true` on the third iteration. It is perfectly all right to reassign a value to the loop variable inside the loop because, as in the case of the `repeat with [loop variable] from [start value] to [stop value]` statement, the repeat loop assigns the next value before each iteration.

It is a good strategy to reassign the `contents of` the loop variable to the loop variable as you write any script using this form of the `repeat` statement, because even experienced scripters forget. You can always go back and remove that line when you're done, if it isn't needed.

Bear in mind, however, that in some cases you might actually prefer to have a reference to an item in the list, rather than its value. This would be true, for example, when you plan to change the value of the item in the list itself, instead of just using it for other purposes. Or you might even plan to delete the item from the list or add another item. You can do this with impunity inside the repeat loop, because AppleScript retains the initial list the first time it encounters the `repeat` statement. It always iterates once for every item in the original list.

You may sometimes want to know whether a repeat loop is currently in its first or last iteration, for example, to perform initialization or cleanup. With the previous form of the `repeat` statement, that is easy because the statement itself contains the start value and the stop value as integers. You can simply test the current value of the loop variable to see whether it is equal to the start or stop value. In the `repeat with [loop variable] in [list]` form, it is almost as easy, because you can refer to the first and last items in the list, as shown in Script 11.16.

```
set employees to {"Bob", "Ted", "Carol", "Alice"}
repeat with employee in employees
    set employee to contents of employee
    if employee is first item of employees then
        display dialog "First: " & employee
    else if employee is last item of employees then
        display dialog "Last: " & employee
    end if
end repeat
```

SCRIPT 11.16

until and while Loops

There are two other forms of repeat loops that are often used, but you can do almost everything you want without them. In our experience, designing repeat loops using these two forms is much more prone to logical errors. There is no reason not to use them if you understand how they work, but we pay little attention to them in this book.

The `repeat until` form uses a Boolean expression. It iterates continuously until the expression returns `true`, and then it moves on to the next statement after the loop.

The `repeat while` form also uses a Boolean expression, but it iterates only while the expression returns `true`, moving on to the next statement after the loop as soon as it becomes `false`. An example of a `repeat while` loop appears as the last script in the "Lists" section of Chapter 18, *Working with Lists and Records*, where it is used to sort the strings in a list into alphabetical order.

What's Next?

In this chapter, you learned how to use several forms of `repeat` statements to perform standardized, repetitive processing of multiple values such as items in a list. In the next chapter, you'll learn how to catch errors in your scripts so that they can recover without a glitch—or at least fail gracefully.

12

Lesson **12**

Error Handlers

You may be surprised to hear that errors aren't necessarily a bad thing in scripts. In fact, some features in AppleScript deliberately generate errors in commonly encountered situations, just because catching an error and dealing with it as if it were an error is the simplest way to accomplish a goal.

To catch errors of any kind, AppleScript provides the `try` statement and its optional `on error` handler. Learn to use them properly with help from this chapter, and errors will become just another tool in your scripting toolkit.

The try Statement

Sometimes the only thing you want to do when your script encounters an error is to make sure the script doesn't crash. People using your script will be much happier if it continues running and doing the job they expected it to do. The simple `try` statement does exactly this.

The following examples involve the `display dialog` command in the Standard Additions scripting addition, which you learned about in Chapter 9, *Communicating with the User*. By default, the dialog it displays has two buttons, OK and Cancel. If you click the Cancel button, the `display dialog` command generates error -128 by design. If you don't catch it in a `try` block, the script simply quits without explanation. This may be exactly what the user expected, but sometimes it can be annoying and confusing if the script quits without offering an explanation.

Sometimes, especially when using the `display dialog` command in a simple script, you don't need to get fancy about figuring out the error number or reporting to the user what happened. You just want the script to go on running instead of quitting on the spot.

Because it doesn't have a `try` block to catch the error generated by the Cancel button, Script 12.1 just quits when you click Cancel. It never gets to the commands following the line on which the error occurs, `beep` and `display dialog`, unless you click OK, which doesn't generate an error.

```
display dialog "Click Cancel and watch what happens."
beep
display dialog ("You just saw a try block at work.") ¬
    buttons {"OK"} default button "OK" -- you never get here!
```
SCRIPT 12.1

Put the first `display dialog` command in a simple `try` block, as shown in Script 12.1, and this time the statements following the error are executed even if you click the Cancel button. The error is ignored.

```
try
    display dialog "Click Cancel and watch what happens."
end try
beep
display dialog ("You just saw a try block at work.") ¬
    buttons {"OK"} default button "OK" -- now you do get here!!
```
SCRIPT 12.2

There are many other situations where a simple **try** block provides a useful solution to a scripting problem, even if other techniques might also be available. Suppose, for example, that you want to write a flash-card script to teach division to a child. You want to ask the child for a number to use as the divisor, but the child might type a non-numeric character or 0, which would cause an error. Rather than criticize the child for making a mistake and perhaps discouraging the next Einstein from pursuing a career in science, you want the script to just move on and ask again. Script 12.3 shows the wrong way to go about it:

```
repeat
    display dialog ("Divide 100 by any number:") ¬
        default answer ("") ¬
        buttons {"OK"} default button "OK"
    set answer to 100 / (text returned of result as number)
    display dialog "The answer is: " & answer ¬
        & return & return & "Try again?"
end repeat
```
SCRIPT 12.3

If the child enters something that isn't a legal divisor, such as 0, the disheartening message shown in Figure 12.1 might appear:

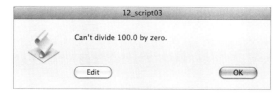

FIGURE 12.1 A typical AppleScript error message.

To avoid the error message, just enclose the body of the repeat loop in a simple **try** block, as in Script 12.4.

> **WARNING** ► If you run this script, it won't quit. You have to press Option+Command+Escape and force quit, as described at the end of this section.

```
repeat
    try
        display dialog ("Divide 100 by any number:") ¬
            default answer ("") ¬
            buttons {"OK"} default button "OK"
        set answer to 100 / (text returned of result as number)
        display dialog "The answer is: " & answer ¬
            & return & return & "Try again?"
    end try
end repeat
```
SCRIPT 12.4

Now, any time the child enters some text or 0, the script simply moves on to the next iteration of the repeat loop and asks again. No scolding allowed.

Notice one important feature of the **try** block illustrated in this example. As soon as the script encounters an error, execution jumps to the next statement following the **try** block, in this case the **end repeat** statement. None of the remaining statements within the **try** block is executed. This means you don't have to restrict the **try** block to only the one statement that might generate an error. You can put as many statements as you like inside the **try** block and count on AppleScript to ignore all of them following any statement that causes an error. You are free to write the script as if it will never generate errors and then enclose the whole thing in one massive **try** block to deal with any errors that do occur. This isn't always the best approach, but you will see a way to make good use of this behavior later in the chapter.

If you run the previous example, however, you might discover that it has a big problem. Once you enter an invalid answer, the script keeps asking again, but the dialog contains only an OK button and you can't quit. If you enter a valid answer to return to the second dialog and click its Cancel button, this just gen-erates another error and takes you right back to the question. If you are run-ning the script in Script Editor, you have to press Option+Command+Escape to open the Force Quit Applications dialog and quit Script Editor.

There's an easy solution to this problem: use the on error handler discussed in the next section.

The on error Handler

AppleScript's optional on error handler is valid only inside a try block. It is an essential part of error handling in most scripts.

The on error handler takes several optional parameters, but we'll discuss only two of them in this book. The others are for advanced users and are rarely seen in practice.

The simplest form of the on error handler uses none of the optional param-eters. The next example, Script 12.5, attempts—unsuccessfully, at first—to use it to solve the problem left over from the previous section:

```
repeat
    try
        display dialog ("Divide 100 by any number:") ¬
            default answer ("") ¬
            buttons {"OK"} default button "OK"
        set answer to 100 / (text returned of result as number)
        display dialog "The answer is: " & answer ¬
            & return & return & "Try again?"
    on error
        return
    end try
end repeat
```
SCRIPT 12.5

Script 12.5 illustrates correct usage of the on error handler—it compiles and runs—but it doesn't solve the problem in a helpful way. When the child enters an invalid divisor, the error generated by the division operation causes execution to jump immediately to the **on error** handler. Since it contains a **return** statement, the script immediately quits. What we wanted to do was to give the child an *opportunity* to quit, not to quit automatically on every mistake. Practice makes perfect, and we want the kid to keep trying!

```
repeat
    try
        display dialog ("Divide 100 by any number:") ¬
            default answer ("") ¬
            buttons {"OK"} default button "OK"
        set answer to 100 / (text returned of result as number)
        try
            display dialog "The answer is: " & answer ¬
                & return & return & "Try again?"
        on error
            return
        end try
    end try
end repeat
```

SCRIPT 12.6

Script 12.6 illustrates another useful feature of **try** blocks: they can be nested. The problem with the previous example was that it was overinclusive; it caught every error, not just the error generated when the child clicked the Cancel button in the second dialog. In Script 12.6, a second **try** block is nested within the outer **try** block, focusing specifically on the second dialog, which is the only dialog that has a Cancel button. Now, the outer **try** block functions as it did originally, allowing the first dialog to be displayed repeatedly without interruption even when an invalid answer is entered, while the second, nested **try** block catches the Cancel button error and quits.

But there is still a problem. The child has no way to get back to the second dialog and its Cancel button, except by entering a valid divisor first. That's not exactly user-friendly design. This is a job for the **on error** handler's optional **number** parameter.

Using the number Parameter

One of the optional parameters to the on error handler is number. In many cases, you know in advance that you want to handle a specific error, and you can find in the documentation (or by experimentation) what error number is generated when that error occurs. In the case of the display dialog command, you already know that clicking the Cancel button generates error -128.

To make the flash-card script as friendly as you can, you need to add a Cancel button to the first dialog so the child can quit at any time. But, when you do that, the outer **try** block won't know the difference between the error caused by an invalid divisor and the error caused by clicking the Cancel button in the first dialog. One approach might be to extend the inner **try** block so it now covers both dialogs and to make sure it quits only on error -128. Here it is, in Script 12.7.

```
repeat
    try
        try
            display dialog ("Divide 100 by any number:") ¬
                default answer ("")
            set answer to 100 ¬
                / (text returned of result as number)
            display dialog "The answer is: " & answer ¬
                & return & return & "Try again?"
        on error number -128
            return
        end try
    end try
end repeat
```
SCRIPT 12.7

Now the script works just the way it should. A wrong answer results in the question being asked again, and clicking the Cancel button in any dialog quits immediately. It works this way because the return statement in the on error handler is executed only when it encounters a -128 error. Thus, the Cancel button gets caught, but the error caused by an invalid divisor passes right by. But there's still room for improvement.

Most of the time, your scripts should use a variable in the number parameter, instead of a literal error number. When the script encounters the on error handler because of an error of some kind, it will automatically set the variable to the number of the current error. Inside the on error handler, you can test the variable and branch to any desired statements depending on the number contained in the variable. This gives you great flexibility to handle a variety of errors, all within a single try block. Script 12.8 is the final flash-card script.

```
repeat
    try
        display dialog ("Divide 100 by any number:") ¬
            default answer ("")
        set answer to 100 ¬
            / (text returned of result as number)
        display dialog "The answer is: " & answer ¬
            & return & return & "Try again?"
    on error number error_number
        if error_number is -128 then return
    end try
end repeat
```
SCRIPT 12.8

If the child clicks Cancel in either the first or the second dialog, the display dialog command generates error -128. AppleScript jumps immediately to the on error handler and stuffs that number into the error_number variable. The statement inside the on error handler tests the variable and, since the result is true, executes the return statement and quits. If the child instead enters an invalid divisor, AppleScript generates an error with some other error number and then jumps to the on error handler and sets the error_number variable to that number. The test in the on error handler returns false, so script execution jumps next to the end repeat statement immediately following the end try statement—and 'round and 'round we go.

Reporting Error Messages

In addition to the `number` parameter, the `on error` handler takes an optional unnamed parameter, called the *direct parameter*. If you provide a variable for this parameter, AppleScript will set it to an error message explaining the error that just occurred. You can use the error message in the body of the `on error` handler to report it to the user, save it to a log file, or sometimes even extract useful information from it. Consider Script 12.9.

```
try
    set divisor to 2 + 3 - 5
    return 100 / divisor
on error error_message number error_number
    display alert ("YIKES! Something's wrong!") ¬
        message error_message ¬
        & (" Error number ") & error_number & "."
end try
```
SCRIPT 12.9

The error message provided by AppleScript allows you to provide more useful information to the user, and you can embellish it as much as you like. Script 12.9 presents the alert shown in Figure 12.2, which has much more potential to offer help than the message in Figure 12.1.

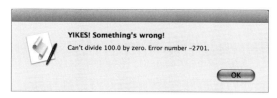

YIKES! Something's wrong!
Can't divide 100.0 by zero. Error number –2701.

OK

FIGURE 12.2 An enhanced error message using an `on error` handler.

Throwing Errors

In all the previous examples, the error numbers and the error messages were supplied to the script from outside the script. Error numbers and messages are often supplied by the system, by the Apple events mechanism underlying

AppleScript, and by applications. Check an application's documentation for a complete list of error messages and numbers that it can generate.

But your scripts are not limited to handling errors provided from outside. It can generate errors of its own by design, complete with their own error messages and numbers. Generating a custom error of your own is called *throwing an error*. Script 12.10 shows an example:

```
set winner to 7
display dialog "Pick a number:" default answer ""
set answer to text returned of result
try
    set whole_number to answer as integer
on error
    error answer & " is not a number." number 901
end try
if whole_number is less than winner then
    error answer & " is too low." number 902
else if whole_number is greater than winner then
    error answer & " is too high." number 903
else
    display dialog "You win!" buttons {"OK"} default button "OK"
end if
```

SCRIPT 12.10

As you see, **error** is an AppleScript command. You can give it an optional *direct parameter* in the form of a string to supply your own custom error message, and you can give it an optional **number** parameter value in the form of an integer to supply your own custom error number. You can supply other optional parameters, as well, but they are designed for advanced users, and we don't cover them in this book.

The previous example shows that you can vary the content of a custom error message by concatenating script variables and strings. This gives you the ability to customize your error messages to make them more informative. If you don't supply a value for the direct parameter, AppleScript will supply an empty string.

The error numbers you choose can be any integer at all, positive or negative. However, it is good practice to avoid error numbers that might be provided by the system or by a targeted application. A good rule of thumb is to use positive numbers only, in a range from 500 to 10000. If you don't supply a custom error number, AppleScript will supply -2700, the generic AppleScript error number.

When your script executes an **error** command, it generates a genuine error. The script stops execution if the command is not in a **try** block, and Script Editor or the system presents an error sheet or alert, just as it would in the case of a divide-by-zero error or a system or application error. For example, run the previous script in Script Editor, and enter **4**. Script Editor presents the sheet shown in Figure 12.3.

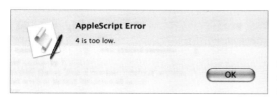

FIGURE 12.3 A standard error sheet from a custom **error** command.

You've learned that it is useful to catch errors by enclosing suspect commands in a **try** block with an optional **on error** handler. Custom errors that your scripts generate can be handled in the same way. Script 12.11 builds on the previous example to provide more information to the user.

```
set winner to 7
try
    display dialog "Pick a number:" default answer ""
    set answer to text returned of result
    try
        set whole_number to answer as integer
    on error
        error answer & " is not a number." number 901
    end try
    if whole_number is less than winner then
        error answer & " is too low." number 902
    else if whole_number is greater than winner then
        error answer & " is too high." number 903
    else
        display dialog ("You win!") ¬
            buttons {"OK"} default button "OK"
    end if
on error error_message number error_number
    display dialog error_message & space ¬
        & "Consult ref #" & error_number & ", then try again!"
end try
```

SCRIPT 12.11

Run Script 12.11, enter **9**, and see the dialog in Figure 12.4 explaining what you should do.

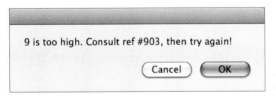

FIGURE 12.4 A custom error dialog from a custom error command.

A Practical Example

When you write more complex scripts, good error handling is indispensable, especially if the scripts will be used by others in some sort of production environment. The users of your scripts probably aren't very computer-savvy. Even if they are, they have work to do, and they don't want your script to get in the way. They will be happier customers if you have anticipated every error they might encounter, especially if you've provided good messages explaining how they can fix any problem themselves and get back to work without having to call you.

Your first instinct in writing a complex script might be to enclose every potentially problematic statement in its own separate `try` block, with its own `on error` handler to present a message to the user. This approach has two significant drawbacks. First, you might overlook a statement that could cause an error in circumstances you didn't consider, resulting in an embarrassing failure without an explanation. Second, your script will quickly become crowded with lengthy compound `try` blocks that make it hard to read and understand the overall logic of the script. It will be a maintenance nightmare for you in the future.

There is a simple solution that most experienced scripters use. Put your entire script inside one long `try` block and then handle all the errors it encounters in one massive `on error` handler at the end. All of the error handling will be concentrated at the end of the script, where it is out of the way when you're trying to work on the script's essential logic. Custom messages can be presented in the `on error` handler for every error that occurs, depending on the error number in the `number` parameter, and a catchall clause at the end of the `on error` handler can help the script fail gracefully in the event an error occurs that you didn't anticipate.

This technique works because AppleScript error handling is hierarchical. If an error occurs inside a subroutine and the subroutine doesn't have its own `try` block, AppleScript looks at the next higher level of the handler calling chain. It keeps proceeding up the chain until it finds a `try` block that handles the error. If you've provided a `try` block enclosing the entire script, any error is guaranteed to end up there if you haven't already caught it at a lower level. You'll learn more about subroutines in Chapter 16, *Subroutines*.

When using this technique, scripters sometimes use a global variable, setting it to a different string for each error. Then they use that variable to report the error in the final **on error** handler. However, it is often easier to use the **error** command to throw custom errors in a complex script. The **error** command allows you to set custom error messages, just as you can do in a variable, but it also lets you invent a large number of custom error numbers to distinguish between all the errors that your script might encounter. You can design these custom error numbers so they make it possible to fine-tune the **on error** handler to suit the specific needs of the script.

You can also combine all of these approaches. You can have a top-level **try** block cover most errors but occasionally place a smaller group of statements in a nested inner **try** block that requires special handling. You can place some messages in variables, especially when you want to use a common phrase as a prefix that applies to a group of errors, while sending custom error messages to the **on error** handler using the **error** command.

Script 12.12 is an example using all of these techniques. It takes you through a tricky job interview.

```
try

    -- initialize
    set script_error_prefix to "An error occurred: "
    set user_error_prefix to "Your answer can't be right. "
    set user_disqualified_prefix to "I'm sorry, you don't qualify."

    -- introduction
    display dialog ("Welcome to Jobs 'R Us.") ¬
        & return & return ¬
        & ("I'll begin by asking you about yourself.") ¬
        & (" Shall we get started?")

    --get birth date
    repeat
        try
```

```
        display dialog ("What year were you born?") ¬
            default answer ""
        set answer to text returned of result
        set birth_year to answer as integer
        exit repeat
    on error number -1700
        display alert script_error_prefix ¬
            message ("You must enter a number.")
    end try
end repeat
set this_year to year of (current date)
if birth_year < (this_year - 65) then
    error user_disqualified_prefix number 5001 -- too old
else if birth_year > this_year then
    error user_error_prefix number 5002 -- future date
else if birth_year > (this_year - 18) then
    error user_disqualified_prefix number 5003 -- too young
end if

-- get current age
repeat
    try
        display dialog ("How old are you?") ¬
            default answer ""
        set answer to text returned of result
        set current_age to answer as integer
        exit repeat
    on error number -1700
        display alert script_error_prefix ¬
            message ("You must enter a number.")
    end try
end repeat
if current_age is not equal to (this_year - birth_year) then
    error user_error_prefix number 5004
end if
```

```
        -- conclusion
        display dialog ("Congratulations. You're hired!") ¬
            buttons {"OK"} default button "OK"


on error error_message number error_number
    if error_number is -128 then
        -- user cancelled
        display dialog ("'Bye. Return again soon!") ¬
            buttons {"OK"} default button "OK"
        return
    else if error_number > 5000 and error_number ≤ 5004 then
        -- user error
        if error_number is 5001 then -- too old
            set full_message to error_message ¬
                & return & return ¬
                & ("We don't hire people over 65.")
        else if error_number is 5002 then -- not yet born
            set full_message to error_message ¬
                & return & return ¬
                & (birth_year & " is in the future.") ¬
                & (" We don't hire time travelers.")
        else if error_number is 5003 then -- too young
            set full_message to error_message ¬
                & return & return ¬
                & ("We don't hire people under 18.")
        else if error_number is 5004 then -- wrong age
            set full_message to error_message ¬
                & return & return ¬
                & ("Your real age is ") ¬
                & this_year - birth_year ¬
                & (". We don't hire people who can't count.")
        end if
        display dialog full_message & (" Go away!") ¬
            buttons {"OK"} default button "OK"
```

```
    else
        -- unexpected error
        display dialog ("An unexpected error occurred.") ¬
            & return & return ¬
            & ("Sorry, but we'll have to stop for now.") ¬
            buttons {"OK"} default button "OK"
    end if
end try
```
SCRIPT 12.12

The entire script is enclosed in a **try** block, with a comprehensive **on error** handler at the end. There are also a couple of small **try** blocks within the outer **try** block to handle localized logic requirements of the script.

The script initializes variables used generally at the outset. These variables contain strings that the script will use as standard prefixes for error messages. There are three strings, one for each of three categories of errors.

After a brief introduction from the interviewer, the script asks for the year when you were born. Since the answer must be a number but you might inadvertently enter non-numeric characters, the script attempts to coerce the answer (which always starts out as text in the **display dialog** command) to an integer. If the coercion fails, AppleScript returns error -1700. Without some help, the script would quit at this point. To make the script more user-friendly, the coercion and related statements are placed inside a localized **try** block, and the **try** block is placed inside a repeat loop. When you enter text that can't be coerced to a number, the associated **on error** handler reminds you to enter a number, and the repeat loop lets you try again. Once you enter text that can be coerced to a number, the coercion works without error, and the script executes the next statement, which exits the repeat loop and moves on.

This is a common pattern for handling inadvertent data entry errors in AppleScript. It's easy for a user to hit an adjacent key by accident, and you don't want that common mistake to force everybody to start all over again. Since this **try** block is in a repeat loop, it must be placed around the specific statements that might cause an error. The **on error** handler can't be placed at the end of the script, because there would be no way to force execution back to the beginning of the repeat loop.

Once you've successfully entered a number, the script goes on to analyze it to make sure you meet the company's hiring policies. If you're too old, you're too young, or you provide a birth date in the future, the script "throws an error" using the appropriate prefix variable and an error number unique to the specific problem. The error is handled in a comprehensive `on error` handler at the end of the script, using the prefix supplied with the `error` command and a message appropriate for the error number. These error numbers amount to business policies embodied in the script.

If you meet the age requirements for this company, the script goes on to ask for your age. This may seem redundant, but it is in fact a sneaky job interviewer's trick to trip you up. This part of the script uses the same techniques you saw earlier to get a number from you, and then it implements a business policy requiring utmost honesty when describing your age. If the answer you give is not consistent with the birth date you gave previously, the script throws another error that is handled in the final `on error` handler.

There are a couple of other points worth noticing in this script.

The introduction dialog and the question dialogs contain a Cancel button to let you duck out of the interview quickly if you don't think it's going well. Pressing Cancel generates error -128, and you want to be sure this error does not get hung up in the wrong `on error` handler. The reason it gets past the inner `try` blocks is that their `on error` handlers explicitly test for error -1700. Error -128 passes right through them, untouched, looking for a higher-level `on error` handler that does handle them. When they get to the final, outer `on error` handler, they are caught by its first `if` clause, which tests explicitly for error -128. There, the script says goodbye and quits.

The next `if` test first checks for the entire range of "business logic" error numbers defined earlier in the script. This allows the script to use a single `display dialog` command at the end of this `if` block. Inner `if` tests check for each error number in turn, setting the `full_message` variable to a message that is appropriate for the specific error number.

Finally, a catchall `else` clause provides a soft landing if the script encounters any other error. We can't think of any way to get to this clause, but it's better to be safe than sorry.

What's Next?

In this chapter, you learned how to make your scripts friendlier to your users by sprinkling `try` blocks and `on error` handlers through them so they don't fail abruptly with incomprehensible technical error messages supplied by the system. You also learned that this feature of AppleScript is not only for handling mistakes made by you or your users but also for implementing business logic as a designed-in feature of your scripts. In the next chapter, you'll assemble everything you've learned up to this point and think about overall design of your scripts. That will bring Part I, *Instant AppleScript*, to a close.

Part **II**

Essential Topics

13

Lesson 13
Script Editor

Part II, *Essential Topics*, begins with Apple's Script Editor, because a utility to compose, edit, compile, and run scripts is absolutely essential to using AppleScript. In this chapter, instead of explaining how scripts work, we'll describe in detail how you actually create them using Script Editor.

Script Editor has been included with AppleScript since the beginning, back in the days of System 7. It was revised to run natively on Mac OS X and to look and feel like a typical Mac OS X application. It nevertheless retains all the features of the original, though reorganized and simplified, and it now includes additional features that make writing, editing, and debugging scripts easier than ever. Script Editor is even scriptable!

Exploring the Script Window

Script Editor is a document-based application. Every script is a separate document, edited in its own window. Figure 13.1 shows all the features of a script window.

FIGURE 13.1 The script window in Script Editor.

Let's review the features of a script window from the top down.

First, across the top of the window beneath the title bar is a standard Mac OS X *toolbar*. The toolbar doesn't contain the formatting tools you might see in a typical text editor, because script formatting is controlled separately, by user-settable AppleScript preferences. Script Editor's mission is to make it easy to compile and test scripts. The toolbar reflects this by putting the principal tools you need to compile and run a script within easy reach of your mouse, relegating a few font and format controls to the menu bar.

By default, the toolbar contains buttons to record, stop, run, and compile scripts. The same four commands are also available in the Script menu with keyboard shortcuts. A fifth button on the right opens a drawer that we'll talk about later.

▶ The Record button places Script Editor into Record Mode to record the actions a user takes in a recordable application such as the Finder. This can be considered an editing button, in a sense, since in Record Mode Script Editor automatically types the text of a script into the script window as it monitors the actions taking place in the application being recorded.

▶ The Stop button stops the recording or playback of a script.

▶ The Run button compiles and runs the script.

▶ The Compile button compiles the script without running it. Use the Compile button to check for syntax errors.

Like other Mac OS X windows with toolbars, the script window's toolbar is customizable. Choose the Customize Toolbar command in the View menu. Figure 13.2 shows the additional tools you can add to the toolbar. Most of them relate to Script Editor's role in compiling, running, and debugging scripts.

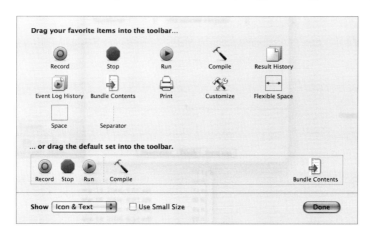

FIGURE 13.2 The Customize Toolbar sheet.

Next, the feature below the toolbar is the *navigation bar*. Like the toolbar, you show and hide the navigation bar using a menu item in the View menu. Use the language pop-up button at the left end of the navigation bar to choose any available Open Scripting Architecture (OSA) language component currently installed on your computer. Depending on what products you've installed, you might see a JavaScript component and one or two AppleScript Debugger components, as well as the standard AppleScript component. Use the elements pop-up menu on the right to select any element in the script window quickly from a list of properties, global variables, and handlers. (This works best if the script has been compiled and saved.) When the insertion point is in a line declaring a property or a global variable or in the first line of a subroutine handler, the title of the elements pop-up menu is the name of that element. Figure 13.3 shows the navigation pop-up open.

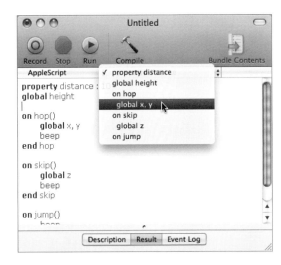

FIGURE 13.3 The navigation bar showing a selected handler.

Under the navigation bar is the content area of the script window. It's a split view. Drag the divider up and down to see more of the top pane or more of the bottom pane or to completely hide either of them. Double-click the divider to drop it all the way to the bottom and hide the lower pane, and double-click it again to restore its original position. Double-click it while holding down the Option key to raise it to the top and hide the upper pane, and double-click it again to restore its position.

The top pane is the *script pane*, where you enter and edit the text of your script, as shown in Figure 13.4.

In the bottom pane, you view various kinds of information about the script using the display control at the bottom of the window. Select the information you want to see in the bottom pane by clicking the control or by using the View menu or a keyboard shortcut. In Figure 13.4, the bottom pane shows the result returned by the script when it was run, because the *Result pane* is selected. This is one of several features of Script Editor that help you test and debug your scripts.

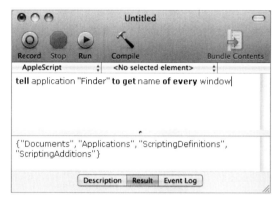

FIGURE 13.4 The script pane and the Result pane.

Another debugging feature appears in the bottom pane when you choose the *Event Log pane*. As you see in Figure 13.5, the Event Log shows each event executed by the script, in turn, followed by its result. You can show additional information in the Event Log by sprinkling your script with **log** commands. This is more useful than the Result pane when you need to monitor the values returned by several steps in a script instead of watching only the last value returned.

FIGURE 13.5 The Event Log pane.

The *Description pane* serves a different purpose altogether. When it is selected, you can type a description of the script in the lower pane of the script window. This description is shown to the user before the script is run, if you save it as an application or application bundle with the Startup Screen option set. Use the Font menu to set the font and size used in the start-up screen. Figure 13.6 shows the Description pane, and Figure 13.7 shows the start-up screen that it creates.

FIGURE 13.6 The Description pane using a custom font and size.

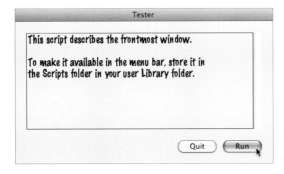

FIGURE 13.7 The start-up screen presenting the script's description.

If you don't like the default size of the script window that Script Editor opens every time you choose New from the File menu, change any script window to the size you prefer, and then choose Save as Default from the Window menu. Set the default location of the window divider and the default lower pane (Description, Result, or Event Log) in every new window the same way.

Writing and Compiling a Script

The text of a script always appears in the upper pane of a split script window. When a script window is first opened, the blinking text insertion caret appears in the script pane, and you can begin typing in it immediately. If you open an existing script and it was not saved as run-only, its text appears in this pane, and you can begin editing it immediately. As you saw earlier, this is also the pane in which the text of a recorded script appears automatically as you perform actions in the application being recorded.

If you try to type something in the window but it doesn't appear, the script pane may be hidden. If that is the case, you'll see the window divider with a dimple near the top of the window, under the toolbar and the navigation bar. Double-click the divider, and the script pane opens so you can type into it.

Don't try to type the text of a script into the bottom pane of a script window while it is set to the Description pane. Script Editor lets you type it there, but nothing happens when you try to run it or compile it.

> **TIP ▶** You can enter common elements of a script, without typing them, by choosing them from a contextual menu while the mouse is over the script pane. See "The Contextual Menu" section later in this chapter for details.

Once you think you're done typing a script—or even if you aren't done but you want to see whether you've made any mistakes yet—click the Compile button. If the script's syntax is valid, it will successfully compile. You'll know it was successful because the formatting and indentation of the script will change to match whatever formatting preferences you've set in Script Editor's Editing and Formatting preferences. (We'll talk more about formatting later in this chapter.)

You'll also know that compiling was successful if you don't see an error message. When you attempt to compile a script containing a syntax error, Script Editor presents a sheet with an informative error message and highlights the offending text. To fix it, dismiss the error sheet and edit the script. Figure 13.8 shows a typical syntax error message.

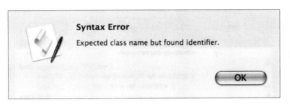

FIGURE 13.8 A syntax error message after attempting to compile a bad script.

Script Editor is pretty smart about AppleScript syntax, but only when you click the Run or Compile button. When you start writing a script, everything you type appears in a single monotonous font, and every new line butts up against the left edge of the window unless you type a tab or space character. If you insert extra spaces or tabs in a line, they all appear faithfully as you typed them. The only formatting that happens automatically while you're typing is line wrap—when the text you're typing hits the right edge of the window, Script Editor automatically starts a new line and moves the last word to the left edge of the window and indents it. Figure 13.9 shows an example of script text that hasn't yet been compiled.

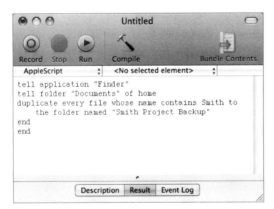

FIGURE 13.9 Text of a script that hasn't yet been compiled.

The magic happens the moment you click Run or Compile. If your syntax is valid, Script Editor automatically indents the text of the script to match the logical nesting of statements inside blocks, and all extra white space is deleted. You control line wrap and the amount of indenting in the Editing pane of Script Editor's Preferences window. Script Editor's editing preferences override any custom indentation you attempt to apply using space or tab characters.

Even better, compiling a script changes its formatting to match the formatting you set in the Formatting pane of the Preferences window. You can set a different font, font size, font color, and style separately for new text and for each of the following syntax elements of a compiled script: operators, language keywords, application keywords, comments, values, variables, and subroutines. Being able to distinguish between these syntax elements at a glance is enormously helpful when reading a script and diagnosing any behavioral problems it may exhibit. Figure 13.10 shows an example of a compiled script with automatic indenting and formatting (you can't see the font colors here because the figure is black and white).

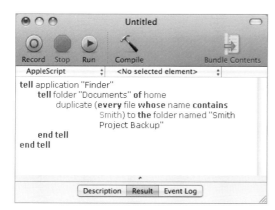

FIGURE 13.10 Text of the same script after it was compiled.

Running a Script

There are many ways to run a script once it's compiled and saved. For example, if you saved it as an application or application bundle, double-click it in the Finder or select it and choose Open from the Finder's File menu. If you saved it as a script or a script bundle in one of the official Scripts folders, choose it from the Script menu in the menu bar to run it. (See Chapter 14, *AppleScript Utility*, for instructions about using the Script menu.)

In Script Editor itself, you can run a script even before you've saved it. Just click the Run button in the script window. If you haven't compiled it yet, Script Editor automatically compiles it and, if successful, runs it. A typical usage pattern when developing a new script or editing an old script is to type some text, hit the Run button, dismiss the error dialog, type some more text, hit the Run button again, dismiss the error dialog, and so on, until you've got it right.

The main advantage of running a script in Script Editor is that you can take advantage of all of Script Editor's debugging features. You've already seen some of them, such as the formatting that Script Editor applies to a script when it's compiled, the Result pane and the Event Log that show the result of script statements when they are run, and Script Editor's ability to select the offending statement when it encounters an error at run time. We discuss others later in this chapter in the "Advanced Features" section.

Saving a Script

You usually write a script because you want to use it again and again to perform some dull or repetitive task or to automate a complex workflow. This implies that you want to save it for future use. Since each script is a document unto itself, you save a script just as you would save any document in any other document-based application. Choose Save or Save As from Script Editor's File menu, and Script Editor presents a familiar dialog asking you where you want to save it and under what name.

Like many applications, Script Editor's Save As dialog contains an area near the bottom where you choose how to save a document. You must make up to three basic choices in Script Editor: the file format, the line endings, and various options. Some choices apply only to particular file formats. Figure 13.11 shows the Save As dialog with the file format set to "script."

First you must choose a file format. You have five choices: script, application, application bundle, script bundle, and text.

Two of the file formats, application bundle and script bundle, were introduced in Mac OS X 10.3 (Panther). These are best thought of as subcategories of the application and script formats, respectively, but they have a special feature in common. Both of them save the script as a native Mac OS X bundle instead of a single file. A bundle looks just like a file on the screen, because it uses Script Editor's standard icon for a script file, a droplet, or an applet. (You'll learn about droplets in Chapter 20, *Droplets*.) In reality, a bundle is a folder that contains other items. As we'll explain later in this chapter, you can store sounds, images, movies, text files, and many other things inside a script bundle or an application bundle and use them in the script. This is a very powerful feature, making it easy to distribute complete automation solutions that are transparent to users.

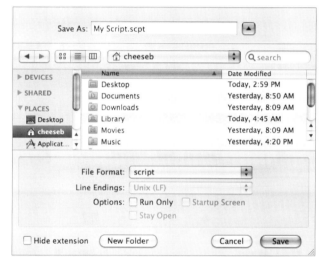

FIGURE 13.11
Script Editor's Save As dialog set to save in the "script" format.

Script Editor automatically adds an appropriate extension to a script file's name when you save it. You can change these name extensions, of course, but we strongly recommend against doing that. Script Editor and other applications recognize a script text file if it has the ".applescript" extension. They recognize the other file formats by the extensions ".scpt" for a script file, ".scptd" for a script bundle, and the standard ".app" for an application file and an application bundle. You can see the extension in the Save As dialog by unchecking the Hide Extension checkbox, as shown in Figure 13.11.

We'll describe each file format in turn, from the simplest to the most complex, because all the other choices depend on your choice of a file format.

Saving as Text

A Script Editor text file contains the text of a script that has not been compiled.

Why would you want to save a script as text, since it isn't compiled and therefore can't be run? There are several reasons. For one, a text file can be opened in any text editor or word processor. Saving a script as text allows you to show it to people who don't have or don't know how to use a script editor, and it may be the most convenient format to use if you're preparing a script for publication. You can even edit a script text file in any text editor or word processor and then copy it back to Script Editor and compile and run it there.

The most important reason for saving a script as a text file, however, is that it lets you save a script that still contains syntax errors and therefore can't be compiled and saved as a script or an application. We all have to sleep now and then, and it is a good idea to save a script-in-progress as a text file overnight even though it hasn't yet reached a stage where it will successfully compile.

Scripts saved as scripts and applications usually also contain the full text of a script, so you can open them and edit them in Script Editor or any other application that recognizes the compiled script and script application formats. Most text editors and word processors don't understand these other script formats, and they will either refuse to open the file or display indecipherable garbage characters.

Once you've decided to save a script as a text file, you have only one other choice to make: the line endings. If you choose another file type, the Line Endings pop-up menu is dimmed and unavailable, as you can see in Figure 13.11. By default, a script text file is saved using UNIX line endings, namely, line feed (LF) characters. You can choose Mac or Windows line endings instead. Mac line endings are carriage return (CR) characters. Windows line endings are a pair of characters—a carriage return followed by a line feed (CRLF).

NOTE ▶ In case you don't know the history, these characters got their names from the earliest days of message transmission by wire. Characters in the ASCII character table from ASCII character 0 to ASCII character 31 are called control characters because they controlled the receiving Teletype machine. They are distinguished from all the other characters, which are called printable characters. The line feed character is ASCII character 10, and the carriage return character is ASCII character 13. The Windows convention of using two characters is said to stem from the fact that a Teletype machine needed extra time to return the carriage return to its starting position. This problem was solved by using a second character, a line feed, to rotate the carriage down one line. The time it took the line feed to do its work also gave the carriage return time to finish its job before the next printable character arrived.

Any line endings should work in Script Editor. Given the UNIX heritage of Mac OS X, it is not surprising that UNIX line endings are the default. The only occasion when you might want to consider other line endings is when the script is going to be used in a text editor or word processor that requires them.

A fourth line ending choice, Preserve Line Endings, is useful when you've opened a script text file from someone else and edited it and you want to be sure to save it with the same line endings it had when you received it.

Figure 13.12 shows the Save As dialog for a text file with the Line Endings pop-up menu open.

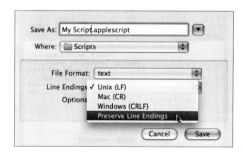

FIGURE 13.12 The Line Endings pop-up menu when saving a script as a text file.

Saving as Script File

A Script Editor script file contains a script that has been compiled. For this reason, most applications that are designed to run scripts can run script files. Such an application is sometimes called a *script runner*. This includes Script Editor itself, of course, and also third-party script editors, Apple's Script menu, and similar third-party utilities. A script file is not an application, however—you cannot run it by double-clicking it in the Finder.

A script file usually includes the full text of the script, so you can read and edit a script file when you open it in Script Editor. Most text editors and word processors can't read the text of a script file, however, so there is no need to choose any particular line endings for it. The Line Endings setting is therefore dimmed. Every script editor can open the text of a script file without regard to line endings.

They can open any script file that wasn't saved with the Run Only option checked, that is. This is the only option available for a script file. When you save it with the Run Only option checked, the text of the script is *not* saved in the file. This option allows you to distribute your scripts without revealing how they work. It protects them against tampering by pranksters, and it protects your hard-earned trade secrets from being stolen by pirates.

There is a downside, however, that most scripters discover the hard way at least once. If you save a script as a run-only script without keeping a text copy, you'll never be able to edit the script again. Its entire text is gone, and there is no practical way to recover it. The moral of this story is that you should always develop your script with its text included and then save a copy in a secure location, perhaps as a text file, before you save the distribution version with the Run Only option checked.

Figure 13.13 shows a script file being saved with the Run Only checkbox checked.

FIGURE 13.13 Setting
the Run Only option
when saving a script
as a script file.

Saving as Application File

Script Editor can also save a script as an application file. When saved as an application file, a script contains the text of the script (if it isn't saved with the Run Only option checked), a compiled script so it can run, and some code that enables it to be run just like any application without the aid of a separate script runner.

A script application does not need the help of a script runner. For example, you can run it by double-clicking it in the Finder or selecting it and choosing Open from the Finder's File menu.

A script application is commonly known as an *applet*. If it contains an *open handler*, it is known as a *droplet* because it can be run by dragging and dropping files and folders onto it. Droplets are discussed in Chapter 20, *Droplets*.

You have three options when you save a script as a script application, as shown in Figure 13.14:

- ▶ The Run Only option works exactly like the Run Only option when saving a script as a script file, discussed in the preceding section.

- ▶ The Startup Screen option, when set, causes an applet to present an introductory alert before it runs, briefly explaining what it does and giving the user the option to quit or to run the applet. This works only with applets; a droplet does not present the start-up screen before running when you drop items on it. You saw how to set up a start-up screen's explanatory message in the description pane of a script window in Figure 13.6, and you saw a start-up screen in Figure 13.7.

▶ The Stay Open option, when set, causes the applet to continue running after it finishes its work. Most Mac applications behave this way by default, but script applications usually quit as soon as they finish their job. By setting this option, you make an applet or droplet work like most applications. It is necessary to set the Stay Open option in order to use certain AppleScript features, such as the idle handler discussed in Chapter 24, Adding Timing Controls to Scripts.

FIGURE 13.14 Setting the Stay Open option when saving a script as a script application.

Saving as Script or Application Bundle

When you save a script as a script bundle or an application bundle, you get all of the options described previously for saving it as a single script file or application file, plus one additional feature that adds great power and flexibility to your scripts.

NOTE ▶ Script bundles and application bundles run only on Mac OS X 10.3 (Panther) and newer.

A script bundle or an application bundle is, behind the scenes, a folder. You can place sounds, images, movies, and document files of many kinds inside it. Then, using the `path to resource` command, your script can get a reference to these internal files and use them. Because a bundle looks like a single file to the user, you can distribute your scripts in the same way you distribute any old-style script. All their support files are hidden away inside the bundle, where the average user can't get at them and needn't bother keeping them organized and available.

Even better, you can distribute your script with custom sounds and other files, without having to worry whether the users have installed the correct support files in their system.

Once you've saved a script as a script bundle or an application bundle, the Bundle Contents button in the script window's toolbar becomes enabled. Click it, and a drawer opens showing the contents of the bundle in an expandable outline, as shown in Figure 13.15.

FIGURE 13.15 The Bundle Contents drawer.

By default, the bundle contains a text file named "description.rtfd," which contains the contents of whatever start-up screen message you set up in the description pane of the script window, and it contains a Scripts folder that contains the script's main script. Double-click any of these items in the drawer to open them in the application that owns them; for example, double-click Text Edit for the "description.rtfd" file and the Finder for any folders. You can edit and save them using the application that owns them. In the Finder, for example, drag additional files into them. Select one of the items in the drawer and use the menu in the Bundle Contents drawer to open them; to reveal them in the Finder; to duplicate, delete, and rename them; and to create new folders, as shown in Figure 13.16.

FIGURE 13.16 The Bundle Content drawer's menu in use.

> TIP ► Another way to open a script bundle or application bundle is to
> place the cursor over the saved file's icon and Control-click to open the
> Finder's contextual menu. Choose the Show Package Contents menu item.
> You have to do it this way in Mac OS X 10.3 (Panther).

Using the path to resource Command

Let's have a little fun with an application bundle. Suppose your creative
instincts tell you that your new script simply must play the system's Tink
sound whenever it starts. You know you can't rely on your users to follow
instructions—just because you tell them to change their system alert sound to
Tink doesn't mean they'll do it. You'll have to force their hands. How? Install a
copy of the Tink sound file in your script bundle, and play it instead of calling
the `beep` command as the script's first command.

To make this work, you must be running Mac OS X 10.4 (Tiger) or newer,
because you're going to use the new `path to resource` command in the Standard
Additions scripting addition. You'll also have to download and install David
Blache's free Play Sound application from Microcosm Software at `http://
microcosmsoftware.com/playsound/`. It's a scriptable faceless background appli-
cation that plays standard AIFF sound files, as well as sounds in other formats.

Here are step-by-step instructions:

1. In Script Editor, create a new script by choosing New from the File menu.

2. Type Script 13.1 into the script window, and compile it.

```
get path to resource "Tink.aiff" in directory "Sounds"
tell application "Play Sound" to play result
```
SCRIPT 13.1

3. Save it as an application bundle by choosing Save As from the File menu.

4. Click the Bundle Contents button in the toolbar to open the Bundle Contents drawer.

5. Using the pop-up menu in the Bundle Contents drawer, create a new folder in the bundle, and name it "Sounds."

6. Use the Finder to open the system's built-in Sounds folder at /System/ Library/Sounds, and locate the file named "Tink.aiff."

7. Drag the "Tink.aiff" file over the name of the new Sounds folder in the script window's Bundle Contents drawer. You'll see the Sounds folder open (the disclosure triangle turns down). When it's positioned properly, drop the "Tink.aiff" file into the Sounds folder. A copy of the file is now safely incorporated into your application bundle. Figure 13.17 shows this step in progress.

FIGURE 13.17 Dragging the "Tink.aiff" sound file into the bundle's new Sounds folder.

8. Compile and save the application bundle again.

9. Using the Finder, double-click your new application bundle, and listen to the Tink sound!

> **TIP** ▶ This script won't work if you run it in Script Editor. The reason for this is that the `path to resource` command looks for the "Tink.aiff" file in the Resources folder of the currently running application bundle by default. When you run a script in Script Editor, the current application is Script Editor, and there's no "Tink.aiff" file in the Script Editor application bundle. It works when you run your new script application by double-clicking it, because then it is the current application and it does contain a copy of "Tink.aiff."

Find and Replace

Script Editor has a Find menu in its Edit menu and a full array of find and replace commands.

Some of the commands in the Find menu amount to navigation commands. In addition to the navigation bar with its pop-up menu letting you select and scroll to specific properties, global variables, and handlers, the Find menu includes several commands to scroll specific parts of a script into view in the script window. There is a Jump to Selection command that scrolls the current selection back into view in case you've scrolled to some other point in your script and need to find your way back quickly, and there are Find Next and Find Previous commands that select and scroll to the next or previous occurrence of the current Find target. Figure 13.18 shows the Find menu.

As convenient as the Find menu is, the real star is the Find dialog that opens in response to the Find command, as shown in Figure 13.19. Use the Find dialog to find any text you enter in the Find text field, either within the entire file or within a selected section of it; you can use the usual options to ignore case and to search for whole words or for text that starts with or contains the text you want to find. Type replacement text in the Replace With field. With the buttons at the bottom of the dialog, replace all occurrences of found text with the replacement text, replace the currently selected occurrence, replace the selected occurrence and find the next occurrence, or simply find backward with the Previous button or forward with the Next button.

FIGURE 13.18 The Find menu.

FIGURE 13.19 The Find dialog in use.

Finally, there is the Find menu's Use Selection for Find command. When you choose it, it doesn't appear to do anything. However, it sets the currently selected text as the text to find, both for the Find Next and Find Previous commands and for the Find dialog itself. Using the Use Selection for Find command and the Find Next and Find Previous commands, you can find every occurrence of the selected text in the entire script without opening the Find dialog.

The Dictionary Browser

You learned a lot about the contents of an AppleScript terminology dictionary in Chapter 2, *Dictionaries*. Here, we'll explain the mechanics of examining a dictionary using Script Editor's dictionary browser. The browser improved dramatically in Mac OS X 10.4 (Tiger).

Open the dictionary browser by choosing Open Dictionary from Script Editor's File menu. After a few moments, a dialog opens presenting a list of all scriptable software on your computer. Select one of the items in the list and click Open, or click the Browse button to open a standard file dialog if you prefer to navigate to a program in a known location. The list shows the kind of each scriptable program—whether application, application (Classic), or scripting addition—and, when you expand the dialog, its version and its path.

To make it easier for you to open the dictionaries of applications you frequently script, use the Library palette discussed in the "Advanced Features" section.

Figure 13.20 shows Script Editor's dictionary browser set to view the Finder's dictionary by suite. The Item class in the Finder items suite is selected. Let's review what you see and what you can do with it.

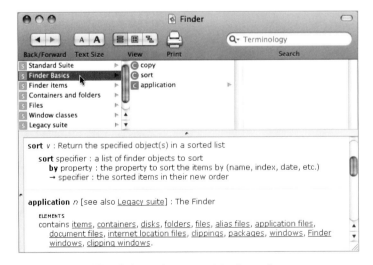

FIGURE 13.20   The dictionary browser set to view suites.

At the top of the browser window is a standard toolbar. To customize it, use the Customize Toolbar command in the View menu. By default, it includes the buttons and search field you see in Figure 13.20. The Back/Forward buttons work like the buttons in a Web browser, retracing your steps as you navigate through the dictionary. The Text Size buttons enlarge or reduce the font size in the main view pane. The Suites, Containment, and Inheritance buttons arrange the browser pane in three different ways, described in a moment. The print button prints the dictionary, and the search field allows you to search for terminology without having to browse for it.

Below the toolbar is the browser pane, which is a standard Mac OS X column view. The browser pane makes it very easy to navigate up and down the suite hierarchy, the containment hierarchy, or the inheritance hierarchy. You see the suite hierarchy's browser in Figure 13.20. Enlarge or reduce the browser pane by dragging the window divider up or down.

Finally, the dictionary pane appears at the bottom of the browser window. Within the dictionary pane, you see most of the contents of a typical dictionary entry for the commands and classes shown. These may include, for a command like the Finder's `find` or `sort`, the following:

- The name of the command

- Its syntactical role (verb)

- A brief description

- How it is used (the command itself, followed by the type and a brief description of any direct parameter it requires)

- A list of parameters with their names, types, and descriptions (optional parameters are in square brackets)

- Any return value (indicated by an arrow), with its type and description

For a class like the Finder's `application` class shown in Figure 13.20, the contents of the dictionary pane may include the following:

▶   Its name

▶   Its syntactical role (noun)

▶   The classes from which it inherits (not shown in Figure 13.20 because the `application` class does not inherit from anything)

▶   A brief explanation of what it is

▶   A list of its elements

▶   A list of its properties, including their names, their data types in parentheses, whether they are read-only ("r/o"), and a brief explanation of their role

▶   A list of the commands to which the class responds

The Elements section includes a list of classes that contain this class ("contained by," not shown in Figure 13.20 because an application is not contained by any other elements) and a list of elements that this class contains ("contains"). Each of the classes in the inheritance list and the elements list is colored blue and underlined to indicate that it is linked to its definition. When you click a link, you are immediately whisked away to that part of the dictionary; click the Back button to return.

The browser pane organizes the dictionary a little differently when you set it to *containment view* or *inheritance view*. Both of those views show only classes, since the concepts of containment and inheritance do not apply to commands in AppleScript. Figure 13.21 shows the containment view. From left to right, the selected classes show that an application contains a folder and a folder contains a file. Figure 13.22 shows the inheritance view. From right to left, the selection shows that a document file inherits elements and properties from a file and shows that a file inherits elements and properties from an item.

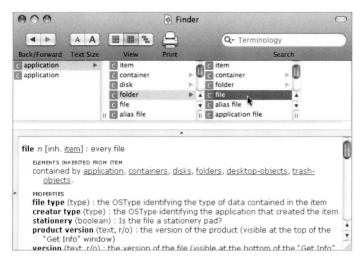

FIGURE 13.21 The containment view of the browser pane.

FIGURE 13.22 The inheritance view of the browser pane.

In Mac OS X 10.4 (Tiger), the dictionary browser gained the ability to include extended comments and explanations about items in a dictionary, including script examples, live links to the Web, and illustrations. These features appear in a dictionary only if the developer includes them. One of the first applications to include these features was PreFab UI Actions, a faceless background application from PreFab Software, Inc., written by one of the authors (Bill Cheeseman). Figure 13.23 shows a portion of its extended dictionary. You can download a free 30-day trial copy of UI Actions to see more of its expanded dictionary at `http://prefabsoftware.com/uiactions/`.

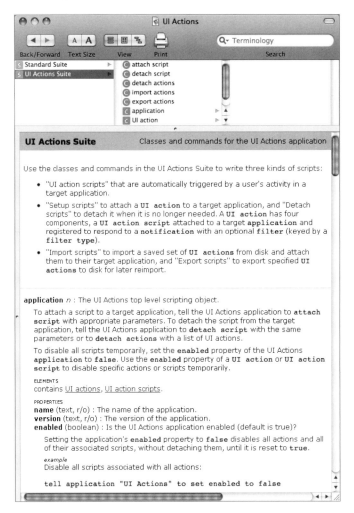

FIGURE 13.23 Extended dictionary features in the PreFab UI Actions scripting addition.

Some of the information available is not shown in Script Editor's dictionary browser. For example, it does not show the reference forms that are supported by particular elements of a class, such as by index and by name, as the old dictionary browser did. The theory is that all classes should support all reference forms although, in practice, some classes do not support some reference forms, and sometimes this is by design.

Third-party script editors may organize dictionaries very differently, and they may even include additional information not shown in Script Editor, such as an element's reference forms. Figure 13.24 shows the dictionary browser in Script Debugger 4 from Late Night Software, available at `http://www.latenightsw.com/sd4/`. Figure 13.25 shows the dictionary viewer in Smile from Satimage, available at `http://www.satimage.fr/software/`.

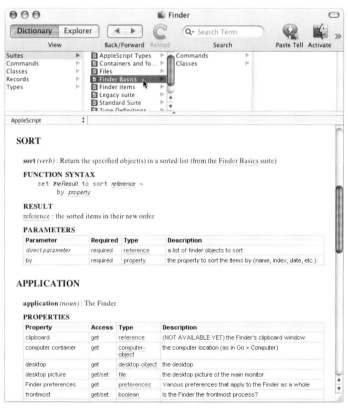

FIGURE 13.24
The dictionary browser in Script Debugger 4.

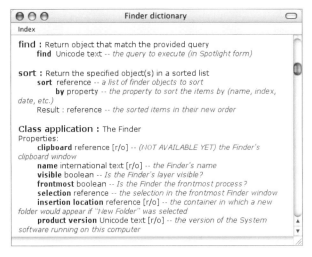

FIGURE 13.25 The dictionary viewer in Smile 3.

Application Preferences

You control several aspects of Script Editor's behavior and appearance using its Preferences window. Open the window by choosing Preferences from the Script Editor menu.

General Preferences

The General preference pane, shown in Figure 13.26, contains a pop-up menu where you choose the default OSA language. It defaults to AppleScript, but others may be available depending on what products you have installed. You can override the default for any one script by choosing a different language in the script window's navigation bar.

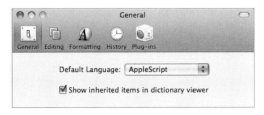

FIGURE 13.26
The General preference pane.

New in Leopard is a General preference setting called "Show inherited items in dictionary viewer." By default, this new setting is off. As a result, when you look at the dictionary entry for a class such as `application`, you see only the elements and properties that belong directly to the `application` class, but you don't see any of the elements and properties that it inherits from the `item` class. You have to remember to look at the `item` class to see the inherited elements and properties. This has proven to be confusing to users over the years, so we recommend you turn this setting on. Then, when you look at the dictionary entry for, say, the `application` class, you will see both its elements and properties and the elements and properties it inherits from the `item` class, each identified according to the class in which it is defined. Figure 13.22, earlier in the chapter, shows the dictionary viewer with this feature turned on.

Turning this setting on or off takes effect only after you quit Script Editor and relaunch it.

Editing Preferences

Use the Editing preference pane, shown in Figure 13.27, to control how script windows wrap and indent lines of script text when you compile a script. If set to wrap lines, you always see every word in every line because long lines wrap around to the next line instead of running beyond the right edge of the window. Indenting wrapped lines by a number of characters reduces the chance you will mistake one long script statement for two or three separate statements.

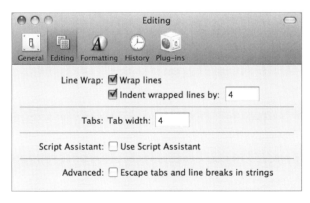

FIGURE 13.27
The Editing preference pane.

You can set the editor to use tabs instead of spaces for indentation and to define the width of a tab in terms of space characters. Turning on the Script Assistant causes Script Editor to suggest terms as you begin to type them. See the "Advanced Features" section for more information about the Script Assistant.

Formatting Preferences

The Formatting preference pane is where you set the font, font size, and font color the dictionary viewer uses for various kinds of syntactical elements in AppleScript, scriptable applications, and scripting additions. The preferences you set here apply to AppleScript formatting throughout the system. If you change a formatting setting here, the same new setting will appear in the preferences of some other script editor, such as Script Debugger or Smile, when you open its preferences.

To change the font and its style and size, select one or more categories in the first column, and then use Script Editor's Font menu to choose a different font, font style, and size, or double-click the category to open the system Font panel. To change the font color, double-click the color swatch in the last column, and choose another color in the system Color palette. The changes take effect immediately in the first column of the Formatting pane. Click Apply to see the new settings take effect in open scripts. The Apply button compiles them and applies the new settings. Click Revert to return to the previous settings. Apple provides some very good defaults, which you can reinstate at any time by clicking Use Defaults.

Figure 13.28 shows the Formatting pane with AppleScript's default settings. (You can't see the colors here because the figure is printed in black and white.)

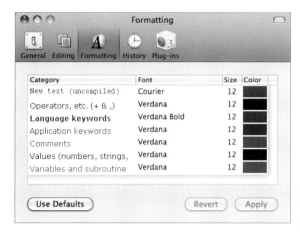

FIGURE 13.28
The Formatting preference pane.

History Preferences

You've already seen the Result pane and the Event Log pane of Script Editor's script window. By setting the options available in the History preference pane, you can keep a collection of recent results and recent event logs to help you track changes in the behavior of a script as you work on it. This is an invaluable aid when debugging your scripts. Figure 13.29 shows the History preference pane.

You enable the history you want to track—results or event logs—by checking one of the boxes, and for each you choose whether to let the history collection continue growing without limit or to restrict it to a fixed number of recent results or event logs.

When the "Log only when visible" setting is unchecked, Script Editor always logs event history, even while the Event Log History window is closed. When it is checked, Script Editor collects event log history only when the Event Log pane is selected in the script window or the Event Log History window is open.

You can run a script with the Result pane selected in the script window to see the overall result of running a script and at the same time examine the most recent event log history in the Event Log History window without running the script again. Without the Event Log History feature, you would have to run the script a second time after selecting the Event Log pane in the script window, because the Event Log pane in the script window is empty if you switch to it after running a script with the Result pane selected, no matter what the setting of "Log only when visible" is.

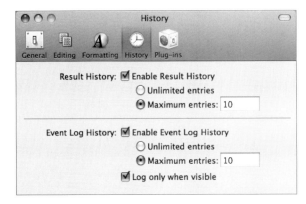

We describe the Result History window and the Event Log History window in the "Advanced Features" section.

Plug-ins Preferences

Figure 13.30 shows the Plug-ins preference pane, displaying one installed third-party Script Editor plug-in. Script Editor comes with a handful of built-in plug-ins, but they aren't listed in the preference pane.

Script Editor supports a plug-in architecture to add new tools to Script Editor. One third-party plug-in for Script Editor is LibrarySE. You can download LibrarySE at `http://scriptbuilders.net/files/libraryseplug inforscripteditor0.9.4.html` (or search for it on the ScriptBuilders site if its version number has changed).

To install a Script Editor plug-in for all users of your computer, drag it to the Script Editor subfolder in the Apple folder of the Library's Application Support folder, at Library > Application Support > Apple > Script Editor. You may have to create the Script Editor folder. Alternatively, install it at the same path in your user Library folder to make it available only to the current user. Next time you launch Script Editor, it will recognize the new plug-in and ask you for permission to enable it, as shown in Figure 13.31.

FIGURE 13.31
The New Plug-in Found dialog.

LibrarySE adds a Library menu to Script Editor's menu bar. This makes it easy to open dictionaries for your favorite scriptable applications directly from a menu, without having to open Script Editor's own Library palette from the Window menu. We describe Script Editor's built-in Library palette in the "Advanced Features" section. The Library menu created by the LibrarySE plug-in appears in Figure 13.32.

FIGURE 13.32
The LibrarySE plug-in's Library menu.

The Contextual Menu

Apple has put to good use the fact that Script Editor is scriptable. Every standard installation of Mac OS X includes a large collection of scripts whose sole purpose is to type standard AppleScript syntax elements into the script window for you. These scripts are available to you in the contextual menu that appears when you click in the script pane of the script window while holding down the Control key or when you click the right button of a two-button mouse. Figure 13.33 shows the contextual menu (yours may differ depending on what software you have installed).

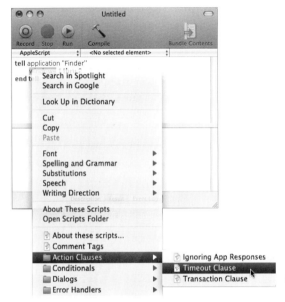

FIGURE 13.33 Script Editor's contextual menu.

These scripts are located in the Script Editor Scripts folder available to all users of the computer, at Library > Scripts > Script Editor Scripts. You open this folder by choosing Open Scripts Folder from the contextual menu. You can edit the provided scripts to customize their behavior. You can even add scripts and subfolders of your own to this folder, using the existing scripts as a model, if you find yourself frequently typing other syntax elements.

The scripts provided by Apple behave a little differently depending on which of them you choose. Some simply paste a few lines of AppleScript text into the script pane at the current insertion point. Others replace selected text with a few lines of AppleScript text. If you haven't selected some text that a script requires you to select, it presents a dialog explaining what you should do. Before doing anything that would destroy existing text, these scripts warn you what will happen. Many of the dialogs include a Help button that opens the Apple Help Viewer. If you don't like what a script did, choose Undo from the Edit menu.

We won't describe all of the provided scripts here, but it is worth spending time on one of the categories to illustrate how they work. Open the others in Script Editor, and examine them to see what they do and how they work.

Repeat Routines

The Repeat Routines submenu in the contextual menu contains four scripts that insert a repeat loop into the script window.

You start by typing a statement that sets a variable to a list, such as:

```
set my_list to {1, 2, 3}
```

Then you select the name of the variable that contains the list of items you want to process—`my_list`, in this example. If you don't select the name of a list variable, select the list itself, including the curly braces enclosing it. Finally, move the mouse over the selected variable name, and click while holding down the Control key to open the contextual menu. Choose the repeat routine you want from the submenu—say, Special Case First & Last—and a complete repeat loop using the selected list variable is immediately inserted into the script at the insertion point. The repeat loop includes a comment within each branch that serves as a placeholder for the statements to be executed in that branch. Replace the placeholders with AppleScript statements, and you're done. Script 13.2 shows the result of the example—everything after the first line was inserted by the contextual menu command:

```
set my_list to {1, 2, 3}
set the item_count to the number of items in my_list
repeat with i from 1 to the item_count
    set this_item to item i of my_list
    if i is 1 then -- first list item
        -- insert actions for: this_item
    else if i is the item_count then -- last list item
        -- insert actions for: this_item
    else -- other list items
        -- insert actions for: this_item
    end if
end repeat
```

SCRIPT 13.2

Advanced Features

We think of a few of Script Editor's features as aiming at more advanced users. We discuss them separately in the following sections.

Library Palette

You saw earlier in this chapter that the File menu includes an Open Dictionary command. After a short pause while it searches the disk, it lists all of your scriptable applications. You then scroll to the application you want and double-click it, or select it and click Open, to open its dictionary. If you prefer, you click Browse and navigate to the application's location to open it. This process is somewhat time-consuming, and it can be annoying if you need to open the same application's dictionary frequently.

Script Editor provides a convenient alternative, the Library palette, shown in Figure 13.34. It is a separate window that you open from Script Editor's Window menu. By default, it lists several scriptable Apple applications. Simply

FIGURE 13.34 The Library palette.

double-click the one you want, or select it and click the Open Dictionary button (it looks like a small stack of books), and its dictionary opens.

A nice feature of the Library palette is the Add Application button (a plus sign). Click it, and a file dialog opens allowing you to navigate to any application or scripting addition and add it to the list. Once it's in the list, you'll never again have to wait for the Open Dictionary dialog to open that application's dictionary.

Select a name in the list, and click the Remove Application button (a minus sign) to remove it.

The New Script button (the standard script emblem) opens a new script window with a prewritten `tell` block addressed to the application selected in the list.

The LibrarySE Script Editor plug-in described in the "Plug-ins Preferences" section earlier includes a palette similar to Script Editor's own Library palette, but the LibrarySE palette includes an additional button in its toolbar to reveal the selected application in the Finder, as shown in Figure 13.35.

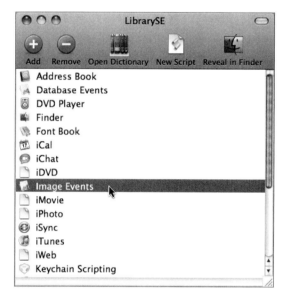

FIGURE 13.35 The LibrarySE plug-in's LibrarySE palette.

Script Assistant

The Script Assistant is a remarkable tool for making it easier to type AppleScript statements into the script pane of the script window. Turn this feature on in the Editing pane of the Preferences window, as described earlier.

The Script Assistant is a *code completion* tool. When it is turned on, any word you start to type in the script pane of Script Editor's script window suddenly offers to type the rest of itself, if Script Editor recognizes it as the beginning of a valid AppleScript term.

Script Editor signals that it has recognized what you might be typing by adding an ellipsis character (three dots). When you see the ellipsis, press the Escape or F5 key on your keyboard or choose Complete from the Edit menu to see a pop-up menu of possible completed terms. Figure 13.36 shows the contextual menu after you type **add**. Then select the term you want by clicking it, or use the up and down arrows to select the next or previous term, and press the Return key. The term you select is immediately typed into the script window. If you don't want to bother with automatic code completion, just keep typing. The ellipsis disappears, and the characters you type take its place.

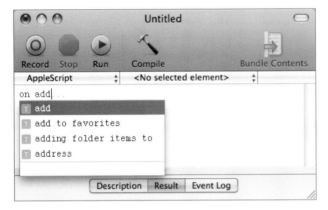

FIGURE 13.36 The contextual menu after typing *add* and pressing the F5 key.

If there is only one possible completion, Script Editor types it in automatically, in dimmed characters, instead of presenting an ellipsis. If you keep typing, the dimmed characters disappear, and the characters you type appear in their place. But if the dimmed characters were exactly what you wanted, simply press the Escape or F5 key, or choose Complete from the Edit menu—they immediately turn dark, and the insertion point jumps to the end of them.

Result History and Event Log History

Depending on the options you set in the History preference pane discussed earlier, you can collect recent results and recent event logs to help you track changes in the behavior of a script as you work on it. This is a powerful debugging tool. Run a script every time you edit it, and then compare the latest result or event log to previous results or event logs.

You open the Result History window and the Event Log History window by choosing them from Script Editor's Window menu. Figure 13.37 shows the Result Log History window, and Figure 13.38 shows the Event Log History window. Simply select the instance you want to examine, and its contents appear to the right. Click Clear History to clear all instances. Click Show Script to return to the script whose history you are examining.

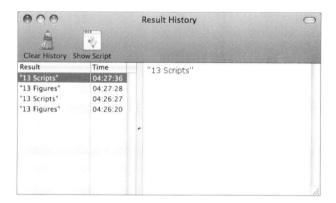

FIGURE 13.37 The Result History window.

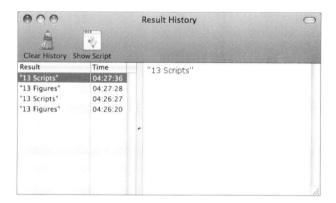

FIGURE 13.38 The Event Log History window.

The Script Editor Application Service

Script Editor provides services to other applications through the Services submenu in the application menu of most applications.

Open any application's application menu—for example, the TextEdit menu in TextEdit—and a few lines down you see the Services submenu. One of the items in it is another submenu named Script Editor. The Script Editor menu contains three commands: Get Result of AppleScript, Make New AppleScript, and Run as AppleScript.

To use any of these three commands, first select one or more lines of text in any text-based application, such as TextEdit. The selected lines should contain valid AppleScript statements.

The Get Result of AppleScript command runs the selected script and replaces the selected text with the result returned by the script. This is a convenient way to do arithmetic in any text editor that supports Services. Type this script into a TextEdit window: **234/16 * pi**. Then select it, and choose Get Result of AppleScript from the Script Editor menu in TextEdit's Services submenu. The selected script is immediately replaced with the number `45.945792558751`.

The Run as AppleScript command also runs a selected script, but it does not change the selected text. Instead, it is useful for running a script that causes some action to occur. For example, instead of using the Finder to navigate to the AppleScript Utility application and launch it, you could simply type **run application "AppleScript Utility"**, select it, and then choose Run as AppleScript from the Services submenu. Note that the quotation marks must be the straight quotation marks expected by AppleScript.

The Make New AppleScript command opens a Script Editor window and pastes the selected text into it. This command does not honor the Default Script Editor setting in AppleScript Utility. It always opens Script Editor.

URL Protocol Support

Script Editor supports Apple's URL Protocol Messaging. It enables you to embed a script in a Web page or in a PDF document in such a way that a reader can click a link to transfer the text of the script directly into Script Editor. This makes it easy to set up Web sites or PDF documents that contain sample AppleScript code for instructional purposes.

Without support for URL Protocol Messaging, the only way for a reader to test a published script is to copy it from the Web page or the PDF document and paste it into Script Editor. Unfortunately, this process often omits required characters or incorporates illegal characters, and the script won't compile. If the script is instead embedded in the Web page or PDF document, the reader simply clicks the link, and the script is automatically pasted into a Script Editor window in proper syntactical form.

URL Protocol Messaging presents no greater security issues than copying and pasting the text of any published script, such as the example scripts on the Web site for this book. The embedded script is not executed until you take affirmative steps to compile and run it, which is equally true if you paste a script from this book's Web site into Script Editor. This means you can take all the time you need to study the text of the script to be sure it is safe before you use it.

Each link contains four sections: the *URL protocol* or scheme, the *application address*, the *action tag*, and the *script tag*. Here's an example:

```
applescript://com.apple.scripteditor?action=new&script=beep
```

The URL protocol is `applescript`. It is separated from the rest of the URL by the familiar colon followed by two slashes, `://`. This protocol is registered with the system. Any link whose URL begins with this protocol is passed to Script Editor for processing.

The application address is an application identifier, such as `com.apple. scripteditor`. Because the application address is specific to one application, URL Protocol Messaging ignores the Default Script Editor setting in AppleScript Utility.

The action tag specifies one of three actions, using the form *action=action type*. The three supported actions are new, to create a new script window containing the script in the script tag; insert, to insert the script into the frontmost script window at the insertion point; and append, to insert the script at the end of the script in the frontmost script window. Use a question mark to separate the application address from the action tag. It looks like this:

```
?action=insert
```

The script tag should be a valid AppleScript script, using the form *script=encoded text*. Special characters such as carriage returns and tabs must be encoded using standard URL encoding, such as %0D for a return character. The & character must separate the action tag and the script tag. For example, the script statement display dialog "Hello" would be set up like this, using %20 for space characters and %22 for straight quotation marks:

```
&script=display%20dialog%20%22Hello!%22
```

Scripting Script Editor

No discussion of Script Editor would be complete without noting that it is itself scriptable, as mentioned earlier. Script Editor implements the AppleScript Standard Suite and Text Suite, as well as a special Script Editor Suite that allows you to control key features of Script Editor. With AppleScript, you can instruct Script Editor to compose or even record custom scripts for you, to check their syntax, to compile them and run them, and to save them to disk. You can also use AppleScript to learn what language was used to write an existing script and whether the language supports compiling or recording.

Apple has made good use of Script Editor's scriptability in Script Editor's contextual menu, as described in "The Contextual Menu" section. A number of scripts in the Script Editor Scripts submenu of the Scripts folder in your local Library folder are addressed directly to Script Editor.

What's Next?

In this chapter, you learned almost everything there is to know about using Script Editor to write, edit, debug, compile, and run your scripts. In the next chapter, you'll learn about a newer application for use with AppleScript, AppleScript Utility.

14

Lesson 14
AppleScript Utility

Mac OS X 10.4 (Tiger) introduced a new application, AppleScript Utility, to collect in one central location several system settings that are relevant to AppleScript. It includes an important new feature, the Default Script Editor setting. The other settings available in AppleScript Utility were (and still are) scattered in various locations, but AppleScript Utility now lets you see and set all of them in a single window for convenience. Best of all, in Leopard AppleScript Utility has become scriptable!

AppleScript Utility is located in the AppleScript folder in your top-level Applications folder. Double-click it to launch it, or choose Open AppleScript Utility from the Script menu. Figure 14.1 shows the main application window.

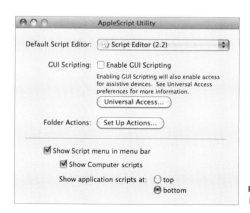

FIGURE 14.1 The AppleScript Utility window.

Default Script Editor

Script Editor has been a standard part of the Mac OS since AppleScript was invented. Although some third-party applications have performed similar functions for almost as long, the Mac OS has until recently behaved as if Script Editor were the only option for editing and debugging scripts.

Now, with AppleScript Utility, you can set any script editor you like to be the default script editor, and the system honors your choice in appropriate ways in many circumstances. For example, when you double-click a script file, the Finder opens it in whatever script editor you have designated as your default script editor. In addition, when an error occurs in a running applet, the Edit button in the error alert, shown in Figure 14.2, opens the script in whatever application you've designated as the default script editor. This is convenient if you prefer to work in a third-party script editor all the time but you frequently use scripts that may have been created using another script editor.

FIGURE 14.2 A bad applet's error alert, with an Edit button. The offending script opens for editing in the default script editor when you click the Edit button.

The most commonly used third-party script editors in Mac OS X are Script Debugger from Late Night Software and Smile from Satimage. Both of them appear along with Apple's Script Editor in the Default Script Editor pop-up menu, if they are installed on your computer, as shown in Figure 14.3.

In addition, the Select command at the bottom of the pop-up menu lets you choose any other third-party editor. The applications that the Select command lets you choose are text editors, for the most part, although you can choose some other applications, such as FileMaker Pro. However, if you choose an application that is not designed to handle the AppleScript statements in a script, you will likely be disappointed. When the script opens in one of these applications, you will probably see mostly garbage (in TextEdit, for example), or you might be warned that the application can't handle the file (in FileMaker Pro, for example).

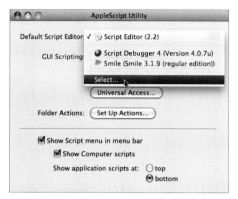

FIGURE 14.3 The Default Script Editor pop-up menu in AppleScript Utility.

Third-party applications that are not themselves script editors can be designed to honor the user's choice of a default script editor. For example, PreFab UI Browser from PreFab Software, which was written by one of the authors (Bill Cheeseman), "sends" automatically generated AppleScript statements directly into a script editor's window. When running under Leopard or Mac OS X 10.4 (Tiger), it uses the default script editor you chose in AppleScript Utility unless you choose a different script editor in UI Browser's Preferences. A free 30-day trial version of UI Browser is available for download at `http://prefabsoftware.com/uibrowser/`. Figure 14.4 shows the relevant portion of UI Browser's Preferences window.

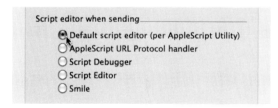

FIGURE 14.4 A section of the AppleScript pane in the PreFab UI Browser Preferences window.

GUI Scripting

GUI Scripting is a special form of AppleScript introduced as a standard part of the system in Mac OS X 10.3 (Panther). It allows you to script unscriptable applications by controlling their UI elements, such as buttons and menu items. See Chapter 28, *GUI Scripting*, for more information about it.

You must enable GUI Scripting before you can use it, because Mac OS X leaves it disabled by default. To enable it manually, check the Enable GUI Scripting checkbox in AppleScript Utility. You can leave it turned on all the time unless you have unusual security concerns.

Enabling GUI Scripting does the same thing that the "Enable access for assistive devices" setting in the Universal Access pane of System Preferences does. GUI Scripting is based on Apple's accessibility technology, as are assistive applications for disabled persons. Turning on one of these settings is the same as turning on the other, and the settings in AppleScript Utility and the Universal Access pane are synchronized. Although a button in AppleScript Utility launches System Preferences and opens its Universal Access pane for you, there is no reason to do this unless you need the other features available in Universal Access.

GUI Scripting can also be turned on automatically using AppleScript. See the "Scripting AppleScript Utility" section later in this chapter and Chapter 28, *GUI Scripting*, for details.

Folder Actions

Folder actions were originally a classic Mac OS technology, but they were introduced into Mac OS X in Mac OS X 10.2 (Jaguar). A folder action allows you to "attach" scripts to a folder in the Finder. The scripts are triggered automatically whenever files and other Finder items are added to the folder or removed from it and whenever changes are made to the folder's window. See Chapter 21, *Folder Actions*, for more information about this feature.

AppleScript Utility's Set Up Actions button launches the Folder Actions Setup application for you. This is convenient if you have AppleScript Utility open. If you don't, you can launch Folder Actions Setup by choosing Configure Folder Actions from the Folder Actions submenu in the Script menu or from the Finder contextual menu, or you can launch it simply by double-clicking Folder Actions Setup in Applications > AppleScript > Folder Actions Setup.

Script Menu

The Script menu is an optional global menu, located in the Menu Extras area at the right end of the menu bar. It lists all the scripts that are stored in the Scripts folder in the current user's Library folder and, optionally, the local Library folder available to all users of the computer. You can run any of these scripts simply by choosing them in the Script menu, even if they are compiled scripts instead of applets. If you prefer to store your scripts in other folders, you can place aliases to them in either of these Scripts folders to make them appear in the Script menu. To activate the Script menu, check the "Show Script menu in menu bar" checkbox in AppleScript Utility.

The main purpose of the Script menu is to give you a convenient way to run scripts that you use frequently, in your day-to-day work. You can create as many folders as you like in either of the Scripts folders to organize your scripts according to specific projects or tasks. Doing this will cause the Script menu to organize them in submenus named for these folders. Double-click any of the submenus to open its folder. Holding down a modifier key while choosing a script in the Script menu helps you manage your scripts. The Option key opens the script in your default script editor; the Shift key reveals the script in the Finder.

The local Scripts folder is referred to as the "Computer" Scripts folder in Leopard; it was called the "Library" Scripts folder in Mac OS X 10.4 (Tiger). In both cases, it refers to the Scripts folder located in the local domain at Library > Scripts. It is created for you when you install Mac OS X, and it is populated with a number of example scripts. The user Scripts folder, unlike the local Scripts folder, is not created when you first install Mac OS X, but you can easily use the Finder to create it yourself in your user Library folder. If you don't, it is created for you automatically the first time you choose Open User Scripts Folder from the Open Scripts Folder menu item in the Script menu.

A subsidiary checkbox in AppleScript Utility, "Show Computer scripts" ("Show Library scripts" in Tiger), allows you to add the scripts that are in the local Scripts folder to the Script menu. If this checkbox is not selected, the Script menu lists only those scripts that are in the user Scripts folder. When it is checked, the local scripts are grouped near the top of the menu, and the user scripts are grouped beneath them. Scripts in the local Scripts folder are available to all users of the computer. However, as long as this folder contains nothing but the Apple example scripts, you might prefer to leave the "Show Computer scripts" setting unchecked.

AppleScript Utility also allows you to choose whether so-called application scripts appear at the top or the bottom of the Script menu. This choice applies only if you have created a special folder named Applications in your user Scripts folder (it doesn't work in the local Scripts folder). You can use the Finder to create this special Applications folder if it doesn't already exist. You create subfolders in this Applications folder and name them after applications. Any scripts placed in one of these subfolders appear in the Script menu only when the corresponding application is active. This helps control the size of the Script menu if you've installed a lot of scripts in it. The scripts appear in a separate group, near the top of the Script menu or at its bottom, under a dimmed heading identifying the application (such as "Finder Scripts" or "TextEdit Scripts"). Figure 14.5 shows an example of this feature in use. This useful feature allows you to have an application-specific script menu even for applications that don't implement a Script menu themselves.

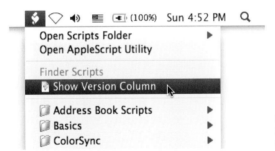

FIGURE 14.5 Part of the Script menu showing Finder Scripts near the top.

Another useful consequence of creating an Applications folder in the user Scripts folder is that the Open Scripts Folder menu item at the top of the Script menu acquires a new submenu, in addition to Open Computer Scripts Folder and Open User Scripts Folder. The third submenu allows you to open the Scripts Folder for the frontmost application, which makes it easy to add new scripts to it. This menu creates the application-specific folder for you automatically in the special Applications folder if it doesn't yet exist. For example, if you have created an Applications folder in your user Scripts folder, then whenever the Finder is active, the third submenu in the Open Scripts Folder menu item is Open Finder Scripts Folder—even if you haven't yet created a folder called "Finder" in the Applications folder.

Scripting AppleScript Utility

In Leopard, AppleScript Utility is itself now scriptable. Here's its dictionary:

```
application n [inh. item] : the AppleScript Utility application
    properties
    default script editor (file) : the editor to be used to open
        scripts
    GUI Scripting enabled (boolean) : Are GUI Scripting events
        currently being processed?
    application scripts position (top/bottom) : the position in
        the Script menu at which the application scripts are
        displayed
    Script menu enabled (boolean) : Is the Script menu installed in
        the menu bar?
    show Computer scripts (boolean) : Are the Computer scripts
        shown in the Script menu?
```

The most exciting aspect of the dictionary is that none of these properties is read-only. Using a script addressed to AppleScript Utility, you can now, in Leopard, set any script editor to be the default script editor, turn on GUI Scripting without having to tell the user to turn it on manually, and configure the Scripts menu in the menu bar.

Script 14.1 is an example that turns on the Script menu. Before running it, launch AppleScript Utility, uncheck the "Show Script menu in menu bar" setting, and leave the AppleScript Utility window where you can see it. If you watch the screen closely, you will see the checkbox become checked and the Script menu appear in the menu bar the moment you run the script.

```
tell application "AppleScript Utility"
    set Script menu enabled to true
end tell
```

SCRIPT 14.1

We'll say more about turning on GUI Scripting via AppleScript in Chapter 28, *GUI Scripting*, and provide some example GUI Scripting scripts.

What's Next?

This chapter covered the use of AppleScript Utility to change various system settings having to do with AppleScript. In the next chapter, you'll start learning about essential scripting topics having to do with the AppleScript language— features of AppleScript and various scripting additions that weren't dealt with in Part I, *Instant AppleScript*, but that are nevertheless essential to practical scripting in the real world.

15

Basics

Data Persistence

What's Next?

Lesson 15
Script Properties

You already know that many application objects in AppleScript have properties. A Finder `disk` object has `capacity` and `free space` properties; an `outgoing message` object in Mail has `content`, `sender`, and `subject` properties; and a Safari `document` object has `source` and `text` properties. These properties have in common the ability to provide information to your scripts and, in many cases, to change application behavior and to store information from your scripts in a persistent way.

In AppleScript, you can think of a script as just another object, and it can have properties, too. The difference is that you define a script's properties yourself and give them any name you like. When you `set` a property in a script to a value or `copy` a value to a script property, the value is saved as data in the script. You can retrieve the value later in the same script, and you can even retrieve it after the script quits by running the script again. Data stored in a script's properties is persistent; that is, AppleScript saves the data in the script itself. Script properties are similar to the global variables you learned about in Chapter 8, *Data Containers, Operators, and Coercions*, but they are specially designed to be useful for storing and accessing persistent data.

In this chapter, you will learn how to use the unique features of script properties, especially data persistence.

Basics

Script properties have a lot in common with variables. You learned about variables in Chapter 8, *Data Containers, Operators, and Coercions*. You define a variable in a script by name; you **set** a variable to a value or **copy** a value to a variable, which your script can retrieve while it is running; and you can give a variable local or global scope.

You can perform all of these actions with properties, too, except that they are global to the script as a whole. You use a property in a script in the same way you use a global variable, with two important differences. First, you always declare a property with an initial value. Second, if your script changes a property's initial value, you can retrieve the changed value every time you run the script.

You define a property by using the key word **property** followed by a unique name, a colon, and an initial value. You retrieve its current value by including its name in a statement. Script 15.1 is a simple example.

```
property version : "1.0"
display dialog "This script is at version " & version
```
SCRIPT 15.1

You can't declare a property just anywhere in a script. For example, you can't declare a property in a subroutine handler, which you will learn about in the next chapter. Script 15.2 won't compile:

```
beep_twice()


to beep_twice()
property beep_count: 2 --> BAD SYNTAX
beep beep_count
end
```
SCRIPT 15.2

The next example, Script 15.3, won't compile, either, because you can't declare a property inside a **tell** block.

```
tell app "Finder"
property front_window: window 1 --> BAD SYNTAX
return front_window
end
```
SCRIPT 15.3

A property is customarily defined at the beginning of a script, but it doesn't have to be. Properties can be defined after other statements, as long as they are at the top level of the script and not in a subroutine handler or `tell` block, and they don't have to be grouped together. One reason they are often defined at the beginning of a script is that they are given initial values. Anyone studying a script will likely understand how it works more easily if all the initial values are listed at the beginning. It may be easier to understand more complex scripts, however, if properties are defined in groups, at the beginning of each section of the script where they are used. Script 15.4 shows this technique.

```
property version : "1.0"
display dialog "This script is at version " & version


property run_count : 0
set run_count to run_count + 1
if run_count is 1 then
    set count_string to "once"
else if run_count is 2 then
    set count_string to "twice"
else
    set count_string to (run_count as string) & " times"
end if
display dialog "This script has been run " & count_string
```
SCRIPT 15.4

Script 15.4 illustrates several other features of properties. A property may be initialized to an "empty" value. In this case, the `run_count` property is set to `0` initially. You change the value of a property by using the `set` command or the `copy` command, just as you do with variables. In this case, the run_count property is incremented by adding 1 to its initial value.

The most important feature of properties, however, is that the new value persists. The first time you run Script 15.4 and click past its first dialog, it displays the run count as "once," as shown in Figure 15.1. The second time you run it, it displays the run count as "twice." The third time, it displays the run count as "3 times," as shown in Figure 15.2. The run_count property retains its value between executions of the script. The current value is saved in memory when the script quits, and it will still be there the next time you run it.

FIGURE 15.1 Displaying the run_count property after the first run.

FIGURE 15.2 Displaying the run_count property after the third run.

> **NOTE** ▶ Every time you recompile a script, its properties' values are erased. The first time you run a script after editing it, the properties are initialized to their defined initial values.

The persistence of properties implies that the initial value is set only the first time the script is run. When it is run again, AppleScript sees that the property already has a value and does not reinitialize it. This is true even if the script changes the initial value after initialization; the changed value is saved and reused when the script is run again. For more details about persistence, see the next section, "Data Persistence."

Properties can be initialized to any type of data supported by AppleScript or by a scriptable application. The example in Script 15.5 uses a list. Notice that the list is initialized to an empty list.

```
property my_list : {}
set end of my_list to time string of (current date)
return my_list
--> after 3 runs, returns: {"6:47:00 AM", "6:47:02 AM", "6:47:04 AM"}
```
SCRIPT 15.5

The next example, Script 15.6, uses a Finder window reference. Although script properties can't be defined within a `tell` block, you can define a property by initializing it to an application property outside a `tell` block by including a reference to the application, as long as it is a simple reference.

```
property front_window : window 1 of application "Finder"
tell application "Finder" to return front_window
```
SCRIPT 15.6

The first time it is run, Script 15.6 assigns to the `front_window` property a Finder reference to the current front window, assuming at least one Finder window was open at the time. If you run it again after bringing some other Finder window to the front, the script still returns a Finder reference to the window that was frontmost the first time you ran the script, because property values are persistent.

As with variables, you can reset a property to another type of value after it is initialized. In the next example, Script 15.7, the `rank` property is initialized to an integer but is then set to a string.

```
property rank : 1
if rank is 1 then set rank to "first class"
display dialog "Mac software is " & rank
```
SCRIPT 15.7

Initializing a property to an empty list or an empty string is a commonly used technique when a property is intended to hold a type of data that doesn't have a convenient or meaningful "empty" value, or whose type is not yet known. Script 15.8 shows this technique.

```
property full_name : {}
set full_name to "Benjamin Franklin"
return last word of full_name
--> returns: "Franklin"
```
SCRIPT 15.8

Data Persistence

You will sometimes hear even experienced scripters say that properties are persistent while variables are not. Don't believe everything you're told, even if the speaker has sterling credentials. Use Script 15.9 to see for yourself that both property values and global variable values persist after a script quits and is rerun.

```
global global_variable
display dialog "Type a word:" default answer ""
set answer to text returned of result
if answer is not "" then
    set global_variable to answer
end if
display dialog global_variable
```
SCRIPT 15.9

Run Script 15.9, and type a word—say, **abracadabra**. Because your answer is not an empty string, the script sets the value of the global variable my_variable to abracadabra and displays it. Then the script quits. Run the script a second time, but don't type anything; leave the text field empty, and just click OK. Like magic, the script displays "abracadabra" again. Clearly, this evidence proves that global variables are persistent.

This doesn't mean you should use global variables when persistence is what you want. As the previous example shows, you have to be careful to initialize the global variable only when it doesn't yet have a value. Otherwise, the variable will be reinitialized every time you run the script, and the value will not be persistent, as a practical matter. Properties discriminate between their uninitialized and initialized states automatically, without requiring you to write any special initialization statements. They are just plain easier to use when you're writing a script.

Local variables are not persistent. Try the same experiment with Script 15.10, and see for yourself. The second time you run the script, typing nothing, you get an error message telling you that the local variable is not defined.

```
local local_variable
display dialog "Type a word:" default answer ""
set answer to text returned of result
if answer is not "" then
    set local_variable to answer
end if
display dialog local_variable
```
SCRIPT 15.10

There are degrees of data persistence, with respect to properties and global variables alike. In your experiments until now, you have probably run and rerun the previous examples in Script Editor, without closing the scripts between runs. If you close the global variable example and then open it and run it again in Script Editor without typing a word, you will discover that the value of the global variable set in the first run has disappeared. In other words, it did not persist after the script was closed. If you run the example using properties, as shown in Script 15.11, you will see the same behavior.

```
property my_property : ""
display dialog "Type a word:" default answer ""
set answer to text returned of result
if answer is not "" then
    set my_property to answer
end if
display dialog my_property
```
SCRIPT 15.11

If, however, you copy the global variable example and the property example into your local Scripts folder and run them from the Script menu, you will discover they are persistent. This is also true if you run them in one of the popular third-party script editors, such as Script Debugger from Late Night Software. If you compile and save the examples as applets using Script Editor or another editor, they are also persistent when you run them in the Finder. The bottom line is that it is a script's execution environment that determines whether global variable and property values are persistent after a script is closed. If they are, then the values are stored to disk, and they will even persist after you shut down your computer and restart it.

An important moral of this chapter is that when writing a script that depends upon persistence, you must be sure to use properties or, if it's convenient, global variables. If the script requires persistence even after a script quits or the computer is restarted, test it in the environment where it will be used and, if necessary, document that values will not persist in some circumstances when it is used in other environments.

Another moral applies only when you are distributing your scripts to others in the form of applets. If you want them to start out fresh the first time they are run on another machine, be sure to compile them just before you distribute them, *and don't run them after you compile them*. If you don't follow this advice, any global variable or property value that was changed when you ran the applet will persist the first time somebody else runs a copy installed on another computer. Depending on the nature of the applet, this could result in an embarrassing breach of confidentiality.

What's Next?

In this chapter, you learned about properties, data containers within a script that allow you to save information for the next time the script is run. In the next chapter, you will learn about subroutine handlers, which allow you to break a complex script into smaller pieces that make it easier to organize a script. Subroutines can also be used and reused within a script to make it smaller and more understandable.

16

Lesson **16**
Subroutines

Anytime a script you're working on starts to get long and complicated, you should think about using *subroutines*. Subroutines are also sometimes referred to as *subroutine handlers* or, simply, *handlers*.

In this chapter, we'll explain subroutines and demonstrate them using a single, long script. The script is fun to use if you have a lot of songs in your iTunes library. It asks you for a "theme"—a word or phrase that might be found in the titles of several of your songs, such as *love* or *crazy*—and creates a new playlist in iTunes gathering them together for easy listening. Alternatively, it creates a text file listing them, saves it to disk, and opens it for your examination.

We'll start with the basics: what a subroutine is, how a subroutine works, and why you should use subroutines. After covering the basics, we'll use the iTunes script to explain by example exactly how subroutines are implemented and used. Finally, we'll explain some of the more complicated aspects of subroutines.

What Is a Subroutine?

A subroutine is a group of AppleScript statements enclosed in a block begin-ning with the keyword on or to and a name identifying the handler. It some-times includes one or more parameters. The block ends with the end keyword followed by the name of the handler. Compiling the script automatically adds the name of the handler after end to help you recognize it when you're looking at the end instead of the beginning of a long handler.

A subroutine is usually fairly short, performing a relatively simple function that is easily encapsulated in a few statements. It is often designed to return a value, but it doesn't have to do so. Script 16.1 is a simple example:

```
on get_input()
    display dialog ("Create or view a playlist of all the tunes") ¬
        & (" in your iTunes library having a common theme.") ¬
        & return & return ¬
        & ("Enter the theme as a word or phrase:") ¬
        default answer "" buttons {"Cancel", "View", "Create"} ¬
        default button "Create"
    return result
end get_input
```
SCRIPT 16.1

The get_input subroutine does what the handler's name suggests. It presents a dialog, using the display dialog command, asking you to type a word or phrase to search for in your iTunes library, and then it returns the result of the command. As you know, the result of the display dialog command when used to get textual input is usually a record containing two properties, the text returned and the button returned.

You could certainly get by without making this a separate subroutine in your script and instead simply call the display dialog command directly in the main body. When you're developing a long script, however, moving the user input statements into a separate subroutine makes it easier to make changes later. For example, you might decide to present a series of dialogs to get more information from the user, concatenate all the answers into a single record, and return that to the caller. If you've started out by making user input a separate subroutine, the only thing you'll have to do later to enhance the script is to make changes to the `get_input` subroutine—and, of course, add statements to use the additional information.

How Does a Subroutine Work?

A subroutine does not run by itself when you run the script. If you typed the `get_input` subroutine into a script, compiled it, and then ran it, nothing would happen, and you would never see the dialog.

Instead, a subroutine runs only when the main script or another subroutine *calls* it by name, passing along any parameters it requires. When it is called, a subroutine executes the statements it contains and returns any return value to the *caller*. Execution then returns to the statement immediately following the call to the subroutine. The caller might use the return value as input to some other command or to set a variable. Script 16.2 contains the same `get_input` subroutine you saw earlier, but it adds commands at the beginning of the script, in its main body, that call the subroutine and display the name of the button you chose.

```
get_input()
display dialog "You chose " & button returned of result


on get_input()
    display dialog ("Create or view a playlist of all the tunes") ¬
        & (" in your iTunes library having a common theme.") ¬
        & return & return ¬
        & ("Enter the theme as a word or phrase:") ¬
        default answer "" buttons {"Cancel", "View", "Create"} ¬
        default button "Create"
    return result
end get_input
```
SCRIPT 16.2

Thus, a script with subroutines consists of two parts, the main body of the script and one or more subroutines. It makes no difference whether the subroutines are placed before or after the main body, but it is common to put the subroutines at the end so that the first thing you see when you look at a script is its main body where the overall logic of the script is located.

The main body of a script is often called an *implicit run handler*, because it is run automatically when you run the script, just as if it were a real *run* handler.

Why Use Subroutines?

There are at least three good reasons to use subroutines.

One reason is to make it easier to understand a long script. Without subroutines, a long script is a monotonous, sometimes mind-boggling flow of commands handling every detail of execution step-by-step from start to finish. With subroutines, by contrast, the main body of a script can be very short, using descriptive names to call handlers located elsewhere in the script that do the actual work. To understand the overall logic of the script, you need only to read its main body. If you've chosen descriptive names for your subroutines, the logic of the script will be very clear from reading the main body alone.

Another reason to use subroutines is that they allow you to isolate all the statements relating to a particular operation in one place, where it is easy to focus on them. If you want to understand smaller pieces of the script's logic, you don't have to read through its main body; instead, you just read the appropriate handler, where all of that specific functionality is located.

A third reason to use subroutines is that they let you condense a repeated operation into a single set of statements that you have to write only once. Instead of retyping the same statements over and over again at various places in the script, you write them once in a subroutine and call the subroutine repeatedly from the main body of the script. This has many advantages. It is easier on you, it reduces the risk of errors in retyping the statements numerous times, and it shortens the script. It makes debugging, maintenance, and revisions much easier, too, because you have to make a change in only one place before testing it everywhere.

An Example Using iTunes

Almost by definition, subroutines require a long and complex example to illustrate their use. In the iTunes script described here, starting with Script 16.3, we'll start by discussing the main body of the script. It is a short series of statements describing the overall logic of the script. The main body begins by getting user input. Most of the remaining statements in the main body call subroutines implemented later in the script to do all the work. The rest of the statements in the main body are control statements determining which subroutines are called based on the user's input. This is a typical design pattern for scripts that use subroutines.

Calling Subroutines

To understand the benefits of subroutines, look at the main body of the iTunes script, Script 16.3. You should be able to figure out what the script does and how it works from just reading this once over lightly.

```
set the input to get_input()
set the theme to the text returned of the input
set the action to the button returned of the input

set the library_ref to init_library()

set the ID_list to find_IDs for the theme
if the ID_list is not {} then
    if the action is "Create" then
        make_playlist out of the ID_list
    else
        get_tunes from the ID_list
        present_playlist for the result
    end if
end if
```

SCRIPT 16.3

First, the script asks you for a theme, calling the `get_input` subroutine you saw earlier. Once you've typed a word or phrase into the dialog and clicked a button to dismiss it, execution jumps from the subroutine back to the next statement in the main body, where the script stores the two entries from the `dialog reply` record into two global variables, `theme` and `action`, for later use.

Then, the main body calls another subroutine, `init_library`, and stores its return value into another global variable, `library_ref`. You will see how the `init_library` subroutine works in a moment. For now, it is enough to tell you that it obtains a reference to your iTunes library. The `library_ref` global variable will be used in other subroutines for several purposes, such as to specify where the script should search for songs having the specified theme. Because it is used pervasively in many subroutines, it is easier to get its value in every subroutine where it's needed as a global variable, instead of passing it into each subroutine as a parameter.

Finally, you get to the guts of the main body. You can readily see that the next group of statements starts by finding the unique IDs for all of the songs in your library that match the theme you requested (`find_IDs for the theme`). The `find_IDs` subroutine returns a list of ID numbers and stores it in another global variable, `ID_list`. It starts with this step because both branches of the next group of statements require the list of IDs. After making sure the list is not empty, the next group of statements uses an `if` test to choose one of two branches, calling appropriate subroutines depending on the button you clicked. If you clicked Create, the first branch makes a playlist containing all of the songs whose IDs are contained in the `ID_list` variable, calling `make_playlist out of the ID_list`. If you clicked View, the `else` branch does two things. First, it gets the songs for each ID stored in `ID_list`, calling `get_tunes from the ID_list`. Second, it presents them to you by calling `present_playlist for the result`.

Examining the main body hasn't told you any details about how each subroutine performs its task. For example, you don't know what's in the `ID_list` variable or how it is presented to you. But you do have a clear idea of the tasks the script performs, the order in which it performs them, and the user choices to which it responds.

Implementing Subroutines

Now let's turn to the subroutines to see exactly what they do.

Recall that the first subroutine, `init_library`, returns a reference to your iTunes library. Writing this subroutine requires a little knowledge of how iTunes organizes the data it stores, but you can figure this out by reading the iTunes dictionary. The dictionary tells you that the **application** object in the iTunes Suite contains, among other things, elements called, collectively, **sources**. The dictionary also tells you that every **source** object has a **kind** property and that a source's **kind** can have one of several enumerated values. The dictionary offers a clue as to which kind of source you want to use: you know you want to create a playlist that draws from every song you have, and the dictionary describes the `library playlist` class as the "master music library playlist." Based on our daily use of iTunes and the fact that the first item in iTunes' source listing in the left pane of the main window is Library, we think you want the first kind in the enumeration, the `library` source. Knowing what you know about AppleScript, you can now write the initialization subroutine that gives your script a global reference to your iTunes library. We've started it for you in Script 16.4.

```
on init_library()
    tell application "iTunes"
        get first source whose kind is library
        return first library playlist of result
    end tell
end init_library
```
SCRIPT 16.4 (before revision)

Here's how Script 16.4 works. In AppleScript, elements are lists of objects. Judging by its dictionary, iTunes may contain many different **source** elements, and within any one **source** element there may be many different `library playlist` elements. For this script, we want only one of the **source** elements and only one `library playlist` element within it. At each level, therefore, we get the first object in the relevant list of elements. You usually get an element having a desired property by getting the first item in the list that has a property with that value, and we do that here in the first line when we get the `first source` `whose kind is library`. Some element lists are composed of objects having a variety of subclasses, and an iTunes `library` is such an object. Since we're interested only in a `library playlist` object, we get the first item in the sublist of library sources of the desired subclass in the second line by getting the `first library playlist` of the result.

Now that this subroutine is written, let's take a look at whether we can improve it. To examine it, we don't have to hunt through a long script looking for the lines where we got the library playlist. We had the foresight to break the script into functional subroutines, and we know at a glance that what we want to study is confined to the `init_library` handler. Looking at Script 16.4 and studying the iTunes dictionary, we realize that library playlists can be identified directly by name without searching the two element lists. We therefore remove the two lines that aren't necessary by commenting them out, which is a common way to save them for future reference in case we eventually decide we want to use them, after all. Then we add the single statement that constitutes the new, more efficient version of the subroutine, shown in Script 16.4.

```
on init_library()
    tell application "iTunes"
        --get first source whose kind is library
        --return first library playlist of result
        return playlist "Library"
    end tell
end init_library
```
SCRIPT 16.4 (after revision)

Returning to the main script, the next subroutine that the main body of the script calls is `find_IDs`. In AppleScript, information is often uniquely identified by an identifier, or ID for short. This is often an integer, but it can be a string or any other kind of value that uniquely identifies each item of information. Unique IDs are especially important in applications that deal with data that might include duplicates. "Covers" are common in the music business—we don't mean the artwork on the packaging, but the recording of the same song by many different artists. When searching a database of songs, you want to be sure to get every cover of a masterpiece such as, say, "Shake That Sh**," so you can't use the title to differentiate between songs. In iTunes, as with many applications, the main differentiator is the ID. Here's the subroutine, in Script 16.5.

```
on find_IDs for my_theme
    global library_ref
    tell application "iTunes"
        try
            return database ID ¬
                of every file track of library_ref ¬
                whose name contains my_theme
        on error error_message number error_number
            tell me to report_error of error_message ¬
                given number:error_number
            return {}
        end try
    end tell
end find_IDs
```
SCRIPT 16.5

This is one of several subroutines that need a reference to the global `library_ref` variable that the script initialized at the beginning, so the variable has to be declared as global in this subroutine, as you will see shortly. The subroutine then uses a *filter reference*, or `whose` clause, to quickly find every file track in the library where its name contains the word or phrase you typed into the opening dialog—what we call the *theme*. The theme was set up as a global variable at the beginning of the script, but it is not accessed as a global variable in this subroutine as `library_ref` was. You could write the subroutine to do it that way, but the theme is used in only this one subroutine so the script is easier to understand if you pass it into the subroutine as a variable. We explain how to use the `for` keyword to pass in the variable in a moment. Here, in the subroutine, the parameter is named `my_theme`, which functions inside the subroutine as a local variable.

If there are no songs with this theme in your iTunes library, iTunes generates an error. The `find_IDs` subroutine catches it immediately in the `on error` handler, calls the `report_error` subroutine shown in Script 16.6 to give you the bad news, and returns an empty list. The main body of the script tests whether the returned list is empty and, if so, bypasses all further processing and quits. This is the first example you've seen of a subroutine calling another subroutine. Subroutines can be called from anywhere in a script, including other subroutines.

```
on report_error of error_message given number:error_number
    global theme
    --display dialog error_message & space & error_number
    display dialog ¬
        ("Your iTunes library doesn't contain any tunes") ¬
            & (" with \"") & theme & ("\" in the title.") ¬
        buttons {"OK"} default button "OK"
end report_error
```
SCRIPT 16.6

The `report_error` subroutine does not actually use the `error_message` and `error_number` parameters passed into it. We've left a statement that does use them in the subroutine, but commented it out, to show how you could use them.

Next, if `ID_list` is not empty and you clicked the Create button, the script creates a playlist in iTunes containing all the tracks with the theme you chose. This happens in the `make_playlist` subroutine, Script 16.7. Because this is the last step in the script if you clicked Create, this subroutine is not designed to return a value.

```
on make_playlist out of ID_list
    global theme
    tell application "iTunes"
        activate
        set new_playlist to make new playlist ¬
            with properties {name:(theme & " theme")}
        repeat with tune_ID in ID_list
            tell me to get_location for tune_ID
```

```
        add {result} to new_playlist
      end repeat
    end tell
end make_playlist
```
SCRIPT 16.7

The `make_playlist` subroutine first activates iTunes so you can view and play the new playlist. It then makes the new playlist, naming it by giving it the name of the theme with the suffix `theme`. A new playlist is empty, so it then loops through every ID in the ID list returned by the `find_IDs` subroutine, getting its location as an alias reference and adding it to the new playlist. Once the new playlist appears in the Sources pane in the main iTunes window, you can click it to view all of its tracks and click the Play button to play them.

The `make_playlist` subroutine has another example of a subroutine calling another subroutine. The `get_location` subroutine in Script 16.8 returns the `location` property of the tune having the ID that was passed into the subroutine in the `tune_ID` parameter. The `location` property is an alias reference. The `make_playlist` subroutine places this result in a list before calling the `add` command, because the `add` command requires a list of alias references.

```
on get_location for tune_ID
    global library_ref
    tell application "iTunes"
        return location of first file track of library_ref ¬
            whose database ID is tune_ID
    end tell
end get_location
```
SCRIPT 16.8

If you clicked the View button instead of the Create button, the script calls the `get_tunes` subroutine in Script 16.9. This subroutine uses the `ID_list` passed in as a parameter to get the `name`, `artist`, `album`, and `year` properties of each track having the designated theme. It assembles these into a list of records and returns it to the main body of the script. In the nomenclature of this script, each "tune" is a record containing these four properties.

```
on get_tunes from ID_list
    set return_list to {}
    repeat with this_ID in ID_list
        set this_name to get_name for this_ID
        set this_artist to get_artist for this_ID
        set this_album to get_album for this_ID
        set this_year to get_year for this_ID
        set tune to {name:this_name, artist:this_artist} ¬
            & {album:this_album, year:this_year}
        set end of return_list to tune
    end repeat
    return return_list
end get_tunes
```

SCRIPT 16.9

Each of the properties of a tune is obtained from iTunes using a subroutine on the same model as get_location.

Finally, the present_playlist subroutine in Script 16.10 creates a formatted text file with the vital information (name, album, artist, and year) for each tune having the designated theme, asks you how to save it, saves it in the location and under the name you provide, and opens it in TextEdit so you can read it immediately. It uses the choose file name command and some of the commands in the File Read/Write suite in the Standard Additions scripting addition to do all this.

```
on present_playlist for tune_list
    global theme
    try
        choose file name with prompt ("Save playlist:") ¬
            default name ("iTunes " & theme & " theme.txt") ¬
            default location (path to documents folder)
        set playlist_alias to result
        set file_ref to ¬
            open for access playlist_alias with write permission
        repeat with tune in tune_list
```

```
            write "Tune: " & name of tune ¬
                & return to file_ref
            write "Album: " & album of tune ¬
                & return to file_ref
            write "Artist: " & artist of tune ¬
                & return to file_ref
            write "Year: " & year of tune ¬
                & return to file_ref
            write return to file_ref
        end repeat
        close access file_ref
        tell application "TextEdit"
            activate
            open playlist_alias
        end tell
    on error
        try
            close access file_ref
        end try
    end try
end present_playlist
```

SCRIPT 16.10

The iTunes Script

Script 16.11 presents the entire iTunes script, including subroutines not printed previously.

```
set input to get_input()
set theme to text returned of input
set action to button returned of input


set library_ref to init_library()


set ID_list to find_IDs for theme
```

```
if ID_list is not {} then
    if action is "Create" then
        make_playlist out of ID_list
    else
        get_tunes from ID_list
        present_playlist for result
    end if
end if

on init_library()
    tell application "iTunes"
        --get first source whose kind is library
        --return first library playlist of result
        return playlist "Library"
    end tell
end init_library

on get_input()
    display dialog ("Create or view a playlist of all the tunes") ¬
        & (" in your iTunes library having a common theme.") ¬
        & return & return ¬
        & ("Enter the theme as a word or phrase:") ¬
        default answer "" buttons {"Cancel", "View", "Create"} ¬
        default button "Create"
    return result
end get_input

on find_IDs for my_theme
    global library_ref
    tell application "iTunes"
        try
            return database ID ¬
                of every file track of library_ref ¬
                whose name contains my_theme
        on error error_message number error_number
```

```
            tell me to report_error of error_message ¬
                given number:error_number
            return {}
        end try
    end tell
end find_IDs


on make_playlist out of ID_list
    global theme
    tell application "iTunes"
        activate
        set new_playlist to make new playlist ¬
            with properties {name:(theme & " theme")}
        repeat with tune_ID in ID_list
            tell me to get_location for tune_ID
            add {result} to new_playlist
        end repeat
    end tell
end make_playlist


on get_location for tune_ID
    global library_ref
    tell application "iTunes"
        return location of first file track of library_ref ¬
            whose database ID is tune_ID
    end tell
end get_location


on get_tunes from ID_list
    set return_list to {}
    repeat with this_ID in ID_list
        set this_name to get_name for this_ID
        set this_artist to get_artist for this_ID
        set this_album to get_album for this_ID
        set this_year to get_year for this_ID
```

```
        set tune to {name:this_name, artist:this_artist} ¬
            & {album:this_album, year:this_year}
        set end of return_list to tune
    end repeat
    return return_list
end get_tunes


on get_name for tune_ID
    global library_ref
    tell application "iTunes"
        return name of first file track of library_ref whose database ID
is tune_ID
    end tell
end get_name


on get_artist for tune_ID
    global library_ref
    tell application "iTunes"
        return artist of first file track of library_ref whose database ID
is tune_ID
    end tell
end get_artist


on get_album for tune_ID
    global library_ref
    tell application "iTunes"
        return album of first file track of library_ref whose database ID
is tune_ID
    end tell
end get_album


on get_year for tune_ID
    global library_ref
    tell application "iTunes"
        return year of first file track of library_ref whose database ID
is tune_ID
```

```
        end tell
    end get_year


    on present_playlist for tune_list
        global theme
        try
            choose file name with prompt ("Save playlist:") ¬
                default name ("iTunes " & theme & " theme.txt") ¬
                default location (path to documents folder)
            set playlist_alias to result
            set file_ref to ¬
                open for access playlist_alias with write permission
            repeat with tune in tune_list
                write "Tune: " & name of tune ¬
                    & return to file_ref
                write "Album: " & album of tune ¬
                    & return to file_ref
                write "Artist: " & artist of tune ¬
                    & return to file_ref
                write "Year: " & year of tune ¬
                    & return to file_ref
                write return to file_ref
            end repeat
            close access file_ref
            tell application "TextEdit"
                activate
                open playlist_alias
            end tell
        on error
            try
                close access file_ref
            end try
        end try
    end present_playlist
```

```
on report_error of error_message given number:error_number
    global theme
    --display dialog error_message & space & error_number
    display dialog ("Your iTunes library contains no tunes") ¬
        & (" with \"") & theme & ("\" in the title.") ¬
        buttons {"OK"} default button "OK"
end report_error
```
SCRIPT 16.11

Subroutine Miscellany

You probably noticed that we didn't explain a few things you see in the iTunes script. For example, the get_input and init_library subroutine names are followed by an empty set of parentheses, while the names of all the other subroutines are followed by a variety of phrases beginning with terms such as for, out of, and from. What's that all about? And global variables were declared in some subroutines but not in others. We describe these and other details of subroutines in the following sections.

Labeled vs. Positional Parameters

Subroutines come in two flavors, those with *labeled parameters* and those with *positional parameters*. You are free to use either flavor. The choice is strictly a matter of taste, so you don't have to answer to anybody when you make your choice. Many scripters think labeled parameters make a script easier to understand because they are more English-like, while others think positional parameters are simpler, perhaps because you don't have to think about which label sounds best for a particular subroutine.

When you define a subroutine, you use a *parameter variable* along with the name of the handler and the leading on or to keyword, with or without a label. For example, in the definition of the make_playlist subroutine in the iTunes script, the label was out of and the parameter variable was ID_list. The parameter variable functions as a local variable within the subroutine, representing the value that was passed by the caller to the subroutine in the parameter.

We used one form of labeled parameters for most of the subroutines in the iTunes example. The phrases `for`, `out of`, and `from` are special labels that are built into AppleScript. There are several others, most of which help make a subroutine call look like a plain English sentence if you name the subroutines with one eye on a grammar book. They include `above`, `against`, `around`, `at`, `into`, `onto`, and more than a dozen others. When you use labeled parameters in this way, the order in which you list them is irrelevant as long as each parameter value is matched up with the correct label. There is one exception to this rule: if a subroutine has a direct parameter, its label must be `of` or `in`, and it must come first in the list.

We won't spend much time on the other form of labeled parameters. Basically, all of the parameters as a group, other than the direct parameter, are preceded by the keyword `given`, and each of the following parameters has a descriptive label you make up yourself to fit the circumstances, followed by a colon and the parameter variable. The `report_error` subroutine is the only instance of this form of labeled parameter in the iTunes example.

The other flavor is the positional parameter. In this flavor, all parameters are passed as parameter variables, separated by commas, inside a pair of parentheses. The order of the parameters matters. Subroutines that have no parameters must include the pair of parentheses with nothing contained in them.

When calling a subroutine, the caller must use the same form of parameters as the definition and the same terminology. A special rule applies when calling Boolean parameters. You can use `with` or `without` with the parameter variable in place of the value. The `with` keyword implies true; `without` implies false. Note that optional parameters are not allowed in AppleScript; subroutine calls must include all the defined parameters.

Return Statements

Subroutines return a value using a `return` statement. It can come at the end of the subroutine or in any control statement such as an `if` test. Whenever it is encountered, execution of the subroutine is immediately terminated and jumps to the statement following the call to the subroutine. If a `return` statement returns a value, the value is passed to the next statement; if not, the subroutine returns the value of the last subroutine statement executed, if it returns a value. In the latter case, scripts often ignore the return value.

Global Variables

You can declare global variables in subroutines, as was done in several of the subroutines in the iTunes script. When you do this, the scope of the global variable is limited to that subroutine; that is, it can be used only within the subroutine. This is why you had to re-declare the `library_ref` global variable in several subroutines in the iTunes example. However, when the subroutine refers to its global variable, it gets any value that was given to the global variable earlier in the script's execution. Because `library_ref` was initialized near the beginning of the script with a call to the `init_library` subroutine, all subroutines that declare a `library_ref` global variable get its value as it was initialized at the outset.

Subroutine Calls in tell Statements

When a subroutine is called inside a `tell` statement, you must take care to inform AppleScript that the subroutine call is not addressed to the target of the `tell` statement. You do this by explicitly telling `me` to perform the subroutine, where `me` is a reserved word that means that script (the target of the `tell` block is called `it` to distinguish it from `me`). Alternatively, you can use the reserved word `my` before the subroutine call or `of me` after it. You saw an example of the `tell me` form in the `find_IDs` subroutine, where the `report_error` subroutine was called within a `tell` block addressed to iTunes. Calling the subroutine there without a `tell me` or `my` qualifier would cause an error, because iTunes doesn't recognize a `find_IDs` command.

Pass-by-Reference Parameters

Just as lists, records, dates, and script objects share memory when you use the **set** command instead of the **copy** command to give them a value, so do they share memory when you pass them in a subroutine parameter. This is a powerful feature of subroutines, since it allows you to make changes to the list inside the subroutine, and the changes magically take effect outside the subroutine. But it is all too easy to introduce bugs into your script without meaning to, if you forget this rule.

What's Next?

In this chapter, you learned how to use subroutines to organize your scripts so they are more understandable and easier to maintain, by breaking them into named groups of statements. In the next chapter, you will learn how to work with text using AppleScript.

17

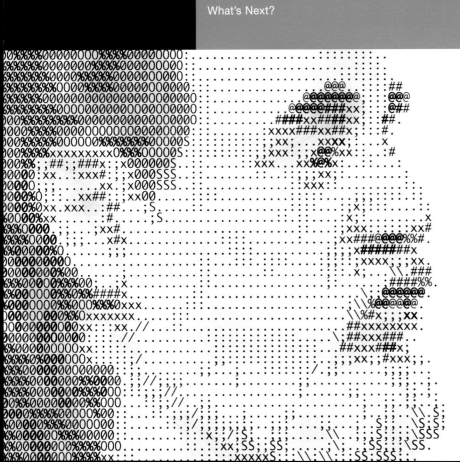

Working with Text

The manipulation of textual data is one of the most common script actions. Nearly every script works with text in some manner, whether it's parsing filenames, creating display messages, or editing word-processing documents. This chapter contains an overview of the standard text tools incorporated into the AppleScript language and how they are used in common practice.

Basics

First of all, what is text? To AppleScript, textual data is a collection of characters. Traditionally in AppleScript, the terms *string* and *text* are often used interchangeably when describing textual data, and we have done so throughout this book. However, when dealing with data types used by text handling commands and properties in AppleScript, it can be important to be more precise, as you will see in the section on "The Many Forms of Text" later in this chapter.

Textual data can be included directly in scripts or read from files, databases, other applications, or even from the clipboard. When included in a script, *textual data is always enclosed within straight quotation marks* to indicate that the characters are *text* and are not terms from the AppleScript language or an application's dictionary.

For example, the word `folder` placed unquoted in a script would be treated by AppleScript as a reference to a scriptable object associated with the file system, namely, a folder, and not as textual data. Try to count the number of characters in `folder` in Script 17.1, and you'll see that AppleScript refuses.

```
get the count of the characters of folder --> BAD SYNTAX
```
SCRIPT 17.1

The script generates an error because it considers the term `folder` to be a scriptable object, not textual data containing characters to be counted. However, when placed within straight quotation marks, the word folder is then considered by AppleScript to be textual data. Try Script 17.2.

```
get the count of the characters of "folder"
--> returns: 6
```
SCRIPT 17.2

The script considers `"folder"` to be textual data. It performs the requested action, returning the number of characters in the word.

Textual data is always placed within quotation marks. Should your textual data contain any straight quotation marks (")as part of the text, they must be individually identified to the script as textual data. For example, try Script 17.3, which attempts to display a message including quotation marks.

```
display dialog ¬
"I always place text inside " " characters." --> BAD SYNTAX
```
SCRIPT 17.3

The script errors when compiled because it considers the interior quotation marks to identify the beginning and end of text passages in the same manner as the outside ones. To indicate that the interior quotation marks are textual data, place a backslash character before each occurrence of a textual quotation mark. This process of individually marking characters is called *escaping a character*, and the backslash character is known as the *escape character*. Now run the script again, modified as shown in Script 17.4.

```
display dialog ¬
    "I always place text inside \" \" characters."
```
SCRIPT 17.4

Note, as shown in Figure 17.1, that the script does not display the backslash characters but only the characters that were *escaped*.

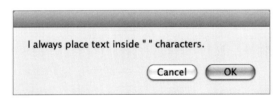

FIGURE 17.1 Escaped quotation marks displayed in a dialog.

In Mac OS X 10.4 (Tiger), another technique was introduced: concatenate segments of a string with the new **quote** constant, described in the later "Concatenation" section.

Finally, if textual data contains a backslash character that is not being used to escape another character, it must be—you guessed it—escaped by placing another backslash character before it, as in Script 17.5. The resulting dialog is shown in Figure 17.2.

```
display dialog ¬
    "Place a backslash (\\) before non-escaping characters."
```
SCRIPT 17.5

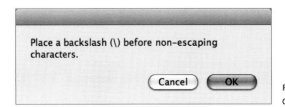

FIGURE 17.2 An escaped escape character displayed in a dialog.

The length Property

A fundamental property of textual data is the number of characters comprising a string or collection of characters. A string's character count is the value of its length property. The use of length is shown in Script 17.6.

```
get the length of "Once upon a time there was a man and his dog."
--> returns: 45
```
SCRIPT 17.6

Concatenation

Combining multiple strings into a single string is a task often performed in scripts. To join two or more strings together, use the *concatenation operator*, which is the ampersand character (&). Try Script 17.7.

```
"I love Macs." & "They are my favorite computers."
--> returns: "I love Macs.They are my favorite computers."
```
SCRIPT 17.7

The two strings have been combined or *concatenated* into a single string. Notice however, that there is no space between the two sentences. This can be easily corrected by including the constant **space** in the concatenation statement, as in Script 17.8.

```
"I love Macs." & space & "They are my favorite computers."
--> returns: "I love Macs. They are my favorite computers."
```
SCRIPT 17.8

Or, with less effort, just add a space at the end of the first string or the beginning of the second string, as we do in Script 17.9.

```
"I love Macs." & " They are my favorite computers."
--> returns: "I love Macs. They are my favorite computers."
```
SCRIPT 17.9

Just as you can include real space characters in a quoted string when composing a script, you can include real tab, return, and newline characters. Even after compiling it, the script itself reflects the formatting of the string that it generates. This technique is often used by scripters as a quick and dirty way to "preview" a formatted string. Script 17.10 is an example.

```
set formattedText to "
Please enter:
    Name:
    Address:"
return formattedText
--> returns:
"
Please enter:
    Name:
    Address:"
```
SCRIPT 17.10

To make the process of joining strings easier and visually cleaner, the AppleScript language reserves four words, each representing a character, which can be concatenated with textual data: space, tab, return, and quote. The last of these, quote, is new in Tiger. The character generated by the term return is the standard Macintosh carriage return character, ASCII character 13. AppleScript doesn't provide a reserved word for newline, ASCII character 10. These special terms can be used freely when combining strings, as in Script 17.11.

```
"Please enter:" & return & tab & "Name:" & return & tab & "Address:"
--> returns:
"Please enter:
    Name:
    Address:"
```
SCRIPT 17.11

There is yet another technique available in AppleScript to embed these so-called control characters into text. Use a single letter representing the control character, such as **t** for tab and **n** for newline, preceded by the escape character, like this: "**\n**" and "**\t**". This technique is so common among advanced users that, in Leopard, Apple has introduced a new "advanced" preference in the Editing pane of Script Editor preferences: "Escape tabs and line breaks in strings." Turn on that preference, and then recompile Script 17.10; before your eyes it turns into this script:

```
set formattedText to "\nPlease enter:\n\tName:\n\tAddress:"
return formattedText
--> returns:
"
Please enter:
    Name:
    Address:"
```
SCRIPT 17.12

If you turn this new Leopard editing preference off again and reopen Script 17.12, it reverts to the embedded control character format shown in Script 17.10, even if you saved Script 17.12 in the meantime. The concatenated reserved word format of Script 17.11 is not affected by this preference setting.

> **TIP** ▶ For those times when your script generates HTML or other structured text, use repeated **set** statements with a single named variable as the container for the text. Include the space, tab, and return terms where needed in the concatenation process to maintain the visual structure of the data, thereby making it easier to parse and locate where other information is inserted into the formatted text, as in this example where the current date string is inserted into the body of a web page:

```
set this_date to the date string of the (current date)
set this_HTML to ""
set this_HTML to this_HTML & "<html>" & return
set this_HTML to this_HTML & tab & "<head>" & return
```

```
set this_HTML to this_HTML & tab & tab & "<title>Date</title>" &
return
set this_HTML to this_HTML & tab & "</head>" & return
set this_HTML to this_HTML & tab & "<body>" & return
set this_HTML to this_HTML & tab & tab & this_date & return
set this_HTML to this_HTML & tab & "</body>" & return
set this_HTML to this_HTML & "</html>"
--> returns:
"<html>
    <head>
        <title>Date</title>
    </head>
    <body>
        Wednesday, August 29, 2007
    </body>
</html>"
```

SCRIPT 17.13

Quoting Text

We've already discussed how to use the escape character to include straight quotation marks in text passages in AppleScript.

There is another approach. When you want to quote an item within a text string, use curly quotation marks ("") instead of straight quotation marks (""). Since curly quotation marks are not used by AppleScript to identify text, they do not require special handling. The opening curly quotation mark is generated by pressing Option+[and the closing curly quotation mark is Shift+Option+[. Some people think curly quotation marks look better in dialogs and alerts, while others prefer straight quotation marks.

The following examples demonstrate how to use curly quotation marks to highlight text in a string. Script 17.14 places the curly quotation marks and the rest of the text in the same string.

```
display dialog "Do you want to open disk "Moria" now?"
```
SCRIPT 17.14

Script 17.15 demonstrates how the contents of a variable can be enclosed in curly quotation marks in a displayed message.

```
set the disk_name to "Moria"
display dialog "Do you want to open disk "" & disk_name & "" now?"
```
SCRIPT 17.15

Both examples produce the same dialog, shown in Figure 17.3.

FIGURE 17.3 Displaying curly quotation marks in a dialog.

The offset Command

The offset command is included in the String Commands suite in the Standard Additions scripting addition. It is used to determine the location of specified text within a string. The offset command has two required parameters: of, followed by the text to be located, and in, followed by the text to search.

Try Script 17.16.

```
offset of "time" in "Once upon a time in a land far away..."
--> returns: 13
```
SCRIPT 17.16

The result of the command is the count of characters up to and including the first character of the search string in the targeted text. In the previous example, the first character of the string "time" in the targeted text is the 13th character from the start of the searched string, and it therefore has an offset value of 13.

The search string does not have to be a complete word or phrase; it can be composed of a single character or multiple characters, as shown in Script 17.17.

```
offset of "p" in "Once upon a time in a land far away..."
--> returns: 7
```
SCRIPT 17.17

The result of the offset command is always the index of the first occurrence of a search string in targeted text. Note that the indexes of multiple matches are not returned; only the index of the first match is, as shown in Script 17.18.

```
offset of "a" in "Once upon a time in a land far away..."
--> returns: 11, not {11, 21, 24, 29, 32, 34}
```
SCRIPT 17.18

If there is no occurrence of a search string in the targeted text, as shown in Script 17.19, the result of the offset command is zero.

```
offset of "z" in "Once upon a time in a land far away..."
--> returns: 0
```
SCRIPT 17.19

This works because indexes in AppleScript are always one-based, so there can't be a character at index 0.

> **TIP** ▶ In Mac OS X version 10.2 and earlier, the offset command always considered the case of the targeted text when looking for matches. This is no longer true. Compare Script 17.20 and Script 17.21.
>
> ```
> offset of "f" in "abcdefABCDEF"
> --> returns: 6 in all versions of Mac OS X
> ```
> **SCRIPT 17.20**
>
> ```
> offset of "F" in "abcdefABCDEF"
> --> returns: 12 in Mac OS X 10.2 (Jaguar) and earlier; otherwise
> returns 6
> ```
> **SCRIPT 17.21**

The offset command did not work with the ignoring case and considering case action clauses in Jaguar and earlier, as shown by Script 17.22.

```
ignoring case
    offset of "F" in "abcdefABCDEF"
end ignoring
--> returns: 12 in Mac OS X 10.2 (Jaguar) and earlier; otherwise
returns 6
```
SCRIPT 17.22

This behavior was fixed in Mac OS X version 10.3 (Panther) and newer. The default is ignoring case, which means scripts written for Mac OS X 10.2 (Jaguar) and older do not work as designed when you run them in Panther, Tiger, and Leopard. You can now use the considering case action clause to replicate the behavior of Jaguar and earlier. The same history applies to the considering diacriticals and ignoring diacriticals clauses; the default is ignoring diacriticals. You will learn more about action clauses in Chapter 19, Action Clauses.

Text and Character Ranges

Sometimes you'll want to identify and extract portions of textual data, such as a name or phone number, from a sentence or paragraph. Any group of contiguous characters can be referenced by using their offset values to indicate where in the target string the range of characters begins and ends. For example, to get the first seven characters in a string, use a script like Script 17.23.

```
characters 1 thru 7 of "5551234 SMITH WILLIAM J"
--> returns: {"5", "5", "5", "1", "2", "3", "4"}
```
SCRIPT 17.23

The result of the script is a list of the characters comprising the range of characters from character 1 through character 7 of the targeted string. To rejoin the list of individual characters and make it a string, you can use the as string coercion as shown in Script 17.24.

```
(characters 1 thru 7 of "5551234 SMITH WILLIAM J") as string
--> returns: "5551234"
```
SCRIPT 17.24

You can make the process of extracting a string from a parent string even easier by asking for a text range instead of a range of characters. Script 17.25 shows how to do this.

```
text 1 thru 7 of "5551234 SMITH WILLIAM J"
--> returns: "5551234"
```
SCRIPT 17.25

When working with text, remember this rule: request a *range of characters* when you want the result as a *list of characters*; request a *range of text* when you want the result to be a *string*.

> **TIP** ▶ As shown in the earlier Script 17.24, a list of characters can be converted to text by using the `as string` coercion. Using the `as text` conversion works interchangeably with `as string`.
>
> The parentheses are required to indicate to the script that it must perform the action of getting characters 1 through 7 before trying to coerce them to a string. As you may remember from algebra class, calculations inside parentheses are performed first and replaced by their result. In this example, the statement inside the parentheses is replaced with its result, a list of characters. That list is then converted to text with the `as string` coercion.

You can combine the use of the `offset` command and the range reference form to extract specific sections of text from strings. For example, let's say you want to extract the name of a file from a file name that includes a name extension, such as "Smith Project.doc.".

First, use the `offset` command to locate and store the index of the dot character in the file name, as shown in Script 17.26.

```
set x to the offset of "." in "Smith Project.doc"
--> returns: 14
```
SCRIPT 17.26

Next, add a line to use the stored offset index value to extract a text range, as shown in Script 17.27.

```
set x to the offset of "." in "Smith Project.doc"
text 1 thru x of "Smith Project.doc"
--> returns: "Smith Project."
```
SCRIPT 17.27

Note that the result is not quite what we wanted, because the returned name still contains the dot character separator. This is because the `offset` value always includes the targeted character, in this case, the dot character. To correct this, add a small bit of math to the script by subtracting 1 from the index to compensate for the first character of the search string, as we do in the final version, Script 17.28.

```
set x to the offset of "." in "Smith Project.doc"
text 1 thru (x - 1) of "Smith Project.doc"
--> returns: "Smith Project"
```
SCRIPT 17.28

Negative Offset Values

The offset of characters in a string can be referenced from either end. For example, the offset of the character "m" in "salmon" is 4 when counted from left to right. It has a negative index value of -3 when counted from right to left. Offset values counting from the left are positive integers, while offset values counting from the right are negative integers. In other words, the character "m" is the fourth character from the beginning of the word "salmon" and the third character from the end.

As you will learn in Chapter 18, *Working with Lists and Records*, the same principle applies to lists. The list item "`Sal`" has an index value of 2 in this list:

```
{"Bob", "Sal", "Carl", "Sue", "Wanda"}
```

It also has a negative index value of -4 when counted from the end.

Negative index values are handy when you want to reference a range of characters in a string that includes the last character. By using a negative index value, it is possible to identify the last character of the string without knowing the string's length.

Here's a string comprising a seven-digit phone number and a person's name. Although the length of the phone number is always seven characters, the name could be of any length:

```
"5551234 SMITH WILLIAM J"
```

In this example, the name of the person always follows the seven-digit number with a space character and continues to the end of the string. To get the offset of the last character, you could use the `length` property and then use the returned value to indicate the text range of the name you want to extract, as shown in Script 17.29.

```
set x to the length of "5551234 SMITH WILLIAM J"
text 9 thru x of "5551234 SMITH WILLIAM J"
--> returns: "SMITH WILLIAM J"
```
SCRIPT 17.29

However, it is simpler to use the negative index value of the last character, which is always -1, to extract the name from the string, as shown in Script 17.30.

```
text 9 thru -1 of "5551234 SMITH WILLIAM J"
--> returns: "SMITH WILLIAM J"
```
SCRIPT 17.30

In summary, Script 17.31 uses both positive and negative index values to extract the name and phone number from the string. Note that the script also uses text ranges and text concatenation to format the phone number. See Figure 17.4 for the result.

```
set the customer_data to "5551234 SMITH WILLIAM J"
set the customer_phone to text 1 thru 7 of the customer_data
set the customer_phone to (text 1 thru 3 of the customer_phone & ¬
    "-" & text 4 thru -1 of the customer_phone)
set the customer_name to text 9 thru -1 of the customer_data
display dialog (customer_name & return & customer_phone)
```
SCRIPT 17.31

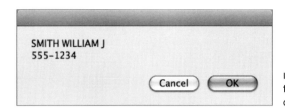

FIGURE 17.4 A dialog displaying text formatted using string commands.

Multiple Occurrences of Text

Sometimes a string you're parsing may contain more than one instance of a search character. For example, `smith.01.jpg` contains two occurrences of the dot character. Separating the file name from the name extension using the offset command to search for a dot character from the left won't work in this example because the `offset` command returns the offset of the first occurrence of an item in a string. In this example, we want the last occurrence of the dot character.

Even though it returns only a single offset, the `offset` command can still help extract the name from the string. Here are some strategies for dealing with this situation.

First, if the search string always has the same length and position in the targeted strings, use negative index values to identify it, as in Scripts 17.32 and 17.33 where the name extension ".jpg" is trimmed from file names.

```
text 1 thru -5 of "smith.01.jpg"
--> returns: "smith.01"
```
SCRIPT 17.32

```
text 1 thru -5 of "observatory.01.jpg"
--> returns: "observatory.01"
```
SCRIPT 17.33

The negative index value was specified with a value that would compensate for the dot character without requiring a subtraction operation. The script doesn't have to subtract 1 because you performed the subtraction in your head before you wrote the script.

Second, if necessary, define the search string to include contiguous characters common to the various search options, as Scripts 17.34 and 17.35 where the name extension could be ".jpg" or ".jpeg".

```
set x to the offset of ".jp" in "smith.01.jpg"
text 1 thru (x - 1) of "smith.01.jpg"
--> returns: "smith.01"
```
SCRIPT 17.34

```
set x to the offset of ".jp" in "smith.01.jpeg"
text 1 thru (x - 1) of "smith.01.jpeg"
--> returns: "smith.01"
```
SCRIPT 17.35

Third, convert the target string to a list of characters, reverse the order of items in the list, coerce the list back into a string, get the offset of the target character(s), and use the returned offset index as a negative value to parse the original target string, as shown in Script 17.36.

```
set the char_list to every character of "car.01.jpeg"
--> returns: {"c", "a", "r", ".", "0", "1", ".", "j", "p", "e", "g"}
set the reversed_list to the reverse of the char_list
--> returns: {"g", "e", "p", "j", ".", "1", "0", ".", "r", "a", "c"}
set the reversed_string to the reversed_list as string
--> returns: "gepj.10.rac"
set x to the offset of "." in the reversed_string
--> returns: 5
-- add 1 to compensate for the first character of the search string
set x to x + 1
-- use the result as a negative offset value
text 1 thru -x of "car.01.jpeg"
--> returns: "car.01"
```
SCRIPT 17.36

Script 17.37 is a shorter version of this approach, reduced to two statements by placing the first steps within parentheses so that they are executed first.

```
set the item_name to "car.01.tif"
set x to the offset of "." in ¬
    (the reverse of every character of the item_name) as string
set this_name to text 1 thru -(x + 1) of the item_name
--> returns: "car.01"
```
SCRIPT 17.37

Use this technique anytime you want to remove text from the end of a string.

The `offset` command is a useful tool for locating and extracting segments from textual data. Another tool for dividing strings into segments is AppleScript's `text item delimiters`, up next.

Text Item Delimiters

One of the most powerful and useful text manipulation tools provided by AppleScript is the ability to change its built-in *text item delimiters*.

Text item delimiters are the characters used to separate sections of textual data in a string. A simple example is one we use every day, namely, the use of the space character as a *delimiter* to separate words in sentences. For example, the words in the sentence "Jane and Bob went shopping." are separated from each other, or *delimited*, by the space character. If they were delimited by hyphens, the sentence would be "Jane-and-Bob-went-shopping."

You can use AppleScript's built-in text item delimiters to extract sections of strings for use elsewhere in your scripts. This technique requires a simple set of actions:

1. Set AppleScript's text item delimiters to the character or string currently used to delimit the targeted string (such as the space character used to delimit the words in a sentence)

2. Perform any desired actions with the targeted string using text item delimiters

3. Set AppleScript's text item delimiters back to their default value (a list containing an empty string identified by two consecutive straight quotation marks: {""}).

For example, Script 17.38 uses AppleScript's text item delimiters to divide the string `"5551234 SMITH WILLIAM J"` into its component parts:

```
set AppleScript's text item delimiters to space
set these_items to the text items of "5551234 SMITH WILLIAM J"
set AppleScript's text item delimiters to {""}
return these_items
--> returns: {"5551234", "SMITH", "WILLIAM", "J"}
```
SCRIPT 17.38

To extract the individual text items from their parent string, the script first sets `AppleScript's text item delimiters` to the character used to delimit the target data, in this example, a space character.

It then asks AppleScript for all the `text items` comprising the string and copies the resulting list into a variable.

Finally, the script resets `AppleScript's text item delimiters` to the default value of a list containing an empty string and then returns the data stored in the variable.

Changing a String's Delimiters

Note that the result of the second line of the previous script is a *list* of the text items that comprise the source string. As you already know, a list of text strings can be coerced into a single string by using the `as string` coercion, as in the following example:

```
{"A", "B", "C", "D", "E"} as string
--> returns: "ABCDE"
```
SCRIPT 17.39

When a list is coerced to a string, the current value for `AppleScript's text item delimiters` is inserted between the list items. In Script 17.39, nothing was inserted between list items since the current value of `AppleScript's text item delimiters` is an empty string. To insert other characters between the list items, first change `AppleScript's text item delimiters` to the desired delimiter values, as in Script 17.40 where a hyphen is placed between each list item.

```
set AppleScript's text item delimiters to "-"
set this_string to {"A", "B", "C", "D", "E"} as string
set AppleScript's text item delimiters to {""}
return this_string
--> returns: "A-B-C-D-E"
```
SCRIPT 17.40

> **NOTE ►** Always restore the default delimiters to a list containing an empty
> string. The default `text item delimiters` is a global value that is used by
> all scripts. If you don't restore this global value in every script, different
> text item delimiters may produce unexpected results in other scripts in
> a variety of circumstances, including whenever a script coerces a list to a
> string.

Text item delimiters can be a single character or a string of characters. For
example, Script 17.41 replaces the space delimiters in the target string with
a combination of hyphens and bullet characters. The script first sets the text
item delimiters to the delimiter used in the target string, extracts the text items,
then sets the text item delimiters to three characters that will replace the spaces
in the target string when the list is coerced back to a string.

```
set AppleScript's text item delimiters to space
set these_items to text items of "5551234 SMITH WILLIAM J"
set AppleScript's text item delimiters to "-•-"
set the new_string to these_items as string
set AppleScript's text item delimiters to {""}
return new_string
--> returns: "5551234-•-SMITH-•-WILLIAM-•-J"
```
SCRIPT 17.41

Using Text Item Delimiters to Extract Data

Using text item delimiters, Script 17.42 is another version of a script shown
earlier in this section that extracts a client name and phone number from
a string.

```
set AppleScript's text item delimiters to space
set these_items to text items of "5551234 SMITH WILLIAM J"
set the client_phone to the first item of these_items
set the client_name to (items 2 thru -1 of these_items) as string
set AppleScript's text item delimiters to {""}
return {client_name, client_phone}
--> returns: {"SMITH WILLIAM J", "5551234"}
```
SCRIPT 17.42

Note the use of the negative index value -1 in the script to indicate the last item in the list of text items.

Using Text Item Delimiters to Replace Data

You can use text item delimiters in a variety of ways. For example, although AppleScript does not have a **replace** command for text manipulation, you can use text item delimiters to locate and replace text within a targeted string.

In Script 17.43, the format tag "[[CUST]]" is replaced with a customer's name in a greeting form by first delimiting the target string with the text tag "[[CUST]]" as the default delimiter and then setting the default delimiter to a customer name, coercing the resulting list of text items to a string, and finally resetting the default text item delimiters to an empty string in a list.

```
set this_greeting to "Thank you [[CUST]] for trying our products!"
set AppleScript's text item delimiters to "[[CUST]]"
set these_items to the text items of this_greeting
set AppleScript's text item delimiters to "Sal"
set this_greeting to these_items as string
set AppleScript's text item delimiters to {""}
return this_greeting
--> returns: "Thank you Sal for trying our products!"
```
SCRIPT 17.43

Replacing special text tags within form letters is a common tool used by database publishers to produce batch mailings, mail merges, catalogs, and other mass-produced print and media materials.

If your script contains multiple statements using text item delimiters to replace text in strings, you can shorten and simplify the script by placing the multiple-step replacement commands in a subroutine and adding it to the end of your script. You learned about subroutines in Chapter 16, *Subroutines*.

The subroutine in Script 17.44 contains the script statements for replacing text in a string with other text. The script calls the subroutine from the main body.

```
set this_greeting to "Thank you [[CUST]] for trying our products!"
set this_greeting to replace_text(this_greeting, "[[CUST]]", "Bob")
--> returns: "Thank you Bob for trying our products!"


on replace_text(this_text, search_string, replacement_string)
    set AppleScript's text item delimiters to the search_string
    set the item_list to every text item of this_text
    set AppleScript's text item delimiters to the replacement_string
    set this_text to the item_list as string
    set AppleScript's text item delimiters to {""}
    return this_text
end replace_text
```

SCRIPT 17.44

Find/Change Limitations

As shown earlier, you can use text item delimiters to find and replace unique text passages in strings. They are not always reliable for finding and replacing words or phrases, however.

For example, Script 17.45 uses the subroutine developed earlier to replace the word "one" with the word "two" in a string.

```
set this_text to "Is one plus one the same as one times one?"
set the new_string to my replace_text(this_text, "one", "two")
--> returns: "Is two plus two the same as two times two?"
```

SCRIPT 17.45

Although the subroutine returned the proper result in this example, it may return unexpected results if the text comprising the word to be located is contained within other words, as in this example where the word "one" is part of the word "someone," as shown in Script 17.46.

```
set this_string to "If someone adds one plus one, what is the result?"
my replace_text(this_string, "one", "two")
--> returns: "If sometwo adds two plus two, what is the result?"
```
SCRIPT 17.46

To avoid this problem in your scripts, keep in mind that text item delimiters examine text, not words.

> **TIP ►** Another issue regarding the use of text item delimiters to replace text in strings is that text item delimiters were always case sensitive in Mac OS X 10.4 (Tiger) and older, but in Leopard they now honor the `considering case` and `ignoring case` action clauses you will learn about in Chapter 19, Action Clauses. The default is `ignoring case`. Thus, in Tiger, Script 17.47, which attempts to replace the word "one" with "two" in an all-uppercase string, fails to do so, but in Leopard it succeeds in changing the text.
>
> ```
> set this_string to "IF SOMEONE ADDS ONE PLUS ONE, WHAT IS THE RESULT?"
> my replace_text(this_string, "one", "two")
> --> returns: "IF SOMEtwo ADDS two PLUS two, WHAT IS THE RESULT?" in
> Leopard; "IF SOMEONE ADDS ONE PLUS ONE, WHAT IS THE RESULT?" in Tiger
> and earlier
> ```
> **SCRIPT 17.47**
>
> As was the case with the `offset` command, you can replicate the old behavior of AppleScript's `text item delimiters` in Leopard by using the `considering case` action clause.
>
> In Leopard, AppleScript's `text item delimiters` now also respond to `considering diacriticals` and `ignoring diacriticals`, defaulting to `ignoring diacriticals`.

Delimiting Paths

Text item delimiters are often used to manipulate file and folder paths in order to construct item references. For example, you can use text item delimiters to create a reference to the containing folder of an item by converting its file reference to a string, extracting the path segments as a list omitting the last one, and rejoining them as a string.

In Script 17.48, a reference to the folder containing a file is created using text item delimiters:

```
set this_file to choose file with prompt "Pick a file:"
--> returns: alias "Macintosh HD:Users:sal:Pictures:green_ipod.jpg"
-- coerce the alias reference to a string
set this_filepath to this_file as string
--> returns: "Macintosh HD:Users:sal:Pictures:green_ipod.jpg"
-- set the delimiter to the character used to separate path segments
set AppleScript's text item delimiters to ":"
-- extract all path segments except the last one by requesting a range
set the path_segments to text items 1 thru -2 of this_filepath
--> returns: {"Macintosh HD", "Users", "sal", "Pictures"}
-- coerce the extracted segments back to a colon-delimited string
set the parent_folderpath to the path_segments as string
--> returns: "Macintosh HD:Users:sal:Pictures"
-- reset the delimiters to the default
set AppleScript's text item delimiters to {""}
-- convert the path to an alias reference
set the parent_folder to the parent_folderpath as alias
--> returns: alias "Macintosh HD:Users:sal:Pictures:"
```
SCRIPT 17.48

Script 17.49 is a more concise version.

```
set this_file to choose file with prompt "Pick a file:"
set AppleScript's text item delimiters to ":"
set the parent_folder to ¬
    (text items 1 thru -2 of (this_file as string)) as string as alias
set AppleScript's text item delimiters to {""}
return the parent_folder
--> returns: alias "Macintosh HD:Users:sal:Pictures:"
```
SCRIPT 17.49

In both versions of the example, the path segments of the parent folder were extracted by specifying a range of items from 1 to -2, because the second-to-last segment is the segment representing the containing folder.

Don't use that example for folder paths, however. To see why, first try Script 17.50, which delimits a reference to a *file* on disk. Run it and pick a file in your Pictures folder.

```
set this_path to choose file
set AppleScript's text item delimiters to ":"
set the path_segments to every text item of (this_path as string)
set AppleScript's text item delimiters to {""}
return the path_segments
--> {"Macintosh HD", "Users", "sal", "Pictures", "green_ipod.jpg"}
```
SCRIPT 17.50

Next, try Script 17l.51, which delimits a reference to a *folder* on disk. Pick your Pictures folder this time.

```
set this_path to choose folder
set AppleScript's text item delimiters to ":"
set the path_segments to every text item of (this_path as string)
set AppleScript's text item delimiters to {""}
return the path_segments
--> returns: {"Macintosh HD", "Users", "sal", "Pictures", ""}
```
SCRIPT 17.51

Both scripts return the same number of path segments. However, the last path segment of the folder path is an empty string. This is because *folder paths always end in a colon*. Compare these two item references:

```
alias "Macintosh HD:Users:sal:Pictures:green_ipod.jpg"
alias "Macintosh HD:Users:sal:Pictures:"
```

Using this knowledge, adjust your script to compensate for the trailing colon in a folder path, as shown in Script 17.52.

```
set this_path to (choose folder) as string
set AppleScript's text item delimiters to ":"
if this_path ends with ":" then -- it's a folder reference
    set the parent_segments to text items 1 thru -3 of this_path
else -- it's a file reference
    set the parent_segments to text items 1 thru -2 of this_path
end if
set this_path to the parent_segments as string
set AppleScript's text item delimiters to {""}
return (this_path as alias)
--> returns: alias "Macintosh HD:Users:sal:Pictures:"
```
SCRIPT 17.52

As written, the script will never reach the `else` branch of the `if` test, because the `choose folder` command doesn't let you choose a file. But in a general-purpose subroutine, which might receive a reference to a file or a folder, it is essential, as shown in the next example.

Script 17.53 is the same script converted to a subroutine that returns the parent folder of folders and files whose references are passed to it.

```
display dialog ("Get the parent folder of a...") ¬
    buttons {"Cancel", "Folder", "File"} default button "File"
if button returned of result is "File" then
    choose file
else
    choose folder
end if
```

```
return parent_directory(result)

on parent_directory(this_item)
    set this_path to this_item as string
    if (the offset of ":" in this_path) ¬
        is equal to (the length of this_path) then -- a volume
        display alert ("You chose a volume") ¬
            message "Volumes don't have containers. Choose a folder."
        return
    end if
    set AppleScript's text item delimiters to ":"
    if this_path ends with ":" then -- a folder
        set the parent_segments to text items 1 thru -3 of this_path
    else -- a file
        set the parent_segments to text items 1 thru -2 of this_path
    end if
    set this_path to the parent_segments as string
    set AppleScript's text item delimiters to {""}
    return (this_path as string as alias)
end parent_directory
```
SCRIPT 17.53

We added a test at the beginning of the subroutine to catch the error generated when the user chooses a volume, which doesn't have a parent folder. The test works because, as you recall, the offset command counts from the left. If the first colon character it encounters is also the last character, you know you have a volume reference.

Using Text Item Delimiters with Other Path Types

You can use text item delimiters with other path types such as POSIX paths or URLs. The following example uses text item delimiters to save an image, currently displayed in the front Safari browser window, to the Desktop.

To follow along with this example, first launch Safari, and go to the Mac OS X AppleScript page at `http://www.apple.com/macosx/features/applescript/`. Then click the image of the Script Editor application icon at the top of the page while holding down the Control key, and choose Open Image in New Window from the contextual menu. The Script Editor icon image opens in a new Safari window.

The first statement in Script 17.54, shown in a moment, retrieves the URL of the page containing the image.

Since Internet URLs are defined as network paths whose segments are delimited by forward slash characters, the script then uses the slash character as the text item delimiter to extract the last path segment, which is the image's file name.

Next, the script creates a file reference to the location and the file name to use for the saved file. To do this, the path of the target parent folder, in this case, the Desktop folder, is coerced to a string, and then the file name is concatenated to the end.

To create a file reference to the file to be created, the concatenation result is copied into a variable, `target_path`, and preceded by the class identifier `file`. This newly created file reference is then used as the parameter for Safari's `save` command.

```
tell application "Safari"
    activate
    -- get the URL of the front window
    set this_URL to URL of document 1
    set AppleScript's text item delimiters to {"/"}
    set the image_name to the last text item of this_URL
    set AppleScript's text item delimiters to {""}
    set the target_path to ¬
        ((path to desktop) as string) & the image_name
    save document 1 in file target_path
end tell
```
SCRIPT 17.54

When you run Script 17.54, `this_URL` is set to the path to the Web site given at the beginning of this section, plus `"images/indextop20050412.jpg"`. The `image_name` variable is then set to `"indextop20050412.jpg"`. Finally, `target_path` is set to `"Macintosh HD:Users:sal:Desktop:indextop20050412.jpg"`.

If you run this script now, you may discover that, at least in some versions of Safari, its `save` command adds another name extension to the downloaded image, ".download", behind your back. You can easily remove this name extension using techniques you've already learned in this chapter.

Characters, Words, and Paragraphs

The AppleScript language recognizes the fundamental structures of text, namely, *characters*, *words*, and *paragraphs*.

For example, enter and run Script 17.55.

```
set this_story to ¬
    "Once upon a time in a village far far away lived a man and his dog."
& return & "Every day the man and his dog would walk from their house by
the ocean down to the beach." & return & "One day while strolling the
sandy beach, the pair came upon a silver dollar gleaming in the afternoon
sun."
--> returns:
"Once upon a time in a village far far away lived a man and his dog.
Every day the man and his dog would walk from their house by the ocean
down to the beach.
One day while strolling the sandy beach, the pair came upon a silver
dollar gleaming in the afternoon sun."
```
SCRIPT 17.55

The result of the script is a short, multiparagraph story we'll use when demonstrating these text elements.

Add a statement after the previous statement, as shown in Script 17.56, and run the script.

```
set this_story to ¬
    "Once upon a time in a village far far away lived a man and his dog."
& return & "Every day the man and his dog would walk from their house by
the ocean down to the beach." & return & "One day while strolling the
sandy beach, the pair came upon a silver dollar gleaming in the afternoon
sun."
count of paragraphs of this_story
--> returns: 3
```

SCRIPT 17.56

AppleScript recognized that the text was divided into three paragraphs. To AppleScript, a paragraph is a section of text delimited by return characters. Add a different line to the original script, as in Script 17.57, and run it.

```
set this_story to ¬
    "Once upon a time in a village far far away lived a man and his dog."
& return & "Every day the man and his dog would walk from their house by
the ocean down to the beach." & return & "One day while strolling the
sandy beach, the pair came upon a silver dollar gleaming in the afternoon
sun."
count of words of this_story
--> returns: 54
```

SCRIPT 17.57

AppleScript recognized that the story text was divided into 54 words. Add the statement shown in Script 17.58 to the original script.

```
set this_story to ¬
    "Once upon a time in a village far far away lived a man and his dog."
& return & "Every day the man and his dog would walk from their house by
the ocean down to the beach." & return & "One day while strolling the
sandy beach, the pair came upon a silver dollar gleaming in the afternoon
sun."
count of characters of this_story
--> returns: 264
```

SCRIPT 17.58

AppleScript recognized that the story text was composed of 264 characters.

Each of these text elements can be extracted from a string using reference forms such as **every**, **first**, and **last**, and text range references, as illustrated by Script 17.59.

```
every paragraph of this_story
--> returns: {"Once upon a time in a village far far away lived a man and
his dog.", "Every day the man and his dog would walk from their house by
the ocean down to the beach.", "One day while strolling the sandy beach
the pair came upon a silver dollar gleaming in the afternoon sun."}
first word of this_story
--> returns: "Once"
last word of this_story
--> returns: "sun"
first word of second paragraph of this_story
--> returns: "Every"
last word of paragraph 2 of this_story
--> returns: "beach"
first character of word 3 of paragraph 2 of this_story
--> returns: "t"
words 3 thru 6 of paragraph 2 of this_story
--> returns: {"the", "man", "and", "his"}
```
SCRIPT 17.59

The **length** property can be used with the individual text elements, as shown in Script 17.60.

```
length of paragraph 3 of this_story
--> returns: 106
length of word 5 of the first paragraph of this_story
--> returns: 2
```
SCRIPT 17.60

Simple true or false comparisons can be performed with the text elements, as shown in Script 17.61.

```
first paragraph of this_story contains "dog"
--> returns: true
last paragraph of this_story begins with "dog"
--> returns: false
```
SCRIPT 17.61

Bad News, Good News...

The current version of AppleScript considers paragraphs and words to be sections of larger text strings—paragraphs are delimited by return characters, and words are delimited by spaces and punctuation. AppleScript does not consider paragraphs, words, and characters to be scriptable objects that can be located by using the values of their properties or elements in searches using a *filter reference*, or `whose` clause. This behavior limits the actions a scripter can take when working with text elements.

For example, add the statement shown in Script 17.62 to the end of the original Script 17.55. It attempts to locate every paragraph in the story whose properties or elements match a specified parameter:

```
set this_story to ¬
    "Once upon a time in a village far far away lived a man and his dog."
& return & "Every day the man and his dog would walk from their house by
the ocean down to the beach." & return & "One day while strolling the
sandy beach, the pair came upon a silver dollar gleaming in the afternoon
sun."
every paragraph of this_story whose first character is "O"
```
SCRIPT 17.62

When run, the statement fails because paragraph elements in the current version of AppleScript are not searchable using their property values. This also means that a text element cannot be the target of commands such as `set`, `duplicate`, or `delete`., as shown by Script 17.63.

```
set this_story to ¬
    "Once upon a time in a village far far away lived a man and his dog."
& return & "Every day the man and his dog would walk from their house by
the ocean down to the beach." & return & "One day while strolling the
sandy beach, the pair came upon a silver dollar gleaming in the afternoon
sun."
set every word of this_story where it is "dog" to "cat"
```

SCRIPT 17.63

And you can't count the occurrences of a particular character in a string, as shown by Script 17.64.

```
count every character of "farm" where it is "f"
```

SCRIPT 17.64

So, how does a script edit text containing words and paragraphs?

Use a scriptable text editor such as Apple's TextEdit. To an application like this, text elements such as characters, words, and paragraphs are scriptable objects with properties and elements that can be manipulated using standard AppleScript tools.

As an example, enter and run Script 17.65, which targets Apple's TextEdit application included with Mac OS X.

```
tell application "TextEdit"
    activate
    make new document at the beginning of documents
    set the text of the front document to ¬
        "Once upon a time in a village far far away lived a man and his
dog." & return & "Every day the man and his dog would walk from their
house by the ocean down to the beach." & return & "One day while strolling
the sandy beach, the pair came upon a silver dollar gleaming in the
afternoon sun."
end tell
```

SCRIPT 17.65

A document containing the sample short story is created. Leave the TextEdit document open and try Script 17.66, which attempts to locate and change a specific word in the story using the set verb.

```
tell application "TextEdit"
    activate
    set every word of the text of ¬
        the front document where it is "dog" to "cat"
end tell
```
SCRIPT 17.66

If you examine the content of the front TextEdit document, you'll see that indeed every occurrence of the word "dog" has been changed to "cat."

Try counting the occurrences of a particular character in the story using Script 17.67.

```
tell application "TextEdit"
    activate
    count of (every character of the text of ¬
        the front document where it is "f")
end tell
--> returns: 4
```
SCRIPT 17.67

With some scriptable text editors, properties pertaining to the formatting of the text can also be manipulated. The example in Script 17.68 changes the size and typeface of the document's contents.

```
tell application "TextEdit"
    activate
    tell the text of the front document
        set the font to "Arial"
        set the size to 17
    end tell
end tell
```
SCRIPT 17.68

The example in Script 17.69 searches the document for every paragraph beginning with a specific character and changes the color of the paragraph to red.

```
tell application "TextEdit"
    activate
    set red_color to {65535, 0, 0}
    tell the text of the front document
        set the color of every paragraph whose ¬
            first character is "O" to the red_color
    end tell
end tell
```
SCRIPT 17.69

> **TIP** ▶ Colors are often defined in terms of their RGB values (RGB stands for red, green, blue). A color's RGB value is a list of three numbers ranging from 0 to 65535. For example, this is the RGB values for yellow: {65535, 65535, 0}. If you're using Mac OS X 10.3 (Panther) or newer, you can use the choose color command to pick a color. The result is the chosen color's RGB value list, as shown in Script 17.70.
>
> ```
> tell application "TextEdit"
>     activate
>     set the chosen_color to choose color
>     tell the text of the front document
>         set the color of every paragraph whose ¬
>             first character is "O" to the chosen_color
>     end tell
> end tell
> ```
> **SCRIPT 17.70**

The Many Forms of Text

In this chapter, we've focused on text without saying much about the many forms of text that are used on computers in the modern era. On the Macintosh, for example, text now usually takes the form of Unicode text.

Unicode is an international standard that is designed for the display and manipulation of digital characters of all kinds, as used in any and all languages. Many thousands of characters are available in Unicode, compared to the 255 available in ASCII. How to deal with each of these forms of text is a vast and somewhat advanced topic, beyond the scope of this book. We will say only a little about it here.

AppleScript has become more and more adept at handling Unicode text over recent years. In Leopard, AppleScript's support for the modern, powerful Unicode standard has reached full fruition. All built-in AppleScript and standard scripting addition commands and properties that deal with text now fully support Unicode.

At the beginning, by contrast, AppleScript emphasized ASCII text. ASCII stands for American Standard Code for Information Interchange. It is a system of numeric codes that represent alphanumeric characters such as *Z* and *3*, and special characters such as *é* and *¢*. The range of numeric codes is from 0 to 255, with 32 to 127 corresponding to the most commonly used characters in the English language.

Along the way from ASCII to Unicode, AppleScript sometimes had a lot of difficulty dealing with these different ways of understanding text. Some commands did not work properly with one form of text or another, and scripters had to resort to bizarre combinations of coercions to deal with textual data of type `string`, `text`, `Unicode text`, and others. Now, in Leopard, a concerted effort has been made to ensure that all commands and properties dealing with textual data are of type `text`, which now consists exclusively of full-blown Unicode text.

Many applications will continue to work best with ASCII textual data for a long time to come, however. So, it is still important for scripters to know how to work with old-style string and text data. We'll discuss how to work with old-style ASCII text first, then turn to Unicode text.

ASCII Textual Data

AppleScript has long had two commands for working with ASCII data: `ASCII character` and `ASCII number`. They are part of the String Commands suite in the Standard Additions scripting addition. They still work in Leopard, but they are now considered legacy commands compared to a new Unicode-friendly technique that we'll describe when we get to the Unicode discussion.

To retrieve the ASCII number of a character, place the character after the term `ASCII number`, as in Script 17.71.

```
ASCII number "X"
--> returns: 88
```
SCRIPT 17.71

To retrieve the ASCII character corresponding to an ASCII number, place the number after the term `ASCII character`, as in Script 17.72.

```
ASCII character 72
--> returns: "H"
```
SCRIPT 17.72

It is useful to be aware of some unique characteristics of ASCII data. The numeric characters 0 through 9 correspond to ASCII numbers 48 through 57:

The uppercase alphabetic characters, such as *A* and *Z*, correspond to ASCII numbers 65 through 90. The lowercase alphabetic characters, such as *a* and *z*, correspond to ASCII numbers 97 through 122.

The traditional return character is ASCII character 13. Since the underpinnings of Mac OS X are UNIX, many of its programs, such as TextEdit and Script Editor, use the standard UNIX linefeed or newline character, ASCII character 10, instead of the traditional Macintosh return character.

Some standard uses for ASCII commands in scripts are changing the case of characters and preparing text for display in HTML pages.

Changing Case

Script 17.73 changes the case of uppercase letters (ASCII numbers 65 through 90) to lowercase characters (ASCII numbers 97 through 122).

The difference between the ASCII codes for uppercase and lowercase number is always 32. To convert a lowercase character to uppercase, *add* 32 to the character's number. To convert an uppercase character to lowercase, *subtract* 32 from the code.

```
set this_string to "THE QUICK BROWN FOX JUMPED OVER THE LAZY DOG."
-- convert to lower case
set the changed_string to ""
repeat with i from 1 to the length of this_string
    set this_character to character i of this_string
    set this_number to (ASCII number this_character)
    if this_number is greater than or equal to 65 and ¬
        this_number is less than or equal to 90 then
        set this_character to (ASCII character (this_number + 32))
    end if
    set the changed_string to the changed_string & this_character
end repeat
return the changed_string
--> returns: "the quick brown fox jumped over the lazy dog."
```
SCRIPT 17.73

To retain the uppercase state of the sentence's starting character, change the third and fourth lines of the previous script as shown in Script 17.74.

```
set this_string to "THE QUICK BROWN FOX JUMPED OVER THE LAZY DOG."
-- convert to lower case
set the changed_string to the first character of this_string
repeat with i from 2 to the length of this_string
    set this_character to character i of this_string
    set this_number to (ASCII number this_character)
    if this_number is greater than or equal to 65 and ¬
        this_number is less than or equal to 90 then
```

```
            set this_character to (ASCII character (this_number + 32))
        end if
        set the changed_string to the changed_string & this_character
    end repeat
    return the changed_string
    --> returns: "The quick brown fox jumped over the lazy dog."
```
SCRIPT 17.74

Script 17.75 changes the case of lowercase characters (ASCII numbers 97 through 122) to uppercase characters (ASCII numbers 65 through 90).

```
set this_string to "The quick brown fox jumped over the lazy dog."
-- convert to upper case
set the changed_string to ""
repeat with i from 1 to the length of this_string
    set this_character to character i of this_string
    set this_number to (ASCII number this_character)
    if this_number is greater than or equal to 97 and ¬
        this_number is less than or equal to 122 then
        set this_character to (ASCII character (this_number - 32))
    end if
    set the changed_string to the changed_string & this_character
end repeat
return the changed_string
--> returns: "THE QUICK BROWN FOX JUMPED OVER THE LAZY DOG."
```
SCRIPT 17.75

Adding ACSII Codes to HTML

The HTML-based pages displayed on the Internet commonly rely on ASCII codes or special character entities to indicate when special characters, such as ©, are to be displayed. These special characters are often referred to as *high ASCII characters*, meaning that their ASCII codes are above the standard printable character range of 32 to 126. Printable high ASCII character codes are between 128 and 255.

To be displayed correctly in standard HTML pages, high ASCII characters must be replaced with special character entities in the following format containing their corresponding ASCII number:

ô

which represents this:

"ô"

Script 17.76 replaces high ASCII characters in a string with their corresponding HTML entities.

```
set this_phrase to "Bob's shoes are so "very" TrenDay™." & ¬
    return & "He should list then on his resumé."
set these_characters to every character of this_phrase
set this_HTML to ""
repeat with i from 1 to the count of these_characters
    set this_character to item i of these_characters
    set the ASCII_number to (ASCII number this_character)
    if the ASCII_number is greater than 126 then
        set this_HTML to this_HTML & ¬
            ("&#" & (the ASCII_number as string) & ";")
    else if the ASCII_number is in {10, 13} then
        set this_HTML to this_HTML & "<BR>"
    else
        set this_HTML to this_HTML & this_character
    end if
end repeat
return this_HTML
--> returns: "Bob&#213;s shoes are so &#210;very&#211;
TrenDay&#170;.<BR>He should list then on his resum&#142;."
```
SCRIPT 17.76

Unicode Textual Data

In Leopard, the `ASCII character` and `ASCII number` commands should be replaced by the terms `character id` and `id`, respectively, if you need to ensure that your scripts will work with languages other than English that use characters outside the ASCII range. Use them the same way the `ASCII character` and `ASCII number` commands are used. To obtain a Unicode character using `character id`, supply the Unicode number of the desired character. To obtain the Unicode number of a specified character, get its `id`. The script examples discussed above will still work with `character id` and `id` because, fortunately, the order and numbering of the first 128 characters are identical in the ASCII and Unicode systems.

The new `character id` and `id` terms even work with multiple characters at once. For example, `id of "Sal"` returns a list of code points, `{83, 97, 108}`, and `character id {66, 105, 108, 108}` returns `"Bill"`. You can use `string id` and `Unicode text id` with a list of code points as alternatives to `character id`, but `text id` does not work at this time.

The numbers, or code points, and their associated Unicode characters are officially listed at the `http://unicode.org` Web site. A convenient access point is the Unicode Character Code Charts by Script page at `http://unicode.org/charts/`, where you can download PDF files for various script systems, such as Basic Latin, General Punctuation, Mathematical Operators, and Geometric Shapes. You can also look up a character by typing its code in a search field on that Web site.

Now that AppleScript fully supports Unicode in Leopard, you no longer have to worry about coercing strings using the `as text`, `as string,` and `as Unicode text` coercions in Leopard. They still compile and run for reasons of backward compatibility, but they all yield Unicode text. All text in AppleScript is now of one class, known as "text." For example, if you compare the dictionaries of the Tiger and Leopard Standard Additions scripting addition, you will see that properties that used to list the type of the return value as `string` now list it as `text`, and the results are fully Unicode compliant. However, keep in mind that applications may still distinguish between the different forms of text.

In Leopard, the type of text is Unicode 16 throughout AppleScript, that is, whether you specify text without a coercion or use the coercion `as text`, `as string`, or `as Unicode text`. When you write a script to run both under Leopard and under Mac OS X 10.4 (Tiger), you should be careful to use a coercion that will yield the type of text your script needs in Tiger. Specifically, when writing scripts for Leopard and Tiger, you may want to use the `as Unicode text` coercion for proper Tiger operation even though the coercion isn't needed to work with Unicode text in Leopard.

One benefit of this modernization of AppleScript's text handling is that scripts should now work equally well no matter what the user's language preferences. You can freely mix Unicode characters from different languages in one script. Another benefit is that string comparisons now work as expected without requiring you to make sure both items are of the same text type. There are some other changes of a more advanced nature that are beyond the scope of this book; you can read about them in Apple's official AppleScript Release Notes for Mac OS X 10.5.

Some of the new text features, such as `id`, work only when your scripts run using AppleScript 2.0.

The summarize Command

Often overlooked, the `summarize` command of the String Commands suite in the Standard Additions scripting addition can be used to encapsulate a long text passage in a few sentences. The command has one parameter, `in`, followed by the number of sentences to be used for the summary.

Script 17.77 is an example that uses the `summarize` command to distill the contents of a story posted on `http://www.whitehouse.gov` regarding the annual pardoning of the national Thanksgiving turkey:

```
set this_story to ¬
    "This year marks the 56th anniversary of the first National
Thanksgiving Turkey presentation. Though live Thanksgiving turkeys were
presented intermittently to presidents since the Lincoln administration,
the current event dates to 1947, when the first National Thanksgiving
Turkey was presented to President Harry Truman.
```

The presentation at times has brushed against broader history. For
example, the November 1963 event was one of President Kennedy's last in
the Rose Garden. President Clinton, in 1996, returned from an Asian summit
and literally went directly to the ceremony.
This year's turkey was picked from among a group of 40 birds hatched on
July 10 in a turkey barn in the Carthage, Missouri area.
A few minor modifications were made to prepare the turkeys for the
presentation. The 40-bird flock was segregated into a special area in the
barn, and the turkeys periodically were hand fed and given additional
interaction with people in an effort to acclimate them to the environment
they will experience in the Rose Garden Ceremony.
By mid-fall, 15 finalists are selected. The week before the presentation,
the National Turkey Federation chooses the National Thanksgiving Turkey
and its alternate to bring to Washington. An alternate is chosen in case
the National Thanksgiving Turkey cannot fulfill the responsibilities of
being the National Turkey.
After the presentation, the turkeys will be taken to Frying Pan Park's
Kidwell Farm where they will reside."

```
summarize this_story in 3
--> returns:
(*
"Though live Thanksgiving turkeys were presented intermittently to
presidents since the Lincoln administration, the current event dates
to 1947, when the first National Thanksgiving Turkey was presented to
President Harry Truman.


...This year's turkey was picked from among a group of 40 birds hatched on
July 10 in a turkey barn in the Carthage, Missouri area.


...The 40-bird flock was segregated into a special area in the barn, and
the turkeys periodically were hand fed and given additional interaction
with people in an effort to acclimate them to the environment they will
experience in the Rose Garden Ceremony.
"
*)
```

SCRIPT 17.77

The `summarize` command often does an adequate job of condensing a story. Script 17.78 is a simple script that uses the command to summarize the contents of the Web page displayed in the front Safari browser window. Note that this script works best with pages displayed in "printer-friendly" mode.

```
tell application "Safari"
    set this_text to the text of document 1
    set this_summary to summarize this_text in 2
    display dialog this_summary buttons {"OK"} default button 1
end tell
```
SCRIPT 17.78

What's Next?

In this chapter, you learned a great deal about AppleScript's built-in capability to handle text, as well as the more powerful text management capabilities of many text editor applications. In the next chapter, you'll learn about working with lists and records.

18

Working with Lists and Records

It is common in AppleScript to organize information of all kinds into lists or records. You've seen them several times already. For example, in Chapter 6, *Information Tools*, you used the `list disks` and `list folders` commands in the Standard Additions scripting addition, and you saw the file information record returned by the `info for` command, also in Standard Additions.

This chapter gives you an overview of operations you can perform with lists and records and demonstrates how they are used in practice.

Lists

Lists are the real workhorses for information management in AppleScript. When you ask the Finder for the `name` of every `item` in the current user's Documents folder, it gives you a *list* of the names of all the folders, documents, and other files in the folder. When you ask Address Book for the `birth date` of every `person` you've entered, it gives you a *list* of birth dates. When you ask the System Events application for the `file` of every `process` running on your computer, it gives you a *list* of alias references. In addition to getting a *list* of every element of an object, some objects return a *list* when you ask for a property. You can even create lists of your own, and they can contain a mixture of different types of information, such as numbers, strings, dates, file references, and even other lists.

A list is useful in many ways. You can insert and delete list items. You can count list items. You can sort list items into a different order. You can search a list to find items of interest. Most important, you can examine each item in a list in turn using a loop to repeat the same operation on every item.

Basics

The `list` class is a built-in AppleScript value class, like `text`, `number`, `date`, and a list's close cousin, `record`. As with these other classes, you can create a new object of the list class simply by executing the appropriate literal expression. You saw in Chapter 17, *Working with Text*, that you can create a string object by enclosing some text in straight double quotation marks, as shown in Script 18.1.

```
"Hi there!"
class of result
--> returns: string
```
SCRIPT 18.1

To create a list object, you do something similar. Instead of enclosing the values in quotation marks, you enclose them in curly braces and separate them with commas, as shown in Script 18.2.

```
{1, 2, 3}
class of result
--> returns: list
```
SCRIPT 18.2

As the example shows, the literal expression of a list is an ordered set of values, separated by commas and enclosed in curly braces. Although you usually think of a list as containing multiple values, a list can contain a single value, as in Script 18.3.

```
{1}
class of result
--> returns: list
```
SCRIPT 18.3

And it can contain no values at all, in which case it is referred to as an *empty list*, as in Script 18.4.

```
{}
class of result
--> returns: list
```
SCRIPT 18.4

A list object can include values of different classes, along with expressions that return a value, such as references to other objects. When the script is executed, it evaluates any expressions and references to obtain their values, and then it returns the result in another comma-delimited, curly brace–enclosed list expression. Script 18.5 is a fanciful example:

```
{1, "two", third word of "one two three", 2 + 2}
--> returns: {1, "two", "three", 4}
```
SCRIPT 18.5

Properties

List objects have a handful of properties. You have already seen the `class` property in some of the previous examples. The `class` property is common to all AppleScript objects, and we won't discuss it further here. The other properties of a list object are its `length`, `rest`, and `reverse`. The last two are unique to lists and can be very convenient.

Length

The `length` property of a list works like the `length` property of textual data, which you learned about in Chapter 17, *Working with Text*. Instead of counting characters, however, it counts the individual comma-separated items in the list, as shown in Script 18.6.

```
{1, "two", third word of "one two three", 2 + 2}
length of result
--> returns: 4
```
SCRIPT 18.6

The `length` property returns the same result as using the `count` command on the list.

Rest

Script 18.7 shows the `rest` property of a list, which returns a list containing all the items in the list remaining after the first item.

```
{1, 2, 3}
rest of result
--> returns: {2, 3}
```
SCRIPT 18.7

This may seem a little odd in the abstract, but when you use the `rest` property in the context for which it is intended, it is perfectly in keeping with the plain-English tradition of AppleScript. Here's why.

Lists are commonly used in repeat loops, where you often want to handle the list's items in succession, one in each iteration of the loop. One way to do this is to process the first item in the list in the first iteration, then process the first item of the remaining items in the next iteration, and so on, until all of the items have been handled. If each iteration of the loop works with the items remaining after the previous iteration, the script can keep processing the first item without incrementing a loop counter.

Script 18.8 is an example that will make this clear:

```
set my_list to {1, 2, 3}
repeat until my_list is {}
    display dialog first item of my_list
    set my_list to the rest of my_list
end repeat
```
SCRIPT 18.8

On the first iteration of the repeat loop, the first item displayed is 1. Click OK, and on the second iteration, the first item is 2 because the script set the `my_list` variable to `the rest of my_list`. Click OK again, and the first item is 3 for the same reason. Click OK again, and the script quits because the list is now empty.

Reverse

The `reverse` property of a list returns—can you guess?—a list containing all the items in the original list in the reverse order, as shown in Script 18.9.

```
reverse of {1, 2, 3}
--> returns: {3, 2, 1}
```
SCRIPT 18.9

Sometimes you might want to process the items in a list in reverse order. Rather than using a loop counter and proceeding backward, you can simply reverse the order of the list at the beginning of the script. This is necessary if you want to use the `rest` property backward, since there is no counterpart to the `rest` property that returns all the items in the list *before* the *last* item.

```
set my_list to {1, 2, 3}

set my_list to reverse of my_list
repeat until my_list is {}
    display dialog first item in my_list
    set my_list to the rest of my_list
end repeat
```
SCRIPT 18.10

Run Script 18.10 and watch as the dialogs count down backward.

Constructing Lists

You often won't have the luxury of using a literal expression to form a list, as you did in the previous examples. Instead, you sometimes must construct a list piecemeal from individual values that your script obtains while it is running.

The fastest way to construct a list is to copy each new item to the **end** or the **beginning** of an existing list. The **end** and **beginning** of a list are special objects that can be used to add new items to the list, one at a time. If you're starting from scratch, the initial list should be an empty list. You would usually do this in a repeat loop, but we'll do it directly in Script 18.11 to illustrate the concept.

```
set new_list to {}
set end of new_list to 1
set end of new_list to 2
set end of new_list to 3
return new_list
--> returns: {1, 2, 3}
```
SCRIPT 18.11

When you're getting the last value in a list instead of setting it, **end** can be used interchangeably with **last item**, **back item**, and **item -1**. All of these references, including **end** when used in this manner, refer to the existing last item in the list, and all of them generate an error if you try to get them from an empty list.

However, those index reference forms are quite different from end when you are inserting an item into a list, as shown in Script 18.12.

```
set new_list to {0}
set last item of new_list to 1
set back item of new_list to 2
set item -1 of new_list to 3
return new_list
--> returns: {3}
```
SCRIPT 18.12

That example started with a one-item list because you can't refer to the first, front, last, or back item of an empty list, whether you're setting it or getting it. When setting the end of a list in Script 18.11, however, AppleScript created a new item in the empty list for you and gave it the specified value. None of the other terms created a new value in Script 18.12, but instead simply substituted the new value for the existing last item in the list. When it finished executing, the list still contained only one item, because AppleScript did not create a new item. Only the end object has this special capability.

To construct a list in reverse order, use the special beginning object instead, as shown in Script 18.13.

```
set new_list to {}
set beginning of new_list to 1
set beginning of new_list to 2
set beginning of new_list to 3
return new_list
--> returns {3, 2, 1}
```
SCRIPT 18.13

There is a second common way to construct lists, concatenation, but it is slower when adding individual items to a list repeatedly. We therefore discuss it in a later section, where you will learn how to combine two existing lists into a single, longer list.

Assigning Lists to Variables

Like all objects, list objects can be assigned to variables using the **set** or **copy** command. Script 18.4 shows how to do this.

```
set mixed_list to {1, "two", third word of "one two three", 2 + 2}
return mixed_list
--> returns: {1, "two", "three", 4}
```
SCRIPT 18.14

With lists, it is important to keep in mind the distinction between **set** and **copy**. Usually, these two commands are interchangeable. But with lists and some other objects—namely, records, dates and script objects—they are very different when used to assign a variable containing an object to another variable. (There is no difference when assigning a literal list expression to a variable, as in the previous example.)

The **set** command assigns a list object in one variable to another variable by referring to the location of the first variable in the computer's memory. The first variable and the second variable end up sharing the same data, because both values are located in the same place in memory. As a result, any changes to one of the variables affects the other variable in the same way.

```
set list_1 to {1, 2, 3}
set list_2 to list_1
set end of list_1 to 4
return list_2
--> returns: {1, 2, 3, 4}
```
SCRIPT 18.15

As you see in Script 18.15, both **list_1** and **list_2** refer to the same object. When you added **4** to the end of **list_1**, it was added to the end of **list_2**, as well. Sometimes this is what you want. But when it isn't what you want, it can be difficult to debug your script if you don't keep this distinction in mind.

The **copy** command creates a new object and copies the contents of the first object to it, as shown in Script 18.16. They are two separate and independent objects, kept in different locations in the computer's memory, so changing one leaves the other unchanged. This is more often what you want, so you should remember to use copy with list variables unless you have some special reason to use set instead.

```
set list_1 to {1, 2, 3}
copy list_1 to list_2
set end of list_1 to 4
return list_2
--> returns: {1, 2, 3}
```
SCRIPT 18.16

The individual items in a list can be assigned to variables, as well. Furthermore, a special shorthand syntax makes it easy to assign every item in a list to multiple variables all at once, in a single statement. Simply include the variable names in curly braces. As many of the values as have corresponding variables are assigned, in matching order, as you see in Script 18.17.

```
set {item_1, item_2, item_3} to {1, 2, 3}
return item_2
--> returns: 2
```
SCRIPT 18.17

Concatenating and Nesting Lists

Two lists can be joined so that all the elements of both become elements in a single, longer list. Alternatively, a list can be inserted into another list. In the latter case, the inserted list retains its identity as a separate list, and it is said to be "nested" within the first list. It is important to keep these two concepts separate. Confusing them can lead to hard-to-find errors in your scripts.

Lists are joined together using the concatenation operator, &, as Script 18.18 demonstrates.

```
set list_1 to {1, 2, 3}
set list_2 to {4, 5, 6}
set list_1 to list_1 & list_2
return list_1
--> returns: {1, 2, 3, 4, 5, 6}
```
SCRIPT 18.18

As mentioned in the "Constructing Lists" section, you can add items to a list repeatedly using concatenation. This works perfectly well, as shown in Script 18.19, but it is relatively slow and should usually be avoided. It creates a completely new list with each statement, instead of adding a single end or beginning object to an existing list.

```
set new_list to {}
set new_list to new_list & 1
set new_list to new_list & 2
set new_list to new_list & 3
return new_list
--> returns: {1, 2, 3}
```
SCRIPT 18.19

A list can be inserted into another list as a nested list using the same techniques you saw in the "Constructing Lists" section. See Script 18.20 for an example.

```
set list_1 to {1, 2, 3}
set list_2 to {4, 5, 6}
set end of list_1 to list_2
return list_1
--> returns: {1, 2, 3, {4, 5, 6}}
```
SCRIPT 18.20

However, you can also insert a list into another list by using concatenation, if what you concatenate to the first list is a list inside a list.

```
set list_1 to {1, 2, 3}
set list_2 to {4, 5, 6}
set list_1 to list_1 & {list_2}
return list_1
--> returns: {1, 2, 3, {4, 5, 6}}
```
SCRIPT 18.21

As you see in Script 18.21, a nested list is expressed as a comma-delimited list in curly braces inside another comma-delimited list in curly braces. The nested list is treated just like any other expression inside a list. You can get its value using any of the techniques described in the "Finding List Items" section later in this chapter. Script 18.22 is an example.

```
get item 4 of {1, 2, 3, {4, 5, 6}}
--> returns: {4, 5, 6}
```
SCRIPT 18.22

A nested list is counted as a single item, as shown in Script 18.23.

```
length of {1, 2, 3, {4, 5, 6}}
--> returns: 4
```
SCRIPT 18.23

Nested lists are more common than you might think, because some frequently encountered data items in AppleScript are lists. For example, in the Finder, the position of an item on the screen is a point, which is a list containing two items, the horizontal and vertical location of the window's upper-left corner. If you ask for the position of several open windows, as in Script 18.24, you get a list of lists.

```
tell application "Finder"
    get position of every window
end tell
--> returns: {{-845, 537}, {-865, 517}}
```
SCRIPT 18.24

Comparing Lists

Any two lists can be compared for equality or inequality to determine whether one list starts with or ends with the other and to determine whether one list contains or is contained by the other.

Equality

Whether two lists are considered equal to one another depends both on the value and on the position of the items they contain. All expressions and references are evaluated before considering the order of the items, as demonstrated in Script 18.25.

```
set list_1 to {1, 2, 3}
set list_2 to {"1" as integer, 1 + 1, length of "abc"}
return list_1 is equal to list_2
--> returns: true
```
SCRIPT 18.25

Starts With or Ends With

One list starts with another list if all the values in the second list appear at the beginning of the first list and in the same order. In fact, instead of a second list, you can have a single value on the right side of the expression. Expressions and references are evaluated first. See Scripts 18.26 and 18.27.

```
set list_1 to {1, 2, 3}
set prefix to {1, 2}
return list_1 begins with prefix
--> returns: true
```
SCRIPT 18.26

```
{1, 2, 3} starts with 1
--> returns: true
```
SCRIPT 18.27

One list ends with another list if all the values in the second list appear at the end of the first list and in the same order. A single value instead of a list can appear on the right. Evaluation occurs first. See Script 18.28.

```
set list_1 to {1, 2, 3}
set suffix to {2, 3}
return list_1 ends with suffix
--> returns: true
```
SCRIPT 18.28

Containment

Whether one list contains or is contained by another list depends on the value of evaluated expressions and references and their order. Instead of asking whether the list on the right is the prefix or suffix of the list on the left, the `contains` operator asks whether it is a sublist at any position in the first list, as shown in Script 18.29. The expression on the right can be a single value instead of a list.

```
set list_1 to {1, 2, 3, 4, 5}
set sub_list to {3, 4}
return list_1 contains sub_list
--> returns: true
```
SCRIPT 18.29

The `contained by` operator simply reverses the sense of the left and right values, as shown in Script 18.30.

```
set list_1 to {1, 2, 3, 4, 5}
set sub_list to {3, 4}
return sub_list is in list_1
--> returns: true
```
SCRIPT 18.30

When you type `is contained by` into the script window and compile it, it compiles to `is in`.

Finding and Replacing List Items

You usually get the value of an individual item of a list by index, as shown in Script 18.31.

```
get item 3 of {"one", "two", "three", 2 + 2}
--> returns: "three"
```
SCRIPT 18.31

This means you can use synonyms such as `first item` and `second item` instead of `item 1` and `item 2`, and you can use `last item` instead of a negative index as in `item -1`. Other synonyms also work, as in `front item` and `back` `item`. As you saw in the "Constructing Lists" section, however, you cannot use `end item` or `beginning item with lists`; instead, you refer simply to their `end` or their `beginning`.

You can also use `middle item`, as well as `some item` to get an item at random.

You also set an item to a particular value by index. This amounts to a replacement operation, shown in Script 18.32.

```
set my_list to {1, 2, 3}
set item 2 of my_list to "two"
return my_list
--> returns: {1, "two", 3}
```
SCRIPT 18.32

You aren't limited to getting one item from a list at a time. You `get` a range of items as shown in Script 18.33.

```
set my_list to {1, 2, 3, 4, 5, 6}
return items 3 thru 5 of my_list
--> returns: {3, 4, 5}
```
SCRIPT 18.33

You can't use the same technique to set a range of items in a list. You must resort to other techniques, such as setting them one at a time in a repeat loop.

Using `every item` with a list returns all the list's values in another list. This is redundant if all of the items in the list are simple values, since executing a list expression returns the values of all its items in another list anyway. If some of the items are expressions or references, however, `every item` evaluates them and returns a list of their values, as does simply executing the list expression.

In the current version of AppleScript, you cannot get a list item relative to another list item. For example, the expression `item before last item of {1, 2, 3}` produces an error. You can't get a list item by name or by ID, either, because list items don't have names or IDs.

The most widely bemoaned omission in the current version of AppleScript is
the inability to use the *filter reference form* with AppleScript lists. AppleScript
lists simply don't support `whose` clauses. If you try to use the statement, `every`
`item of {1, 2, 3} where it is less than 3`, for example, you get an error.

> TIP ▶ You can extract items from a list by class, but this is not, strictly
> speaking, an example of the filter reference form. The statement `get every`
> `string of {1, "two", "three", 2 + 2}` returns `{"two", "three"}`, and the
> statement `get second integer of {1, "two", "three", 2 + 2}` returns 4.

Lists in Applications

To this point, the examples of AppleScript lists have been based on scripts
you create yourself. Many applications return values in lists, too, especially
when you ask for every element of a particular application class, such as
`every document` or `every window`. As you will see, however, many applications
can do more with the listed values than AppleScript alone can do. This section
explores a few examples. We'll start with the Finder in Script 18.34.

```
set docs_path to path to applications folder
tell application "Finder"
    get every application file of docs_path
end tell
--> returns: {application file "Address Book.app" of folder "Applications"
of startup disk of application "Finder", application file "Automator.
app" of folder "Applications" of startup disk of application "Finder",
application file "Backup.app" of folder "Applications" of startup disk
of application "Finder", application file "Calculator.app" of folder
"Applications" of startup disk of application "Finder", application file
"Chess.app" of folder "Applications" of startup disk of application
"Finder", application file "Dashboard.app" of folder "Applications" of
startup disk of application "Finder", ...}
```
SCRIPT 18.34

We've truncated the return value because of space considerations, but you get the idea: the Finder can produce a list of objects of a kind that it alone knows about, such as application files in a folder. The question for discussion is this: does the Finder permit you to do more with the values in this list than AppleScript does with other lists? Let's run some experiments to see. Start with Script 18.35.

```
set docs_path to path to applications folder
tell application "Finder"
    get class of every application file of docs_path
end tell
--> returns: {application file, application file, application file,
application file, application file, application file, ...}
```
SCRIPT 18.35

That seems like a reasonable result, but it isn't what you saw when you got the class of an AppleScript list in the examples at the beginning of this chapter. There, the scripts returned list, that is, the class of the list object, not a list containing the class of every object in the list. Let's change that last script a little, in Script 18.36, and see what happens.

```
set docs_path to path to applications folder
tell application "Finder"
    get every application file of docs_path
    return class of result
end tell
--> returns: list
```
SCRIPT 18.36

As you see, the Finder assembled the listed values differently in the first of these two examples, where you asked the Finder for the class of every application file directly, in the same statement that got the values from the Finder. In the second example—where you got every application file from the Finder in the form of a list first and then operated on the result—AppleScript took over and did things its own way, even inside the Finder tell block.

You may have guessed by now what is happening. In the first example, the Finder was being asked to do all the work of assembling a list containing the `class` property of every application file in the folder. The Finder returned the result in a list only *after* it had done all the internal work of finding the application files (excluding any items in the folder that were not application files) and getting the `class` property of each of them. In the second example, the Finder was being asked only to assemble a list containing references to the application files themselves. As you saw in the opening script in this section, the result of that command was a list containing file references, not a list containing classes. Since the result was a list, asking for its `class` property yields `list`, the class of the result.

This difference in behavior is important when you use an application to perform more elaborate tasks, such as getting a property of a filtered list of objects. Recall that AppleScript lists by themselves do not support `whose` clauses. However, many applications are very good at getting, for example, the name of every object that meets test criteria such as `greater than 0` or `comes before date "April 15, 2008"`. Using a `whose` clause to filter application elements within the application can be many times faster than using an AppleScript repeat loop to filter the elements after they have been assembled into a list containing all of the elements. To avoid errors, however, you must be very careful to make sure you are asking the application to do the filtering, and not asking AppleScript to filter a list.

For example, Script 18.37 fails with an error because AppleScript is trying to do something with the list that AppleScript doesn't know how to do (if the error sheet runs off the bottom of your screen, just hit the Return key to dismiss it):

```
set docs_path to path to applications folder
tell application "Finder"
    get every item of docs_path
    return every item of result whose name starts with "A" --> ERROR
end tell
```
SCRIPT 18.37

Change the script slightly, in Script 18.38, and it works!

```
set docs_path to path to applications folder
tell application "Finder"
    get every item of docs_path whose name starts with "A"
end tell
--> returns: {application file "Address Book.app" of folder "Applications"
of startup disk of application "Finder", folder "AppleScript" of folder
"Applications" of startup disk of application "Finder", application file
"Automator.app" of folder "Applications" of startup disk of application
"Finder"}
```

SCRIPT 18.38

This same principle applies to all Finder properties and elements. For example, you can get the name of every application file if you do it the right way, shown in Script 18.39.

```
set docs_path to path to applications folder
tell application "Finder"
    get name of every application file of docs_path ¬
        whose name starts with "A"
end tell
 --> returns: {"Address Book.app", "Automator.app"}
```

SCRIPT 18.39

Other applications raise the same issue. For example, the first of the following two TextEdit scripts, Script 18.40, works, but the second, Script 18.41, doesn't. Open several blank windows in TextEdit before running these scripts.

```
tell application "TextEdit"
    get name of every window
end tell
--> returns: {"Untitled 5", "Untitled 4", "Untitled 3", "Untitled 2"}
```

SCRIPT 18.40

```
tell application "TextEdit"
    get every window
    get name of every item of result --> ERROR
end tell
```
SCRIPT 18.41

Using Lists

Using a list often involves manipulating it in some fashion, such as deleting an item from a list, inserting an item at a specified place in the list, or sorting it into some useful order. AppleScript doesn't have any built-in commands to implement these behaviors, so you will have to use other techniques, such as the repeat loops you learned about in Chapter 11, *The Repeat Loop*.

Offset of an Item in a List

Lists are ordered, by definition, and it is often important to know where a particular item is located within a list. As you learned in the earlier "Finding and Replacing List Items" section, an item's location is represented by its index. Indexes are one-based throughout AppleScript because that is how people count things in the real world. It is therefore usually best, for consistency, to maintain that convention in scripts where you compute an item's position. Unlike the string type in AppleScript, an AppleScript list does not recognize an offset command. You must therefore write one yourself if you need to know the index of a list item. Script 18.42 is an example.

```
set this_list to {"Sal", "Sue", "Bob", "Carl"}
list_position("Carl", this_list)
--> returns: 4

on list_position(this_item, this_list)
    repeat with i from 1 to the count of this_list
        if item i of this_list is this_item then return i
    end repeat
    return 0
end list_position
```
SCRIPT 18.42

In the example, execution loops through a list using the `repeat with [loopVariable] from [startValue] to [stop value]` syntax you learned about in Chapter 11, *The Repeat Loop*. The `with` clause in the example has no explicit `by` parameter, so it automatically increments the value of the loop variable by 1 on each pass through the loop. The loop variable is often called a *counter variable*, for good reason, because it counts the items in the list one by one. When the item with the specified value is found, the script simply returns the value of the loop variable, which is the current count of iterations completed. The return value is one-based because the `with` clause started with 1. The script returns this value as soon as the specified value is found, breaking out of the repeat loop. Thus, the script completes execution more quickly if the specified value is nearer the beginning of the list.

If the specified value is not found in the list, the script returns 0, just as the `offset` command does in the case of a string. The script knows that nothing was found when it reaches the stop value of the repeat loop and still hasn't found a match. Since 0 is not a legal index value in a one-based index system, returning 0 when nothing is found is a convenient convention. Scripts using this handler can rely on a value of 0 to mean that the specified value is not in the list, for example, by testing the return value for 0 and behaving differently if nothing was found.

One useful way to use an item's location in a list is to arrange related items of information in multiple lists having a parallel order. For example, if a list of names is maintained in the same order as a separate list of telephone numbers, you can get the phone number of a particular person by finding the position of that person in the first list and then getting the phone number in the same position in the other list. Script 18.43 uses the earlier `list_position` handler to cross-reference the phone list.

```
set the name_list to {"Sal", "Sue", "Bob", "Carl"}
set the phone_list to {"5-5874", "5-2435", "5-9008", "5-1037"}

set the chosen_person to choose from list the name_list ¬
    with prompt "Choose a person:"
if the chosen_person is false then return "user cancelled"
set the phone_number to ¬
    item (list_position((chosen_person as string), ¬
        name_list)) of the phone_list
```

```
display dialog ¬
    "The phone extension for " & chosen_person & ¬
    " is " & phone_number & "." buttons {"OK"} default button 1

on list_position(this_item, this_list)
    repeat with i from 1 to the count of this_list
        if item i of this_list is this_item then return i
    end repeat
    return 0
end list_position
```
SCRIPT 18.43

The list_position subroutine handler used in the two previous examples
assumes that there are no duplicates in the list. If there are duplicates, it returns
the first match and ignores any others. Often, however, your scripts need to
know about duplicates. For example, there may be several people named Sue
in your phone list, and you probably want to be able to see the phone numbers
of all of them so you can pick the right one. To do this, modify the handler to
add a parameter specifying whether to return duplicates, and use that parameter
to decide what to do, as shown in Script 18.44.

```
set this_list to {"Sal", "Sue", "Bob", "Carl", "Sue"}
list_positions(this_list, "Sue", true)
--> returns: {2, 5}

on list_positions(this_list, this_item, list_all)
    set the offset_list to {}
    repeat with i from 1 to the count of this_list
        if item i of this_list is this_item then
            set the end of the offset_list to i
            if list_all is false then ¬
                return item 1 of offset_list
        end if
    end repeat
    if list_all is false and offset_list is {} then return 0
    return the offset_list
end list_positions
```
SCRIPT 18.44

The only difference between the handler in Script 18.44 and the previous handler is that this handler uses the new `list_all` parameter to decide whether to keep searching for instances of `this_item` after the first instance is found. If the `list_all` parameter is false, the handler always returns the result as a number, even if it is 0, just as the previous version of the handler did. But if `list_all` is true, the handler always returns the indexes of found items in a list, even when there is only one of them. If none are found, it returns an empty list instead of 0. When you use this script with `list_all` set to true, you must make sure your script is prepared to handle the case of an empty list. Then, if the result is not empty, you must extract the individual item or items in the list to use them, for example, to get corresponding items in a parallel list.

Count of Duplicate Items in a List

Counting duplicate items in a list uses the same principles, but the handler is simpler because you know you always want to scan the entire list looking for duplicates. See Script 18.45.

```
set this_list to {"Sal", "Sue", "Bob", "Carl", "Sue"}
count_matches(this_list, "Sue")
--> returns: 2


on count_matches(this_list, this_item)
    set the match_counter to 0
    repeat with i from 1 to the count of this_list
        if item i of this_list is this_item then ¬
            set the match_counter to the match_counter + 1
    end repeat
    return the match_counter
end count_matches
```

SCRIPT 18.45

Insert Items into a List by Position

Things get a little harder when you want to insert a new item into an existing list at a specified location. In the following example, Script 18.46, the `insert_item` handler has three parameters: the list into which you will insert an item, the item to be inserted, and the position at which it is to be inserted. The `insert_position` parameter should be set to the index that the inserted item will have in the final list. For example, if the `insert_position` is 1, the new item will be inserted at the beginning of the list—before the original first item, if the original list is not empty.

The handler returns false if nothing is inserted. Depending on how you want to use it, you might prefer to change it so the handler returns the original list, unchanged, when nothing is inserted. The conditions under which the script inserts nothing and returns false are defined in the initial statements of the handler, namely, when the `insert_position` parameter is 0 or when it is greater than the length of the list plus 1. It also handles a negative `insert_position`, which counts backward from the end of the list.

The guts of the handler usually performs the insertion operation by breaking the original list into two pieces at `insert_position`, adding the new item to the end of the first part and concatenating the two lists into a single list with the new item at the designated location. In the special case where the `insert_position` is at the beginning or the end of the original list, it isn't necessary to split the list, and the new item is simply added to the `beginning` or `end`.

All of this is done in the last `else` clause of the handler, where the `insert_position` is a positive integer greater than 0 (an `insertion_position` of 0 was handled separately earlier in the handler). The handler checks for an `insert_position` of less than 0 first, which requires slightly more complicated logic including reversing the list twice.

```
set this_list to {"Sal", "Sue", "Bob", "Carl"}
set this_list to insert_item(this_list, "Wanda", 3)
--> returns: {"Sal", "Sue", "Wanda", "Bob", "Carl"}

on insert_item(this_list, this_item, insert_position)
    set the list_count to the count of this_list

    if the insert_position is 0 then
        return false
    else if the insert_position is less than 0 then
        if (the insert_position * -1) is greater than ¬
            (the list_count + 1) then return false
    else
        if the insert_position is greater than ¬
            (the list_count + 1) then return false
    end if

    if the insert_position is less than 0 then
        if (the insert_position * -1) is the (list_count + 1) then
            set the beginning of this_list to this_item
        else
            set this_list to the reverse of this_list
            set the insert_position to (insert_position * -1)
            set this_list to ¬
                ((items 1 thru (insert_position - 1)) ¬
                    of this_list) ¬
                    & this_item ¬
                & ((items insert_position thru -1) ¬
                of this_list)
            set this_list to the reverse of this_list
        end if
    else
        if the insert_position is 1 then
            set the beginning of this_list to this_item
        else if the insert_position is (the list_count + 1) then
            set the end of this_list to this_item
        else
            set this_list to ¬
```

```
                ((items 1 thru (insert_position - 1)) ¬
                        of this_list) ¬
                        & this_item & ¬
                ((items insert_position thru -1) ¬
                        of this_list)
            end if
        end if
        return this_list
end insert_item
```

SCRIPT 18.46

> **NOTE ▶** We inserted extra parentheses in this example to make the logic
> clearer and also to ensure that the script was formatted properly to fit
> within the margins of the book.

Replace Items in a List by Matching

You saw in the "Finding and Replacing List Items" section that you can replace
an item in a list by index if you know its position ahead of time. Script 18.47 is
a script that replaces items by matching a search string when you don't know
the position of matching items in advance.

```
set this_list to {"Sal", "Sue", "Bob", "Carl", "Sue"}
replace_matches(this_list, "Sue", "Wanda", false)
--> returns: {"Sal", "Wanda", "Bob", "Carl", "Sue"}

on replace_matches(this_list, match_item, replacement_item, replace_all)
    repeat with i from 1 to the count of this_list
        set this_item to item i of this_list
        if this_item is the match_item then
            set item i of this_list to the replacement_item
            if replace_all is false then exit repeat
        end if
    end repeat
    return this_list
end replace_matches
```

SCRIPT 18.47

That was very simple. You just looped through the original list, replacing items that match by index. If `replace_all` was false, you exited the repeat loop immediately after finding the first match. At the end, you returned the original list with any replacements.

Delete Items in a List by Matching

Deleting items in a list is more complicated because you have to build up a new list that does not contain matching items, instead of simply resetting their values in place in the original list. Script 18.48 shows one way to do it.

```
set this_list to {"Sal", "Sue", "Bob", "Carl", "Sue"}
delete_matches(this_list, "Sue", false)
--> returns: {"Sal", "Bob", "Carl", "Sue"}

on delete_matches(this_list, match_item, delete_all)
    set return_list to {}
    repeat length of this_list times
        set this_item to item 1 of this_list
        if this_item is not match_item then ¬
            set end of return_list to this_item
        set this_list to rest of this_list
        if this_item is match_item and delete_all is false then
            set return_list to return_list & this_list
            exit repeat
        end if
    end repeat
    return return_list
end delete_matches
```
SCRIPT 18.48

Here, you processed the first item in the list on each pass through the repeat loop, making sure to set the list to the remaining items in the list on each pass using the list object's **rest** property. By keeping track of the remaining items in the list, you were able to terminate execution quickly after you found the first match, if the `delete_all` parameter was set to false. You did this by concatenating the separate return list that was being built up, one item at a time, with the rest of the original loop, all at once instead of one item at a time.

Sort Items in a List

No discussion of lists is complete without a method to sort the list. The handlers in these scripts sort string items into alphabetical order.

There are many sorting algorithms, and it is important to make the right choice when the list you want to sort is very long. In AppleScript, however, if you have a very long list to sort, you should consider finding a third-party scripting addition or application that is faster than an AppleScript `repeat` loop. For a shorter list—say, up to a few hundred items—you may find that speed isn't an issue and an AppleScript sort routine using a `repeat` loop is fast enough.

The handler shown next, in Script 18.49, is offered first because its logic is fairly easy to understand, which isn't true of most sorting algorithms. It processes all the items in the list in an outer repeat loop. A nested inner repeat loop scans the entire list looking for the "smallest" value (the value that comes first, alphabetically) and adds it to a separate return list. The return list starts out empty, but on each pass through the outer loop the smallest remaining item in the original list is identified and added to the end of the return list. A separate list, containing the indexes of all the items already added to the return list, is maintained in order to avoid adding an item to the return list that is already in it. By the time it's all over, the return list contains every item from the original list, sorted in ascending ASCII order.

The handler is called by the main script to display a list of composers sorted in alphabetical order using the `choose from list` command in the Standard Additions scripting addition.

```
set the composer_list to {"Ellington", "Copland", "Bach", "Mozart"}
choose from list ASCII_Sort(the composer_list)

on ASCII_Sort(my_list)
    set the index_list to {}
    set the sorted_list to {}
    repeat (the number of items in my_list) times
        set the low_item to ""
        repeat with i from 1 to (number of items in my_list)
            if i is not in the index_list then
                set this_item to item i of my_list
                if the low_item is "" then
                    set the low_item to this_item
                    set the low_item_index to i
                else if this_item comes before low_item then
                    set the low_item to this_item
                    set the low_item_index to i
                end if
            end if
        end repeat
        set the end of sorted_list to the low_item
        set the end of the index_list to the low_item_index
    end repeat
    return the sorted_list
end ASCII_Sort
```

SCRIPT 18.49

A better script is the optimized "Bubble Sort" shown next, in Script 18.50. It is still considered inefficient in computer science circles, but for most AppleScript applications it is perfectly good. A classic Bubble Sort makes one pass through the original list in an outer loop, just as in the previous example. In a nested inner loop, it compares each pair of items in succession, swapping them in place if they're out of order. On each pass through the outer loop, the "largest" item in the list filters up to the top, like a bubble rising in water. In the optimized Script 18.50, additional steps are taken to remember whether swaps are no longer needed above a certain index and whether the list is already completely sorted, before the outer list has completed all of its iterations. This allows the script to complete its work and return the sorted list more quickly in some circumstances.

One reason that this script is faster is that it can detect when the list is completely sorted. Another reason is that it sorts the list in place using AppleScript's ability to set the value of an item in a list by index directly and quickly. It does not require a separate return list.

```
set the composer_list to {"Ellington", "Copland", "Bach", "Mozart"}
choose from list Bubble_Sort(the composer_list)


on Bubble_Sort(my_list)
    set last_swap_position to length of my_list
    repeat while last_swap_position is greater than 0
        set comparisons_needed to last_swap_position - 1
        set last_swap_position to 0
        repeat with i from 1 to comparisons_needed
            if item i of my_list > item (i + 1) of my_list then
                set swap_item to item i of my_list
                set item i of my_list ¬
                    to item (i + 1) of my_list
                set item (i + 1) of my_list to swap_item
                set last_swap_position to i
            end if
        end repeat
    end repeat
    return my_list
end Bubble_Sort
```

SCRIPT 18.50

Coercing Lists to Strings and Back

When you're working with lists of strings, it can be useful to coerce the list to a string. You've already seen how this works with a single-item list, shown in Script 18.51.

```
get {"Word"} as string
--> returns: "Word"
```
SCRIPT 18.51

When you do this with a longer list, the words end up jumbled into a single word, as shown in Script 18.52.

```
get {"Sal", "Sue", "Carl", "Bob"} as string
--> returns: "SalSueCarlBob"
```
SCRIPT 18.52

To get a more useful string—say, to report the values in a dialog—use AppleScript's `text item delimiters` property, as shown in Script 18.53. It is customary to save the old `text item delimiters` first and restore them at the end in order to provide a consistent base delimiter in case another coercion will be performed later. The default value is a list with an empty string: {""}.

```
set old_delimiters to AppleScript's text item delimiters
set AppleScript's text item delimiters to {", "}
set my_friends to {"Sal", "Sue", "Carl", "Bob"} as string
set AppleScript's text item delimiters to old_delimiters
return my_friends
--> returns: "Sal, Sue, Carl, Bob"
```
SCRIPT 18.53

In the previous example, you temporarily replaced the old delimiters with a two-character delimiter consisting of a comma followed by a space. When the `as string` coercion was applied to the list, it automatically separated each list item with the new delimiters.

If you ponder this for a moment, you will realize why the initial attempt to coerce the list ended up running all the list items together. In reality, it was separating each item with the default built-in delimiter, which is an empty string and therefore doesn't show up on the screen. This highlights the reason why it is customary to save and restore AppleScript's `text item delimiters` when changing them. If you attempt to coerce some other list to a string later, you might be surprised at what gets used as a delimiter if you haven't taken care to follow the customary practice. You can't completely protect yourself by taking care to set the text item delimiters every time you plan to perform a coercion because, as you've seen before, AppleScript sometimes performs implicit coercions and you might not recognize in advance all of the circumstances in which that can happen. The problem can even rear its head in other scripts, since `text item delimiters` is a global property of AppleScript and persists even when running separate scripts.

AppleScript also honors the `text item delimiters` property when you want to turn a string back into a list. You don't do this with a coercion, but by getting the `text items` of the string after setting appropriate `text item delimiters`. For example, to get a list containing all the words in a sentence, set `text item delimiters` to a space, as shown in Script 18.54.

```
set old_delimiters to AppleScript's text item delimiters
set AppleScript's text item delimiters to {space}
set word_list to text items of "I can't get no satisfaction"
set AppleScript's text item delimiters to old_delimiters
return word_list
--> returns: {"I", "can't", "get", "no", "satisfaction"}
```
SCRIPT 18.54

You can use the same technique to separate many standard-format strings into their elements. Script 18.55, for example, lists all the elements of a POSIX path:

```
set old_delimiters to AppleScript's text item delimiters
set AppleScript's text item delimiters to {"/"}
set item_list to text items of POSIX path of (path to scripting additions
folder from user domain)
set AppleScript's text item delimiters to old_delimiters
return item_list
--> returns: {"", "Users", "sal", "Library", "ScriptingAdditions", ""}
```
SCRIPT 18.55

Technically, the `text item delimiters` global property is a list of strings, but it has always been true that only the first string in the list is used. Many scripters don't bother to include the curly braces, since AppleScript coerces the string to a single-item list automatically before passing it along to the `text item delimiters` property.

Records

Records are a close cousin to lists. Instead of an ordered list of unnamed values, a record is an *unordered* set of *named* values referred to as *properties*. Because a record is unordered, you don't get its properties by index or in a repeat loop using indexed access. Instead, you get its properties individually, by name. For this reason, of course, you need to know all of the names it uses to label the values of its properties. In the case of records you've created in your own scripts, that's easy. For the names used in records returned by applications, you need to consult the application's dictionary or documentation.

The great advantage of records when scripting is that access to information organized as a record is unambiguous and self-explanatory. When you want the name of an employee, you ask explicitly for the `name` property of an `employee` record.

In the following sections, we'll cover aspects of records that distinguish them from lists, but we will skip aspects where their behavior is similar to that of lists.

Basics

Like the `list` class, the `record` class is a built-in AppleScript value class. You can create a new object of the record class simply by executing the appropriate literal expression.

A record looks something like a list, in that its entries are separated by commas and enclosed in a pair of curly braces. What's different is that every entry in a record is preceded by a label and a colon, like this: `{name:"Joe", gender:"male", age:27}`. You get the value of an entry by its label, as in Script 18.56

```
set employee to {name:"Joe", gender:"male", age:27}
get gender of employee
--> returns: "male"
```
SCRIPT 18.56

Each label-value pair is referred to as a *property*.

To see that the order of properties in a record is unimportant, run Script 18.57, in which the same label-value pairs appear in a different order in the literal expression that creates the record object. The result is the same as in the previous example.

```
set employee to {gender:"male", name:"Joe", age:27}
get gender of employee
--> returns: "male"
```
SCRIPT 18.57

A record object, like a list object, can contain values of any class, as well as expressions that return values. The expressions are evaluated when the script is executed. Records, like lists, can also contain nested records (as well as nested lists).

Your scripts will often use multiple records that have the same structure. For example, a script relating to a company's employees is likely to encounter several record objects relating to different employees. It is not uncommon, for example, for scripts to process similar records in a list by using a repeat loop.

Because of this, it is helpful to write your scripts in such a way that the properties of every employee record have the same labels, such as `name` and `age`. Since AppleScript is a very loosely typed language, there is nothing except practicality to stop you from putting a `name` property in one employee record, a `pseudonym` property in another, and a `nom_de_plume` property in a third. You will pay the price for your lack of discipline, however, when it comes time to process multiple employee records in a list in a repeat loop. For example, you will want to refer to the `name` property of each employee using the same label, `name`, in each iteration of the loop.

If one of the records in a list of similar records does not have a value for a particular label, you can either leave that property out or provide a default or "empty" value for it. In either case, you will have to design your script so that it can detect and deal with a missing or default value when it runs across one. For example, an employee record could contain the properties `{gender:"male", age:27}` if the name is not available, or it could contain the properties `{name:"", gender:"male", age:27}`, using an empty string as the default value of the `name` property. This is merely a design decision. The logic of your script will differ depending on the decision you make. For example, attempting to get the `name` of an employee when you left that property out of the record generates an error, so you would have to be prepared to catch this error in a `try` block.

Properties

A record recognizes only a `class` property and a `length` property, apart from the custom properties you put into the record yourself. These built-in properties behave differently than the custom properties. For example, the `class` and `length` properties of a record are always present. Also, they aren't counted along with custom properties when you get the `length` of a record, as demonstrated by Script 18.58.

```
set employee to {name:"Joe", gender:"male", age:27}
get length of employee
--> returns: 3
```
SCRIPT 18.58

Class

It is important to discuss the **class** property of a record briefly, because it does not always return **record** as its result.

Applications can return objects that look and act like records in every way but that AppleScript reports as being a different class. For example, a **Finder window** object in the Finder has three properties, **icon view options**, **list view options**, and **column view options**, which the dictionary describes as having data types with corresponding names: **icon view options**, **list view options**, and **column view options**.

When you get the **class** property of the **icon view options** property of a **Finder window** object, for example, the result is **icon view options**. Run Script 18.59 while at least one Finder window is open:

```
tell application "Finder"
    get class of icon view options of window 1
end tell
--> returns: icon view options
```
SCRIPT 18.59

You wouldn't know from the return value that this is a record. But when you get the properties of the **icon view options** property of the window, as in Script 18.60, you find that it is a record. Its **class** property is included in the record, and it has a value of **icon view options**.

```
tell application "Finder"
    get properties of icon view options of window 1
end tell
--> returns: {class:icon view options, arrangement:not arranged, icon
size:128, shows item info:false, shows icon preview:false, text size:12,
label position:bottom, color:{0, 0, 0}}
```
SCRIPT 18.60

The **class** property of this kind of application property can be used in a script to identify the kind of record the script is currently working on. This is important because, for example, a Finder window's **icon view options** property contains a different set of properties than its `list view options` property. See the properties of the `list view options` property in Script 18.61.

```
tell application "Finder"
    get properties of list view options of window 1
end tell
--> returns: {class:list view options, calculates folder sizes:false, icon
size:small, sort column:column id name column of list view options of
Finder window id 5 of application "Finder", uses relative dates:true}
```
SCRIPT 18.61

Script 18.62 is a script that needs to check the class of a view options record to avoid an error.

```
tell application "Finder"
    repeat with options in ¬
        {icon view options of window 1, ¬
            list view options of window 1, ¬
            column view options of window 1}
        if class of options is list view options then ¬
            return calculates folder sizes of options
    end repeat
end tell
--> returns: false
```
SCRIPT 18.62

Length

The `length` property of a record counts the individual properties, or label-value pairs, in a record. It returns the same value as using the `count` command, as shown in Script 18.63.

```
set employee to {name:"Joe", gender:"male", age:27}
get length of employee
--> returns: 3
```
SCRIPT 18.63

Constructing Records

In addition to creating a record by executing a literal record expression, you can add individual properties to an existing record at any time. However, you don't add a property to a record by setting the new property, as you might think.

If a property with the given label already exists, you change its value to a new value, replacing the old value, by using the **set** command as shown in Script 18.64. This is similar to replacing an existing list item by setting the item by index.

```
set employee to {name:"Jane", gender:"female", age:24}
set age of employee to 25
return employee
--> returns: {name:"Jane", gender:"female", age:25}
```
SCRIPT 18.64

However, you can do this only when a property with the given label already exists. If you try to set a property to a value in a record that doesn't already have a property with that label, you get an error, as shown in Script 18.65.

```
set employee to {name:"Jane", gender:"female", age:24}
set citizenship of employee to "U.S.A." --> BAD SYNTAX
return employee
```
SCRIPT 18.65

What you must do instead is concatenate the original record and a new record containing only the new property, as in Script 18.66.

```
set employee to {name:"Jane", gender:"female", age:24}
set employee to employee & {citizenship:"U.S.A."}
return employee
--> returns: {name:"Jane", gender:"female", age:24, citizenship:"U.S.A."}
```
SCRIPT 18.66

This is similar to using concatenation to add values to a list. Records don't have a mechanism to add new record properties the way you set the `beginning` or end of a list, because records aren't ordered—they don't have a `beginning` object or an `end` object.

Concatenating Records

As noted earlier, records can be concatenated to other records. This is the only way to add properties to an existing record.

When you concatenate records, you are not limited to adding only one property at a time. You can add multiple new properties at once to an existing record by concatenating lengthy records as shown in Script 18.67.

```
set employee to {name:"Ernest", gender:"male", age:62}
set benefits to {annual_pension:35000, retirement_age:65}
set employee to employee & benefits
return employee
--> returns: {name:"Ernest", gender:"male", age:62, annual_pension:35000,
retirement_age:65}
```
SCRIPT 18.67

Watch out when you concatenate records that contain properties with the same label. You will be surprised to learn that the property in the first record trumps the property in the second record. That is, the value of the property in the first record is not replaced, and the value of the property in the second record is ignored, as shown in Script 18.68.

```
set employee to {name:"Ernest", age:62}
set employee to employee & {age:24}
return employee
--> returns: {name:"Ernest", age:62}
```
SCRIPT 18.68

The only way to change the value of an existing property is to `set` it directly.

Comparing Records

Any two records can be compared for equality or inequality and to determine whether one record contains or is contained by the other. You cannot determine whether one record starts with or ends with another record, because records are not ordered.

Equality

Two records are considered equal if they have the same number of properties, the properties have the same labels, and the values of the labeled properties are the same. Expressions and references are evaluated. The order of properties need not be the same.

Containment

One record contains another record if all the properties in the second record are included in the first record and the values are equal. Their order does not matter.

Coercing Records to Lists

You can coerce any record to a list, but the labels of the record properties are lost. For that reason, there is no way to coerce a list back to a record. Script 18.69 shows what happens to a record stripped of its labels.

```
set employee to {name:"Felicity", gender:"female", age:32}
return employee as list
--> returns: {"Felicity", "female", 32}
```
SCRIPT 18.69

Coercing a record to a list allows you to iterate through all of its property values in a repeat loop, something you can't do with a record. Script 18.70 encounters an error when you run it, because you can't use the index reference form to extract a property value from a record.

```
set employee to {name:"Felicity", gender:"female", age:32}
repeat with my_value in employee
    get contents of my_value --> BAD SYNTAX
end repeat
```
SCRIPT 18.70

Just coerce the record to a list, and Script 18.71 works.

```
set employee to {name:"Felicity", gender:"female", age:32}
repeat with my_value in employee as list
    get contents of my_value
end repeat
--> returns: 32, which is the last value in the list
```
SCRIPT 18.71

The coercion also works with records returned by AppleScript commands and properties. For example, the `get volume settings` command in the Standard Additions scripting addition returns a record that might look like the example in Script 18.72.

```
get volume settings
--> returns: {output volume:39, input volume:30, alert volume:100, output muted:false}
```
SCRIPT 18.72

Coerce it to a list, and you get the result of Script 18.73.

```
(get volume settings) as list
--> returns: {39, 30, 100, false}
```
SCRIPT 18.73

Because the list returned by such a command is always ordered in the same way, you can reliably retrieve specific values from the list as we do in Script 18.74.

```
(get volume settings) as list
set my_alert_volume to item 3 of result
--> returns: 100
```
SCRIPT 18.74

This might prove useful if you want to iterate through all the settings in a repeat loop. You can also easily set a bunch of variables to all of the values in the record with a single statement, as in Script 18.75.

```
copy ((get volume settings) as list) to ¬
    {my_output_volume, ¬
        my_input_volume, ¬
        my_alert_volume, ¬
        my_output_muted}
return my_input_volume
--> returns: 30
```
SCRIPT 18.75

What's Next?

In this chapter, you learned all about lists and records, the two important data manipulation classes in AppleScript. In the next chapter, you'll learn about action clauses that control how AppleScript behaves when comparing text and when encountering application commands that have crashed.

19

Considering and Ignoring

With Timeout

What's Next?

Lesson 19
Action Clauses

AppleScript makes assumptions about many things you probably take for granted, such as that string comparisons are usually performed without regard to capitalization. These assumptions are similar to preference settings in an application. They are set by default to the behavior you might expect most of the time, so you usually don't have to think about them. But they may not always be appropriate for a particular task, and AppleScript lets you change them.

For example, when you compare two words, AppleScript assumes you don't care about capitalization. But what if you're working with proper names, and you want to pick out every reference to some guy named Carpenter in an article about building houses? It would be useful in that context to be able to tell AppleScript to notice the difference between carpenter and Carpenter. Otherwise, you would have to write an elaborate handler to compare the ASCII or Unicode number of the first character of each word to see whether it falls in the range of uppercase letters.

Or you might have noticed that your scripts sometimes generate an error if they have to wait a long time for a complicated application process to come to an end—say, when Photoshop is processing a high-resolution image. AppleScript makes an assumption about how long it should wait before jumping to the conclusion that the script has gotten hung up on an application error, but its assumption is sometimes unwarranted. It would be useful if you could tell AppleScript to be more patient when you're scripting an operation that you know is slow.

AppleScript doesn't require you to deal with issues like these in a traditional Preferences dialog, because you need finer-grained control over attributes such as case. You might want to change one of these settings for one operation in a script while leaving the default behavior in place for the rest of the script. In addition, you might want your scripts to be portable to another computer where you don't have control of the user's Preferences. You have to be able to override the defaults in your script on a case-by-case basis, and the behavior of your script should be obvious to anyone reading its text.

AppleScript lets you deal with many of these issues by using a special syntax to control *attributes* such as the `case` of characters in comparison operations. You enclose the relevant portions of your script in a `considering` block or an `ignoring` block, as shown in Script 19.1.

```
considering case
    "carpenter" is equal to "Carpenter"
end considering
--> Returns: false
```
SCRIPT 19.1

You can use several attributes in `considering` and `ignoring` clauses. Some of them default to `ignoring`, while others default to `considering`. There is no harm in specifying the default behavior of an attribute, but you don't have to do it. For example, Script 19.2 works as expected, but the enclosing `ignoring` clause is unnecessary because AppleScript ignores `case` by default:

```
ignoring case
    "carpenter" is equal to "Carpenter"
end ignoring
--> Returns: true
```
SCRIPT 19.2

You use slightly different syntax to change how long AppleScript waits for a command addressed to an application, or to a scripting addition in certain circumstances, using a `with timeout` clause. By default, AppleScript waits 2 minutes (120 seconds). Script 19.3 shows how you can temporarily shorten or lengthen the default timeout interval

```
tell application "TextEdit"
    activate
    with timeout of 5 seconds
        display dialog ("Quick, type a word:") default answer ""
    end timeout
    beep
end tell
```
SCRIPT 19.3

If you run Script 19.3 as a compiled script in Script Editor as written, without using a **try** block, the alert sheet shown in Figure 19.1 appears if you wait more than the allotted time to click a button. When you dismiss the alert, the script quits without executing the commands following the `with timeout` block. You'll find out how to handle the timeout error more effectively near the end of this chapter.

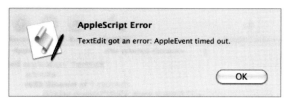

AppleScript Error

TextEdit got an error: AppleEvent timed out.

OK

FIGURE 19.1 An AppleScript timeout error sheet.

Considering and Ignoring

Table 19.1 lists all the attributes that can be controlled with `considering` and `ignoring` clauses, indicating the default behavior of each.

TABLE 19.1 Attributes for Ignoring and Considering Clauses

Considering	Ignoring
application responses*	case
diacriticals	expansion†
hyphens	numeric strings°
punctuation	
white space	

* The `restart`, `shut down`, `log out`, and `sleep` commands ignore `application responses` by default.

†Not supported in Leopard.

° New in Mac OS X 10.4 (Tiger).

Comparison Operations

Seven of these eight attributes—all of them except `application responses`—can be considered or ignored only in comparison operations between text objects. The concept of a comparison operation is fairly broad. It obviously includes determining whether two strings are equal or one of them comes before or after the other alphabetically. But it also includes what are sometimes called *containment operations*, such as determining whether a text object such as a paragraph contains a specified word.

Furthermore, these attributes apply only to comparisons performed by AppleScript. Comparisons performed by an application or by the system do not honor `considering` and `ignoring` clauses using these attributes. Instead, they treat uppercase and lowercase according to their own internal rules, which can differ from one application to the next.

At least theoretically, these distinctions can lead to big surprises if you don't remember or understand them. They can lead to buggy scripts, because an attempt to use a `considering` or `ignoring` clause with an operation that is not one of the applicable comparisons, or with a comparison operation performed by an application or the system, is silently ignored, without generating an error. Testing the behavior of your scripts with text having differing attributes is the only way to be sure the script is correct.

In practice, however, these rules won't often trip you up. AppleScript usually performs comparison operations itself after getting the value of an object from an application. As a result, scripts that tell an application to compare one word to another, for example, almost always work in accordance with a `considering` or `ignoring` clause.

Consider the TextEdit examples in Scripts 19.4, 19.5 and 19.6, all of which do honor the `considering` and `ignoring` clauses. To use them, first create a new TextEdit document containing two words, *carpenter* and *Carpenter*, one with an initial lowercase letter and the other with an initial uppercase letter, and make sure it is the frontmost document in TextEdit. You can see from the results that all of these scripts honor the AppleScript rules for the `case` attribute.

```
tell application "TextEdit"
    tell document 1
        word 1 is equal to word 2
    end tell
end tell
--> Returns: true
```
SCRIPT 19.4

```
tell application "TextEdit"
    tell document 1
        ignoring case
            word 1 is equal to word 2
        end ignoring
    end tell
end tell
--> Returns: true
```
SCRIPT 19.5

```
tell application "TextEdit"
    tell document 1
        considering case
            word 1 is equal to word 2
        end considering
    end tell
end tell
-->Returns: false
```
SCRIPT 19.6

One area where you may frequently encounter problems is in whose clauses.
In at least the common sense of the word, each of Scripts 19.7, 19.8 and 19.9 is
performing a comparison operation between it and "carpenter", and we know
that the comparison is being performed by the application because AppleScript
by itself does not implement whose clauses. Obviously, the last of these three
scripts is ignoring the considering case clause, and it does not generate an
error even though the result is wrong.

```
tell application "TextEdit"
    tell document 1
        get every word ¬
            where it is equal to "carpenter"
    end tell
end tell
--> Returns: {"carpenter", "Carpenter"}
```
SCRIPT 19.7

```
tell application "TextEdit"
    tell document 1
        ignoring case
            get every word ¬
                where it is equal to "carpenter"
        end ignoring
    end tell
end tell
--> Returns: {"carpenter", "Carpenter"}
```
SCRIPT 19.8

```
tell application "TextEdit"
    tell document 1
        considering case
            get every word ¬
                where it is equal to "carpenter"
        end considering
    end tell
end tell
--> Returns: {"carpenter", "Carpenter"} WRONG!
```
SCRIPT 19.9

The inability to apply `considering` and `ignoring` clauses in `whose` clauses can be a serious impediment. Application `whose` clauses are usually very fast because they are written by the application's developer and are therefore savvy about the application's internal data structures. If your script has to consider attributes taking into account the case of characters in string comparisons, however, it must resort to repeat loops, which are relatively slow, unless the application developer has dealt with this issue in the application.

Combined and Nested Clauses

`considering` and `ignoring` clauses can be combined. To include several attributes of one type, say, `ignoring`, list them using commas. Compiling will change the last comma to `and`:

`ignoring white space, hyphens and punctuation`

Join `considering` attributes to `ignoring` attributes in a single clause using `but`:

`considering case but ignoring white space`

`considering` and `ignoring` clauses can also be nested. When nested blocks are in conflict, the inner block prevails. For example, one of several comparisons in an outer `considering case` block can be placed in a nested inner `ignoring case` block to restore it alone to the default behavior of the `case` attribute. If there is no conflict, nested blocks are additive. For example, if the outer block ignores `case` and the inner block ignores `hyphens`, any comparisons in the inner block will ignore both `case` and `hyphens`.

The Attributes

In this section, we discuss all of the available attributes.

Application Responses

The `application responses` attribute, unlike all the others, applies only to commands that are addressed to an application. This includes faceless background applications but not scripting additions. Most commands addressed to an application consider the `application responses` attribute by default, so you must place them in an `ignoring application responses` block to override the default behavior.

Starting with AppleScript 1.9 in Mac OS X 10.2.3 (Jaguar), the `restart`, `shut down`, `log out`, and `sleep` commands ignore the `application responses` attribute by default. Prior to version 1.9, `restart`, `shut down`, and `log out` considered this attribute by default, which led to an amusing conundrum. Since the application that was running a script using these commands could not quit until the script completed execution but the script could not complete execution until the application running it responded to the command by quitting, the script would hang unless you used these commands in an explicit `ignoring application responses` block.

The default behavior, `considering application responses`, in effect causes a script to pause execution when each Apple event is sent to an application and to resume execution when the target application sends a reply event back indicating either that the command completed executing successfully or that it encountered an error. You usually don't notice any delay, because most application commands complete execution quickly.

However, some commands can take a long time to execute, for example, when querying a very large database or rendering a complex image, and you may want the script to move on to other tasks without waiting. Place the command in an `ignoring application responses` block. For example, on a fast computer with lots of RAM installed, you might want a script to run several database queries at once without waiting for each to return a result. Any script that does this must take account of the fact that errors will not be heeded. Also, the results must be made available outside the script, for example, by saving a file to disk through some other means once it is done. Any script that simply sets up the screen for reading, perhaps by loading a Web site on a computer with a slow Internet connection, is a candidate for an `ignoring application responses` clause.

> **TIP** ► A `with timeout` clause may be preferable to deal with long-running application processes, and it is the only way to deal with long-running scripting addition processes launched inside an application process.

Case

The `case` attribute relates only to the capitalization of letters. It has nothing to do with whether the Shift or Caps Lock key is down.

Comparisons performed by AppleScript ignore `case` by default, so strings that differ only in the capitalization of letters are treated as if they were equal. You must use `considering case` to override the default behavior.

Beginning with Mac OS X 10.3 (Panther), the `offset` command in the String Commands suite in the Standard Additions scripting addition honors `considering case` and `ignoring case` statements. Previously, it did not, and it always considered case. Since AppleScript ignores the `case` attribute by default, the behavior of older scripts that use `offset` may have changed if they relied on the old default behavior of the `offset` command. To make them behave as originally designed, add `considering case` clauses to these older scripts.

Beginning with Leopard, `AppleScript's text item delimiters` also honors `considering case` and `ignoring case` statements. Previously, as with the `offset` command, it did not, and it always considered case. Existing scripts that depend on the old behavior may have to be revised for Leopard by adding `considering case` clauses because the default is `ignoring case`. The `considering` or `ignoring` block must enclose both the statement that sets the `text item delimiters` and the statement that performs the comparison.

The `case` attribute applies only to comparisons performed by AppleScript, as described in the earlier "Comparison Operations" section, and by the `offset` command in the String Commands suite in the Standard Additions scripting addition and when using `AppleScript's text item delimiters` in Leopard. For examples using the `offset` command and `AppleScript's text item delimiters`, see Chapter 17, *Working with Text*.

Diacriticals

Diacritical marks are the marks that appear above some letters in some languages, such as in naïve and résumé.

Comparisons performed by AppleScript consider `diacriticals` by default, so strings that differ in the presence or absence of diacritical marks are treated as unequal. You must use `ignoring diacriticals` to override the default behavior.

Beginning with Mac OS X 10.3 (Panther), the `offset` command in the String Commands suite in the Standard Additions scripting addition honors `considering diacriticals` and `ignoring diacriticals` statements. Previously, it did not, and it always considered diacriticals. Since AppleScript considers the `diacriticals` attribute by default, unlike the `case` attribute, the behavior of older scripts that use `offset` will not change with respect to the diacriticals attribute.

Beginning with Leopard, `AppleScript's text item delimiters` also honors `considering diacriticals` and `ignoring diacriticals` statements. Previously, as with the `offset` command, it did not, and it always considered diacriticals. Since the new default behavior and the old behavior are identical, existing scripts that depend on the old behavior of the `diacriticals` attribute need not be revised for Leopard. The `considering` or `ignoring` block, if you use it, must enclose both the statement that sets the `text item delimiters` and the statement that performs the comparison.

The `diacriticals` attribute applies only to comparisons performed by AppleScript, as described in the earlier "Comparison Operations" section, and by the `offset` command in the String Commands suite in the Standard Additions scripting addition and when using `AppleScript's text item delimiters` in Leopard. For examples using the `offset` command and `AppleScript's text item delimiters`, see Chapter 17, *Working with Text*.

Expansion

The `expansion` attribute relates to characters such as æ and Œ, which are often expanded into character pairs such as ae and OE. This attribute is no longer supported, and existing scripts using it will not compile or run under Leopard. We discuss it here because it was available under Mac OS X 10.4 (Tiger) and older versions of the OS.

Comparisons performed by AppleScript ignore `expansion` by default, so strings that differ only in the use of these characters instead of the corresponding double characters are treated as if they were equal. You must use `considering expansion` to override the default behavior. Under Leopard, since the `expansion` attribute is no longer supported, comparisons of strings will always treat expanded and unexpanded characters as unequal.

The `expansion` attribute applies only to comparisons performed by AppleScript, as described in the earlier "Comparison Operations" section.

Hyphens

The `hyphens` attribute relates to hyphenated words. Within an `ignoring hyphens` block, hyphens are treated as if they were not present, so that *over-worked* and *overworked* are treated as equal. Note that this attribute has nothing to do with space characters, so that *over-worked* and *over worked* are considered unequal in any event.

Comparisons performed by AppleScript consider `hyphens` by default, so strings containing hyphens are treated as unequal to the corresponding strings without the hyphens. You must use `ignoring hyphens` to override the default behavior.

The `hyphens` attribute applies only to comparisons performed by AppleScript, as described in the "Comparison Operations" section.

Numeric Strings

Beginning with Mac OS X 10.4 (Tiger), a new attribute, `numeric strings`, has been added to the list of attributes with which `considering` and `ignoring` blocks can be used. This was necessary because the version of AppleScript installed with Tiger was 1.10—the tenth minor version of AppleScript 1. Without this new attribute, alphabetical comparisons of AppleScript version strings would treat AppleScript 1.10 as coming before the previous version, AppleScript 1.9.2. Since a number of other applications use a similar versioning scheme, where the so-called minor and bugfix version numbers can range as high as 15, this new attribute has broader significance, as well.

Comparisons performed by AppleScript ignore `numeric strings` by default, so 1.10 is treated as coming before 1.9. You must use `considering numeric strings` to override the default behavior. You will probably always (and only) do this when comparing standard-format version strings.

The `numeric strings` attribute applies only to comparisons performed by AppleScript, as described in the earlier "Comparison Operations" section.

Punctuation

The `punctuation` attribute relates to these punctuation marks: . , ? : ; ! \ ' " ` . Within an `ignoring punctuation` block, they are treated as if they were not present.

Comparisons performed by AppleScript consider `punctuation` by default, so the strings "Why?" and "Why" are treated as unequal. You must use `ignoring punctuation` to override the default behavior.

The `punctuation` attribute applies only to comparisons performed by AppleScript, as described in the earlier "Comparison Operations" section.

White Space

The `white space` attribute relates to the space, tab, newline and return characters. Within an `ignoring white space` block, they are treated as if they were not present.

Comparisons performed by AppleScript consider `white space` by default, so, for example, strings with and without leading or trailing spaces are treated as unequal even if they are otherwise identical, as are strings containing words that are separated by tabs, newline characters and returns. You must use `ignoring white space` to override the default behavior.

The `white space` attribute applies only to comparisons performed by AppleScript, as described in the earlier "Comparison Operations" section.

With Timeout

Sometimes you may want to lengthen the default timeout interval, and sometimes you may want to shorten it.

Extending the Timeout Interval

A `with timeout` clause is often essential when you use AppleScript to issue a long-running command to an application (or to a scripting addition within an application `tell` block or whose direct parameter is an application process), because the script quits with a timeout error as soon as the default two-minute timeout interval has expired without a reply event from the application. The two-minute timeout interval doesn't matter if your script does nothing more than, say, open a document on the screen that you want to read. But if your script needs to do something when the command finishes executing, such as saving a digital photo that the target application was processing, then you need a `with timeout` clause to extend the default timeout interval.

It usually isn't a good idea to try to determine exactly how long the process will run in an attempt to extend the timeout interval by just enough to let the process complete. Different computers process data at significantly different speeds, and even the same computer can run slower or faster depending on what other processes are running. Sometimes you can establish a reasonable order of magnitude plus a safety margin—say, five or six minutes instead of an hour. But often it is best to set such a long interval that it amounts to forever—say, a week. Script 19.10 shows how to do this.

```
tell application "Adobe Photoshop CS3"
    with timeout of weeks seconds -- 604800 seconds
        -- perform a very slow process
    end timeout
end tell
```
SCRIPT 19.10

> **NOTE** ▸ The longest available timeout interval is 8,947,848 seconds, or a
> little more than 3 months. If you type a larger integer into a `with timeout`
> clause, it will compile to `8947848 seconds`.

Don't make the mistake of thinking that a long `with timeout` interval will cause
your script to sit there for a week, doing nothing after the process completes
execution. A `with timeout` clause is not the same as a `delay` command. It does
not cause your script to pause for the timeout interval. In fact, if the long-
running command inside the `with timeout` block finishes executing sooner
and sends the script a reply event, the script immediately takes up where it
left off. This may happen after only a few seconds or minutes, and the script
immediately goes on to save the processed photo or do whatever remains to be
done. Then, assuming it was not saved as a stay-open application, it quits even
though the timeout interval is nowhere near expiring.

> **TIP** ▸ Instead of lengthening the default timeout interval, you can put
> a long-running application command inside an `ignoring application`
> `responses` block. The script continues executing immediately, without
> waiting for a reply event or an error from the target application, and the
> timeout interval is therefore never exceeded. The script's behavior will be
> different in other ways, as well, and it may not be appropriate to do this
> in all cases. For example, you won't hear about freezes or any other errors.
> Furthermore, your script won't be able to process the results of the process
> when it does complete.

In short, the job of a `with timeout` clause is only to stave off an unwanted
timeout error. The only penalty you might suffer when using a long timeout
interval is that you won't hear about it right away when the target application
freezes because of an unexpected problem. In that situation, the script looks

like it is still running (in fact, it is still running) because it has not yet received a reply event. The possibility of an unexpected freeze is the only reason for you to try to keep the timeout interval as short as possible in light of a reasonable estimate of the likely run time of the process. If you intend to run your script overnight, for example, and it is expected to take only an hour to complete, it would nevertheless be a good idea to set the timeout interval to eight hours. That will allow the process to run to completion even if you underestimated how much time it needed, but if the target application does freeze, you will see a timeout error message when you get to work the next morning.

Shortening the Timeout Interval

In other situations, you might want to shorten the timeout interval from its default two-minute duration. This is unlikely to be useful when running a process in an application context, because the script will always continue on to its next command as soon as the target application returns a reply event even if the default two minutes have not expired. That is, it won't make the script run any faster. Besides, two minutes isn't all that long to wait to learn that the target application froze, which is a rare occurrence. However, there might be circumstances where you want to force the user to respond to a dialog in less than two minutes, perhaps, for example, to enter a password without allowing the user time to look it up in a stolen address book.

Near the beginning of this chapter, you saw a script that reported a timeout error if you waited more than five seconds to respond to a dialog presented by the `display dialog` command. The timeout error caused the script to quit as soon as you dismissed the error sheet, without executing any commands following the `with timeout` block.

It would be much more useful to catch the timeout error and give the user an opportunity to recover. Applying what you learned in Chapter 12, *Error Handlers*, you might end up with the little game shown in Script 19.11.

```
tell application "TextEdit"
    activate
    repeat
        try
            with timeout of 5 seconds
                display dialog ("Quick, type a word:") ¬
                    default answer "" giving up after 5
            end timeout
            if text returned of result is "" then
                display alert "You cheated! 'Bye."
                exit repeat
            end if
        on error number error_number
            if error_number is -128 then exit repeat
            delay 1
            beep
            display alert ("You weren't quick enough!") ¬
                message ("Respond in 5 seconds. Try again!")
        end try
    end repeat
end tell
```

SCRIPT 19.11

Run the script and try to respond within five seconds. If you type any character and click OK in time, you'll get to try again thanks to the repeat loop enclosing the entire script. If you click OK without typing a character, you're disqualified for cheating.

But if you wait more than five seconds, you are treated to some interesting techniques for using the `display dialog` command in a `with timeout` block. You know from running the earlier script that the dialog does not go away when the timeout error occurs. This is true even if the dialog is displayed in a `try` block, because there is no convenient way to dismiss the dialog in the `on error` handler. To make the dialog go away when the timeout interval expires, the new, enhanced script uses the `display dialog` command's optional `giving` `up after` parameter to dismiss it automatically at the moment the timeout interval expires. Since you didn't respond within the allotted time, the timeout error causes script execution to branch to the `on error` handler. In the `on error` handler, a `delay 1` statement is necessary to give AppleScript a moment before displaying the error alert. If you omit the `delay 1` statement, the script gets into an anomalous state, and you have to force quit Script Editor by pressing Option+Command+Escape (Command+period won't work).

Now you can play the game endlessly, getting another chance every time you miss the timeout interval. You can, of course, quit the game at any time by clicking Cancel—as long as you do it within five seconds!

What's Next?

This chapter covered several ways in which your scripts can vary the default behavior of AppleScript, both when comparing text and when waiting for an application to respond to commands directed to it. In the next chapter, you'll learn how to write droplets—stay-open AppleScript applications that process files dropped on them.

20

Lesson **20**

Droplets

With this chapter, you'll begin to learn about a variety of AppleScript techniques you can use to react to actions somebody performs on your computer, such as adding a file to a folder.

It is often useful to write scripts that run automatically and immediately in reaction to events such as this in order to help you decide how to respond or to take care of menial tasks without requiring your personal attention. For example, you might write a script that automatically updates a log file or presents an alert every time somebody on your office network adds a file to the Drop Box folder in your Public folder. Or you might write a script that immediately asks you which tracks to add to your iTunes library when you insert an audio CD.

Scripts like these are especially useful in complex workflows, where you chain multiple scripts together in such a way that each script runs automatically as soon as the previous script finishes its part of the job.

You'll start in this chapter—after a brief introduction to event handlers in general—by learning about a feature that has existed in AppleScript since the beginning, droplets. A droplet is an ordinary AppleScript script application, or applet, except that it includes an *open handler*. The presence of the open handler in a script application tells the system that this script is a droplet. The system gives it a distinctive icon shown in Figure 20.1, alerting you that it does something special: a downward-pointing arrow. When you drop one or more Finder items on it, the droplet immediately launches, if it isn't already running, and its open handler is executed. It knows which items you dropped, passing a list of aliases to them in the open handler's parameter, so you can easily tell it to process them in any way you find useful.

FIGURE 20.1 A droplet icon.

Event Handlers and Applets

Scripts that are saved as applications or application bundles are commonly known as script applications or *applets*.

You can include special handlers in an applet that are called by the system when a user performs certain actions on the computer. These handlers are sometimes called *command handlers*, because another script can call them the same way it might call a scriptable application's commands. They are sometimes called *event handlers*, because they respond to events sent to them by the system.

The built-in AppleScript event handlers are `run`, `reopen`, `idle`, `quit`, and `open`:

▶ The run handler is triggered in response to a user action that runs a script—for example, double-clicking the applet's icon. The run handler is the only event handler that can be implicit. Any script statements at the top level of a script are considered to be in an implicit run handler, but you can put them all in an explicit run handler if you prefer.

▶ The reopen handler is triggered in response to some of the same user actions that trigger the run handler, but only if the applet is already running. In that situation, the run handler is not called.

▶ The idle handler is like the dog that didn't bark. It is called periodically when the user doesn't do something with the computer—in other words, when the computer is idle. You'll learn about idle handlers in Chapter 24, Adding Timing Controls to Scripts.

▶ The quit handler is triggered in response to a user action that quits a script.

▶ The open handler, which is the subject of this chapter, is triggered in response to the user's dropping one or more Finder items onto the applet's icon. An applet with an open handler is called a droplet.

Droplets need not be saved as "stay-open" applications, but they often are, as shown in Figure 20.2, so that they can continue running in case the user wants to drop more items without wasting the time it takes for the droplet to launch again.

FIGURE 20.2 Saving a stay-open applet in Script Editor.

Event handlers in applets and droplets differ from the subroutine handlers you learned about in Chapter 16, *Subroutines*, in that they do not require parentheses. You define them and call them without parentheses, just as you would call any scriptable application's commands without parentheses. For the one event handler that takes a parameter, **open**, you simply provide a variable name following the command name, as you would with a scriptable application's commands that take parameters. You use the variable name within the handler just as you would use any subroutine parameter.

The Open Handler

The open handler takes a single parameter. Anytime you drop one or more Finder items on an applet that has an open handler, the system calls the handler and sets the value of its parameter to a list of alias references to the items you dropped. You can drop folders, disks, and files of any kind on a droplet, and the list contains an alias reference to each of them. The parameter value is a list even if you drop a single item, so you should remember to get the alias reference out of the list before trying to use it.

Script 20.1 is a simple droplet to illustrate the form of an open handler. It does nothing but report the number of Finder items dropped on it. When you compile it, be sure to save it as an application or an application bundle. Test it by dragging one or more files, folders, or disks onto the droplet's icon, and see it display the number of items dropped. If you dropped a single item, you will see the count is 1. If you drop several items, you will see an exact count of all of them.

```
on open my_items
    display dialog ("Count of items dropped: ") ¬
        & (count my_items) ¬
        buttons {"OK"} default button "OK"
end open
```
SCRIPT 20.1

Screening for File Types

Many open handlers are intended to work only with files of a specific type, only with folders, or, perhaps rarely, only with disks. A robust droplet should make sure the user dropped the right kind of items on it, instead of failing with an uncaught error. Because there is no way to prevent someone from dropping a whole bunch of files, folders and disks on your droplet, you have to deal with all of these possibilities in every droplet you write. To do this, you usually have to use a **repeat** loop to process the dropped files one at a time, since the parameter to the open handler is a list. Within the **repeat** loop, you test various properties of each item in turn.

Script 20.2 is an example that opens photos of three kinds—JPEG, TIFF, and GIF—in Preview and ignores anything else that is dropped on it. For example, although Preview is perfectly capable of opening PDF files, this script screens them out because we're interested in only certain kinds of photos. The script illustrates the preferred way to determine the type of object that was dropped on a droplet and to filter out unwanted items under Leopard and Mac OS X 10.4 (Tiger). We'll show you a similar technique that's suitable for use in Mac OS X 10.3 (Panther) and earlier a little later.

```
property UTI_list : ¬
    {"public.jpeg", "public.tiff", "com.compuserve.gif"}
on open these_items
    repeat with i from 1 to the count of these_items
        set this_item to item i of these_items
        set the item_info to info for this_item
        if (folder of the item_info is false) and ¬
            (the type identifier of the item_info ¬
                is in the UTI_list) then
            tell application "Preview" to open this_item
        end if
    end repeat
end open
```
SCRIPT 20.2

This script is meant only to open files, so the first thing it has to do is screen out any folders and disks that might be dropped on it. The `info for` command in the Standard Additions scripting addition is perfect for this task. Since the `folder` property in the `file information` record returned by the `info for` command is `true` if the item is either a folder or a disk, you can kill two birds with one property. (If you revise this script to use the System Events application instead of the `info for` command, as is recommended for Leopard, you will have to restructure its logic slightly because System Events does not have a Boolean `folder` property.)

Next, once you know you have a file, you must test it to be sure it is a JPEG, TIFF, or GIF file. How you do this differs depending on which version of the Mac OS your script is expected to run on.

Uniform Type Identifiers (UTIs)

In Mac OS X 10.4 (Tiger), the newest mechanism to determine file types, *Uniform Type Identifiers*, or *UTIs*, came into full flower. We first discussed UTIs in Chapter 9, *Communicating with the User*, in connection with the `of type` parameter to the `choose file` command. To remind you, UTI's are dot-delimited strings, such as "public.jpeg," "public.tiff," and "com.compuserve.gif." As you saw in the previous example, you can learn a file's UTI by getting the `type identifier` property of the `file information` record returned by the `info for` command. The `type identifier` property was introduced in Tiger. It is also available as a property of a `file` in the System Events application.

UTIs are based on an hierarchical structure where, for example, a specific type identifier such as "com.compuserve.gif" may also have a higher-level or more general type identifier to which it *conforms*, such as "public.image." Unfortunately, unlike the `of type` parameter to the `choose file` command, the `info for` command does not permit a script to check for the most general image UTI, "public.image," instead of the more specific "com.compuserve.gif." There is no generalized AppleScript command to determine whether a specific UTI conforms to a more general UTI. When using the `info for` command, you must therefore check for all the specific types you want to handle.

The list of recognized public and private UTIs is long, and it grows longer daily as developers invent new file types and give them new UTIs. Duplication of UTIs is prevented because new public types can be created only by Apple and because private types always include the developer's name, as in "com.compuserve.gif." The system is very robust, and it brings great flexibility and reliability to file typing in Tiger.

The topic of UTIs is too big to take on in this book in detail. For an introduction, read the *Uniform Type Identifiers Overview* document on the Apple developer Web site at `http://developer.apple.com`. It includes several tables listing all the common UTIs and explains their hierarchical structure.

File Types and Name Extensions

Over the years before Tiger, the Mac OS evolved several different ways to determine a file's type. In the classic Mac OS, files carried information about their type and the application that "owned" them internally. The `info for` command's `file information` record gave you this information in its `file type` property, using short strings such as "JPEG," "TIFF" and "GIF." This mechanism remained the principal means to determine a file's type in the earliest versions of Mac OS X, but the use of name extensions began to flower in order to make the Mac OS more compatible with file type conventions used on other operating systems. The `info for` command's `file information` record was given a new property way back in Mac OS X 10.1, the `name extension` property, to accommodate this trend. Typical name extensions were "jpg," "jpeg," "tif," "tiff," and "gif," all separated from the file name by a *dot* separator. Because some Mac OS X files began to omit the internal type indicator reflected in the `file type` property, while others hadn't yet acquired the name extension reflected in the `name extension` property, it became necessary to test both for a file's `file type` and for its `name extension` properties to determine a file's type. The new UTI system checks for an internal file type and a name extension automatically as part of its algorithm for establishing the file's UTI, but you can't use the `type identifier` property when running on Mac OS X 10.3 (Panther) or older.

In scripts that will run under Mac OS X 10.3 (Panther) and older, therefore, you should always check for both the `file type` and the `name extension` to be sure you catch all files that use either technique. A script that does this should also work correctly in Leopard and Tiger. Script 20.3 is the previous script modified for Panther and earlier.

> **TIP** ▶ Don't forget to supply spaces as needed to pad a shorter file type string out to the required four characters. If you supply a three-character string in the list by accident, the actual four-character file type won't be found in the list.

```
property type_list : {"JPEG", "TIFF", "GIFf"}
property extension_list : {"jpg", "jpeg", "tif", "tiff", "gif"}
on open these_items
    repeat with i from 1 to the count of these_items
        set this_item to item i of these_items
        set the item_info to info for this_item
        if (folder of the item_info is false) and ¬
            ((the file type of the item_info ¬
                is in the type_list) or ¬
                (the name extension of the item_info ¬
                    is in the extension_list)) then
            tell application "Preview" to open this_item
        end if
    end repeat
end open
```
SCRIPT 20.3

In this example, the script first checks the `file type` property of the `file information` record returned by the `info for` command and determines whether it is included in the `type_list` property initialized at the top of the script. Because some newer photo files don't have traditional file type information embedded within them, the script also checks the `name extension` property of the `file information` record to see whether it is included in the `extension_list` property. Using the logical operator `or`, the script tells Preview to open the photo if either test is true.

Processing Folders

In the previous script, you screened out folders. Often, however, you want to process folders. The same basic logical structure applies, but files are screened out and folders are processed. In the handler shown in Script 20.4, all processing of folders is handled in the `process_folder` subroutine, which is left blank here because this is a skeleton droplet for illustration purposes only.

```
on open these_items
    repeat with i from 1 to the count of these_items
        set this_item to item i of these_items
        set the item_info to info for this_item
        if folder of the item_info is true then
            process_folder(this_item)
        end if
    end repeat
end open


on process_folder(this_item)
    -- this_item is an alias reference to a folder
    -- FOLDER PROCESSING STATEMENTS GO HERE
end process_folder
```
SCRIPT 20.4

Processing Items in Subfolders

The first examples in this chapter were a little rigid about screening out folders, and the most recent example was too rigid about processing nothing but folders. Many people organize their photos in folders, subfolders, and subsubfolders, and a more convenient droplet would take this common practice into account by processing files *and* folders, all in one droplet.

Script 20.5 is a droplet that allows folders as well as files to be dropped on it. When it encounters a folder, it looks at all the items in the folder to see whether any of them qualify for processing. If one of those folders contains a folder, it looks at all the items in it, too, and... well, you get the drift.

The open handler in this example is familiar. It is identical in logical structure to the open handler in the UTI version of the first major example in this chapter. However, instead of screening out folders when it finds them, it calls the `process_folder` subroutine to process them. Also, instead of opening photo files right in the open handler, it opens them in a separate subroutine called `process_items`. This is efficient because photos are opened both from the open handler and from the `process_folder` subroutine. There is no reason to write the processing steps twice when you can do it once in a subroutine and call the subroutine twice.

```
property UTI_list : ¬
    {"public.jpeg", "public.tiff", "com.compuserve.gif"}


on open these_items
    repeat with i from 1 to the count of these_items
        set this_item to (item i of these_items)
        set the item_info to info for this_item
        if folder of the item_info is true then
            process_folder(this_item)
        else if (the type identifier of the item_info ¬
            is in the UTI_list) then
            process_item(this_item)
        end if
    end repeat
end open


on process_folder(this_folder)
    set these_items to list folder this_folder without invisibles
    repeat with i from 1 to the count of these_items
        set this_item to alias ((this_folder as text) ¬
            & (item i of these_items))
        set the item_info to info for this_item
        if folder of the item_info is true then
            process_folder(this_item)
        else if (the type identifier of the item_info ¬
            is in the UTI_list) then
            process_item(this_item)
        end if
    end repeat
end process_folder


on process_item(this_item)
    tell application "Preview" to open this_item
end process_item
```
SCRIPT 20.5

By far the most interesting part of this script is the `process_folder` subroutine. Its logical structure is almost identical to that of the open handler, but there are a few differences.

The parameter to the `process_folder` subroutine is an alias reference to a folder, not a list of alias references like the list that the open handler's parameter variable contained. Our goal is to use the same logic in the `process_folder` subroutine that we used in the open handler, so we have to create a list of all the items in the folder that is organized like the list originally passed to the open handler. To do this, the script uses the `list folder` command in the Standard Additions scripting addition to get a list of all the items in the folder (leaving out invisible items). At the beginning of each iteration of the repeat loop, it concatenates the folder reference and the item reference from the `list folder` command to create a full reference to each item in the subfolder.

Now the script does a remarkable thing: it reproduces the logic of the repeat loop in the open handler exactly, calling the `process_folder` subroutine every time it finds a more deeply nested subfolder. Calling a subroutine from itself is known as *recursion*. Whenever a data structure is itself recursive, as in the case of the nested folders the droplet is traversing, it is often appropriate to process it using recursive subroutine calls. The nested subroutine calls burrow deeper and deeper into the stack of nested folders, opening qualifying photos as they go, popping back up out of the stack for air occasionally when they run out of items to process in one folder and then diving back down as soon as they find another nested folder. By the time it's finished, the droplet has traversed every subfolder in the original list of items dropped on the droplet, opening every qualifying photo no matter how deeply nested in subsubfolders or deeper.

You've probably noticed that the script can be made even shorter, because there are two identical groups of processing statements. We left them separate initially to make the logic of the script clearer. Script 20.6 is the same script, condensed.

```
property UTI_list : ¬
    {"public.jpeg", "public.tiff", "com.compuserve.gif"}

on open these_items
    repeat with i from 1 to the count of these_items
        set this_item to (item i of these_items)
        set the item_info to info for this_item
        do_processing(this_item, item_info)
    end repeat
end open

on process_folder(this_folder)
    set these_items to list folder this_folder without invisibles
    repeat with i from 1 to the count of these_items
        set this_item to alias ((this_folder as text) ¬
            & (item i of these_items))
        set the item_info to info for this_item
        do_processing(this_item, item_info)
    end repeat
end process_folder

on process_item(this_item)
    tell application "Preview" to open this_item
end process_item

on do_processing(this_item, item_info)
    if folder of the item_info is true then
        process_folder(this_item)
    else if (the type identifier of the item_info ¬
        is in the UTI_list) then
        process_item(this_item)
    end if
end do_processing
```

SCRIPT 20.6

Alias Files and Droplets

None of the droplet examples in this chapter checks to see whether you dropped an alias file on the droplet. The reason may surprise you: an open handler's parameter variable *never* contains a reference to an alias file. Really. Even when you deliberately drop an alias file on it. Don't believe it? Try dropping an alias file on the droplet shown as Script 20.7, and you'll see that it always returns false. Testing the `alias` property of the information record returned by the `info for` command in the Standard Additions scripting addition *always returns false in a droplet*.

```
on open my_files
    get info for item 1 of my_files
    display dialog alias of result
end open
```
SCRIPT 20.7

When thinking about this conundrum, take care to distinguish between an *alias file* and an *alias reference*. An open handler's parameter is a list of alias references, which are AppleScript objects. An alias file is a file system object. It turns out that AppleScript *always* resolves an alias file when one is dropped on a droplet, before triggering the droplet and sending any information to the open handler's parameter variable. Only after AppleScript locates the alias file's `original item` does it launch the droplet, and then it passes a reference to the `original item` into the open handler. The parameter to the open handler therefore always contains an alias reference to the original file, folder, or disk, never to the alias file itself.

When you think about it, this makes perfect sense for almost every use to which you might want to put a droplet. In the second droplet in this chapter, for example, you tested each dropped item to see whether it was a folder or disk. If you drop an alias file pointing to a folder or disk, then AppleScript finds its original item, and the script identifies the `original item` as a folder or disk and screens it out—which is just what you want, since your script opens only photos. If you drop an alias file pointing to a JPEG, TIFF, or GIF file, AppleScript finds the `original item`, and your script identifies it as a JPEG,

TIFF, or GIF file and opens it in Preview—which is, likewise, just what you want. Perfect! You never have to worry about alias files when writing droplets. They just work.

Well, almost. There are a couple of issues.

For one, if you ever want to write a droplet that does something with an alias file itself, such as determining when it (the alias file, not its original item) was created, you're stuck. You can't get there from here.

Finally, if you try to drop a disconnected, or orphaned, alias file on a droplet, AppleScript won't be able to find its `original item` because, by definition, it has none. In the old days, AppleScript would treat this as an error. Now, AppleScript is much smarter. The droplet won't highlight when an orphaned alias file is dragged over it, and it won't accept the drop. You don't have to worry about trying to catch the error and alert the user, because the droplet won't even run.

The open, run, and reopen Commands

There is a love-hate relationship between the open handler and the run handler. They go together, but they don't work together.

They have in common the fact that running a script application for the first time triggers one or the other. But, even when both are present, only one of them is called. When you double-click a script application with a run handler, or when you select it and then open it using the Finder's File menu, the system launches it and calls its run handler; it does not call the open handler, even if one is present. When you drop a file onto a script application with an open handler, the system launches it and calls its open handler; it does not call the run handler, even if one is present. To avoid confusing these two command handlers, remember that the term `open` refers to opening the Finder items that are dropped on a droplet. It does not refer to opening the droplet itself from the Finder's File menu, which triggers the run handler instead of the open handler.

TIP ▸ These rules apply even when the run handler is an implicit run handler. When a script contains some statements at the top level, they are considered to be in a run handler even if they are not enclosed in an on run block. Thus, the system does not run them when an item is dropped on a droplet.

Because the open handler and the run handler share the distinction of being the first part of a script to run when a droplet or an applet is first run, it is where you should set up or initialize any conditions that are required to make sure the script works as designed.

Unlike the run handler, the open handler is not limited to use when a droplet is first run. The system calls an open handler every time items are dropped on the droplet, even if it is already running. If you anticipate dropping items on a droplet frequently during a work session, you should leave it running. It will work faster every time you drop items on it, because it won't need to take time to launch again.

Although the system does not call a run handler if you double-click a stay-open applet that is already running, you can achieve the same effect by including a *reopen handler* in the applet. The reopen handler does nothing when you first run an applet. It also does nothing when you drop an item on a droplet, even though it incorporates the word *open*. Instead, the system triggers the reopen handler only when you attempt to run an already-running script by double-clicking it or by opening it from the Finder's File menu. The reopen handler therefore serves either of two purposes: it can be used to run the run handler by calling it explicitly whenever a stay-open applet is double-clicked while it is already running, or it can be used on those occasions when you need special behavior when you double-click a running applet.

Script 20.8 is a script that implements an explicit run handler, an open handler, and a reopen handler. To see the rules described previously in action, try dropping Finder items on it before and after it is running, double-clicking it in the Finder when it is not running, and double-clicking it after it is already running. Because it includes a reopen handler, be sure to save it as a stay-open application or application bundle.

```
on run
    report("Run handler")
end run


on open my_items
    report("Open handler")
end open


on reopen
    report("Reopen handler")
end reopen


on report(message)
    display dialog message buttons {"OK"} default button "OK"
end report
```
SCRIPT 20.8

Finally, Script 20.9 is a complex example making good use of the ability to incorporate a run handler, an open handler, and a reopen handler, all in one script. Think of it as a poor man's implementation of preferences for a droplet. It uses a run handler to allow you to double-click it to set up the properties of the script that control its behavior when it is used as a droplet. Run the script by double-clicking it whenever you want to save a different set of properties, and then drop Finder items on it when you want to process them according to the current settings. It includes a reopen handler whose only purpose is to run the run handler even if the script is already running when you double-click it. Without this, a user is likely to be stymied when double-clicking an already-running script, because nothing would happen and the reason would not be obvious to most users.

This droplet is similar to the previous examples, but in addition to adding the ability to set preferences, it optionally presents an alert when a file of the wrong type is encountered.

```
property UTI_list : ¬
    {"public.jpeg", "public.tiff", "com.compuserve.gif"}
property post_alert : true

on run
    repeat
        display dialog ("My File Processing Droplet") ¬
            & return & return ¬
            & ("Post User Alert: ") & (post_alert as text) ¬
            buttons {"Cancel", "Set Prefs", "Done"} ¬
            default button 3
        if the button returned of the result is "Set Prefs" then
            display dialog ¬
                ("Should this droplet post an alert ") ¬
                    & ("when items it can't handle ") ¬
                & ("are dropped onto it?") ¬
                & return & return ¬
                & ("Current Status: ") ¬
                & (post_alert as text) ¬
                buttons {"Cancel", "False", "True"}
            if the button returned of the result is "False" then
                set post_alert to false
            else
                set post_alert to true
            end if
        else
            return "done"
        end if
    end repeat
end run

on reopen
    run
end reopen
```

```
on open these_items
    repeat with i from 1 to the count of these_items
        set this_item to item i of these_items
        set the item_info to info for this_item
        if (folder of the item_info is false) and ¬
            (the type identifier of the item_info ¬
                is in the UTI_list) then
            process_item(this_item)
        else if post_alert is true then
            set old_delimiters ¬
                to AppleScript's text item delimiters
            set AppleScript's text item delimiters to {", "}
            set the display_list to UTI_list as string
            set AppleScript's text item delimiters ¬
                to old_delimiters
            tell application ¬
                (path to frontmost application as string)
                beep
                display dialog ¬
                    ("This droplet only processes ") ¬
                        & ("files of type:") ¬
                    & return & return ¬
                    & display_list ¬
                    giving up after 15 ¬
                    buttons {"OK"} default button "OK"
            end tell
        end if
    end repeat
end open

on process_item(this_item)
    tell application "Preview" to open this_item
end process_item
```
SCRIPT 20.9

What's Next?

In this chapter, you took the first step toward writing scripts that react to events occurring on your computer—specifically, when you drop Finder items on an AppleScript droplet. In the next chapter you will learn about actions that a script can take automatically when you add Finder items to a folder, by attaching scripts called *folder actions* to folders.

21

The Two Faces of Folder Actions

Using Folder Actions

What's Next?

Lesson **21**
Folder Actions

Until you learned about droplets in the previous chapter, you had written scripts that run when you tell them to run. You click the Run button in a Script Editor window, or you double-click an applet. Even droplets require you to take an affirmative step, dropping a document on a droplet in the Finder. These techniques and others like them are very useful, because they allow you to reduce a complex and time-consuming series of steps to a single step. But all of them have one thing in common: if you don't remember to perform the user action that runs your script, your script just sits there. Scripts like this take automation only halfway.

Wouldn't it be great if your scripts were smart enough to run by themselves, whenever they're needed? Then you would have reduced that complex and time-consuming series of steps not just to a single step but to no steps at all! If you put a lot of effort into writing a script that automatically sorts your photos into separate folders by type, wouldn't it take a load off your mind if you didn't have to remember to run it every time you saved a photo you've finished editing? And then there are all those things that happen on your computer that you don't even know about. If you're on a network and co-workers sometimes put files in the Drop Box folder in your Public folder, wouldn't you like to know about it right away instead of having to remember to open your Drop Box folder every few minutes?

AppleScript comes with a variety of tools that take automation to this next level. In this chapter, you'll use folder actions to run scripts automatically when the contents or state of a folder changes. In other chapters, you'll use similar techniques to run scripts automatically, for example, when midnight rolls around. Third-party utilities add still more tools that use AppleScript to help you manage your computer even when you aren't paying attention.

The Two Faces of Folder Actions

Setting up a folder action takes two steps: you write a folder action script, and you attach it to a target folder so that it runs automatically whenever the folder changes. What makes using folder actions different from ordinary scripting is that you have to perform these steps only once, when you're setting up a folder action script. After that, folder action scripts run by themselves every time they're supposed to run—today, next week, and next year—until you turn them off. (There is a third step, enabling folder actions on your computer, but you have to do that only once, and then you can forget about it.)

A folder action script is an ordinary AppleScript script that can use all the techniques you've already learned about, but it has an additional feature. It contains one or more special handlers, called *folder action event handlers*, that run when they are triggered by a change in the target folder. The AppleScript terminology suite that defines these special handlers is the Folder Actions suite, which is located in the Standard Additions scripting addition. Because these event handlers are defined in a scripting addition that is installed as part of Mac OS X, they are always available.

You can attach a folder action script to a target folder in several ways: you can use a convenient application provided by Apple called Folder Actions Setup, you can use a menu item in a Finder contextual menu or in the Script menu, or you can write a script to do it.

Folder Actions Setup is installed as part of Mac OS X. It is located in the AppleScript folder in the top-level Applications folder. It offers a simple, intuitive user interface that lets you choose the target folder and the folder action script or scripts to attach to it.

If you prefer to automate the process of attaching a folder action script to a target folder, you can write a script using the commands that are defined in a second Folder Actions Suite, this one located in the System Events application. The System Events application is part of Mac OS X and defines many important AppleScript objects and commands. It is located in the CoreServices folder of the System Library folder, at System > Library > CoreServices.

Writing a Folder Action Script

A folder action script does not require a run handler or an open handler, because it isn't run by a user the way an ordinary script is run. Instead, it contains one or more folder actions event handlers. If any of these handlers are included in the script, they are triggered automatically when the corresponding events occur in the target folder. You must compile your scripts and save them as compiled scripts. You must store them in a special Folder Action Scripts folder, either in the Scripts folder in the local Library folder or in the Scripts folder in the current user's Library folder. (Create the Folder Action Scripts folder yourself if it doesn't already exist.) The Folder Action Scripts folder is treated specially, in that its contents are not displayed in the Script menu because a folder action script isn't meant to be run by a user.

Using the folder actions event handlers, you can design your script to be triggered not only by changes to the contents of the target folder—adding files to it or removing files from it—but also by changes to the position and size of the target folder's window and by opening and closing it. The window does not have to be open to trigger these event handlers (except for the `closing folder window for` event, of course).

Mac OS X comes with several example folder action scripts preinstalled. Look for them in the AppleScript folder of the top-level Applications folder. You will see they use a naming convention that is helpful in understanding their purpose. For example, the "add - new item alert.scpt" script responds to the `adding folder items to` event, and it presents an alert when a new item is added to the target folder. This naming convention is not required, and it would not be appropriate for a script that contains multiple event handlers. Study these example scripts to see how several different kinds of folder action scripts work.

The adding folder items to Event

To trigger your script whenever a user adds one or more items to the target folder, include an `adding folder items to` event handler.

The direct parameter should be any variable name you like, such as `target_folder`. You can use this as a local variable in the body of the handler. It contains an alias reference to the target folder once the handler is triggered by adding an item to the target folder. Most of the folder action event handlers have a direct parameter that works the same way.

This event handler has another parameter, `after receiving`, which should also be a variable name, such as `added_items`. In the body of the handler, you can use this variable to get a list of alias references to the item or items that were added to the folder, whether they were document files, application files, other folders, or any other kind of Finder item.

The handler is triggered every time one or more items are dragged into the target folder and also whenever a new item is saved into the target folder or created in it.

A simple `adding folder items to` event handler might look like the example shown in Script 21.1. It displays a dialog containing the name of the item that was added to the target folder, or the name of the first item if several items were added. (It doesn't need to check to make sure at least one item was added, because the fact that it was triggered guarantees this.)

```
on adding folder items to target_folder after receiving added_items
    get info for item 1 of added_items
    display dialog name of result
end adding folder items to
```
SCRIPT 21.1

The removing folder items from Event

To trigger your script whenever a user removes one or more items from the target folder, include a `removing folder items from` event handler. Use it the same way you use the `adding folder items to` event handler, including a direct parameter that is a variable name such as `target_folder`.

The second parameter is `after losing`. Use it with a variable name such as `removed_items`, just as you did with the `after receiving` parameter to the `adding folder items to` handler. In the body of the handler, you can use this variable to obtain a list of references to the item or items that were removed from the folder. If the items were removed from the target folder by dragging them somewhere else on the same disk, the references will be alias references pointing to their new locations. If they were deleted permanently, the dictionary states that only the names as strings will be available. However, if they are moved to the trash, the variable contains alias references to them in the trash.

Script 21.2 is a simple `removing folder items from` event handler. It displays a dialog containing the complete path to the item that was removed from the target folder or the path to the first item if several items were removed.

```
on removing folder items from target_folder after losing removed_items
    get item 1 of removed_items
    display dialog result as string
end removing folder items from
```
SCRIPT 21.2

The moving folder window for Event

To trigger your script whenever a user moves or resizes the target window, include a `moving folder window for` event handler. Use a variable name such as `target_folder` as the direct parameter.

> **NOTE** ▶ In older versions of Mac OS X, the `moving folder window for` event handler was triggered only if the toolbar of the target folder's window was hidden. This issue was fixed in Mac OS X 10.4 (Tiger), and the handler is now triggered in Tiger and Leopard even if the toolbar is showing.

This event handler has a second parameter, `from`, which should also be a variable name, such as `start_coordinates`. In the body of the handler, you can use this variable to obtain the starting coordinates of the window, before a user moved or resized it. This is useful if your script needs to provide an option to change the folder back to its original position or size. As the dictionary notes, you can get the coordinates of its final resting place from the Finder using the alias reference to the target folder from the direct parameter.

Script 21.3 is a `moving folder window for` event handler that moves the target window back to its original position and size every time a user moves or resizes it. Attached to all the Finder windows in a kiosk, this script would prevent users from rearranging the desktop.

```
property master_coordinates : {}
on moving folder window for target_folder from start_coordinates
    if master_coordinates is {} then
        set master_coordinates to start_coordinates
    end if
    tell application "Finder"
        set bounds of window of target_folder to master_coordinates
    end tell
end moving folder window for
```
SCRIPT 21.3

When a folder action script tells the Finder to change the bounds of the target folder's window, the scripted move does not trigger the script again. (This is a good thing, because otherwise the script would be triggered again and again until it crashed.) As a result, the script does not notice the new coordinates the next time a user moves or resizes the window. Instead, it keeps using as its starting coordinates the position and size that a user last set by manually moving the window. The earlier example script works around this behavior by saving the initial starting coordinates in a persistent property and using the saved property from then on. To reset the initial starting coordinates, turn off the script temporarily in Folder Actions Setup, place the window where you want it, recompile and save the script to reset the property, and then turn the script back on in Folder Actions Setup.

The opening folder and closing folder Events

To trigger your script whenever a user opens or closes the target folder, include an `opening folder` or `closing folder` event handler. Use a variable name such as `target_folder` as the direct parameter. Neither of these handlers has a second parameter.

For examples of folder action scripts that use these event handlers, look at the example folder action scripts that are installed with Mac OS X, in the AppleScript folder in the Applications folder.

Attaching a Folder Action Script

To use a folder action script after you've written or acquired one, you must attach it to its intended target folder or folders and make sure it is turned on. When you no longer need it, you can turn it off temporarily or remove it (that is, detach it) from its target folder.

In Mac OS X, folder action scripts attached by a user work only when that user is logged in to allow different users to set up their folder action scripts separately. This means scripts attached to removable or shared disks will work only for the user who attached them.

There are several ways to attach a folder action script in Mac OS X.

Folder Actions Setup

Folder Actions Setup is often the most convenient way to attach and remove folder action scripts, especially when you're managing several of them at once. It provides an easy-to-use graphical user interface, shown in Figure 21.1.

FIGURE 21.1 The Folder Actions Setup window.

To use Folder Actions Setup, you must save your folder action scripts in one of the standard locations, the Folder Action Scripts folder in the Scripts folder in either the local Library folder or the current user's Library folder. Create the Folder Action Scripts folder yourself if it does not already exist. If you've turned on the "Show Script menu in menu bar" option in the AppleScript Utility, you can open either of these folders quickly by choosing Open Computer Scripts Folder or Open User Scripts Folder from the Open Scripts Folder menu item at the top of the Script menu. Placing your folder action scripts in one of these folders ensures that Folder Actions Setup includes them in its Choose a Script to Attach sheet, described in a moment.

Folder Actions Setup is simple to use. Launch it by double-clicking it in the AppleScript folder in the Applications folder or, if the AppleScript Utility is running, click the Set Up Actions button. Alternatively, you can choose Configure Folder Actions from the contextual menu while a Finder item is selected, or you can choose Configure Folder Actions from the Folder Actions submenu in the Script menu.

In the Folder Actions Setup window, click the + button under the table on the left (the Folders with Actions table) to open a standard file browser sheet, navigate to the desired target folder, and click Open. The Choose a Script to Attach sheet opens immediately, listing all the scripts in the standard Folder Action

Scripts folders. Choose one or more of them and click Attach, and you're done. If you want to attach a script to a folder that is already listed in the table, select the folder, and then click the + button under the table on the right (the Script table) to open the Choose a Script to Attach sheet.

The checkboxes in the On columns of both tables are automatically checked to enable the newly attached script. Uncheck a checkbox in the On column in the Script table to temporarily disable a script, or uncheck a checkbox in the Folders with Actions table to temporarily disable all scripts attached to a specific folder. Click the - button under the Script table to remove a script, and click the - button under the Folders with Actions table to remove all scripts that are attached to a specific folder.

In Leopard, Folder Actions Setup is scriptable. For the most part, it duplicates AppleScript functionality that was already available in the System Events application and remains available there in Leopard. The details of both are discussed later in this chapter.

The Contextual Menu

For quick, on-the-fly management of folder action scripts for individual volumes or folders, use the Finder's contextual menu.

Place the mouse over the volume or folder icon in the Finder to which you want to attach a script, click while holding down the Control key, and then choose Attach a Folder Action. The Choose a File dialog opens, in which you can choose any script file in order to attach it to the volume or folder.

> TIP ▶ The Choose a File dialog should open by default to the current user's Folder Action Scripts folder. You can navigate to a script anywhere on your computer and choose it, but don't let this fool you into thinking that you can attach a script that is located outside one of the standard Folder Action Scripts folders. If you try this, the target folder will look as though it has an attached script when you look at it in Folder Actions Setup, but the script will never be triggered. Also, the contextual menu for the target folder will not include the Remove a Folder Action and Edit a Folder Action commands that it usually includes when used with a folder having attached scripts.

When you use the contextual menu on a volume or folder already having one or more attached folder action scripts, it includes Remove a Folder Action and Edit a Folder Action commands that allow you to remove or edit selected folder actions.

The Script Menu

The Folder Actions menu item in the Script menu provides commands that are similar to those in the contextual menu. However, they run scripts that are installed as part of Mac OS X, and their behavior is a little different from that of the similar contextual menu commands. Note that the Folder Actions menu item appears only if you have enabled the "Show Computer scripts" setting in AppleScript Utility.

The Attach Script to Folder command opens a free-standing list window that is similar to Folder Actions Setup's Choose a Script to Attach sheet. Select one or more scripts from the list, and click OK. A Choose a Folder dialog then opens. Navigate to the folder to which you want to attach the script or scripts, and click OK.

The Remove Folder Actions command presents a window listing all folders that have scripts attached. Choose one or more of them, and click OK. It then presents a series of separate windows, one for each folder you chose, listing all scripts that are attached to the folder. Select one or more of the attached scripts, and click OK to remove them.

> **NOTE** ▶ If Folder Actions Setup is open while you use these commands, it may appear to freeze. Just wait a while, and it will eventually notice the changes and update its window.

The Script menu does not include an Edit a Folder Action Script command corresponding to the command of that name in the contextual menu.

AppleScript

The System Events application contains a Folder Actions Suite defining a set of classes and commands for managing folder actions using AppleScript. For examples showing how some of them are used, study the scripts installed as part of Mac OS X in the AppleScript folder in the Applications folder. The Example Scripts folder is actually an alias file pointing to the Folder Action Scripts folder in the Scripts folder in the local Library folder.

In addition to basic commands to `attach action to`, `remove action from`, and `edit action of`, the Folder Actions Suite defines an `attached scripts` command that lists all folder action scripts attached to a given folder. It also defines an object model consisting of two classes, `folder action` and `script`, each of which has a settable `enabled` property and read-only properties to get the `name` and `path` of a `folder action` or a `script`, the `volume` of a `folder action` and the `POSIX path` of a `script`. The `folder action` class also has a `scripts` element that lists all folder action scripts contained by it. The `folder action` and `script` classes are also defined in the Folder Actions Setup Suite in Folder Actions Setup in Leopard.

In addition, the System Events Suite defines two properties of its `application` object that are useful when writing scripts to manage folder actions, `Folder Action scripts folder` and `folder actions enabled`, as well as the `folder action` element that lists all existing `folder action` objects in the file system. The `folder actions enabled` property and the `folder action` element are also defined in the Folder Actions Setup Suite in Folder Actions Setup in Leopard.

In this connection, you might well ask what a `folder action` object is, exactly. To find the answer, run a script to `tell application "System Events" to get every folder action`. You'll discover from the result returned by that statement that a `folder action` is an object in the application that contains one or more folder action scripts and links all of them to a given folder. A `folder action` object takes the name of the folder with which it is associated.

Oddly, there can be more than one `folder action` object associated with a given folder, all of them having the same name. This fact is reflected in Folder Actions Setup, where you can add a folder more than once and connect different folder action scripts to each of them.

TIP ▶ The attached scripts command in the Folder Actions Suite is supposed to list all the scripts attached to the specified folder, but in fact it lists only the scripts that are attached to the first `folder action` object associated with the folder. To write a bulletproof script to get all the scripts that are attached to a folder, check for multiple `folder action` objects for that folder, and get all of the scripts contained by all of them. The Finder contextual menu commands Remove a Folder Action and Edit a Folder Action also list only those scripts that are attached to the first `folder action` object; you must use the Folder Actions Setup application or write a script to remove any scripts attached to a second folder action.

Using these classes and commands in the System Events dictionary, it is possible to write a sophisticated application having all the features of the Folder Actions Setup utility provided by Apple. In fact, one of us (Bill Cheeseman) did exactly that for the classic Mac OS many years ago. If you plan to write scripts that use these commands, you will find it useful to add System Events to the Script Editor's Library window, so that you won't have to dig down to the CoreServices folder in the System Library folder every time you need to look at the dictionary.

Using Folder Actions

You must enable folder actions generally in order to use this important AppleScript technology.

To enable folder actions, launch Folder Actions Setup, and if the Enable Folder Actions checkbox is unchecked, click it. This launches the System Events application in the background if it's not already running, and it sets up System Events so that it can trigger any attached folder action scripts that are turned on. Unchecking the Enable Folder Actions checkbox does not cause System Events to quit immediately, because it may be in use by another technology, but it does render all folder action scripts inoperative until you turn it on again. Disabling folder actions with the menu and script commands described next behaves the same way.

In Mac OS X 10.4 (Tiger), enabling folder actions adds the System Events application to the Login Items pane in the Accounts pane of System Preferences, and disabling it removes System Events from Login Items. Once launched, System Events remains running indefinitely by default, even if you set the `quit delay` property of the System Events `application` object to a positive value instead of the default 0. Some users have noticed that problems may crop up on the computer while Folder Actions is enabled in Tiger, so it may be prudent to leave it turned off when not needed.

> **TIP** ▶ If all of your folder action scripts stop working, System Events might have crashed. Click the Enable Folder Actions checkbox in Folder Actions Setup once or twice to relaunch it and turn folder actions back on. You can launch the Activity Monitor in the Utilities folder in the Applications folder to see whether System Events is running.

Folder actions and System Events behave differently in Leopard. System Events is not added to the Login Items pane when you turn on folder actions, but it does run automatically whenever it is needed, for example, when folder actions is enabled. By default on Leopard, it quits automatically after five minutes (300 seconds) of inactivity, unless folder actions is turned on. You can change this interval by setting the `quit delay` property of the System Events `application` object. Setting `quit delay` to 0 causes System Events to remain running at all times. Folder actions has been improved in a variety of ways in Leopard, and it appears to be very solid. For example, in Leopard you can now attach a script bundle as a folder action.

The Folder Actions submenu in the Script menu contains Enable Folder Actions and Disable Folder Actions commands that you can use instead of Folder Actions Setup, and the Finder contextual menu contains a command that toggles between Enable Folder Actions and Disable Folder Actions.

You can also use AppleScript to enable and disable folder actions generally, as well as checking its current state, using the `folder actions enabled` property of the `application` object in the System Events Suite. In Leopard, the `folder actions enabled` property can also be scripted using the `application` object in the Folder Actions Setup Suite in Folder Actions Setup.

What Is Folder Actions Good For?

The brief examples shown earlier only hint at the power and utility of folder actions.

Folder action scripts are perfectly suited to automated workflows that use "watch folders" or "drop boxes" to control and manipulate document files as they move from step to step in a complex production process. For example, suppose you are the editor of a real estate agency's weekly catalog of available houses, and you need to process photos as you receive them from several agents, each of whom uses a different kind of camera with different settings. The first folder in your workflow might have an attached script that moves digital photographs to separate folders by type as you download them from one of the cameras. Each of those folders might have a unique script attached that performs type-specific manipulations to each photo as it is added to the folder and then sends it to a final folder. The final folder might have a script attached that places each photo into the next available slot in the catalog as it is added. What would otherwise have been a time-consuming and labor-intensive project now requires you only to download the photos when each agent returns to the office and, when the deadline approaches, print the catalog.

Differences from Mac OS 9

Folder actions began life in the classic Mac OS and is fully functional under Mac OS 9 in the Classic environment in earlier versions of Mac OS X. It was introduced in Mac OS X with version 10.2 (Jaguar). The AppleScript commands are identical in Mac OS 9 and Mac OS X, but differences in the Finder require that many Mac OS 9 folder action scripts be revised for use in Mac OS X.

Folder action scripts attached to folders in the Classic environment work only for the user who attached them.

The badges that appear on folders having attached scripts in Mac OS 9 do not exist in Mac OS X. To determine quickly whether a Mac OS X folder has attached scripts, open the contextual menu, and look for the Remove a Folder Action and Edit a Folder Action commands.

What's Next?

This chapter covered how to use folder actions to trigger scripts automatically whenever items are added to a folder or removed from it or other changes are made to the folder's window. In the next chapter, you'll learn about Image Events.

22

The Big Picture

What's Next?

Image Events

The world of the modern computer user is filled with pictures. Images from the Internet, images in your mail messages, images from your cell phone, images from your camera—they're everywhere. Manipulating and sharing images is a big part of what we do with our computers.

Most scripters don't realize that Mac OS X includes powerful built-in scriptable image-processing tools that work independently of any well-known photo software. In this chapter, you'll learn how to scale, crop, rotate, pad, flip, and convert images, and you don't need anything but AppleScript.

The Big Picture

Not to bore you with the details, but it may be useful to know the story behind the story....

Mac OS X contains an image-processing framework called Core Image. This framework is responsible for most of the image processing done by the operating system and software such as iPhoto or Aperture. The power of this framework is made available to shell scripts through a command-line utility called Scriptable Image Processing Server (SIPS). Another interface to this utility is a small application in the System > Library > CoreServices folder named Image Events.

Image Events: The Application

AppleScript uses the Image Events application to control the SIPS architecture. Image Events has no visual interface and presents no menus, windows, or dialogs for user interaction. It is intended to run invisibly as a background process, accessible only via AppleScript commands.

The scripting dictionary for Image Events, detailing its scriptable objects and commands, can be accessed from the Library palette in the Script Editor application.

The script suites included in the Image Events dictionary are as follows:

- ▶ **Standard Suite:** This suite includes the standard objects and commands used by most scriptable applications. However, unlike other applications, Image Events runs as an invisible process with no user interface, so only a few commands from this suite, such as `close` and `quit`, are relevant.

- ▶ **Text Suite:** This default suite is included in most scriptable applications and is used for manipulating text objects. Since Image Events does not currently support any text classes, this suite is not used.

- ▶ **Disk-Folder-File Suite:** This suite is used for locating files and folders on disk. The classes and commands from this suite make it possible to locate, open, or delete files and folders using the Image Events application instead of the Finder.

▶ **Image Suite:** This suite contains the properties and commands for manipulating image files.

▶ **Image Events Suite:** This suite contains the properties of the Image Events application itself.

Let's examine some practical uses of the Image Events application by focusing on the Image Suite.

Image Properties

Like all scriptable objects, images have properties that define them, such as their dimensions, their color space, and their resolution. The `image` class of the Image Suite of the Image Events dictionary contains these and other properties:

▶ `bit depth` (`best/black & white/color/four colors/four grays/grayscale/ millions of colors/millions of colors plus/sixteen colors/sixteen grays/thousands of colors/two hundred fifty six colors/two hundred fifty six grays, r/o`):

   bit depth of the image's color representation

▶ `color space` (`CMYK/Eight channel/Eight color/Five channel/Five color/ Gray/Lab/Named/RGB/Seven channel/Seven color/Six channel/Six color/ XYZ, r/o`):

   color space of the image's color representation

▶ `dimensions` (`list, r/o`):

   the width and height of the image, respectively, in pixels

▶ `embedded profile` (`profile, r/o`):

   the profile, if any, embedded in the image

▶ `file type` (`BMP/GIF/JPEG/JPEG2/MacPaint/PDF/Photoshop/PICT/PNG/PSD/ QuickTime Image/SGI/Text/TGA/TIFF, r/o`):

   file type of the image's file

▶ `image file` (`file, r/o`):

   the file that contains the image

- ▶ location (`disk item, r/o`):

  the folder or disk that encloses the file that contains the image

- ▶ name (`text, r/o`):

  the name of the image

- ▶ resolution (`list, r/o`):

  the horizontal and vertical pixel density of the image, respectively, in dots per inch

You can access these read-only properties easily using the Image Events application.

Getting the Properties of an Image

To extract the value of a property of an image, your script must contain the following steps:

1. Start the Image Events application using the `launch` verb. Do not use the `activate` verb because the Image Events application has no user interface and runs invisibly.

2. A file reference to the target image must be passed to the `open` command within an Image Events `tell` block. Doing so loads the image data from the image file. Once the image data has been successfully accessed, the script returns a reference to the opened image, which can be stored in a variable for use elsewhere in the script.

3. The value of the properties of the loaded image can be extracted.

4. The image data is purged from memory by using the `close` command targeting the opened image data.

Script 22.1 extracts the value of a single image property using the procedures outlined above.

```
set this_file to choose file without invisibles
try
    tell application "Image Events"
        -- start the Image Events application
        launch
        -- open the image file
        set this_image to open this_file
        -- extract the property value
        copy the resolution of this_image to {H_res, V_res}
        -- purge the open image data
        close this_image
    end tell
    display dialog "Resolution: " & (H_res as string)
on error error_message
    display dialog error_message
end try
```
SCRIPT 22.1

Use the previous steps when designing all of your Image Events scripts.

> **IMPORTANT:** The file formats supported by Image Events for read access are PICT, Photoshop, BMP, QuickTime Image, GIF, JPEG, MacPaint, JPEG2, SGI, PSD, TGA, PDF, PNG, and TIFF. Some of these formats are not supported for writing or saving.

The properties of an image can be queried individually as shown in the previous script or extracted together by getting the value of the `properties` property, which is returned as an AppleScript *record,* a comma-delimited list of *key-value* pairs, each with a property and its corresponding value delimited by a colon character:

```
{embedded profile:missing value, image file:file "Aluminum:Library:Desktop
Pictures:Flow 1.jpg" of application "Image Events", color space:RGB,
name:"Flow 1.jpg", bit depth:millions of colors, resolution:{72.0, 72.0},
location:folder "Aluminum:Library:Desktop Pictures:" of application "Image
Events", dimensions:{1600, 1024}, class:image, file type:JPEG}
```

In a script, it is faster to extract the property values from the properties record than to query the Image Events application for each property. Script 22.2 uses this technique to display the dialog containing the property values for a chosen image shown in Figure 22.1.

```
set this_file to choose file without invisibles
try
    tell application "Image Events"
        -- start the Image Events application
        launch
        -- open the image file
        set this_image to open this_file
        -- extract the properties record
        set the props_rec to the properties of this_image
        -- purge the open image data
        close this_image
        -- extract the property values from the record
        set the image_info to ""
        set the image_info to the image_info & ¬
            "Name: " & (name of props_rec) & return
        set the image_info to the image_info & ¬
            "File: " & (path of image file of props_rec) & return
        set the image_info to the image_info & ¬
            "Location: " & (path of location of props_rec) & return
        set the image_info to the image_info & ¬
            "File Type: " & (file type of props_rec) & return
        set the image_info to the image_info & ¬
            "Bit Depth: " & (bit depth of props_rec) & return
        set the image_info to the image_info & ¬
            "Res: " & item 1 of (resolution of props_rec) & return
        set the image_info to the image_info & ¬
            "Color Space: " & (color space of props_rec) & return
        copy (dimensions of props_rec) to {X, Y}
        set the image_info to the image_info & ¬
            "Dimemsions: " & X & ", " & Y
    end tell
```

```
    display dialog image_info
on error error_message
    display dialog error_message
end try
```
SCRIPT 22.2

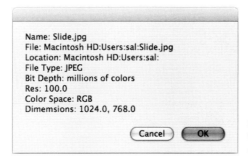

FIGURE 22.1 A dialog displaying
the Image Event properties for a
chosen image.

Note that in the previous script, the value of the `image file` and `location`
properties required additional handling to convert them into a text string. By
default, these properties return file references, such as this:

```
file "Macintosh HD:Users:sal:Slide.jpg" of application "Image Events"
```

An Image Events file reference cannot be coerced into a string by using the **as
string** coercion:

```
image file of the props_rec as string
--> error: "Can't make file \"Macintosh HD:Users:sal:Slide.jpg\" of
application \"Image Events\" into type string."
```

To convert an Image Events file reference to a text path, access either the `path`
or the `POSIX path` of the file reference.

The first returns an HFS colon-delineated path:

```
path of image file of props_rec
--> returns: "Macintosh HD:Users:sal:Slide.jpg"
```

and the second returns a UNIX slash-delineated path:

```
POSIX path of image file of props_rec
--> returns: "/Users/sal/Slide.jpg"
```

Manipulating Images

Altering images has become a common task in our digital world, and AppleScript can make manipulating groups of images a simple procedure. The following section reviews each of the image manipulation commands in the Image Suite.

To manipulate an image, your scripts must contain the following steps.

1. Start the Image Events application using the `launch` verb. Do not use the `activate` verb because the Image Events application has no user interface and runs invisibly.

2. A file reference to the target image must be passed to the `open` command within an Image Events `tell` block. Doing so will load the image data from the image file. Once the image data has been successfully accessed, the script will return a reference to the opened image, which can be stored in a variable for use elsewhere in the script.

3. Apply any manipulation commands to the image data.

4. Save the altered data back into the source file or to another file.

5. The image data is purged from memory by using the `close` command targeting the opened image data.

These steps are used in all of the following examples.

Flipping an Image

```
flip v : Flip an image
    flip specifier : the object for the command
        [horizontal boolean] : flip horizontally
        [vertical boolean] : flip vertically
```

The `flip` command is used to reverse the axis of an image. It has two options for the required parameter: `horizontal` for changing the axis of the image on a horizontal plane and `vertical` for changing the axis of the image on a vertical plane. Script 22.3 is an example.

```
set this_file to choose file without invisibles
try
    tell application "Image Events"
        -- start the Image Events application
        launch
        -- open the image file
        set this_image to open this_file
        -- perform the manipulation
        flip this_image with horizontal
        -- save the changes
        save this_image with icon
        -- purge the open image data
        close this_image
    end tell
on error error_message
    display dialog error_message
end try
```

SCRIPT 22.3

You can even flip in both directions at the same time by including both parameters in the flip command, as shown in Figure 22.2:

```
flip this_image with horizontal and vertical
```

FIGURE 22.2 Use of the `flip` command. From left to right: Normal, horizontal flip, vertical flip, both directions.

Also, here are a couple of things to note regarding the **save** command in the previous script:

First, the command takes an optional parameter of **in**, followed by a path, either in HFS or POSIX format, to a file to be created. Since the **in** parameter was not used in the previous example, the script will save the altered image data back into the source image file. We'll examine the save command in detail later in this chapter.

Second, the example script uses the optional **icon** parameter to indicate to Image Events to generate a new icon for the altered image file when it is saved. The icon will be a standard Mac OS X image icon.

Rotating an Image

```
rotate v : Rotate an image
    rotate specifier : the object for the command
        to angle real : rotate using an angle
```

The **rotate** command is used to rotate an image clockwise around its center point. The value for the **to angle** parameter is a positive integer from 1 to 359.

To convert a negative rotation angle (counterclockwise values), such as -90, to a positive value, add 360:

-90 + 360 = 270

Note that images rotated to values other than 90, 180, or 270 will have their "nonimage" areas padded with black pixels to maintain the resulting image shape as a rectangle.

To rotate an image, follow the same steps as the previous script, as shown in Script 22.4 and Figure 22.3.

```
set this_file to choose file without invisibles
try
    tell application "Image Events"
        -- start the Image Events application
        launch
```

```
        -- open the image file
        set this_image to open this_file
        -- perform action
        rotate this_image to angle 270
        -- save the changes
        save this_image with icon
        -- purge the open image data
        close this_image
    end tell
on error error_message
    display dialog error_message
end try
```

SCRIPT 22.4

FIGURE 22.3 Use of the rotate command. From left to right: Normal, rotated 270 degrees or -90 degrees (90 degrees counterclockwise), rotated 45 degrees (note the automatic padding of the space around the rotated image).

Scaling an Image

```
scale v : Scale an image
    scale specifier : the object for the command
        [by factor real] : scale using a scalefactor
        [to size integer] : scale using a max width/length
```

Scaling an image will proportionally increase or decrease the dimensions of an image, as shown in Figure 22.4. The scaling process will not change the resolution of an image. In other words, an image with a resolution of 72 DPI, scaled to 50 percent of its current dimensions, will still have a resolution of 72 DPI. An image with a resolution of 300 DPI, scaled to 200 percent of its current dimensions, will still have a resolution of 300 DPI.

The `scale` command must include one of two parameters, indicating the method used to calculate the scale and the amount of scaling to apply.

If you choose to scale the image based on a percentage of its current dimensions, the value you provide for the `by factor` parameter is a number indicating the percentage of scaling to apply. The value 1 is equivalent to 100 percent. The value .5 is 50 percent. The value 1.5 is 150 percent, and so on. Use this formula to determine the scaling factor: `desired percentage * .01`.

If you choose to scale the image to a specific dimension, the value you provide for the `to size` parameter is a single integer indicating the new value for longest dimension to be scaled (either height or width, whichever is longer).

Here are some script examples using each method. First, Script 22.5 scales an image by percentage.

```
set this_file to choose file without invisibles
try
    tell application "Image Events"
        -- start the Image Events application
        launch
        -- open the image file
        set this_image to open this_file
        -- perform action
        scale this_image by factor 0.5
        -- save the changes
        save this_image with icon
        -- purge the open image data
        close this_image
    end tell
```

```
on error error_message
    display dialog error_message
end try
```
SCRIPT 22.5

FIGURE 22.4 Use of the scale command. From left to right: Normal, scaled to 50 percent, normal, scaled to 50 percent.

Scaling by percentage is a simple matter of entering the percentage factor as the value for the **by** factor parameter of the scale command. If you want to scale the image to a specific dimension, use the **to** size parameter.

This parameter takes only one value, namely, the length to be assigned to the longest side of the image. If you want the longest side of an image to be scaled to a specific length, then the script is straightforward as in Script 22.6 where the image is proportionally scaled so that its longest side is 128 pixels in length:

```
set this_file to choose file without invisibles
set the target_length to 128
try
    tell application "Image Events"
        -- start the Image Events application
        launch
        -- open the image file
        set this_image to open this_file
        -- perform action
        scale this_image to size target_length
```

```
        -- save the changes
        save this_image with icon
        -- purge the open image data
        close this_image
    end tell
on error error_message
    display dialog error_message
end try
```

SCRIPT 22.6

However, if you want the shortest side of an image to be a specific length, then you'll have to add a calculation to the script to determine the new length for the longest side of the image, based on the current length of the shortest side of the image. Script 22.7 shows how. See Figure 22.5 for the result.

```
set this_file to choose file without invisibles
set the target_length to 128
try
    tell application "Image Events"
        -- start the Image Events application
        launch
        -- open the image file
        set this_image to open this_file
        -- get dimensions of the image
        copy dimensions of this_image to {W, H}
        -- determine the shortest side and then
        -- calculate the new length for the longer side
        if W is less than H then
            set the scale_length to (H * target_length) / W
            set the scale_length to ¬
                round scale_length rounding as taught in school
        else
            set the scale_length to (W * target_length) / H
            set the scale_length to ¬
                round scale_length rounding as taught in school
```

```
        end if
        -- perform action
        scale this_image to size scale_length
        -- save the changes
        save this_image with icon
        -- purge the open image data
        close this_image
    end tell
on error error_message
    display dialog error_message
end try
```

SCRIPT 22.7

FIGURE 22.5 Use of the scale command. From left to right: Normal, longest side scaled to 128 pixels, shortest side scaled to 128 pixels.

Note that the previous script used the value of the `dimensions` property of the image to determine the appropriate action to take. Scripts will often examine image properties like `dimensions`, `color space`, and `file type` to intelligently process them in workflows.

Also notice the use of the `round` command in the previous script example. It is used to deal with fractions of a pixel by rounding the values appropriately, or as the optional `rounding` parameter says: `as taught in school`.

Padding an Image

```
pad v : Pad an image
    pad specifier : the object for the command
        to dimensions list : the width and height of the new image,
            respectively, in pixels, as a pair of integers
    [with pad color list] the RGB color values with which to pad the
        new image, as a list of integers
```

Padding an image adds black space around the image to the dimensions provided in the script command, as seen in Figure 22.6. The padding is black by default, but in Leopard you can optionally specify any other padding color. This is similar in function to growing or shrinking the image canvas in Adobe Photoshop. Padding is often used to put a border around images or every image in a group of images the same size, regardless of their original orientation.

The `pad` command takes a list of two integers for the `to dimensions` parameter: the new width (in pixels) for the image and the new height for the image. See Script 22.8 for an example.

```
set this_file to choose file without invisibles
try
    tell application "Image Events"
        -- start the Image Events application
        launch
        -- open the image file
        set this_image to open this_file
        -- perform action
        pad this_image to dimensions {640, 480}
        -- save the changes
        save this_image with icon
        -- purge the open image data
        close this_image
```

```
    end tell
on error error_message
    display dialog error_message
end try
```
SCRIPT 22.8

The result of the `pad` command depends upon the dimensions of the image in relation to the dimensions of the pad area. If the image dimensions are smaller than the pad area, the image will be surrounded by an area of black pixels. If the image dimensions are larger than the pad area, then the image will be cropped to match the pad area. Both effects are shown in Figure 22.6.

FIGURE 22.6 Use of the pad command. From left to right: Normal, image is smaller than the indicated pad area, image is larger than the indicated pad area.

There are three approaches you can use to prevent an image from being cropped during a pad:

▶ Don't alter the current image dimensions, and add a pad area based on the indicated pad proportions (aspect ratio), such as 4 x 3 or 16 x 9.

▶ Use the current image dimensions as the starting point for determining and adding a pad area, and then scale the image to fit the desired pad size.

▶ Use the `scale` command to resize the image to fit within the desired pad dimensions and then add padding.

The first method uses the current image dimensions and provided pad area proportions to calculate and apply the padding. Script 22.9 demonstrates this technique by padding images to letterbox (16 x 9) format. See the result in Figure 22.7.

```
set this_file to choose file without invisibles
-- indicate the proportions for the pad area
set H_proportion to 16
set V_proportion to 9
try
    tell application "Image Events"
        -- start the Image Events application
        launch
        -- open the image file
        set this_image to open this_file
        -- get dimensions of the image
        copy dimensions of this_image to {W, H}
        -- calculate pad dimensions
        if H_proportion is greater than V_proportion then
            set the new_W to (H * H_proportion) / V_proportion
            set pad_dimensions to {new_W, H}
        else
            set the new_H to (W * V_proportion) / H_proportion
            set pad_dimensions to {W, new_H}
        end if
        -- perform action
        pad this_image to dimensions pad_dimensions
        -- save the changes
        save this_image with icon
        -- purge the open image data
        close this_image
    end tell
on error error_message
    display dialog error_message
end try
```

SCRIPT 22.9

FIGURE 22.7 Use of the pad command to pad images to a 16:9 ratio. From left to right: Vertical 3:4 image, horizontal 4:3 image, square 1:1 image.

The second approach uses the current dimensions of the image, and the proportions of the provided target pad dimensions, as the basis for determining the pad area. Once the image has been padded proportionally, it is scaled to fit the target padding dimensions, as shown in Script 22.10.

```
set this_file to choose file without invisibles
-- indicate the final dimensions for the padded image
set target_W to 960
set target_H to 540
try
    tell application "Image Events"
        -- start the Image Events application
        launch
        -- open the image file
        set this_image to open this_file
        -- get dimensions of the image
        copy dimensions of this_image to {W, H}
        -- calculate pad dimensions
        if target_W is greater than target_H then
            set the new_W to (H * target_W) / target_H
            set pad_dimensions to {new_W, H}
            set the scale_dimension to target_W
        else
            set the new_H to (W * target_H) / target_W
            set pad_dimensions to {W, new_H}
            set the scale_dimension to target_H
        end if
        -- perform action
```

```
            pad this_image to dimensions pad_dimensions
            -- save the changes
            save this_image with icon
            -- perform action
            scale this_image to size scale_dimension
            -- save the changes
            save this_image with icon
            -- purge the open image data
            close this_image
        end tell
    on error error_message
        display dialog error_message
    end try
```

SCRIPT 22.10

Note that in the previous script, the image is saved twice: once after the padding has been applied, and once after the scaling has been applied. This is necessary when a scale procedure follows a padding procedure.

The third approach begins by scaling the image to fit within the target pad area and then adds the padding to the scaled image, as shown in Script 22.11.

```
set this_file to choose file without invisibles
-- indicate the final dimensions for the padded image
set target_W to 960
set target_H to 540
try
    tell application "Image Events"
        -- start the Image Events application
        launch
        -- open the image file
        set this_image to open this_file
        -- get dimensions of the image
        copy dimensions of this_image to {W, H}
        -- calculate scaling
        if target_W is greater than target_H then
```

```
        if W is greater than H then
            set the scale_length to (W * target_H) / H
            set the scale_length to ¬
                round scale_length rounding as taught in school
        else
            set the scale_length to target_H
        end if
    else if target_H is greater than target_W then
        if H is greater than W then
            set the scale_length to (H * target_W) / W
            set the scale_length to ¬
                round scale_length rounding as taught in school
        else
            set the scale_length to target_W
        end if
    else -- square pad area
        set the scale_length to target_H
    end if
    -- perform action
    scale this_image to size scale_length
    -- perform action
    pad this_image to dimensions {target_W, target_H}
    -- save the changes
    save this_image with icon
    -- purge the open image data
    close this_image
    end tell
on error error_message
    display dialog error_message
end try
```

SCRIPT 22.11

Note that unlike the script for the second technique, this script does not require an additional **save** command since the padding process occurs after scaling the image.

Framing Images

An interesting use of the pad command is to create a border around images. This can be done by indicating the thickness of the border in pixels or as a percentage of the overall size of the image, as shown in Figure 22.8.

FIGURE 22.8 Use of the pad command to add a frame whose thickness is fixed number of pixels.

Script 22.12 adds a frame, whose width is the indicated number of pixels, around an image. Note that the thickness of the frame on each side of the image is the indicated number of pixels. If you want to add a frame that increases the width or height of the image by only 12 pixels, use half that amount, 6 pixels, as the value for the frame_TH variable.

```
set this_file to choose file without invisibles
set the frame_TH to 12
try
    tell application "Image Events"
        -- start the Image Events application
        launch
        -- open the image file
        set this_image to open this_file
        -- get dimensions of the image
        copy dimensions of this_image to {W, H}
        -- perform action
        pad this_image ¬
            to dimensions {W + frame_TH, H + frame_TH}
        -- save the changes
        save this_image with icon
```

```
        -- purge the open image data
        close this_image
    end tell
on error error_message
    display dialog error_message
end try
```

SCRIPT 22.12

Script 22.13 adds a frame, whose width is a percentage of the overall size of the image based on the length of the distance between the opposing ends of the image. See Figure 22.9 for the result.

```
set this_file to choose file without invisibles
set the TH_factor to 0.05 -- 5%
try
    tell application "Image Events"
        -- start the Image Events application
        launch
        -- open the image file
        set this_image to open this_file
        -- get dimensions of the image
        copy dimensions of this_image to {W, H}
        -- determine the length of the hypotenuse
        set the HY_length to ((W ^ 2) + (H ^ 2)) ^ 0.5
        -- determine the frame thickness
        set frame_TH to HY_length * TH_factor
        -- perform action
        pad this_image ¬
            to dimensions {W + frame_TH, H + frame_TH}
        -- save the changes
        save this_image with icon
        -- purge the open image data
        close this_image
    end tell
on error error_message
    display dialog error_message
end try
```

SCRIPT 22.13

FIGURE 22.9 Use of the pad command to add a frame whose thickness is based on a percentage of their overall size. Note that the height of each image (excluding the thickness of the frame) is the same. The frame thickness of each image varies because the size of the images vary.

Cropping an Image

```
crop v : Crop an image
    crop specifier : the object for the command
        to dimensions list : the width and height of the new image,
            respectively, in pixels, as a pair of integers
```

Cropping an image removes pixels around the outside of an image. The crop command automatically centers the cropped area in the image.

The to dimensions parameter of the crop command takes as its value a list of two integers: the new width (in pixels) for the image and the new height for the image as shown in Script 22.14.

```
set this_file to choose file without invisibles
set the crop_W to 640
set the crop_H to 480
try
    tell application "Image Events"
        -- start the Image Events application
        launch
        -- open the image file
        set this_image to open this_file
        -- perform action
```

```
        crop this_image to dimensions {crop_W, crop_H}
        -- save the changes
        save this_image with icon
        -- purge the open image data
        close this_image
    end tell
on error error_message
    display dialog error_message
end try
```

SCRIPT 22.14

Most often, the crop command is used to trim the outside edges of images. This technique can be accomplished by specifying the number of pixels to crop or the percentage of pixels to crop.

Script 22.15 crops the indicated number of pixels from the height and width of an image, as shown in Figure 22.10.

```
set this_file to choose file without invisibles
set the vertical_crop to 24
set the horizontal_crop to 48
try
    tell application "Image Events"
        -- start the Image Events application
        launch
        -- open the image file
        set this_image to open this_file
        -- get dimensions of the image
        copy dimensions of this_image to {W, H}
        -- perform action
        crop this_image ¬
            to dimensions {W - horizontal_crop, H - vertical_crop}
        -- save the changes
        save this_image with icon
        -- purge the open image data
        close this_image
```

```
        end tell
on error error_message
    display dialog error_message
end try
```

SCRIPT 22.15

FIGURE 22.10 Use of the crop command to crop pixels from the width and height of an image.

Instead of cropping by indicating a specific number of pixels, you can crop by a percentage of the image width and height as shown in Script 22.16 and Figure 22.11.

```
set this_file to choose file without invisibles
set the vertical_crop to 0
set the horizontal_crop to 0.32 -- 32%
try
    tell application "Image Events"
        -- start the Image Events application
        launch
        -- open the image file
        set this_image to open this_file
        -- get dimensions of the image
        copy dimensions of this_image to {W, H}
        -- perform action
```

```
        crop this_image to dimensions ¬
            {W - (W * horizontal_crop), H - (H * vertical_crop)}
        -- save the changes
        save this_image with icon
        -- purge the open image data
        close this_image
    end tell
on error error_message
    display dialog error_message
end try
```

SCRIPT 22.16

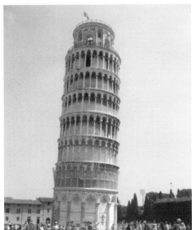

FIGURE 22.11 Cropping an image by percentage.

Another interesting use of the **crop** command is to convert images to letterbox format, whose dimensions are in 16 x 9 proportion. You can crop the middle section from some horizontal and vertical images to display in HD format. This technique works only for images whose main content is centered in the image.

Script 22.17 extracts an image section in letterbox format. The result is shown in Figures 22.12 and 22.13.

```
set this_file to choose file without invisibles
try
    tell application "Image Events"
        -- start the Image Events application
        launch
        -- open the image file
        set this_image to open this_file
        -- get dimensions of the image
        copy dimensions of this_image to {W, H}
        -- determine the letterbox area
        set crop_W to W
        -- calcluate the 16:9 proportions
        set crop_H to (W * 9) / 16
        -- perform action
        crop this_image to dimensions {crop_W, crop_H}
        -- save the changes
        save this_image with icon
        -- purge the open image data
        close this_image
    end tell
on error error_message
    display dialog error_message
end try
```

SCRIPT 22.17

FIGURE 22.12 Using the crop command to extract a section in letterbox proportions from a horizontal image.

FIGURE 22.13 Using the crop command to extract a section in letterbox proportions from a vertical image.

File Conversion

```
save v : Save an image to a file in one of various formats
    save specifier : the object for the command
        [as (BMP/JPEG/JPEG2/PICT/PNG/PSD/QuickTime Image/TIFF)] :
            file type in which to save the image (default is to make
            no change)
        [icon boolean] : Shall an icon be added? (default is false )
        [in disk item] : file path in which to save the image, in
            HFS     or POSIX form
        [PackBits boolean] : Are the bytes to be compressed with
            PackBits? ( default is false, applies only to TIFF )
        [with compression level high/low/medium] : specifies the
            compression level of the resultant file ( applies only to
            JPEG )
    --> alias
```

When working with images, it is common to make duplicates in various file formats and to convert images between formats. The **save** command in Image Events can accomplish this easily.

The supported file formats for *reading* an image with the Image Events application are as follows: PICT, BMP, QuickTime Image, GIF, JPEG, MacPaint, JPEG2, SGI, PSD, TGA, Text, PDF, PNG, and TIFF.

The supported file formats for *saving* an image with the Image Events application are as follows: JPEG2, TIFF, JPEG, PICT, BMP, PSD, PNG, and QuickTime Image.

> **IMPORTANT:** When saving image data in a format other than its original format, always save the image data to a new file; do not attempt to save the image data into the existing source file.

Script 22.18 relies on user interaction to convert a chosen image file to a TIFF image.

```
set this_file to choose file without invisibles
set the target_file to (choose file name default name "newimage.tif")
-- convert file reference in alias format to path string
set the target_path to the target_file as Unicode text
try
    tell application "Image Events"
        -- start the Image Events application
        launch
        -- open the image file
        set this_image to open this_file
        -- save in new file
        save this_image as TIFF in target_path with icon
        -- purge the open image data
        close this_image
    end tell
on error error_message
    display dialog error_message
end try
```
SCRIPT 22.18

Note in the previous script that the reference to the destination file must be converted to an HFS path string or a POSIX path, because the **in** parameter of the save command will not accept file references generated by methods other than its own Disk-Folder-File suite.

Script 22.19 "converts" an image to another format by saving a copy of the image in the same parent directory as the source image and then deleting the original image. Note that the derive_filename subroutine is particularly useful for determining the name for the new file based on the original filename using a different name extension, such as "tif," "jpg," and so on. Use it in your scripts when you need to create or save a file that may have preexisting copies in the destination folder.

Be sure to change the value of the new_format and nme_ext properties to your desired file format and name extension.

```
set this_file to choose file without invisibles
try
    tell application "Image Events"
        -- start the Image Events application
        launch
        set the new_format to TIFF
        set the nme_ext to "tif"
        -- derive new name for the new image file
        copy my derive_filename(this_file, nme_ext, "-", "") ¬
            to {new_name, target_HFSpath}
        -- open the image file
        set this_image to open this_file
        -- save in new file. The result is a file ref to the new file
        set the new_image to save this_image ¬
            as new_format in file target_HFSpath with icon
        -- purge the open image data
        close this_image
    end tell
    tell application "Finder"
        -- delete the original file
        delete this_file
    end tell
```

```
on error error_message
    display dialog error_message
end try


on derive_filename(this_item, new_extension, increment_separator, target_
folder)
    -- A sub-routine used for deriving the name and path of a new file
using the name of an existing file
    -- Pass in file ref in alias format, the new name extension, an
increment separator, and any target directory (in alias format)
    -- Name and HFS path for new file are returned. The name is
incremented if a file exists in the target location.
    -- Pass a null string for the target directory to use the item's
parent directory
    -- Pass a null string for the new name extension to use the item's
current name extension
    tell application "Finder"
        if target_folder is "" then
            set the target_folder to ¬
                the container of this_item
        end if
        set the file_name to the name of this_item
        set file_extension to the name extension of this_item
        if the file_extension is "" then
            set the trimmed_name to the file_name
            set extension_separator to ""
        else
            set the trimmed_name to ¬
                text 1 thru -((length of file_extension) + 2) ¬
                    of the file_name
            set extension_separator to "."
        end if
        if the new_extension is "" then
            set target_name to file_name
            set target_extension to file_extension
```

```
            else
                set target_extension to new_extension
                set target_name to ¬
                    (the trimmed_name & extension_separator & ¬
                        target_extension) as Unicode text
            end if
            if (exists document file target_name ¬
                of target_folder) then
                set the name_increment to 1
                repeat
                    set the new_name to ¬
                        (the trimmed_name & increment_separator & ¬
                            (name_increment as Unicode text) & ¬
                            extension_separator & ¬
                            target_extension) as Unicode text
                    if not (exists document file new_name ¬
                        of the target_folder) then
                        set the target_HFSpath to ¬
                            ((target_folder as Unicode text) & ¬
                                new_name)
                        return {new_name, target_HFSpath}
                    else
                        set the name_increment to ¬
                            the name_increment + 1
                    end if
                end repeat
            else
                set the target_HFSpath to ¬
                    ((target_folder as Unicode text) & target_name)
                return {target_name, target_HFSpath}
            end if
        end tell
end derive_filename
```

SCRIPT 22.19

You can use a variation of the previous file conversion script to create a thumbnail image from a source image for use on a Web site. Note that Script 22.20 uses the derive_filename subroutine that is contained in the previous example:

```
set this_file to choose file without invisibles
try
    tell application "Image Events"
        -- start the Image Events application
        launch
        set the new_format to PNG
        set the nme_ext to "png"
        set the thumb_size to 128
        -- derive new name for the new image file
        copy my derive_filename(this_file, nme_ext, "-", "") ¬
            to {new_name, target_HFSpath}
        -- open the image file
        set this_image to open this_file
        -- scale to thumnail size
        scale this_image to size thumb_size
        -- save in new file. The result is a file ref to the new file
        set the new_image to save this_image ¬
            as new_format in file target_HFSpath with icon
        -- purge the open image data
        close this_image
    end tell
    tell application "Finder"
        -- delete the original file
        delete this_file
    end tell
on error error_message
    display dialog error_message
end try
```

SCRIPT 22.20

Extracting Metadata

Metadata is information that is embedded in or associated with image files. For example, cameras often include information within each image they produce about the make and model of the camera used, the f-stop used, the exposure time, the color space, and the date the image was taken. This set of metadata is often referred to as the Exchangeable Image File Format (EXIF) data. Images in JPEG or TIFF format usually support the inclusion of EXIF data.

A subset of this information can be extracted from images using Image Events, as demonstrated in Script 22.21 and Figure 22.14.

```
set this_file to choose file without invisibles
try
    tell application "Image Events"
        -- start the Image Events application
        launch
        -- open the image file
        set this_image to open this_file
        -- extract the metadata values
        tell this_image
            repeat with i from 1 to the count of metadata tags
                try
                    set this_tag to metadata tag i
                    set the tag_name to the name of this_tag
                    set the tag_value to the value of this_tag
                    if i is 1 then
                        set the tag_text to ¬
                            tag_name & ": " & tag_value
                    else
                        set the tag_text to the tag_text & ¬
                            return & tag_name & ": " & tag_value
                    end if
                on error
                    if the tag_name is "profile" then
```

```
                    set the tag_text to the tag_text & ¬
                        return & tag_name & ": " & ¬
                        name of tag_value
                end if
            end try
        end repeat
    end tell
    -- purge the open image data
    close this_image
  end tell
  display dialog tag_text
on error error_message
  display dialog error_message
end try
```

SCRIPT 22.21

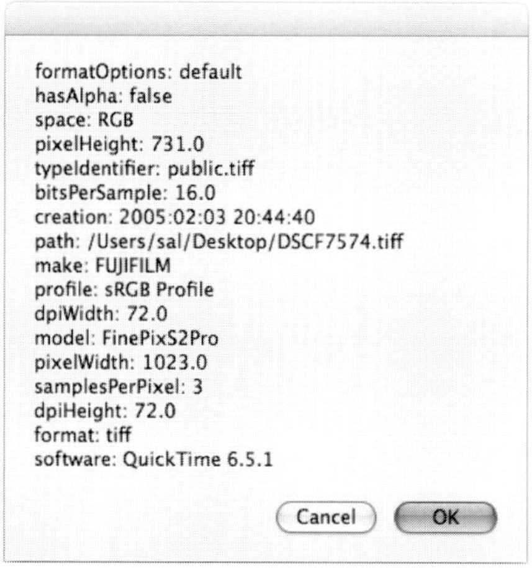

```
formatOptions: default
hasAlpha: false
space: RGB
pixelHeight: 731.0
typeIdentifier: public.tiff
bitsPerSample: 16.0
creation: 2005:02:03 20:44:40
path: /Users/sal/Desktop/DSCF7574.tiff
make: FUJIFILM
profile: sRGB Profile
dpiWidth: 72.0
model: FinePixS2Pro
pixelWidth: 1023.0
samplesPerPixel: 3
dpiHeight: 72.0
format: tiff
software: QuickTime 6.5.1

          Cancel      OK
```

FIGURE 22.14 The metadata tags and values from a chosen image.

Script 22.22 is a shorter script that extracts the value for a single metadata tag.

```
set this_file to choose file without invisibles
try
    tell application "Image Events"
        -- start the Image Events application
```

```
    launch
    -- open the image file
    set this_image to open this_file
    -- extract the value for the metadata tag
    tell this_image
        set the camera_type to ¬
            the value of metadata tag "model"
    end tell
    -- purge the open image data
    close this_image
  end tell
  display dialog camera_type
on error error_message
  display dialog error_message
end try
```

SCRIPT 22.22

Note that support for metadata in Image Events is limited. The values of the metadata tags can be read but they cannot be written. And they do not include other common metadata sets such as International Press Telecommunications Council (IPTC).

However, Mac OS X 10.4 (Tiger) introduced a system-wide metadata architecture called Spotlight. It makes it extremely simple to read the metadata of files and to search for related documents, e-mails, and so on. AppleScript can use the Spotlight frameworks to read the combined metadata of any image. It accomplishes this through scripting Spotlight's built-in command-line tool `mdls`.

This process is covered in detail in Chapter 29, *Scripting the Shell*.

What's Next?

This chapter covered the use of Image Events to manipulate images. In the next chapter, you'll learn about Database Events, a similar application focused on manipulating collections of data.

23

Database Events

Mac OS X 10.4 (Tiger) introduced a simple database application for use with AppleScript known as Database Events. Database Events is a scriptable background application located in the CoreServices folder of the System Library folder at System > Library > CoreServices, along with the Finder and the System Events and Image Events scriptable background applications discussed in previous chapters.

Using the Database Events application's terminology, your scripts can create and access databases containing information saved as records, with fields that you define. Until now, scripters have often stored persistent information in small documents using the File Read/Write suite in the Standard Additions scripting addition. The new Database and Database Events suites in the Database Events application provide a much simpler tool that is both more powerful and easier to use.

Database Events uses CoreData and the open source SQLite database engine, which is built into Mac OS X. SQLite is powerful, fast, professional-level database software, and it forms the backbone of Mac OS X's CoreData technology. Database Events hides SQLite's complexity, turning it into a perfect lightweight information manager for AppleScript.

The Object Model

To examine the classes and commands in the Database Events application, open its dictionary. In Leopard, you should find it listed in Script Editor's Library window. In Tiger, if you anticipate using it often, add it to Script Editor's Library window if it isn't already there. To do this, choose the Library command from Script Editor's Window menu. When the Library window opens, click the Add button (the round button with a plus sign), navigate to System > Library > CoreServices, select Database Events, and then click Open. When you see Database Events added to the Library window, select it and click the Library window's Open button (the button that looks like a stack of books). The Database Events dictionary opens, and you can examine it at your leisure.

A database is a collection of records. The database is kept in memory unless you choose to store it using the `save` command, as described in a moment. Each `record` is a named collection of fields, and each `field` contains a named item of information. In AppleScript terms, a `database` object is an `element` of the Database Events application, a `record` is an `element` of a `database`, and a `field` is an `element` of a `record`. There can be an unlimited number of data-bases, records, and fields, and you use any AppleScript reference form to refer to them, such as by name or by index. You retrieve the values of fields and records matching complex search criteria by using AppleScript's filter reference form (`whose` clauses).

The only properties of a `field` are its `id`, its `name`, and its `value`. The `id` prop-erty was added to the dictionary in Leopard. It is a unique number assigned automatically when you create the field. The `id` and `name` properties are marked read-only, which means you aren't supposed to change them after the field is created. You can set the `value` property at any time to any simple data type known to AppleScript, and you can change its value whenever you like. Because different fields can have the same `name` and the `value` of a field can be changed, you may find it useful to use the `id` in your scripts to ensure that you are referring to a specific field.

The only properties of a `record` are its `id` and its `name`. The `id`, like the `id` of a `field`, is a unique read-only number assigned automatically when you create a `record.` The `name` property is also marked read-only. When you create a new record, Database Events automatically creates in it a special field labeled "name" with a value equal to the name of the record. In other words, the value of a record's `name` property and the value of its `name` field are identical.

The only properties of a `database` are its `name` and its `location`. Both properties are marked read-only. When you save a database without specifying its `location`, it is saved in the Databases folder of the current user's Documents folder by default. If it doesn't already exist, the Databases folder is created automatically for you when you save your first database. This design enhances the simplicity of Database Events, because it frees you from having to manage storage locations.

Looking at the Database Events Suite, you see that the Database Events application has a special property, `quit delay`, which controls how long the application continues running if you do not quit sooner. By default, it quits automatically after five minutes of inactivity, just like the Image Events application discussed in the previous chapter and the System Events application discussed in Chapter 21, *Folder Actions*. Be careful about letting the Database Events application quit automatically, because the contents of all open databases will be lost if you have not saved them. This is not a problem if you're using the database as a temporary, in-memory data store while a script is running, because you expect the data to disappear when you're done with it. But if you mean to create a database that will remain available the next time you run Database Events, be sure to save it whenever you add or modify data. You can specify a different duration by setting the `quit delay` property to any number of seconds. Setting it to 0 causes the application to remain running indefinitely. The `quit delay` property reverts to the default 300 seconds the next time you run Database Events.

The Database Events application responds to the commands in the Standard Suite. The `make` and `save` commands play especially important roles.

Usage

Suppose you want to keep track of your personal collection of classic science fiction movies using Database Events. You can do this with some simple scripts shown in this chapter.

What Is a Database Object?

Before beginning, we must explain some basic principles underlying Database Events that affect how you create and refer to databases: from AppleScript's point of view, *a database object exists only if a database is currently open*. This is true even if the database already exists on disk as a database file.

This is nothing new. It's true of just about every document in every document-based application. It can be a little confusing when you first start working with Database Events, however, because Database Events hides most of the document management busywork required of you by other document-based applications. It's easy to forget that a database in Database Events is just another document. Here's how it works.

You end up with an open **database** object when you create a new database from scratch in memory and when you open an existing database from disk into memory. If you haven't yet created or opened a database, any attempt to refer to a **database** object will fail, as shown by Scripts 23.1, 23.2 and 23.3. This is true even if the database file exists in the Databases folder of your Documents folder.

```
tell application "Database Events"
    get database 1 --> ERROR
end tell
```
SCRIPT 23.1

```
tell application "Database Events"
    get database "Movie Collection" --> ERROR
end tell
```
SCRIPT 23.2

```
tell application "Database Events"
    get databases 1 thru 2 --> ERROR
end tell
```
SCRIPT 23.3

To avoid the error generated by these examples, ask Database Events to tell you whether a database is currently open, as we do in Scripts 23.4 and 23.5. This will prove useful when we get started with the sci-fi classics movie database, in just a moment.

```
tell application "Database Events"
    exists database 1
end tell
--> returns: false
```
SCRIPT 23.4

```
tell application "Database Events"
    database "Movie Collection" exists
end tell
--> returns: false
```
SCRIPT 23.5

Even if a database file is not currently open, it may exist on disk. One way to learn whether a database file exists on disk is to ask the Finder or the System Events application. Script 23.6 returns false if you run it now, because the database hasn't yet been saved. The Databases folder may not even exist. As you work your way through this chapter, you will save the "Movie Collection.dbev" file in a new Databases folder. If you then come back to Script 23.6 and run it again, it will return true:

```
tell application "System Events"
    exists file "Movie Collection.dbev" of ¬
        folder "Databases" of documents folder
end tell
--> returns: false
```
SCRIPT 23.6

Database Events, like many applications, is able to access its own documents on disk, so you don't have to resort to the Finder or System Events. Database Events addresses a database file by its POSIX path, although you wouldn't know this from examining its dictionary. You can determine whether a database file exists in the default location on disk by using a POSIX path like ~/Documents/Databases/Movie Collection.dbev. For general purposes, use a script like Script 23.7:

```
tell application "Database Events"
    exists database (POSIX path of (path to documents folder) ¬
        & "Databases/Movie Collection.dbev")
 end tell
--> returns: false
```
SCRIPT 23.7

Again, if you run Script 23.7 after completing this chapter, it will return true.

Take special note of the fact that, if the database file does exist on disk, referring to it by its POSIX path in this fashion automatically opens it, bringing the database into memory. This is in keeping with the design of Database Events, which hides the gory details of document management and makes it very easy to use a database in your scripts. In fact, you must use the POSIX path to open a database file on disk; any other reference form, such as an alias reference, will not work. We will use this important feature of Database Events in the coming sections.

> **TIP ▶** Never use the open command with a POSIX path reference to a database file in Mac OS X 10.4 (Tiger). The POSIX path itself opens the database file, and the open command opens it again. You end up with two copies of the database, each having the same name open in memory at once. This issue has been fixed in Leopard. See the "Opening an Existing Database" section later in this chapter for more information.

Creating a New Database

When you're ready to start working with a new database, your first task is to create it. It's usually a good idea to give it a name immediately. Also, if you're going to type these scripts by hand as you read along, you should make the Database Events application continue running for longer than the default five minutes. Script 23.8 gets you started:

```
tell application "Database Events"
    set quit delay to 0 -- run indefinitely
    make new database with properties {name:"Movie Collection"}
end tell
--> returns: database "Movie Collection" of application "Database Events"
```
SCRIPT 23.8

The Database Events dictionary indicates that a `database` object's `name` property is read-only, but as you see in this script, you can nevertheless set its `name` when you create it.

> TIP ▸ You can make a new database without assigning a name to it. When you write information to it or read information from it, simply refer to it by index, for example, `database 1`. This works well if you don't intend to save the database. However, if you do plan to save it, it is best to give it a name when you create it. If you save a database that doesn't have a name, Database Events saves it as a file named "Databases.dbev" at the root level of your Documents folder. You can access the contents of "Databases.dbev" later, but it may become confusing if information from different scripts is added to a single database lacking a distinctive name. We recommend you use unnamed database objects only if they will hold temporary data to be discarded when the script is done.

Now return to the beginning of this chapter and run Script 23.1 again. It returns a reference to the database, `database "Movie Collection" of application "Database Events"`, because the database has been created and it is now open. For the same reason, Script 23.2 returns a reference to the database, and Scripts 23.4 and 23.5 return `true`. Script 23.3, which asks for a range of databases, still produces an error because only one database is open.

Wait a minute, though. Are you sure this first attempt at creating a new database is going to work correctly in all circumstances? For example, if you use Script 23.8 as the basis for a script that you or somebody else will run repeatedly, will you always know that a `database` object named Movie Collection isn't already open?

No, you won't. In fact, Database Events allows you to create multiple databases having the same name, just as it allows you to create multiple fields with the same name. If you run Script 23.8 twice, that's exactly what you end up with. Try it. Run Script 23.8 again, and then run the simple test shown in Script 23.9:

```
tell application "Database Events"
    get every database
end tell
--> returns: {database "Movie Collection" of application "Database
Events", database "Movie Collection" of application "Database Events"}
```
SCRIPT 23.9

If you run Script 23.3 now, it returns the same list of two database references instead of causing an error, because now there are two databases open and the range of `databases 1 thru 2` exists. These are in fact two separate database objects; they are not two references to the same database object. For example, adding a record to one of them does not add it to the other.

This is not what you intended, in all likelihood, and you probably won't have any way to distinguish two databases with the same name. Harking back to our introductory comments, you can protect against this by making sure you always check whether a `database` object with the specified name is already open, as shown in Script 23.10:

```
tell application "Database Events"
    set quit delay to 0 -- run indefinitely
    if not (database "Movie Collection" exists) then
        make new database with properties {name: "Movie Collection"}
    end if
end tell
```
SCRIPT 23.10

There's still a problem, though. How can you be sure that a database file named Movie Collection does not already exist on disk? If it does, you probably want to open it instead of creating a new, empty database with the same name.

You can protect against all of these eventualities by checking for the disk file before creating a new database from scratch. This final version of the script, Script 23.11, is a routine that you should usually run before creating a new database if there is any chance at all that a database with the specified name already exists in memory or in the default Databases folder on disk. This makes use of the principles we discussed in our introductory comments.

```
tell application "Database Events"
    set quit delay to 0 -- run indefinitely
    if not (database "Movie Collection" exists) then
        if not (exists database ¬
            (POSIX path of (path to documents folder) ¬
                & "Databases/Movie Collection.dbev")) then
            make new database ¬
                with properties {name:"Movie Collection"}
            save result
        end if
    end if
end tell
```

SCRIPT 23.11

If you study this script closely, you'll see that we've made use of the fact that a reference to an existing database file on disk using its POSIX path actually opens the file. First, we check whether a **database** object named Movie Collection is open in memory. If it is open, we move along because that is presumably the database we want to use. Referring to the database *by name* like this does *not* open any database file on disk having the same name. If the database isn't open in memory, we next check whether it exists as a file on disk in the default location, using the POSIX path property. If it does exist as a file, the POSIX path reference automatically opens the file. The **exists** command returns true, and we move along because the desired **database** object is now open in memory. Only if both tests return **false**—the Movie Collection database does not exist in memory or on disk—do we reach the statement that creates a new Movie Collection `database` object from scratch.

No matter how many times you run this script, only one Movie Collection `database` object will be open in memory. Moreover, it will always be the same database that exists on disk, if there is already a Movie Collection database file on disk.

> **NOTE** ▶ This script is dependent on the behavior of a POSIX path reference to the database file in the current version of Database Events. If that behavior should change in a future version so that it no longer opens a database file, the script will require revision.

You may also notice that we slipped another statement into the inner `if` block in Script 23.11, namely, `save result`. We'll discuss the reason for this in the "Saving a Database" section later in this chapter. For now, just take it on faith that whenever you create a new database that is meant to stick around after the script quits, it is a good idea to save it immediately, right after creating it, instead of waiting until later. The `save` command automatically creates the Databases folder, if it does not already exist, and then it saves the new database to disk in the Databases folder. You should save it again and again every time you add information to the database or change information already in the database.

Storing Information in a Database

Before proceeding, you need to get the Database Events application back to its default state. Run the next script, Script 23.12, which tells the Database Events application to quit. This removes the multiple Movie Collection databases from memory. Just to be safe, you should now also delete the Movie Collection database file from the disk, if one was already created. Then run Script 23.11, earlier in the chapter, to create a single empty Movie Collection database.

```
tell application "Database Events" to quit
```
SCRIPT 23.12

NOTE ▶ Throughout the rest of this chapter, we assume that the Database Events application remains running and the Movie Collection database remains open. This assumption should be true if you use the final version of the script in the previous section, Script 23.11, to create the new Movie Collection database. If any of these scripts doesn't work, it is probably because the application quit or the database was closed in the meantime. To fix the problem, run Script 23.11 again to reopen the database so you can work through this chapter with it open.

Now you're ready to enter your first movie into the database. Every movie in your collection will be stored in a separate record of its own. You should give every new record a memorable name that will make it easy for you to peruse your collection next Saturday evening when all your Trekkie friends come over. The movie's title is the obvious choice, as shown in Script 23.13.

```
tell application "Database Events"
    tell database "Movie Collection"
        make new record ¬
            with properties {name:"The Man Who Fell to Earth"}
        save
    end tell
end tell
```
SCRIPT 23.13

Although the dictionary indicates that a `record` object's `name` property is read-only, you can set it when you create it. In fact, you must do so, because Database Events won't let you create a new record without specifying a `name` property, even though the dictionary says the `make` command's `with properties` parameter is optional.

The `make new record` command in Script 23.13 returns `record id 164722150 of database "Movie Collection" of application "Database Events"` as its result. You can store this record reference in a variable and use it in subsequent statements to add fields to the record. The `record id` returned when you run the script will probably be different from the `record id` shown here.

In Script 23.13, we saved the database immediately after adding the new record to it. It is a good practice to save a database immediately after making a change or a group of changes to it in order to be sure changes are not lost if Database Events automatically quits a moment later or the power fails. In addition, as you will learn shortly, you should always make sure a database was saved before you look up information in it.

You can create multiple records with the same name. Records with duplicate names may be appropriate, depending on the nature of the data kept in the database. For example, remakes of popular movies are common. The example script therefore does not test for the existence of another record with the same name. Because of this, it is your responsibility to make sure the script is not run more than once. In a script that gets the names of new records from the user interactively, you might want to detect the duplicate name and ask the user whether it is intentional. To do this, use the techniques you learned in Chapter 9, *Communicating with the User*.

As the dictionary indicates, the `name` property of a record is also a field named `name`, which is created for you automatically when you create a record with a `name` property. To see that this is so, run Script 23.14.

```
tell application "Database Events"
    tell database "Movie Collection"
        get properties of field 1 of record 1
    end tell
end tell
--> returns: {class:field, id 210255593, name:"name", value:"The Man Who
Fell to Earth"}
```
SCRIPT 23.14

The structure of a Database Events **record** object is extremely flexible. You can add fields without restriction using any names you like. As a result, it is up to you to exercise the discipline required to maintain consistent naming conventions and a consistent structure. Script 23.15 adds several fields to the record for the stars of the movie.

```
tell application "Database Events"
    tell database "Movie Collection"
        tell record "The Man Who Fell to Earth"
            make new field with properties ¬
                {name:"actor", value:"David Bowie"}
            make new field with properties ¬
                {name:"actor", value:"Rip Torn"}
            make new field with properties ¬
                {name:"actor", value:"Candy Clark"}
            make new field with properties ¬
                {name:"actor", value:"Buck Henry"}
        end tell
        save
    end tell
end tell
```
SCRIPT 23.15

As you see, you can add as many fields as you like with the same name—in this example, actor. Like most movies, this science fiction cult classic has more than one actor.

Before we turn to data retrieval, we'll add a few more movies in Script 23.16 to make the database interesting. We'll also add a new field to track the director of each movie.

To delete a record from the database, use the **delete** command. We won't show you such a script here because we don't want to delete any of these wonderful movies.

```
tell application "Database Events"
    tell database "Movie Collection"
        tell record "The Man Who Fell to Earth"
            make new field with properties ¬
                {name:"director", value:"Nicolas Roeg"}
        end tell
        make new record ¬
            with properties {name:"Blade Runner"}
        tell record "Blade Runner"
            make new field with properties ¬
                {name:"actor", value:"Harrison Ford"}
            make new field with properties ¬
                {name:"actor", value:"Daryl Hannah"}
            make new field with properties ¬
                {name:"director", value:"Ridley Scott"}
        end tell
        make new record ¬
            with properties {name:"Alien"}
        tell record "Alien"
            make new field with properties ¬
                {name:"actor", value:"Sigourney Weaver"}
            make new field with properties ¬
                {name:"director", value:"Ridley Scott"}
        end tell
        save
    end tell
end tell
```

SCRIPT 23.16

To change the value of an existing field, replacing the old value, simply look up the field and set its `value` property to the new value. For Ridley Scott's upcoming third remake of *Blade Runner*, for example, change the name of the lead actor from Harrison Ford to the new star in Script 23.17.

```
tell application "Database Events"
    tell database "Movie Collection"
        save
        tell record "Blade Runner"
            set value of first field where its name is ¬
                "actor" and its value is ¬
                "Harrison Ford" to "Sal Soghoian"
        end tell
        save
        get properties of every field of record "Blade Runner"
    end tell
end tell
--> result: {{class:field, id:210522068, name:"name", value:"Blade
Runner"}, {class:field, id:210522069, name:"actor", value:"Sal Soghoian"},
{class:field, id:210522070, name:"actor", value:"Daryl Hannah"},
{class:field, id:210522071, name:"director", value:"Ridley Scott"}}
```
SCRIPT 23.17

At the beginning of Script 23.17, before looking up the record we wanted to change, we told the database to **save** itself. We did this because the Database Events application may return incorrect results from searches unless previous additions and changes to the database were saved to disk before the search is conducted. In this example, if you had not saved the database, the script would incorrectly find the field whose value is `"Daryl Hannah"` and change her to `"Sal"`, which we're sure would not please Ms. Hannah. Saving it immediately before a search is the surest way to get the correct result, but you can omit this step prior to a search if you make a habit of saving scripts after every change or group of changes, as we did in Scripts 23.13, 23.15, and 23.16 (and as we did after making Sal a movie star in Script 23.17).

NOTE ▶ In Mac OS X 10.4 (Tiger), attempting to change the values of the read-only properties of a field, a record, or the database itself does not generate an error. The result is not always what you would expect, and we therefore recommend you take care not to attempt to change any of the read-only properties. In the case of a database's `location` property and a record's `id` property, the attempt is simply ignored and the original value remains unchanged. However, in other cases, the value is changed, not always in the way the script specifies, and the database may become unusable. If you try to change an existing field's `name` property, the name may be removed. Thereafter, its name is reported as `missing value`, and you can't reset it to the original name. You can also change the `name` properties of an existing record and even an existing database. In the case of a record, it works correctly as if it were not marked read-only, and saving the database makes the change permanent. Changing a record's name may make it more difficult to retrieve the data, however, unless you keep track of the new name. Although you can change the name of a database, the database is still saved to disk under the original name. If you then open it from disk while the database is still open, it nevertheless reports that its name is the new name, presumably because it uses the value that is still in memory. When you close it and reopen it from disk, the original name is restored.

At least some of this behavior has changed in Leopard, with the read-only properties acting as if they were read-write. Changing any of these properties will likely interfere with your ability to retrieve information from the database, and we recommend against it.

Retrieving Information from a Database

Retrieving information from a database is, at its simplest, a matter of getting the values of its properties. Just as you can **set** the value of a named field, you can **get** its value. Script 23.18 retrieves the name of the director of *Alien*. It works as written because most movies have only one director. If the movie had two directors, Script 23.18 would get only the first director's name.

```
tell application "Database Events"
    get value of field "director" of ¬
        record "Alien" of database "Movie Collection"
end tell
--> result: "Ridley Scott"
```
SCRIPT 23.18

To get the name of every actor in a movie, run a script like Script 23.19 that uses a whose clause to extract all of the fields named actor:

```
 tell application "Database Events"
    tell database "Movie Collection"
        tell record "The Man Who Fell to Earth"
            get value of every field whose name is "actor"
        end tell
    end tell
end tell
--> returns: {"David Bowie", "Rip Torn", "Candy Clark", "Buck Henry"}
```
SCRIPT 23.19

With only a little more effort, in Script 23.20 you can get the name of every movie in your collection that was directed by Ridley Scott:

```
tell application "Database Events"
    tell database "Movie Collection"
        get name of every record where ¬
            value of field "director" of it is "Ridley Scott"
    end tell
end tell
--> Returns: {"Blade Runner", "Alien"}
```
SCRIPT 23.20

For even more complex searches, use a compound whose clause, as in Script 23.21.

```
tell application "Database Events"
    tell database "Movie Collection"
        get name of every record where ¬
            (value of field "director" of it is "Ridley Scott") ¬
                and ¬
            (value of every field whose name is "actor") ¬
                contains "Daryl Hannah"
    end tell
end tell
--> Returns: {"Blade Runner"}
```
SCRIPT 23.21

You may find the last test in Script 23.21 puzzling. What the last test does, first, is to execute the statement in parentheses, value of every field whose name is "actor". This statement is executed once for the first movie record and again for every subsequent record as the script's request for the name of every record meeting the specified tests is evaluated. Each time it is executed, it generates a list containing the names of all the actors in the single movie currently being examined. For each move in turn, it then applies the contains "Daryl Hannah" test to the list of actors' names. If the current list of actors' names includes "Daryl Hannah", the script tentatively adds the movie record to the list of movie records that will eventually be returned by the script as a whole. When the script completes its evaluation of every record in the database, it returns a final list containing only those movie records that satisfy both the last test and the first test, value of field director of it is "Ridley Scott". As with all whose clauses, it is actually the target application, Database Events, that is evaluating these statements, and it is very fast.

We omitted the save command at the beginning of each of these scripts because we assume you're following along and haven't changed the database, which was already saved after the last change, in Script 23.17. But remember what we said earlier: save a database whenever you change it, and make sure it has been saved before you perform any searches on it.

Saving a Database

Unless you're using a database transiently, only for the duration of a single run of the script, you need to save it so you can retrieve information from it later. Saving it is simple, as you've already seen, because all **database** objects are saved in a standard **location** by default, which you do not have to specify. You've already specified its **name** property, and that's the name under which it will be saved. The **save** command automatically creates the Databases folder if necessary; adds the required name extension, which is the ".dbev" extension, to the database name; and saves the new file in the default location.

You can create a database and save it to a location other than the default location, if you want. Since a **database** object's **location** property is read-only, you should not change it after the database has been created. Instead, you should decide where to keep it at the outset and set its custom location while creating it. To create a new database on the user's Desktop, for example, run Script 23.22, which is a variant of Script 23.11. The location is the path to the folder or disk that will contain the new database file, not to the database file itself.

```
tell application "Database Events"
    set quit delay to 0 -- run indefinitely
    if not (exists database "My Bottlecap Collection") then
        if not (exists database ¬
            (POSIX path of (path to desktop folder) ¬
                & "My Bottlecap Collection.dbev")) then
            set db_path to path to desktop folder
            make new database ¬
                with properties ¬
                {name:"My Bottlecap Collection", location:db_path}
            save result
        end if
    end if
end tell
```

SCRIPT 23.22

The Database Events dictionary describes the `location` property as an *alias reference*, such as the reference returned by the `path to` command or a user interaction command like `choose folder`. True to the dictionary, you must specify an alias reference in the `location` property of the new database when you create it, as you did in Script 23.22. It remains the case, however, that you must use a POSIX path to open an existing database, as described in the "What Is a Database?" section earlier in the chapter. This is why, in Script 23.22, you see both styles, a POSIX path to open the database if it already exists on disk and an alias reference to specify its location if you have to create it. Like a number of things in AppleScript, this is an apparent inconsistency that you just have to remember.

> **NOTE ▶** Although you must use an alias reference when you `set` the
> `location` property of a database, when you `get` the `location` in Mac OS X
> 10.4 (Tiger), you get a POSIX path instead of an alias reference.

You can close the database and quit Database Events now. Quitting when you're done with Database Events is a good idea if you set its `quit delay` property to 0 to keep it open indefinitely. Quitting will eliminate whatever overhead your system incurs while it is running in the background. Script 23.23 does the trick:

```
tell application "Database Events"
    tell database "Movie Collection" to close saving yes
    quit
end tell
```
SCRIPT 23.23

Opening an Existing Database

A saved database is of no use if you can't open it again later. The dictionary is a little misleading. It indicates that the Standard Suite's `open` command can be used with an alias reference to the database file, but nothing happens when you do this. In fact, the `open` command works only with the POSIX path to the file, as shown in Script 23.24:

```
tell application "Database Events"
    open database "~/Documents/Databases/Movie Collection.dbev"
end tell
```
SCRIPT 23.24

Unfortunately, in Mac OS X 10.4 (Tiger), if you run Script 23.24 and then run a test script that gets **every database**, you'll discover that two **database** objects with the same name were opened in memory at once. The reason for this is that the POSIX path reference to the database opened the database once, as you know, and then the **open** command opened it again. In addition, when it is used with a POSIX path, we find that the **open** command sometimes doesn't work at all in Tiger, seemingly at random. A solution to these issues is to omit the **open** command and just use the POSIX path reference by itself. You should use Script 23.25 in Tiger, instead of Script 23.24.

```
tell application "Database Events"
    database "~/Documents/Databases/Movie Collection.dbev"
end tell
```
SCRIPT 23.25

Leopard has fixed this problem, so you can safely use an **open database** command with a POSIX path in Leopard, as in Script 23.24. Script 23.25 works in Leopard as well.

The Presidents Database

For examples of more complex Database Events scripting techniques, go to the book's Web site and download the Presidents Database Scripts.

What's Next?

This chapter covered the use of the Database Events scriptable background application to store and retrieve information in a powerful and flexible scriptable database using AppleScript. In the next chapter, you'll learn how to use the AppleScript idle handler and other techniques to use timing controls in scripts.

24

Adding Timing Controls to Scripts

There's an old saying that "timing is everything." Although this phrase is usually used when describing one's life choices, it sometimes applies to AppleScript, too. Controlling the speed and timing of your scripts is essential when automating tasks that

▶ require a momentary pause, such as while a window opens or a Web page loads; or

▶ occur over a period of time or at specific times, such as a script that downloads your e-mail at 2 p.m. and 5 p.m. every day.

In this chapter, we'll examine techniques and strategies for addressing time requirements in scripts.

The delay Command

The most basic form of time manipulation is adding a pause to a script by using the `delay` command from the Standard Additions scripting addition. This command is used to insert a pause of a specified duration into a script.

Enter and run Script 24.1. The first time you run it, there is a natural-feeling pause between the first sentence and the second. But the second time you run it, notice that the second statement executes immediately after the first. Depending on the voice used by the script, this might make the simulated conversation seem a bit forced and unnatural. The pause during the first run was an accidental result of AppleScript taking time to process the command. The conversation was more hurried on the second run because AppleScript remembered the processing that it had taken the time to perform the first time.

```
say "Hello."
say "What is your name?"
```
SCRIPT 24.1

To inject some "space" into the conversation every time the script is run, we'll add a pause after the greeting by using the `delay` command. To use this command, place the number of seconds for the desired pause after the verb `delay`, as in Script 24.2.

```
say "Hello."
delay 1
say "What is your name?"
```
SCRIPT 24.2

The script now has more measured pacing. If it seems too long, change the delay to 0.5 seconds and try it again.

The `delay` command is a useful tool for adding short pauses into scripts. The value for its timing parameter is in whole numbers or, starting with Mac OS X 10.3 (Panther), decimal values such as 0.5.

Using the delay Command to Watch

Scripts can silently observe the actions of applications and then perform tasks when specified conditions occur, such as when a Web page has finished loading in a Safari browser window. Although a "watch" script can be written with the `delay` command, it must be organized carefully to avoid becoming stuck in an endless loop.

Let's write a script that loads a Web page in the Safari browser application and then extracts the text of the loaded page. Open an empty browser window in Safari, and then run Script 24.3:

```
tell application "Safari"
    set the URL of the front document to "http://www.apple.com/"
    set this_data to the text of document 1
end tell
```
SCRIPT 24.3

If you run Script 24.3 when Safari isn't already running or there is no window open in Safari, it may generate an error because the application hasn't launched or the document hasn't opened by the time the second statement executes. Even if you launched Safari and opened an empty document manually before running the script, it may return an empty string as the value of `this_data`. This is expected behavior, because the Safari application does not wait for the page to load before continuing the script. The second statement, which attempts to extract the text from a page that isn't yet loaded, is executed immediately after the first line and returns an empty string because all it sees is the empty Safari window you started with.

To enable the script to function as intended, it must include a check to see whether the browser window has completed the loading process before attempting to extract the text of the Web page. We can use the `delay` command within a repeat loop to perform a series of checks over time to determine when the target Web page has successfully loaded in the browser window, as in Script 24.4:

```
tell application "Safari"
    set the URL of the front document to "http://www.cnn.com/"
    delay 1 -- let the page begin to load before checking
    repeat
        -- use Safari's 'do JavaScript' to check a page's status
        if (do JavaScript "document.readyState" in document 1) ¬
            is "complete" then exit repeat
        delay 1 -- wait a second before checking again
    end repeat
    beep
    set this_data to the text of document 1
end tell
```

SCRIPT 24.4

Although Script 24.4 may work and appears to be a proper solution, it includes the common mistake of placing the delay command within an open-ended repeat loop. Thus, it does not provide a way to stop the script if there is a problem accessing the target URL address. If Safari never loads the Web site, the script will continue executing the repeat loop endlessly.

Placing a limit on the total number of status checks done within the repeat loop prevents the script from remaining in an endless loop. In Script 24.5, the repeat loop is set to increment 60 times, after which the script is stopped by throwing an error. This technique prevents a "runaway script" from taking over your computer.

```
tell application "Safari"
    set the URL of the front document to "http://www.cnn.com/"
    delay 1 -- let the page begin to load before checking
    repeat with i from 1 to 60 -- the number of times to check
        if (do JavaScript "document.readyState" in document 1) ¬
            is "complete" then
            exit repeat
        else if i is 60 then -- there was a problem loading the page
            error number -128
        else
```

```
        delay 1
      end if
    end repeat
    beep
    set this_data to the text of document 1
end tell
```
SCRIPT 24.5

While the script is paused because of the `delay` command, it does not prevent other applications and processes on your computer from continuing to run. You therefore needn't worry that a script containing a `delay` command will slow down the computer's ongoing work. To see that this is true, you could start a long-running process, such as an Adobe Photoshop action on a high-resolution photograph, then run Script 24.5. You would see that the Photoshop action continues to do its work without a noticeable slowdown.

The Idle Handler

One purpose of automation is to make your life easier by freeing you from the drudgery of executing repetitive tasks. Using AppleScript, you can create special "assistants" that perform tasks for you throughout the day, such as monitoring a project's status, checking specific Web sites and servers for updates, or creating daily and hourly reports.

Scripts designed to perform repeated actions over time are often implemented as stay-open AppleScript applications, or *applets*. To perform an action at timed intervals, these applets use a special subroutine called an *idle handler*.

You learned about subroutines in Chapter 16, *Subroutines*. They are sections of AppleScript code that execute when they are called by another statement in a script or by an application. They are often tied to events, such as launching a script or dragging items onto a droplet. These events trigger event handlers in your scripts written to address these specific events.

An idle handler is a special subroutine used by scripts to perform repeated actions over time. It is constructed so that it performs an action immediately and then pauses for a specified duration until it performs the action again. You specify the duration of the pause between calls to an idle handler in seconds.

As with other handlers, an idle handler begins with an opening statement—in this case, `on idle`—and ends with a closing statement—`end idle`. It must be placed outside any `tell` blocks. Script 24.6 shows the basic structure of the idle handler.

```
 on idle
    -- action goes here
    return 3 -- number of seconds to pause before repeating
end idle
```
SCRIPT 24.6

Repeated Actions Over Time

As an example, let's create a simple script that performs an action repeatedly. In a new script window in Script Editor, enter and compile Script 24.7 without saving or running it.

```
on idle
    display dialog "Hello." buttons {"OK"} default button 1
    return 3
end idle
```
SCRIPT 24.7

Judging from the statements in this script, it should display a dialog, and then it should wait three seconds after you confirm the dialog before displaying the dialog again. Right?

Now, run the script by clicking the Run button in Script Editor.

Nothing happens. *Idle handlers do not work when executed in the Script Editor.* For the idle handler to function, its host script must be saved as a script application, or applet, that is designed to stay open after it is launched.

Save the example script to the Desktop as an application with the Stay Open checkbox in the save sheet selected, as shown in Figure 24.1.

FIGURE 24.1 Saving a script as a stay-open applet.

Switch to the Desktop, and launch the script. It displays the dialog repeatedly over time, always three seconds after you dismiss the dialog by clicking OK. To stop the script, make the applet the frontmost application, and press Command+Q to quit, or you can click and hold its icon in the Dock and choose Quit from the pop-up menu while the dialog is not showing.

The applet does not perform its action every three seconds. Instead, it performs its action three seconds *after* you click OK. The length of time required to perform the indicated action (clicking OK) *plus* the duration of the indicated delay determines the total length of time between repetitions.

In other words, the applet, with a three-second delay, does not repeat 20 times per minute. It takes more than a minute to repeat 20 times, because the length of time the dialogs are allowed to remain on-screen before you click OK adds to the time required to execute the repeated actions.

> **NOTE** ▶ You can achieve the same effect by using a `delay` command in a repeat loop, as shown in the previous section.

Incrementing a Counter

Since the applet runs in stay-open mode, it can store information on an ongoing basis. Quit the previous applet, write a new script (Script 24.8), save it as a stay-open applet, and then run it by double-clicking it in the Finder.

```
property display_count : 0
on idle
    set the display_count to the display_count + 1
    display dialog "Hello, this dialog has been displayed " & ¬
        (display_count as string) & ¬
        " times." buttons {"OK"} default button 1
    return 3
end idle
```
SCRIPT 24.8

As the applet runs, it displays a running total of the number of times the dialog has been presented, as shown in Figure 24.2.

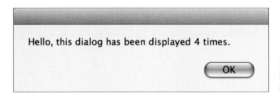

Hello, this dialog has been displayed 4 times.

OK

FIGURE 24.2 The dialog displaying the number of times the applet has been run.

The applet keeps track of how many times the dialog is presented by storing the loop count in a property whose value is incremented each time the idle handler is executed. You learned about persistent properties in Chapter 15, *Script Properties*.

What Time Is It?

Scripts that perform actions at specific times of day require ongoing knowledge of the current date and time. AppleScript has two methods for determining a point in time: the current date command and the date method of the UNIX shell. We'll include a quick overview of them here.

The current date command is part of the Standard Additions scripting addition. It can be used anywhere within a script. Enter and run Script 24.9.

```
set this_moment to (the current date)
--> returns: date "Thursday, August 16, 2007 4:53:52 PM"
```
SCRIPT 24.9

The result of this command is a *date object* that contains all the information AppleScript can tell you about a specific moment in time. Several properties can be extracted from the date object, as in the example statements shown in Script 24.10 (the results you see will differ). Comment out every statement in the script except the one you want to run by typing two hyphens at the beginning of each statement, and then run the script to see its result.

```
set this_moment to (the current date)
--> date "Thursday, June 5, 2003 3:48:08 PM"
date string of this_moment
--> "Thursday, June 5, 2003"
short date string of this_moment
--> "06/06/03"
time string of this_moment
--> "3:48:08 PM"
month of this_moment
--> June
(month of this_moment) as string
--> "June"
(month of this_moment) as number
--> 6
day of this_moment
--> 5
year of this_moment
--> 2003
time of this_moment -- returns seconds from midnight
--> 56888
(time of this_moment) / hours
--> 15.802222222222
(time of this_moment) / minutes
--> 948.133333333333
```
SCRIPT 24.10

The date method of the UNIX shell also provides quick access to the current date and time by executing the do shell script AppleScript command with the UNIX shell command date as its parameter, as shown in Script 24.11.

```
do shell script "date"
--> "Thu Jun 5 15:56:34 HST 2003"
do shell script "date +'%d'"
--> returns the current day as string: "05"
do shell script "date +'%m'"
--> returns the current month as string: "06"
do shell script "date +'%y'"
--> returns the current year as string: "03"
do shell script "date +'%H'"
--> returns the current hour as string: "15"
do shell script "date +'%M'"
--> returns the current minute as string: "56"
do shell script "date +'%S'"
--> returns the current hour as string: "34"
do shell script "date +'%m/%d/%y'"
--> returns the current date string separated by slashes: "06/05/03"
do shell script "date +'%H:%M:%S'"
--> returns the current time string separated by colons: "15:56:34"
```
SCRIPT 24.11

The following examples incorporate a variety of the date and time access techniques described in this chapter.

Webcam Watcher Example

As an example of how to use an idle handler to gather data over time, Script 24.12 periodically downloads the current view from the Web camera overlooking the UCLA observatory in the hills outside Los Angeles, California. This script requires an active connection to the Internet.

Copy the script to a new script window, and save it as an applet named Webcam Watcher with the Stay Open option selected. Place the applet in a new folder named Webcam in your home directory. Once the script is started, it will periodically download Webcam images to a folder it creates daily in its parent folder. An image is shown in Figure 24.3.

```
on idle
    try
        set target_URL to ¬
            "http://www.astro.ucla.edu/~obs/images/towercam.jpg"
        -- get the current date and time as a numeric text string
        set the date_string to (do shell script "date +'%m%d%y'")
        --> returns current date without delimiters: 051203
        set the time_string to (do shell script "date +'%H%M%S'")
        --> returns current time without delimiters: 095151
        set the file_name to date_string & time_string & ".jpg"
        --> returns something like: 051203095151.jpg
        -- use the 'path to' command to get location of this applet
        set this_app to the path to me
        --> alias "Macintosh HD:Users:sal:Wecam:Webcam Watcher.app"
        tell application "Finder"
            -- get the location of the folder containing this applet
            set parent_folder to the container of this_app
            --> returns: alias "Macintosh HD:Users:sal:Wecam:"
            -- check to see if a folder for the current day exists
            if not (exists folder date_string of parent_folder) then
                make new folder at parent_folder ¬
                    with properties {name:date_string}
            end if
        end tell
        -- create a file path using the parent folder,
        -- the current date, and the file name
        set the target_file to ((parent_folder as string) & ¬
            date_string & ":" & file_name)
        -- download the webcam image to the parent folder
        tell application "URL Access Scripting"
            download the target_URL to ¬
```

```
                    file target_file replacing yes ¬
                    with progress and unpacking
                ignoring application responses
                    quit
                end ignoring
            end tell
            beep 2
        end try
        -- tell the script to wait 300 seconds (5 minutes) before repeating
        return 300
    end idle
```
SCRIPT 24.12

FIGURE 24.3 The UCLA observatory Web camera view.

Actions at a Specific Time

Using an idle handler, it is possible to create applets that perform actions at or near a specific time, such as on the hour, at midnight, or at 5:13 PM. These applets work by checking the current time periodically to see whether it matches targeted times that are declared in minutes. Don't forget to save them as stay-open applications; we won't remind you again.

The first example, Script 24.13, performs an action at specified times during every hour.

```
on idle
    set the target_minutes to {0, 15, 30, 45}
    -- a list of integers between 0 and 59. 0 is on the hour
    set current_minute to (do shell script "date +'%M'") as number
    if the current_minute is in the target_minutes then
        -- do action
        say "If you're thinking it's the time 4 a break you're " & ¬
            "correct if you're hungry 4 a snack " & ¬
            "you'd better hurry up!" using "Cellos"
        -- delay until the target minute has passed
        repeat
            set this_minute to ¬
                ((do shell script "date +'%M'") as number)
            if this_minute is not the current_minute then exit repeat
            delay 10
        end repeat
    end if
    return 45
end idle
```

SCRIPT 24.13

The targeted times of the hour are included in the list assigned to the variable named target_minutes. The values for this list are integers representing the minutes of an hour and can be any number between 0 and 59. For example, 0 is the top of the hour, 15 is a quarter after the hour, and so on. To have the script execute only once during an hour, place only one integer in the list.

To sense time changes, this script uses the do shell script command to access the current minute and then coerces the result to an integer. This value is then checked against the list of targeted minutes. If the list contains the current minute value, the script executes the designated action; otherwise, it returns an idle delay of 45 seconds.

Also note the use of the `delay` loop in the script to make sure the action is performed only once for a targeted minute.

As with the previous example, save the script as an applet with the Stay Open option enabled.

The next example, Script 24.14, demonstrates how to target specific times during the day. As with Script 24.13, this script uses minutes as the measuring increment. However, in this script, a specific minute is identified as the number of seconds from midnight to the targeted minute. The number of seconds is always rounded down to the nearest minute.

For example, 15 minutes after midnight would be equal to 15 x 60 (seconds) or 900, and 2 AM would be described as 2 (hours) x 3600 (seconds per hour), or 7200. The formula for calculating a specific minute in time is as follows:

```
(hours * 3600) + (minutes * 60) = target time
```
So 7:47 AM would be:

```
(7 * 3600) + (47 * 60) = 28020
```
The formula is based on a 24-hour clock, so 7:47 PM is considered to be 19:47, or as follows:

```
(19 * 3600) + (47 * 60) = 71220
```
The following example is an outline to use when creating your own scripts for performing daily actions. To use the script, place any targeted time values in the `target_times` list. The script uses the `time` property of the `current date` (returned as the number of seconds from midnight) to determine when to execute the indicated actions.

As with Script 24.13, Script 24.14 returns an idle delay of 45 seconds if no match is made. Note that both examples are accurate within the range of a minute, not to a specific second.

```
on idle
    set the target_times to {}
    -- EX: {25500, 41400, 58200} = {7:05 AM, 11:30 AM, 4:10 PM}
    set the current_time to ¬
        ((the time of the (current date)) div 60) * 60
```

```
    if the current_time is in the target_times then

        -- ACTIONS GO HERE

        -- delay until the target minute has passed
        repeat
            set this_time to ¬
                (((the time of the (current date)) div 60) * 60)
            if this_time is not the current_time then exit repeat
            delay 10
        end repeat
    end if
    return 45
end idle
```

SCRIPT 24.14

The Movie Maker Script

Here's an example of an applet that executes an action at a specific time of day. This Movie Maker script works with the Webcam Watcher script to take a day's images and convert them to a time-lapse movie using the QuickTime Player application.

As with the previous examples, save Script 24.15 as an application with the Stay Open option checked. Place it in the same folder as the Webcam Watcher script, and launch it when you start the Webcam Watcher script. At 12:01 AM, the script will create a movie file from the previous day's Web cam images and place the movie file in the same folder as the source images. A frame from the resulting movie is shown in Figure 24.4.

When it is launched, the script first executes the statements in the implicit run handler before beginning the idle loop. In this example, the script presents a confirmation dialog before storing the current date string in the variable date_string and entering the idle handler.

```
global date_string

activate
display dialog "Movie Builder" buttons {"Quit", "Start"} default button 2
if the button returned of the result is "Quit" then
    tell me to quit
end if
-- get the current date and time as a numeric text string
set the date_string to (do shell script "date +'%m%d%y'")
-- returns current date without delimiters: 051203

on idle
    try
        set the target_times to {60} -- 12:01 AM
        set the current_time to ¬
            ((time of the (current date)) div 60) * 60
        if the current_time is in the target_times then
            -- get the path to the applet
            set this_app to the path to me
            tell application "Finder"
                -- get the location of the folder containing this applet
                set parent_folder to the container of this_app
                -- Look for a folder containing the day's images
                if not ¬
                    (exists folder date_string of parent_folder) then
                    error "no source folder found"
                end if
                set the source_folder to ¬
                    (folder date_string of the parent_folder)
                set the source_image to ¬
                    (the first file of source_folder whose ¬
                        file type is "JPEG" or ¬
                        name extension is "jpg") as alias
            end tell
            tell application "QuickTime Player"
                activate
                stop every document
```

```
            close every document saving no
            open image sequence source_image frames per second 6
            tell document 1
                if not (exists annotation "Full Name") then
                    make new annotation with properties ¬
                        {name:"Full Name", full text:¬
                            (date_string & space & "Time Lapse")}
                else
                    set the full text of annotation "Full Name" to ¬
                        (date_string & space & "Time Lapse")
                end if
            end tell
            set the new_file to ¬
                ((source_folder as string) & ¬
                    date_string & ".mov")
            save document 1 in file new_file as self contained
            close document 1 saving no
        end tell
        -- delay until the target minute has passed
        repeat
            set this_time to ¬
                (((the time of the (current date)) div 60) * 60)
            if this_time is not the current_time then exit repeat
            delay 10
        end repeat
        -- reset the stored date string to the new day
        set the date_string to (do shell script "date +'%m%d%y'")
    end if
on error error_message
    display dialog error_message buttons ¬
        {"Quit"} default button 1 giving up after 120
    tell me to quit
end try
return 45
end idle
```

SCRIPT 24.15

FIGURE 24.4 A frame from a time-lapse movie of the UCLA observatory Web camera.

The Easy Way: Use iCal

Perhaps the easiest way to have scripts execute at a specific time is to tell an application to run them for you. iCal supports executing scripts as an event action. As with any iCal event, scripts can be set to execute once, hourly, daily, or on any schedule you choose.

To assign a script to be an event action, perform the following steps. Step 5 is shown in Figure 24.5.

1. Compile and save the script as a compiled script or an applet.

2. Launch iCal, double-click the target date in the main iCal window to create a new event, double-click the new event, and click the Edit button. The New Event window opens.

3. Using the first pop-up menu in the "alarm" section of the window, set the alarm type to **Open file**. The Open file iCal action "opens" a file. In this example, it will recognize that the file you specify in step 4 is a script and run it when the specified time arrives.

4. Using the second pop-up menu in the "alarm" section of the window, choose the Other command, and, in the file dialog, choose the script file you saved in step 1.

5. To enable the script to execute at a designated time, use the third pop-up menu in the "alarm" section of the window to, and fill in the date and time to a moment a couple of minutes from now.

6. Set the repetition, if any, of the event with the repeat pop-up menu.

FIGURE 24.5 Setting a script as the alarm in iCal's New Event drawer.

That's all you do. The iCal application does not have to be running to run the script. The computer, however, must be awake and not shut down or in sleep mode.

Audio Alarm Clock Script

To enable iCal to be used as an audio alarm clock, save Script 24.16, and assign it using the previous instructions. The iCal application will run the script at the appointed time, and the script will launch the iTunes application and play a random song from a playlist.

```
try
    tell application "iTunes"
        launch
        set the playlist_names to the name of every playlist
        if playlist_names contains "Audio Alarm" then
            set this_track to some track of playlist "Audio Alarm"
        else if the playlist_names contains "Top 25 Most Played" then
            set this_track to ¬
                some track of playlist "Top 25 Most Played"
        else
            set this_track to some track of playlist "Library"
        end if
        play this_track
    end tell
end try
```
SCRIPT 24.16

What's Next?

In this chapter, you learned a variety of techniques using AppleScript to trigger actions at intervals and at specific times of day. In the next chapter, you will learn about built-in AppleScript unit conversions, which you can use to convert a value between various measures, such as inches to centimeters.

25

Lesson **25**

Unit Coercions

Pop quiz:

▸ How many centimeters in an inch?

▸ How many liters in a gallon?

▸ How many yards in a kilometer?

▸ What is 39 degrees Fahrenheit, in Celsius?

If you're like us, you probably couldn't answer any but the first question (2.54 centimeters per inch). Unless we use these calculations regularly, we're liable to be a bit rusty converting values between measurement systems.

Fortunately for us, on the rare occasions when we need to convert measurement units, AppleScript provides built-in tools that make us look like we really know our stuff. Unit coercions can make even the most complex conversion easy.

Unit coercions work in the same manner as the standard coercions we've used throughout this book, such as number to text, text to number, list to string, record to list, and so on. The difference is that unit coercions involve unit types and standard measures including distance, volume, weight, and temperature.

In this chapter, we'll examine how to coerce between unit types and how to perform basic calculations involving different units of measurement.

Distance

AppleScript has built-in unit coercions for the English (British Imperial System) and metric systems of measurement. The unit types for distance measurements include inches, feet, yards, and miles for the English system and centimeters, meters, and kilometers for the metric system.

Coercions can be made within systems, such as from yards to feet or from meters to centimeters, or between systems, such as from kilometers to miles.

Before we begin, it is essential to note that you cannot turn a numeric value into a unit measurement simply by placing the name of the units after the number, as in `5 miles` or `12 kilometers`. AppleScript won't compile a script like Script 25.1.

```
5 miles --> BAD SYNTAX
```
SCRIPT 25.1

Instead, numeric values must be coerced into unit measurements, which is why this chapter is called *Unit Coercions*.

Let's begin our examination of unit coercions by coercing a numeric value into a distance measurement of the unit type `miles`. Enter and run Script 25.2.

```
1 as miles
```
SCRIPT 25.2

The result as displayed in the Result pane of Script Editor is as follows:

```
--> returns: miles 1.0
```

You've coerced the numeric value 1 to the distance measurement of `miles` `1.0` by placing the unit coercion `as miles` after the number in the script. The script now views the result as a distance measurement in the unit type of `miles` and not as the numeric value `1`.

To demonstrate this, let's examine the result of the extended coercion shown in Script 25.3 as we coerce the numeric value 1 first to `miles` and then to `yards`.

```
1 as miles as yards
--> returns: yards 1760.0
```
SCRIPT 25.3

The result, `yards` `1760.0`, shows that the initial numeric value of 1 was coerced to `miles`, because a mile is composed of 1,760 yards (we remembered that!).

Try another double coercion, this time to `feet` , as shown in Script 25.4.

```
1 as miles as feet
--> returns: feet 5280.0
```
SCRIPT 25.4

And another to `inches`, as shown in Script 25.5.

```
1 as miles as inches
--> returns: inches 6.336E+4
```
SCRIPT 25.5

Unit coercions work in both directions, from the larger units to smaller units and from smaller units to larger units, as shown in Scripts 25.6 and 25.7.

```
0.625 as miles as yards
--> returns: yards 1100.0
```
SCRIPT 25.6

```
1100 as yards as miles
--> returns: miles 0.625
```
SCRIPT 25.7

NOTE ▶ Some versions of AppleScript prior to Mac OS X 10.3 (Panther) may return a value for inches that is off by an extremely small amount. You may see this if you run Script 25.8 in Mac OS X 10.2 (Jaguar).

```
1 as feet as inches
--> returns: inches 11.999999981758
```
SCRIPT 25.8

This error can easily be remedied by using the round command, demonstrated in Script 25.9.

```
(round (1 as feet as inches)) as inches
--> returns: inches 12.0
```
SCRIPT 25.9

The extra coercion back to inches at the end of the statement is necessary, because the rounding process automatically coerces the unit measurement to a number before rounding.

Coercing Between Systems

Unit values are converted into measurements from other measurement systems by placing a unit coercion to the target system after the initial coercion, as in Scripts 25.10, 25.11, 25.12, and 25.13.

```
-- miles to kilometers
1.75 as miles as kilometers
--> returns: kilometers 2.816352
```
SCRIPT 25.10

```
-- kilometers to miles
2 as kilometers as miles
--> returns: miles 1.242742384475
```
SCRIPT 25.11

```
-- miles to meters
1.5 as miles as meters
--> returns: meters 2414.016
```
SCRIPT 25.12

```
-- centimeters to yards
12345 as centimeters as yards
--> returns: yards 135.0065617979
```
SCRIPT 25.13

Calculations with Unit Coercions

Performing calculations with unit coercions is not quite the same as adding, subtracting, multiplying, or dividing numbers. The process is not difficult, but it does require a few extra steps.

For example, run Script 25.14, which attempts to add 75 feet and 14 feet together:

```
(75 as feet) + (14 as feet) --> ERROR
```
SCRIPT 25.14

When the script is executed, an error message is displayed by Script Editor declaring that the script can't make the unit measurement **feet 75.0** into a number, as shown in Figure 25.1.

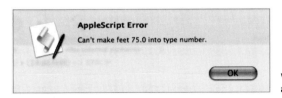

FIGURE 25.1 Error message when attempting arithmetic with a unit type.

In other words, the result of the first part of the script, where the number 75 is coerced into a unit measurement of **feet 75.0**, cannot be used in a numeric calculation. Calculations can involve only numbers, not unit types.

To enable the addition of two unit values, each unit value must be coerced into a numeric value before adding them together. Script 25.15 works.

```
(75 as feet as number) + (14 as feet as number)
```
SCRIPT 25.15

The result of the calculation is now the numeric value 89.0.

To complete the process, the calculation result can be coerced back to the original unit type, in this case feet. To accomplish this, place the entire script within parentheses, and apply another coercion to the end of the statement. The result is a unit measurement in feet, as shown in Script 25.16.

```
((75 as feet as number) + (14 as feet as number)) as feet
--> returns: feet 89.0
```
SCRIPT 25.16

> **TIP** ▶ When performing calculations with unit types, place each set of coercions within its own set of parentheses. Doing so will clearly delineate the elements of the calculation.
>
> Remember your algebra: calculations inside parentheses are performed first and then are replaced by their result. Therefore, Script 25.16, although written in one line, is actually executed in these steps.
>
> ```
> ((75 as feet as number) + (14 as feet as number)) as feet
> (75.0 + 14.0) as feet
> (89.0) as feet
> --> result: feet 89.0
> ```
> **SCRIPT 25.17**

You can also perform calculations involving unit types from different measurement systems. For example, how far is 1.5 miles plus 2.5 kilometers? Script 25.18 shows a first, incorrect attempt to find the answer.

```
(1.5 as miles) + (2.5 as kilometers) --> ERROR
```
SCRIPT 25.18

As you knew in advance, Script 25.18 doesn't work. The calculation requires multiple coercions, beginning with the coercion of the unit types to a common unit type, depending on the measurement system you want for the answer. For this example, we want the answer in `miles`, so we start by coercing the unit measurement in `kilometers` into `miles`, as shown in Script 25.19.

```
(1.5 as miles) + (2.5 as kilometers as miles) --> ERROR
```
SCRIPT 25.19

The next step is to convert the unit measurements to numeric values, as shown in Script 25.20.

```
(1.5 as miles as number) + (2.5 as kilometers as miles as number)
--> returns: 3.053427980593
```
SCRIPT 25.20

The script works now, but it returns a numeric value. The final step, in Script 25.21, is to coerce the resulting numeric value to the desired unit type of `miles`. Note that the entire calculation is placed within parentheses with the final coercion outside the parentheses.

```
((1.5 as miles as number) + (2.5 as kilometers as miles as number)) ¬
    as miles
```
SCRIPT 25.21

When the script is executed, the result, in `miles`, is as follows:

```
--> returns: miles 3.053427980593
```
The same technique, written to return the result in `kilometers`, would be Script 25.22.

```
((1.5 as miles as kilometers as number) + ¬
    (2.5 as kilometers as number)) as kilometers
--> returns: kilometers 4.914016
```
SCRIPT 25.22

Comparisons

Performing a comparison between two unit measurements involves the same procedure as calculations: each unit measurement must first be coerced into a common unit type (if they are not already in the same unit type) and then into a numeric value.

For example, the comparison in Script 25.23 produces an error indicating that the script cannot perform a mathematical procedure on the provided unit measurements.

```
1.5 as miles is greater than 2.0 as kilometers --> ERROR
```
SCRIPT 25.23

To compare the two measurements, first coerce one into the unit type of the other, as in Script 25.24.

```
(1.5 as miles as kilometers) ¬
    is greater than 2.0 as kilometers --> ERROR
```
SCRIPT 25.24

Then coerce both unit measurements to numeric values. The comparison can now be made, and Script 25.25 returns a Boolean value (`true` or `false`) indicating the result of the comparison.

```
(1.5 as miles as kilometers as number) is greater than ¬
    (2.0 as kilometers as number)
--> returns: true
```
SCRIPT 25.25

Is the script result correct? We can always check the result with the coercion shown in Script 25.26.

```
2.0 as kilometers as miles
--> returns: miles 1.242742386364
```
SCRIPT 25.26

Well, 1.5 is greater than 1.242742384475, so the comparison was true.

Script 25.27 is a handy miles converter script that converts any amount in miles into several other units, as shown in Figure 25.2.

```
display dialog "Enter number of miles to convert:" default answer ""
set the miles_val to text returned of the result as number as miles
display dialog "MILES CONVERTER" & return & return & ¬
    (miles_val as string) & " miles is equal to:" & return & ¬
    "Yards: " & (miles_val as yards as string) & return & ¬
    "Feet: " & (miles_val as feet as string) & return & ¬
    "Inches: " & (miles_val as inches as string) & return & ¬
    "Kilometers: " & (miles_val as kilometers as string) & return & ¬
    "Meters: " & (miles_val as meters as string) & return & ¬
    "Centimeters: " & (miles_val as centimeters as string) ¬
        buttons {"OK"} default button 1
```

SCRIPT 25.27

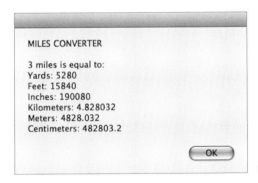

FIGURE 25.2 The miles converter script at work.

Volume

AppleScript provides unit coercions for volume measurements in the English unit types of quarts and gallons, and the metric unit type of liters.

Note that the pints unit type is not supported, although at two pints per quart it's easy to calculate in your head if needed.

Script 25.28 is an example coercion from **gallons** to **liters**.

```
2.3 as gallons as liters
--> returns: liters 8.7064476
```
SCRIPT 25.28

Script 25.29 converts **liters** to **quarts**:.

```
8 as liters as quarts
--> returns: quarts 8.453505193094
```
SCRIPT 25.29

An important caveat regarding volume measurements involves the unit type of **ounces**. Although **ounces** are commonly used in volume measurements, AppleScript reserves the **ounces** unit type for weight measurements only, so the coercion in Script 25.30 fails with an error.

```
1 as quarts as ounces --> ERROR
```
SCRIPT 25.30

AppleScript provides unit coercions for several cubic volume measurements, including **cubic centimeters**, **cubic meters**, **cubic inches**, **cubic feet**, and **cubic yards**. Scripts 25.31 and 25.32 show examples.

```
3 as cubic feet as cubic meters
--> returns: cubic meters 0.084950539776
```
SCRIPT 25.31

```
3 as cubic meters as cubic feet
--> returns: cubic feet 105.944000164466
```
SCRIPT 25.32

Weight

AppleScript provides unit coercions for weight measurements in the English unit types of ounces and pounds and in the metric unit types of grams and kilograms. For examples, see Scripts 25.33 and 25.34.

```
1 as ounces as grams
--> returns: grams 28.349525
```
SCRIPT 25.33

```
3100 as grams as pounds
--> returns: pounds 6.834329675718
```
SCRIPT 25.34

Tons are not included as a unit type. There is no single definition of a ton.

Temperature

AppleScript provides unit coercions for temperature measurements in the Fahrenheit, Celsius (Centigrade), and Kelvin systems. See Scripts 25.35 and 25.36.

```
32 as degrees Fahrenheit as degrees Celsius
--> returns: degrees Celsius 0.0
```
SCRIPT 25.35

```
0 as degrees Kelvin as degrees Fahrenheit
--> returns: degrees Fahrenheit -459.67
```
SCRIPT 25.36

Script 25.37 is a useful temperature converter script that converts a temperature as a number to any temperature measurement unit. Figures 25.3 and 25.4 show the temperature converter script in action.

```
display dialog "Enter the amount and choose the temperature system:"
default answer ¬
    "" buttons {"Kelvin", "Celsius", "Fahrenheit"} default button 3
copy the result as list to {text_returned, button_pressed}
set the default_value to the text_returned as number
if the button_pressed is "Kelvin" then
    set the dialog_message to ¬
        ("Kelvin: " & default_value & return & ¬
            "Fahrenheit: " & (default_value as degrees Kelvin ¬
            as degrees Fahrenheit as number) as string) & return & ¬
        "Celsius: " & (default_value as degrees Kelvin ¬
        as degrees Celsius as number) as string
else if the button_pressed is "Celsius" then
    set the dialog_message to ¬
        ("Celsius: " & default_value & return & ¬
            "Fahrenheit: " & (default_value as degrees Celsius ¬
            as degrees Fahrenheit as number) as string) & return & ¬
        "Kelvin: " & (default_value as degrees Celsius ¬
        as degrees Kelvin as number) as string
else
    set the dialog_message to ¬
        ("Fahrenheit: " & default_value & return & ¬
            "Kelvin: " & (default_value as degrees Fahrenheit ¬
            as degrees Kelvin as number) as string) & return & ¬
        "Celsius: " & (default_value as degrees Fahrenheit ¬
        as degrees Celsius as number) as string
end if
display dialog dialog_message buttons {"OK"} default button 1
```
SCRIPT 25.37

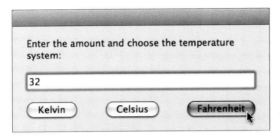

FIGURE 25.3 The temperature converter script converting to Fahrenheit.

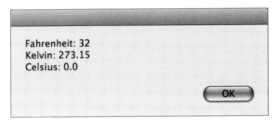

FIGURE 25.4 The temperature converter script displaying the result.

What's Next?

In this chapter, you learned how to coerce numbers into a variety of standard units of measurement. In the next chapter, you'll learn about units of measurement relating to time.

26

Lesson 26
The date Object

In Chapter 24, *Adding Timing Controls to Scripts*, you got a brief introduction to the `current date` command in the Standard Additions scripting addition and the `date` command of the UNIX shell. Here, we'll show you how to use date and time arithmetic and to compare dates to make better use of your time.

Knowing what day and time it is right now is only the beginning. You often have a second date, and you want to know how much time has passed since then or how much time will pass until then. For example, given your birthday, how old are you right now? Given the deadline for your next term paper, how much time do you have left to finish it? Or given a period of time in which to accomplish something, you want to know when it's due. For example, you just found a parking ticket on your windshield, and it says you have 30 days to pay the fine. What due date should you mark on your calendar? Or maybe you want a stopwatch to tell you how long the ads last in the middle of your favorite TV show.

Date and Time Tools

AppleScript comes with a full toolkit for calculating date and time intervals and performing every other calculation and comparison you might need in order to travel down the river of time. Let's start by exploring the details, and then we'll write a spiffy deadline calculator.

The Date Class and Its Properties

In Chapter 24, Script 24.9 showed you that the `current date` command returns a value that looks like this:

```
set this_moment to (the current date)
--> returns: date "Thursday, August 16, 2007 4:53:52 PM"
```

The term `date` in the return value is a tip-off that this is not just a string describing the day, date, and time. In fact, it is a `date` object, based on a built-in AppleScript data type having equal standing with other data types such as `number` and `list`. The term `date` together with the quoted text following it in the example is simply AppleScript's preferred form for expressing the value of a `date` object.

Although Script Editor does not show you a dictionary for built-in AppleScript classes, there is something that amounts to a dictionary buried deep in the system. You can read it in some third-party script editors such as Script Debugger from Late Night Software. Table 26.1 lists all the properties of the `date` class.

Every one of these properties has a value, so you can always extract these details from any date. You saw in Script 24.10 in Chapter 24, for example, that `year of (current date)` returns the year as an integer, such as `2007`.

Most of the properties you might need in order to perform date calculations and comparisons are ordinary integers, namely, `day`, `year`, `hours`, `minutes`, and `seconds`. The `hours` property is based on a 24-hour clock. The `time` in seconds since midnight is also available as an integer. These integers may already suggest to you how to perform date arithmetic using AppleScript, but an integer for the month is missing. You'll see how to deal with this omission shortly.

TABLE 26.1 Properties of the Date Class

Property	Value Type	Description
date string	text	The date portion of a date-time value as text
day	integer	The day of the month of a date
hours	integer	The hours of a date-time value
minutes	integer	The minutes of a date-time value
month	month	The month of a date
seconds	integer	The seconds of a date-time value
short date string	text	The date portion of a date-time value as text
time	integer	The time since midnight of a date
time string	text	The time portion of a date-time value as text
weekday	weekday	The day of a week of a date
year	integer	The year of a date

Three of the properties are text objects: date string, short date string, and time string. You can also coerce the entire date object to a string containing both the date and the time. As strings, these are suitable for display of any date or time in human-readable format. For example, the statement short date string of (current date) returns a date like this: "2005-12-29". The format of the string depends on how you have set the Dates and Times formats in the Formats pane of the International pane in System Preferences. The example just shown is in the YYYY-MM-DD format prescribed by an international standard, ISO 8601:2004, which is unambiguous across national boundaries and languages. It guarantees that dates sorted in alphabetical order will automatically be in chronological order, as well.

> **TIP** ► Never write scripts using a date object on the assumption that these string properties will appear in the same format on someone else's computer. For example, don't perform date arithmetic on values you obtain by breaking down a date string into separate pieces using text item delimiters. Not only might the separate pieces be in a different order on another computer, but the delimiters might also be different. For the same reason, never alphabetize dates to get them into chronological order unless you have taken steps to ensure that they are in ISO 8601:2004 format.

But what, you may ask, are the properties that are listed in Table 26.1 as month and weekday types? The answer is that they are classes containing lists of constants named for the 12 months of the year and the 7 days of the week, in English; for example, `April` and `August`, and `Monday` and `Friday`.

Since AppleScript constants can be coerced to strings, it is easy to get the month or the weekday of any date object in a form suitable for display. For example, the statement `month of (current date) as string` might return `"December"`, and `weekday of (current date) as string` might return `"Wednesday"`.

Similarly, the `month` and `weekday` constants can be coerced to integers. Using this technique, you now see how to obtain the month as an integer in order to perform date arithmetic and comparisons. For example, the statement `month of (current date) as integer` returns `12` if this month is December. Likewise, the statement `weekday of (current date) as integer` returns `5` if today is Thursday, based on the built-in assumption that Sunday is the first day of the week. This allows you to perform date arithmetic based on weeks and weekdays as opposed to days of the month.

Notice that an AppleScript date object always uses the Gregorian calendar.

Setting a Date

When you want to use a specific, literal date in AppleScript, we recommend you use the standard date format, like this: `date "Thursday, August 16, 2007 4:53:52 PM"`.

It usually isn't convenient to include the day of the week, because you probably don't know what it is if the date is more than a few days in the past or the future. Happily, you can leave out parts, such as the day of the week and the time of day. When you compile the script, AppleScript supplies missing parts as appropriate default values, and it changes the text of your script to AppleScript's preferred standard format if it isn't already in that format. For example, if you type `set start_date to date "December 29, 2005"`, compiling will change the statement to `set start_date to date "Thursday, December 29, 2005 12:00:00 AM"`. It is useful to see the full date when you compile the script, because it allows you to verify that all of the properties of the date object will be set as you want them.

Omitted values are supplied according to somewhat complex default rules described in the AppleScript Language Guide. The most important rules to remember are that the omitted time defaults to `12:00:00 AM` (midnight at the beginning of the day) if you provide the date, and the omitted date defaults to the current date if you supply the time. The missing values are provided when you click the Compile button.

Once you have set a date in a variable as a `date` object, the script can modify it by setting any of its properties. When you set its `month` property, you can use either a month constant such as `August` or an integer such as 8. The others are all integers. If you attempt to set the weekday and you guess wrong, the erroneous input value is ignored and AppleScript does the right thing, setting the actual weekday to correspond to the date you provided.

You can also set a date and time by setting the time of a specified date, using `of`, `relative to`, or `in`. For example, if you type `date "12:00 pm" relative to date "December 29, 2005"`, compiling will change the text to `date "Thursday, December 29, 2005 12:00:00 PM"`.

> **TIP** ▶ Best practices suggest you always set literal dates in your scripts using AppleScript's preferred format. Using one of the formats set in the Formats pane of the International pane in System Preferences on the computer you are using to write the script might also work, but in our experience this isn't always reliable, and the rules may change between versions of the operating system. If you don't use AppleScript's preferred format, parts you omit may be supplied as incorrect values or it might simply fail to work. For example, in Mac OS X 10.4 (Tiger), if your short date format is set to the ISO 8601:2004 format and you type `set current_date to "12/29/05"` using the format commonly used in the United States, compiling will incorrectly change your script's text to `set current_date to date "Thursday, December 29, 2005 12:29:05 PM"`, where the supplied time is incorrect (it should be `"12:00:00 AM"`). In Leopard, if your short date format is set to the ISO 8601:2004 format and you type `set current_date to "2005-12-29"`, it simply doesn't work, but typing `set current_date to "12/29/05"` does work. If you attempt to set a date using a literal string that bears no resemblance to a date and time, it simply won't compile.

Date Constants, Commands and Operators

To use dates and date arithmetic in AppleScript, the tools available to you include a variety of constants, commands and operators.

Date Constants

In addition to the constants returned by the month and weekday properties of a date object, AppleScript recognizes the constants minutes, hours, days, and weeks. These return integers representing the number of seconds in a minute (60), an hour (3600), a day (86400), and a week (604800), respectively. They are convenient for converting any value that is expressed in seconds to the equivalent value in minutes, hours, days, or weeks so that you don't have to remember or calculate that a week, for example, contains 60 x 60 x 24 x 7 seconds. Converting to and from seconds is a common task, because most of the date commands and date arithmetic use seconds for consistency, while most user input and display is more easily understood (by humans) in hours and minutes or days and weeks.

You can easily convert a value given, say, as a number of days to the equivalent number of seconds by multiplying the first value by the constant days. These statements both define the variable fortnight to be the same value, 1209600 seconds:

```
set fortnight to 2 * weeks
set fortnight to 14 * days
```

Similarly, you convert a value given as a number of seconds to the equivalent value in, say, hours, by dividing the first value by the constant hours. When converting a number of seconds to minutes, hours, or some other unit of time in this manner, it is usually best to use the div command. The result is truncated to an integer value representing the largest number of whole minutes, hours, and so on, fitting within the given number of seconds. For example, 91 div minutes returns 1 minute. You get the remainder by using the mod command. For example, 91 mod minutes returns 31 seconds. Script 26.1 accepts the number of seconds entered by the user and displays it as minutes and seconds.

```
display dialog ¬
    "Enter the number of seconds:" default answer ""
set user_answer to text returned of result as integer
set display_minutes to user_answer div minutes
set display_seconds to user_answer mod minutes
display dialog (display_minutes as string) ¬
    & " minutes, " & display_seconds & ¬
    " seconds." buttons {"OK"} default button "OK"
```
SCRIPT 26.1

If you prefer a decimal notation, use the / operator.

> **NOTE ▸** We refer to minutes, hours, days, and weeks as constants. In real-
> ity, they are global properties, and they are better described as predefined
> variables because you can reset them to other values. You might illustrate
> Einstein's time dilation effect, for example, by setting minutes to 59 instead
> of 60, and AppleScript will dutifully use the new value when your scripts
> perform date arithmetic. In regular usage, it is a bad idea to set any of
> these predefined variables to another value. The new value will mess up
> date arithmetic in the same script and also in all other scripts, because
> these are, in fact, global properties.

Date Commands

You have seen one command relating to date objects already, the current
date command in the Standard Additions scripting addition. It is of primary
importance for any script that needs to calculate or display dates or times relative to the current date and time.

The only other standard AppleScript command relating to date objects is
time to GMT, also in Standard Additions. This command returns the number
of seconds between your time zone, as set in the Time Zone pane in the Date
& Time pane of System Preferences, and Greenwich mean time. For example,
in a city such as Boston in the Eastern time zone, the statement get time to
GMT div hours returns -5, meaning that if it is 12 PM (noon) in Greenwich,
England, it must be 7 AM in Boston, Massachusetts, in the United States. This

command is essential when doing date arithmetic or comparing dates involving more than one time zone. For example, Script 26.2 could be used by a daytime trans-Atlantic flyer to calculate the total travel time from London.

```
display dialog ("Enter the departure time in London") ¬
    & (" in the format HH:MM AM or PM:") default answer ""
set departure_time to date (text returned of result)
display dialog ("Enter the arrival time where you are") ¬
    & (" in the format HH:MM AM or PM:") default answer ""
set arrival_time to (date (text returned of result))
set travel_duration to ¬
    arrival_time - departure_time - (time to GMT)
display dialog ("The flight lasted about ") ¬
    & travel_duration div hours & ¬
    " hours." buttons {"OK"} default button "OK"
```

SCRIPT 26.2

To use the script, make sure your time zone is set to the time zone of your arrival location in the Date & Time pane of System Preferences before running the script. Then enter the local time in London upon departure in the first dialog (say, **07:00 PM**), and enter the time where you arrive in local time in the second dialog (say, **09:00 PM**).

In a real-world script dealing with dates and times, you should take additional steps to deal with the realities of time, such as the transition from one day to the next and the fact that (in our experience of this universe, at least) time flows in only one direction. For example, you would want to verify the format of each entered string to ensure that it is a valid time string. You would also want to verify the reasonableness of the values entered (for example, arrival must come after departure, taking account of the time zone difference). In addition, this script sets the `departure_time` and `arrival_time` variables using only the time of day. AppleScript supplies the current date as the default date, and the script as written therefore works correctly only if departure and arrival occur on the same day.

Date Operators

In AppleScript, you need *operators* to do arithmetic and perform comparisons, and date arithmetic and comparisons are no exception.

The + operator you use to add numbers is also used for adding a time interval (in seconds) to a date to get a new date. Likewise, the - operator you use to subtract numbers is also used for subtracting two dates to get a time interval (in seconds) or subtracting a time interval (in seconds) from a date to get a new date.

You use any of the comparison operators =, ≠, >, ≥, <, and ≤ to compare dates. In addition, two of these operators have synonyms that are especially useful to enable you to use plain English when comparing dates. For example, you don't usually ask whether "November *is less than* December"; instead, you ask whether "November *comes before* December." AppleScript lets you use `comes before` and `comes after` as synonyms for the < and > operators, respectively. You can also use these synonyms when comparing other types of data, for example, to test the rule of number theory illustrated by Script 26.3.

```
1 comes before 2
--> returns: true
```
SCRIPT 26.3

We suggested previously that the travel time script should perform a reality check to ensure that the arrival time occurs after the departure time, taking into account the time zones. To do this, you might want to change the example so that the `arrival_time` variable is adjusted to London time before calculating `travel_duration`. Then you could easily insert a new line to test whether the arrival time comes after the departure time. The new script would use the - operator to subtract a time interval—namely, `time to GMT`—from the arrival time, and it would use the `comes after` synonym for the > operator to perform the reality check. Script 26.4 is the new version, with the important changes highlighted.

```
display dialog ("Enter the departure time in London") ¬
    & (" in the format HH:MM AM or PM:") default answer ""
set departure_time to date (text returned of result)
display dialog ("Enter the arrival time where you are") ¬
    & (" in the format HH:MM AM or PM:") default answer ""
set arrival_time to (date (text returned of result)) ¬
    - (time to GMT)
if arrival_time comes after departure_time then
    set travel_duration to arrival_time - departure_time
    display dialog ("The flight lasted about ") ¬
        & travel_duration div hours & ¬
        " hours." buttons {"OK"} default button "OK"
else
    display dialog ("You're a time traveler!") ¬
        buttons {"OK"} default button "OK"
end if
```

SCRIPT 26.4

An ISO 8601:2004 Converter

We talked earlier about the ISO 8601:2004 international date format standard, warning you not to count on an alphabetical arrangement of dates being in chronological order without first verifying that they are all in the ISO format. Script 26.5 is a handy tool to convert any **date** object to the ISO format (we use the **current date** command here only as a convenient way to give the script a **date** object to work with).

```
set now to current date
set delimiter to "-"
set year_string to year of now as string
set month_string to month of now as integer as string
if length of month_string is 1 then
    set month_string to "0" & month_string
end if
set day_string to day of now as string
```

```
if length of day_string is 1 then
    set day_string to "0" & day_string
end if
return year_string & delimiter ¬
    & month_string & delimiter ¬
    & day_string
```

SCRIPT 26.5

A Deadline Calculator

Next is the nifty script we promised at the beginning of this chapter, Script 26.6.
It calculates a deadline using many of the techniques you've learned in this
chapter. Enter the number of days until the deadline expires, and it displays
the deadline as a date. Enter the deadline as a date, instead, and it displays the
number of days until the deadline expires. An explanation of the script's logic
follows the script.

```
repeat
    -- initialize variables
    set now to date (date string of (current date))
    set input_interval to 0
    set input_deadline to now
    set invalid_entry to false

    -- get user input
    set user_input to text returned of ¬
        (display dialog ("Enter days to calculate deadline,") ¬
            & return & (" or enter deadline to calculate days:") ¬
            default answer "")
    if user_input is "" then
        display dialog ("You entered nothing.") ¬
            & return & return & "Try again?"
    else
        try
            set input_interval to user_input as integer
```

```
        if input_interval is less than 0 then
            set error_message to ¬
                ("\"" & user_input & "\"") ¬
                    & (" is in the past.") ¬
                & return & return & "Try again?"
            try
                display dialog error_message
            on error number -128 -- user canceled
                exit repeat
            end try
        end if
    on error
        try
            set input_deadline to date (user_input)
            if input_deadline comes before now then
                set error_message to ¬
                    ("\"" & user_input & "\"") ¬
                        & (" is in the past.") ¬
                    & return & return & "Try again?"
                try
                    display dialog error_message
                on error number -128 -- user canceled
                    exit repeat
                end try
            end if
        on error
            set invalid_entry to true
            set error_message to ¬
                ("\"" & user_input & "\"") ¬
                    & (" isn't a number or date.") ¬
                & return & return & "Try again?"
            try
                display dialog error_message
            on error number -128 -- user canceled
                exit repeat
```

```
                        end try
                    end try
                end try


                -- calculate and display answer
                if not invalid_entry then
                    if input_interval is 0 and input_deadline is now then
                        display dialog "YIKES! The deadline is TODAY!"
                    else if input_interval is greater than 0 then
                        if input_interval is 1 then
                            set output_deadline to "TOMORROW!"
                        else
                            set output_deadline to date string of ¬
                                (now + (input_interval * days))
                        end if
                        display dialog "The deadline is " & output_deadline
                    else if input_deadline comes after now then
                        set output_interval to ¬
                            (input_deadline - now) div days
                        if output_interval is 1 then
                            set when_phrase to "TOMORROW!"
                        else
                            set when_phrase ¬
                                to "in " & output_interval & " days."
                        end if
                        display dialog "The deadline expires " & when_phrase
                    end if
                end if
            end if
    end repeat
```

SCRIPT 26.6

The entire deadline calculator script is embedded in an endless **repeat** loop to make it easy to calculate several deadlines in one session. When you're done, click Cancel. As you know, the Cancel button in the dialog displayed by the `display dialog` command generates error -128, and the error automatically exits the `repeat` loop unless the dialog is being displayed in a `try` block. When it is being displayed in a `try` block, the script checks for error -128 and calls `exit repeat` explicitly. Since there are no commands after the end of the `repeat` loop, the script then quits.

After initializing key variables at the beginning of the `repeat` loop, the script gets user input using the `display dialog` command with the `default answer` parameter. Instead of asking the user first whether to calculate the deadline from the number of days remaining or, instead, to calculate the number of days remaining from the deadline, the script just looks at the user's input and exercises intelligent judgment about what the user wants.

If the user entered nothing, the script points this out and lets the user try again. The logic of the script bypasses the section that calculates and displays the result, because that section is in the `else` branch of the `if` block. The use of an `else` branch is required in this situation because AppleScript does not have a command to continue to the next iteration of the repeat loop, as many programming languages do.

In case the user entered a number, the script attempts to coerce the input text in the `text returned` property of the dialog reply record to an integer. If the user entered some text that can't be coerced to an integer, AppleScript generates an error. Since this dialog is displayed in a `try` block, it immediately branches to the `on error` handler, bypassing the statements that deal with user input of a negative integer. The `on error` handler contains another part of the script, which checks whether the user entered a date—we'll discuss more about that later in the chapter. If the coercion to an integer does work, the script remains in the `try` block and goes on to check the integer to make sure it is not less than zero. A negative value would yield a date in the past, so the script displays an error message asking the user to try again. If the user clicks OK, the script flows to the section that calculates and displays the result. However, no result is calculated or displayed because that section of the script checks for a positive number of days before displaying anything.

Finally, if the user input is successfully coerced to a positive number, the final section of the script calculates and displays the deadline. It does this by using the days constant to convert the input number of days to the equivalent number of seconds and the + operator to add the number of days to the current date.

If the user did not enter a number, the coercion error described earlier causes execution to flow to an on error handler. This on error handler contains a nested try block that uses logic similar to the number calculation to test whether the user entered a date. If the user's input cannot be coerced to a date object, execution jumps to another on error handler that displays a message explaining that the user's input was neither a number nor a date and asks the user whether to try again. If the user clicks OK, the script's logic does flow to the section that calculates and displays a result, but nothing happens because that section of the script tests whether the user input is a number or a date. By definition it is neither, since the attempts to coerce it to a number or a date failed, and execution goes to the next iteration of the repeat loop.

Finally, if the user input is successfully coerced to a date, the final section of the script calculates and displays the number of days remaining. It does this by using the - operator to get the number of seconds between the deadline and the current date and the days constant to convert that to a time interval expressed in days.

One line deserves special mention:

```
set now to date (date string of (current date))
```

This statement sets now to the current date, but it omits the current time in order to allow date comparisons to be made on a standardized basis. To do this, it relies on the fact that AppleScript automatically supplies a time of 12:00:00 AM (midnight at the beginning of the day) when the time property of a date object is omitted. Otherwise, testing whether a deadline comes before the current date would return true if you ran the script any time after midnight. An important feature of this line is that it uses the date string property of the date object returned by the current date command to create the new date object for the now variable. The string returned by the date string property is guaranteed to be in the proper format, thus avoiding the portability problems that can occur when a script that uses a literal date value is run on another computer with different international date format settings.

A Day of Year Calculator

Some people like to know how many days have passed in the current year. Using AppleScript date arithmetic, it is easy to satisfy their curiosity. We'll show you several ways to calculate the day of the year (DOY).

First, Script 26.7 is the brute-force approach.

```
set current_date to the current date
set year_string to (the year of current_date)
set year_start to "January 1 " & year_string
set year_start to date year_start
set DOY to (((current_date - year_start) / (1 * days)) div 1) + 1
```
SCRIPT 26.7

This script first gets the current date. Next, it builds up a string for the first day of this year in a format that AppleScript recognizes, and then converts it to another date object. It then subtracts the two to get the amount of time that has passed since the beginning of the year in seconds, and it divides by the **days** constant to convert the value in seconds to the equivalent value in days. Finally, it must deal with the fact that the **current date** command includes the time of day, which usually isn't midnight at the beginning of the day. This would usually result in a DOY value containing a fractional day, since the script uses the **/** operator instead of the **div** operator. The script takes care of this problem by using the **div** operator to eliminate the fractional part and adding **1** to get the current day. The current day isn't yet done, but it must be counted to get the correct DOY.

We can make several improvements to the first example, using the features of the AppleScript **date** object to eliminate the string concatenation and division operations. Script 26.8 is our first attempt at improvement.

```
set current_date to date (date string of (current date))
set year_string to (the year of current_date)
set year_start to "January 1 " & year_string
set year_start to date year_start
set DOY to ((current_date - year_start) div days) + 1
```
SCRIPT 26.8

In the first statement, we used the trick described in the "Deadline Calculator" section to eliminate the time of day from the current date. By starting with midnight at the beginning of the current date, we eliminate the issue of the fractional day. As a result, in the final statement in Script 26.8 we are able to convert seconds to days using a single `div` operator, eliminating the `/` operation. We also shortened the redundant statement `1 * days` to `days`, eliminating an unneeded multiplication operation. But we still use three lines to build up the date object representing the beginning of the year.

Using new features of the `date` object introduced in Mac OS X 10.4 (Tiger), we are able to achieve our final script, Script 26.9.

```
set current_date to date (date string of (current date))
copy current_date to year_start
set month of year_start to 1
set day of year_start to 1
set DOY to ((current_date - year_start) div days) + 1
```
SCRIPT 26.9

This version uses no string objects or concatenation. Instead, it makes a separate copy of the `current_date` object and then resets two of its properties, `month` and `day`, to the integer values for the month of January and the first day of the year. The script uses `copy` rather than `set` because, as you learned in Chapter 8, *Data Containers, Operators, and Coercions*, this makes `year_start` an independent variable whose value we can change without simultaneously changing the value of the `current_date` variable. It is convenient to start with the `current_date` object created in the first line, because it already has its time of day set to midnight. If we had started with a full `date` object, we would have needed another line to set its `time` property to 0.

What's Next?

This chapter covered how to use the `date` object and related commands and constants to do date arithmetic and perform date comparisons. In the next chapter, you'll learn all about networking and AppleScript.

27

Lesson **27**

Connecting to Network Servers

Scripted workflows often must mount and unmount volumes on networks. Communication with network servers is handled by a variety of communication methods or *protocols*.

AppleScript is able to connect to any file server that can be accessed via the Connect to Server command in the Finder's Go menu, including iDisks and servers that support the AFP, WebDAV, Windows (SMB, Samba, CIFS), or FTP protocols. In this chapter, we will examine how to mount remote volumes using each of these communication protocols.

The mount volume Command

The `mount volume` command in the Standard Additions scripting addition is used to access volumes and directories located on network servers. Here is the dictionary listing for the `mount volume` command, in the File Commands suite. It has a direct parameter and four optional parameters:

```
mount volume: Mount the specified volume
    mount volume text
        -- the name or URL path (e.g. 'afp://server/volume/') of the
           volume to mount
        on server text
           -- the server on which the volume resides; omit
              if URL path provided
        [in AppleTalk zone text]
           -- the AppleTalk zone in which the server resides; omit
              if URL path provided
        [as user name text]
           -- the user name with which to log in to the server; omit
              for guest access
        [with password text]
           -- the password for the user name; omit for guest access
```

The first parameter is not shown in square brackets to indicate that it is normally a required parameter. As the description states, it is optional only in the sense that it should not be provided when the volume to mount is specified by a URL path. The other parameters are optional, as indicated by the square brackets, except that, again, the AppleTalk zone should not be provided when the volume to mount is specified by a URL path.

This command can be used to access network servers supporting a variety of communication protocols, as discussed in the next several sections.

WebDAV

Web-based Distributed Authoring and Versioning (WebDAV) is a connection and transfer method based on Hypertext Transfer Protocol (HTTP). HTTP is the protocol employed by the vast majority of Internet servers to display Web pages and media files. HTTP supports access to WebDAV file servers. It is used by Apple's .Mac service as one of two protocols for mounting and managing iDisks.

To mount a WebDAV server using the mount volume command, follow the command with the HTTP-based URL of the server volume. For example, Script 27.1 shows the mount volume command using the URL of an iDisk.

```
mount volume "http://idisk.mac.com/<your_name>/"
```
SCRIPT 27.1

When the script is executed, a WebDAV authentication dialog, shown in Figure 27.1, is automatically presented (unless you have already saved your password in your keychain). Enter the correct user name and password to gain access to the server.

FIGURE 27.1 Sal enters his password to mount his iDisk.

By default, the mount volume command returns a reference. It cannot proceed to the next line in the script until either the target volume is mounted or an error occurs. Once the server has successfully been accessed, a reference to the mounted volume is returned to the script and it continues.

```
--> returns: file "<your_name>:"
```

The returned reference is a *path reference* to the mounted volume. To convert this reference to one that is usable by other applications and commands, coerce it to an *alias reference* by using the as alias coercion. Script 27.2 is an example of this technique.

```
try
    set this_volume to ¬
        (mount volume "http://idisk.mac.com/<your_name>/") as alias
on error
    display dialog ("There was a problem mounting the volume.") ¬
        buttons {"Cancel"} default button 1
end try
--> returns: alias "<your_name>:"
```
SCRIPT 27.2

The alias reference to the mounted volume can now be used with the Finder or any other application.

The `mount volume` command is placed inside parentheses so that it executes first, and the result of the command is then coerced to an alias reference, which is assigned as the value of the variable `this_volume`.

WebDAV: User Name and Password

To mount a WebDAV volume without user interaction, include the appropriate values for the `as user name` and `with password` parameters in the statement, as shown in Script 27.3.

```
mount volume "http://idisk.mac.com/<your_name>/" as user name ¬
    "<your_name>" with password "<your_password>"
```
SCRIPT 27.3

The volume mounts without any authentication dialogs.

WebDAV: iDisk Public Folders

When mounting an iDisk Public folder using the WebDAV protocol, it is not necessary to include a user name or a password if the account owner has set the account preferences to allow guest access. Just follow the command with the URL to the .Mac user's Public folder, as in Script 27.4.

```
mount volume "http://idisk.mac.com/<your_name>/Public/"
--> returns: file "<your_name>-Public:"
```
SCRIPT 27.4

You can control access to your iDisk's Public folder in the .Mac System Preferences pane, as shown in Figure 27.2.

FIGURE 27.2 Bill getting ready to protect his iDisk Public folder with a password in System Preferences.

Script 27.5 uses the mount volume command with the WebDAV protocol to access the Public folder of any .Mac account. Simply enter the name of the target .Mac account in the dialog.

```
try
    display dialog "Mount .Mac Public Folder" & return & return & ¬
        "Enter the name of .Mac account:" default answer ""
    set the account_name to the text returned of the result
    mount volume ("http://idisk.mac.com/") ¬
        & account_name & "/Public/"
on error error_message number error_number
    if the error_number is not -128 then
        display dialog error_message buttons {"OK"} default button 1
    end if
end try
```
SCRIPT 27.5

Script 27.6 is another version of the same script, with an option to pick from a list of favorite .Mac accounts instead of entering the account name.

```
set the favorite_servers to {"saltbox", "steveroo"}
try
    display dialog "Mount .Mac Public Folder" & return & return & ¬
        "Enter the name of .Mac account:" default answer ¬
        "" buttons {"Cancel", "Favorites", "Go!"} default button 3
    copy the result as list to {account_name, button_pressed}
    if the button_pressed is "Favorites" then
        set the account_name to ¬
            (choose from list favorite_servers ¬
                with prompt "Pick the .Mac Account:") as string
        if the account_name is "false" then error number -128
    end if
    set this_volume to (mount volume ("http://idisk.mac.com/" & ¬
        account_name & "/Public/")) as alias
    tell application "Finder"
        activate
        open this_volume
    end tell
on error error_message number error_number
    if the error_number is not -128 then
        display dialog error_message buttons {"OK"} default button 1
    end if
end try
```
SCRIPT 27.6

FTP

File Transfer Protocol (FTP) is a protocol used on the Internet for sending and retrieving files. When a URL or address begins with `ftp://`, it usually indicates that a file will be transferred from a server to the connecting computer or that the FTP volume will be accessed.

Mac OS X 10.2 (Jaguar) added support for FTP access via the Finder's Connect to Server command. This same support was added to the mount volume command.

Note that the FTP support in Mac OS X 10.2 and 10.3 is not for downloading or uploading files. It is for mounting an FTP server volume in read-only mode from which files can be copied to your computer.

Script 27.7 is an example that connects to a public FTP server (one that doesn't require a user name or password).

```
mount volume "ftp://ftp.apple.com"
```
SCRIPT 27.7

Script 27.8 connects to a specific folder on the public FTP server.

```
mount volume "ftp://ftp.apple.com/developer/MacOSX/"
```
SCRIPT 27.8

FTP: User Name and Password

Naturally, most FTP servers are not so freely accessible. If the target of the mount volume command is an FTP server requiring a user name and password, an authentication dialog is automatically displayed when the mount volume command is executed.

To connect without an authentication dialog, use the as user name and with password parameters with their appropriate values. Script 27.9 shows how, but it won't actually work because of the fanciful password.

```
mount volume "ftp://ftp.apple.com/developer/MacOSX/" as user name ¬
    "sal" with password "schmoo1234"
```
SCRIPT 27.9

TIP ▶ On some kinds of servers, the `as user name` and `using password` parameters may not work to bypass the login dialog. In those instances, try adding the name and password in the target URL, as shown in Script 27.10. The server should mount just as it would if an authentication dialog were completed.

```
mount volume ¬
    "ftp://<your_name>:<your_password>@ftp.apple.com"
```
SCRIPT 27.10

AFP

AppleTalk Filing Protocol (AFP) is one of the oldest supported connection methods in the Mac OS. It employs the standard authentication methods shown in the previous protocol examples, as shown in Scripts 27.11, 27.12, and 27.13.

```
-- using the optional parameters
mount volume "afp://idisk.mac.com/<your_name>/" as user name ¬
    "<your_name>" with password "<your_password>"
```
SCRIPT 27.11

```
-- including username and password in the URL
mount volume "afp://<your_name>:<your_password>@idisk.mac.com/<your_
name>/"
```
SCRIPT 27.12

```
-- using the decimal form of the IP address of the host server
mount volume "afp://55.555.555.55/volume_name/" as user name ¬
    "<your_name>" with password "<your_password>"
```
SCRIPT 27.13

TIP ▶ The iDisk Public folder cannot be accessed via AFP. Script 27.14 does not work. In fact, it hangs. If you run it in Script Editor, you will have to force quit Script Editor to recover.

```
mount volume "afp://idisk.mac.com/<your_name>/Public/"
```
SCRIPT 27.14

To mount the Public folder, use WebDAV instead, as in Script 27.15.

```
mount volume "http://idisk.mac.com/<your_name>/Public/"
```
SCRIPT 27.15

SMB Protocol

Many of us work in multiplatform environments with computers running Microsoft systems and servers. The `mount volume` command also supports Microsoft's Server Message Block (SMB) protocol. Using this protocol you can mount a Windows server volume.

The syntax for SMB access employs a target URL beginning with `smb://` followed by the server address and the name of the share point on the host computer, as shown in Script 17.16.

```
mount volume "smb://server.domain.com/<share_name>"
```
SCRIPT 27.16

When the script is executed, Mac OS X presents an authentication dialog.

To mount a SMB volume without an authentication dialog, include the user name and password in the target URL, as in Script 17.17.

```
mount volume ¬
    "smb://<your_name>:<your_password@server.domain.com/share_name"
```
SCRIPT 27.17

Unmounting Volumes

The easiest way to unmount a volume is to instruct the Finder to `eject` the mounted volume. For example, if the iDisk public folder is currently mounted, Script 27.18 ejects it.

```
tell application "Finder" to eject alias "<your_name>-Public:"
```
SCRIPT 27.18

Since a disk is a scriptable object in both the Finder and System Events dictionaries, it can be the target of `whose` clause queries, as in Script 27.19.

```
tell application "Finder" to ¬
    eject (first disk whose name ends with "Public")
```
SCRIPT 27.19

Disk Contents

The `mount volume` command is for mounting volumes. It cannot be used to download or upload items to servers. You can, however, accomplish essentially the same goal by first mounting a remote volume and then using the Finder to copy items from or add items to the mounted server (assuming you have permission to do so).

Here are some examples of this technique using the WebDAV protocol and your iDisk. Script 27.20 copies an item from a Public folder.

```
try
    mount volume "http://idisk.mac.com/<your_name>/Public"
    set this_idisk to result as alias
    tell application "Finder"
        duplicate document file "sal.jpg" of this_idisk to ¬
            the desktop with replacing
        eject this_idisk
    end tell
```

```
on error error_message
    display dialog error_message buttons {"OK"} default button 1
end try
```
SCRIPT 27.20

This same script can easily be adapted to become a *droplet* for copying items dragged onto it to the Public folder of your iDisk. To make a droplet, add an *open handler* to a script and save it as an application.

We'll show you three versions of the droplet. The first, Script 27.21, presents an authentication dialog, unless you have already saved your iDisk password to your keychain.

```
-- WITH AUTHENTICATION DIALOG
on open these_items
    try
        set the user_name to "<your_name>"
        set this_idisk to ¬
            (mount volume "http://idisk.mac.com/" & ¬
                user_name & "/") as alias
        tell application "Finder"
            duplicate these_items to ¬
                folder "Public" of this_idisk with replacing
            eject this_idisk
        end tell
    on error error_message
        display dialog error_message buttons {"OK"} default button 1
    end try
end open
```
SCRIPT 27.21

Script 27.22 presents a dialog requesting your password.

```
-- WITH PASSWORD INPUT DIALOG
on open these_items
    try
        set the user_name to "<your_name>"
        display dialog "Enter the iDisk password for "" & ¬
            user_name & "":" default answer "" with hidden answer
        set this_password to the text returned of the result
        set this_idisk to ¬
            (mount volume ("http://idisk.mac.com/" & ¬
                user_name & "/") as user name ¬
                user_name with password this_password) as alias
        tell application "Finder"
            duplicate these_items to ¬
                folder "Public" of this_idisk with replacing
            eject this_idisk
        end tell
    on error error_message
        display dialog error_message buttons {"OK"} default button 1
    end try
end open
```

SCRIPT 27.22

Script 27.23 presents no dialog in advance, because it provides the user name and password directly.

```
-- WITH NO DIALOGS
on open these_items
    try
        set the user_name to "<your_name>"
        set this_password to "<your_password>"
        set this_idisk to ¬
            (mount volume ("http://idisk.mac.com/" & user_name & ¬
                "/") as user name ¬
                user_name with password this_password) as alias
```

```
        tell application "Finder"
            duplicate these_items to ¬
                folder "Public" of this_idisk with replacing
            eject this_idisk
        end tell
    on error error_message
        display dialog error_message buttons {"OK"} default button 1
    end try
end open
```

SCRIPT 27.23

Disk Properties

Should you want to find out information about a mounted volume, the Finder's disk object gives you access to basic data about the disk.

Here is a section of the Finder's dictionary for the disk class. A disk object inherits some of the standard properties of a container in addition to having the following unique properties:

id (integer, r/o) : the unique id for this disk (unchanged while disk remains connected and Finder remains running)

capacity (double integer, r/o) : the total number of bytes (free or used) on the disk

free space (double integer, r/o) : the number of free bytes left on the disk

ejectable (boolean, r/o) : Can the media be ejected (floppies, CD's, and so on)?

local volume (boolean, r/o) : Is the media a local volume (as opposed to a file server)?

startup (boolean, r/o) : Is this disk the boot disk?

format (Mac OS format/Mac OS Extended format/UFS format/NFS format/audio format/ProDOS format/MSDOS format/NTFS format/ISO 9660 format/High Sierra format/QuickTake format/Apple Photo format/AppleShare format/UDF format/ WebDAV format/FTP format/Packet-written UDF format/Xsan format/unknown format, r/o) : the filesystem format of this disk journaling enabled (**boolean, r/o**) : Does this disk do file system **journaling?**

ignore privileges (**boolean**) : Ignore permissions on this disk?

Script 27.24 uses the Finder's **disk** properties to get the size and free space of any iDisk that allows access to its Public folder. The resulting dialog is shown in Figure 27.3.

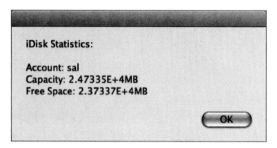

iDisk Statistics:

Account: sal
Capacity: 2.47335E+4MB
Free Space: 2.37337E+4MB

OK

FIGURE 27.3 A dialog displaying the size and free space of an iDisk.

```
try
    display dialog "Enter the .Mac account name:" default answer ""
    set the account_name to the text returned of the result
    set this_disk to (mount volume "http://idisk.mac.com/" & ¬
        account_name & "/Public/") as alias
    tell application "Finder"
        open this_disk
        delay 5
        set the free_space to ¬
            (((the free space of this_disk) div 104800) * 0.1)
        set the disk_capacity to ¬
            (((the capacity of this_disk) div 104800) * 0.1)
        eject this_disk
    end tell
    display dialog "iDisk Statistics: " & return & return & ¬
        "Account: " & account_name & return & ¬
        "Capacity: " & (disk_capacity as string) & "MB" & return & ¬
        "Free Space: " & (free_space as string) & ¬
        "MB" buttons {"OK"} default button 1
```

```
on error error_message
    display dialog error_message buttons {"OK"} default button 1
end try
```
SCRIPT 27.24

What's Next?

In this chapter, you learned how to mount and unmount disks on a network and over the Internet and how to upload and download files. In the next chapter, we'll give you a quick tour of the highlights of GUI Scripting.

28

GUI Scripting in a Nutshell

Advanced GUI Scripting Topics

What's Next?

Lesson **28**

GUI Scripting

AppleScript controls applications by sending them messages called *Apple events*. When a scriptable application receives an Apple event, it determines what the message wants it to do, and then it performs the requested action. The scripts you write are rarely designed to address or control the user interface elements of an application, such as a text field or window, because that isn't AppleScript's normal focus. Usually, you use AppleScript to get at an application's underlying data. You rely on the application's scripting dictionary to learn what elements and properties of the application can be addressed and controlled, as you learned in Chapter 2, *Dictionaries*.

But what if an application is not scriptable—in other words, what if it doesn't have a dictionary? How do you control it? Can it be scripted at all?

The answer is yes—sort of.

To control applications that aren't scriptable, AppleScript provides a special technology called Graphical User Interface Scripting, or *GUI Scripting*. (People in the know routinely pronounce it "gooey scripting" without cracking a smile.) Unlike regular AppleScript, which addresses the internal elements and properties of an application, GUI Scripting controls an application the same way you do, by pushing buttons, choosing menu items, typing text into input fields, and so on. Although it is not as dependable, flexible, and fast as traditional scripting, GUI Scripting can be a handy last resort for solving your automation workflow issues.

Introduced as a standard feature in Mac OS X 10.3 (Panther), GUI Scripting is designed specifically to read and control all of the user interface elements, or *UI elements*, in an application, such as its buttons and menu items. The remarkable thing about GUI Scripting is that it uses AppleScript to control features in an application that can't be manipulated by traditional AppleScript techniques—either because the dictionary of the target application does not define the classes and commands needed to do what you want, or because the target application is not scriptable at all in the traditional sense.

Every native Mac OS X application whose UI elements were written using standard Apple user interface techniques is scriptable with GUI Scripting. You can also use GUI Scripting with applications that were written using older toolkits or that have custom UI elements, if they were revised to support Apple's accessibility standards. Still, when you use GUI Scripting, you have to be aware that it won't work with every UI element in every application.

You may hear experienced scripters say that GUI Scripting should be used only as a last resort. They're right. GUI Scripting is certainly appropriate, and very useful, when you simply can't accomplish a task using traditional AppleScript techniques. But you should always check first to see whether you can do it with the classes and commands defined in the target application's dictionary. The application's designed-in AppleScript support is likely to be significantly faster for many tasks, and it is also probably much more in tune with the specific data structures and features implemented by the application.

GUI Scripting in a Nutshell

With those caveats behind us, let's take a whirlwind tour of GUI Scripting.

Enable GUI Scripting

First, you must enable GUI Scripting. It is disabled by default on new installations of Mac OS X, as part of Apple's industry-leading effort to make its computers as secure as possible for the average user.

One way to turn on GUI Scripting is to do it manually. Open the AppleScript folder in the top-level Applications folder, and double-click AppleScript Utility to launch it. Then check the Enable GUI Scripting check box, and quit. After authenticating with your password, GUI Scripting is turned on (or off, if you unchecked the check box). As you learned in Chapter 14, *AppleScript Utility*, you can also turn on GUI Scripting manually in the Universal Access pane of System Preferences, using the "Enable access for assistive devices" setting. GUI Scripting uses Apple's accessibility technology to work its magic, and these two settings control the same switch. For most users, there is no reason why you shouldn't just leave GUI Scripting turned on from now on.

The whole point of AppleScript is automation, so we aren't satisfied with the manual solution. Now we'll show you how to turn on GUI Scripting automatically, without asking your users to interrupt what they're doing in order to turn it on manually. For security reasons, the AppleScript commands discussed here ask the user to authorize it before actually flipping the GUI Scripting switch, but that is simply a matter of entering an administrator password in an authentication dialog and hitting the Return key to dismiss it.

First, recall we mentioned in Chapter 14 that AppleScript Utility is now scriptable in Leopard. One of its newly scriptable features is its `GUI Scripting enabled` application property. Script 28.1 is a simple handler you can call in any script to turn GUI Scripting on or off. As you will see in a moment, this script isn't quite ready for prime time, but it works. We'll show you a better way shortly.

```
enableGUIScripting(true)
beep
-- GUI Scripting statements go here

to enableGUIScripting(switch)
    tell application "AppleScript Utility"
        set GUI Scripting enabled to switch
    end tell
end enableGUIScripting
```

SCRIPT 28.1

If you run the script while GUI Scripting is turned off, three things happen. To notice all three of them, leave the AppleScript Utility window open in a corner of your screen, where you can see it. First, your computer beeps. Second, a dialog appears just above the center of your screen, saying "System Events requires that you type your password." The script didn't tell AppleScript Utility to present this authentication dialog, but AppleScript Utility makes it happen, anyway, every time you try to change the GUI Scripting Enabled setting. Third, after you've authenticated yourself and authorized the action by typing your password and clicking OK, a checkmark appears in the Enable GUI Scripting check box in the AppleScript Utility window.

That's just fine if all you want your script to do is to turn on GUI Scripting. But what if you want your script to begin executing some GUI Scripting statements right after you've entered your password? It won't work, because the script continues running to its end while the authentication dialog is on the screen, without giving you a chance to complete the authentication process and turn GUI Scripting on. You saw this when the computer ran the beep command before you authenticated. Any GUI Scripting statements you might add to the script where the comment says "GUI Scripting statements go here" will be reached before GUI Scripting is turned on, and the script will fail with an error because GUI Scripting is still disabled when the script tries to run those statements.

What to do? You could experiment with various techniques to pause execution of the script until the dialog is dismissed and GUI Scripting is enabled.

But we've saved you the trouble. Try as we might, we can't find an effective way to do this with AppleScript Utility and still cover all the possible scenarios, such as clicking the Cancel button to dismiss the authentication dialog. The main problem, as it turns out, is that the authentication dialog is presented by the System Events application, not by AppleScript Utility. The authentication dialog is not scriptable, and AppleScript Utility has no way to know that you haven't yet entered your password.

The solution lies in telling a different application, the System Events application, to turn on GUI Scripting for you. It is a little-known fact, but this capability was introduced and is available in Mac OS X 10.4 (Tiger), as well as being available in Leopard. Remember, as we said earlier, that the GUI Scripting Enabled setting in AppleScript Utility controls the same switch as the "Enable access for assistive devices" setting in the Universal Access pane of System Preferences. GUI Scripting is based on Apple's accessibility technology, which focuses on control of UI elements in every standard Mac OS X application. The switch that turns this accessibility feature on and off can also be set using the UI elements enabled application property disclosed in the System Events application's scripting terminology dictionary.

Script 28.2 is a new version of Script 28.1, modified to use the System Events application. This script works in Tiger and Leopard.

```
enableGUIScripting(true)
beep
-- GUI Scripting statements go here

to enableGUIScripting(switch)
    tell application "System Events"
        set UI elements enabled to switch
    end tell
end enableGUIScripting
```

SCRIPT 28.2

Run this script, and you'll immediately notice that the beep command doesn't run until after you dismiss the authentication dialog. This is so even if you dismiss the dialog by clicking Cancel instead of OK. If you have the AppleScript

Utility or Universal Access window open and click OK in the authentication dialog, you'll also notice that the beep sounds only after the GUI Scripting or accessibility check box becomes checked. Therefore, any GUI Scripting statements you add to the script in place of the "GUI Scripting statements go here" comment will run *after* GUI Scripting has been enabled. For this reason, you will almost always want to use the System Events application version of this handler, shown in Script 28.2.

The new script works this way because the System Events application presents the authentication dialog, and System Events honors the `considering application responses` action clause by default, as do most scriptable applications, as you learned in Chapter 19, *Action Clauses*. Although AppleScript Utility also honors the default `considering application responses` action clause, AppleScript Utility does not monitor the System Events application that presents the dialog. As a result, the AppleScript Utility version of the script immediately runs to its conclusion even though the System Events authentication dialog is still open, whereas the System Events application dutifully waits until the dialog is dismissed before proceeding.

You may have noticed that there is still a usability issue with this version of the script: you had to click the authentication dialog to bring it to the front before you could type your password. We usually think of System Events as a background application with no traditional user interface, but like many such applications, it is capable of presenting a user interface when it needs to, such as when it presents the authentication dialog.

The cure, therefore, is to use an `activate` command to bring System Events to the front. When you run the revised version of the script, Script 28.3, you can immediately start typing your password without first clicking in the authentication dialog.

```
enableGUIScripting(true)
beep
-- GUI Scripting statements go here

to enableGUIScripting(switch)
    tell application "System Events"
```

```
        activate
        set UI elements enabled to switch
    end tell
end enableGUIScripting
```

SCRIPT 28.3

One final usability issue must be addressed. As written, the revised version of the script doesn't give the main body of the script a clue as to whether the user clicked Cancel or OK in the authentication dialog, or what the final state of GUI Scripting might be. If the user clicked Cancel instead of turning GUI Scripting on, or if the handler failed to turn it on for any other reason, any subsequent attempt to execute GUI Scripting statements will fail because GUI Scripting won't be enabled.

To fix this issue, we'll add a feature that is common to many handlers, as shown in Script 28.4. We'll cause the handler to return a Boolean result of `true` or `false` to tell the caller whether GUI Scripting is now enabled or disabled, respectively. Notice that we changed the name of the handler slightly so that its grammatical sense is that of a property (an adjective describing state) rather than a command (a verb telling the script to perform an action).

```
if enabledGUIScripting(true) then
    -- GUI Scripting statements go here
    display dialog "GUI Scripting is enabled"
else
    -- non-GUI Scripting statements go here
    display dialog "GUI Scripting is disabled"
end if


on enabledGUIScripting(switch)
    tell application "System Events"
        activate
        set UI elements enabled to switch
        return UI elements enabled
    end tell
end enabledGUIScripting
```

SCRIPT 28.4

The reported state of `GUI Scripting enabled` may be `true` even if the user canceled authentication, if it was already on when the handler was called. That is, the handler reports the *state* of GUI Scripting, not the *success or failure* of the handler in changing its state. This final version of the handler can be called under any circumstances, and it will always correctly report the current state of GUI Scripting immediately after you call the handler. We recommend you include this handler in virtually every GUI Scripting script you write.

> **NOTE** ▶ There is a cosmetic glitch in Tiger, whereby the AppleScript Utility check box does not change state if its window is open when you run this script. The actual system setting is correct, however, and the check box reflects the correct value if you quit AppleScript Utility and relaunch it. This window would not ordinarily be open while you're running GUI Scripting scripts, and the cosmetic issue has been resolved in Leopard.

You can even use this handler in scripts that are intended to run without human intervention, if GUI Scripting is already turned on, because the System Events application does not present the authentication dialog at all if it sees that GUI Scripting is already configured in accordance with the command. We could nevertheless have embedded the entire body of the handler in an `if` block, testing whether the `switch` parameter and the `current GUI Scripting`–enabled setting are different, in order to prevent the script from bringing System Events to the front unless it would actually change the `GUI Scripting enabled` setting. However, the script will bring System Events to the front whenever it needs to change the setting, so there is no point in including this test in most circumstances. If your script wants to keep some other application frontmost before and after this handler is called, the script must save a reference to the frontmost application before calling the handler and activate it afterward. This is a common design pattern in scripts that contain handlers addressed to utility applications.

As shown earlier, your script should call the handler at the beginning of the script with the parameter set to `true` to turn GUI Scripting on. If you are in a security-sensitive environment, call it again at the end of the script with the parameter set to `false` to turn GUI Scripting off.

Ensuring That System Events Is Running

In the "Using Folder Actions" section of Chapter 21, *Folder Actions*, we talked at some length about the System Events application and its behavior with respect to Folder Actions. We're going to repeat some of that discussion here, because System Events also plays a pivotal role in GUI Scripting. Not only can you use System Events to turn on GUI Scripting, but you need it in order to control the UI elements of target applications. We will explain how System Events does this in a moment.

But first, how do you make sure System Events is running when you run a GUI Scripting script? The answer, as you learned in Chapter 21, is that System Events runs whenever it is needed. When Folder Actions is turned on, System Events launches. Similarly, when a script executes the `tell application "System Events"` statement that is required in every GUI Scripting script, System Events launches. That's all there is to it.

In Mac OS X 10.4 (Tiger), once System Events is launched, it keeps running. In Leopard this has changed. By default, System Events quits automatically if it isn't used for five minutes (300 seconds), unless Folder Actions is turned on or a script has set the System Events `application` object's `quit delay` property to another value. In either version of the OS, it doesn't matter to GUI Scripting because the next script that runs the `tell application "System Events"` statement will relaunch System Events.

It is unlikely that the time it takes System Events to launch will be noticeable when you run a GUI Scripting script. But if you're determined to milk every ounce of speed out of your computer that you can, run a script that tells the System Events application to `set quit delay to 0`. This causes System Events to remain running until you explicitly tell it to quit.

Take Control of a Target Application

Next, you might ask, where is the terminology for GUI Scripting defined, if it works with target applications that don't even have a dictionary? You will find the answer in the System Events application, hidden away in the CoreServices folder in the System Library folder, alongside the Finder and other core system applications, at System > Library > CoreServices > System Events.

System Events is scriptable, and its dictionary contains many suites of AppleScript classes and commands, including several that are new in Leopard. You have encountered some of them already in this book, including the Folder Actions Suite. The one you need to understand in order to use GUI Scripting is the Processes Suite. System Events gives AppleScript access to all application processes that are currently running. Using this unique ability to look inside running applications, System Events is able to read and control virtually all of their UI elements.

You might also ask how you can write a `tell` block that targets both the System Events application and the target application at the same time. We gave you a hint in the previous paragraph. To the System Events application, any application process is nothing more than an object, just as a window or a document is an object to the Finder. Nested `tell` blocks are common in scripts that send multiple commands to all manner of objects, such as windows and documents. Therefore, all you have to do is tell System Events to tell an application process object to do something with one of its UI elements, exactly the same way you might tell a word processing application to tell its first document to get its first paragraph.

To show you how this looks, Script 28.5 is the skeleton for every GUI Scripting script. This script happens to target the Preview application process. It contains standard nested `tell` blocks.

```
activate application "Preview"
tell application "System Events"
    tell process "Preview"
        --GUI SCRIPTING STATEMENTS
    end tell
end tell
```
SCRIPT 28.5

The first line isn't always necessary. However, some GUI Scripting commands work only when the application you're trying to control is frontmost so that all of its UI elements are visible and active. It's therefore a good idea to activate the target application in every GUI Scripting script, before addressing any commands to System Events and the target application's process object. Once you have the script working, you can try it without the first line to see whether it still works and whether you want to keep some other application in front while your script is running.

We'll use the Preview application for most of our examples, because Preview is not a scriptable application in its own right. Where we use another application, even if it is scriptable, it will be to control some aspect of it that isn't covered by its built-in scripting interface.

Traverse a Target Application's UI Element Hierarchy

The System Events application's Processes Suite defines a large number of classes referring to various kinds of UI elements. These are the objects you will use to control a targeted application. They include many everyday UI elements that you're accustomed to clicking, such as buttons, check boxes, menus, and menu items. They also include familiar containers, such as windows, drawers, sheets, tables, and text areas. The list includes just about every kind of user control and display area known to Mac OS X, including color wells, sliders, and tab groups.

An application's UI element objects are organized in a containment hierarchy that reflects their arrangement on the screen. The top-level or *root* object is the target application itself. Most applications have, at the next level, one or more windows and a single menu bar. Each window contains a variety of UI elements, such as pop-up menus and text fields, as well as other objects that are themselves containers, such as text areas and tables. The menu bar has its own hierarchy, containing menu bar items, menus, and menu items. As you will see, it is appropriate to think of every object in these hierarchies as having a *parent* (except for the application, which is the root object) and one or more *children* (except for the UI elements at the end of every branch, which are known as *leaf* elements).

Turning this hierarchy into an AppleScript reference is straightforward, if not always obvious. Here is an example from the Preview Preferences window:

```
text field 1 of tab group 1 of window "Preview Preferences"
```

And here is another example, this one from Preview's menu bar:

```
menu item "Crop" of menu 1 of menu bar item "Tools" of menu bar 1
```

Get and Set a UI Element's Properties

All of these UI element objects inherit from a common `UI element` class and therefore share common elements and properties. The ability to set some of these properties is one of the features that enable GUI Scripting to control an application through its user interface. Since this is only an overview of GUI Scripting, we will limit this discussion to the most useful features.

Some of the properties of every UI element are strictly informational. For example, you can get a UI element's `role`, which is a simple Unicode text string like "button" or "window." You can also get its `subrole`, which is often empty but sometimes contains useful information to distinguish between different kinds of UI elements that have a common role, such as "standard window" and "floating window." Many UI elements in newer applications also have a more detailed `description` and some `help` text. You can also get a UI element's `title`. Not every UI element has a title, but you can always use its `index` to refer to it if it doesn't have a title. For most kinds of UI elements, you can get its `position` and `size` on the screen.

For our purposes, however, the more interesting properties of a UI element are the ones you can `set`. For example, you can usually find out whether a UI element is `enabled` and `selected`, but sometimes you can also `set` its `enabled` or `selected` property. You will probably have to experiment to find out exactly how each application responds when you attempt to set one of its properties.

By far the most important property of a UI element for our purposes is its `value`. If a UI element has a value, you can `get` it. The System Events dictionary says the value is an integer. However, depending on the UI element, it might be a number, a Unicode text string, a date, or something else. The `value` property can be very useful when you want to know the value of something that is displayed in a UI element of an application. We'll use the Preview and TextEdit applications for examples of the `value` property, because their Preferences windows have several different kinds of UI elements and some of them have settable values.

Script 28.6 gets the name of the current user of Preview. This works only in the version of Preview that ships with Leopard, because Preview has undergone a number of changes since Mac OS X 10.4 (Tiger). The result will of course be different on your computer, although the current user of Preview need not be the same as the current user of the computer.

```
activate application "Preview"
tell application "System Events"
    tell process "Preview"
        keystroke "," using {command down}
        tell tab group 1 of window "Preview Preferences"
            click radio button "General"
            get value of text field 1
        end tell
    end tell
end tell
--> returns: "Bill Cheeseman"
```
SCRIPT 28.6

Pretty amazing, when you consider that Preview supposedly isn't scriptable!

In the script, the GUI Scripting `keystroke` command is used first to open Preview's Preferences window. It does this by sending the comma key to the Preview application with the Command key down, just as if you had typed a comma while holding down the Command key on the keyboard. In GUI Scripting, this is how you send keyboard shortcuts to an application. Most applications designate Command-, (Command+comma) as the keyboard shortcut to open their Preferences windows.

The script then clicks the General tab in the tab control at the top of the Preferences window. It does this by sending GUI Scripting's `click` command to what GUI Scripting knows as `radio button 1` or `radio button "General"` of the tab group. A general principle of GUI Scripting is that controls must be visible before you can script them, just as they would have to be visible in order to control them with your mouse or keyboard. Tab group 1 contains the text field we're interested in, so the script has to make the text field visible before continuing, which it does by selecting the General pane.

Finally, the script addresses the first text field in `tab group 1` of the Preferences window to get at its current attributes. The script gets the `value` property of the text field.

Script 28.7 is a script that changes the user by setting the value of the text field.

```
activate application "Preview"
tell application "System Events"
    tell process "Preview"
        keystroke "," using {command down}
        tell tab group 1 of window "Preview Preferences"
            click radio button "General"
            tell text field 1
                set value to "Sal Soghoian"
            end tell
        end tell
    end tell
end tell
```

SCRIPT 28.7

Run the script. If the Preferences window was already open and visible, you'll see the value of the text field change in a snap, while you watch. If it wasn't already open, the script launches Preview and opens the Preferences window, and it changes the text field's value so fast that you might miss the action.

Script 28.8 accomplishes the same thing using a different GUI Scripting technique, typing Sal's name into the text field one character at a time, instead of setting the **value** of the text field all at once.

```
activate application "Preview"
tell application "System Events"
    tell process "Preview"
        keystroke "," using {command down}
        tell tab group 1 of window "Preview Preferences"
            click radio button "General"
            select text field 1
        end tell
        keystroke "Sal Soghoian"
    end tell
end tell
```
SCRIPT 28.8

You should understand two points about Script 28.8. First, the **keystroke** command was not addressed to the text field, but to the **application** object itself. That's how typing works in Mac OS X: you type some letters on the keyboard while an application is frontmost, and they appear in whichever text container currently has keyboard focus in that application. Second, that's why we included the **select text field 1** statement. It wasn't actually needed in this script, because there is only one text field in the Preferences window and so it automatically has focus. But in other circumstances you should use this technique in a window with several text fields to make sure the **keystroke** command's typing goes to the correct text field.

It is important to know about both of these techniques for entering text into a text field using GUI Scripting, because some applications respond to one technique and others to the other technique.

Script 28.9 is another example, this time using TextEdit. This script works both in Tiger and in Leopard.

```
activate application "TextEdit"
tell application "System Events"
    tell process "TextEdit"
        keystroke "," using {command down}
        delay 1
        click radio button ("New Document") ¬
            of tab group 1 of window "Preferences"
        delay 1
        tell text field 1 of tab group 1 of window "Preferences"
            set value to "80"
        end tell
    end tell
end tell
```

SCRIPT 28.9

TextEdit is scriptable up to a point, but you sure can't do that using its dictionary!

The script calls AppleScript's delay command twice to pause execution for one second. This may not be necessary if you have a fast computer, but on slower computers GUI Scripting sometimes needs to give the application a bit of time to complete its performance of an action. In general, if a GUI Scripting script doesn't work when you think it should, try inserting delay 1 in strategic places to see whether that solves the problem.

The result of getting the value of a text field is a text string, not a number. That's why the script sets the value of the text field to the string "80" instead of the number 80.

Perform Actions on a UI Element

Setting the value of a UI element is all well and good, but there are many UI elements whose `value` property cannot be set. How do you control them?

True to the basic concept behind GUI Scripting, you do what you would do in the user interface: you `click` them. The `click` command is one of a very small number of commands that can be performed using GUI Scripting, but these commands are all that you need. You saw the `click` command in action earlier, but now we'll switch back to Preview to show other examples of its use.

Script 28.10 tries, without success, to set the value of the "Respect Image and screen DPI for scale" check box in the Images tab view of the Preview Preferences window under Leopard. The script doesn't cause an error, but it doesn't work, either. The reason is that the value of a check box can be read using the `get` command, but it usually can't be changed using the `set` command.

```
activate application "Preview"
tell application "System Events"
    tell process "Preview"
        keystroke "," using {command down}
        tell tab group 1 of window "Preview Preferences"
            click radio button "Images"
            tell checkbox "Respect image and screen DPI for scale"
                set value to 1 -- nothing happens
            end tell
        end tell
    end tell
end tell
```
SCRIPT 28.10

The value of a check box is in fact an integer, as the UI element entry in the System Events dictionary tells you. When a check box is checked, its value is 1; when unchecked, it's 0. But you can't set its value. Instead, you have to click it. Script 28.11 does work!

```
activate application "Preview"
tell application "System Events"
    tell process "Preview"
        keystroke "," using {command down}
        tell tab group 1 of window "Preview Preferences"
            click radio button "Images"
            tell checkbox "Respect image and screen DPI for scale"
                if value is not 1 then click -- it works!
            end tell
        end tell
    end tell
end tell
```

SCRIPT 28.11

Tabs, radio buttons, and pop-up menus all work the same way. To find out
which radio button in a radio group is selected, find the radio button that has
a value of 1 instead of 0. But you can't set this value. You already know what to
do: click the radio button you want.

Choosing a menu item in any menu is a little more complicated, because GUI
Scripting can't click a menu item until the menu is open and visible on the
screen. To click a menu item, you have to click the menu first to open it. Script
28.12 zooms in on a picture, assuming the front window holds a picture.

```
activate application "Preview"
tell application "System Events"
    tell process "Preview"
        tell menu "View" of menu bar 1
            click
            click menu item "Zoom In"
        end tell
    end tell
end tell
```

SCRIPT 28.12

An alternative way to execute a command in a menu item is to use the **keystroke** command. As you saw already, it can be used to send a keyboard shortcut to any application. This is often better than clicking a menu to open it and then clicking a menu item, but of course it works only with menu items that have keyboard shortcuts. When sending shortcuts that are alphabetical characters, always send the lowercase letter; otherwise, GUI Scripting will think the Shift key is down, and it won't work. Script 28.13 quits Preview using this technique.

```
activate application "Preview"
tell application "System Events"
    tell process "Preview"
        keystroke "q" using {command down}
    end tell
end tell
```
SCRIPT 28.13

And that concludes our whirlwind tour of GUI Scripting.

Advanced GUI Scripting Topics

There is a great deal more to GUI Scripting than you have seen here, but this will get you started. Here are a few glimpses of what to look forward to when you explore this topic in greater depth.

GUI Scripting is built on top of Apple's accessibility technology. The accessibility features of Mac OS X were developed to make the UI elements in any application available to assistive applications, which allow people who are disabled to use the Mac's graphical user interface with screen readers and a variety of input devices. VoiceOver, introduced in Mac OS X 10.4 (Tiger), is one example of a screen reader.

Several classes and commands in the System Events Processes Suite make it possible to use special accessibility terminology with GUI Scripting. The accessibility terminology is a little different from what you saw in the basic GUI Scripting examples given earlier. For example, you can *perform* an *action*.

These two GUI Scripting statements do the same thing: `click button 1` and `tell button 1 to perform action "AXPress"`. The more technical accessibility form of GUI Scripting statements sometimes works better than the standard GUI Scripting terminology. You can also accomplish some tasks using the accessibility terminology that aren't otherwise possible. For example, to determine whether the value property of a UI element is settable, try this: `get settable of attribute "AXValue" of text field 1`. You can even write scripts that navigate the entire UI element hierarchy. The key to doing this is to use the "AXParent" and "AXChildren" attributes.

One of the most difficult aspects of GUI Scripting is understanding the containment hierarchy of the UI elements in a particular application. For example, there are sometimes hidden UI elements in the hierarchy that have to be included in a reference to a particular UI element. Also, if a UI element doesn't have a title, you have to refer to it by index, but there is no easy way to find out what the index is if there are multiple UI elements of the same type in one container. With some effort, you can run test scripts to learn how to write a valid reference to a UI element. A popular commercial product that makes this much easier is UI Browser, from PreFab Software, written by one of us (Bill Cheeseman). UI Browser displays an application's UI element containment hierarchy in an easy-to-understand format, complete with all UI element titles and indexes. It also tells you which attributes are settable and which aren't, and it lists all the actions that a UI element recognizes. It even generates GUI Scripting statements for you, which you can paste into your favorite script editor or "send" directly to a window in the default script editor. Visit `http://prefabsoftware.com/uibrowser/` to learn more about it.

What's Next?

This chapter touched on the high points of GUI Scripting, a special AppleScript technology that allows you to control the user interface of almost any application, even if it is not scriptable in its own right. In the next chapter, you'll learn how to script the command line using UNIX shell commands.

29

Turn On the Spotlight

What's Next?

Lesson **29**

Scripting the Shell

It has been a while since Mac OS X was created, and many Mac users don't remember Mac OS 9, Mac OS 8, or System 7. To them, multitasking has always been the way the OS works, and transparent windows have always been the norm. But in reality, Mac OS X is an evolving merger of two operating systems, the classic Mac OS and BSD UNIX. Apple has done an amazing job of combining the strengths of both into an attractive, easy-to-use OS with strong underpinnings and a robust set of frameworks and tools.

AppleScript debuted in System 7 as a system-wide scripting language inspired by HyperTalk, the scripting language used by HyperCard. AppleScript came free with System 7 Pro and for only $15 more you could purchase the scriptable Finder, which came on its own 400KB floppy. It wasn't until System 7.5 that a scriptable Finder was part of the standard OS install. And from System 7.5 to Mac OS 9, AppleScript was the only user scripting language built into the OS—until Mac OS X was created, that is.

For at least ten years before the birth of AppleScript, UNIX-based operating systems were controlled by entering text commands in a special text input window. These commands were used to create, edit, and delete files, folders, and messages; run applications; and perform the general functions of the OS. All of these tasks were accomplished by entering text into the "command line" from within the Terminal application.

These two languages are designed very differently: AppleScript is English-like and verbose, while command-line scripting (as it is commonly called) has a syntax that is very terse and nonconversational. For example, a script to duplicate the PDF files in your Documents folder to a folder on the Desktop would look like this in AppleScript:

```
tell application "Finder" to duplicate ¬
    (every document file of folder "Documents" of home ¬
        whose kind is "PDF Document") to folder "Backup"
```

And it would look like this in UNIX:

```
cp ~/Documents/*.pdf ~/Desktop/Backup
```

AppleScript uses the Finder application to perform the copy process, while the UNIX command uses a command line interpreter called a *shell* to control the file system. That's why it's called *shell scripting* when referring to the UNIX command line.

The AppleScript language is full of verbs and nouns, while, at first glance, shell scripts appear to be full of cryptic combinations of letters and symbols. However, the various UNIX utilities and shells that ship with Mac OS X offer thousands of powerful and useful commands that are accessible to AppleScript scripters through a special AppleScript command called `do shell script`. This command is part of the Standard Additions scripting addition, and it provides a powerful bridge for scripters to take advantage of many hidden abilities in the OS. With a bit of effort, you can learn enough shell commands to be slightly dangerous.

This chapter will not attempt to provide a complete overview of all of the abilities of the `do shell script` command but will instead highlight a few ways to use the command to augment the abilities of AppleScript. For a complete overview of the command, read Apple Technical Note TN2065, which can be viewed online at `http://developer.apple.com/technotes/tn2002/tn2065.html`.

Read the Manual

The first UNIX command we're going to examine creates calendars. It's called `cal`. To execute this command using AppleScript, place it after the `do shell script` command in a new script window, as shown in Script 29.1. Note that UNIX commands are always placed within quotation marks, since all shell commands are text strings.

```
do shell script "cal"
```
SCRIPT 29.1

When the script is run, AppleScript passes the command to the UNIX shell and returns the result to the script. In this case, the result is a block of text formatted as a calendar for the current month!

```
"    August 2007
Su Mo Tu We Th Fr Sa
          1  2  3  4
 5  6  7  8  9 10 11
12 13 14 15 16 17 18
19 20 21 22 23 24 25
26 27 28 29 30 31
"
```

Now that's cool, but can the command do more? Maybe, but how do you find out how to use it to its fullest abilities?

As you've previously learned, the various objects, properties, and commands used by a scriptable application are outlined and defined in its scripting dictionary, accessed from within the Script Editor application. However, for UNIX commands, they are described in technical documents called man pages (short for *manual* pages) that are usually accessed and displayed within the Terminal application.

Since we're AppleScript gurus, we'd rather write a script that will retrieve the text of a man page and display it with proper formatting in a new TextEdit document. Copy Script 29.2 into a new script window and run it,

```
set the manual_text to (do shell script "man cal | col -b")
tell application "TextEdit"
    activate
    set this_document to ¬
        make new document with properties {text:manual_text}
    set the properties of the text of this_document to ¬
        {size:12, color:{0, 0, 0}, font:"Courier"}
    set the bounds of window 1 to {0, 22, 612, 792}
end tell
```
SCRIPT 29.2

A new TextEdit document opens containing the manual page for the `cal` command.

```
CAL(1)      BSD General Commands Manual     CAL(1)

NAME
    cal -- displays a calendar

SYNOPSIS
    cal [-jy] [[month]     year]

DESCRIPTION
    cal displays a simple calendar.  If arguments are not specified, the
    current month is displayed.  The options are as follows:

    -j    Display julian dates (days one-based, numbered from January 1).

    -y    Display a calendar for the current year.

    A single parameter specifies the year (1 - 9999) to be displayed; note
    the year must be fully specified: ''cal 89'' will not display a calendar
    for 1989.
    Two parameters denote the month (1 - 12) and year.  If no
    parameters are specified, the current month's calendar is displayed.
```

A year starts on Jan 1.

The Gregorian Reformation is assumed to have occurred in 1752 on the 3rd of September. By this time, most countries had recognized the reformation (although a few did not recognize it until the early 1900's.) Ten days following that date were eliminated by the reformation, so the calendar for that month is a bit unusual.

HISTORY
A cal command appeared in Version 6 AT&T UNIX.

BSD   April 28, 1995   BSD

As you can see from the command's description, a number of optional arguments are used with the `cal` command. One of them is -j to display the dates as integers from the start of the year rather than from the start of each month. Run Script 29.3 to see how it works.

```
do shell script "cal -j"
```
SCRIPT 29.3

Another is -y to display the calendar for the current year, as shown in Script 29.4.

```
do shell script "cal -y"
```
SCRIPT 29.4

Used together, the command string would look like Script 29.5. Note that arguments are always separated from the command by a space and usually preceded by a dash.

```
do shell script "cal -jy"
```
SCRIPT 29.5

To get the calendar for a specific year, place the full year string after the command (don't forget to add the space after the command), as in Script 29.6.

```
do shell script "cal 1952"
```
SCRIPT 29.6

To get the calendar for a specific month, place the number of the month and the full year string after the command, as shown in Script 29.7.

```
do shell script "cal 1 1952"
```
SCRIPT 29.7

A common use of the `do shell script` command is to retrieve information or settings and then incorporate that data into regular AppleScript scripts. Now that you understand some of the parameters to the `cal` command, look at Script 29.8. It creates a printable calendar for the current month. It uses the same method as the previous script for accessing man pages, retrieving the data, and displaying it in a new TextEdit document.

```
set the command_result to (do shell script "cal")
tell application "TextEdit"
    activate
    set this_document to ¬
        make new document with properties {text:command_result}
    set properties of text of this_document to ¬
        {size:50.0, color:{0, 0, 65535}, font:"Courier"}
    set the bounds of window 1 to {0, 22, 792, 612}
end tell
```
SCRIPT 29.8

> **TIP ▶** When printing the resulting document, set the page orientation to landscape in the Print Setup dialog.

Script 29.9 a variant of Script 29.8 that creates a calendar for the entire year.

```
set the command_result to (do shell script "cal -y")
tell application "TextEdit"
    activate
    set this_document to ¬
        make new document with properties {text:command_result}
    set properties of text of this_document to ¬
        {size:15.0, color:{0, 0, 65535}, font:"Courier"}
    set bounds of window 1 to {0, 22, 612, 792}
end tell
```
SCRIPT 29.9

In addition to using the data resulting from a do shell script command, you can use information generated from AppleScript to generate the command string dynamically. For example, Script 29.10 creates a printable calendar for the next month.

```
set the temp_date to the current date
set day of the temp_date to 1
set month of the temp_date to ¬
    ((month of the temp_date) as integer) + 1
set the month_value to ¬
    month of the temp_date as integer as string
set the year_value to (year of temp_date) as string
set the manual_text to ¬
    (do shell script "cal " & month_value & space & year_value)
tell application "TextEdit"
    activate
    set this_document to ¬
        make new document with properties {text:manual_text}
    set properties of text of this_document to ¬
        {size:50.0, color:{0, 0, 65535}, font:"Courier"}
    set bounds of window 1 to {0, 22, 792, 612}
end tell
```

SCRIPT 29.10

The values used in the command string are first derived in AppleScript and then stored in AppleScript variables that are used to create the complete command string.

You can incorporate the use of do shell script commands within standard AppleScript constructs, such as the repeat loop in Script 29.11 to generate calendars for the next twelve months.

```
set the temp_date to the current date
set day of the temp_date to 1
set H to 0
set V to 0
set offset_increment to 22
repeat 12 times
    set month of the temp_date to ¬
        ((month of the temp_date) as integer) + 1
    set the month_value to ¬
        month of the temp_date as integer as string
    set the year_value to (year of temp_date) as string
    set the manual_text to ¬
        (do shell script "cal " & month_value & space & year_value)
    tell application "TextEdit"
        activate
        set this_document to ¬
            make new document with properties {text:manual_text}
        set properties of text of this_document to ¬
            {size:50.0, color:{0, 0, 65535}, font:"Courier"}
        set bounds of window 1 to {0 + H, 22 + V, 792 + H, 612 + V}
    end tell
    set H to H + offset_increment
    set V to V + offset_increment
end repeat
```

SCRIPT 29.11

You can even incorporate information provided by AppleScript's user interaction commands to generate a command string. Enter Script 29.12 in a new script window, and save it as "Display Man Page." The script prompts you to enter the name of the shell command you want to review and then uses that name to generate a man page in TextEdit.

```
display dialog "Enter the UNIX command:" default answer ""
set the UNIX_command to the text returned of the result
set the manual_text to ¬
    (do shell script "man " & UNIX_command & " | col -b")
tell application "TextEdit"
    activate
    set this_document to ¬
        make new document with properties {text:manual_text}
    set properties of text of this_document to ¬
        {size:12, color:{0, 0, 0}, font:"Courier"}
    set the bounds of window 1 to {0, 22, 612, 792}
end tell
```

SCRIPT 29.12

We'll use this script to continue our exploration of the do shell script command.

Date and Time

The UNIX date command is a very useful tool for generating a wide variety of formatted date and time strings. Unlike the AppleScript date record object that can be easily altered via mathematical calculations, the result of the UNIX date command is static text. Use Script 29.12 to view the man page for this command.

To return the current date and time, use the date command without any optional parameters, as in Script 29.13.

```
do shell script "date"
--> returns: "Tue Feb 27 17:02:55 PST 2007"
```

SCRIPT 29.13

To create a formatted date string (sometimes referred to as a *date slug*), follow the command with a plus character (+) and the format placeholders for the various date elements, enclosed in single quotation marks or escaped double quotation marks. Format placeholders consist of a single character preceded by a percent character. Refer to this command's man page for a list of the format placeholders.

For example, the format string for current month, day, and year, delimited by dashes is shown in Script 29.14.

```
do shell script "date '+%m-%d-%Y'"
--> returns: "02-27-2007"
```
SCRIPT 29.14

To generate the current time string, delimited by colons, use the format string shown in Script 29.15.

```
do shell script "date '+%H:%M:%S'"
--> returns: 17:02:55
```
SCRIPT 29.15

> **NOTE** ▶ Using delimiting characters and/or extra text is optional. The command will work the same even with the formatting placeholders put adjacent to each other: %H%M%S.

You can add other nonplaceholder text within the format string and even add new lines by including %n within the string, as shown in Script 29.16.

```
do shell script "date '+DATE: %m-%d-%Y%nTIME: %H:%M:%S'"
--> returns: "DATE: 02-27-2007
             TIME: 17:25:19"
```
SCRIPT 29.16

Script 29.17 shows one more use of the date command that involves the interesting technique of inserting a UNIX command within other UNIX command strings. Using this technique, you can generate the parameters to create a calendar for the current month by placing the date command within the command string for the cal command.

```
do shell script "cal $(date '+%m %Y')"
```
SCRIPT 29.17

As with AppleScript, the command within the parentheses is executed first and replaced with its result, which is then used to supply the parameters for the main command. You'll find this technique is often used when the `date` command is combined with other commands to generate unique names for files. Note the use and placement of the dollar sign and parentheses to indicate that another command follows.

Screen Capture

Even though the `screencapture` command is unique to Mac OS X and is not found in the standard UNIX set of commands used by other operating systems, it provides an excellent way to control the screen capture tools built into the OS.

To use the command, simply follow it with a POSIX path to the new file to be created on disk, as shown in Script 29.18. Note that the default format for the captured image is PNG.

```
do shell script "screencapture ~/Desktop/screen.png"
```
SCRIPT 29.18

If you would rather put the screen capture on the clipboard, use the argument -c as in Script 29.19.

```
do shell script "screencapture -c"
```
SCRIPT 29.19

Additionally, you can control the format of the captured image by inserting the argument -t, followed by the abbreviation for the file type of the image, into the command string, as shown in Script 29.20. If you are creating an image on disk, be sure that the name extension for the image file matches the type indicator.

```
do shell script "screencapture -ttif ~/Desktop/screen.tif"
```
SCRIPT 29.20

The available file types include TIFF (tif), JPEG (jpg), PNG (png), PDF (pdf), BMP (bmp), and PICT (pict). Script 29.21 captures the screen to the clipboard in PDF format.

```
do shell script "screencapture -ctpdf"
```
SCRIPT 29.21

By default, capturing the screen to a file overwrites any existing file of the same name. If you want each screen capture to have a unique name, insert the `date` command into the command string to generate a name suffix based on the current date and/or time. Script 29.22 shows how.

```
do shell script ¬
    "screencapture ~/Desktop/screen-$(date '+%m%d%Y-%H%M%S').png"
--> screen-02282007-051006.png
```
SCRIPT 29.22

The `screencapture` command can be used interactively by adding the `-i` argument to the command string, as in Script 29.23. In this mode, you can capture the screen by selection or window. Pressing the Control key causes the screenshot to go to the clipboard, and pressing the spacebar toggles between mouse selection and window selection modes. Pressing the Escape key or pressing Command+. (Command+period) cancels the interactive screenshot.

```
do shell script "screencapture -ic"
```
SCRIPT 29.23

The command includes other arguments for starting the interactive session with a window selection cursor (`-W`) and for turning off the camera sound (`-x`). Script 29.24 uses the `say` command to prompt the user to select the window to capture.

```
say "Select a window."
do shell script "screencapture -iWc"
```
SCRIPT 29.24

Using this command, you can easily create a set of customized screen capture tools to aid you when you're documenting a book or report. Script 29.25

takes a screen capture of a window, saved as a unique file in the OS temporary folder, and then opens it for editing in the Preview application.

```
set date_slug to do shell script "date '+%m%d%Y-%H%M%S'"
set the file_name to "screen-" & date_slug & ".png"
say "Select a window."
try
    do shell script "screencapture -iW tmp/" & file_name & ¬
        ";open -b com.apple.Preview tmp/" & file_name
end try
```
SCRIPT 29.25

Note the use of the open command to open the file in an application with a bundle identifier of com.apple.Preview (Preview). This second command string follows the first command string and employs a semicolon character to indicate that another command string follows.

If you want to open the screen capture file in a new outgoing message in the Mail application, simply change the bundle identifier to com.apple.Mail, as shown in Script 29.26.

```
set date_slug to do shell script "date '+%m%d%Y-%H%M%S'"
set the file_name to "screen-" & date_slug & ".png"
say "Select a window."
try
    do shell script "screencapture -iW tmp/" & file_name & ¬
        ";open -b com.apple.Mail tmp/" & file_name
end try
```
SCRIPT 29.26

Script 29.27 is Sal's personal script for capturing the screen or a selection to file. It first prompts you for a name and location for the screen capture file and then uses the file's name extension to determine the image format for the created file. After prompting you to choose between capturing the screen or a selection, it asks whether you want to open the image file in Preview, Mail, or nothing. Enjoy!

```
set the default_name to "untitled"
repeat
    set the target_file to ¬
        (choose file name with prompt ¬
            ("Name & location for the screen capture. " & ¬
                "Format is determined by the name extension:") ¬
                default name default_name) as Unicode text
    try
        set the name_extension to text -4 thru -1 of the target_file
        if the name_extension is not in ¬
            {".tif", ".jpg", ".png", ".pdf", ".bmp", ".pct"} then
            error
        else
            if the target_file ends with ".pct" then
                set the file_type to "pict"
            else
                set the file_type to ¬
                    text -3 thru -1 of the target_file
            end if
            set the target_path to the quoted form of ¬
                the POSIX path of the target_file
            exit repeat
        end if
    on error
        set AppleScript's text item delimiters to ":"
        set the default_name to the last text item of the target_file
        set AppleScript's text item delimiters to ""

        display dialog "The file name "" & default_name & ¬
            "" must end with one of these name extensions:" & ¬
            return & return & ¬
            ".tif, .jpg, .png, .pdf, .bmp, or .pct" & ¬
            return & return & ¬
            "The format of the image file is determined by ¬
            the name extension you use." buttons ¬
```

```
                {"OK"} default button 1 with icon 2
    end try
end repeat
display dialog "Capture method:" buttons ¬
    {"Cancel", "Screen", "Selection"} default button 3
set the capture_method to the button returned of the result
if the capture_method is "Screen" then
    do shell script ¬
        ("screencapture -t" & file_type & space & target_path)
else
    say "select a region or window."
    do shell script ¬
        ("screencapture -it" & file_type & space & target_path)
end if
display dialog "Open file with:" buttons ¬
    {"None", "Mail", "Preview"} default button 3
set the target_application to the button returned of the result
if the target_application is "Mail" then
    tell application "Mail"
        activate
        open target_file
    end tell
else if the target_application is "Preview" then
    tell application "Preview"
        activate
        open target_file
    end tell
end if
```

SCRIPT 29.27

For those of you who like to monitor remote computers, Script 29.28 shows you how to take a full-screen capture periodically and send it in an e-mail to a specified address. Change the recipient to somebody you know, and save the script as a stay-open application. You can adjust the idle time to whatever interval you want.

```
on idle
    try
        set date_slug to do shell script "date '+%m%d%Y-%H%M%S'"
        set the file_name to "screen-" & date_slug & ".png"
        do shell script "screencapture -tpng tmp/" & file_name
        tell application "Mail"
            set this_message to ¬
                make new outgoing message with properties ¬
                    {subject:"Screen Capture"}
            tell this_message
                make new to recipient with properties ¬
                    {name:"Animal Friend", address:"seal@zoo.com"}
            end tell
            tell contents of this_message
                make new attachment with properties ¬
                    {file name:("tmp/" & file_name)}
            end tell
            set visible of this_message to true
            send this_message
        end tell
    end try
    return 3600 -- one hour
end idle
```
SCRIPT 29.28

Turn On the Spotlight

The term *information age* is often used nowadays when referring to the torrent of digital data that runs through our lives. The amount of data that resides on our ever-larger hard drives is quickly becoming more than we can manage through traditional methods of navigating complex hierarchies of folders with complex naming and labeling schemes. We're quickly becoming overwhelmed with data…overwhelmed with data…overwhelmed with data….

In Mac OS X 10.4 (Tiger), Apple introduced a groundbreaking architecture for storing and retrieving information about the items on your computer. It appropriately named this new tool Spotlight, because in the same way a light makes it easier to see in the dark, Spotlight makes it easier to find your way through the maze of information on your computer. It does this by collecting and saving *metadata*.

A common definition of the term *metadata* is "data about data." The data on our computers, such as documents, images, and messages, have properties, or *attributes*, that define their use and construction. All files share some common properties such as name, size, creation and modification dates, and file types. But metadata extends the standard set of attributes to focus on those pertinent to the particular file type.

For example, digital image files taken by cameras have attributes such as camera, f-stop, aperture, orientation, and color space. They can also contain user-defined attributes such as caption, byline, headline, author, editor, and so on.

Audio files played on iPods have metadata attributes such as artist, album, beats per minute, and genre. Every kind of file can have metadata associated with it, regardless of the kind of file it is, and Spotlight can retrieve that information for you to use.

Reading the Tea Leaves...

There currently is no native AppleScript interface to Spotlight, but it does have a command-line utility named `mdls` for reading metadata from a file. `mdls` stands for *metadata list*. It generates a paragraph-delimited list of every metadata tag and its corresponding value.

Script 29.29 uses AppleScript's `do shell script` command to get a list of all the Spotlight metadata attributes, and their values, from a JPEG image.

```
set this_file to choose file of type "public.jpeg" without invisibles
do shell script ("mdls " & ¬
    the quoted form of the POSIX path of this_file)
```
SCRIPT 29.29

The result of this script is a list of Spotlight metadata attribute tags and their values returned as paragraph-delimited text:

```
/Users/sal/Desktop/SQUARE.JPG -------------
kMDItemAcquisitionMake          = "Canon"
kMDItemAcquisitionModel         = "Canon PowerShot S500"
kMDItemAperture                 = 3.34375
kMDItemAttributeChangeDate      = 2007-02-23 17:35:25 -0800
kMDItemAuthors                  = ("Sal Soghoian")
kMDItemBitsPerSample            = 32
kMDItemColorSpace               = "RGB"
kMDItemContentCreationDate      = 2006-07-31 05:25:36 -0700
kMDItemContentModificationDate  = 2007-02-23 17:35:04 -0800
kMDItemContentType              = "public.jpeg"
kMDItemContentTypeTree          = ("public.jpeg", "public.image", "public.
data", "public.item", "public.content")
kMDItemCopyright                = "2006 Nyhthawk Productions"
kMDItemCreator                  = "Adobe Photoshop CS2 Macintosh"
kMDItemDescription              = "A door knocker in Florence, Italy."
kMDItemDisplayName              = "SQUARE.JPG"
kMDItemEXIFVersion              = "2.2"
kMDItemExposureTimeSeconds      = 0.125
kMDItemFlashOnOff               = 0
kMDItemFocalLength              = 9.09375
kMDItemFSContentChangeDate      = 2007-02-23 17:35:04 -0800
kMDItemFSCreationDate           = 2006-07-31 05:25:36 -0700
kMDItemFSCreatorCode            = 0
kMDItemFSFinderFlags            = 1024
kMDItemFSInvisible              = 0
kMDItemFSIsExtensionHidden      = 0
kMDItemFSLabel                  = 0
kMDItemFSName                   = "SQUARE.JPG"
kMDItemFSNodeCount              = 0
kMDItemFSOwnerGroupID           = 0
```

```
kMDItemFSOwnerUserID         = 501
kMDItemFSSize                = 991115
kMDItemFSTypeCode            = 0
kMDItemHasAlphaChannel       = 0
kMDItemID                    = 653224
kMDItemKeywords              = (door, knocker, vacation, Florence,
Italy)
kMDItemKind                  = "JPEG Image"
kMDItemLastUsedDate          = 2007-02-23 17:35:25 -0800
kMDItemOrientation           = 0
kMDItemPixelHeight           = 1024
kMDItemPixelWidth            = 1024
kMDItemProfileName           = "Camera RGB Profile"
kMDItemRedEyeOnOff           = 0
kMDItemResolutionHeightDPI   = 72
kMDItemResolutionWidthDPI    = 72
kMDItemTitle                 = "Door Knocker"
kMDItemUsedDates             = (2007-02-23 17:35:04 -0800, 2007-02-23
16:00:00 -0800)
```

That's a lot of information! And some of it is pretty obscure. For example, it includes the attribute tag `kMDItemRedEyeOnOff`, whose value is `0`, meaning automatic red-eye adjustment is off. (In the world of command-line results for Boolean values, `0` is false, and `1` is true.)

Note that every image may not have the same set of metadata attributes. It depends on the camera, the editing software, and the user as to what tags are applied to a file.

To make it easier to extract specific metadata without parsing large amounts of text, the `mdls` command has an optional parameter that lets you extract the metadata for a specific attribute key. To get the value for a specific tag, follow the command `mdls` with a space, the parameter `-name`, followed by a space, the attribute name, another space, and finally the POSIX path to the target file, as shown in Script 29.30.

```
Set this_result to do shell script ¬
    "mdls -name kMDItemAcquisitionModel ~/Desktop/SQUARE.JPG"
```
SCRIPT 29.30

If the target file contains the indicated attribute, the result is a line of text consisting of the tag name followed by an equal sign and the tag value:

`"kMDItemAcquisitionModel = \"Canon PowerShot S500\""`
If the file does not contain the attribute, the command generates an error.

If the provided POSIX path points to a file that doesn't exist, the **do shell script** command generates an error. You will need to incorporate an error handler in your script if there is a possibility the paths used do not refer to existing files, as in Script 29.31. The error dialog is shown in Figure 29.1.

```
try
    do shell script ¬
        "mdls -name kMDItemAcquisitionModel ~/Desktop/Missing.jpg"
on error error_message
    display dialog (error_message) with icon 2
end try
```
SCRIPT 29.31

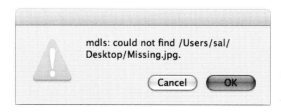

FIGURE 29.1 If the passed POSIX path points to a nonexistent file, the `mdls` command errors.

The other example scripts in this chapter assume that the passed POSIX paths point to existing images.

For advanced metadata extraction of attributes whose values are lists, dates, and numbers, use the three AppleScript subroutines shown in Script 29.32. With them, you can extract the value of any Spotlight metadata tag that has been applied to an image. These routines convert the data to its proper AppleScript format, such as list, integer, and number.

```
on get_metadata(this_file, attribute_key)
    set this_result to ¬
        (do shell script ("mdls -name " & attribute_key & ¬
            space & (quoted form of the POSIX path of this_file)))
    if the (count of paragraphs of this_result) is 0 then
        -- attribute not available
        return ""
    else
        -- get offset of = in result
        set x to the offset of "=" in this_result
        set result_string to (text from (x + 2) to -1 of this_result)
        if the result_string is "(null)" then
            return missing value
        else if the result_string begins with "\"" and ¬
            the result_string ends with "\"" then
            -- STRING
            -- remove encasing quotes
            return (text 2 thru -2 of result_string)
        else if the result_string begins with "(" and ¬
            the result_string ends with ")" and ¬
            (count of paragraphs of result_string) ¬
                is greater than 1 then
            -- MULTIPLE-LINE LIST
            -- remove open paren, return, and 4 spaces
            -- remove close return and paren
            set edit_string to (text 7 thru -3 of result_string)
            set AppleScript's text item delimiters to ("," & return)
            set the these_items to ¬
                every text item of the edit_string
            set AppleScript's text item delimiters to ""
            return my cleanup(these_items)
        else if the result_string begins with "(" and ¬
            the result_string ends with ")" then
            -- SINGLE-LINE LIST
            -- remove encasing parens
```

```applescript
                    set edit_string to (text 2 thru -2 of result_string)
                    set AppleScript's text item delimiters to ", "
                    set these_items to every text item of the edit_string
                    set AppleScript's text item delimiters to ""
                    return my cleanup(these_items)
                else if the attribute_key ends with "Date" then
                    -- DATE
                    return result_string
                else
                    -- NUMBER OR LIST
                    if result_string contains "." then
                        return result_string as number
                    else
                        return result_string as integer
                    end if
                end if
            end if
        end if
end get_metadata

on cleanup(this_list)
    -- remove leading and trailing spaces
    set this_list to my trim_list_items(this_list, " ", 2)
    -- remove leading and trailing quotes
    set this_list to my strip_quotes(this_list)
end cleanup

on strip_quotes(this_list)
    repeat with i from 1 to the count of this_list
        set this_item to item i of this_list
        if this_item begins with "\"" and ¬
            this_item ends with "\"" then
            set item i of this_list to ¬
                text 2 thru -2 of this_item
        end if
    end repeat
```

```
        return this_list
    end strip_quotes


    on trim_list_items(this_list, trim_chars, trim_indicator)
        repeat with i from 1 to the count of this_list
            set this_text to item i of this_list
            -- 0 = beginning, 1 = end, 2 = both
            set x to the length of the trim_chars
            -- TRIM BEGINNING
            if the trim_indicator is in {0, 2} then
                repeat while this_text begins with the trim_chars
                    try
                        set this_text to characters (x + 1) thru -1 of this_
text as string
                    on error
                        -- the text contains nothing but the trim characters
                        return ""
                    end try
                end repeat
            end if
            -- TRIM ENDING
            if the trim_indicator is in {1, 2} then
                repeat while this_text ends with the trim_chars
                    try
                        set this_text to characters 1 thru -(x + 1) of this_
text as string
                    on error
                        -- the text contains nothing but the trim characters
                        return ""
                    end try
                end repeat
            end if
            set item i of this_list to this_text
        end repeat
        return this_list
```

```
        end trim_list_items

on convert_UNIX_dates(passed_data)
    -- "2007-02-23 17:35:04 -0800" to date record
    if the class of the passed_data is list then
        set is_list to true
        if passed_data is {} then return {}
    else
        set is_list to false
        if passed_data is "" then return ""
    end if

    set passed_data to passed_data as list
    set the date_records to {}
    repeat with i from 1 to the count of the passed_data
        try
            set this_UNIX_date to item i of the passed_data
            set AppleScript's text item delimiters to space
            copy every text item of this_UNIX_date to ¬
                {date_string, time_string, zone_string}
            set AppleScript's text item delimiters to ""

            set AppleScript's text item delimiters to "-"
            copy every text item of date_string to ¬
                {this_year, this_month, this_day}
            set AppleScript's text item delimiters to ""

            set AppleScript's text item delimiters to ":"
            copy every text item of time_string to ¬
                {this_hour, this_minute, this_second}
            set AppleScript's text item delimiters to ""

            set temp_date to the current date
            set year of the temp_date to this_year as integer
            set month of the temp_date to this_month as integer
```

```
            set day of the temp_date to this_day as integer
            set hours of the temp_date to this_hour as integer
            set minutes of the temp_date to this_minute as integer
            set seconds of the temp_date to this_second as integer

            set the end of the date_records to the temp_date
        end try
    end repeat

    if is_list is true then
        return the date_records
    else
        if the date_records is {} then return ""
        return item 1 of the date_records
    end if
end convert_UNIX_dates
```

SCRIPT 29.32

With those subroutines added at the bottom of your script, you can call them to extract only the metadata you need, as in Script 29.33, which extracts the caption from a JPEG image file.

```
set this_file to choose file of type "public.jpeg" without invisibles
set the image_caption to ¬
    my get_metadata(this_file, "kMDItemDescription")
--> "A door knocker in Florence, Italy."
```

SCRIPT 29.33

Script 29.34 extracts the assigned keywords.

```
set this_file to choose file of type "public.jpeg" without invisibles
set these_keywords to ¬
    my get_metadata(this_file, "kMDItemKeywords")
--> {"door", "knocker", "vacation", "Florence", "Italy"}
```

SCRIPT 29.34

Script 29.35 extracts a list of dates and times that the image has been opened.

```
set this_file to choose file of type "public.jpeg" without invisibles
set the use_dates to ¬
    my get_metadata(this_file, "kMDItemUsedDates")
--> {"2007-02-23 17:35:04 -0800", "2007-02-23 16:00:00 -0800", "2007-02-24
16:00:00 -0800", "2007-02-28 16:00:00 -0800"}
```
SCRIPT 29.35

The result of Script 29.35 is a list of UNIX date strings. If you want to convert them to AppleScript date records, use the convert_UNIX_dates subroutine shown in Script 29.32, which accepts a single UNIX date string or a list of UNIX date strings.

```
set the use_dates to my convert_UNIX_dates(use_dates)
--> {date "Friday, February 23, 2007 5:35:04 PM", date "Friday, February
23, 2007 4:00:00 PM", date "Saturday, February 24, 2007 4:00:00 PM", date
"Wednesday, February 28, 2007 4:00:00 PM"}
```
SCRIPT 29.36

For your reference, here are some tables of some commonly used metadata attribute keys. You can find the complete list online at http://developer.apple.com/documentation/Carbon/Reference/MetadataAttributesRef/MetadataAttrRef.html. Table 29.1 lists the image metadata attribute keys, Table 29.2 lists the common metadata attribute keys (IPTC), Table 29.3 lists the file system metadata attribute keys, and Table 29.4 lists the file metadata attribute keys.

TABLE 29.1 Image Metadata Attribute Keys

Key	Type	Description
kMDItemAcquisitionMake	String	Manufacturer of the device used to acquire the document contents.
kMDItemAcquisitionModel	String	Model of the device used to acquire the document contents.

Key	Type	Description
kMDItemAlbum	String	Title for the collection containing this item. This is analogous to a record label or photo album.
kMDItemAperture	Number	Aperture setting used to acquire the document contents. This unit is the APEX value.
kMDItemBitsPerSample	Number	Number of bits per sample. For example, the bit depth of an image (8-bit, 16-bit etc.) or the bit depth per audio sample of uncompressed audio data (8, 16, 24, 32, 64, etc.).
kMDItemColorSpace	String	Color space model used by the document contents. For example, "RGB", "CMYK", "YUV", or "YCbCr".
kMDItemEXIFVersion	String	Version of the EXIF header used to generate the metadata.
kMDItemExposureMode	Number: 0 (auto exposure), 1 (Manual Exposure), 2 (Auto Bracket)	Exposure mode used to acquire the document contents.
kMDItemExposureProgram	String: Manual, Normal, etc.	Type of exposure program used by the camera to acquire the document contents. Possible values include Manual, Normal, Aperture priority, etc.

Table continues on next page

TABLE 29.1 Image Metadata Attribute Keys *(continued)*

Key	Type	Description
kMDItemExposureTimeSeconds	Number	Exposure time used to capture the document contents.
kMDItemExposureTimeString	Date String	Time when the document contents were captured. Typically this corresponds to when a photograph is exposed.
kMDItemFNumber	Number	Diameter of the aperture relative to the effective focal length of the lens.
kMDItemFlashOnOff	Number (Boolean)	Whether a camera flash was used to capture the document contents.
kMDItemFocalLength	Number	Actual focal length of the lens, in millimeters.
kMDItemHasAlphaChannel	Number (Boolean)	Whether the image has an alpha channel.
kMDItemISOSpeed	Number	ISO speed used to acquire the document contents. For example, 100, 200, 400, etc.
kMDItemLayerNames	List of Strings	Names of the layers in the file.
kMDItemMaxAperture	Number	Smallest F number of the lens in APEX value units, usually in the range of 00.00 to 99.99.
kMDItemMeteringMode	String: Unknown, Average, CenterWeightedAverage, Spot, MultiSpot, Pattern, Partial	Metering mode used to acquire the image.

Key	Type	Description
kMDItemOrientation	Number: 0 (landscape), 1 (portrait)	Orientation of the document contents.
kMDItemPixelHeight	Number	Height, in pixels, of the contents. For example, the image height or the video frame height.
kMDItemPixelWidth	Number	Width, in pixels, of the contents. For example, the image width or the video frame width.
kMDItemProfileName	String	Name of the color profile used by the document contents.
kMDItemRedEyeOnOff	Number (Boolean): 0 (no red-eye reduction mode or unknown), 1 (red-eye reduction used)	Red whether red-eye reduction was used to take the picture.
kMDItemResolutionHeightDPI	Number	Resolution height, in DPI, of the item.
kMDItemResolutionWidthDPI	Number	Resolution width, in DPI, of the item.
kMDItemWhiteBalance	Number: 0 (auto white balance), 1 (manual)	White balance setting of the camera when the picture was taken.

TABLE 29.2 Common Metadata Attribute Keys (IPTC)

Key	Type	Description
kMDItemAuthors	List of Strings	Byline
kMDItemCity	String	Identifies city of origin according to guidelines established by the provider. For example, "New York", "Cupertino", or "Toronto".
kMDItemContactKeywords	List	A list of contacts that are associated with this document, not including the authors.
kMDItemCopyright	String	Copyright owner of the file contents.
kMDItemCountry	String	The full, publishable name of the country or primary location where the intellectual property of the item was created, according to guidelines of the provider.
kMDItemCreator	String	Name of the application used to create the document content. For example, "Pages" or "Keynote".
kMDItemDescription	String	Caption
kMDItemHeadline	String	Publishable entry providing a synopsis of the contents of the item. For example, "Apple Introduces the iPod Photo".
kMDItemKeywords	List of Strings	Keywords associated with this file. For example, "Birthday", "Important", etc.

kMDItemStateOrProvince	String	Province or state of origin according to guidelines established by the provider. For example, "CA", "Ontario", or "Sussex".
kMDItemTitle	String	Title of the item. For example, this could be the title of a document, the name of a song, or the subject of an e-mail message.

TABLE 29.3 File System Metadata Attribute Keys

Key	Type	Description
kMDItemFSContentChangeDate	Date String	Date the file contents last changed.
kMDItemFSCreationDate	Date String	Date that the contents of the file were created.
kMDItemFSInvisible	Number (Boolean)	Whether the file is invisible.
kMDItemFSIsExtensionHidden	Number (Boolean)	Whether the file extension of the file is hidden.
kMDItemFSLabel	Number	Index of the Finder label of the file. Possible values are 0 through 7.
kMDItemFSName	String	File name of the item.
kMDItemFSNodeCount	Number	Number of files in a directory.
kMDItemFSOwnerGroupID	Number	Group ID of the owner of the file.
kMDItemFSOwnerUserID	Number	User ID of the owner of the file.
kMDItemFSSize	Number	Size, in bytes, of the file on disk.
kMDItemPath	String	Complete path to the file. This value of this attribute can be retrieved but can't be used in a query or used to sort search results.

TABLE 29.4 File Metadata Attribute Keys (Other)

Key	Type	Description
kMDItemKind	String	The kind identifier string. Such as, "JPEG Image"
kMDItemLastUsedDate	Date String	The date of the last time the document was opened.
kMDItemDisplayName	String	The name of the file as displayed in the Finder.
kMDItemAttributeChangeDate	Date String	The date of the last time a metadata attribute was changed.
kMDItemContentType	String	Uniform Type Identifier of the file. For example, a JPEG image file will have a value of public.jpeg. The value of this attribute is set by the Spotlight importer. Changes to this value are lost when the file attributes are next imported. This attribute is marked as nosearch. You must specify this attribute key explicitly in a query in order for its contents to be searched.
kMDItemContentTypeTree	List of Strings	Uniform Type Identifier hierarchy of the file. For example, a JPEG image file will return an array containing "public.jpeg", "public.image", and "public.data". The value of this attribute is set by the Spotlight importer. Changes to this value are lost when the file attributes are next imported. This attribute is marked as nosearch. You must specify this attribute key explicitly in a query in order for its contents to be searched.
kMDItemCreator	String	Software used to create the document.

The `mdls` command is used to access the value of assigned metadata attributes, not to set them. Metadata attributes are usually set in a document when it is opened in an application for editing.

Finding the Needle...

Extracting the metadata from files is very useful, but it's not the only thing that Spotlight does. Finding items on your computer is Spotlight's most powerful feature.

There's a command line utility for using Spotlight to locate items by matching the value of their metadata attributes to a set of values outlined in a *query string*. This command is appropriately named `mdfind` and provides a great way to enhance the functionality of your scripts.

To use the command, you simply follow the command with a space and a query string that details your search parameters. Try Script 29.37.

```
set the search_result to ¬
    do shell script ("mdfind 'kMDItemCopyright == \"Apple\"w'")
```
SCRIPT 29.37

The result is a very long paragraph-delimited list of POSIX paths to all the disk items on your computer that have the word *Apple* in their copyright strings:

```
/Applications/Utilities/Disk Utility.app
/Applications/Utilities/Network Utility.app
/Applications/Utilities/System Profiler.app
/Applications/Utilities/Terminal.app
/System/Library/Fonts/Apple LiGothic Medium.dfont
/System/Library/Fonts/AppleGothic.dfont
/System/Library/Fonts/AquaKanaBold.otf
/System/Library/Fonts/AquaKanaRegular.otf
/System/Library/Fonts/Courier.dfont
etc…
```

Let's refine the search query string to locate all of the Apple fonts on your computer. See Script 29.38.

```
set the search_result to ¬
    do shell script ("mdfind 'kMDItemCopyright == \"Apple\"w &&
kMDItemContentTypeTree == public.font'")
```
SCRIPT 29.38

The result is a long paragraph-delimited list of POSIX paths to the Apple font files on your computer:

```
/System/Library/Fonts/Apple LiGothic Medium.dfont
/System/Library/Fonts/AppleGothic.dfont
/System/Library/Fonts/AquaKanaBold.otf
/System/Library/Fonts/AquaKanaRegular.otf
/System/Library/Fonts/Courier.dfont
/System/Library/Fonts/Geneva.dfont
/System/Library/Fonts/Helvetica.dfont
/System/Library/Fonts/Keyboard.dfont
/System/Library/Fonts/LastResort.dfont
etc…
```

Script 29.39 is one more variation on the same script.

```
set the search_result to ¬
    do shell script ("mdfind 'kMDItemCopyright == \"Apple\"w &&
kMDItemContentTypeTree == com.apple.application'")
```
SCRIPT 29.39

The result of this version is a long paragraph-delimited list of POSIX paths to the Apple applications on your system:

```
/Applications/Utilities/Disk Utility.app
/Applications/Utilities/Network Utility.app
/Applications/Utilities/System Profiler.app
/Applications/Utilities/Terminal.app
/Applications/Internet Connect.app
```

```
/Applications/Utilities/Bluetooth File Exchange.app
/Applications/Utilities/Keychain Access.app
/Applications/Utilities/NetInfo Manager.app
/Applications/Utilities/ODBC Administrator.app
/Applications/Utilities/Printer Setup Utility.app
/Applications/QuickTime Player.app
/Applications/iDVD.app
etc…
```

To convert the resulting list of POSIX paths to an AppleScript list of file references in alias format, place the subroutine shown in Script 29.40 at the bottom
of your script.

```
on convert_POSIX(passed_data)
    if the class of passed_data is string then
        try
            return (passed_data as POSIX file as alias)
        on error
            return ""
        end try
    else
        set these_items to {}
        repeat with i from 1 to the count of the passed_data
            try
                set this_path to item i of the passed_data
                set the end of these_items to ¬
                    (this_path as POSIX file as alias)
            end try
        end repeat
        return these_items
    end if
end convert_POSIX
```

SCRIPT 29.40

Pass to it an AppleScript list of POSIX paths derived from the paragraph-delimited query results, as shown in Script 29.41.

```
set the search_result to ¬
    do shell script ("mdfind 'kMDItemCopyright == \"Apple\"w &&
kMDItemContentTypeTree == com.apple.application'")
if the search_result is "" then
    set search_result to {}
else
    set the search_result to every paragraph of the search_result
    set the search_result to my convert_POSIX(search_result)
end if
```

SCRIPT 29.41

The result of the subroutine is an AppleScript list of file references in alias format:

```
{alias "Macintosh HD:Applications:Utilities:Disk Utility.app:", alias
"Macintosh HD:Applications:Utilities:Network Utility.app:", alias
"Macintosh HD:Applications:Utilities:System Profiler.app:", alias
"Macintosh HD:Applications:Utilities:Terminal.app:", alias "Macintosh
HD:Applications:Internet Connect.app:", alias "Macintosh HD:Applications:U
tilities:Bluetooth File Exchange.app:", alias "Macintosh HD:Applications:
Utilities:Keychain Access.app:", alias "Macintosh HD:Applications:Utiliti
es:NetInfo Manager.app:", alias "Macintosh HD:Applications:Utilities:ODBC
Administrator.app:", alias "Macintosh HD:Applications:Utilities:Printe
r Setup Utility.app:", alias "Macintosh HD:Applications:QuickTime Player.
app:", etc.}
```

By default, all Spotlight searches are global, across the entire system (except it excludes the System and invisible folders). If you want to limit the search location to a specific folder hierarchy, use the optional -onlyin parameter to limit the scope of the search. Place the parameter after the mdfind command, and follow it with a POSIX path to the folder to search and the query string (don't forget to separate all the command string components with spaces). Script 29.42 is an example that searches the Pictures folder, and every folder it contains, for TIFF images whose name begins with *D*.

```
do shell script ¬
    "mdfind -onlyin ~/Pictures 'kMDItemFSName == \"D*.tif\"'"
```
SCRIPT 39.42

Refining the Search Parameters

The real power of the command line to control Spotlight is unleashed by learning how to create the necessary query strings to locate the items you want to process. Let's examine how to best define a query.

The basic format of a query string is this:

```
(attribute) space (comparison operator) space (value)
```

like this:

```
'kMDItemCopyright == \"Apple\"'
```

A couple of things to note:

▶ Enclose the entire query in single quotation marks. That's because it's a query string, and in AppleScript, text strings are always quoted. Since the query string is used with the `do shell script` command, which also takes a string as its parameter, the query string is a string within a string. Since the outer quotation marks are double quotes, we use single quotation marks on the inside string.

▶ In the previous example, the attribute value is a text string. So (you guessed it), the attribute value must be quoted. However, since we've already used double quotes to enclose the `do shell script` command string, we need to escape the inner double quotes by placing a backslash character before each of them. This tells the Script Editor to ignore their use when trying to compile the script command.

It's no big deal; you just have to remember to make these adjustments when the Spotlight command is executed from AppleScript instead of the Terminal application.

The comparison operator in the previous example is two adjacent equal signs (==), which means *equal to*. You can use other comparison operators as well. Here's a list:

Operator	Description
==	Equal
!=	Not equal
<	Less than (available for numeric values and dates only)
>	Greater than (available for numeric values and dates only)
<=	Less than or equal (available for numeric values and dates only)
>=	Greater than or equal (available for numeric values and dates only)

Script 29.43 shows some example query strings using these operators.

```
do shell script "mdfind 'kMDItemFSLabel == 0'"
-- items that have no Finder label assigned to them

do shell script "mdfind 'kMDItemFSLabel != 0'"
-- items that have a Finder label assigned to them

do shell script "mdfind 'kMDItemPixelHeight < 1000'"
-- images whose height is less than 1000 pixels

do shell script "mdfind 'kMDItemPixelWidth > 1000'"
-- images whose width is greater than 1000 pixels

do shell script "mdfind 'kMDItemPixelHeight <= 1000'"
-- images whose height is less than or equal to 1000 pixels

do shell script "mdfind 'kMDItemPixelWidth >= 1000'"
-- images whose width is greater than or equal to 1000 pixels
```
SCRIPT 29.43

In addition, the `mdfind` command also supports these modifiers, wildcard characters, and time variables, as shown in Scripts 29.44, 29.45, and 29.46.

Here's how string modifiers work:

Search String	Result
`"Paris"`	Matches *Paris* but not *paris* or *I love Paris*
`"Paris"c`	Matches *Paris* and *paris* but not *I love Paris*
`"Paris"wc`	Matches *Paris*, *paris*, *I love Paris*, *paris-france.jpg*, but not *Comparison*

```
do shell script ¬
    "mdfind -onlyin ~/Pictures 'kMDItemDescription == \"Florence\"w'"
```
SCRIPT 29.44

Here's how the wildcard character (*) works:

Search String	Result
`"paris*"`	Matches attribute values that begin with *paris*; for example, matches *paris* and *parisol*, but not *comparison*
`"*paris"`	Matches attribute values that end with *paris*
`"*paris*"`	Matches attributes that contain *paris* anywhere within the value; for example, matches *paris*, *parisol*, and *Comparison*
`"paris"`	Matches attribute values that are exactly equal to *paris*

```
do shell script ¬
    "mdfind -onlyin ~/Pictures 'kMDItemFSName == \"D*.tif\"'"
```
SCRIPT 29.45

Here's how the time variables work:

Time Variable	Description
`$time.now`	The current date and time
`$time.today`	The current date
`$time.yesterday`	Yesterday's date
`$time.this_week`	Dates in the current week

```
do shell script "mdfind 'kMDItemFSContentChangeDate > $time.today'"
```

And here's how compound search structures work:

```
do shell script "'(kMDItemAuthors == \"Sal\"wc || kMDItemAuthors ==
\"Bill\"wc) &&
 (kMDItemContentType == \"audio\"wc || kMDItemContentType ==
\"video\"wc)'"
```
SCRIPT 29.46

There is much more than we can detail in this chapter. One final point we should make, however, is that you no longer have to worry about malicious scripters who might try to tell an application on a remote computer on the network to **do shell script**. Leopard doesn't allow that to happen.

For a comprehensive overview of how to construct Spotlight search queries, download Apple's online guide in PDF format available at `http://developer.apple.com/documentation/Carbon/Conceptual/SpotlightQuery/SpotlightQuery.pdf`.

Script 29.47 shows one last example. Can you figure out what it searches for?

```
set the search_result to ¬
    do shell script ("mdfind -onlyin ~/Documents
'kMDItemFSContentChangeDate > $time.today && kMDItemContentTypeTree ==
public.image'")
```
SCRIPT 29.47

It locates all the image files in the Documents directory that were changed today.

What's Next?

In this chapter, you learned how to use AppleScript's `do shell script` command to add the immense power of *shell scripting* to your AppleScript tool chest. In the next chapter, we'll briefly describe a few other advanced features of AppleScript before bringing this book to a close and letting you loose to use AppleScript on your own.

30

Object-Oriented Scripting

FaceSpan and AppleScript Studio

Automator

What's Next?

Lesson **30**
Advanced Topics

This book doesn't cover everything there is to know about AppleScript. You've learned a lot—enough, we hope, to enable you to do just about anything you might like in the way of automating repetitive tasks that are best left to the computer. But you have a lot to look forward to, should you decide to continue the journey.

In this chapter, we give you just a peek at some of the more advanced tools that are available to AppleScripters.

First, there are advanced features in AppleScript itself that we haven't covered. The most interesting of them is AppleScript's support for a technology that computer scientists call *object-oriented programming*. We'll give you a taste of it here.

Next, you've probably noticed that AppleScript's facilities for putting a sophisticated user interface on a script are, shall we say, somewhat limited. The `display dialog` command and its siblings let you put up a simple dialog with some text, two or three buttons, and a text field, but that's about it as far as user interaction is concerned. A few years ago, Apple addressed this issue by releasing AppleScript Studio, a development environment that you can use to build complete, full-featured Mac OS X applications using AppleScript. You may not realize that some of the professional-quality applications you use today may actually have been written in the AppleScript language using AppleScript Studio. We'll tell you a bit about AppleScript Studio and another AppleScript-based development tool, FaceSpan.

Finally, the most exciting recent development in the AppleScript world is Automator. Even though AppleScript is a fairly simple and straightforward scripting language using what often looks strikingly like plain English terminology, many people who would like to automate some of their tasks lack the time or inclination to learn AppleScript. Now, with Automator, a huge number of AppleScript-based actions have been written and are freely available from Apple and a number of third-party Web sites. Actions are short scripts that perform concise, easily explained tasks, either on their own or in conjunction with applications. You string them together into an Automator workflow using a convenient drag-and-drop user interface, and without any scripting at all you've built a script to do just about anything you want.

Object-Oriented Scripting

In this book, you've read a little about the AppleScript *object model*, which is a way to structure an application's terminology so that scripts can access and manipulate the application's data flexibly and powerfully using objects having properties and commands.

It isn't just scriptable applications that can take advantage of this approach. You can construct your scripts, too, so that they implement objects. AppleScript recognizes the `script` class, which you can use to create a `script` object having properties, as well as commands that operate on them.

Now that you know these objects are called *scripts*, you can begin to relax because you realize that you already know a lot about them. The scripts you've been writing throughout this book are themselves **script** objects, with properties and commands. The only thing more to learn about script objects is that you can also create them inside a script.

We'll give you a simple example in Script 30.1, instead of a lot of theory and explanation, just to show you what they look like. As you'll see, the basic idea is to create objects in a script that emulate, or model, real-world objects. Each of them has properties and commands that represent attributes and actions characteristic of the corresponding real-world object. If you set them up right, their use can be highly intuitive and natural.

```
property boy : ""
property girl : ""


on run
    init_talkers()
    recite_poem()
end run

to init_talkers()
    if class of boy is not script then ¬
        set boy to make_talker("Junior")
    if class of girl is not script then ¬
        set girl to make_talker("Princess")
end init_talkers

to recite_poem()
    tell boy to recite("One two, buckle my shoe.")
    tell girl to recite("Three four, knock at the door.")
    tell boy to recite("Five six, pick up sticks.")
    tell girl to recite("Seven eight, lay them straight.")
    tell boy to recite("Nine ten, a good fat hen.")
end recite_poem
```

```
to make_talker(voice_name)
    script talker
        property voice : voice_name
        to recite(stanza)
            say stanza using voice
        end recite
    end script
    return talker
end make_talker
```
SCRIPT 30.1

In Script 30.1, you declare two properties, boy and girl. They start out empty, but in the init_talkers handler you call the make_talker handler twice to initialize them. The make_talker handler creates a "talker" script object and returns it so that the init_talkers handler can assign one to the boy and one to the girl. The boy and the girl are now script objects, each having a built-in voice and the ability to use it to recite stanzas from a little rhyme.

In the make_talker handler, you see the script object itself. It is declared the same way you declare a local variable, except you use the keyword script instead of local. The script object is declared in a block, terminated by an end script statement. Within the script block, you declare properties and handlers, just as you have done in the scripts you have written throughout this book. Here, each talker script object has a single property, characteristic of everybody who talks, namely, a voice. Each talker script object also knows how to perform a characteristic action, namely, to recite a stanza of a poem. The make_talker handler is an *object constructor*. The script object declared inside the handler does not actually exist until the handler is run. When run, the handler creates an object conforming to this script declaration and returns it to the caller, where it is assigned to the boy or girl property. When a talker object is created, the make_talker handler sets its voice_name property to the voice that was passed into the handler from the caller.

In the recite_poem handler, you see how easy and natural it is to use the two objects you created. You don't have to remind them what voice to use, because each of them was born with a specific voice. And you don't have to explain to them what reciting a stanza is all about, because each of them was born with the knowledge that he or she should `say` the stanza `using` his or her own `voice`. You just tell one `talker` object or the other to `recite` the next stanza, and it belts it out using the `voice` it was born with.

Script objects can be much bigger and more sophisticated than this. Not only can they have many properties and handlers, but script objects can have *parent* objects. The child object *inherits* properties and handlers from its *parent*, but it can modify them and declare additional properties and handlers of its own. It can even *override* its parent's handlers in order to act appropriately based on its own unique characteristics. Thus, you could declare a complex object such as a `shape` that knows in an abstract way how to return the number of sides it has but that has no idea how many sides that might be for any particular shape Then you could declare child objects such as a `triangle` and a `square` that inherit this handler and smartly return 3 or 4, respectively, when asked. The fun only starts there. Look into `script` objects in more detail if you're intrigued by this brief introduction.

FaceSpan and AppleScript Studio

Way back when AppleScript was first released, about 15 years ago, a tool called Frontmost came with it. Apple described Frontmost then as an application "that allows you to create sophisticated user interfaces for AppleScript applications," and it did exactly that, in an elegant and easy-to-use way. Eventually, it became known as FaceSpan, and it has recently become available for Mac OS X from Late Night Software, the developer of another important AppleScript tool mentioned from time to time in this book, *Script Debugger*. Late Night Software has described FaceSpan 4 as an "AppleScript-based Rapid Application Development (RAD) tool for constructing Mac OS X applications." You'll find it on the Web at `http://www.latenightsw.com/fs4/`. Version 5 of FaceSpan is well along in development, and it holds great promise.

During the period before FaceSpan was ported to Mac OS X, Apple recognized the need for a tool to enable scripters to build applications with a full-fledged Aqua user interface using AppleScript, and AppleScript Studio was born in

2001. Like FaceSpan, it allows scripters to create applications native to Mac OS X using AppleScript, complete with an Aqua-compliant user interface with menus, windows, dialogs, sheets, buttons, sliders, text views, text fields, and a host of other user controls that are not ordinarily available to AppleScript.

AppleScript Studio is not a stand-alone product. Instead, it is a collection of tools that are incorporated into Apple's software development package known collectively as *Xcode Tools*. Xcode Tools comes as part of every retail copy of Mac OS X, although it is not installed by default. It is the software development package used by Apple and most Macintosh developers to write programs of all kinds, including major commercial products that are written in a variety of programming languages.

What AppleScript Studio added to Xcode Tools was the ability to use AppleScript as a language having full citizenship alongside C, C++, Objective-C, and other programming languages. To write an AppleScript-based application using Xcode Tools, you use two of the tools in particular. Xcode is an integrated development environment (IDE) incorporating a professional-level code editor, compiler, debugger and linker. A companion tool, Interface Builder, is a powerful graphical design tool that enables you to build your application's user interface by dragging user interface elements from a palette, sizing and positioning them on your screen, and connecting them to the code you create in Xcode.

AppleScript Studio and its development tools can be daunting for scripters who have not had experience using high-powered programmer's tools, because the tools' user interfaces are not exactly intuitive and the tools include many complexities that will be of no use to the typical scripter. FaceSpan, by contrast, has a long tradition of providing an eminently understandable interface combined with enormous power focused specifically on scripters and their needs and aspirations.

Both AppleScript Studio and FaceSpan produce a finished product that is a native Mac OS X application in every respect, built under the hood using the same Apple Cocoa frameworks that underpin most applications newly developed for the Mac since Mac OS X was first released.

This is not the place to detail how AppleScript Studio and FaceSpan work, but we will show you a little of each of them in use. These screenshots are taken from example application projects that ship with FaceSpan and Xcode Tools, respectively.

FaceSpan

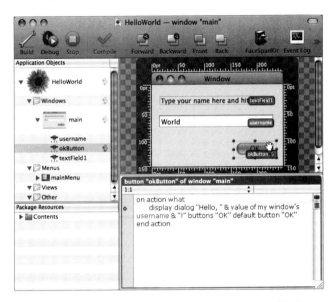

FIGURE 30.1 FaceSpan's project window, integrating objects, design, and scripts.

FIGURE 30.2 FaceSpan's views Library.

AppleScript Studio

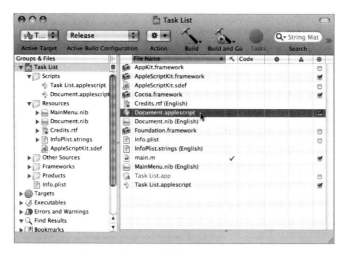

FIGURE 30.3 Xcode's Groups & Files window.

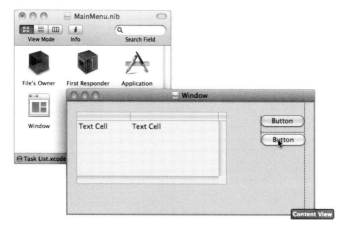

FIGURE 30.4 An Interface Builder application window during design.

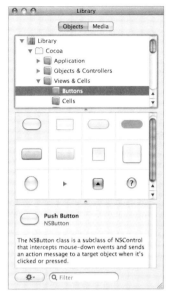

FIGURE 30.5 Interface Builder's views Library.

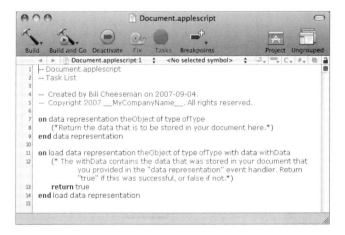

FIGURE 30.6 Xcode's script editing window.

Automator

Apple released Automator to great excitement with Mac OS X 10.4 (Tiger) in 2005. A flood of *Automator actions* were released at the same time, both by Apple and by third-party developers, and the outpouring of new actions has not abated since then.

Developers of scriptable applications have been quick to release actions that work with their own products for several reasons. Foremost among them is the competitive spirit. The developer community perceives that offering a set of useful Automator actions along with the main application gives a product a competitive advantage in the marketplace. For the same reason, more and more developers are making their applications scriptable for the first time so they can jump on the Automator bandwagon. In addition, Automator actions are very easy to write, and they make it genuinely convenient for users to create scripted workflows. The developer who can convince the marketplace to incorporate a product into a business-critical workflow is a developer who will lock in his customer base.

Automator is based on an application of the same name, where you find and select Automator actions and build up a workflow graphically using a drag-and-drop user interface. Instead of writing AppleScript statements to control the behavior of each action in the workflow, you choose items from pop-up menus, fill in text fields, and click buttons—a simple, everyday experience for any Mac user. Figure 30.7 shows a workflow in the process of being built in Automator.

It isn't hard for a developer to write Automator actions. In fact, anybody can write an action using AppleScript if the target application is scriptable, because scriptable applications have terminology dictionaries that make their scripting interfaces public.

Advanced users can write Automator actions using other programming languages, such as Objective-C. However, the developer of an action written this way must have access to the programming interface of the application, so this method is generally confined to developers who control the application code.

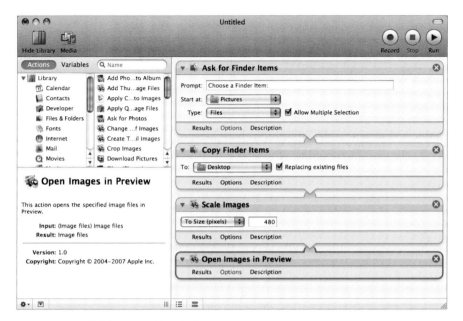

FIGURE 30.7 Building a workflow in Automator.

To learn more about Automator, visit: http://automator.us.

What's Next?

In this chapter, we told you just a little about advanced topics in AppleScript to get you interested in pursuing AppleScript to a deeper and even more productive level. With this, you've completed both Part I, *Instant AppleScript*, and Part II, *Essential Topics*.

What's next? That's for you to decide! We hope we've gotten you off to a good start.

Index